SCENTS AND SENSIBILITY

SCENTS &
SENSIBILITY

*Perfume in Victorian
Literary Culture*

CATHERINE MAXWELL

OXFORD
UNIVERSITY PRESS

OXFORD
UNIVERSITY PRESS

Great Clarendon Street, Oxford, OX2 6DP,
United Kingdom

Oxford University Press is a department of the University of Oxford.
It furthers the University's objective of excellence in research, scholarship,
and education by publishing worldwide. Oxford is a registered trade mark of
Oxford University Press in the UK and in certain other countries

© Catherine Maxwell 2017

Published in the United States of America by Oxford University Press
198 Madison Avenue, New York, NY 10016, United States of America

British Library Cataloguing in Publication Data
Data available

Library of Congress Control Number: 2017936255

ISBN 978–0–19–870175–0

Printed in Great Britain by
Clays Ltd, St Ives plc

For Philip Bullock
and
Sara Lyons

Acknowledgements

I would like to thank the Leverhulme Trust for its award of a Major Research Fellowship (2014–2016), which allowed me the time to write this monograph, to my referees—Dennis Denisoff, Hilary Fraser, and Yopie Prins—for generously supporting my application, and to Maria Delgado, Colin Jones, and Clair Wills for kindly reading my proposal and offering feedback. I would also to express my gratitude to the School of English and Drama at Queen Mary for its support of my project, and to all my colleagues in the School and its administrative team who have encouraged me or lent practical assistance, with special thanks to Michèle Barrett and Markman Ellis as respective Heads of School, to Paul Hamilton and David Colclough as successive Heads of English, to my appraisers Jerry Brotton and Julia Boffey, and to Huw Marsh, the School Research Manager, and Pat Hamilton for helping with the practicalities of both my application and the award period.

I am most grateful to the following individuals and institutions for inviting me to present portions of my research at their conferences and symposia: Jason Hall and Alex Murray, 'Decadent Poetics' at Exeter University (2011); Luisa Calè and Stefano Evangelista, 'Romanticism at the Fin de Siècle', Trinity College, Oxford (2013); Christine Atha, 'The Affective Turn', Royal College of Art (2014); Alice Condé, Jane Desmarais, Angela Dunstan, and Jessica Gossling, 'Decadence and the Senses', Goldsmiths, London (2014); Sarah Parker, Marion Thain, and Ana Vadillo, 'The Michael Field Centenary Conference', IES, Senate House, London (2014); Line Cottegnies, Catherine Lanone, and Marc Porée, 'Remembering through the Senses', Université Sorbonne Nouvelle Paris 3 (2014); Kate Hext and Alex Murray, 'Aestheticism and Decadence in the Age of Modernism', IES, Senate House (2015); Elisa Bizzotto and Stefano Evangelista, 'Arthur Symons: Writing across Arts and Cultures', IUAV, Venice (2015); Will Tullett (King's College, London), 'Remembrance of Perfumes Past', V&A, London (2016); Laura Kilbride, Orla Polten, and Alex Wong, 'Swinburne's *Poems and Ballads*', St John's, Cambridge (2016). I would also like to thank the following for kindly inviting me to present talks and seminar papers: Vic King and Brian Hinton, Dimbola Museum and Art Gallery, Isle of Wight (2013); Giuseppe Albano and Luca Caddia, Keats-Shelley House, Rome (2015); Elisabeth Angel-Pérez, Françoise Sammarcelli, and Charlotte Ribeyrol, the VALE séminaire général, Université Paris-Sorbonne (2015); Sophie Gilmartin and Matt Ingleby, the London Inter-collegiate Nineteenth-Century Seminar, IES, Senate House (2016), and to the organizers of graduate seminars at the University of Kent (2011), University of Edinburgh (2013), University of Exeter at Falmouth (2014), and University of Oxford (2015).

I thank all those who kindly provided information or answered queries including Michele Barrett, Denyse Beaulieu, Amanda and Simon Brooke of Grossmith, London, Robin Darwall-Smith, Lesley Higgins, Rohan McWilliam, Takako Mendl, Amanda Paxton, Michael Richardson at Bristol Special Collections, Clive

Simmonds, Evelyn Welch, and Stephen Wildman. I would also like to acknowledge Peter Henderson, Walpole Librarian at the King's School, Canterbury; Senate House Library Special Collections; perfumer Thomas Fontaine and the staff of the Osmothèque, Versailles.

It gives me great pleasure to acknowledge all those who read and commented on my published articles or work in progress: John Bailey, Susan Barbour, Brooke Belldon, Julia Boffey, Rowan Boyson, Christina Bradstreet, Clare Brant, Dennis Denisoff, Jenny Dunlop, Angie Dunstan, Markman Ellis, David Howes, Caro Greville, Katy Mullin, Stephen Nelson, Francis O'Gorman, Lizzie Ostrom (aka 'Odette Toilette'), Eric Takens-Milne, Ben Wakefield, and Rose Wood. Special thanks are due to those who generously offered detailed feedback on specific chapters or portions of this book: Isobel Armstrong, Shahidha Bari, Philip Bullock, Mary Condé, Michael Craske, Santanu Das, Stefano Evangelista, Nick Freeman, Paul Hamilton, Suzanne Hobson, Matt Ingleby, Daichi Ishikawa, Sara Lyons, Sarah Parker, Jennifer Potter, Claire Preston, Amber Regis, Chris Reid, Charlotte Ribeyrol, Marion Thain, Melissa Tricoire, Sarah Wood, and Ana Vadillo. I am especially grateful to Philip Bullock and Stefano Evangelista who prompted me to turn what started off as a chapter into this book, to Sara Lyons who heroically read nearly all of the manuscript and was a constant source of encouragement, and to Mary Condé and Sarah Wood who were wonderfully attentive readers and offered much valued support in the final stages of this project.

I extend my warm thanks to Leonie Sturge-Moore and Charmian O'Neil for kind permission to quote or refer to manuscript material relating to Michael Field and to the British and Bodleian libraries for permission to use this material. Portions of this monograph have appeared in a different form in a number of publications, and I hereby acknowledge Palgrave Macmillan, the *Pater Newsletter*, Legenda and the Modern Humanities Research Association as original sources and am grateful for permission to reuse material. I offer special thanks to the editors of these works—Jason Hall, Alex Murray, Lene Østermark-Johansen, Alice Condé, and Jane Desmarais—for their valued comments and feedback. I also acknowledge, for the provision of specific images and the permission to use them, the British and Bodleian Libraries, Bristol University Special Collections, the Fitzwilliam Museum, Cambridge, and the V&A. I am especially grateful to Grossmith, London, Johann Maria Farina, Cologne, Keats-Shelley House, Rome, and the Pérez Simón Collection, Mexico, for allowing me to publish photographs owned by them free of charge. I also thank the London Library (especially Amanda Stebbings and Mary Gillies) for graciously allowing me to photograph items in its collection, with the responsibility for copyright being my own. Warm thanks to Daichi Ishikawa who was unfailingly helpful in taking these and other photographs for me. I thank the New Directions Publishing Corp (US) and Carcanet Press Limited (UK) for permission to cite H.D.'s poem 'Sheltered Garden', copyright the Estate of Hilda Doolittle; The Society of Authors, the King's School, Canterbury, and Special Collections, Senate House Library, University of London, for brief reference to the manuscripts of Compton Mackenzie; and Faber and Faber Ltd (UK) and Harcourt Mifflin Harcourt (US) to cite excerpts from the poetry of T. S. Eliot (*Collected Poems*

1909–1962 by T. S. Eliot. Copyright 1936 by Houghton Mifflin Harcourt Publishing Company. Copyright © renewed 1964 by Thomas Stearns Eliot. Reprinted by permission of Harcourt Mifflin Harcourt Publishing Company. All rights reserved.)

Finally I offer my sincere thanks to Jacqueline Norton, my commissioning editor at OUP, for her support for this project, and to Ellie Collins and Aimee Wright for their kind assistance, and my deep gratitude to Luca Caddia and Charlotte Ribeyrol for their generosity and kindness as hosts in Rome and Paris respectively, to friends at Perfume Lovers London, and to my family, especially my mother Teresa Maxwell and my sister Isobel Maxwell.

Contents

List of Figures

List of Plates

Notes on the Texts

Unless otherwise indicated, the following editions are used throughout with page references supplied in the text.

PJK The Poems of John Keats, ed. Miriam Allott (London and New York: Longman, 1970)

SPP Shelley's Poetry and Prose, ed. Donald H. Reiman and Sharon B. Powers (New York and London: Norton, 1977)

Poems The Collected Poetical Works of Algernon Charles Swinburne, 6 vols (London: Chatto & Windus, 1904)

PBA Algernon Charles Swinburne, *Poems and Ballads and Atalanta in Calydon*, ed. Kenneth Haynes (London: Penguin Books, 2000)

DG Oscar Wilde, *The Picture of Dorian Gray*, ed. Michael Patrick Gillespie, Norton Critical Editions (New York and London: W. W. Norton, 2007)

All references to Shakespeare are to *The Norton Shakespeare, Based on the Oxford Edition*, ed. Stephen Greenblatt et al., 2nd edn (New York and London: W. W. Norton & Co., 2008).

I use the following editions of works by Walter Pater:

Ren The Renaissance: Studies in Art and Poetry (The 1893 Text), ed. Donald L. Hill (Berkeley, CA: University of California Press, 1980)

GL Gaston de Latour: The Revised Text, ed. Gerald Monsman (Greensboro, NC: ELT Press, 1995)

SR Studies in the History of the Renaissance (1873), ed. Matthew Beaumont (Oxford: Oxford University Press, 2010)

ME Marius the Epicurean, ed. Gerald Monsman (Kansas City, MO: Valancourt Books, 2008)

IP Imaginary Portraits, ed. Lene Østermark-Johansen (London: Modern Humanities Research Association, 2014)

All other references are to *The Library Edition of the Works of Walter Pater* (London: Macmillan, 1910): *A Appreciations, GS Greek Studies, MS Miscellaneous Studies, EG Essays from The Guardian, PP Plato and Platonism.*

TSL The Swinburne Letters, ed. Cecil Y. Lang, 6 vols (New Haven, CT, and London: Yale and Oxford University Presses, 1959–62)

UL The Uncollected Letters of Algernon Charles Swinburne, ed. Terry Meyers, 3 vols (London: Pickering & Chatto, 2005)

LJAS The Letters of John Addington Symonds, ed. Herbert M. Schueller and Robert L. Peters, 3 vols (Detroit, MI: Wayne State University Press, 1967–9)

CL The Complete Letters of Oscar Wilde, ed. Merlin Holland and Rupert Hart-Davis (London: Fourth Estate, 2000)

All references to Works and Days, the multi-volume shared diary of Katharine Bradley and Edith Cooper, are to the manuscripts held by the British Library, now freely available online via the Digital Archives of the Victorian Lives and Letters Consortium. The digitized diaries are temporarily housed online at http://tundra. csd.sc.edu/vllc/field_diaries, although it should be noted that my transcriptions, taken from the original MSS, use the original numbered MS pages and not the page numbers provided for the digitized version.

Most of the nineteenth-century texts referred to in this book, including many of the perfume texts, can be freely accessed and downloaded from http://www.archive. org. When referring to G. W. Septimus Piesse's *Art of Perfumery*, which appeared in five editions (1855, 1856, 1862, 1879, 1891), I have used the edition in which the passage cited appears for the first time, the implication being, unless otherwise specified, that it appears, albeit in variant form, in the subsequent editions. Full publication details of these separate editions are provided in the Bibliography.

Introduction

Reflecting on smell's ability to transport the mind and emotions, the psychologist Havelock Ellis noted in 1905 how many literary writers had described it 'as, above all others, the sense of imagination'.[1] This book, the first to examine the role played by scent and perfume in Victorian literary culture, is a reconceptualization of the imagination that reinstates its hidden links with the historically neglected sense of smell. Smell's evocative capacity, its connection to atmosphere and memory, make it a potent means of registering the particularity of a historical and cultural moment. Perfume, the exaltation of smell through the olfactory enhancement of the environment and the body, engages the imagination through the creation, projection, and influence of different kinds of identity, mood, and aura. Perfume-associated notions of imaginative influence and identity are central to this project, which explores the unfamiliar scented world of Victorian literature. It concentrates on the many aesthetic and decadent texts where fragrance is most strongly indicated, but also notes important anticipations in Shelley and Keats and earlier Victorians like Browning and Gaskell, in addition to documenting the suspicion of perfume evinced by many early and mid-Victorian novelists.

The primary emphasis of this study is on literature and literary analysis, but with reference throughout to the historical and material context. Victorian fragrance is a surprisingly under-researched field, with histories of perfume generally focused on nineteenth-century France. While France has always been the undisputed centre of the modern perfume industry, the tendency to engage almost exclusively with French tastes and fashions has meant that there is comparatively little documentation of the British experience. Britain's thriving and commercially successful perfume culture from the mid-nineteenth century onwards is rarely acknowledged.

This book investigates Victorian tastes in perfume for men and women with regard to both personal adornment and the wider environment. By 'perfume' I mean a pleasing scent relished for pleasure's sake. While in many cases this refers to scented goods or products, it also refers to 'naturals': flowers, plants, or naturally occurring odorous substances admired for their fragrance. While such natural fragrance often finds its way into perfumery, it also has significance in its own right, forming part of an individual's specific scent preferences. Thus, scented naturals, along with floral ornaments such as corsages and buttonholes, are included in this study with manufactured perfume, soap, and toiletries, and reference to

---

[1] Havelock Ellis, 'Section II: Smell', in *Studies in the Psychology of Sex: Sexual Selection in Man* (Philadelphia, PA: F. A. Davis Company, 1906), p. 55.

such things as aromatic jewellery; the scenting of garments, linen, fans, furniture, books, and paper; aromatic salts, perfumed snuff and tobacco; potpourri, pastilles, and incense. In addition to literary sources, this study draws on material such as perfume manuals and perfumers' guides, etiquette guides, beauty and hygiene manuals, advertising, works on floriculture and gardening, journalism, diaries, letters, interviews, memoirs, and biographies.

Aesthetic interest in perfume, first noticeable during the 1860s and intensifying throughout the subsequent decades of the century, almost certainly owes something to the development and expansion of British perfumery immediately prior to this in the 1850s. First published in 1855, *The Art of Perfumery* by the well-known London perfumer G. W. Septimus Piesse proved so popular that it had reached its third edition by 1862, when its author wrote that 'the exportation of perfumery has exactly doubled in value since the date of the first edition of this work'.[2] In this new edition Piesse noted how the perfumery trade had been boosted by Gladstone's removal of the soap tax in 1853, and observed that flowers grown in warmer climates like jasmine, tuberose, and acacia 'are now easily imported for manufacture into England', and that 'Tropical produce, together with musk, ambergris, castor [castoreum] and other raw materials for the perfumer's laboratory, comes to the British market before it reaches Continental cities.'[3] While bemoaning excise duties 'on spirits of wine' (perfumer's alcohol) that diminished the commercial success of exported English perfume, Piesse declared confidently 'England now produces the finest perfumery in the world.'[4] While this is undoubtedly something of a hyperbolic patriotic boast, British perfumery products were respected and sold internationally by the early 1860s. English toilet soap in particular had a worldwide reputation and English lavender oil, obtained from the extensive lavender fields at Hitchin, Hertfordshire, and Mitcham, Surrey, was thought to be unsurpassed, and a vital ingredient for any superior lavender water.

Piesse's confidence in British perfume was supported by Eugene Rimmel, another major British perfumer. In *The Book of Perfumes* (1865), a work based on articles previously published in the *Englishwoman's Magazine*, Rimmel reported that there were currently about sixty manufacturers of perfumery in London.[5] With London central to the trade in raw materials for perfumery and with a flourishing perfume industry of its own, there is good reason for his statement that 'London and Paris may be called the head-quarters of perfumery.'[6] Of these two books, Piesse's is the more specialized, containing numerous perfume recipes, and addressing itself more directly to the would-be perfumer, but both are very accessible and contain histories of perfume studded with illustrative quotation from literature. Both proved popular—Rimmel's book reached its fifth edition in 1867, while Piesse's much larger tome went through two more updated editions (1879, 1891)

---

[2] G. W. Septimus Piesse, *The Art of Perfumery and the Methods of Obtaining the Odours of Plants*, 3rd edn (1855; London: Longman, Brown, Green, & Longmans, 1862), p. xi.

[3] Ibid., p. viii.   [4] Ibid., p. x.

[5] Eugene Rimmel, *The Book of Perfumes* (London: Chapman & Hall, 1865), p. 233. Rimmel's preface is dated 15 December 1864, but the first edition carries the date 1865.

[6] Ibid., p. 233.

before the end of the century.[7] While there is no evidence that they were read by any of the authors discussed in this study, they testify to a growing interest in perfume and its production throughout the second half of the nineteenth century, something supported by the articles on perfume and perfumery that regularly appear in British journals and periodicals from mid-century onwards.[8]

If aestheticism, the leading late Victorian intellectual, artistic, and cultural movement of the period 1860 to 1900, which promotes 'the cult of beauty', coincides with an upsurge of interest in perfumery in Britain, then decadence, aestheticism's more rarefied offshoot, flowering in the 1880s and 1890s, deepens that relationship. Notions of beauty favouring the artificial over the natural overlap with the discovery and use of synthetic fragrance materials and the concomitant birth of the modern perfume industry in the 1880s. Early synthetics like coumarin, heliotropin, and ionones that add to the artifice of perfumery certainly have relevance to some of the perfumes liked or mentioned by decadent writers like Oscar Wilde and Arthur Symons.

Indeed, British aesthetic and decadent literature, with its watchword of 'art for art's sake' and its commitment to pleasure, is the perfect partner for the artifice of perfumery, since they share the desire to improve on nature. 'Nature has good intentions [...] but [...] she cannot carry them out', as Wilde's spokesman, Vivian, famously remarks in his dialogue 'The Decay of Lying' (1889).[9] Smell as both sense and sensation has often been deprecated for its association with a rude or raw physicality at odds with civilized manners and values, but perfume transcends that rawness, or is the sublimation of it into a higher-level experience. The cultivation of scented flowers and the wearing of perfume, enhancing both one's environment and individual attractiveness, show the triumph of pleasure over necessity. For the skilled perfumer, precise replication of a natural fragrance is not only impossible but pointless; his art is to add complexity and interest in a refinement of nature. Perfume signifies elite culture; a luxury product afforded only by the wealthy, it creates an aura of exclusivity that announces the superior status of its wearer, marking him or her off from the common mass of humanity. It is thus an ideal accessory for the aesthete or the decadent who elevates art, imagination, and culture over nature, and regards himself as a member of a higher order. The partnership of decadence and perfumery and their supremacy over nature is perfectly illustrated by an anecdote concerning Wilde's 'Sphinx', Ada Leverson, whom Aubrey Beardsley asked to come early for a party so that she could help him 'scent the flowers'. When she arrived, she found him busily spraying the gardenia and tuberoses with opopanax,

---

[7] Rimmel also published a French edition of his book *Le Livre des Parfums* (Paris: E. Dentu, 1870), translated by himself, in which he corrected various errors and omissions.

[8] See, for example, Eliza Lynn Linton, 'Perfumes', *Household Words* 15.363 (7 March 1857), 236–40; 'Britannia's Smelling Bottle', *Once a Week* (8 December 1860), 665–8; 'Flower Farming', *Cornhill Magazine* 10.58 (October 1864), 427–33; 'Flower Farming and Perfume Manufacturing', *Illustrated Review* 2.137 (August 1874), 90–1; Anne Hathaway, 'Scent and Scent Bottles', *Woman's World* 2 (1889), 321–5; Emma Brewer, 'Petal to Perfume', *Strand Magazine* 16.92 (August 1898), 232–5; Jacques Boyer, 'The Perfume Trade', *The Idler* 23 (September 1903), 434–41.

[9] 'The Decay of Lying', in *Oscar Wilde: The Major Works*, ed. Isobel Murray (Oxford: Oxford University Press, 2000), p. 215.

and he 'handed her a spray of frangipane for the stephanotis'.[10] Culture is still a factor even for those more conservative aesthetes who prefer natural scents to perfumed products; the flowers they enjoy are frequently enhanced with mythic or literary association, or may be of the hothouse variety, or only to be found in foreign lands. Whether blooming at home or abroad, the flowers cherished by the epicurean aesthete require his time and leisure to search them out for rapt contemplation.

I say 'his' advisedly for the majority of the authors I discuss are male, which is ironic in that there is almost no secondary literature on Victorian men's use of perfume. While conservative convention proscribed perfume for men, it is clear that urban sophisticates, dandies, bohemians, and male aesthetes and decadents were keenly interested in scent and enjoyed deploying it in different ways. One of the key themes of this study is the emergence of the *olfactif,* the cultivated individual with a refined sense of smell, very evident in the poetry and prose of the poet and critic Algernon Charles Swinburne, and emulated by aesthetic successors like Walter Pater, Edmund Gosse, John Addington Symonds, Lafcadio Hearn, Wilde, and Symons. Previously a heightened sense of smell might be attributed to class and gentility—witness Elizabeth Gaskell's Lady Ludlow declaring that 'nothing showed birth like a keen susceptibility of smell'—or more conventionally to feminine sensitivity, since women have traditionally been regarded as more olfactorily responsive.[11] But after 1860 this heightened sense bears witness to the innately superior receptivity of the aesthete. He usurps the place of those ancient female followers of Dionysus who, in the words of Walter Pater, 'experience most directly the influence of things which touch thought through the senses' (*GS*, p. 57).

As this study demonstrates, leading male aesthetic writers like Swinburne, Pater, Symonds, Gosse, Wilde, and Symons pride themselves on their sensitivity to fragrance and present themselves as *olfactifs,* a pose also adopted by decadent minor poets like Mark André Raffalovich and Theodore Wratislaw. Awareness of scent and perfume pervades their writing in many different ways, signifying diverse though often interrelated things such as style, atmosphere, influence, sexuality, sensibility, spirituality, refinement, individuality, and the aura of personality, dandyism, modernity, and memory. Conversely, cultural suspicion of 'effete' or 'effeminate' male aesthetes, coupled with popular prejudice against men who use scent, is commonly seen in contemporary reviews along with the critical detection and disapproval of inappropriately 'perfumed style'.

---

[10] Osbert Sitwell, 'Ada Leverson', in *Noble Essences or Courteous Revelations: An Autobiography* (London: Macmillan, 1950), p. 137.

[11] Elizabeth Gaskell, 'My Lady Ludlow', in *My Lady Ludlow and Other Stories,* ed. Edgar Wright (Oxford: Oxford University Press, 1989), p. 38. Rachel Herz in *The Scent of Desire: Discovering Our Enigmatic Sense of Smell* (New York and London: Harper Perennial, 2008), p. 130, suggests that a woman's sense of smell is better than a man's but only during that part of her cycle when conception is possible. Avery Gilbert in *What the Nose Knows: The Science of Smell in Everyday Life* (New York: Crown Publishers, 2008) acknowledges female superiority in smell ability but suggests that this 'is partly due to women having higher verbal fluency' (p. 53), meaning that they can describe smells better than men.

Nonetheless, I make numerous references to female writers throughout my first chapter with special attention paid to Gaskell. The poet A. Mary F. Robinson (Mary Robinson) features in Chapter 5. The female aesthetes Katharine Bradley and Edith Cooper, the aunt and niece who wrote poetry and drama under the name Michael Field, get a weighty chapter of their own, which draws substantially on archival material taken from their manuscript diaries. For both these women perfume was a source of constant pleasure, as it was not for Virginia Woolf, who appears in a final chapter devoted to the 'drydown' of scented Victorian literature in the early twentieth century. Here Woolf's dislike of perfume is contrasted with the enthusiasm shown for it by Katherine Mansfield and Ottoline Morrell, and her near male contemporary, the novelist Compton Mackenzie, who was far more influenced by the literature and culture of the *fin de siècle*.

Influence is a preoccupation of this study, not least because, in addition to their familiarity with each other's work, many of the aesthetic writers named knew each other personally, or had at least corresponded. Swinburne, Pater, and Symonds knew each other through their connections with Oxford, and all three were friends with Gosse. Symonds's ill-health, which took him to Switzerland in 1880, meant that he had fewer social opportunities, but he adored Mary Robinson, a favourite correspondent of his, and exchanged letters with Swinburne, Wilde, and Symons. A voracious reader, he read (and occasionally reviewed) work by them and by his other aesthetic peers. Pater spent time in Swinburne's company during the early 1870s and was subsequently friends with Wilde, Robinson, Raffalovich, and Bradley and Cooper. Bradley and Cooper also had significant friendships with Wilde and Symons and later with Raffalovich. Gosse, a key figure in London literary circles, was known to all of these, as was Wilde, who may not have met Symonds in person, but had met just about everyone else including the young poet Theodore Wratislaw. Symons knew everyone, with the exception of Lafcadio Hearn, something of an outsider in that he left England for America in 1869, never to return. But even Hearn, although he never met any of his fellow aesthetes, had certainly read Swinburne, Pater, Symonds, and Gosse, and knew of Wilde as a promulgator of aestheticism.

My interest in tracing patterns of literary influence, apparent in my earlier monographs *The Female Sublime from Milton to Swinburne: Bearing Blindness* (2001) and *Second Sight: The Visionary Imagination in Late Victorian Literature* (2008), has proved particularly relevant, since my exploration of smell-memory and perfume nostalgia has revealed that many texts about scent and memory reference earlier texts on the same subject.[12] Perfume's connection with imaginative influence, memory, and personal identity is central to this book, so special attention is given to way literary texts figuratively reinforce these links, describing processes of writing and composition in recurrent metaphoric images of flowers, air, atmosphere, breath, inhalation, and inspiration. Whether approving or otherwise, those instances where

---

[12] Catherine Maxwell, *The Female Sublime from Milton to Swinburne: Bearing Blindness* (Manchester: Manchester University Press, 2001); *Second Sight: The Visionary Imagination in Late Victorian Literature* (Manchester: Manchester University Press, 2008).

the style or atmosphere of aesthetic or other literary texts is characterized as 'scented' or 'perfumed', are also of particular interest. While hostile critics employ such language and images pejoratively, aesthetic writers themselves, encouraged by the example of predecessors like Shelley, use them to signal what they find admirable in a writer.

It is often asserted—without much foundation—that smell is an elusive sense and that smells are hard to describe because we possess a limited olfactory vocabulary. Debunking this claim as 'pretty weak', the smell scientist Avery Gilbert asserts, 'Tar, fish, grapefruit—every smelly thing in the world is a potential adjective.'[13] (Actually there is also a perfectly serviceable technical vocabulary to describe scents, but most people are simply not familiar with terms like 'camphoraceous', 'butyric', 'aldehydic', 'indolic', 'ozonic', 'phenolic', and 'vanillic'.) However, this supposed deficiency of language does not seem to have deterred nineteenth-century writers any more than it does the many modern perfume consumers who log on to internet perfume sites like Fragrantica or Basenotes to contribute their impressions of the perfumes they sample or who formalize these responses at greater length in regular personal blogs. Victorian writers were influenced by each other and earlier writers, just as modern bloggers and reviewers are undoubtedly influenced by Luca Turin and Tania Sanchez's milestone book *Perfumes: The A–Z Guide* (2008, 2009), which pioneered a witty, eloquent, and evocatively impressionistic way of writing about perfume. In recent years the volume of writing on perfume has gone a long way to disproving William Ian Miller's 1997 claim that 'the olfactory and the gustatory reduce us to saying little more than yum or yuck'.[14] Arguably, far from finding a language for odour inaccessible or hard to grasp, the literate perfumista or perfume aficionado experiences perfumes as partially mediated through the scented veil of language she inherits from her perfume guides or mentors, or perhaps from literature in general. In its turn, *Perfumes: The A–Z Guide* may itself owe something to Victorian aesthetic 'impressionistic' prose; Sanchez declares in her introduction that 'The arts appeal in various ways to our various senses, and if you want to think long and hard about such things, I recommend reading Walter Pater.'[15]

The books on perfumery by Piesse and Rimmel frequently cite literary texts, especially poetry—Shakespeare and Milton are favourite sources—to gloss particular scents, or to introduce different topics, or to serve as chapter epigraphs. This is a practice still found, if somewhat more sporadically, in modern books on perfume or on smell, suggesting that literature is still often seen as perfume's ally. For example, select literary quotation appears scattered throughout Roy Genders's *A History of Scent* (1972) and David G. Williams's *Perfumes of Yesterday* (2004), while even a recent popular guide, *The Perfume Bible* (2014), cites Arthur Symons's 'Memory' ('As a perfume doth remain | In the folds where it hath lain').[16] The citation of literary texts is also a feature of more meditative reflections like *Essence*

---

[13] Gilbert, *What the Nose Knows*, pp. 126–7.
[14] William Ian Miller, *The Anatomy of Disgust* (Cambridge, MA: Harvard University Press, 1997), p. 67.
[15] Luca Turin and Tania Sanchez, *Perfumes: The A–Z Guide* (London: Profile Books, 2009), p. 8.
[16] Roy Genders, *A History of Scent* (London: Hamish Hamilton, 1972); David G. Williams, *Perfumes of Yesterday* (Port Washington, NY, and Weymouth: Micelle Press, 2004); Josephine Fairley and Lorna

and Alchemy: A Natural History of Perfume (2001) and *Fragrant: The Secret Life of Scent* (2014), both by the natural perfumer Mandy Aftel.[17] As well as citing literary sources, Aftel appends to *Essence and Alchemy* an extensive bibliography of books on smell, scent, and perfume.

Reading about perfume, whether this involves literary or specialist sources, is thus intrinsically bound up with its appreciation, as indeed is writing. As the perfumer Karen Gilbert instructs, 'When "training your nose," write down detailed notes on everything you smell and how you perceive it personally.'[18] New perfume lovers and apprentice perfumers are regularly encouraged to fix the identity of scents and perfumes in their memories through mental and imagistic associations recorded in written notes. Jean-Claude Ellena, the in-house perfumer for Hermès, recommends notebooks 'for recording performance (intensity, long-lastingness, volatility, stability) and sensory qualities (odors that are bright, dark, dense, thin, light, heavy, soft, harsh, warm, gentle, etc.)'.[19] Avery Gilbert notes that 'verbal skills boost performance on tests of odor memory and odor identification', while *The Perfume Bible* emphasizes the importance of 'putting words to aromas', citing 'our scientist friend, Professor George Dodd', founder of the Olfaction Research Group at Warwick University, who explains that, in linking words with smells, '"You actually strengthen the neural pathways in the brain itself and, in turn, that helps you to become better at smelling things."'[20]

Another more extensive kind of writing about perfume is the modern perfume memoir such as Denyse Beaulieu's *The Perfume Lover* (2012), Alyssa Harad's *Coming to My Senses* (2012), and Jo Malone's *My Story* (2016), in which the subject details not only her love of perfume but also traces the emergence of that love through a personal history irradiated by key encounters with or memories of scent.[21] Shorter individual reminiscences about smell and scent frequently appear in internet blogs—while Jean-Claude Ellena provides a personal account from the rather more specialized viewpoint of a perfumer in his *The Diary of a Nose: A Year in the Life of a Parfumeur* (2012).[22] Again such writing has progenitors in literary

McKay, *The Perfume Bible* (London: Kyle Books, 2014), p. 69. For a discussion of Symons's 'Memory', see Chapter 7 in this book.

[17] Mandy Aftel, *Essence and Alchemy: A Natural History of Perfume* (New York: North Point Press, 2001); *Fragrant: The Secret Life of Scent* (New York: Riverhead Books, 2014).

[18] Karen Gilbert, *Perfume: The Art and Craft of Fragrance* (London and New York: Cico Books, 2013), p. 59.

[19] Jean-Claude Ellena, *Perfume: The Alchemy of Scent*, tr. John Crisp (New York: Arcade Publishing, 2011), p. 41.

[20] Gilbert, *What the Nose Knows*, p. 53; Fairley and McKay, *The Perfume Bible*, p. 7.

[21] Denyse Beaulieu, *The Perfume Lover: A Personal History of Scent* (London: HarperCollins, 2012); Alyssa Harad, *Coming to My Senses: A Story of Perfume, Pleasure, and an Unlikely Bride* (New York: Viking, 2012); and Jo Malone, *My Story* (London and New York: Simon and Schuster, 2016). A poignant counter-example is Bonnie Blodgett's *Remembering Smell* (Boston, MA, and New York: Houghton Mifflin Harcourt, 2010) in which, the writer, a keen gardener and cook, mourns her sense of smell when, following a severe cold, she experienced first phantosmia (phantom malodour), followed by anosmia (total loss of smell).

[22] A good example of such reminiscence is regularly supplied by 'Lemon Wedge' writing for 'Aroma Folio', the blog of the specialist London perfumery store Les Senteurs. See http://www.lessenteurs. wordpress.com. See also Jean-Claude Ellena, *The Diary of a Nose: A Year in the Life of a Parfumeur*, tr. Adriana Hunter (London: Particular Books, 2012).

texts—not just the frequently cited example of Marcel Proust's madeleine in the opening volume of his *Remembrance of Things Past* (1913), but earlier works such as Wilde's *The Picture of Dorian Gray* (1890, 1891), in which Dorian's life is vividly punctuated by an olfactory accompaniment, Pater's quasi-autobiographical portrait 'The Child in the House' (1878), and, even earlier, 'The History of a Child' (1836), another semi-fictional memoir by the Romantic poet Letitia Elizabeth Landon, known as 'L.E.L.'.[23] I provide further examples in two early twentieth-novels by Compton Mackenzie that, looking back to the late Victorian era, present significant moments in the lives of his protagonists intimately associated with smell and scent. Borrowing a term coined by the perfumer writer and historian David Pybus, we might call such writers 'aromancers', in that they narrate for us often entrancing stories or romances about scent and smell that revive or conjure up the past.[24]

This study concentrates on those who think of themselves as *olfactifs*, but most perfumers or expert 'noses' do not regard themselves as innately olfactorily gifted, remarking that development of one's sense of smell is a matter of practice and, in the case of an apprentice perfumer, rigorous daily training to recognize and evaluate the hundreds of naturals and synthetics from which perfumes are composed. Yet, although they start with much the same abilities as everyone else, trained perfumers are capable of olfactory feats that seem astonishing to most ordinary people. Jean-Claude Ellena comments: 'As an apprentice I learned not only to distinguish between the odor of a jasmine concrete from Egypt, Italy, or Grasse in France, but to identify what kind of vaporator had been used to produce the absolute: one made of copper, tin, stainless steel, or glass.'[25] But even ordinary individuals, assuming that they have normal olfactory function, should find that the more focused they are on smelling things, the better at it they become. While human olfactory ability is considerably less impressive than that of animals, a little application can yield startling results, as revealed in the engaging experiments of the Nobel Prize-winning physicist Richard P. Feynman, who found he could identify by smell quite easily which book from a bookcase had been most recently handled, much to the incredulity of his friends.[26] Then there are the findings of Charles Foster who, in his extraordinary book *Being a Beast* (2016), describes a July spent in rural Wales with his young son, attempting to inhabit the sensory world of the badger:

> We bustled and grunted and elbowed and pushed and pressed our noses into the ground. And even *we* smelt something: the citrusy piss of the voles in their runs within the grass; the distant marine tang of a slug trail, like a winter rock pool; the crushed

[23] Walter Pater, 'The Child in the House' (1878), originally collected in *MS* (1895). Text used throughout is *IP*, pp. 83–99; L.E.L [Letitia Landon], 'The History of a Child', in *Traits and Trials of Early Life* (London: H. Colburn, 1836), pp. 281–312, and in *Letitia Elizabeth Landon: Selected Writings*, ed. Jerome McGann and Daniel Riess (Peterborough, ON: Broadview Press), pp. 147–59.
[24] David Pybus, ed., *Transports of Delight: An Aromatic Journey in Verse from East to West on the Wings of Perfume* (Folkestone: Global Oriental Ltd, 2007), p. ix.
[25] Ellena, *Perfume: The Alchemy of Scent*, p. 15.
[26] Richard P. Feynman, 'Testing Bloodhounds', in *Surely You're Joking, Mr Feynman! Adventures of a Curious Character as Told to Ralph Leighton*, ed. Edward Hutchings (New York: W. W. Norton & Co., 1985), pp. 104–6.

laurel of a frog; the dustiness of a toad; the sharp musk of a weasel; the blunter musk of an otter; and the fox, whose smell is red to the least synaesthetic man alive.[27]

Smell, because it seems the least necessary of our senses, is vastly underused by many people, with odour often barely noticed. Yet it is also commonplace to hear complaints about the lack of smell in modern 'sanitized' daily life, complaints that seem groundless to those trying to resurrect what Helen Keller called 'the fallen angel' of our senses, and indeed Ellena asserts, 'I know of nothing that has no smell.'[28] While the principal writers examined in this study may not approach the level of olfactory acuity reached by a perfumer, it is clear that fragrance plays a vital role in their imaginative lives, and once alerted to this, readers can hardly fail to notice the numerous allusions to scent in aesthetic and decadent writing. Additionally, exploring a text's all too often unacknowledged or hidden links with the sense of smell offers a different, more intimate contact with its author and the particularity of his or her creative imagination.

Notions of 'the body' and 'embodiment' have been increasingly popular in literary-critical studies over the last twenty years, but discussion of these topics has often been abstract, drawing on a predominantly psychoanalytic and theoretical vocabulary with surprisingly little reference to actual sensory and sensuous experience. More recently there has been greater direct interest in the senses, provoked by landmark cultural-historical studies like Alain Corbin's *The Foul and the Fragrant* (1986) and *Aroma: The Cultural History of Smell* by Constance Classen, David Howes, and Anthony Synnott (1994).[29] However, most literary studies that have made reference to the senses in the nineteenth century have tended to concentrate on sight, hearing, or, more recently, touch.[30] William Cohen's *Embodied: Victorian Literature and the Senses* (2009), which explores 'the interior, subjective experience of self and sensation', is a case in point, often privileging touch, but commenting relatively little on smell and thus, albeit unintentionally, confirming its lowly position in the traditional hierarchy of the senses.[31]

---

[27] Charles Foster, *Being a Beast* (London: Profile Books Ltd, 2016), p. 48.

[28] Helen Keller, 'Smell, the Fallen Angel', in *The World I Live In* (New York: The Century Co., 1908), p. 64; Ellena, *Perfume: The Alchemy of Scent*, p. 14.

[29] Alain Corbin's *The Foul and the Fragrant*, first published in French as *Le Miasme et la jonquille: l'odorat et l'imaginaire social, XVIII–XIXe siècles* (1982), has had a number of changes in subtitle since it first appeared in English translation, these being *The Sense of Smell and Social Image in Modern France* (Leamington Spa: Berg, 1986), *Odour and the French Social Imagination* (London: Picador, 1994), and *Odour and the Social Imagination* (London and Basingstoke: Papermac, 1996), this last being the edition I use throughout. See also Constance Classen, David Howes, and Anthony Synnott, *Aroma: The Cultural History of Smell* (New York: Routledge, 1994).

[30] See, as representative recent examples, for sight, Kate Flint, *The Victorians and the Visual Imagination* (Cambridge and New York: Cambridge University Press, 2000), Luisa Calè and Patrizia di Bello, eds., *Illustrations, Optics and Objects in Nineteenth-Century Literary and Visual Cultures* (London and Basingstoke: Palgrave Macmillan 2010); for hearing, John M. Picker, *Victorian Soundscapes* (Oxford: Oxford University Press, 2003); for touch, Lene Østermark-Johansen, *Walter Pater and the Language of Sculpture* (Farnham and Burlington, VT: Ashgate, 2011), and Heather Tilley's recent guest-edited issue *The Victorian Tactile Imagination* for the internet journal *19: Interdisciplinary Studies in the Long Nineteenth Century* 19 (2014), freely accessible at http://www.19.bbk.ac.uk.

[31] William Cohen, *Embodied: Victorian Literature and the Senses* (Minneapolis, MN: University of Minnesota Press, 2009), p. 16.

Of those few books that deal with smell and literature, Hans Rindisbacher's seminal study *The Smell of Books: A Cultural-Historical Study of Olfactory Perception in Literature* (1992) includes a brief discussion of Wilde's *Dorian Gray* but is otherwise preoccupied with continental writers like Leo Tolstoy, Fyodor Dostoyevsky, J. K. Huysmans, and Rainer Maria Rilke.[32] Janice Carlisle's *Common Scents: Comparative Encounters in High-Victorian Culture* (2004), to date the only book devoted to smell in Victorian literature, deals specifically with prose fiction of the 1860s, with class and gender its major focus.[33] Carlisle deftly shows how the social class of fictional characters is indicated by their different relations to odour, and as her title suggests, she is particularly interested in everyday odours like those of food and lower middle-class trades. Although she discusses how polite middle- and upper-class femininity is often signalled by natural flower fragrance, there is little reference to perfumery in her study. While nineteenth-century French literature has long been noted for its many references to perfume, as observed by Richard Stamelman in his magisterial, beautifully illustrated monograph *Perfume: Joy, Obsession, Scandal, Sin* (2006), up till now there has been no sustained attempt to examine scent in Victorian literature.[34] The art historian Christina Bradstreet has published a suggestive article on smell and perfume in Victorian painting and another on an early twentieth-century 'perfume concert', and there is some valuable research on perfume in periods predating the nineteenth century—in particular the Renaissance and eighteenth century—by academics like Holly Dugan, Clare Brant, and William Tullett, but even here the emphasis is predominantly historical rather than literary.[35]

The relatively modest amount of research that touches on olfaction in the nineteenth century has mostly dealt with 'bad smells', privileging odour associated with labour, industry, urban development, inadequate hygiene, and poverty, something that is also a feature of studies dealing with earlier historical periods.[36] There seems to be a gleeful delight in portraying periods earlier than our own as innately

---

[32] Hans J. Rindisbacher, *The Smell of Books: A Cultural-Historical Study of Olfactory Perception in Literature* (Ann Arbor, MI: University of Michigan Press, 1992).

[33] Janice Carlisle, *Common Scents: Comparative Encounters in High-Victorian Culture* (New York: Oxford University Press, 2004).

[34] Richard Stamelman, *Perfume: Joy, Obsession, Scandal, Sin* (New York: Rizzoli, 2006).

[35] Christina Bradstreet, '"Wicked with Roses": Floral Femininity and the Erotics of Scent', *Nineteenth-Century Art Worldwide* 6 (2007), freely accessible online at http://www.19thc-artworld-wide.org, and 'A Trip to Japan in Sixteen Minutes: Sadakichi Hartmann's Perfume Concerts', in *Art, History and the Senses: 1830 to the Present*, ed. Patrizia di Bello and Gabriel Koureas (Farnham and Burlington, VT: Ashgate, 2010), pp. 51–64; Holly Dugan, *The Ephemeral History of Perfume: Scent and Sense in Early Modern England* (Baltimore, MD: Johns Hopkins University Press, 2011); Clare Brant, 'Fume and Perfume: Some Eighteenth-Century Uses of Smell', *Journal of British Studies* 43 (2004), 444–63; William Tullett, 'The Macaroni's "Ambrosial Essences": Perfume, Identity and Public Space in Nineteenth-Century England', *Journal for Eighteenth-Century Studies* 38 (2015), 163–80.

[36] See, for example, Stephen Halliday, *The Great Stink of London: Sir Joseph Bazalgette and the Cleansing of the Victorian Metropolis* (Stroud: Sutton, 1999) and *The Great Filth: The War against Disease in Victorian London* (Stroud: Sutton, 2007); William A. Cohen and Ryan Johnson, eds., *Filth: Dirt, Disgust and Modern Life* (Minneapolis, MN: University of Minnesota Press, 2005); Victoria Kelley, *Soap and Water: Cleanliness, Dirt and the Working Classes in Victorian and Edwardian Britain* (London: I. B. Tauris, 2010); Lee Jackson, *Dirty Old London: The Victorian Fight against Filth* (New Haven, CT: Yale University Press, 2014); Sabine Schülting, *Dirt in Victorian Literature and*

malodorous, a trait exploited by the popular children's series 'Smelly Old History' by Mary Dobson, which includes such titles as *Medieval Muck*, *Tudor Odours*, *Reeking Royals*, and *Victorian Vapours*.[37] Countering such a trend, the early modern historian Mark Jenner has argued that our assumptions about things like the street cleanliness of bygone eras are often mistaken, and may well misrepresent earlier standards of hygiene.[38] The social historian Ruth Goodman, who has made several experimental attempts at 'living in the past', also notes the tendency of 'modern writers and historians' to assume that 'people were dreadfully malodorous in the past, before modern washing with water', adding, 'My own experience makes me sceptical about their claims.'[39] This is not to deny that many aspects of, say, urban life in 1560 or 1860 would be shockingly unacceptable to modern olfactory sensibilities, although time travellers from the past might well be appalled by modern ambient odours to which we are inured, like traffic fumes and chemical smells. Moreover, the inclination to represent past eras as noisome and our own time as inoffensively odorous and thus superior, seems part of that larger tendency observed by the medical historian Jonathan Reinarz to use smell to mark out one group from another, 'Christian from the heathen, [...] blacks from whites, women from men, virgins from harlots, artisans from aristocracy', with the privileged or socially empowered denigrating as rank and foul-smelling those deemed lesser beings.[40]

Although this study notes the sometimes less than fragrant components that help make up a pleasing scent or perfume, its focus on pleasurable odours means that it generally steers clear of discussing stinks, stenches, and the less savoury smells of the Victorian era. Moreover, although it mentions various scientific and para-scientific writers such as George Wilson, Charles H. Piesse, Grant Allen, Gustav Jäger, and Havelock Ellis, it is not intended to be a review of nineteenth-century theories of olfaction as these have almost negligible impact on the way aesthetic authors—predominantly influenced by literary texts—think and write about scent and perfume.[41] Its emphasis falls more on the development of perfume tastes and trends. Like all objects connected with taste, perfume is subject to fashion and evolution, as vividly demonstrated by Lizzie Ostrom in her *Perfume: A Century of Scents* (2015), which examines the period 1900–99.[42] Victorian fragrance is no

Culture (London: Routledge, 2016). See also Emily Cockaigne, *Hubbub: Filth, Noise and Stench in England, 1600–1770* (New Haven, CT, and London: Yale University Press, 2007).

[37] Mary Dobson, *Medieval Muck* (Oxford: Oxford University Press, 1997), *Tudor Odours* (1997), *Reeking Royals* (1998), and *Victorian Vapours* (1997).

[38] Mark Jenner, 'Civilization and Deodorization? Smell in Early Modern English Culture', in *Civil Histories: Essays Presented to Sir Keith Thomas*, ed. Peter Burke, Brian A. Harrison, and Paul Slack (Oxford: Oxford University Press, 2000), pp. 127–44; 131–2.

[39] Ruth Goodman, *How to be a Victorian: A Dawn-to-Dusk Guide to Everyday Life* (London: Viking, 2013), p. 15. See also her *How to be a Tudor: A Dawn-to-Dusk Guide to Everyday Life* (London: Viking, 2015).

[40] Jonathan Reinarz, *Past Scents: Historical Perspectives on Smell* (Urbana, Chicago, and Springfield, IL: University of Illinois Press, 2014), p. 18.

[41] Rowan Boyson's 'Wordsworth's Anosmia', *La Questione Romantica* 3.2 (2014), 63–80, contains some useful reference to late eighteenth-century and early nineteenth-century scientific works on smell (pp. 65–7).

[42] Lizzie Ostrom, *Perfume: A Century of Scents* (London: Hutchinson, 2015).

exception and this broadly chronological study takes note of the way shifting social trends and attitudes dictated who wore what and when. As a luxury product often seen to connote elite values, perfume is perhaps especially susceptible to the process of debasement, with formerly esteemed fragrances falling from grace if they are perceived as becoming too popular or common, a process that speeds up towards the end of the nineteenth century, when, because of increased production and new cheaper aroma chemicals, perfume became more affordable to those on lower incomes. Moreover, while the twentieth century is predominantly seen as the period when new synthetics, technical innovation, and sophisticated advertising raise perfume to new heights, ideas about scent and perfume expressed in Victorian literary texts can be seen to anticipate major perfume trends and perfume stories post-1900.

This book opens with 'Top Notes: Victorian Perfume Contexts', a chapter that, after a brief discussion of Eugene Rimmel and Septimus Piesse, two major manufacturers and promoters of perfume, provides an overview of fragrance use for both men and women and debunks some popular myths and assumptions. It subsequently explores attitudes towards perfume in nineteenth-century literary culture, noting the negative coverage of perfume use in early and mid-Victorian fiction with special reference to the figure of the scented dandy, a figure who makes a return at the *fin de siècle*. In contrast, as shown in the second part of this chapter, Victorian poetry is more positive, reflecting the influential perfumed legacy of Romanticism and, in particular, Shelley, a key precursor for many aesthetic and decadent writers. An illustrative reading of Edmund Gosse's sonnet 'Perfume' shows how its language is saturated with echoes from both Shelley and Keats. After a brief discussion of the 'hothouse' atmosphere of aestheticism, decadence, and the *fin de siècle*, the chapter concludes with reference to the aggressive reaction of male modernists, and in particular, T. S. Eliot, to a Romantic and Victorian culture seen as decadent, feminine, and perfumed. In exploring Eliot's response, I indicate his unease with perfume while showing how his writing reveals its own fragrant memories of Shelley.

'Perfumed Melodies, Violet Memories' is one of two chapters that focus on the scent of single flower, here the violet. Although often associated with the modest Victorian maiden, the violet has an alternative literary genealogy that links its scent not just to memory and death but also specifically to music and poetry. After tracking its influential literary origins in Shakespeare and Bacon, I show how violet scent encrypts memories of Shelley and Keats that haunt the Victorian imagination. I trace that memorial scent as it permeates various later Victorian lyrics to be finally exhaled in a sonnet of 1901 by Katharine Bradley.

Many of the following chapters in this book fall into two parts, in that I pair writers who illustrate a particular trend or tendency in the way they write about perfume. Chapter 3, 'Les Fleurs du Mâle', is a study of the founding figures of British aestheticism, the poet Algernon Charles Swinburne and the Oxford don and essayist Walter Pater, and discusses how they embraced the identity of the aesthetic *olfactif*, the cultivation of scent sensitivity, and the notion of the scented ambience or perfumed atmosphere produced by individual writers and literary or cultural schools, with this reflected in their influential critical prose. Swinburne's notorious collection *Poems and Ballads* (1866) apparently revels in heady exotic perfumes, influenced by Baudelaire's *Les Fleurs du mal* (1857), yet already evinces some ambivalence about those heavy scents; his own taste for light airy florals and dislike of animalic musk clearly emerges in his subsequent poetry and prose as he distances himself from Baudelaire. While such preference looks as if it might conform to conservative mid-Victorian taste, Swinburne's own associations with his favoured scents are anything but conventional. Walter Pater, another lover of delicate floral fragrance, refines Swinburne's perception of the 'scent' of literature into a subtler critical language. I examine Pater's 'flair', his 'distinctive olfactory discernment', in his personal tastes and his adoption of the role of *flaireur* both in his creative writing and his appreciation of other authors. Pater's influential notion of the 'scented essence' of a literary work would be taken up by admirers like Wilde and Symons, while his own writing was noted by his readers and critics for its unmistakable perfume.

The smell of the human body is something that speaks intimately to the very nature of perfume, which references and alludes to corporeal odours as much as it camouflages them. 'Scent, the Body, and the Cosmopolitan *Flaireur*' focuses on the cosmopolitan *flaireur*, the sophisticated citizen of the world who relishes the fragrance of travel, represented by the historian and classicist John Addington Symonds and the journalist and critic Lafcadio Hearn, his junior by ten years. Appreciators respectively of male and female body scents, both Symonds and Hearn write enthusiastically about the perfumes of the places they visit and the bodies they encounter there, but they are also keen consumers of the literature of other lands, both past and present, savoured by them for its release of distinctive male and female fragrances.

'Carnal Flowers, Charnel Flowers', serves as an entr'acte and focuses again on a single flower scent, this time one very much associated with the stronger fragrance of decadence. Contrasting with the more delicate scent of the violet explored in Chapter 2 is the powerful perfume of the tuberose, an exotic hothouse flower. Starting with Shelley, I track its heady fragrance through a range of texts to concentrate on three poems by late Victorian minor poets—Mark André Raffalovich, Mary Robinson, and Theodore Wratislaw—and show how the scent of the tuberose is bound up with dangerous or voluptuous pleasures, with love, eroticism, criminality, and death.

'Michael Field's Fragrant Imagination' establishes the importance of perfume to the female aesthetes Katharine Bradley and Edith Cooper and shows how it plays a significant role both in the poetry produced by Bradley and in entries in the women's shared diary, especially those written by Cooper. Often exchanged in the form of gifts and scented flowers, perfume is strongly associated by both women with love but also with poetic creativity, as in Bradley's verse, which celebrates her tender amatory feelings for Cooper but also her deep affection for the artist Charles Ricketts. The chapter concludes with a reading of one of Bradley's most accomplished poems, which can be regarded as a poetic scented signature, expressing the essence of Michael Field.

'Dandies and Decadents' examines the decadent *olfactif* as represented by Oscar Wilde and the poet and critic Arthur Symons who, unlike various other men discussed in this book, enjoyed wearing perfume and understood how it helped shape their identities as dandies and sophisticated men about town. Both allude to perfumes that contain synthetic ingredients. Wilde's notions of perfume as an accompaniment to the decadent scented lifestyle and a sign of decadent sexual identity are explored in *Dorian Gray* and in *Teleny* (1893), an anonymously authored novel often associated with him. Such forms of decadent expression are rudely interrupted by his imprisonment in 1895, but the idea of perfume abides with him during his prison years as an important ideal and consolation. In Symons's poetry and prose strong or recognizable perfumes of the period are evoked for scrutiny or contemplation or permeate the memory, calling attention to themselves as markers of decadent modernity. For Symons, perfume identified with memory does not fade, an idea borne out by his critical appreciation of the perfume of particular literary texts, lyric poetry especially, and celebrated in his own verse.

All perfumes have an evolutionary trajectory, with the final stage of application known as the 'drydown', when the base notes (the heavier molecules which are slower to take flight) come into their own. In the last phases of the drydown, the perfume becomes a ghost of itself. Sillage, a French word applied to the wake left by a ship, is the name perfumers give to the scent trail that a perfume wearer leaves behind in the air. In my concluding chapter, 'Victorian Drydown and Sillage', I consider the reception of the Victorian perfumed legacy by examining two contrasting early twentieth-century literary responses to perfume and decadence by Virginia Woolf and Compton Mackenzie. Close examination of Woolf's rejection of Victorianism, part of a modernist backlash also apparent in writers like T. S. Eliot and Ezra Pound, shows that she had little personal contact with the literary and artistic culture of decadence. Her puritanism and distrust of perfume also emerges in diary entries recording her deep disapproval of women who wear it. Although she never became a perfume lover, Woolf's novel *Flush* (1933) allows her a rapprochement with Victorian literature and smell, and a subsequent memoir, 'Sketch of the Past', shows her gradually becoming more accommodating of her sensory self. In contrast with Woolf, Compton Mackenzie, critic, essayist, and author of over forty novels, had a much more relaxed and tolerant attitude towards Victorianism, decadence, perfume, and smell, and a strong personal attachment to the literature of the *fin de siècle*. Counterpointing Woolf's often aggressive and puritanical modernism, Mackenzie's more liberal response to the perfume of aestheticism, decadence, and the *fin de siècle* is expressed in his autobiography, various essays, and his two most important early novels *Carnival* (1912) and *Sinister Street* (1913–14). Their lives punctuated by scent and smell, Mackenzie's protagonists Jenny Pearl and Michael Fane reveal his skill as an aromancer, adept at using smell memories and impressions, as well as the social and cultural contexts of perfume, to underscore the key moments and experiences in an individual's life.

Modern perfume lovers are also attuned to the way scent acts as an accompaniment to their lives, and the current huge increase of interest in buying, collecting, and reading about perfume makes this a pertinent moment for this book. Ever larger numbers of people consume blogs like Perfume Shrine, Persolaise, Bois de Jasmin, Grain de Musc, The Candy Perfume Boy, The Scented Salamander, Now Smell This, Perfume Smellin' Things, and Perfume Posse (to name some of the most popular), and attend perfume events to learn more about perfume ingredients and the huge range of contemporary perfumes. This in turn has led to increased interest in vintage and historical perfumes, seen in books like Lizzie Ostrom's *Perfume: A Century of Scents* and Barbara Herman's *Scent and Subversion: Decoding a Century of Provocative Perfume* (2013).[43] For those curious to smell the perfumed past, 'vintage sessions', lectures, and study days afford the opportunity to smell rare perfumes, perfume recreations, and now hard-to-access ingredients like musk, civet, and ambergris, as do the conferences, seminars, and private consultations at the Osmothèque, the world's leading perfume museum at Versailles, which houses an unrivalled collection of vintage perfume, and fragrances painstakingly recreated according to the original formulae.[44] Guerlain's flagship store on the Champs-Élysées also offers the chance to smell past masterpieces as recreated by its head perfumer Thierry Wasser and his assistant Frédéric Sacone. It is therefore now possible to experience perfumes made before 1900.

Calling perfume 'the unseen, unforgettable fashion accessory', Coco Chanel famously wrote that it 'heralds your arrival and prolongs your departure'.[45] I hope to alert my reader to that prolonged departure and to argue that, although it is perhaps a little fainter, there is no reason why we cannot catch and savour the still perceptible traces of the late Victorian sillage.

[43] Barbara Herman, *Scent and Subversion: Decoding a Century of Provocative Perfume* (Guildford, CT: Lyons Press, 2013).

[44] For example, the V&A study day 'Remembrance of Perfumes Past', 19 March 2016, which, in addition to featuring talks by a range of speakers on different periods from the Renaissance to the twentieth century, included illustrative perfume samples and recreations made by the historical perfumer Stephen Nelson.

[45] Coco Chanel, quoted in Priscilla Tucker, 'Scented with Success', *New York Herald Tribune* (18 October 1964), section 2, p. 4.

1

Top Notes
Victorian Perfume Contexts

BRITANNIA'S SMELLING BOTTLE

Hell, Heaven, and the French Connection

The word 'smell' tends to suggest bad rather than good odours. *Chambers Dictionary* glosses the noun as 'a pleasant or (often) unpleasant scent' and the intransitive verb as 'to have an odour (*esp* unpleasant)', and certainly to say someone 'smells' is never complimentary. A whiff of bad odour emanates from the etymology of the word, as 'smell', deriving from Middle English 'smel', is allied to Dutch and Low German words meaning 'to smoulder'.[1] In *Aromatics and the Soul* (1923), Dan McKenzie links 'smell' to 'a German dialect word for hell—*smela*—which in turn is itself akin to the Bohemian *smola*, resin or pitch', thus evoking the place associated with sulphurous fumes and the stench of corruption.[2] Such ominous associations remind us that before the identification of germs as a source of disease (something that did not occur till the 1870s), infection was widely understood to be communicated by 'miasmas', noxious smells associated with filth. However, as Constance Classen observes, with the evolution of microbial research, odours became 'inessential'.[3] She notes too how this downgrading was reinforced by 'the dominant philosophic trends of the Enlightenment', remarking that 'Condillac thought smell to be the sense that "contribute[s] least to the operations of the human mind." Kant dismissed smell as the most dispensable of the senses, one which did not even merit aesthetic cultivation.'[4] Such attitudes are echoed at the end of the nineteenth century by the social commentator Max Nordau, who in *Degeneration* (1892), his jeremiad on the late nineteenth century, wrote that:

> [T]he sense of smell has scarcely any further share in man's knowledge. He obtains his impressions of the external world no longer by the nose, but principally by the eye and ear. [...] a 'symphony of perfumes' in the Des Esseintes sense can, therefore, no longer give the impression of moral beauty, this being an idea which is elaborated by the

---

[1] See *Chambers Dictionary* (Edinburgh: Chambers Harrap Ltd, 1993), also *An Etymological Dictionary of the English Language*, ed. Rev. Walter W. Skeat, 4th edn (Oxford: Clarendon Press, 1910).

[2] Dan McKenzie, *Aromatics and the Soul* (London: William Heinemann, 1923), p. 73.

[3] Classen, Howes, and Synnott, *Aroma*, p. 89.

[4] Constance Classen, *The Color of Angels: Cosmology, Gender and the Aesthetic Imagination* (New York and London: Routledge, 1998), p. 58.

centres of conception. [...] Smellers among degenerates represent an atavism going back, not only to the primeval period of man, but infinitely more remote still, to an epoch anterior to man.[5]

Deprecated as one of the lower senses, smell, too often associated with a primitive corporeality, is a potential embarrassment to a hygienic, rational, modern-day society. Yet while smell as both sense and sensation can connote a rude or raw physicality at odds with civilized manners and values, it can also signal the transcending or sublimation of that rawness. Perfume, the antithesis of the low infernal smells of dirt and disease, lifts the mind and the spirit far above the mere baseline of existence. The studied appreciation of appealing natural fragrances, or their synthesis, imitation, and elevation in the artifice of perfume, suggests a leisured refinement and the luxury of contemplation. Smell may have originally have served to alert humans to beneficial or dangerous foods, substances, and places, and aided basic sexual attraction, but once survival was assured, it found new employment. From antiquity, religious rites have used scent in the form of offerings of flowers and incense—burnt spices, oils, and resins—'perfume' deriving from the Latin *per fumum*, meaning 'through smoke'. Those scented fumes aspiring heavenwards help elevate the mind, lifting one's consciousness to meditation on the divine.

Perfume has also served a number of practical purposes. Alain Corbin and others have explained how, from the seventeenth through to the mid-eighteenth century, when washing was thought (not without reason) to be dangerous, and disease to spread through miasma, perfume was believed not only to camouflage bad odours but also to purge corruption.[6] As Richard Stamelman writes: 'Fragrance was thought of as therapeutic; it strengthened the body and renewed the mind as well as disinfected the contaminated air.'[7] During the course of the nineteenth century, belief in the specifically medicinal powers of fragrance had diminished well before the advent of germ theory. However, many literary and other texts retain a preoccupation with 'bad', 'stale', or 'foul' air as opposed to 'good', 'health-giving' air, with scientific and hygiene specialists still anxious to point out the links between bad smells and dirt as the source of disease. In *Olfactics and the Physical Senses* (1887) Charles H. Piesse, son of the perfumer Septimus Piesse and a Fellow of the Institute of Chemistry, warned that 'Dirt and bad smells are inseparable, and where they are disease rapidly follows.'[8] At the start of the twentieth century, the health and hygiene campaigner Florence Stacpoole was of the same opinion and

[5] Max Nordau, *Degeneration*, tr. George L. Mosse (Lincoln, NE, and London: University of Nebraska Press, 1993), p. 503. The text is the 1895 English translation of the second German edition.

[6] Corbin, *The Foul and the Fragrant*, pp. 61–6.   [7] Stamelman, *Perfume*, p. 61.

[8] Charles H. Piesse, *Olfactics and the Physical Senses* (London: Piesse and Lubin, 1887), p. 117. Charles Henry Piesse (1846–1908) was an analytical chemist, a member of the Royal College of Surgeons, a Fellow of the Institute of Chemistry, and a member of the Chemical and Medical Societies of London. He was also a Public Analyst—that is, a scientist with a responsibility for ensuring public health with regard to food, water, and other environmental matters. He kept up the family interest in olfaction and perfume, updating the *Art of Perfumery* for its fifth edition of 1891. He was appointed Consul-General of Monaco by Queen Victoria in April 1889. In addition to *Olfactics*, he contributed

was even more graphic: 'When you perceive a bad smell something unclean, and perhaps something poisonous, touches you. It is a warning.'[9]

Some belief in the physically beneficial effects of fragrance was evidently still current. In the fourth edition of the *Art of Perfumery* (1879), Septimus Piesse had cited the advice of the Italian physiologist Paolo Mantegazza to cultivate herbs and odorous flowers '"in marshy districts and in places infected with animal emanations"'.[10] In his *Olfactics*, Charles H. Piesse postulated that the benefits of the purest air owed a debt to natural fragrance, and declared: 'The perfumes of nature we believe to be one of the many means of giving health and enjoyment. In what way they act on the system cannot be decided, but that they do act in some way beneficially is abundantly evident.'[11] He also observed 'that men engaged in the trade of manufacturing perfumes are apparently remarkably protected from any species of infectious disease', noting that the 'same phenomenon' had been observed of those working with coal tar.[12] Even today the therapeutic view of fragrance has not been wholly superseded. Belief in its healing power still informs modern aromatherapy, and some odours do have physical and mental benefits, as borne out by the many people suffering from colds or flu who inhale vaporized eucalyptus or camphor to ease nasal congestion. More generally, however, belief in the therapeutic power of fragrance has been absorbed into the widespread feeling that perfume, whether worn on the body or used to scent a room, subtly alters or enhances mood for the better and so contributes to pleasure.

Enjoyment and personal gratification have always been integral to the use of perfume, apart from its possible practical or religious application. In his *Physiological Aesthetics* (1877), Grant Allen proposed that an important precondition of 'the æsthetically beautiful' and 'Æsthetic Feelings' was their distance from 'life-serving function': while 'the fragrance of fruits and spices' very nearly achieved this, sweet floral odours 'are in almost every respect raised into the æsthetic class'.[13] To those of an aesthetic disposition, the cultivation of scented flowers and the wearing of perfume in the form of fragrant garlands, infused fabrics, or essences applied to the hair or skin, show the triumph of pleasure over necessity. Nature loses its urgent claim upon us as natural things are dissolved, dematerialized into essences that have no purpose but to please. That pleasure is complex; for perfume, an invisible presence, can evoke images not only of the natural substances from which it is derived but also a host of personal associations, emotions, and memories specific to the individual.

The modern notion of perfume's spiritual refinement and part transcendence of the material world finds a champion in Richard Le Gallienne, a *fin-de-siècle* poet

the entry on perfumery to the *Encyclopædia Britannica* (9th edition), as well as a practical guide to brewing beer, *Chemistry in the Brewing-Room* (1877).

[9] Florence Stacpoole, *A Healthy Home and How to Keep It* (London: Wells Gardener, Darton & Co., 1905), p. 39.

[10] Piesse, *Art of Perfumery*, 4th edn (1879), p. 54.   [11] Piesse, *Olfactics*, pp. 104–5, 108.

[12] Ibid., p. 105.

[13] Grant Allen, *Physiological Æsthetics* (London: Henry S. King, 1877), pp. 39, 84.

and novelist whose views, in direct contrast to those of Nordau, can be found in his short monograph *The Romance of Perfume* published in 1925:

> The mysterious connection between perfume and the soul seems to have been one of the earliest intuitions of man groping dimly after an understanding of that strange side of himself that eludes the eye and the ear, and after which the hands reach in vain. [...] As perfume seems to be the soul of a flower, so the spirit in man has seemed in all ages to be the evasive immortal essence of his mortal body. Some philosophers indeed, have placed the soul in the olfactory nerve, and the sense of smell has always been recognized as the most ethereal of the senses. All that is sacred, pure, and innocent in man, all that suggests his starry origin and destiny, seems in some way to be most poignantly hinted at in perfume. Not merely fancifully and symbolically, but actually. The deeds of a good man are said to 'smell sweet and blossom in the dust,' and the innocence of children, the pure thoughts of youth, the holiness of saintly men and women are known to give off a sensible fragrance to their very bodies. 'The odour of sanctity' is no mere phrase. It has been over and over again attested as a fact.[14]

In less lofty tones, Havelock Ellis in his analysis of smell declared that 'our olfactory experiences' generate:

> [B]y-sensations [...] of no great practical significance, but of considerable emotional significance from their variety, their intimacy, their associational facility, their remote ancestral reverberations through our brains [...] It is the existence of these characteristics—at once so vague and so specific, so useless and so intimate—which led various writers to describe the sense of smell as, above all others, the sense of imagination.[15]

A potent stimulus to the imagination, perfume has inevitably attracted the attention of poets and novelists such as Charles Baudelaire, J. K. Huysmans, and Marcel Proust. The interest of these particular writers in perfume is unsurprising in that France was, as it still is, the centre of the modern perfume industry. This industry had grown from its beginnings in the mid-sixteenth century when Catherine de' Medici, wife of Henry II, encouraged the manufacture of scented gloves in the south-eastern town of Grasse, ideally situated for the cultivation of aromatic herbs and flowers. The taste for scented leather goods declined as demand increased for perfumes and perfume materials. Grasse became world renowned for its perfume ingredients, supplying both these and high-quality scented goods to the markets of Paris and beyond. Although taste dictated different trends in fragrance at particular historical moments, perfume remained a staple in fashionable French court and aristocratic life. By the nineteenth century, when it began to be produced on a more industrial commercial scale, it was an established upper-class and bourgeois accoutrement. By 1865 there were an estimated 120 perfumers working in Paris, employing about 3,000 men and women, while perfume use was boosted by the rail link, established mid-century between Grasse and Paris, which encouraged the commercial distribution of perfumes throughout the country.[16] French writers thus reflect perfume's accepted place in daily life for the monied classes.

---

[14] Richard Le Gallienne, *The Romance of Perfume* (New York and Paris: Richard Hudnut, 1925), p. 8.
[15] Ellis, 'Section II: Smell', p. 55.
[16] Rimmel, *The Book of Perfumes*, p. 235; Stamelman, *Perfume*, p. 96.

Perfume's role in nineteenth-century French culture is well established, but this chapter demonstrates the importance of fragrance to the Victorians and their literature, and shows that, despite the omissions and generalizations of existing histories, Britain had a rich and thriving perfume culture in place by 1860. Although various aesthetic and decadent authors explored in this book may not have worn perfume themselves, they responded to natural scent and manufactured perfume within a context where its use was valued, varied, and widespread. While—in contrast to poetry and aesthetic and decadent literature—there was some ambivalence or even suspicion of perfume expressed in early and mid-Victorian fiction, it is wrong to assume that most middle and upper-class Victorians were similarly dubious or unenthusiastic, that women wore only light florals, and that men avoided perfume altogether. In broaching these topics I open with a snapshot of the British perfume industry during the nineteenth century to show its health and vigour, and foreground Eugene Rimmel and Septimus Piesse, two figures instrumental in promoting Victorian perfume.

Princes of Perfumery

The eighteenth century had seen the establishment of a number of important London perfumers: William Bayley (1711), Juan Floris (1730), Charles Lillie in the 1730s, the House of Cleaver (1770), which, bought out by William Yardley, would become the House of Yardley, Andrew Pears (1789), and James Atkinson (1799). All of these founding figures, with the exception of Floris, who was Minorcan, were British-born. Lillie, who, according to his trade card, seems also to have had an establishment in Barcelona, is known as the author of *The British Perfumer*, one of the first books on perfumery.[17] In the early nineteenth century the ranks of British perfumery were swelled by Truefitt & Hill (1805), Eugene Rimmel (1834), John Grossmith (1835), Septimus Piesse and Wilhelm Lubin (1855), and, post-1860, by William Penhaligon (1870), William Thomas (who founded the Crown Perfumery in 1872), George Trumper (1875), and James Bronnley (1884), to name but some of the major players.[18] Most (with the exception of Lillie and Piesse and Lubin) are still trading today, although some are relaunched companies like Atkinsons (revived 2013) and Grossmith (revived in 2009 by a descendant, Simon Brooke, and his wife Amanda); some have been taken over or subsumed by other firms (Rimmel by Coty); and some operate under different names: for example, John Price, founded in 1677, which later became Price & Gosnell, but is now John Gosnell & Co., Ltd. Although fewer in number

---

[17] Now in the British Museum, Charles Lillie's trade card (Museum no: 1910,1208.14), bearing the handwritten date 1736 on the verso and advertising an impressive number of wares, can be freely accessed at http://www.britishmuseum.org. Published in 1822, Lillie's book was actually assembled from manuscripts left by him after his death in the 1740s. See William Tullett, 'Review of Jonathan Reinarz's *Past Scents*', *Reviews in History* (2014), review no. 1648: http://www.history.ac.uk/reviews/review/1648.

[18] See John Bailey, Helen Hill, Yvonne Hockey, and Matthew Williams, eds., *British Perfumery: A Fragrant History: Celebrating 50 Years of the British Society of Perfumers* (Frome: British Society of Perfumers, 2013), p. 8.

than their French counterparts, British perfumers regularly gained awards and commendations at the international exhibitions and world fairs that, following in the wake of the Crystal Palace Exhibition of 1851, were popular throughout the second half of the nineteenth century.

Prominent among those award winners was Atkinsons, one of the most important nineteenth-century perfumery houses, with James Atkinson becoming Official Perfumer to the Royal Court of England in 1826. By 1832 the house produced more than forty perfumes and the company moved to 24 Old Bond Street where it remained till well into the twentieth century, its premises being splendidly rebuilt after a fire in 1926. In 1837, starting a trend of launching a perfume to tie in with a significant royal event, it produced two perfumes, Bouquet de la Reine and Coronation Bouquet, to celebrate Victoria's accession to the throne. Atkinsons's achievements included a medal at the International Exhibition held in London in 1862, a silver medal at the Paris Exhibition in 1867, and a gold medal for its eau de cologne at the Paris International Exhibition of 1878.[19] Its successes culminated with the award of the Grand Prix at the Paris Exhibition of 1900, at which point, the company took out a full-page advertisement in the *Chemist and Druggist*, proudly drawing attention to this prize, which it declared as 'The Highest Possible Award' and 'The only "Grand Prix" ever accorded to English Perfumery' (although Pears also won a 'Grand Prix' for its soap the same year).[20]

Two of the best-known perfumers in Victorian London were Eugene Rimmel (1820–1887) and Septimus Piesse (1820–1882) of Piesse and Lubin. Both would achieve leading roles in the industry not only through their books on perfumery but also through their advertising and international distribution of a large range of perfumed goods. Known as 'the Napoleon of Sweet Scents' and 'the Prince of Perfumers', Rimmel was French-born, but took British citizenship in September 1857 and made a considerable contribution to British perfumery, which he championed vigorously.[21] His father, Hyacinthe Mars Rimmel, who had trained under Pierre-François Lubin, perfumer to the Empress Josephine, came to London after accepting an invitation to manage the business of M. Joseph Delcroix, a noted perfumer in New Bond Street.[22] In 1834, at the tender age of fourteen, Eugene joined his father as his apprentice when Rimmel Senior set up his own perfumery in Albemarle Street. Eugene took over the firm shortly after his marriage in 1842, and in 1858, he moved to 96 The Strand, premises that had originally belonged to

---

[19] Ibid., p. 20.

[20] See the *Chemist and Druggist* (25 August 1900), supplement, 5; *Chemist and Druggist* (25 August 1900), 340.

[21] Sources include *Oxford Dictionary of National Biography*, Rimmel's obituary in the *Chemist and Druggist* (5 March 1887), 291–2; 'The Prince of Perfumers', *New York Times* (15 March 1887), 4; and other various newspaper notices of his death including the *Aberdeen Weekly Journal* (28 February 1887), 5, and 'A Napoleon of Sweet Scents', *Pall Mall Gazette* (1 March 1887), 4. See the *Pall Mall Gazette* (4 March 1887), 9, for a notice of Rimmel's funeral.

[22] J. Delcroix & Co. was a well-known West End perfumery company with a perfume manufactory in Grasse. Its products are mentioned in Thackeray's *Pendennis* (1848–50). See William Makepeace Thackeray, *The History of Pendennis*, ed. John Sutherland (Oxford: Oxford University Press, 1994), p. 244 (ch. 20).

Charles Lillie. This would become his home till his death, but he subsequently also owned shops at 24 Cornhill, at 128 Regent Street, as well as a shop in Paris at 17 Boulevard des Italiens, and flower farms and distilleries in Nice. Rimmel's factory employed both men and women, and he was proud to be the first perfumer in England to use female labour. Now best known for his beauty products, including the first commercial non-toxic mascara, his signature 'toilet vinegar' was originally one of his best-sellers, but he also sold an extensive range of soaps, perfumes, and other scented goods including fans, jewels, calendars, books, Christmas cards, valentines, and crackers. By the 1850s he was exporting these to Europe, the Americas, and throughout the British Empire.

A canny salesman and showman, Rimmel was adept at advertising his wares through clever ploys like scented theatre programmes and imaginative public displays. At the Great Exhibition of 1851, a key attraction was Rimmel's 'perfume fountain', while at the 1862 International Exhibition he exhibited his 'perfume vaporizer', a device designed to emit vaporized perfume oils to scent public spaces like ballrooms, theatres, and hospitals, which was also used on Queen Victoria's yacht. (Smaller versions of the vaporizer were available for domestic use.) At the 1862 International Exhibition he served alongside Septimus Piesse on the jury for the perfumery section and drew up the report, which asserted that 'the British manufacturers of perfumery make a very creditable show, which manifests great improvements in that trade since 1851'. Jurors were not eligible for an award but Rimmel generously noted the 'extensive collection of perfumes of excellent quality' displayed by Piesse and Lubin, commenting that the firm 'would undoubtedly have been entitled to a medal' in ordinary circumstances.[23] In 1868 he published his *Recollections of the Paris Exhibition of 1867* in which he complained that 'a great injustice was shown by the Jury, to English perfumers, only one silver medal having been allotted to them', while the British perfumery products 'are quite equal in quality and nearly so in importance to those of the French'. That sole silver medal was awarded to Atkinsons, but Rimmel declared that 'instead of wasting silver medals on Belgian, German and Russian perfumers, whose productions were very inferior, [...] it would have been more judicious to bestow them on some really deserving British manufacturers', naming Pears and 'S. Piesse' among those he thought worthy of such an award.[24]

Although Rimmel has an entry in the *Oxford Dictionary of National Biography*, this is not something awarded Septimus Piesse, who arguably did as much to boost the role of perfumery in Victorian Britain.[25] In spite of his foreign-sounding name,

[23] *International Exhibition 1862: Reports of the Juries on the Subjects of the Thirty-Six Classes into which the Exhibition was Divided* (London: Printed for the Society of Arts, 1863). See 'Report on Class IV, Section D: Perfumery', pp. 1–13; 7. Apart from Atkinsons, award winners included Bayley and Co., R. Low and Son, Pears, and Yardley (see p. 11).

[24] Eugene Rimmel, *Recollections of the Paris Exhibition of 1867* (London: Chapman & Hall, 1868), p. 298.

[25] Subsequent information taken from the entry in Frederick Boase, *Modern British Biography containing Many Thousand Concise Memoirs of Persons who have Died since the Year 1850*, 2 vols (Truro: Netherton & Worth for the author, 1897), and the obituary in the *Chemist and Druggist* (15 November 1882), 496–7.

he was the British-born son of Charles A. J. Piesse, chief clerk in the war office. He qualified as an analytical chemist after studying at University College, London, and was first employed by Atkinsons and then by another well-known London perfumer, Francis Henry Breidenbach, before going into partnership in 1855 with Wilhelm Lubin at 2 New Bond Street. The large cellars under the street housed the firm's famous 'Laboratory of Flowers', atmospherically described in G. L. M. Strauss's *England's Workshops* (1864), which contained various stills and a soap boiler, and an adjacent vast cool storeroom of pomades, oils, ottos, and extracts.[26] Piesse seems to have been the driving force and public face of the company while Lubin remains a shadowy figure. Although seemingly unrelated to the famous perfumer Lubin of Paris, his name nonetheless lent the company a certain cachet.[27] At all events he was replaced as partner by James Phillips, with that subsequent partnership dissolved in November 1873, when Piesse became sole owner of the firm.[28] Like Rimmel, Piesse and Lubin owned flower farms near Nice, as well as lavender farms at Mitcham, Surrey, and warehouses in London docks where perfumed spirits for export were made. Piesse's marketing skills have recently been noted by Andrew Kettler, who has suggested that in promoting the firm's famous 'Frangipanni' perfume, Piesse invented the romantic story of the botanist Mercutio Frangipani who supposedly accompanied Columbus on his voyage to the West Indies, and smelt off the coast of Antigua the fragrance of *Plumeria alba*, later called frangipani. This story appears in Piesse's *Art of Perfumery* (1862) and subsequent editions, and has been repeated in many other perfume histories ever since.[29]

Piesse's obituary in the *Chemist and Druggist* also pays tribute to his marketing skills, which included the use of catchy, even cheeky, English names for his perfumes like Box His Ears, Stolen Kisses, and Kiss-me-Quick (see Figure 1.1).[30] He is also often noted for his theory of what he called 'the gamut of odours', with the word 'gamut' used in its musical sense to signify 'a complete scale of musical notes'. Introduced into the third edition of the *Art of Perfumery*, this was basically a classification of perfume odours, with similar-smelling perfumes forming 'an octave of odours like an octave in music'. This supported his perception that 'certain perfumes coincide, like the keys of an instrument. Such as almond, heliotrope,

---

[26] G. L. M. Strauss, *England's Workshops* (London: Groombridge & Sons, 1864), pp. 171–8. An otto (or attar) is a fragrant essential oil.

[27] Piesse's obituary in the *Chemist and Druggist* implies that Piesse met Lubin through his amateur interest in conjuring.

[28] See the Notice in the *London Gazette* (21 November 1873), 5289.

[29] See Andrew Kettler, 'Making the Synthetic Epic: Septimus Piesse, the Manufacturing of Mercutio Frangipani, and Olfactory Renaissance in Victorian England', *The Senses and Society* 10.1 (2015), 5–25. Kettler's interesting though often rather confusingly presented findings are marred by some errors and misinformation. For example, he gives the dates not of the British but the later American editions of Piesse's *Art of Perfumery*, assumes that Wilhelm Lubin is 'an elite Paris manufacturer of perfumes', and makes unwarranted assumptions about the 'repression of the sense of smell within Victorian sensual education' (p. 6). Piesse's 'Frangipanni' perfume, which in sachet form contains musk, orris, vertiver, and ottos of rose, neroli, and sandalwood, is supposed to smell like the plumeria (or frangipani) flower. See Piesse, *Art of Perfumery* (1855), p. 138. Civet is added to the mix in the 2nd edition (1856), p. 215.

[30] Obituary, *Chemist and Druggist* (15 November 1882), 496.

PIESSE & LUBIN,

BOUQUETS AND NOSEGAYS

FOR SCENTING THE HANDKERCHIEF.

Frangipanni Bouquet
Stolen Kisses—1861
New Bond-street Nosegay
Bouquet Millefleurs
Her Majesty's Perfume
Empress Eugenie's do.
Kiss-me-Quick
Bouquet du Nepoleon III
Royal Hunt Bouquet
Jockey Club Perfume
Yacht Club Nosegay
Ess Bouquet
The Guards' Bouquet
Excelsior, an American
  Perfume
Wild Flowers
H.R.H. Prince of Wales'
  Perfume
  (Smallest bottle of this fra-
  grance is 20s.)
Bouquet d'Amour
Rondeletia

Albion Nosegay,
  with which " Britannia "
  Scents her Handkerchief
Early Spring Flowers
Our Village Nosegay
Marechale
The Naval Nosegay
Piesse's Posy
Flowers of Erin
Alhambra Perfume
Perfume of Paradise
The Flower of the Day
Bouquet of all Nations
St. Valentine's Nosegay
Mousselaine
Bosphorus Bouquet
  from the Valley of Sweet
  Waters.
Prince Arthur's Choice
The Cottage Flower
Curious Essence
Eau de Chypre
Forget-me-not
Fleur de Mauve
Box HIS EARS
  The Sequel to Stolen
  Kisses.

Sold in Bottles, 2s. 6d., 5s., 10s., and 40s. each.   Purchasers taking an assortment of half-a-dozen will
  be charged at a reduced price.

New perfumes every season.

The **Sportman's Perfumes,** Three Bottles in
  a Box, 7s., consisting of Royal Hunt Bouquet, the
  Newmarket Jockey Club, and Yacht Club Nosegay.

Perfumery Factors,

Figure 1.1 'Bouquets and Nosegays', *Piesse and Lubin's Toilet Almanack for 1861*, p. 6. John Johnson Collection: Labels 3 (88) (courtesy of The Bodleian Libraries, The University of Oxford)

vanilla, and clematis blend together, each producing different degrees of a nearly similar impression.'[31] Piesse speculatively and diagrammatically assigned a range of perfumes across the notes of the treble and bass clefs, suggesting that 'If a perfumer desires to make a bouquet from primitive odours, he must take such odours as chord together, the perfume will then be harmonious.' He then suggested how a perfumer might make harmonious bouquets of different 'chords'.[32]

Piesse's son, Charles, referred to his father's 'gamut of odours' as 'the odophone'.[33] This word has since often been applied to the notion of a musical instrument like an organ that emits perfume instead of (or as well as) sound when its notes are pressed but there is no indication that either Piesse had such an instrument in mind. However, just before mentioning his father's theory in his *Olfactics*, Charles Piesse had quoted Dr George Wilson (a chemist and Regius Professor of Technology at Edinburgh University), who in 1856 had written

> Let those who doubt this visit a scientific chemist's laboratory and examine his specimens one by one, and they will easily satisfy themselves that a fac-simile of the largest church organ might be readily constructed, in which each organ-pipe, sounding a different note, should be represented by a phial exhaling, when opened, a different odour.[34]

It is perhaps this statement that has led to the common misconception that Piesse's 'odophone' is an olfactory musical instrument.[35] However, Piesse's terminology may have been responsible for the naming of the 'perfumer's organ', the traditional semi-circular tiered workstation where a perfumer selected and blended his materials, which was used predominantly from the latter half of the nineteenth century to the early years of the twentieth.[36]

The specifics of Piesse's system of classification may not have been adopted, but his analogy of perfume with music was influential and is now widely accepted as a descriptive strategy, with perfumers and perfume lovers alluding to perfume 'top', 'middle', and 'base notes', to 'accords', and 'harmonious compositions'. In the fourth edition of his book, Piesse acknowledged that his association of music and perfume had been anticipated in literature: 'Several of our poets have been singularly happy in their allusions to the analogy which exists between music and odour', citing in support of this Keats, Shelley, and Shakespeare, authors we will

---

[31] Piesse, *Art of Perfumery*, 3rd edn (1862), p. 25.   [32] Ibid., pp. 27, 30.

[33] Charles H. Piesse, entry on 'Perfumery' for the *Encyclopædia Britannica*, 9th edn (1875–89), cited in *Olfactics*, pp. 92–102, with 'the odophone' mentioned pp. 97–8.

[34] George Wilson, *The Five Gateways of Knowledge* (London and New York: Macmillan & Co., 1856), p. 61, cited by Piesse, *Olfactics*, p. 83. Piesse incorrectly states the date of Wilson's pronouncement as 1857.

[35] In J. K. Huysman's *A Rebours* (1884), the decadent hero Des Esseintes has a flavour organ, which he calls a 'mouth organ', in which flavours correspond to notes, while in the twentieth century Aldous Huxley would portray a musical 'scent organ' in his novel *Brave New World* (1932). See J. K. Huysmans, *Against Nature*, tr. Robert Baldick (Harmondsworth: Penguin, 1959), p. 58. The notion of a 'scent-symphony' is also central to James Huneker's story 'The Eighth Deadly Sin', in his collection *Visionaries* (New York: Charles Scribner's Sons, 1905), pp. 23–43. My thanks to Alex Murray for this last reference.

[36] Stamelman, *Perfume*, p. 44.

return to in due course.[37] Piesse's theory is underpinned by a belief in a vibrational theory of smell, by analogy with contemporary vibrational theories of colour and sound: 'My view of the case induces me to conclude that true theory of odours by viewing them as imponderable agents, affecting the nervous system by special vibrations, as colours affect the eye, and sound the ear.'[38] (The idea of vibration as a smell mechanism persisted into the twentieth century but is no longer credited by most smell scientists, a controversial exception being the bio-physicist Luca Turin, who has proposed a vibrational theory based on inelastic electron tunnelling.)[39]

In early nineteenth-century England, chemistry, according to David Knight, was 'a very popular science, which lent itself to demonstration lectures, was accessible, and cut across any "two cultures" divide' (i.e. art and science).[40] Still, while notable for outstanding chemists like Humphry Davy, John Dalton, Joseph Priestley, William Wollaston, and Michael Faraday, England lacked the more institutional academic culture of France, Germany, or even Scotland. Yet it was still possible to acquire training as a chemist, for Pierre-François-Pascal Guerlain studied chemistry in London before opening his first perfume store in Paris on the rue de Rivoli in 1828.[41] Chemistry began to acquire more recognition as a formal academic discipline in the 1840s when Septimus Piesse was studying at University College, and both he and his son Charles belonged to the new breed of professional, academically trained chemists. William Perkin, the British chemist best known for the invention of mauve, the first aniline dye, was also of this new generation of chemists, entering the recently founded Royal College of Chemistry in 1853. He too would make a signal contribution to perfumery when he synthesized coumarin in 1868. An essence naturally derived from tonka beans, coumarin has a sweet vanilla and hay-like aroma and is a key ingredient in men's fougère fragrances but is costly to extract. Perkin's discovery would lead to the first fragrance containing a synthetic chemical odorant, Fougère Royale by Houbigant, which appeared in 1882.[42] During 1875–7, Perkin would also synthesize cinnamic acid used in synthetic indigo dye, the perfumery industry, and as a flavorant. His discoveries would encourage the development of further synthetics such heliotropin (which

[37] Piesse, *Art of Perfumery*, 4th edn (1879), p. 51.

[38] Piesse, *Art of Perfumery*, 3rd edn (1862), p. 42.

[39] See Chandler Burr's account of Turin's ideas in *The Emperor of Scent: A Story of Perfume, Obsession, and the Last Mystery of the Senses* (London: Arrow Books, 2004) and Luca Turin, *The Secret of Scent: Adventures in Perfume and the Science of Smell* (New York: HarperCollins, 2006).

[40] David Knight, 'Chemistry on an Onshore Island: Britain 1789–1840', in *The Making of the Chemist: The Social History of Chemistry in Europe, 1789–1914*, ed. David Knight and Helge Kragh (Cambridge: Cambridge University Press, 1998), p. 106.

[41] Susan Irvine, *Perfume: The Creation and Allure of Classic Fragrances* (New York and Avenel, NJ: Crescent Books, 1995), p. 94; Roja Dove, *The Essence of Perfume* (London: Black Dog Publishing, 2008), p. 27.

[42] David H. Pybus, 'The History of Aroma Chemistry and Perfume', in *The Chemistry of Fragrances*, ed. Charles Sell, 2nd edn (Cambridge: Royal Society of Chemistry 2006), p. 19. For Fougère Royale, see Stamelman, *Perfume*, p. 96. Some sources, like Turin and Sanchez, *Perfumes: The A–Z Guide*, p. 24, give the date for Fougère Royale as 1881, while the perfumer Patricia de Nicolai gives it as 1884. See her article 'A Smelling Trip into the Past: The Influence of Synthetic Materials on the History of Perfume', *Chemistry and Biodiversity* 5 (2008), 1137–46; 1137.

has the vanillic cherry-almond smell of heliotrope flowers) discovered by Rudolph Fittig and W. H. Mielk in 1869; vanillin, synthetic vanilla, one of the most important synthetic fragrance ingredients, by Karl Reimer and Ferdinand Tiemann in 1874; and ionone, a synthetic violet-smelling ketone, discovered by Tiemann and Paul Kruger in 1893.[43] Synthetic coumarin, heliotropin, vanillin, and artificial musk are all mentioned in Piesse's *Art of Perfumery* (1891).[44] In its coverage of the Paris Exhibition of 1900, the *Chemist and Druggist* noted that 'synthetic perfumes are well illustrated, and are proving objects of much curiosity to the general public', drawing attention to specimens of citral, linalool, geraniol, and ionone.[45]

In our twenty-first-century 'green' culture that privileges the 'natural' over the 'artificial', synthetic materials tend to be regarded as inferior, and consumers are often disconcerted to find that their favourite perfumes are composed mostly, if not solely, from synthetics, not realizing the considerable artistic freedom that they give the perfumer. However, this was not necessarily the view at the end of the nineteenth century, as can be seen from a Piesse and Lubin advertisement of 1896 that boldly promotes a range of 'Synthetic Scents' that includes violet, lily of the valley, heliotrope, lilac, and jonquil (see Figure 1.2). This advertisement proudly testifies to the perfumes' 'non-evanescence' and asserts 'a triumph of the science of the Parfumeur-Chimiste over Nature', a sentiment that echoes the boasts of decadent artists to improve on nature, reminding us that literary and cultural decadence coincides with the discovery and use of synthetic fragrance materials.[46]

Perfume Use in the Victorian Period

Although advertisements for perfumes and other scented goods are commonly found in Victorian journals, especially towards the end of the nineteenth century, it is much harder to source perfumer's trade catalogues. However, a good example dating from 1861 is the almanac produced by Piesse and Lubin. Even at this point, when the newly invigorated perfume industry was just getting into its stride, this almanac has twenty pages devoted to perfumes, pomades, soaps, scented cosmetics including lotions, powders, face creams, and hair oil, sachet powders for scenting

[43] See Pybus, 'History of Aroma Chemistry', p. 21; Eugénie Briot, 'From Industry to Luxury: French Perfume in the Nineteenth Century', *Business History Review* 85 (Summer 2011), 281.

[44] Piesse, *Art of Perfumery* (1891), pp. 130, 220–1, 224, 275. A more specialized scientific account of these and the recently discovered ionone can be found in the two volumes of Charles Sawer's *Odorographia* (1892, 1894), while *Practical Perfumery*, a booklet of 1896, shows much interest in the use of synthetics and, in addition to those mentioned, contains brief descriptions of benzoic aldehyde, citral, nitrobenzol, safrol, and terpineol. See Charles Sawer, *Odorographia: A Natural History of Raw Materials and Drugs Used in the Perfume Industry*, 2 vols (London: Gurney & Jackson, 1892–4), 1. 5–10 (artificial musk), 137–8 (coumarin), 162–73 (vanillin), 188–9 (heliotropin); 2. 456 (ionone). See the Section 'Artificial and Refined Perfumes', in Anon., *Practical Perfumery by An Expert*, 3rd edn (London: The British and Colonial Druggist, 1896), pp. 37–42.

[45] *Chemist and Druggist* (30 June 1900), 1094.

[46] *Illustrated London News* (14 November 1896), 645; *Graphic* (6 March 1897), 307. At this time Piesse and Lubin was run by Septimus's eldest son, George Chaplin Nicolson Piesse (1847–1920), notable for his interests in boxing, racing, and gambling. The business seems to have continued till 1929, after which it disappears from the London Post Office Directory.

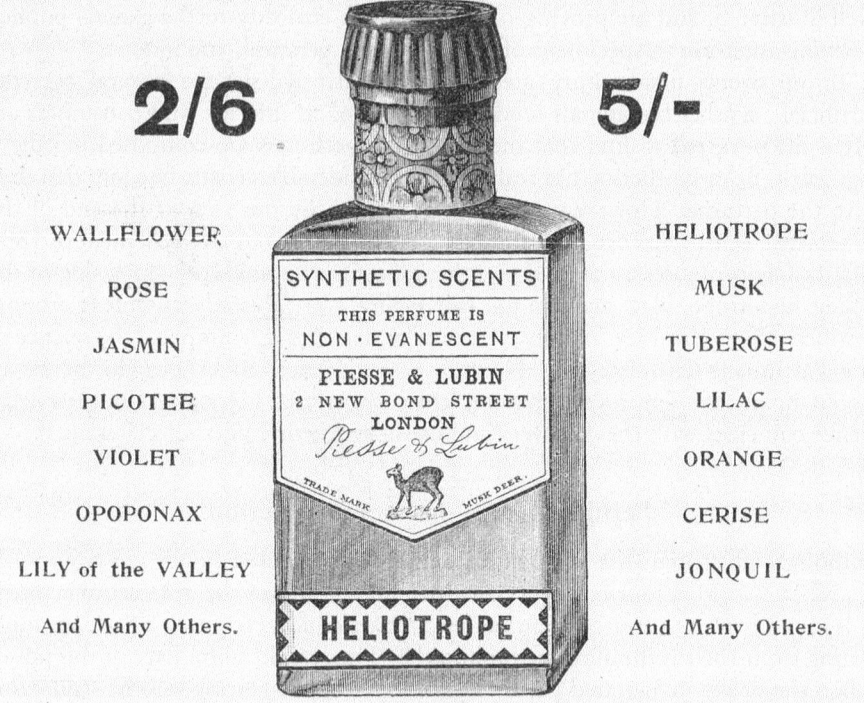

Figure 1.2 Advertisement for Piesse and Lubin 'Synthetic Scents' featuring 'Heliotrope', *Graphic* (6 March 1897), p. 307 (detail), N. 2288 b. 7 (vol. 55) (courtesy of The Bodleian Libraries, The University of Oxford)

clothes and linens, incense and other devices to help fragrance rooms, perfumed syrups, breath lozenges, perfumed toothpaste, smelling bottles, customized gift sets, fancy glass bottles, jars, and containers. In addition to asserting proudly that 'Agents for Piesse & Lubin's perfumery will be found in every city where the English language is spoken', the catalogue also indicates that its goods can be bought by mail order, meaning that they were not restricted to metropolitan consumers.[47] Certainly Piesse and Lubin products were being sold in America and Australia by this date.

This almanac also provides evidence that usage does not necessarily conform to the kinds of advice meted out by etiquette guides of the period. Victorian women in particular were urged to favour only light and delicate floral fragrances and avoid perfumes that contain animalic extracts such as musk and civet. Eugene Rimmel himself advised them to:

> [U]se simple extracts of flowers which can never hurt you, in preference to com-pounds, which generally contain musk and other ingredients likely to affect the head. Above all, avoid strong, coarse perfumes; and remember, that if a woman's temper may be told from her handwriting, her good taste and good breeding may as easily be ascer-tained by the perfume she uses. Whilst a *lady* charms us with the delicate ethereal fragrance she sheds around her, aspiring vulgarity will as surely betray itself by a *mou-choir* redolent of common perfumes.[48]

Animalic scents—musk, civet, ambergris, and castoreum—used in perfumery up to the mid-twentieth century, are nowadays banned substances in Europe and the English-speaking world for animal protection reasons. Musk is a secretion from an abdominal gland of the Tibetan male musk deer located in a sac or 'pod' between the genitals and the navel, and civet a secretion from the anal glands of the Ethiopian civet cat. Ambergris, a grey tarry substance, is an intestinal secretion produced by the sperm whale, usually collected from beaches, while castoreum comes from the abdominal gland of the beaver.[49] Harsh, pungent, even repellent in their raw state, such substances, when diluted, take on a more benign fragrant character, and add sensuality, depth, and staying power to perfume. Musk and civet had been very popular in the eighteenth century but these substances fell out of favour in the nineteenth century. In Elizabeth Gaskell's novella *My Lady Ludlow*, first published in 1858, but set just after 1805, her aristocratic heroine, who prides herself on her 'keen susceptibility of smell', despises musk:

> We never named musk in her presence, her antipathy to it was so well understood through the household: her opinion on the subject was believed to be, that no scent

---

[47] *Piesse & Lubin's Toilet Almanack for 1861*, 32 pp. John Johnson Collection, Bodleian Library, Oxford. The John Johnson Collection is available online through subscribing libraries.

[48] Rimmel, *The Book of Perfumes*, pp. 238–9.

[49] For animalics, see Chandler Burr, *The Perfect Scent: A Year Inside the Perfume Industry in Paris and New York* (New York: Picador, 2007), pp. 248–9, although Burr, like many commentators, refers to ambergris as 'rancid whale vomit' (p. 249), which does not represent the most recent scientific opinion that ambergris is excreted rather than vomited by the whale and may even be the cause of its death, provoking an intestinal rupture, and eventually floating free of the carcass. See Christopher Kemp, *Floating Gold: A Natural (and Unnatural) History of Ambergris* (Chicago and London: University of Chicago Press, 2014), pp. 11–13, 15.

derived from an animal could ever be of a sufficiently pure nature to give pleasure to any person of good family, where, of course, the delicate perceptions of the senses had been cultivated for generations.[50]

Referring to a decrease in the use of 'strong perfumes' favoured by earlier eras, Dr Anna Kingsford asserted in 1886 that 'Even musk and patchouli are now out of mode, and their use in society would be generally regarded as a breach of good taste.'[51]

It is customary to claim that musk and civet were shunned by the Victorians who thought them too overpowering, with a possible deleterious effect on the nervous system. The American handbook *Our Deportment* (1879) declared that 'Musk and patchouli should always be avoided as to people of a sensitive temperament, their odor is exceedingly disagreeable.'[52] According to Susan Irvine, musk 'long held the reputation of giving women "the vapours"', and indeed in 1899, the American beauty adviser, Harriet Hubbard Ayer, opined that 'hysteria is inevitably aggravated and frequently caused by the odor of musk, and the use of this perfume should be forbidden delicate girls and women'.[53] Like Lady Ludlow, refined Victorians supposedly also rejected essences like musk and civet for their unsavoury associations with animal body parts, not to mention their aphrodisiacal sensuality that hints at bodily and sexual odours and man's 'lower nature'. Musk, for example, can be used to evoke a skin note in perfume, sometimes with a suggestion of sweat, and certainly Ayer thought that 'A high-bred woman does not associate herself with musk.'[54] The sensuality of musk meant that it was sometimes regarded as used by women of dubious character, a prejudice borne out by literary texts like Ellen Wood's *East Lynne* (1861), in which the overdressed 'brazen hussy' Afy Hallijohn carries 'a swinging handkerchief of lace, redolent of musk'.[55]

However, unbeknown to purchasers, small amounts of animalic substances were used in most Victorian perfumes as fixatives. Furthermore, there was obviously also a market for perfumes that contained larger amounts, whether this was advertised or not. In the first and subsequent editions of *The Art of Perfumery*, Septimus Piesse declared

> It is a fashion of the present day for people to say 'that they do not like musk'; but, nevertheless, from experience in one of the largest manufacturing perfumatories in

[50] Gaskell, 'My Lady Ludlow', p. 38. The story was originally published in *Household Words* in 1858, and then subsequently in *Round the Sofa* in 1859. In the story, Lady Ludlow refers to an officer recently wounded in the Battle of Trafalgar (p. 171), which took place in 1805, and the narrator refers to 'the byroads of fifty years ago' (p. 6). However, Gaskell inadvertently upset the chronology in *Round the Sofa* by inserting a new frame narrative that implies the story was set back even further in the past than its internal evidence would suggest.

[51] Anna Kingsford, *Health, Beauty, and the Toilet: Letters to Ladies from a Lady Doctor* (London and New York: Frederick Warne & Co., 1886), p. 108.

[52] Anon., *Our Deportment, or the Manners, Conduct and Dress of the Most Refined American Society* (Detroit, MI: F. B. Dickerson, 1879), p. 345.

[53] Irvine, *Perfume: The Creation and Allure of Classic Fragrances*, p. 51; Harriet Hubbard Ayer, *Harriet Hubbard Ayer's Book: A Complete and Authentic Treatise on the Laws of Health and Beauty* (New York: Home Topics Book Company, 1899), pp. 453, 454.

[54] Ayer, *Harriet Hubbard Ayer's Book*, p. 454.

[55] Ellen Wood, *East Lynne*, ed. Elisabeth Jay (Oxford: Oxford University Press, 2005), p. 529 (ch. 52).

Europe, we are of opinion that the public taste for musk is as great as any perfumer desires. Those substances containing it always take the preference in ready sale—so long as the vendor takes care to assure his customer 'that there is no musk in it'.[56]

In the same year, 1855, Queen Victoria is said to have raised eyebrows on a trip to France when she wore a perfume with a detectable hint of musk.[57] This was possibly Ess Bouquet (Essence of Bouquet), said to be her favourite perfume.[58] However, some Victorian customers were clearly willing to purchase more obviously animalic fragrances, for in the 1861 Piesse and Lubin almanac, the list of 'Concentrated Essences of Flowers for Perfuming the Handkerchief' includes perfumes named simply 'musk', 'civet', and 'ambergris' (see Figure 1.3).[59]

If they mention Victorian fragrance at all, standard perfume histories press home the message that Victorians, and in particular the mid-Victorians, preferred light florals.[60] However, the evidence of almanacs such as Piesse and Lubin's again suggests that what might be considered 'good etiquette' is not necessarily representative of actual practice. The list of 'Concentrated Essences' includes the stronger florals such as tuberose, jasmine, and lily that well-bred women were supposed to avoid or, according to Mrs A. Walker, an early Victorian commentator, use only in careful moderation.[61] Class and 'good breeding' are definitely factors here. Gaskell's Lady Ludlow dislikes 'Attar of roses': 'She said it reminded her of the city and of the merchants' wives, over-rich, over-heavy in its perfume. And lilies of valley somehow fell under the same condemnation. [...] everything was refined about them but the smell. That was too strong.'[62] At the opposite end of the century, Harriet Hubbard Ayer also thought there was a 'danger lurking in flower scents', and that to some women 'the heavy odors are like strains of sensuous music and in their results the reverse of elevating'.[63] Refined Victorian women were supposed to favour delicate scents like violet, with Ayer proposing that the 'high-bred woman' 'select the most delicate of violet extracts, and so assimilate her personality with the flower as always to recall it'.[64]

While it may have been the convention to prefer more delicate scents, there was clearly a ready market for stronger perfumes, which increased as the century

---

[56] Piesse, *Art of Perfumery* (1855), p. 100.

[57] See Stamelman, *Perfume*, p. 95; Corbin, *The Foul and the Fragrant*, p. 284, note 129.

[58] For Victoria and Ess Bouquet, see C. J. S. Thompson, *The Mystery and Lure of Perfume* (London: John Lane, 1927), p. 168; Jill Jesse, 'Perfume', in William Kaufmann, *Perfume*, A Dutton Visual Book (New York: E. P. Dutton, 1974), p. 110. Although, as Piesse notes, Ess Bouquet was famously associated with the firm Thomas Bayley and Co., the name was commonly used for a generic type of perfume with citrus top notes of bergamot and lemon, and additional ingredients of rose, orris, and ambergris, but with variations often containing musk in the base. See Piesse, *Art of Perfumery* (1855), p. 118. See also Williams, *Perfumes of Yesterday*, p. 168.

[59] *Piesse & Lubin's Toilet Almanack for 1861*, p. 4.

[60] See Irvine, *Perfume: The Creation and Allure of Classic Fragrances*, p. 24.

[61] See Mrs A. Walker, *Female Beauty as Preserved by Regimen, Cleanliness and Dress* (London: Thomas Hood, 1837), p. 423. Mrs Walker thought that 'the sense of smell in women is remarkable for its exquisite susceptibility' and that they should also avoid, among other things, 'an apartment overcharged with the odour of certain flowers, and generally speaking all scents too active or too penetrating' (pp. 125, 126).

[62] Gaskell, 'My Lady Ludow', p. 39.   [63] Ayer, *Harriet Hubbard Ayer's Book*, p. 454.

[64] Ibid.

CONCENTRATED

ESSENCES OF FLOWERS,

FOR PERFUMING THE HANDKERCHIEF.

Magnolia	Jonquil	Lotus of Egypt
White Rose	Lily of the Valley	Rezeda
Cedrat	Lemon Thyme	Provence Rose
Pergalaria	Orange Blossom	Mignionette
Sweet Briar	Fragrant Phlox	Tea Rose
Winter Green	Eau de Portugal	Santal Wood
Neroly	Sweet Pea	White Lilac
Bergamotte	Tuberose	Syringa
Meadow Queen	Clove Pink	Citron
Spring Violet	Heliotrope	Stephanotis
Citronella	Lemon	Hoya-Bella
Wood Violet	Ambergris	Kus-Kus
Volkameria	Jessamine	Vitivert
Limette	Verbena Leaf	Myrtle
Musk	Honeysuckle	Patchouly
Lavender	Wattle Bud	Water Lily
Civet	Acacia	Narcissus
Geranium	Clematis	Erica Odorata
Cedar Wood	Wallflower	Allamandra
Moss Rose	Narcissus	Hyacinth

Sold in Stoppered Bottles, 2s. 6d., 5s., 10s., 20s., and
40s. each. Purchasers taking an assortment of
three, will be charged at a reduced price.

~~~~~~

The Wedding Perfumes,

Three Bottles in a Box, 7s., or Three Boxes, 20s.,
containing Orange Blossom, Lily and Myrtle.

Valentine Sachets, very chaste, 4s. each.

Perfumery Factors,

Figure 1.3 'Concentrated Essences of Flowers for Perfuming the Handkerchief', *Piesse and Lubin's Toilet Almanack for 1861*, p. 4. John Johnson Collection: Labels 3 (88) (courtesy of The Bodleian Libraries, The University of Oxford)

progressed. In France, perfume tastes underwent considerable change during the nineteenth century. Animalics having gone out of fashion in the mid-eighteenth century, there was a brief resurgence in their use in the very early nineteenth century because such heavy scents were beloved by Napoleon's first wife Josephine and her entourage. But, according to Richard Stamelman, after the fall of the Napoleonic Empire, 'delicate scents reasserted themselves', with Romanticism nourishing 'a taste for light gentle, and floral fragrances in harmony with the delicate odors of nature'.[65] Later on the French Second Empire (1852–70) saw a revival of animalics and the use of stronger exotic scents such as vertiver and patchouli. The English fashion designer Charles Worth, relocating to Paris in 1858, complained about his clients' overuse of heavy perfumes, which gave him migraines.[66] This suggests that English fragrances of the time were generally lighter.

As we shall see in Chapters 3 and 4, the older generation of English aesthetes—Swinburne, Pater, Symonds—tended to shun strong fragrances and animalics and to prefer lighter scents (which is not to say that their interpretation or relish of those scents is at all conventional or predictable). Nonetheless, by the early 1860s there was evidently demand for the stronger scents listed in Piesse and Lubin's almanac, and heavier perfumes became increasingly more popular in England, especially with the rise of decadence and the corresponding taste for exotic headier-smelling blooms like the lily and tuberose. Exoticism was also a factor in the rise of headier 'Eastern-inspired' fragrances like Grossmith's Hasu-No-Hana (1888), which supposedly evoked the scent of the Japanese lotus lily, and Phūl-Nānā (1891), which took the gold medal at the 1895 Universal Exhibition in Amsterdam, and was marketed as 'a bouquet of India's choicest flowers' (see Plate 1).[67] Dr Theodor Koller, author of a handbook on cosmetics, claimed in 1902 that 'English people prefer strong scents, so for this reason the flower perfumes are usually strengthened by addition of ambergris, musk, storax, benzoe [sic], cumarin, and patchouli'.[68] French perfume, too, could be purchased in major English cities, and the trade journal, the *Chemist and Druggist*, names a number of specialist shops that sold the more elite brands, while in the 1890s department stores such as Harrods and the Army and Navy stocked a range of the most popular French and English brands.[69]

Perfume was predominantly worn on the handkerchief rather than on the skin, although for some perfume users actual practice might depart from convention. In Austin Dobson's poem of 1866, 'Incognita', the unchaperoned coquettish young

[65] Stamelman, *Perfume*, p. 63.   [66] Ibid., p. 95.

[67] Grossmith London, *Overview*, advertising booklet (Winter 2014), pp. 5, 6.

[68] Theodor Koller, *Cosmetics: A Handbook of the Manufacture, Employment, and Testing of All Cosmetic Materials and Cosmetic Specialities*, tr. Charles Salter (London: Scott, Greenwood & Co., 1902), p. 9.

[69] See, for example, *Victorian Shopping: A Facsimile of the Harrod's Stores 1895 Issue of the Price List*, introduced by Alison Adburgham (Newton Abbot: David & Charles, 1972), pp. 1108–9, which lists many brands, including Bertrand Frères, Atkinsons, Bayleys, the Crown Perfumery, Gosnell, Grossmith, Houbigant, Piesse and Lubin, Pinaud, Piver, and Roger et Gallet. The list of perfume brands in the Army and Navy Stores catalogue for 1898 (accessible at the British Library) is very similar to that of Harrods.

woman who flirts with the male speaker during a train journey 'sprinkled herself with "Ess Bouquet"'.[70] By the 1890s sprays were coming into vogue, as can be seen in the advertisements for Lance perfumes in which a lady mischievously and flirtatiously sprays an approaching gentleman with a portable pen-like spray (see Figure 1.4).[71] In *Le Cabinet de toilette* (1891), translated as *The Lady's Dressing-Room* (1892), Baroness Staffe suggested that a refined woman should be identified with a signature fragrance, which should permeate all her clothes and possessions. The resultant perfume aura appears almost as an emanation of a woman's essential femininity:

> Without being over-scented, which is a mistake, it is well to perfume your linen and all your garments with a light and delicate odour—of one kind only—from head to foot. This enhances your attractions. I repeat that every woman should reject a mixture of scents. She should choose a perfume, and keep to it. All her belongings, her books, her note-paper, her boudoir, the cushions of her carriage (in the eighteenth century they used to be stuffed with sweet-scented herbs, called 'herbes de Montpellier'), her clothes, the smallest things she uses, should give out the same sweet fragrance.[72]

This fragrance was to be achieved by the use of sachets (small silk, muslin, or cambric bags containing scented powders or dried flowers and herbs) and impregnated drawer liners. Sachets in the form of little silk bags and ornamental envelopes were widely available for purchase throughout the Victorian period, and Septimus Piesse also provides details of various receipts for sachet powders in his *Art of Perfumery*.[73] Advertisements from the late 1890s indicate that scented artificial flowers were popular ornaments for women as well as perfumed buttons and 'repandrines', scented ribbons that could be sewn into garments.[74] Throughout the period women might also wear a perfume locket or other kinds of aromatic jewellery that usually contained either solid perfume in the form of scented wax or a small piece of sponge impregnated with perfume.[75] In 1845 Elizabeth Barrett

---

[70] Austin Dobson, 'Incognita', *The Englishwoman's Domestic Magazine* (October 1866), repr. in Dobson, *Vignettes in Rhyme and Vers de Société* (London: Henry S. King, 1873), p. 148.

[71] See also *Victorian Shopping*, p. 1109: 'Sprays and Scent diffusers.—A large assortment of plain, cut, and ornamental glass always in stock, prices from 1/0 upwards.'

[72] La Baronne Staffe, *Le Cabinet de toilette* (Paris: Victor-Havard, 1891); Baroness Staffe, *The Lady's Dressing-Room*, tr. Lady Colin Campbell (London: Cassell & Co., 1892), pp. 324–5. See also *My Lady's Dressing Room*, adapted from the French by Harriet Hubbard Ayer (New York: Cassell Publishing Company, 1892), p. 370.

[73] Piesse, *Art of Perfumery* (1855), pp. 137–40.

[74] See the *Chemist and Druggist* (2 November 1900), 42, for an advertisement by Marshalls' Ltd, retailing 'The Latest Novelty' 'The Button Sachet'—'a button artistic in appearance and of delicate and lasting perfume', and (24 November 1900), p. 32, for an advertisement for a 'Buttonhole Flower'— 'Lifelike Appearance and Natural Perfumes'. Piesse and Lubin's 'Repandrines' scented with peau d'espagne can be found in the Perfumery sections of the Army and Navy Stores Catalogues for 1899, 1900, and 1901, held by the British Library. 'Artificial Perfumed Flowers for Dress, Table Decoration, &c', including buttonholes, and 'Repandrines' can also be found in *Yesterday's Shopping: The Army & Navy Stores Catalogue 1907: A Facsimile of the Amy & Navy Co-operative Society's 1907 Issue of Rules of the Society and Price List of Articles Sold at the Stores*, introduced by Alison Adburgham (Newton Abbot: David & Charles, 1969), pp. 529, 530.

[75] Annette Green and Linda Dyett, *Secrets of Aromatic Jewelry* (Paris: Flammarion, 1998), pp. 94, 101.

Figure 1.4 Advertisement for Lance perfume sprays, *The Lady* (2 December 1897), p. 831. (Photo: Daichi Ishikawa, courtesy of the London Library)

wrote to Robert Browning about the lock of his hair given her as a love token: 'So I put the hair into [the] locket, which I wear habitually, and which never had hair before—the natural use of it being for perfume:—and this is the best perfume for all hours.'[76] As will be seen in Chapter 6, the artist Charles Ricketts presented the poet Katharine Bradley with an ornate aromatic ring of his own design. More prosaically one could buy from Piesse and Lubin, as displayed at the International Exhibition of 1862, 'fountain finger-rings' that emitted a jet of perfume when pressed.[77] Many ladies also carried a smelling bottle or, in the earlier nineteenth century, a vinaigrette, a small perforated container holding smelling salts or a perfumed vinegar to ward off faintness or to hold to one's nose to protect against bad smells.[78]

By the mid-nineteenth century, perfume was firmly regarded as an accessory to personal hygiene and not a substitute for it, and the era saw huge advances in sanitation and in standards of personal cleanliness, giving rise to the oft-cited mantra

[76] Elizabeth Barrett, Letter of 12 December 1845, *The Letters of Robert Browning and Elizabeth Barrett Barrett 1845–1846*, ed. Elvan Kintner, 2 vols (Cambridge, MA: The Belknap Press of Harvard University Press, 1962), 1. 320.

[77] See Edward McDermott, *The Popular Guide to the International Exhibition of 1862* (London: W. H. Smith & Son, 1862), p. 137, and Piesse, *Art of Perfumery*, 3rd edn (1862), p. 225, and subsequent editions.

[78] See Green and Dyett, *Secrets of Aromatic Jewelry*, pp. 106–12; Eileen Ellenbogen, *English Vinaigrettes* (Cambridge: The Golden Head Press, 1956), pp. 9, 10.

'cleanliness is next to godliness'.[79] *The Habits of Good Society*, a popular etiquette manual first published in 1859 and regularly reprinted up to 1890, averred that 'Cleanliness is a duty to one's-self for the sake of health and to one's neighbour for the sake of agreeableness.'[80] Soap had been taxed since 1712, but in 1853 Gladstone's repeal of this tax made it more affordable and substantially increased its production as both a luxury and an everyday commodity. At the 1862 International Exhibition, English toilet soap was considered to be the best on show, and three years later Eugene Rimmel affirmed that the 'English toilet soaps are the best that can be made'.[81] There was an astonishing variety of toilet soap available—the Army and Navy Stores catalogue for 1899 lists over seventy brands alone, with most brands supplying a range of different scents.[82] For those who could not afford these, there were cheaper general-purpose soaps made from animal fats and caustic soda. Lever Brothers introduced its popular Sunlight Soap, made from vegetable oils and glycerin in 1884, and in 1894, Lifebuoy, the first mass-produced carbolic soap, valued for its disinfectant deodorizing qualities.

Personal cleanliness now became associated with health, self-esteem, and respect-ability. Whereas previously bathing, especially immersion, had been viewed with suspicion and even fear, an enhanced medical understanding of hygiene and germ theory valued it as an essential sanitary measure with therapeutic benefits. Increasingly, educated, affluent people adopted regimes that included daily bath-ing—character-forming cold baths for public schoolboys and gentlemen, and warm or tepid baths for women, invalids, and infants.[83] The aspirant lower-middle and respectable working-class, unable to afford bathrooms, daily baths, and the time and labour involved in drawing and heating water, most likely bathed once a week in a tin tub, but many embraced the daily ritual of a full body-wash at the washstand or with soap and a single jug of hot water. Ruth Goodman refers to 'the stand-up wash' as 'the main form of personal hygiene and start of most people's daily routine'.[84] In 1869, *Cassell's Household Guide* pronounced that 'there can be no question that the best possible results follow the use of soap to the arm-pits, the groin and parts about, and the feet, each day'.[85]

Although deodorants in the modern sense of the word did not exist, discerning Victorian consumers could use scented products such as dusting powder to dimin-ish the odour of perspiration, and both women and men might also sponge or dab underarms or corsage with neat or diluted eau de cologne or other kinds of light

---

[79] Thus, for example, the American medical commentator John V. Shoemaker, writing in 1890 in a monograph published in both Britain and the US: 'cleanliness is one of the concomitants of self-respect. It is next to godliness because it is a species of godliness, and may, in turn, through stimulating self-respect, cause godliness to rise to greater heights.' See his *Heredity, Health and Personal Beauty* (London and Philadelphia, PA: F. A. Davis, 1890), pp. 180–1.

[80] *The Habits of Good Society: A Handbook of Etiquette* (London: John Hogg, 1859), p. 102.

[81] Rimmel, *The Book of Perfumes*, p. 237.

[82] *The Army and Navy Stores Catalogue* (15 March 1899), pp. 33–7. British Library.

[83] David J. Eveleigh, *Bogs, Baths and Basins: The Story of Domestic Sanitation* (Stroud: Sutton Publishing, 2002), p. 64.

[84] Goodman, *How to be a Victorian*, p. 10.

[85] *Cassell's Household Guide*, 2 vols (London: Cassell, Petter, and Galpin, 1869), 1. 45.

toilet water as the alcohol would kill the bacteria that creates malodour. For those on lower incomes, Goodman lists as alternatives plain powdered starch or talc bought by weight and, in place of toilet water, a wipe with a cloth dipped in ammonia or in vinegar, this last being slightly less effective but gentler on the skin.[86] By 1890 there was a substantial range of quality goods available to the well-heeled. In a chapter on 'Cosmetic Treatment and Cosmetic Articles', John V. Shoemaker writes that 'no one can object to the refreshing employment of the finer perfumes', and recommends particular brands of scented products. Thus, for scented dusting powder, he approves 'Lubin's rose and violet powders, Pinaud's *millefleurs* powder, Chardin's maréchale powder, Piesse and Lubin's pistachio-nut powder, Rimmel's *ylang-ylang* powder, Piver's *rose-blanche* powder, and Low's rose-leaf powder'.[87] Produced by many companies, 'violet powder', made of finely ground orris (iris) root, which smells like violets, was probably the most widely used dusting powder, and was regularly used by women and approved for sprinkling on babies and infants. Shoemaker specifies as 'Good toilet waters' 'Farina cologne, *eau de violette, eau de Kananga, eau de lavande, lait d'Iris, eau des Mandarins*'.[88] For those who needed more drastic treatment for body odour, there were medicated soaps—Shoemaker mentions several such as 'eucalyptol, napthol, salicylic-acid, witch-hazel, and tannin soap' for 'fetid perspiration', as well as a number of 'home remedies' for 'excessive or odorous perspiration' that could be dusted or dabbed on the skin.[89]

Bad breath was also a concern: *The Habits of Good Society* asserted that it was 'a Christian duty to keep your teeth clean', and indicated the likely fall in one's attractiveness to the opposite sex if this counsel was not heeded.[90] While the less well-off might use simply salt or soot, commercial 'dentifrice' was available made of ground chalk, powdered cuttlefish, or coral, and flavoured with ingredients like myrrh or camphor.[91] Later in the century it was possible to buy breath-sweets or cachous in a wide range of perfumed flavours such as heliotrope, wallflower, jasmine, and honeysuckle; a number of perfumers like Grossmith produced not only soap, sachets, and dusting powder containing their best-selling perfumes but also toothpastes and cachous.[92]

Hair washing was certainly less frequent than now, partly due to anxieties about taking a chill with damp hair, a genuine concern when indoor heating could be minimal and it was difficult to dry women's long tresses. Many Victorian commentators recommended only occasional washes but twice-daily rigorous brushing and combing to distribute the natural oils and remove dirt. *The Habits of Good Society* urged men, who had much shorter hair, 'to wash the head daily', and suggested

---

[86] Goodman, *How to be a Victorian*, p. 19.

[87] Shoemaker, *Heredity, Health and Personal Beauty*, p. 401.   [88] Ibid.

[89] Ibid., pp. 409–10, 419. See, for example, a receipt for half an ounce of 'oleate of zinc' and three drachms of powdered boracic acid.

[90] *The Habits of Good Society*, p. 108.   [91] Goodman, *How to be a Victorian*, pp. 23–5.

[92] See the advertisement for Gibson's Floral Cachous in the *Chemist and Druggist* (10 November 1900), 21, and the praise of Grossmith's products scented with Hasu-No-Hana, including dentifrice, in *Myra's Journal* (1 December 1895), 13.

that for women 'There is no risk [...] if done in warm weather, and well dried by a fire.'[93] Septimus Piesse lists a few receipts for hair washes in his *Art of Perfumery*, and a very simple hair wash might be made with rosemary steeped in boiling water.[94] Weak vinegar and water, or a mild ammonia solution might also be used, or alternatively a little soap, applied sparingly, as it could make hair dry and brittle and the scalp sore.[95] Pomades or pomatums consisting of inodorous lard, suet, or beeswax perfumed with floral extracts, resins, or spices were popular aids for styling or controlling the hair, as were scented oils, and these would make the hair manageable again after washing. Again Piesse supplies a number of receipts.[96] By the end of the century, middle-class women were advised to wash their hair at least once a week with soap and water or have it shampooed by a hairdresser.[97]

Perfume and scented goods were luxury items, particularly in the early Victorian period, although they became more affordable as the century progressed. In *Mary Barton* (1848), set in the 1840s, Elizabeth Gaskell draws a sharp distinction between the wealthy, like Amy Carson, the daughter of the mill-owner, who declares she 'can't live without flowers and scents' and the city's poorer working-class community, many of whom could barely afford the necessities of life. Amy's brother Harry and her father buy her 'eau de Portugal' (a refreshing toilet water composed of citrus oils and rose otto), and a choice rose costing a half a guinea, and Harry buys expensive fragrant roses and lilies of the valley to woo Mary Barton. While Amy is making her request for the rose, a hungry mill-worker sits downstairs amid the appetizing smells of the Carsons' kitchen waiting to apply for 'an infirmary order' from his employer for a sick workmate.[98]

Yet although perfume might not have been a priority for the urban poor, those living in country areas would have ready access to scented wild or cottage-garden flowers and herbs. In 1901 Harry Roberts wrote 'there is no pleasure more democratic as that which is yielded by the fragrance of flowers and leaves'.[99] F. W. Burbidge in *The Book of the Scented Garden* (1905) writes: 'Old men have told me of the days when women placed sprigs of Costmary, Ladslove, Rosemary, and Lavender, with perhaps a flower or two, in their bosoms when they went to church in the stifling hot summer days.'[100] Similar practices continued well into the twentieth century, as Amy Stewart Fraser recalls of her Edwardian Scottish childhood, how 'before entering church', 'The women-folk in the Glen' used to pick a sprig of sweet briar (a wild rose with apple-scented leaves); 'a still older custom was to carry a Sabbath

---

[93] *The Habits of Good Society*, p. 126.

[94] Piesse, *Art of Perfumery* (1855), pp. 196–208, 230–1.

[95] See *The Habits of Good Society*, p. 126; Goodman, *How to be a Victorian*, p. 118.

[96] Piesse, *Art of Perfumery* (1855), pp. 196–208, 230–1.

[97] C. J. S. Thompson, *The Cult of Beauty: A Handbook of Personal Hygiene* (London: Walter Scott, 1894), p. 114.

[98] Elizabeth Gaskell, *Mary Barton*, ed. Shirley Foster (Oxford: Oxford University Press, 2006), pp. 67–8 (ch. 6).

[99] Harry Roberts, *The Book of Old-Fashioned Flowers: A Handbook of Practical Gardening* (London and New York: John Lane, 1901), p. 17.

[100] F. W. Burbidge, *The Book of the Scented Garden* (London and New York: John Lane, 1905), p. 7.

posy of sweet-smelling herbs and flowers such as appleringie, tansy, and the buds of the unforgettable, old-fashioned Scotch rose'.[101]

Country men might also wear scented flowers or herbs in their buttonholes although the fastidious Lady Ludlow is disapproving of those who wear southernwood (another name for 'lad's-love', a strongly camphoraceous herb), and bergamot, a wild plant of the mint family with aromatic foliage whose scent is similar to that of the bergamot oranges used to flavour Earl Grey tea:

> She considered these two latter as betraying a vulgar taste in the person who chose to gather or wear them. She was sorry to notice sprigs of them in the button-hole of any young man in whom she took an interest, either because he was engaged to a servant of hers or otherwise, as he came out of church on a Sunday afternoon. She was afraid that he liked coarse pleasures.[102]

She herself enjoys the more delicate fragrance of lavender and sweet woodroof (sweet woodruff), both herbs dried for potpourri and also used to scent linen and other fabrics and preserve them from insects.

Gaskell's own fondness for fragrance, 'which I value so in a flower', is clear in her other novels and stories, which demonstrate how country folk and ordinary working people relish natural scents and incorporate them into their lives, an example being the 'great sweet-scented-leaved geranium' that 'fills the air with fragrance' in Alice Rose's modest Monkshaven home in *Sylvia's Lovers* (1863).[103] When Alice's daughter Hester opens the lid of chest in which she stores her Sunday cloak, 'a sweet scent of dried lavender and rose-leaves came out'. The country garden of Sylvia's family home is 'planted with berry-bushes for use, and southernwood and sweet-briar for sweetness of smell'.[104] Gaskell's earlier novels, like *Mary Barton* and *North and South* (1854–5), make much of the contrast between the fragrant fresh air of the country and the smoky polluted atmosphere of towns and cities. After time spent in London, Margaret Hale is quick to defend the atmosphere of her native Helstone against her mother's charge of dampness: "'No—no, mamma, it is not that: it is delicious air. It smells of the freshest, purest fragrance, after the smokiness of Harley Street.'" Relocated to industrial Milton, the Hales notice how 'Nearer to the town, the air had a faint taste and smell of smoke; perhaps, after all, more a loss of the fragrance of grass and herbage than any positive taste or smell.'[105]

When the recently bereaved Margaret visits Helstone again after time spent in Milton, Gaskell depicts the kindly ministrations of the landlady of the local inn, who is keen to offer aromatic homely pleasures like 'an armful of lavender-scented towels', and who declares "'It's only this very morning I plunged some fresh-gathered

---

[101] Amy Stewart Fraser, *Roses in December: Edwardian Reflections* (London: Routledge & Kegan Paul, 1981), p. 39.
[102] Gaskell, 'My Lady Ludlow', pp. 38–9.
[103] Letter of 7 December 1857, *Letters of Mrs Gaskell*, ed. J. A. V. Chapple and A. Pollard (Manchester: Manchester University Press, 1966), p. 492.
[104] Elizabeth Gaskell, *Sylvia's Lovers*, ed. Francis O'Gorman (Oxford: Oxford University Press, 2014), pp. 72, 75, 202 (chs 7, 20).
[105] Elizabeth Gaskell, *North and South*, ed. Angus Easson (Oxford: Oxford University Press, 1982), pp. 41, 59 (chs 5, 7).

roses head downward in the water-jug, for, thought I, perhaps some one will be coming, and there's nothing so sweet as spring-water scented by a musk rose or two.'"[106] Similarly, in *Cranford* (1851–3), little scented gifts, homemade by the genteel though modestly circumstanced ladies of the town, betoken thoughtful kindness: 'the rose-leaves that were gathered ere they fell, to make into a pot-pourri for some one who had no garden; the little bundles of lavender flowers sent to strew the drawers of some town-dweller, or to burn in the chamber of some invalid'.[107] A touching if more extravagant gift of natural scent occurs in Gaskell's story 'My French Master' (1853), set just after the French Revolution, where the narrator's father is a gentleman farmer:

> Our house was situated on the edge of the forest; our fields were, in fact, cleared out of it. It was not good land for clover; but my father would always sow one particular field with clover seed, because my mother was so fond of the fragrant scent in her evening walks.[108]

Gaskell tends to be among those Victorian writers who favour pure natural scents against the artificiality of perfume, another influential proponent being the Victorian art critic and sage John Ruskin. Although more preoccupied by sight, Ruskin touches on smell in the second volume (1846) of his compendious *Modern Painters* (5 vols, 1843–60) when he expatiates on how 'the lower pleasures may be elevated in rank':

> Thus Aristotle has subtly noted, that 'we call not men intemperate so much with respect to the scents of roses or herb-perfumes as of ointments and of condiments', (though the reason that he gives for this be futile enough.) For the fact is, that of scents artificially prepared the extreme desire is intemperance, but of natural and God-given scents, which take their part in the harmony and pleasantness of creation, there can hardly be intemperance; not that there is any absolute difference between the two kinds, but that these are likely to be received with gratitude and joyfulness rather than those, so that we despise the seeking of essences and unguents, but not the sowing of violets along our garden banks.[109]

Yet, although Ruskin thinks that 'scents artificially prepared' promote intemperance, he rather surprisingly finds that there is no 'absolute difference' between natural and artificial scents, and, mindful of the perfumes of the Bible, allows that 'all things may be elevated by affection, as the spikenard of Mary, and in the Song of Solomon, the myrrh upon the handles of the lock, and that of Isaac concerning his son'. Nonetheless, Ruskin's general mistrust of 'artificial' perfumes suggests he would not have approved their use by his male contemporaries. While this mistrust

---

[106] Gaskell, *North and South*, pp. 387, 386 (vol. 2, ch. 21).

[107] Elizabeth Gaskell, *Cranford*, ed. Elizabeth Porges Watson (Oxford: Oxford University Press, 1980), p. 15 (ch. 2).

[108] Elizabeth Gaskell, 'My French Master' (1853), in *Cousin Phillis and Other Stories*, ed. Heather Glen (Oxford: Oxford University Press, 2010), p. 70 (ch. 1).

[109] John Ruskin, *Modern Painters*, vol. 2 (Part 3: 'Of Ideas of Beauty', Section 1: 'Of the Theoretic Faculty', ch. 2, subsection 7). See *The Library Edition of the Works of John Ruskin*, ed. E. T. Cook and A. Wedderburn, 39 vols (London: George Allen, 1903–12), 4. 47.

puts him in the company of many conservative commentators during the Victorian period, such views were far from universal.

Victorian Men and Perfume

It is often assumed that Victorian men did not use perfume and certainly the official position is that it was not considered good form. The male author of *The Habits of Good Society* advises gentlemen that 'The ancients followed up the bath by anointing the body, and athletic exercise. The former is a mistake; the latter an excellent practice', and he opines that 'As to pomatum, Macassar, and other inventions of the hairdresser, I have only to say, that, if used at all, it should be in moderation, and never sufficiently to make their scent perceptible in good society.'[110] Another guide, *Etiquette for Ladies and Gentlemen* (1876), is more emphatic, crisply instructing its male readers 'Use no perfumes.'[111] *The Gentleman's Art of Dressing with Economy* of the same year decrees that 'it is a positive sin for the sterner sex to dissipate their coin in cosmetics and perfumed investments'.[112] In 1909 in his weekly feature 'The Outer Man' in the journal *The Modern Man*, the columnist Captain L. H. Saunders answers the question 'Should men use scent?' with the terse response: 'a man who smells of scent is a ridiculous person, and to call him effeminate is to put things in their mildest form'.[113] Aytoun Ellis writes in his history of perfume:

> Up to [the First World War] [...] it was considered effeminate and the worst of taste for a man to use perfume and at most this had to be restricted to a Cologne after-shave lotion. Few were rash enough to allow the barber to scent the hair with violet oil or his honey and flowers; a spray with bay rum or cantharides [hair tonics] was the limit, the vast majority curtly refusing this or even a dusting of scented talcum powder after shaving.[114]

However, after his stiff rejoinder, Captain Saunders backpedals energetically:

> all the same, one may enjoy the benefits of scent without reeking of it in public. [...] I must confess to always having scent on my toilet table, and to using it for various purposes. I have no respect for the man who drenches his handkerchief with scent and flourishes it broadcast. But yet scent may have its uses as part of a man's toilet equipment.[115]

In his novel *69 Birnam Road*, set at the turn of the nineteenth into the twentieth century, William Pett Ridge portrays suburban City men who nostalgically recall 'youthful days in the country, when one had a suit kept for Sunday, and one's hair

---

[110] *The Habits of Good Society*, pp. 107, 117.
[111] *Etiquette for Ladies and Gentlemen* (London and New York: Frederick Warne & Co., 1876), p. 79.
[112] *The Gentleman's Art of Dressing with Economy by a Lounger at the Clubs* (London: Frederick Warne, 1876), pp. 96–7.
[113] Captain L. H. Saunders, 'The Outer Man', *Modern Man* (13 March 1909), 24.
[114] Aytoun Ellis, *The Essence of Beauty: A History of Perfume and Cosmetics* (London: Secker & Warburg, 1960), p. 195.
[115] Saunders, 'The Outer Man', p. 24.

was pomatumed and curled, and a handkerchief scented with lavender water'.[116] Those who thought applying perfume to their handkerchief was effete would, in spite of Ellis's rebuttal, have experienced perfume in other ways, as even Brown Windsor, a traditional quality soap of the kind favoured by gentlemen, was scented with lavender, rosemary, thyme, cassia, caraway, and cloves.[117] As Pett Ridge implies, many men would also use a scented hair oil, pomatum, or bear's grease to slick down their hair. Scented bear's grease, famously associated with Atkinsons, which used the bear for its trademark, was a popular choice for men. When Thackeray's young dandy Arthur Pendennis wears it, his friend complains he is 'scented like a barber'.[118] The Pre-Raphaelite painter Holman Hunt scented his hair and beard with sandalwood oil, a perfume that had a powerful effect on his second wife, Edith Waugh. Kissed by Hunt as a girl of nineteen at his first wedding in 1865, she found 'The effect of this brotherly kiss and the scent of the sandalwood oil [...] so overpowering that had she not been "so well brought up, she would have fainted"'.[119] Gentlemen would also probably use as an aftershave or deodorant eau de cologne, which was such a Victorian staple most people hardly regarded it as a perfume. (Prior to the Victorian period, the Regency dandy Beau Brummell, who shunned perfumes, counted eau de cologne among his 'comestibles'.[120]) Some used other scented light toilet waters. Violet Trefusis, daughter of the King's mistress, recalled that in the early 1900s Edward VII 'smelt deliciously of cigars and *eau de Portugal'*.[121]

Many gentlemen wore a buttonhole or boutonnière, as can be seen in portraits and photographs of the period. In his book *Domestic Floriculture* (1874), F. W. Burbidge observes that 'Button-hole bouquets and coat-flowers are now becoming very fashionable, and when tastefully made up, they certainly form charming little ornaments for evening dress.'[122] Although most guides are silent on the topic, Lady Constance Howard, in *Etiquette: What to Do, and How to Do It* (1885), advises gentlemen: 'A buttonhole of some favourite flower is always worn, morning and evening', while Anne Hassard includes instructions on making 'Button-hole Bouquets' in her book on domestic floral decorations.[123] Famous buttonhole wearers included the Liberal Unionist MP Sir Joseph Chamberlain, whose trademark orchid buttonholes were sent down to him in London from his

[116] William Pett Ridge, *69 Birnam Road* (London: Hodder & Stoughton, 1908), p. 316.

[117] See Piesse, *Art of Perfumery* (1855), p. 166.

[118] Thackeray, *The History of Pendennis*, p. 589 (ch. 47).

[119] Diana Holman-Hunt, *My Grandfather, His Wives and Loves* (1969; London: Columbus Books, 1987), p. 244.

[120] Ian Kelly, *Beau Brummell: The Ultimate Dandy* (London: Sceptre, 2005), p. 161.

[121] Violet Trefusis, *Don't Look Round* (London: Hamish Hamilton, 1952), p. 33.

[122] F. W. Burbidge, *Domestic Floriculture: Window-Gardening and Floral Decorations* (Edinburgh and London: William Blackwood & Sons, 1874), p. 127. A buttonhole is usually a small posy of flowers with foliage and a 'coat-flower', a single flower, though for convenience I use the word 'buttonhole' to cover both.

[123] Lady Constance Howard, *Etiquette: What to Do, and How to Do It* (London: F. V. White, 1885), p. 166; Anne Hassard, *Floral Decorations for the Dwelling House: A Practical Guide for the Home Arrangement of Plants and Flowers* (London: Macmillan, 1875), pp. 80–8.

orchid houses at Highbury Hall in Birmingham.[124] Another was Oscar Wilde who, lamenting the conservatism and uniformity of men's dress in a letter to the *Daily Telegraph* (2 February 1891), declared that 'The little note of individualism that makes dress delightful can only be attained nowadays by the colour and treatment of the flower one wears' (*CL*, p. 465). In 1910 the *Modern Man*, definitely more of a 'lad's mag' than a publication for dandies, cited a West End florist, who observed 'that the trade in button-holes was nothing to what it was in the past', and, looking back to the nineteenth century, noted 'Then every well dressed man sported one.' The same article also observes that 'The favourite flowers, barring the orchid and the rose, would appear to be the carnation, the gardenia, and the tuberose', all flowers that are heavily scented.[125] Another popular and sweetly scented choice for Victorian buttonholes was violets—either the more expensive imported Parma violets or native Devon violets, with the latter, when in season, widely available from street flower-girls for a few pence, so often worn by city workers with more modest incomes.[126]

Even that masculine preserve the smoking room might carry traces of perfume as snuff was often scented with spices and essential oils such as rose, bergamot, violet, and lavender, and pipe tobacco might be scented with similar oils and spices blended with tinctures of musk, civet, or ambergris.[127] (Towards the end of the nineteenth century ladies who daringly smoked cigarettes might, if they wished, opt for a brand scented with violet or rose.[128]) Gentlemen wanting to dispel the odour of stale tobacco smoke might burn Piesse and Lubin's scented ribbon, impregnated with benzoin, myrrh, orris, musk, and rose otto, and known as 'Ruban de Bruges', or a similar product by Rimmel known as 'Persian Fumigating Ribbon'.[129]

While most Victorian men may have limited their contact with scent to such uses, those who saw themselves as urbane or bohemian men, or identified as dandies, certainly did wear more. Atkinsons's notable clients included not only royalty like the Prince of Wales (the future Edward VII), but Sir Robert Peel, and the Dukes of Wellington and Marlborough, while C. J. S. Thompson refers to a ledger belonging 'to one of the oldest Court Perfumers in London', which lists three prime ministers—Lord Palmerston, Lord John Russell, and Mr George Canning—as 'among those who used a considerable amount of perfume'.[130] Other notable perfume wearers were the novelist and MP Edward Bulwer-Lytton, and

---

[124] Peter T. Marsh, *Joseph Chamberlain: Entrepreneur in Politics* (New Haven, CT: Yale University Press, 1994), p. 140.

[125] 'Judging a Man by his Button-hole', *The Modern Man* (15 January 1910), 22.

[126] Mark Griffiths, 'Sweet Tenants of the Shade', *The Garden* 125 (February 2001), 91.

[127] James B. Lutterman, *The Tobacco Manufacturers' Manual: A Vade-Mecum for the Allied Industries* (London: [The author], 1887), pp. 93–105; John Arlott, *The Snuff Shop* (London: Michael Joseph, 1974), p. 34.

[128] See the advertisement for 'White Rose' cigarettes in *The Smoker* (5 March 1892), 175, which, when smoked, 'diffuse a delicate perfume of "White Rose"'. See, too, the advertisement for Ogden's 'Otto de Rose' cigarettes, *The Smoker* (9 April 1892), 224.

[129] See *Piesse & Lubin's Toilet Almanack for 1861*, p. 28 and Figure 6.1.

[130] Bailey et al., eds., *British Perfumery: A Fragrant History*, p. 22; Thompson, *The Mystery and Lure of Perfume*, p. 168.

the novelist and future Prime Minister Benjamin Disraeli, who was singled out as a dandified young man in the 1830s for his extravagant costume and for having 'a person redolent of perfume'.[131] The hero of his novel *The Young Duke* (1831) has 'a white silk waistcoat lined in rose, buttoned with pink topaz, sprayed with essence of violet'.[132] According to Disraeli's wife, Mary Anne, he was also 'passionately fond of flowers', relishing the scented bouquets sent him by Queen Victoria, and he thanked Sarah Brydges Willyams for a gift of roses 'with a perfume so exquisite— witht. wh: latter charm the rarest and the fairest flowers have little spell for me'.[133] Anthony Trollope transferred the scent associated with the dandified Disraeli to his fiction, which he found artificial and over-theatrical—'Through it all there is a feeling of stage properties, a smell of hair oil'—and he thought that Disraeli's later novel *Lothair* (1870) in particular emanated that 'flavour of hair oil, that feeling of false jewels'.[134]

Thackeray mocked Disraeli's friend, the notorious dandy Bulwer-Lytton, in similar terms when reviewing his novel *Ernest Maltravers* (1837): 'If he would but leave off scents for his handkerchief, and oil for his hair [...] how much might be made of him yet.'[135] Bulwer-Lytton's eponymous Pelham, from his novel of 1828, is, remarks Ellen Moers:

> [A]n amateur of perfume, approving its use by women (he meets his future wife outside a perfumer's shop) and by men. He himself cannot concentrate until he has sum- moned a servant 'for my poodle and some *eau de Cologne*' and he recommends the serving of perfumes with dessert. 'In confectionary (delicate invention of the Sylphs), we imitate the forms of the rose and the jessamine; why not their odours too? What is nature without its scents?'[136]

The scented dandy features in other early novels of the period. Thackeray, who enjoys satirizing such figures, portrays Arthur Pendennis 'sprinkling himself with eau-de-Cologne, and carefully scenting his hair and whiskers with that odoriferous water', and intimates he has 'a partiality for rings, jewellery and fine raiment' and 'perfumed baths'.[137] In the same novel Percy Sibwright, a ladies' man of poetical

---

[131] Christopher Hibbert, *Disraeli: A Personal History* (London: Harper Collins, 2004), pp. 65, 74.

[132] The paraphrase is Ellen Moers's, from *The Dandy: Brummell to Beerbohm* (London: Secker & Warburg, 1960), p. 102. See Benjamin Disraeli, *The Young Duke*, 3 vols (London: H. Colburn and R. Bentley, 1831), 1. 210–11.

[133] William Kuhn, *The Politics of Pleasure: A Portrait of Benjamin Disraeli* (London: Free Press, 2006), p. 291. Letter of 23 April 1854, *Benjamin Disraeli: Letters*, ed. J. A. W. Gunn et al., 9 vols to date (Toronto and London: University of Toronto Press, 1982–), 6: *Letters 1852–1856*, ed. M. G. Wiebe, Mary S. Millar, and Ann Robson (1997), 237.

[134] Anthony Trollope, *An Autobiography*, ed. P. D. Edwards (Oxford: Oxford University Press, 1999), pp. 259, 260.

[135] William Makepeace Thackeray, 'Our Batch of Novels for Christmas 1837', *Fraser's Magazine* (January 1838), in *Stray Papers by William Makepeace Thackeray*, ed. Lew Melville (London: Hutchinson & Co., 1901), p. 292.

[136] See Moers, *The Dandy*, p. 81. *Pelham* was first published anonymously by the then Edward Bulwer. See *Pelham; or, The Adventures of a Gentleman*, 3 vols (London: Henry Colburn, 1828), 2. 41–2, 150, 218.

[137] Thackeray, *The History of Pendennis*, pp. 900, 217 (chs 69, 18). The second quotation also cited in Moers, *The Dandy*, p. 207.

tendencies, is found to have in his bedroom 'a museum of scent, pomatum, and bear's-grease pots, quite curious to examine'.[138]

Late Victorian dandies kept up this perfumed tradition. In 1882 when the young Wilde was interviewed in New Orleans on his American tour, he made sure he was surrounded by carefully selected props that announced his decadent dandy status—'yellow-bound novels in the French language, [...] a bundle of cigarettes and a bottle of cologne water'—perfume being an essential part of his self-presentation.[139] Wilde's close friend Ada Leverson, whom he called 'Sphinx', created her own comic version of the *fin-de-siècle* dandy in Cecil Carington, an attitudinizing fop who features in a number of short stories and who memorably updates Pelham's request for 'my poodle and some *eau de Cologne*' by declaring to his valet, 'Collins, [...] take away this eau-de-cologne. It's corked.'[140] In her biography of her mother, Violet Wyndham describes Ada's Mayfair luncheons and dinner parties, remembering 'On the hall table, top hats, some of them smelling sweetly of hair oil', and declaring 'Scent was much used by dandies on their hair.'[141] Henry Paget, the extravagant fifth Marquess of Anglesey (1875–1905), was probably the most famous and outrageous late nineteenth-century dandy. According to H. Montgomery Hyde, 'when he walked along Piccadilly or the Champs Elysées, he invariably carried a snow-white, pink-ribboned poodle in his arms, who was just as abundantly scented with patchouli and *eau d'Espagne* [sic] as his master'.[142]

Studies of nineteenth-century dandyism have usually concentrated on men's dress and manners, ignoring the 'invisible' perfume aura that was the male dandy's extension of his personality, an aura previously suggested by synonyms for 'dandy', like the French 'muscadin' (a man who wears musk perfume) or the English 'jessamy' (a man who wears jasmine perfume).[143] Commenting on fragrances worn by Victorian men, Luca Turin remarks: 'Fragrances in these days were more unisex than they are now. The classic British masculine of the late Victorian period was a musky, powdery floral, typically rather sweet. Perhaps the best surviving example of the genre is Penhaligon's Hammam Bouquet (1872), still eminently wearable.'[144] With a more evident interest and investment in perfume than other men, dandies demonstrate their membership of an elite group and signal their taste and refinement. Wilde would have enjoyed Turin's modern-day description of perfume as

---

[138] Thackeray, *The History of Pendennis*, p. 666 (ch. 52).

[139] 'Oscar Wilde: A Visit to the Apostle of Modern Art', *Daily Picayune* (16 June 1882), in E. H. Mikhail, ed., *Oscar Wilde: Interviews and Recollections*, 2 vols (London and Basingstoke: Macmillan, 1979), 1. 89.

[140] Ada Leverson, 'The Quest of Sorrow', *Yellow Book* 5 (April 1895), 325–35; 329.

[141] Violet Wyndham, *The Sphinx and her Circle: A Biographical Sketch of Ada Leverson 1862–1933* (London: André Deutsch, 1963), p. 58.

[142] H. Montgomery Hyde, *The Other Love: An Historical and Contemporary Survey of Homosexuality in Britain* (London: Heinemann, 1970), p. 154.

[143] 'Muscadin' later came to denote a member of the group of dandyish Parisian streetfighters of the Thermidorian Reaction during the French Revolution. 'Jessamy' is derived from 'jessamine', an old-fashioned word for 'jasmine'. See the satirical print 'A Jessamy' (1790) in the British Museum (Museum no: 1876,1014.63).

[144] Turin and Sanchez, *Perfumes: The A–Z Guide*, p. 23.

'the most portable form of intelligence'.[145] Yet although perfume was worn and enjoyed by many urbane, eminent, and distinguished men, there was ambivalence and hostility about male perfume use, which filters through into literary texts of the period. While aesthetic and decadent writers are fascinated by perfume, men's use of it is often suspect, particularly in earlier Victorian fiction. The perfumed man is frequently a comic figure, but his perfume may also hint that he is untrustworthy, an upstart, cad, or a bounder, or possibly something even more sinister than that.

In Bad Odour

For a number of Victorian novelists scent is the accessory of the overdressed fop. In *Pickwick Papers* (1836), Dickens has fun with the person of Angelo Cyrus Bantam, Esq.:

> His linen was of the very whitest, finest, and stiffest; his wig of the glossiest, blackest, and curliest. His snuff was princes' mixture; his scent *bouquet du roi*. His features were contracted into a perpetual smile; and his teeth were in such perfect order that it was difficult at a small distance to tell the real from the false.

Later Dickens mocks the stockbroker Wilkins Flasher, Esq. and his friend Mr Simmons: 'Both gentlemen had very open waistcoats and very rolling collars, and very small boots, and very big rings, and very little watches, and very large guard-chains, and symmetrical inexpressibles [trousers], and scented pocket-handkerchiefs.'[146] The gauche young baronet, Sir Louis Scatcherd, in Anthony Trollope's *Doctor Thorne* (1858), overdresses. Trying to make an impression on Mary Thorne, 'he carried a scented handkerchief in his hand; he had rings on his fingers, and carbuncle studs in his shirt, and he smelt as sweet as patchouli could make him'.[147]

In *Wives and Daughters* (1864–6), Elizabeth Gaskell draws a contrast between the sons of Squire Hamley, the delicate, refined Osborne who does not appreciate the smell of his father's cattle, and his manlier, good-hearted, but more rough and ready brother Roger. When Roger joins the Squire, who is smoking 'strong tobacco', his father remarks sardonically, '"It will make your clothes smell. You'll have to borrow Osborne's scents to sweeten yourself."' Roger eventually marries the heroine, Molly Gibson, after initially preferring her stepsister Cynthia. Molly's father, Dr Gibson, is wryly satirical about the man Cynthia finally chooses as her husband: '"I don't wonder she preferred him to Roger Hamley. Such scents! such gloves! And then his hair and his cravat!"'[148] If Gaskell implies men's use of scent

---

[145] Luca Turin, quoted in Burr, *The Emperor of Scent*, p. 309.

[146] Charles Dickens, *Pickwick Papers*, ed. James Kinsley (Oxford: Oxford University Press, 1988), pp. 445, 698–9 (chs 35, 55).

[147] Anthony Trollope, *Doctor Thorne*, ed. David Skilton (Oxford: Oxford University Press, 1980), p. 449–50 (ch. 34).

[148] Elizabeth Gaskell, *Wives and Daughters*, ed. Angus Easson (Oxford: Oxford University Press, 1987), pp. 274–5, 635 (chs 23, 56).

is an affectation, then elsewhere it can hint at something not wholly trustworthy, as in *Vanity Fair* (1847–8), where Thackeray sets up a similar but more troubling contrast between the two men who provide Amelia Sedley's love interest: the dandified, vain, and perfidious George Osborne who wipes his face 'with a large yellow bandanna pocket-handkerchief that was prodigiously scented' and his friend, the clumsy but noble Major Dobbin.[149]

Scent as something to be despised and distrusted in a man, an elegant odorous screen that camouflages and hints at a less than fragrant moral interior, can be found in various early to mid-Victorian fictions. In Dickens's *Barnaby Rudge* (1841), Mr (later Sir) John Chester, a vain, selfish man who opposes his son's love match, affects aristocratic airs and scented snuff, and calls for scent to perfume the room after being visited by lesser beings.[150] In Tennyson's dramatic poem *Maud* (1855), Maud's brother, who opposes her romance with the narrator, is described by him as 'a dandy-despot' and an 'oil'd and curl'd Assyrian bull | Smelling of musk and of insolence', and later he complains 'his essences turned the live air sick'.[151] The well-to-do, foppish Stephen Guest of George Eliot's *The Mill on the Floss* (1860), distinguished by his 'diamond ring, attar of roses, and air of nonchalant leisure, at twelve o'clock in the day', abandons his fiancée to lead the heroine Maggie Tulliver astray, while in Ellen Wood's *East Lynne* (1861), the overdressed rake Frank Levison with his 'perfumed hands' and handkerchief 'not entirely guilt-less of scent' is not only a heartless seducer who elopes with the married Lady Isabel Vane and subsequently deserts her and their unborn child, but is a murderer to boot.[152] The female narrator of Gaskell's tale 'The Grey Woman' (1861) is dis-comfited by her early impressions of her suitor, the wealthy dandy Monsieur de la Tourelle. Pressured into marrying him, she recollects when she is immured in his secluded château in the Vosges,

> noticing one or two things in these rooms, then seen by me for the first time. I remem-ber the sweet perfume that hung in the air, the scent bottles of silver that decked his toilet-table, and the whole apparatus for bathing and dressing, more luxurious even than those which he had provided for me.[153]

M. de la Tourelle's perfumed aura of elegance masks his brutality as he turns out to be a member of a murderous criminal gang, and his wife escapes his clutches only to live in terror for the rest of her life. Perfume has another uneasy association with criminality in Dickens's *Great Expectations* (1861), in which the lawyer, Mr Jaggers, is always washing his hands with scented soap as if to disguise the taint

---

[149] William Makepeace Thackeray, *Vanity Fair*, ed. John Sutherland (Oxford: Oxford University Press, 1983), p. 261 (ch. 22).

[150] Charles Dickens, *Barnaby Rudge*, ed. Clive Hurst (Oxford: Oxford University Press, 2003), pp. 196, 347 (chs 23, 43).

[151] Alfred Tennyson, 'Maud', in *Tennyson: A Selected Edition*, ed. Christopher Ricks (Harlow: Longman, 1989), pp. 533, 544.

[152] George Eliot, *The Mill on the Floss*, ed. Gordon S. Haight (Oxford: Oxford University Press, 1996), p. 364 (bk 6, ch. 1); Wood, *East Lynne*, pp. 55, 192 (chs 6, 19).

[153] Elizabeth Gaskell, 'The Grey Woman', in *A Dark Night's Work and Other Stories*, ed. Suzanne Lewis (Oxford: Oxford University Press, 1992), p. 271.

of his dealings with the criminal classes. Even as a child Pip is bothered by this smell, which at a later date announces Jaggers's very presence in the room.[154]

To appreciate the impact of Wilde's *The Picture of Dorian Gray* (1890, 1891) with its portrayal of men's uninhibited and unapologetic pleasure in scent we need to see it in the context of such prejudice. But if men in early or mid-Victorian fiction incur ridicule, disapproval, or suspicion for using perfume, women fare little better. The scented letter—writing paper perfumed with civet or peau d'espagne was popular in the period—is associated with the adventuress like Becky Sharp in *Vanity Fair* or the manipulations of the 'noxious siren', Signora Neroni in Trollope's *Barchester Towers* (1857).[155] Women who affect rich or heavy scents are invariably loose, devious, or damaged, and meet with special censure. In *Jane Eyre* (1847), Rochester tells Jane how he discovers the faithlessness of his French mistress Céline Varens when he stops by her apartment one evening to wait for her return:

> I sat down in her boudoir; happy to breathe the air consecrated so lately by her presence. No,—I exaggerate; I never thought there was any consecrating virtue about her: it was rather a sort of pastille perfume she had left; a scent of musk and amber, than an odour of sanctity. I was just beginning to stifle with the fumes of conservatory flowers and sprinkled essences, when I bethought myself to open the window and step out on to the balcony.[156]

On the balcony he overhears Céline returning with another male admirer, but her 'unwholesome' reputation has already been communicated to the reader by her dubious taste in sensual animalic perfume. In contrast Jane is associated with natural scents which, on the evening Rochester proposes, swirl romantically about her, punctuated only by the 'subtle, well-known scent' of his cigar, a properly masculine note: 'Sweet-briar and southern-wood, jasmine, pink, and rose have long been yielding their evening sacrifice of incense; this new scent is neither of shrub nor flower; it is—I know it well—it is Mr. Rochester's cigar.'[157]

In Mary Braddon's sensation novel *Lady Audley's Secret* (1862), we encounter another heavily scented boudoir belonging to another dubious woman. Lady Audley, a beguiling, doll-like blonde who has married a much older wealthy widower, is actually a bigamist who will attempt to murder her first husband. While she is absent from home, her new nephew Robert Audley and his friend George Talboys, her unwitting first husband, enter her private chamber:

> She had left the house in a hurry on her unlooked-for journey to London, and the whole of her glittering toilette apparatus lay about on the marble dressing-table. The

---

[154] Charles Dickens, *Great Expectations*, ed. Margaret Cardwell (Oxford: Oxford University Press, 2008), pp. 75–6, 192, 202 (ch. 11; bk 2, ch. 7; bk 2 ch. 10).

[155] See Piesse, *Art of Perfumery* (1855), pp. 144–5; Thackeray, *Vanity Fair*, p. 672 (ch. 53); Anthony Trollope, *Barchester Towers*, ed. John Sutherland (Oxford: Oxford University Press, 1996), p. 196 (ch. 44).

[156] Charlotte Brontë, *Jane Eyre*, ed. Margaret Smith (Oxford: Oxford University Press, 2000), p. 140 (bk 1, ch. 15).

[157] Ibid., p. 248 (bk 2, ch. 8).

atmosphere of the room was almost oppressive from the rich odours of perfumes in bottles whose gold stoppers had not been replaced. A bunch of hot-house flowers was withering upon a tiny writing-table.[158]

Like Céline's boudoir, Lady Audley's room is oppressively scented not just by perfumes but by exotic 'hot-house' flowers, the products of another artificial atmosphere. While such artifice will be embraced and celebrated in later decadent texts, here it hints at its female owner's lack of naturalness, her questionable morality, and her duplicity.[159]

The pernicious, stifling, scented boudoir recurs in a late Victorian best-seller, Marie Corelli's *The Sorrows of Satan* (1895) in which Geoffrey Tempest, an aspirant but failed novelist, rises to fame and fortune after becoming a friend of Prince Lucio Rimânez, the devil in earthly form. During his ascent Tempest marries the cold but beautiful Lady Sibyl Elton who falls in love with Rimânez and eventually commits suicide at her toilet table by taking poison. Accompanied by Mavis Clare, a pure-hearted woman friend, Tempest discovers his wife's corpse in her boudoir and orders Mavis to quit the room: 'This air is contaminated—it will poison you! The perfume of Paris and the effluvia of death intermingled are sufficient to breed a pestilence!'[160] Dying, Lady Sibyl has soaked a handkerchief with perfume to ease 'this sick swooning sensation', the scent making her recollect the shop where she bought it in Paris.[161] As in *Jane Eyre*, there is a contrast between the bad woman who wears foreign perfume and the good woman, who is associated with natural English scents—Mavis's 'delicate attractiveness' is compared to the 'breath of honeysuckle' that delights 'the wayfarer with sweet fragrance'.[162] Tempest associates his wife's perfume with her corruption, thinking as he leaves her corpse that 'the perfume in the room had a grave-like earthy smell'.[163]

The perversity of perfume is given substance by a small number of Victorian women who imbibed scent for its alcohol content. In 'The Girl of the Period', her notorious indictment of fast and flashy female types, Eliza Lynn Linton condemns '*la femme passée* of to-day', the showy, pleasure-seeking older woman encountered 'at balls and fêtes and afternoon At Homes', who gives off a frenetic intensity 'perhaps the pupils dilated by belladonna; perhaps a false and fatal brilliancy for the moment given by opium, or by eau de cologne, of which she has a store in her carriage, and drinks as she passes from ball to ball'.[164] Towards the end of the century there was also a craze for subcutaneous perfume injections, a fashionable Parisian practice reported in the *Chemist and Druggist* for September 1898.[165]

---

[158] Mary Elizabeth Braddon, *Lady Audley's Secret*, ed. David Skilton (Oxford: Oxford University Press, 1987), p. 69 (ch. 8).

[159] The woman's scented boudoir, its secrets, and its entry or penetration by the male voyeur reprise an influential eighteenth-century topos explored by Tita Chico in *Designing Women: The Dressing Room in Eighteenth-Century English Literature and Culture* (Lewisburg, PA: Bucknell University Press, 2005). My thanks to Chris Reid for this reference.

[160] Marie Corelli, *The Sorrows of Satan* (Oxford: Oxford University Press, 1998), p. 316 (ch. 34).

[161] Ibid., p. 335 (ch. 36).   [162] Ibid., p. 183 (ch. 19).   [163] Ibid., p. 340 (ch. 36).

[164] Eliza Lynn Linton, *The Girl of the Period*, 2 vols (London: Richard Bentley & Son, 1883), 1. 313.

[165] See 'The Latest Fashion', in the *Chemist and Druggist* (24 September 1898), 522. For another account focused on French literature and culture, see Cheryl Krueger's essay, 'Decadent Perfume

In her long confessional suicide letter, Lady Sibyl reveals that her moral degeneration has been accelerated by addiction to what we might see as another kind of scented imbibing, namely the consumption of poetry and, in particular, Swinburne's verse, which 'poisoned my thoughts forever'.[166] Formerly a lover of poetry—we learn she read Shelley, Keats, and Byron avidly as a girl—she now condemns its 'strained aestheticism and unbridled sensualism'.[167] Like Wilde's Dorian Gray intoxicated by Lord Henry's poisonous yellow book, Sibyl is 'poisoned' by an influential literary text—here Swinburne's verses, so often associated with scent: 'I drank in the poet's own fiendish contempt of God.'[168] While Corelli does not explicitly develop the links between poetry, perfume, and poison, it is hard not to see her novel, which follows in the wake of *Dorian Gray*, as a reaction to what she perceived as corrupt (and implicitly) perfumed aestheticism and decadence.

THE SCENT OF VICTORIAN POETRY

If much Victorian fiction is suspicious of perfume, the picture is usually different when it comes to poets and poetry, which have a much stronger alliance with fragrance, not least because, as will be shown in this section, the figurative language of lyrical thought and creativity involves metaphors connected with scent. At a more literal level, unapologetic reference to manufactured perfume appears in poetry throughout the nineteenth century, though is particularly conspicuous in the *fin de siècle*. Male poets or their poetic personae also have greater license to express a full and uninhibited enjoyment in natural scents, something that tends to be more of a female prerogative in fiction. In 1877 Grant Allen acknowledged that the experience of appreciating scented flowers can 'arouse feelings so nearly approaching the æsthetic level, we naturally find their ideal representative entering into the composition of Poetry', and he adds that 'we cannot doubt that some part in the poetical effectiveness of fragrant flowers must be attributed to the sense of smell'.[169] Allen suggested that '*lily of the valley* excites in us not only an ideal consciousness of the flower, but also a very slight wave of that pleasurable feeling which an actual lily produces in us through the senses of sight and smell'. He also thought that '*Fragrant, sweet, perfumed, scented, odorous*, and all other words denoting pleasant sensations of smell are highly poetic', but that words 'denoting ill odours, such as *stench, stinking* etc' were 'so highly unpoetical that they almost defy introduction into Poetry'. He was sceptical that poetry could accommodate, among other things, 'modern drinks and perfumes', classing them among those terms he considered 'from their very newness, unpoetical', and giving as examples

---

under the Skin and through the Page', *Modern Languages Open* (28 October 2014), http://www.modernlanguagesopen.org/index.php/mlo/article/view/36http://www.modernlanguagesopen.org/index.php/mlo/article/view/36.

[166] Corelli, *The Sorrows of Satan*, p. 327 (ch. 35).　　　[167] Ibid., p. 334 (ch. 36).
[168] Ibid., p. 325 (ch. 35).　　　[169] Allen, *Physiological Æsthetics*, p. 83.

'Jockey-club, millefleurs, or frangipanni.'[170] Although Allen is thought-provoking on the fragrant suggestiveness of poetic language, his olfactory and literary tastes are conservative. By 1877 he was already behind the times as the American writer Charles Godfrey Leland had published 'Frangipani' among 'Poems of Perfume' in his collection *The Music-Lesson of Confucius* (1872) and Austin Dobson had name-checked 'Ess Bouquet' in his poems 'A City Flower' (1864) and 'Incognita' (1866).[171] Back in 1840 Robert Browning challenged assumptions about the poetic use of 'stinks' and 'ill odours' by employing an olfactory metaphor that Allen almost certainly would have found objectionable.

In the conclusion to *Sordello*, his long and notoriously testing narrative poem about the thirteenth-century Italian troubadour Sordello da Goito, Browning uses the uncompromising odour of raw musk as a synonym for the distinctive difficulty of his poetry:

> friends,
> Wake up; the ghost's gone, and the story ends
> I'd fain hope, sweetly—seeing, peri or ghoul,
> That spirits are conjectured fair or foul,
> Evil or good, judicious authors think,
> According as they vanish in a stink
> Or in a perfume: friends, be frank: ye snuff
> Civet, I warrant: really? Like enough—
> Merely the savour's rareness—any nose
> May ravage with impunity a rose—
> Rifle a musk-pod and 'twill ache like yours:
> I'd tell you that same pungency ensures
> An after-gust—but that were overbold:
> Who would has heard Sordello's story told.[172]

Bidding farewell to his protagonist, Browning reminds his readers of the tradition that spirits, when they disappear, are judged benign or otherwise on the basis of the fragrant or noisome smell ('stink') they leave behind them. He quizzes his readers as to what they smell at the end of his poem, guessing that they scent something akin to the powerful animalics musk and civet that were supposedly no longer acceptable and that many Victorians professed to dislike. A freshly opened musk-pod which contains grains of musk has a pungent ammoniacal odour, and musk must be smelt diluted or in small quantities to be fully enjoyed. But Browning

---

[170] Ibid., pp. 247, 252, 268.

[171] Charles Godfrey Leland, 'Frangipani', in *The Music-Lesson of Confucius* (London: Trübner & Co., 1872), pp. 26–8. A poem titled 'Mercutio Frangipanni', attributed to John Cargill Brough, appears in the appendix to Piesse's *Art of Perfumery*, 4th edn (1879), pp. 490–1. For comment on this, see Kettler's 'Making the Synthetic Epic', p. 16. The decadent poet Theodore Wratislaw also includes a poem titled 'Frangipani', dealing with the modern perfume, in his *Caprices* (London: Gay and Bird, 1893), p. 35. Austin Dobson, 'A City Flower', originally published in *Temple Bar* (December 1864), and reprinted in *Vignettes in Rhyme*, p. 143.

[172] Robert Browning, *Sordello*, in *The Poems of Browning*, ed. John Woolford and Daniel Karlin, 4 vols to date (London and New York: Longman, 1991–), 1. 768.

seems to embrace the fact that his poetry, like raw unadulterated musk, has a complex and challenging smell that might make the smeller's nose 'ache'.[173] He does not want his readers to let its perfume simply wash over them like the more immediately appealing, less demanding, and more conventionally acceptable scent of a rose. (He would later complain that Rossetti's verses were '*scented* with poetry, as it were—like trifles of various sorts you take out of a cedar or sandal-wood box', adding 'you know I hate the effeminacy of his school', and thus suggesting a gendered distinction between his own virile, animalic-smelling poetry and the more superficially fragrant but effeminate 'trifles' of the younger poet.[174]) The pungent strength of his work, that complex musky smell of difficulty, he hopes (rather than asserts), will send his readers back for an 'after-gust' or second inhalation, or will remain with them so that they continue to get whiffs of it after the book is closed. Musk is a fixative and, remarking on its 'diffusiveness', Septimus Piesse notes that 'everything in its vicinity soon becomes affected by it, and long retains its odour, although not in actual contact with it'.[175] Browning's speaker seems to hope that his poetry fixes itself in his readers' consciousness and memory, and continues to diffuse its influence through their thoughts.

Both George Wilson and Charles Piesse write about the potential to train the sense of smell, with Piesse in particular urging olfactory education on the grounds of health, hygiene, and aesthetic pleasure.[176] Browning educates his readers' olfactory and literary sensibility by exposing them to a strong perfume that many find repellent. However, a key text cited by both Wilson and Piesse proposes an educative model that Allen would have found far more acceptable, in which the reader is urged to learn 'what be the flowers and plants that do best perfume the air'.[177] During the later nineteenth century Francis Bacon's essay 'Of Gardens' of 1625, which evocatively describes the different sweet scents of flowers, had become something of a literary touchstone, and was also often quoted in books on floriculture and floral fragrance.[178] Piesse glosses Bacon's essay: 'In cultivating our sense of smell it is not, however, sufficient to enjoy the perfume of flowers generally, but we must teach ourselves one flower from another equally by smell as by sight.'[179] Yet, through its literary mediation, Bacon's discussion of floral scent was also read as

---

[173] Gervais Chardon, perfumer to Napoleon and Josephine, claimed that that the smell of raw musk could bring about haemorrhage and that, for this reason, hunters protected their mouth and nose with linen masks. See Genders, *A History of Scent*, p. 218.

[174] Browning to Isa Blagden, 19 June 1870, in *Dearest Isa: Robert Browning's Letters to Isa Blagden*, ed. Edward C. McAleer (Austin, TX, and Edinburgh: University of Texas Press and Edinburgh University Press, 1951), p. 336.

[175] Piesse, *Art of Perfumery* (1855), p. 100.

[176] Wilson, *Gateways*, p. 60; Piesse, *Olfactics*, pp. 66–91.

[177] Francis Bacon, 'Of Gardens', in *The Major Works*, ed. Brian Vickers (Oxford: Oxford University Press, 2002), p. 431.

[178] See, for example, The Rev. Henry N. Ellacombe, *The Plant-Lore and Garden Craft of Shakespeare* (London: W. Satchell & Co., 1884), pp. 137, 281–2, 306; E. V. Boyle, *Days and Hours in a Garden* (London: Elliot Stock, 1884), title page epigraph, and pp. 18, 152; Donald McDonald, *Sweet-Scented Flowers and Fragrant Leaves* (New York: Charles Scribner's Sons, 1895), p. xvii; Roberts, *The Book of Old-Fashioned Flowers*, p. 6.

[179] Piesse, *Olfactics*, p. 91. Interestingly, Piesse's gloss is accidentally enclosed in quotation marks, suggesting it is a continuation of Bacon's essay. Wilson also quotes Bacon's essay (*Gateways*, p. 77).

containing a test of innate olfactory sensibility. Bacon lists as one of the sweetest smells after violets and the musk rose 'the strawberry-leaves dying, which [yield] a most excellent cordial smell'.[180] It may be that his 'strawberry-leaves' were of a different order from later varieties, but most people find it difficult, if not impossible, to detect this fragrance, something Gaskell had fun with when her Lady Ludlow claimed the ability to smell it as a mark of gentle birth and enjoined her young companion to savour it:

> But the great hereditary faculty on which my lady piqued herself, and with reason, for I never met with any other person who possessed it, was the power she had of perceiving the delicious odour arising from a bed of strawberries in the late autumn, when the leaves were all fading and dying. 'Bacon's Essays' was one of the few books that lay about in my lady's room; and if you took it up and opened it carelessly, it was sure to fall apart at his 'Essay on Gardens.' 'Listen,' her ladyship would say, 'to what that great philosopher and statesman says [...]. "Then the strawberry leaves, dying with a most excellent cordial smell." Now the Hanburys can always smell this excellent cordial odour, and very delicious and refreshing it is. You see, in Lord Bacon's time, there had not been so many intermarriages between the court and the city [...]. So the old families have gifts and powers of a different and higher class to what the other orders have. My dear, remember that you try if you can smell the scent of dying strawberry-leaves in this next autumn. You have some of Ursula Hanbury's blood in you, and that gives you a chance.'
>
> But when October came, I sniffed and sniffed, and all to no purpose; and my lady—who had watched the little experiment rather anxiously—had to give me up as a hybrid. I was mortified, I confess, and thought that it was in some ostentation of her own powers that she ordered the gardener to plant a border of strawberries on that side of the terrace that lay under her windows.[181]

Although comic in nature, Gaskell's treatment of this 'most excellent cordial smell' helped enshrine it as a mark not so much of the aristocrat but of the *olfactif*. Answering the question raised by the garden writer Henry Arthur Bright—'whether any one now living can smell the scent of dying Strawberry leaves?'—Swinburne rises to this olfactory challenge: 'My impression is that I *do* know quite well the soft slight aroma of dying strawberry leaves distinct in its dim aroma from all others', while John Addington Symonds declares, 'I can smell the perfume of dried wild strawberry leaves, & seek places often here where it is exhaled under pines.'[182] For both writers the ability to smell this rare scent redolent with literary allusion is an indicator of poetic or aesthetic sensibility.

The pattern of the hypersensitive poet who delights in fragrance had already been laid down by the Romantics, especially Keats and Shelley. It is hard to open one of Keats's longer poems at random and not find a reference to sweet odours,

[180] Bacon, 'Of Gardens', p. 431.　　　[181] Gaskell, 'My Lady Ludlow', pp. 39–40.
[182] Henry A. Bright, *A Year in a Lancashire Garden* (London: Macmillan & Co., 1879), p. 98; Swinburne, *TSL* 4. 122 (6 January 1880); Symonds, *LJAS* 2. 957 (31 October 1884). The Rev. Henry Ellacombe is among those who admit to not being able to smell this fragrance (*The Plant-Lore and Garden Craft of Shakespeare*, p. 282), whereas Gertrude Jekyll, in *Wood and Garden: Notes and Thoughts, Practical and Critical, of a Working Amateur* (London: Longmans, Green & Co., 1899), calls it 'the best sweet smell of all the year' (p. 235).

whether these are floral scents, incense, or perfumes. Alert to the way olfactory sensation heightens atmosphere, he takes pleasure in perfumed fabrics like Madeline's loosened 'fragrant bodice' and her 'blanchèd linen, smooth and lavendered' in 'The Eve of St Agnes', while his Isabella lovingly wraps her dead lover's head in a scented scarf, 'sweet with the dews | Of precious flowers plucked in Araby' (*PJK*, pp. 468, 470, 347). He guesses the flowers around him in 'Ode to a Nightingale' by recognizing their scents in the 'embalmèd darkness' (*PJK*, p. 528). In his sonnet 'To a Friend who sent me some roses', he reports 'feast[ing] on the fragrancy' of a wild musk-rose, yet realizes its scent is surpassed by a later gift, telling the giver, 'But when, O Wells, thy roses came to me, | My sense with their deliciousness was spelled' (*PJK*, p. 47). Like Keats, Shelley also responded strongly to the spell of flower fragrance. He writes to Clair Clairmont about his 'excessive susceptibility of nature': 'You will ask naturally enough where I find any pleasure? The wind, the light, the air, the smell of a flower affects me with violent emotions.'[183] Peter Butter writes:

> Just as birds were primarily sources of melody to him, so flowers were loved above all for their scent. For music and scent are not static nor confined to any one place; they flow, pervade, interpenetrate and produce a sensation of dissolution, of floating. Synaesthesia of music and scent are quite common—more common in Shelley, I should think, than in any other poet—and are especially associated with moments of love.[184]

Both Shelley and Keats were important to the poets explored later in this study, with Shelley especially significant. Arguably the most powerful influence on Swinburne, the writer responsible for triggering olfactory aestheticism in the second half of the nineteenth century, Shelley also leaves his mark on Symonds, Raffalovich, Wilde, Michael Field, and Symons. His poetry, often characterized by Victorian readers as ethereal, has a special affinity with perfume. In 1869 Swinburne described Shelley's romanticism as 'coloured by contact with nature, but not born of it', his 'aim' being to 'render the effect of a thing rather than a thing itself, the soul and spirit of life rather than the living form, the growth rather than the thing grown'.[185] Shelley's perceived shift away from materiality to a preoccupation with the characteristic effect or soul of a thing is particularly noticeable in his images of perfume, an invisible essence that suggests the 'effect' or 'soul' of a flower without its material presence. Sensory, though insubstantial, and yet powerfully evocative, calling not only on the absent flower but also a host of associated images specific to the individual, perfume is, unsurprisingly for Shelley, a perfect analogue for poetry. In 'A Defence of Poetry', he declares poetry 'the perfect and consummate surface and bloom of things; it is as the odour and colour of the rose to the texture of the elements which compose it, as the form and splendour of unfaded beauty to the secrets of anatomy and corruption' (*SPP*, p. 503). In 'To a Sky-Lark', the audible but invisible bird, an ideal version of the solitary but influential poet, is

---

[183] Shelley, Letter of 16 January 1821, *Letters of Percy Shelley*, ed. F. L. Jones, 2 vols (Oxford: Oxford University Press, 1964), 2. 265.

[184] Peter Butter, *Shelley's Idols of the Cave* (Edinburgh: Edinburgh University Press, 1954), p. 73.

[185] Swinburne, 'Notes on the Text of Shelley', in *Essays and Studies* (London: Chatto & Windus, 1875), p. 219.

compared to a series of things obscured from sight but visible or sensible in their effects. This series culminates in the image of the 'embowered' unseen rose, whose wafted perfume betrays its presence:

> Like a rose embowered
>> In its own green leaves—
> By warm winds deflowered—
>> Till the scent it gives
> Makes faint with too much sweet these heavy-winged thieves.　(*SPP*, p. 227)

Again the scent of the rose is poetry, here carried off by the warm winds and thus exerting an influence that goes beyond its immediate point of origin. Shelley was himself compared to a perfume by his friend Thomas Jefferson Hogg: 'Shelley was fugitive, volatile; he evaporated like ether, his nature being ethereal; he suddenly escaped like some fragrant essence, evanescent as a quintessence.'[186] And Shelley would be like the perfume of his rose, carried afar to inspire his Victorian successors.

For Symonds, who wrote a critical monograph on the poet, Shelley's poetry is itself a distillate, and he asserts that 'Shelley [...] pierced through things to their spiritual essence. The actual world was less for him than that which lies within it and beyond it', and in a general essay on poetry he remarks that the 'sweetness' of Shelley's poetry is 'volatilised'.[187] W. B. Yeats, who in 1898, thought that 'We are about to substitute once more the distillation of alchemy for the analyses of chemistry', 'filling our thoughts with the essences of things and not with things', two years later characterized Shelley as a 'poet of essences and pure ideas', noting his 'spiritual essences whose shadows are the delights of all the senses'.[188] For Arthur Symons, 'Shelley's [imagination] is that which disembodies, filling mortal things with unearthly essences.' Later in the same essay he declares,

> His poetry, more than that of any other poet, is the poetry of the soul, and nothing in his poetry reminds us that he had a body at all, except as a nerve sensitive to light, colour, music, and perfume. [...] Poetry was his atmosphere, he drew his breath in it as in his native element.[189]

Poets, too, celebrated Shelley as a 'fragrant essence'. In a commemorative sonnet from his *Lyrics* of 1897, the American poet John Banister Tabb affirmed that 'Thy spirit gave | A fragrance to all nature', while William Watson, in 'Shelley's Centenary', honoured:

> Shelley, the cloud-begot, who grew
> Nourished on air, and sun, and dew,

[186] Thomas Jefferson Hogg, *The Life of Percy Bysshe Shelley*, 2 vols (London: Edward Moxon, 1858), 2. 46.
[187] John Addington Symonds, *Shelley*, English Men of Letters, 2nd edn (London: Macmillan & Co., 1887), p. 125; 'A Comparison of Elizabethan with Victorian Poetry', in *Essays Speculative and Suggestive* (London: John Murray, 1890), p. 386.
[188] W. B. Yeats, 'The Autumn of the Body', in *Essays and Introductions* (London: Macmillan, 1961), p. 193; 'The Philosophy of Shelley's Poetry', ibid., pp. 87, 75.
[189] Arthur Symons, 'Shelley', *Atlantic Monthly* 100 (September 1907), 347–56; 350, 353, collected in *The Romantic Movement in English Poetry* (Archibald Constable & Co., 1909), pp. 275, 281.

Into that Essence whence he drew
His life and lyre
Was fittingly resolved anew
Through wave and fire.[190]

Edmund Gosse (1859–1928), also reflecting on Shelley's legacy in 1892, his
centenary year, declared that 'We must throw ourselves back to what we were at
twenty and recollect how dazzling, how fresh, how full of colour, and melody, and
odour, this poetry seemed to be.'[191] Gosse, the friend and biographer of Swinburne,
is a good example of an aesthetic poet keen to identify himself as an *olfactif* by signalling his Romantic inheritance. Gosse had encountered Romantic poetry as a schoolboy
of sixteen when 'Keats entirely captivated me'. Although initially repelled by Shelley's
'Queen Mab', he was soon writing 'odes that were imitations of those in "Prometheus
Unbound"' and a poem of homage titled 'Elegy on the anniversary of the burial of
Shelley'.[192] In 1871, aged twenty-one, he met various members of the Pre-Raphaelite
Circle, including Dante Gabriel and William Michael Rossetti and, more importantly,
Swinburne who would make a lasting impact on him. Two years later he published
his first book of verse, *On Viol and Flute* (1873). Reviewing the revised edition of
this volume, which included Gosse's best work up to 1879, Walter Pater observed,
'The memories of a large range of poetic reading are blent into one methodical music',
adding that 'a large compass of beautiful thought and expression, from poetry old and
new, have become to him matter malleable anew for a further and finer reach of literary
art'.[193] Both editions contain 'Perfume', a sonnet heavy with the olfactory language of
Romanticism, which can be read as a validation of Gosse's poetic credentials:

What gift for passionate lovers shall we find?
Not flowers nor books of verse suffice for me,
But splinters of the odorous cedar-tree,
And tufts of pine-buds, oozy in the wind;
Give me young shoots of aromatic rind,
Or samphire, redolent of sand and sea,
For all such fragrances I deem to be
Fit with my sharp desires to be combined.
My heart is like a poet, whose one room,
Scented with Latakia faint and fine,
Dried rose-leaves, and spilt attar, and old wine,
From curtained windows gathers its warm gloom
Round all but one sweet picture, where incline
His thoughts and fancies mingled with perfume.[194]

---

[190] John Banister Tabb, 'Shelley', in *Lyrics* (Boston, MA: Small Maynard & Co, 1897), p. 186;
William Watson, 'Shelley's Centenary', in *The Poems of William Watson*, new edn (London and
New York: Macmillan & Co., 1893), p. 18. (The centenary of Shelley's birth fell on 4 August 1892.)
[191] Edmund Gosse, 'Shelley in 1892', in *Questions at Issue* (London: William Heinemann, 1893),
pp. 210–11.
[192] Edmund Gosse, *Father and Son*, ed. Michael Newton (Oxford: Oxford University Press, 2004),
pp. 168, 171; Ann Thwaite, *Edmund Gosse: A Literary Life* (Oxford: Oxford University Press, 1985), p. 52.
[193] Walter Pater, 'Mr Gosse's Poems' (29 October 1890), *EG*, p. 112. The revised edition of *On Viol
and Flute*, which omits poems from the 1873 edition, was published in 1890.
[194] Edmund Gosse, 'Perfume', in *On Viol and Flute* (London: Henry S. King & Co., 1873), p. 96.

Arguing that perfume rather than flowers or poetry suits the mood of the 'passionate lover', the speaker calls for aromatic gifts that atmospherically complement his 'sharp desires'. The scents listed in the octave—cedar wood, pine resin, cinnamon, and samphire—are energizing or stimulating rather than soothing or narcotic, deriving from trees and plants rather than the sweeter florals more usually associated with femininity, with the implication that this bouquet of woody, green, spicy, and marine notes has more of a 'sharp' masculine ambience. Although the speaker has refused books of verse as a present, the scents that he lists have connections to both Keats and Shelley, and so evoke not only fresh or tonic vegetal scents but also the literary texts that mediate them. Gosse's 'splinters of the odorous cedar-tree' suggest the cedar fragments or splinters used to protect clothes against moths, but also the 'odorous cedar bark' in Shelley's 'The Sensitive-Plant' (*SPP*, pp. 215). The pine-buds, sticky with the sharp fresh smell of sap, recall the 'odours' of pine trees in 'Mont Blanc' (*SPP*, p. 90), as well as Shelley's fondness for licking pine resin from the bark of trees, a habit that scandalized his friend Hogg.[195] The 'young shoots of aromatic rind' are most likely cinnamon, the dried inner bark of shoots from the cinnamon tree, and used in sweet and savoury foods. Shelley mentions this spice as one of the aromatic fuels that blaze in the hearth of his Witch of Atlas (*SPP*, p. 355), and Keats as a flavouring in the 'lucent syrops' Porphyro prepares for Madeline (*PJK*, p. 471). 'Samphire', a sea-cliff-dwelling plant used as a vegetable, with an intense carrot or parsley-like flavour, conjures up Shakespeare's famous image of the samphire gatherer in *King Lear*, but also Keats's use of this image in a letter to Benjamin Haydon when he pictures himself as a young poet: 'I am "one that gathers Samphire dreadful trade" the Cliff of Poesy Towers above me.'[196] For the young Gosse, himself a poet in the making, Keats's analogy seems very appropriate.

Gosse strengthens the link with poetry in his sonnet's sestet, as we move from the fragrance of the exterior natural world to the more closeted scented interior of the speaker's heart, which he compares both to a poet and the poet's room, its curtains drawn against the outside world. The embowered poet who is also a lover recalls the solitary poet 'hidden in the light of thought' and the cloistered 'love-laden' maiden of Shelley's 'To a Sky-Lark', both of whom, in their seclusion, produce 'hymns' or 'music' that influence the world around them (*SPP*, p. 227). In his treatment of the poet's room, Gosse is most likely thinking of John Donne's 'The Good Morrow', which puns on the Italian word 'stanza' meaning both a 'room' and a 'poetic verse': 'For love, all love of other sights controls, | And makes one little room an every where.' Donne uses the same punning expression 'little room' for both the quickened womb of the Virgin Mary and the sonnet form, in the second of his Holy Sonnets.[197] The 'little room' that is the speaker's heart, the lover-poet's chamber, and Gosse's sonnet is also a place where perfume becomes

[195] Hogg, *The Life of Percy Bysshe Shelley*, 2. 354.
[196] Shakespeare, *King Lear*, 4. 6. 11–16; Keats, Letter to Benjamin Haydon (10, 11 May 1817) in *John Keats: The Major Works*, ed. Elizabeth Cook (Oxford: Oxford University Press, 2001), p. 354.
[197] John Donne, 'The Good Morrow', Holy Sonnet 2: 'Annunciation', in *The Complete English Poems*, ed. A. J. Smith (Harmondsworth: Penguin Books, 1973), pp. 60, 306.

inextricable from the 'thoughts and fancies' that make up amatory poetry—poetry exemplified by Keats's lovers Isabella and Lorenzo, 'Twin roses', who 'share | The inward fragrance of each other's heart' (*PJK*, p. 331).

The scents of the sestet arise from odorous materials that generally require more processing than those of the octave, resulting in products like tobacco, potpourri, fragrant essential oil, and wine. (Latakia is a strong smoky fragrant pipe tobacco named after the Syrian port city where it originated.) Processing renders all of these substances more concentrated and potent. Tobacco is stronger for being cured. Depending on the variety of rose, dried petals are often more fragrant than fresh ones, and a dusting with ground orris-root helps preserve their fragrance. An attar (from the Arabic word meaning 'scent') is a highly concentrated essential oil, often of roses, obtained by distillation and frequently aged to improve its fragrance. Grape juice, fermented and aged to make wine, is dramatically transformed and intensified in its taste and aroma. As Gosse strengthens the connections between perfume and poetry, he makes this headier concentration of aroma compatible with the condensation and development of thought expected in a sonnet's sestet.

Tobacco would become a popular note in twentieth-century perfumes, although here, with 'old wine', it helps offset the sweeter odours of dried rose leaves and attar, once more emphasizing the masculinity of the poet. For Gosse, strictly brought up within the Plymouth Brethren sect, the smell of tobacco is an early memory of a house rented by his bachelor uncles and suggests bohemian masculine freedom: 'Their house had a strange, delicious smell, so unlike anything I smelt anywhere else, that it used to fill my eyes with tears of mysterious pleasure. I know now that this was the odour of cigars, tobacco being a species of incense tabooed at home on the highest religious grounds.'[198] The 'Dried rose-leaves' evoke the Shelleyan rose leaves of 'Music, when soft voices die' where, preserved and still aromatic, they are analogues for the 'thoughts'—most likely written 'leaves' or pages, and perhaps love poems—that offer comfort after their author has departed:

> Rose leaves, when the rose is dead,
> Are heaped for the beloved's bed—
> And so thy thoughts, when thou art gone
> Love itself shall slumber on....   (*SPP*, p. 442)

While the particularity of 'split attar' is elusive, Shelley, in his whimsical 'Wine of the Fairies', writes of drinking in the scent of the sweet briar or eglantine rose— 'I am drunk on honey wine | Of the moon-unfolded eglantine', and imagines it 'spilt on the summer earth' where it fills with mirth the dreams of sleeping bats, dormice, and moles.[199] As for 'old wine', Keats, in his marginalia on Milton's *Paradise Lost*, imagines that the 'finest parts of the Poem' were produced by Milton 'solacing himself with cups of old wine', and in 'Ode to a Nightingale' he desires to drink a long-stored vintage to escape the demands of the present moment (*PJK*, pp. 525–6).[200]

---

[198] Gosse, *Father and Son*, p. 14.

[199] Fragment: 'Wine of the Fairies', in *Shelley: Poetical Works*, ed. Thomas Hutchinson, rev. G. M. Matthews (Oxford: Oxford University Press, 1970), p. 587.

[200] 'Marginalia on *Paradise Lost*', in *John Keats: The Major Works*, p. 336.

Scent that provokes dreams and wine that inspires poetry or reverie are thus Romantic precursors for the poet's 'thoughts and fancies mingled with perfume'. The perfumes habitually used or savoured during the poet's occupation of his room have created for him a characteristic olfactory aura that has become hard to separate from the aura of his creative thought, and mingled together, perfume and meditation become a form of incense offered before the painting of his muse and beloved.

In his biography Gosse presents a snapshot of himself as nascent *olfactif* when he recalls his experiences of being obliged to visit the poor in rural Devon as a boy of nine (around 1858):

> I dreaded and loathed the smells of their cottages. One had to run over the whole gamut of odours, some so faint that they embraced the nostril with a fairy kiss, others bluntly gross, of the 'knock-you-down' order; some sweet, with a dreadful sourness; some bitter, with a smack of rancid hair-oil. There were fine manly smells of the pigsty and the open drain, and these prided themselves on being all they seemed to be; but there were also feminine odours, masquerading as you knew not what, in which penny whiffs, vials of balm and opoponax, seemed to have become tainted, vaguely, with the residue of the slop-pail. It was not, I think, that the villagers were particularly dirty, but those were days before the invention of sanitary science, and my poor young nose was morbidly, nay ridiculously sensitive. I often came home from 'visiting the saints' absolutely incapable of eating the milk-sop, with brown sugar strewn over it, which was my evening meal.[201]

Contrasting with both the delicate scents of the country evoked by Gaskell and the Romantic fragrance of his sonnet, Gosse's rustic 'gamut of odours'—a phrase that suggests he may possibly have read Piesse—is more of a sensory assault. Although the cottagers do own some inexpensive perfumes—'vials of balm and opoponax'— for him the combination of their cheapness, aspiration, and tainted nature militate against any pleasure, and his recoil from the battery of aggressive and insinuating odours illustrates the plight of the scent-sensitive.

Gosse's status as *olfactif* is fitting for his role as a critic, poet, and man of letters whose literary circle would include a host of aesthetic and decadent writers. Towards the close of his memoir, when he relates how as a young adult he broke free from his father's strict religious surveillance, perfume is a contributing factor. As he implies, it seems far from coincidental that the symbolic moment of protest when he resists his father's intrusive interrogation occurs in a Victorian hothouse:

> There was a morning, in the hot-house at home, among the gorgeous waxen orchids which reminded my Father of the tropics in his youth, when my forbearance or my timidity gave way. The enervated air, soaked with the intoxicating perfumes of all those voluptuous flowers, may have been partly responsible for my outburst.[202]

If the passage intimates that Gosse needs to break out of the 'hot-house' to escape his father's stifling influence, it also suggests that the 'intoxicating perfumes of those voluptuous flowers', flowers of pleasure evocative of Baudelairean decadent

---

[201] Gosse, *Father and Son*, p. 78.   [202] Gosse, *Father and Son*, pp. 183–4 ('Epilogue').

fleurs du mal, infiltrate his consciousness, prompting a rejection of asceticism for the freedoms of life and literature in bohemian London.

Strange Flowers and Heavy Odours of the Hothouse

It was Swinburne who popularized the idea of the perfumed atmosphere of aestheticism when, in his 1862 review, he described Baudelaire's *Les Fleurs du mal* (2nd edn 1861), as having 'a heavy heated temperature with dangerous hothouse scents in it'.[203] Although he would prove keen to leave the Baudelairean hothouse behind him, Swinburne's metaphor endured, allowing successors like Oscar Wilde to recycle it when he reviewed Mark André Raffalovich's poetic collection *Tuberose and Meadowsweet* (1885) in March 1885: 'To say of these poems that they are unhealthy, and bring with them the heavy odours of the hothouse, is to point out neither their defect, nor their merit, but their quality merely.'[204] Stanley Addleshaw, reviewing Arthur Symons's *Silhouettes* (1892) in *The Spirit Lamp*, takes up the baton— 'Nearly every poem in the book is unhealthy, the atmosphere is that of the hothouse'—and he adds, 'These are the orchids of the muse, and he who loves wild-flowers may not approach them.' Yet Addleshaw makes clear that this not a disparagement but an invitation to an elite—'the chosen few who love their Baudelaire as well as their Matthew Arnold; to whom the air of the hot-house laden with the over-powering perfume of exotics is as welcome as the breezes that blow over the sea-bound meadows'.[205]

The contrast between wild flowers and hothouse exotics recurs in 'Theodora' (1895), a decadent short story by 'Victoria Cross', which features an attractively androgynous and sexually assured young woman. The male narrator suggests that Theodora represents the class of women he prefers, that of the 'hothouse gardenia', as opposed to 'the opening primrose type of woman' or 'the simple violet'.[206] The same contrast, in which different kinds of flowers double for types of women, occurs in Theodore Wratislaw's sonnet 'Hothouse Flowers' from his collection *Orchids* (1896). Wild flowers or ordinary garden flowers 'Please less than flowers glass-hid from frosts and snows | For whom an alien heat makes festival.' Presumably such indulged and cosseted exotics, 'flowers reared by man's careful art, | Of heady scents and colours', include courtesans, mistresses, and femmes fatales.[207]

In *The Eighteen Nineties* (1912), one of the earliest critical studies of *fin-de-siècle* decadence, Holbrook Jackson invoked perfume when he characterized the aims of the writers of the era: 'In their search for reality, and their desire to extend the

[203] Algernon Swinburne, 'Charles Baudelaire', in *Swinburne as Critic*, ed. Clyde K. Hyder (London: Routledge & Kegan Paul, 1972), p. 29.

[204] Oscar Wilde, 'A Bevy of Poets', in *The Complete Works of Oscar Wilde*, vol. 6: *Journalism Part 1*, ed. John Stokes and Mark Turner (Oxford: Oxford University Press, 2013), pp. 44–7; 46.

[205] Stanley Addleshaw, 'A Short Note upon a New Volume of Poems' (Review of Arthur Symons, *Silhouettes*), *The Spirit Lamp* 2.4 (6 December 1892), 118.

[206] Victoria Cross, 'Theodora', originally published in the *Yellow Book* 4 (1895), collected in *Daughters of Decadence: Women Writers of the Fin de Siècle*, ed. Elaine Showalter (London: Virago Press, 1993), p. 12.

[207] Theodore Wratislaw, 'Hothouse Flowers', in *Orchids* (London: Leonard Smithers, 1896), p. 23.

boundaries of sensation, the writers of the Eighteen Nineties sought to capture and steep their art in what was sensuous and luscious, in all that was coloured and perfumed.'[208] That perfume became a hothouse odour when Jackson discussed what he identified as the pervasive 'femininity' of the period's minor poetry, a sexually ambiguous quality reminiscent of Cross's androgynous Theodora:

> There was an unusual femininity about it; not the femininity of women, nor yet the feminine primness of men; it was more a mingling of what is effeminate in both sexes. This was the genuine minor note, and it was abnormal—a form of hermaphroditism. But it has left no single poem as a monument to itself. It was never so near corporeality as that. It was a passing mood which gave the poetry of the hour a hothouse fragrance; a perfume faint yet unmistakable and strange.[209]

Bernard Muddiman, following Jackson, similarly detected a sexual note, explicitly of French origin, in the perfumed literature of the nineties: 'In those days a genital restiveness which came over from France started the sex equation. A hothouse fragrance swept across the pudibond wastes of our literature', and he comments a page later that that 'The nineties, indeed, are a pleasant flower-garden over which many strange perfumes float.'[210] The 'pleasant flower-garden' sounds less oppressive than the hothouse, although its scents may be just as troubling. Laurence Binyon, striking the pose of the *olfactif*, concludes his poem 'May Evening' from his *Porphyrion* of 1898, with the lines:

> And perfumes tender, sweet, intense
> Enter me like a delicate blade.
> The lilac odour wounds my sense,
> Of the rich rose I am afraid.[211]

Synaesthesia also informs his earlier 'Midsummer Vigil', where, acknowledging how 'the garden's perfumes thrill me | Like a touch or whispered name', he claims, as a tribute to his beloved, 'This intoxicating sweetness | That the perfumed air exhales'.[212]

Muddiman may have hinted at French influences for nineties literature but when he decided that its 'predominant keynote' was 'a keen sense of that strangeness of proportion which Bacon notes as a characteristic of what he called beauty', he indicated an English precursor: 'It has become disseminated like a perfume from the writings of Pater in the men who came after him.'[213] It is certainly true that Swinburne's perfumed legacy, a legacy spiced by Baudelaire, is more widely disseminated by Pater, and the 'strange flowers' and 'curious odours' of his Conclusion to *Studies in the History of the Renaissance* (1873) (*SR*, p. 120) undoubtedly revive

---

[208] Holbrook Jackson, *The Eighteen Nineties: A Review of Art and Ideas at the End of the Nineteenth Century* (London: Grant Richards, 1912), p. 138.

[209] Jackson, *The Eighteen-Nineties*, pp. 162–3.

[210] Bernard Muddiman, *Men of the Nineties* (London: Henry Danielson, 1920), pp. 132, 133–4.

[211] Laurence Binyon, 'May Evening', in *Porphyrion and Other Poems* (London: Grant Richards, 1898), p. 121.

[212] Laurence Binyon, 'Midsummer Vigil', in *Lyric Poems* (London: Elkin Mathews and John Lane, 1894), pp. 57, 58.

[213] Muddiman, *Men of the Nineties*, p. 135.

in texts such as Aubrey Beardsley's erotic novella, *Under the Hill*, first published as a serial in *The Savoy* (1896). On the opening page of its first chapter, the Abbé Fanfreluche pauses outside the portal to the palace of Helen, where wave 'drowsily strange flowers, heavy with perfume, dripping with odours'.[214]

The story of perfumed aesthetic and decadent literature, starting with Swinburne and Pater, unfolds in the chapters that follow. The contrasting twentieth-century responses of Virginia Woolf and Compton Mackenzie that conclude this study take place during a period of aggressive reaction against the Victorians by male modernists like T. S. Eliot, Ezra Pound, and Wyndham Lewis, who had little tolerance for aestheticism and decadence. Wyndham Lewis, in his controversial *Men without Art* (1934), declared Pater 'the fountain-head' of the decadent culture he despised and condemned him along with various other male writers for possessing an 'essentially feminine' sensibility, while T. S. Eliot, in his Clark lecture on 'Donne and the Middle Ages', given at Trinity, Cambridge, in 1926, finds a hint of hothouse odour and 'femininity' not just in Pater but in a host of Victorian male prose writers not usually classed together:

> In much English prose, even of the finest, of the nineteenth century, I find more than a trace of intellectual psychologism, and just the faintest undefinable perfume of femininity. I find it in Newman and Frances Bradley as well as in Ruskin and Pater. Or it is as if such prose had been written in a low fever; there is a slight temperature to it.[215]

Elsewhere Eliot yearns for authentic Tudor stench to counteract the decadent scent and sentiment he believes has contaminated criticism: 'I have just been given a decadent work of sentiment on the "New Elizabethans" which makes me feel that some of the sewers of the elder period ought to be aired. Damn Lamb, Swinburne, J. A. Symonds.'[216] Symonds also famously contributes to the sickly sweet inundation of decadent writing on the Renaissance in one of Eliot's cancelled *Waste Land* drafts: 'Fresca was baptised in a soapy sea | Of Symonds—Walter Pater—Vernon Lee'.[217]

Yet Eliot's fastidious sensitivity to the Victorian sillage, 'the faintest undefinable perfume of femininity', suggests he may be an *olfactif manqué*, and certainly in his poetry there are some odd returns. I conclude this chapter by noting how the ghost of a faint Romantic perfume clings to some of his writing. When he famously damned Swinburne with faint praise in his essay of 1920, it is curious that in criticizing the supposed lack of music in Swinburne's poetry, he brings in Shelley by way of contrast. For Eliot also disliked Shelley's poetry, finding it 'an affair of adolescence' and 'almost unreadable', so it is odd to see his full citation of that

[214] Aubrey Beardsley, *Under the Hill: A Romantic Story* (Chapters 1, 2, 3), *The Savoy* 1 (January 1896), 156.

[215] Wyndham Lewis, *Men without Art*, ed. Seamus Cooney (Santa Rosa: Black Sparrow Press, 1987), p. 145; T. S. Eliot, *The Varieties of Metaphysical Poetry*, ed. Ronald Schuchard (London: Faber & Faber, 1993), pp. 67–92; 92.

[216] Eliot to Edgar Jepson (12 March 1919), *The Letters of T. S. Eliot*, ed. Valerie Eliot and Hugh Haughton, rev. edn, 6 vols to date (London: Faber & Faber, 2009–), 1: *1898–1923*, 320.

[217] T. S. Eliot, *The Waste Land: An Editorial Composite*, in *The Poems of T. S. Eliot*, ed. Christopher Ricks and Jim McCue, 2 vols (London: Faber & Faber, 2015), 1. 333.

quintessentially Romantic feminine lyric, 'Music, when soft voices die' with its enduringly fragrant 'rose-leaves'.[218] Those 'rose-leaves' will recur in Eliot's 'Burnt Norton', in which the 'echoes' of words and memories disturb 'the dust on a bowl of rose-leaves'.[219] A year earlier in a less well-known essay, 'Kipling Redivivus' (1919), Eliot had made the same disparaging comparison, contrasting 'Swinburne's "songs" with verse which demands the voice and the instrument, with Shelley's "Music, when soft voices die"'.[220] Here, when mentioning this lyric for the first time, Eliot's phrase 'the voice and the instrument' is an additional unacknowledged quotation from Shelley's 'The Sensitive-Plant' (*SPP*, p. 211) where these words describe the synaesthetic musical effect of the fragrance of grass and flowers.

As a boy, Eliot, keen to own Shelley's poems, bought a copy by 'stealing' two dollars from money given him by his father for winning a Latin prize.[221] Associated perhaps with illicit or guilty pleasure, Shelley was, however, more than 'an affair of adolescence', and Eliot would compound his crime by future thefts. It is unsurprising then that, in the words of 'Burnt Norton', 'Other echoes | Inhabit the garden'.[222] Some of his earliest poems, published in the *Harvard Advocate*, have auditory and olfactory echoes of a mingled Romantic and decadent lyricism, as in the concluding lines of 'Before Morning': 'Fragrance of bloom and fragrance of decay | Fresh flowers, withered flowers, flowers of dawn'.[223] Reference to the 'withered flowers' of this lyric, or the 'withered petals' and 'wreath' of 'faded' roses of 'Song' ('When we came home across the hill') may seem generic enough, although 'withered' for Shelley is a word significantly associated with the passage of time, with memory, decay, and, on occasion, renewal.[224] We might recall the poetic 'votive wreaths of withered memory' that open 'Epipsychidion', along with the later reference to 'years that heap | Their withered hours, like leaves, on our decay' (*SPP*, pp. 374, 387), or Shelley identifying himself and implicitly John Keats with the sun-scorched 'withering flower' of 'Adonais' (*SPP*, p. 400), or imagining himself as a 'withered flower' to be revived by the odorous 'healing rain' of Jane Williams.[225] Certainly Shelley's 'withered leaves', like those of his 'Ode to the West Wind' (*SPP*, p. 223), helped 'quicken [the] new birth' of Eliot's earliest poetry.

Other echoes create further disturbance. Reference to fragrance in Eliot's works often seems to be accompanied by anxiety, as if, to quote from 'A Game of Chess', perfume might 'drown the sense in odours'—a Shelleyan formulation, derived from

---

[218] For Eliot's dislike of Shelley, see his lecture 'Shelley and Keats' (17 February 1933), in *The Use of Poetry and the Use of Criticism* (London: Faber, 1933), pp. 87–102; 89, 96. T. S. Eliot, 'Swinburne as Poet', in *The Sacred Wood: Essays on Poetry and Criticism* (London and New York: Methuen, 1960), pp. 146–7; 89, 88.

[219] T. S. Eliot, 'Burnt Norton', from *Four Quartets*, in *The Poems*, 1. 179.

[220] Eliot, 'Kipling Redivivus', *Athenæum* 4645 (9 May 1919), 297–8; 297.

[221] Eliot, Letter to his mother (10 July 1919), in *Letters of T. S. Eliot*, 1. 376. George Franklin suggests that Eliot thereafter associated Shelley with 'guilt and pleasure' in 'Instances of Meeting: Shelley and Eliot: A Study in Affinity', *ELH* 61 (1994), 956.

[222] T. S. Eliot, 'Burnt Norton', in *The Poems*, 1. 179.

[223] T. S. Eliot, 'Before Morning', in *The Poems*, 1. 231.

[224] T. S. Eliot, 'Song' ('When we came home'), in *The Poems*, 1. 231.

[225] 'The Magnetic Lady to her Patient', in *Shelley: Poetical Works*, p. 667.

Prometheus Unbound.[226] Used by Eliot, it suggests a fear of being intellectually and perhaps poetically overwhelmed in an environment oppressively redolent of the past:

> In vials of ivory or coloured glass
> Unstoppered, lurked her strange synthetic perfumes,
> Unguent, powdered, or liquid—troubled, confused
> And drowned the sense in odours; stirred by the air
> That freshened from the window, these ascended
> In fattening the prolonged candle-flames, [...].[227]

Although 'A Game of Chess' starts with an ironic echo of an Elizabethan text, Shakespeare's *Antony and Cleopatra* ('The Chair she sat in'), the ensuing description with its catalogue of rich and esoteric properties—'sevenbranched candelabra', jewels in 'satin cases', 'vials' of perfume—sounds far more like the elaborate hot-house interiors found in nineteenth-century decadent texts such as *A Rebours* or *Under the Hill*.[228] (Huysmans's dandy hero Des Esseintes rarely leaves his luxurious house, is a connoisseur of jewels and perfumes, and will use only real wax candles for illumination; the toilette scene of Beardsley's Helen, complete with 'perfume and powder in delicate flacons and frail cassolettes', is lit, in the accompanying illustration, by a huge candelabra.[229]) Eliot's word 'synthetic', as applied to the 'perfumes', could denote either 'modern', 'artificial', or more simply 'compounded from various sources', though the hint of artifice together with the word 'strange'— associated so powerfully with Swinburne, Pater, and their followers—helps give this passage a whiff of decadence that recalls the 'curious odours' sought out and savoured by the Paterian aesthete.

Eliot's elaborate description of the ornate dressing-room eventually gives way to a portrayal of its neurotic female inhabitant. She owes something to Vivienne Haigh-Wood, his highly strung first wife whom Virginia Woolf, no fan of fragrance, described as 'so scented, so powdered, so egotistic, so morbid'.[230] Anxious and querulous—'"Speak to me. Why do you never speak? Speak"'—the overwrought woman becomes the neurasthenic product of an over-luxurious, decadent, or degenerate culture.[231] It is, after all, the *fin-de-siècle* degenerate or turn-of-the

---

[226] See *Prometheus Unbound*, IV, *ll.* 253–61 (*SPP*, p. 201) where Panthea describes how 'the multi-tudinous Orb' combines 'wild odour', 'music', and 'emerald light' into 'one aerial mass | Which drowns the sense'.

[227] T. S. Eliot, 'A Game of Chess' (from 'The Waste Land'), in *The Poems*, 1. 58.

[228] Shakespeare, *Antony and Cleopatra*, 2. 2. 196–224.

[229] Huysmans, *Against Nature*, pp. 35, 54–6, 118–29, 76; Beardsley, *Under the Hill*, pp. 160–4 (ch. 2); p. 160. Eliot's editors, Christopher Ricks and Jim McCue, cite among other passages for comparison Wilde's *Dorian Gray* (whose hero owes much to Des Esseintes) and the 'hothouse' boudoir scene from Braddon's *Lady Audley's Secret*, which I quoted earlier in this chapter. See *The Poems of T. S. Eliot*, 1. 624, 625. Like Braddon, both Beardsley and Eliot can also be seen as continuators of the eighteenth-century dressing-room theme explored by Tita Chico in *Designing Women*.

[230] Virginia Woolf, *Diary of Virginia Woolf*, ed. Anne Oliver Bell and Andrew McNeillie, 5 vols (London: Hogarth Press, 1977–84), 2. 304 (21 June 1924).

[231] Eliot, 'A Game of Chess', 1. 59. However, Eliot's poetry suggests an equal aversion to the nat-ural odour of the female body as revealed by his queasy distaste for 'female smells in shuttered rooms', the distilled 'rank [...] feline smell' of 'Grishkin in a drawing-room', or the 'hearty female stench' that

century neurasthenic, as characterized respectively by Nordau and Ellis, who displays a heightened sensitivity to smell. Eliot's female subject, a modern Mariana embowered in the remnants of the past, seems to bring together his anxieties about being smothered by a Romantic and Victorian literary culture he identified as decadent, feminine, perfumed, and enervating. In decrying or parodying such a culture, often in ways that paradoxically reveal a strong underlying dependence on it, Eliot aligns himself not only with his male modernist peers but also with a more mainstream conservative and reactionary Victorian critical tradition that rejects the perfume of aesthetic and decadent writing.

Long before 'A Game of Chess', Eliot's poetic unease with perfume hangs in the air. Even the natural scent of daffodils 'Smelling of earth and rain' can suddenly become oppressive:

> And again
> The insistent sweet perfume
> And the impressions it preserves
> Irritate the imagination
> Or the nerves.[232]

Preserving 'impressions', perfume triggers an earlier memory or association that acts as an irritant, and it is the 'insistent sweet' impressions of scented poems by Shelley and others that haunt, irritate, and stimulate Eliot's imagination. That ability of smells or scents to hold onto or revive past memories, an ability celebrated in 'Music, when soft voices die', is the topic of Chapter 2 in which older literary echoes, and Shelley in particular, exert a pervasive olfactory influence on Victorian poetry.

Ezra Pound wisely advised him to cut from the draft of *The Waste Land*. See 'Rhapsody on a Windy Night' and 'Whispers of Immortality', in *The Poems*, 1. 20, 48; 'Odours, confected by the cunning French, | Disguise the good old hearty female stench', in *The Waste Land: An Editorial Composite*, in *The Poems*, 1. 333.

[232] T. S. Eliot, 'Easter: Sensations of April', in *The Poems*, 1. 242.

2

Perfumed Melodies, Violet Memories
Scent and Remembrance in the
Nineteenth Century

> When from a long-distant past nothing subsists, after the people are dead, after the things are broken and scattered, taste and smell alone, more fragile but more enduring, more unsubstantial, more persistent, more faithful, remain poised a long time, like souls, remembering, waiting, hoping, amid the ruins of all the rest.[1]

The best-known pronouncement on olfactory recall—Proust's famous reflection on recovering memory through scent, inspired by the taste and smell of a madeleine soaked in a spoonful of tea—has sparked a continuing debate among modern smell scientists. In one camp are what Avery Gilbert calls the 'Proust boosters'—key figures like Trygg Engen and Rachel Herz—who work on 'odor memory'.[2] Like Rudyard Kipling who declared that 'Smells are surer than sounds or sights | To make your heart-strings crack', Herz, in her recent popular study *The Scent of Desire*, claims that

> Our memories triggered by odors are distinctive in one important way: their emotionality. We list more emotions, rate our emotions as having greater intensity, report our memories as being more emotionally laden, and state that we feel more strongly a sense of being back in the original time and place when a scent elicits the past than when that same event is triggered in any other way.[3]

In the other camp are sceptics like Gilbert himself, who cites research that contradicts Herz's findings, and the bio-physicist and perfume expert Luca Turin, who declares: 'The first reaction of most people when the subject of smell comes up is to mention its "evocative" power and to illustrate it with an anecdote about Granny's perfume. But the peculiar thing about smell cannot be that it evokes memories, because just about everything does.'[4]

My interest lies less with this specifically scientific debate and more with the literary history of smell memory, which, as Gilbert points out, extends much

---

[1] Marcel Proust, *In Search of Lost Time*, tr. C. K. Moncrieff and Terence Kilmartin, rev. D. J. Enright, 6 vols (London: Vintage, 2002), 1: *Swann's Way*, 54.

[2] See ch. 10: 'Recovered Memories', in Gilbert, *What the Nose Knows*, pp. 189–204.

[3] Rudyard Kipling, 'Lichtenberg', in *The Five Nations* (London: Methuen, 1903), p. 191; Herz, *The Scent of Desire*, p. 67.

[4] Luca Turin, *The Secret of Scent: Adventures in Perfume and the Science of Smell* (New York: HarperCollins, 2006), p. 14.

further back than Proust. Gilbert cites a number of American and continental authors who recorded similar perceptions, including Edgar Allan Poe, Nathaniel Hawthorne, and Oliver Wendell Holmes writing in the 1840s and 1850s, as well as the French geologist and botanist Louis-François Ramond de Carbonnières, whose study, *Observations Made in the Pyrenees* of 1789, contains a passage known to Proust and very likely to have influenced him:

> There is a somewhat in perfumes which powerfully awakens the memory of the past. Nothing so soon recalls to the mind a beloved spot, a regretted situation, or moments whose passage has been deeply recorded in the heart, though lightly in the memory. The fragrance of a violet restores us to the enjoyment of many springs.[5]

Gilbert also mentions a number of early twentieth-century articles exploring smell-memory published before Proust brought out his novel. In fact, journalistic interest in the topic can be found much earlier in the nineteenth century, as can be seen in an article entitled 'Scent Memories' by Francis Jacox, published in the Victorian periodical *Bentley's Miscellany* in 1863.[6] In this essay Jacox lists a considerable number of literary scent memory references, principally derived from British writers such as Charles Lamb, Wordsworth, Tennyson, and Elizabeth Gaskell; however, he also cites non-British authors including Oliver Wendell Holmes and Ramond de Carbonnières, both mentioned by Gilbert.

Whether one believes that memories cued by smell are more potent or more emotionally charged than other sense-induced memories, it is clear that many nineteenth-century writers believed this to be the case. Jacox cites the narrator of Gaskell's novel *Ruth* (1853): 'I think scents affect and quicken the memory more than either sights and sounds', and he opens his essay with a slightly adapted unattributed quotation from Holmes's *The Autocrat of the Breakfast-Table* (1858): 'Somebody has said that memory, imagination, old sentiments and associations, are more readily reached through the sense of Smell than by almost any other channel.'[7] In his original essay, Holmes introduces this statement by calling it 'another of these continually recurring remarks', and he adds 'I have said it, and heard it many times, and occasionally met with something like it in books, somewhere in Bulwer's novels, I think, and in one of the works of Mr. Olmsted, I know.'[8]

I am particularly interested in the way literary scent memories themselves often seem to reference earlier literary scent memories or a tradition of scent memory.

---

[5] Gilbert does not provide full references but the original sources of the passages he cites can be found as follows: Edgar Allan Poe, Item 048, 'Marginalia (Part 2)', *Democratic Review* 15 (December 1844), 581; Nathaniel Hawthorne, *The House of the Seven Gables* (Boston, MA: Ticknor, Reed, & Fields, 1851), p. 121 (ch. 7); Oliver Wendell Holmes, *The Autocrat of the Breakfast-Table* (Boston, MA: Phillips, Sampson and Company, 1858), pp. 85–7 (ch. 4); Louis-François Ramond, *Travels in the Pyrenees*, tr. F. Gold (London: Longman, Hurst, Rees, Orme & Browne, 1813), p. 112.

[6] Francis Jacox, 'Scent Memories', *Bentley's Miscellany* 54 (1863), 360–6.

[7] Jacox does not provide full references in 'Scent Memories', but they are as follows: Elizabeth Gaskell, *Ruth: A Novel*, 3 vols (London: Chapman & Hall, 1853), 1. 121 (ch. 4), cited by Jacox, p. 361; Wendell Holmes, *The Autocrat of the Breakfast-Table*, p. 83 (ch. 4), cited by Jacox, p. 360. For a recent edition of Gaskell's novel, see *Ruth*, ed. Alan Shelston (Oxford: Oxford University Press, 1983), p. 60.

[8] Wendell Holmes, *The Autocrat of the Breakfast-Table*, p. 83.

This chapter explores a particular literary memory trail created by an iconic floral scent—that of the violet, an extremely popular flower in the nineteenth century. *Viola odorata*, the wild sweet violet with purple or white flowers, is native to Britain, flowering from March into April. In *Our Village* (1824), her collected sketches of rural life, Mary Russell Mitford memorably describes the gathering of wild violets, a ritual known as 'violeting':

> Now a few yards farther, and I reach the bank. Ah! I smell them already—their exquisite perfume steams and lingers in this moist heavy air. Through this little gate, and along the green south bank of this green wheat-field, and they burst upon me, the lovely violets, in tenfold loveliness. The ground is covered with them, white and purple, enamelling the short dewy grass, looking but the more vividly coloured under the dull, leaden sky. There they lie by hundreds, by thousands.[9]

Cultivated varieties of sweet violet may have blue, reddish, pink, or even yellow flowers, though the purple and white varieties are especially noted for their fragrance and cherished by gardeners (see Plate 2).[10] John Gerard, the sixteenth-century herbalist, had declared that violets were morally inspiring, able 'to admonish and stir up a man to that which is comely & honest'.[11] By the Victorian period the small, sweet, purple blossoms, often hidden among the plant's leaves or other vegetation, had long been viewed as a symbol for an endearingly shy and modest maidenliness. The 'shrinking violet', a development of this idea, is typically a timid or self-effacing woman, loth to assert herself or her views, the expression possibly deriving from Leigh Hunt's 1820 description of woodland flowers—'and here and there by the thorny underwood a shrinking violet' and Thomas Moore's 1817 poetic description of a maiden who 'steals timidly away, | Shrinking as violets do in summer's ray'.[12] The stereotype of the bashful maiden became increasingly dated towards the end of the century; the male narrator of Victoria Cross's *fin-de-siècle* story 'Theodora' announces that 'the girl who does or wishes to suggest the modest violet unfolding beneath the rural hedge[,] had never had a charm for me'.[13] Nonetheless, violets were often to seen to embody feminine virtue, and their perfume—delicate, sweet, fresh, powdery, with some woody notes—was deemed to be the natural choice for a lady, hence Harriet Hubbard Ayer's recommendation that the 'high-bred woman' 'select the most delicate of violet extracts, and so assimilate her personality with the flower as always to recall it'.[14]

Violets were worn by both men and women either as buttonholes or pinned to a coat or dress, providing city-dwellers with a welcome gust of rural sweetness. In

[9] Mary Russell Mitford, 'Walks in the Country: Violeting', in *Our Village: Sketches of Rural Character and Scenery* (London: G. and W. B. Whittaker, 1824), p. 105. Entry dated 27 March.

[10] For an overview, see Roy E. Coombs, *Violets: The History and Cultivation of Scented Violets* (London: B. T. Batsford, 2003).

[11] John Gerard, *The Herball or Generall Historie of Plants* (London: Printed by John Norton, 1597), p. 698.

[12] Leigh Hunt, 'Ronald of the Perfect Hand', *The Indicator* 20 (Wednesday, 23 February 1820), 153–60; 158; Thomas Moore, *Lalla Rookh: An Oriental Romance* (London: Longman, Hurst, Rees, Orme & Brown, 1817), p. 65.

[13] Victoria Cross, 'Theodora', in *Daughters of Decadence*, p. 12.

[14] Ayer, *Harriet Hubbard Ayer's Book*, p. 454.

a poem of 1864 Austin Dobson portrays a male speaker, trapped in the heat of a London summer, pining after the remembered scent of violets: 'And when about Rimmel's the perfumes play, | I smell no sweetness of "Ess Bouquet" | But violets hid in the green.'[15] In season, violets grown in Devon and the South West were sent up daily by train from railway stations like Clevedon in Somerset, where, as reported by the local paper in 1883, wafts of violet perfume eddied out of the parcels office 'to the astonishment of strangers'.[16] In cities like London they were sold cheaply on the streets; in 1894 the American investigative reporter Elizabeth Banks, masquerading as a flower-girl, reports selling them for 'a penny a bunch', inadvertently undercutting the regular price of tuppence.[17] In New York in 1877 there was also a fad for chewing violet flowers as breath sweeteners, though candied or crystallized violets and other violet-flavoured sweets were widely available.[18]

Violet perfume was much in demand throughout the Victorian period, although, ironically for a scent strongly associated with nature, most of it would have had very little contact with real violets. Essential oil of violets or violet absolute is difficult to obtain and extremely costly, so while more expensive brands might include a tiny amount, most violet perfume would be made using orris-root (iris root), which has a violet odour, in an alcoholic extract. More affordable, though still expensive, is violet leaf absolute, which has a cut-leaf or cucumber smell and might also be added to obtain a fresh green note, possibly justifying the claims of companies like Mülhens who declared that their product was 'Distilled from freshly gathered Rhine Violets' or the Crown Perfumery who claimed their perfume was 'Distilled from the Natural Flowers of the Riviera' (see Figure 2.1). In 1893 the violet-smelling compound ionone (a ketone) was discovered, which would be widely used in violet perfumes, although its price, at least initially, was very high.[19] It was later synthesized into two isomeric compounds, alpha-ionone and beta-ionone, which suggest different aspects of violet scent, the first being more floral, the second more woody. These could be used in varying proportions to create different violet effects. Discovery of ionone substantially increased the production of and demand for violet fragrance in the 1890s, and it remained popular well into the twentieth century.

One of the characteristics of ionone both in its synthetic and natural form is that it quickly tires and desensitizes the nose, temporarily turning off the olfactory receptors so that the odour of violets seems to disappear, only to reappear a

[15] Dobson, 'A City Flower', in *Vignettes in Rhyme*, p. 143.

[16] Jennifer Davies, *The Victorian Flower Gardener* (London: BBC Books, 1991), p. 159; Mark Griffiths, 'Sweet Tenants of the Shade', p. 91.

[17] Elizabeth Banks, 'How the Other Half Lives: The Flower Girl', *English Illustrated Magazine* (June 1894), 925–31; 928, 930, reprinted in Elizabeth Banks, 'A Day with the Flower-Girls', in *Campaigns of Curiosity: Journalistic Adventures of an American Girl in London* (Chicago and New York: F. Tennyson Neely, 1894), pp. 139–52; 144, 147.

[18] Amy Stewart, *Gilding the Lily: Inside the Cut Flower Industry* (London: Portobello, 2009), p. 59. Stewart cites a *New York Times* article of January 1877.

[19] Messrs Schimmel & Co.'s report for October 1894, cited in Ernest J. Parry, *The Chemistry of Essential Oils and Artificial Perfumes*, 2nd edn (London: Scott, Greenwood & Co., 1908), p. 491: 'The opinion, which is frequently expressed, that the price of ionone solution will probably be reduced before long is not justified.'

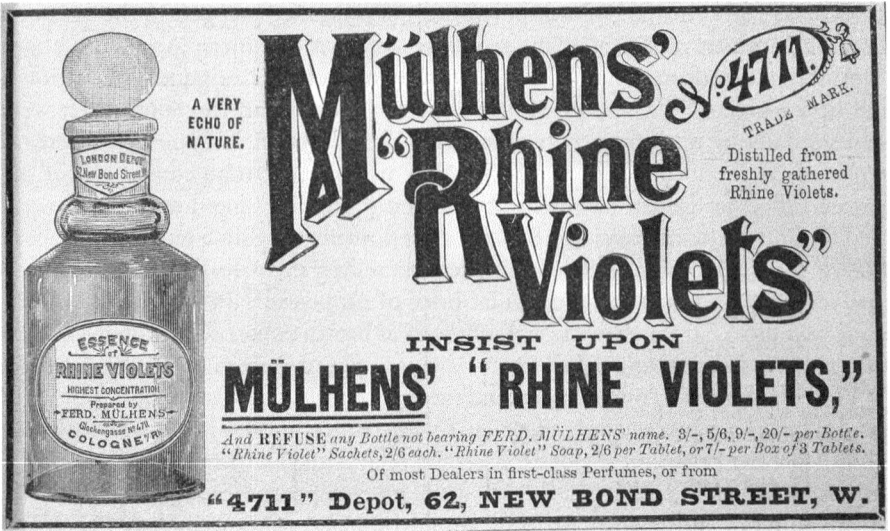

Figure 2.1 Advertisement for Mülhens's Rhine Violets, *Illustrated London News* (29 May 1897), p. 755. (Photo: Daichi Ishikawa, courtesy of the London Library)

while later. Hence the perception of the fleeting smell of violets and Laertes's description of a violet's fragrance in *Hamlet*—'sweet, not lasting, | The perfume and suppliance of a minute'.[20] Shortly after the discovery of ionone, Messrs Schimmel & Co., leading suppliers of essential oils and synthetic fragrances, observed that the 'blunting of the olfactory nerves' led some people to complain that 'ionone has no odour at all', and noted that the same 'nasal delusion' was common when 'smelling freshly gathered violets'.[21] The twentieth-century British perfumer W. A. Poucher said that of all the odours that tired the nose, violets were the worst offenders, and that 'After an hour's work on violets, "intense olfactory fatigue" set in, and the professional nose forgot every smell it ever learned—except, that is, for violets.'[22]

The 'forgetting' and reappearance of violet fragrance seems fitting for a scent that has particularly strong associations with memory and commemoration. Eschewing the more conventional link with the violet of maidenly modesty, this chapter traces an alternative literary genealogy that links the scent of the violet to song and remembrance, and has ultimately more to do with the figure of the fair and fated young man than the demure young woman. We have already encountered Ramond de Carbonnières's sentiment that 'The fragrance of a violet restores us to the enjoyment of many springs', and Jacox cites two other nineteenth-century violet quotations that emphasize the mnemonic power of violet fragrance. The first,

---

[20] Shakespeare, *Hamlet*, 1. 3. 8–9.
[21] Messrs Schimmel & Co., cited in Parry, *The Chemistry of Essential Oils*, pp. 492–3.
[22] Roly Smith, *A Camera in the Hills: The Life and Work of W. A. Poucher* (London: Frances Lincoln Publishers, 2008), p. 79.

by the American sculptor and writer William Wetmore Story, is taken from his poem 'The Violet':

> Oh! faint delicious spring-time violet,
> > Thine odor, like a key,
> Turns noiselessly in memory's wards to let
> > A thought of sorrow free.[23]

The second, by Alfred Tennyson, comes from his early poem 'A Dream of Fair Women' (1833):

> The smell of violets, hidden in the green,
> > Poured back into my empty soul and frame
> The times when I remember to have been
> > Joyful and free from blame.[24]

For Tennyson's speaker, who dreams that he is walking through a wood at dawn, the scent of the violet, as for Ramond de Carbonnières, recalls happy memories, although the recollection of a more innocent time seems tinged with some wistfulness at its passing. In Story's poem the scent of the violets prompts a memory that triggers sorrow. The rest of the poem (not quoted by Jacox) intimates that this is the memory of the speaker's lost love—'Oh vanished Joy! Oh Love, that art no more'—and in the final stanza, the speaker directly links the flower's smell to the emotional, almost physical, force of the memory:

> O violet! thy odor through my brain
> > Hath searched, and stung to grief
> This sunny day, as if a curse did stain
> > Thy velvet leaf.[25]

The violet, a spring flower punctually expressing renewed life after the bleakness of winter and hope of the warmer seasons to come, necessarily reminds us of bygone springs and their attendant joys and losses. Even Luca Turin, ever sceptical about scent memory, evinces a lyrical nostalgia about the smell of violets declaring that 'The peculiarly poetic combination of warm, sweet, floral and woody notes carries within it a mixture of delicacy and brutality which, to my mind at least, is an allegory of childhood.'[26] The connection between violet scent and recollection, especially the recollection of something lost, dead, or buried, is also experienced by Wilde's Dorian Gray, who, in his famous experimentation with perfumes:

> [S]aw that there was no mood of the mind that had not its counterpart in the sensuous life, and set himself to discover their true relations, wondering what there was in frankincense that made one mystical, and in ambergris that stirred one's passions, and in violets that woke the memory of dead romances.   (*DG*, p. 111)

---

[23] William Wetmore Story, 'The Violet', in *Poems* (Boston, MA: Little, Brown & Co., 1856), pp. 224–5 (p. 224), cited by Jacox, 'Scent Memories', p. 361.
[24] Alfred Tennyson, 'A Dream of Fair Women' (stanza 26), in *Poems* (London: Edward Moxon, 1833), p. 128, cited by Jacox, 'Scent Memories', p. 361. See also *Tennyson: A Selected Edition*, p. 84.
[25] Story, 'The Violet', p. 225.   [26] Turin, *The Secret of Scent*, p. 62.

The link between violet fragrance, death, and commemoration is an old one. Violets, which among other things signify mourning, were traditionally used for funerary purposes, protecting mourners from poisonous exhalations from the grave. Charles M. Skinner writes that in antiquity, 'when a Greek was buried his body was concealed with violets, and they were also placed about his grave or tomb so that the dread receptacle was carpeted with color and fragrance'.[27] Michael Ferber writes:

> On 22 March, at the beginning of spring, the Romans celebrated the *dies violaris*, the day on which violets were put on graves, probably to betoken the renewal of life here or hereafter. The violet's appearance in early spring, its brief life, and its dark blood-like color lent it naturally to the cult of the dead.[28]

In one of his satires, the first-century Latin poet Persius mocks dinner-party guests who, following the trite recitation of a poet's verses, declare: 'oh, now, out of those shades, out of the tomb and the oh-so-blessed cinders, will not violets spring?'[29] Persius is ironic but this influential verse probably informs the cry of the bereaved Laertes in Shakespeare's *Hamlet* when he declares of his sister, Ophelia, 'And from her fair and unpolluted flesh | May violets spring!'[30] According to Sir James Frazer's *The Golden Bough*, violets are supposed to have sprung from the blood of Attis, a fair young man beloved by the goddess Cybele, who killed himself under a pine tree by an act of self-castration. His death was annually commemorated in ritual by the priests of the goddess, who would carry a violet-decked pine tree to her shrine.[31] A much later non-classical tradition suggests that violets sprang from the blood of the Greek hero Ajax after he committed suicide.[32] Blood as a generating source for the flower also occurs, though more light-heartedly, in a poem by the Renaissance aristocrat Lorenzo de' Medici,

[27] Charles M. Skinner, *Myths and Legends of Flowers, Trees, Fruits and Plants in all Ages and all Climes* (Philadelphia, PA, and London: J. B. Lippincott, 1911), p. 280.

[28] Michael Ferber, 'Violets', in *A Dictionary of Literary Symbols* (Cambridge: Cambridge University Press, 2007), pp. 224–6 (p. 225). The *dies violaris* was also known as a *violatio, dies violae*, or *dies violationis* 'day of the violet [-adornment]'.

[29] *nunc non e manibus illis, | nunc non e tumulo fortunataque favilla | nascentur violae?* Persius, *Satires* 1. 38–40. See Kenneth J. Reckford, *Recognizing Persius* (Princeton, NJ, and Oxford: Princeton University Press, 2009), p. 42.

[30] William Shakespeare, *Hamlet*, 5. 1. 222–3.

[31] Sir James George Frazer, 'The Myth and Ritual of Attis', in *Adonis, Attis, Osiris: Studies in the History of Oriental Religion* (London: Macmillan & Co. Ltd, 1906), pp. 166, 169. (This forms part of the expanded third edition of *The Golden Bough*.) Frazer draws on Ovid, *Fasti* 4. 283ff., 5. 226, and Arnobius 5. 7.

[32] See Edward Young's poem 'The Instalment' (1726): 'As when stern Ajax pour'd a purple flood | The violet rose, fair daughter of his blood', in *The Complete Works of Edward Young to which is Prefixed a Life of the Author by John Doran*, 2 vols (London: William Tegg & Co., 1854), 1. 342. Ovid relates that a purple flower springs from the blood of Ajax after his suicide (*Metamorphoses* 13. 394–6), although he identifies the flower with the hyacinth. See Ovid, *Metamorphoses*, tr. Frank Justus Miller, 2 vols, 3rd edn (London and New York: W. Heinemann and G. P. Putnam's Sons, 1977–84), 2. 256–7. Pausanias in his *Description of Greece*, 1. 35. 4, says that the flower is white tinged with red. See *Description of Greece*, tr. W. H. S. Jones, 4 vols (Cambridge, MA, and London: Harvard University Press and W. Heinemann, 1918), 1. 189.

who suggested that violets sprang from Venus' blood when she pricked her foot on a thorn.[33]

Certainly violets are one of the flowers, along with the rose and myrtle, associated with Venus, who is described as 'violet-crowned' in the second Homeric Hymn to Aphrodite (Hymn 6. 18). But violets also commemorate other iconic figures. One major tradition reads the ancient Greek word for violet, 'ion' (ἴον), as deriving from Io, a mistress of the god Zeus. He concealed her from his jealous wife Hera by turning her into a white heifer. Scented violets supposedly sprang up where she trod or were made to bloom to feed her. According to this story, and a popular etymology that dates back at the very least to the late sixteenth century and Gerard's *Herball* (1597), 'io' lingers on in the modern word 'violet'.[34] Michael Ferber says that along with several flowers the violet belonged to Persephone, and Ovid mentions violets with lilies as the flowers gathered by Proserpina (Persephone) when she was snatched to the Underworld by Hades.[35] The Muses were described by a number of Greek poets as 'violet-crowned', an epithet also famously used by Pindar of the ancient city of Athens, which he called 'sleek and violet-crowned'.[36] The sweet violet was the symbol of Athens but it is also a flower associated with the Greek poet Sappho, who mentions violets in a number of her Fragments. Violets were among the flowers worn in scented garlands by the Greeks at banquets and on other special occasions and, in one of Sappho's Fragments (Fragment 94), woven crowns of violets are for her a memory of the 'beautiful times' she shared with one of her female lovers, while Sappho herself was described by the lyric poet Alcaeus as 'violet-haired' or 'violet-crowned'.[37]

'Theirs was the violet weaving-bliss' is a line in the opening poem of *Long Ago* (1889), a late Victorian verse collection, which commemorates Sappho and her loves, by the poetic couple Katharine Bradley and Edith Cooper, who wrote together as Michael Field.[38] Michael Field's Sappho, presumably remembering the violet wreaths and their weavers, declares in another of the poems in this collection: 'With my dead lovers memory is not dead; | On me they call from many a violet-bed'.[39] In the nineteenth century, women poets who love women celebrate that love by remembering Sappho and her violets. Another late Victorian English poet, Mary Robinson, gives her partner Vernon Lee (real name Violet Paget) a presentation copy of her poems inscribed with a private lyric that begins 'Violets are for Sappho's

---

[33] Lorenzo de' Medici, 'Violets', tr. Felicia Hemans, in *The Poetical Works of Mrs Hemans* (London: Henry Frowde, n.d.), p. 707.

[34] Gerard, *Herball*, p. 701.

[35] Ferber, *A Dictionary of Literary Symbols*, p. 224; Ovid, *Metamorphoses*, 5. 393.

[36] Ferber, *A Dictionary of Literary Symbols*, p. 225.

[37] *If Not, Winter: Fragments of Sappho*, tr. Anne Carson (Vintage Books, 2003), p. 185. In Alcaeus' Fragment 384, *ioplokos* ('with strands of hair in violet') is now usually translated 'violet-haired'. See *Greek Lyric Poetry*, tr. David Campbell, Loeb Classical Library, 5 vols (Cambridge, MA, and London: Harvard University Press, 1982–93), 1. 405. John Addington Symonds cites Alcaeus addressing Sappho as 'Violet-crowned' in his *Studies of the Greek Poets*, 2 vols (London: Smith, Elder, & Co., 1873–76), 1. 134.

[38] Michael Field, Poem 1: 'They plaited garlands in their time', in *Long Ago* (London: George Bell & Sons, 1889), p. 3.

[39] Michael Field, Poem 40: 'Me thou forgettest', in *Long Ago*, p. 60.

wear'.[40] Similarly inspired by Sappho, the Anglo-American poet, who wrote in French under the name Renée Vivien, adopted the violet as her symbol in memory of her first lover Violet Shilleto, and was known as the 'Muse of the Violets'.[41]

A much later, probably nineteenth-century, tradition associates violets and their fragrance with the archetypal mythic poet Orpheus. In her book *Dante's Garden* of 1898, Rosemary Cotes writes:

> The violet is dedicated to Orpheus with his lute, and the legend also leads us into a realm of music. [...] When Orpheus, with his lute, charmed all the birds and beasts, and woods and mountains, the flowers also arose, and danced in a magic circle round him. And when he sank down, wearied, upon a bank to sleep, upon the spot where his enchanted lute had fallen there sprang into bloom the first violet, which, though the embodiment of purest music, yet is for ever mute, and nestles down amidst its leaves, listening to the everlasting harmonies of Nature.[42]

This passage is echoed by the American folklorist, Katharine M. Beals, in 1917, and then by a noted English garden writer, Eleanour Sinclair Rohde, in 1931, who says:

> Violets preserve in their scent the memory of Orpheus, for one day, being weary, he sank to sleep on a mossy bank, and where his enchanted lute fell, there blossomed the first violet. The magic music of his lute still haunts the scent of violets.[43]

'To his music plants and flowers | Ever sprung' writes Shakespeare of Orpheus in a famous lyric in his play *Henry VIII* (*c*.1613).[44] Although I have found no references earlier than 1898 specifically linking Orpheus and the violet, there are a number of famous texts that link music and violet fragrance. For example, in Francis Bacon's 'Of Gardens' (1625), he declares, 'And because the breath of flowers is far sweeter in the air (where it comes and goes like the warbling of music) than in the hand, therefore nothing is more fit for that delight, than to know what be the flowers and plants that do best perfume the air.' And he goes on to claim 'That which, above all others yields the sweetest smell in the air, is the violet, specially the white double violet, which comes twice a year; about the middle of April, and then about Bartholomew-tide.'[45] Bacon may have been recalling Shakespeare's *Twelfth*

---

[40] The presentation copy of Agnes Mary Frances Robinson's *The Crowned Hippolytus* (London: C. Kegan Paul, 1881) that bears this inscription is in the Norman Colbeck Collection at the University of British Columbia. See *A Bookman's Catalogue: The Norman Colbeck Collection of Nineteenth-Century and Edwardian Poetry and Belles Lettres*, ed. T. Bose and Paul Tiessen, 2 vols (Vancouver: UBC Press, 1987), 1. 234.

[41] *The Muse of the Violets: Poems of Renée Vivien*, tr. Margaret Porter and Catharine Kroger, with a preface by Mme Louise Faure-Favier, tr. Jeanette Forster (Baltic City, MO: The Naiad Press, 1977), p. 7. In 'Let us go to Mytilene', Vivien writes of 'The shadow of Sappho, weaving violets' (p. 61).

[42] Rosemary A. Cotes, *Dante's Garden, with Legends of the Flowers* (London: Methuen & Co, 1898), p. 64.

[43] Katharine M. Beals, *Flower Lore and Legend* (New York: Henry Holt & Co., 1917), p. 46; Eleanour Sinclair Rohde, *The Scented Garden* (London: The Medici Society, 1931), p. 31; originally published in *Spectator* (22 February 1930), as 'Primroses and Violets', 12.

[44] Shakespeare, *Henry VII*, 3. 1. 6–7. In *The Norton Shakespeare* the play appears under the title *All is True*.

[45] Bacon, 'Of Gardens', p. 431.

Night (1601–2), which opens with Duke Orsino's famous speech 'If music be the food of love', a speech that explicitly compares 'sweet music' with a breeze bearing the fragrance of violets:

> If music be the food of love, play on,
> Give me excess of it that, surfeiting,
> The appetite may sicken and so die.
> That strain again, it had a dying fall.
> O, it came o'er my ear like the sweet sound
> That breathes upon a bank of violets,
> Stealing and giving odour![46]

It is at this point that I want to concentrate on tracing a particular violet-fragranced memory trail associated with Shelley, who often seems to be recalling both Shakespeare and his idol Francis Bacon in his fondness for musical fragrant flowers. In a number of his poems floral scent is a figure for poetry, which is seen as surviving or outlasting the actual flower. In his fragmentary poem 'Music', he implies that music, which we may also read as 'poetry', and which he compares to the 'scent of a violet withered up', has an afterlife beyond its creator or point of origin. Thus we are told 'And the violet lay dead while the odour flew | On the wings of the wind o'er the waters blue'.[47] Similarly, in 'Music, when soft voices die', just as music abides in the auditory memory, the scent of flowers also endures when they fade, being absorbed by, preserved in, and indeed helping constitute what we might call our 'olfactory memory':

> Music, when soft voices die,
> Vibrates in the memory.—
> Odours, when sweet violets sicken,
> Live within the sense they quicken.   (*SPP*, p. 442)

For Shelley, music and scent are partnered and, in the synaesthesia for which he is famous, the one can be experienced as the other. Writing to Thomas Love Peacock about the Coliseum, he declares that

> it is overgrown with anemones, wall flowers, & violets, whose stalks pierce the starry moss, & with radiant blue flowers, whose names I know not, & which scatter thro the air the divinest odour which as you recline under the shade of the ruin produces a sensation of voluptuous faintness like the combinations of sweet music.[48]

In 'The Sensitive-Plant' he implies that a music produced by plants, inaudible to the human ear, might be experienced as perfume:

> And the hyacinth purple, and white, and blue,
> Which flung from its bells a sweet peal anew
> Of music so delicate, soft and intense,
> It was felt like an odour within the sense.   (*SPP*, p. 211)

---

[46] Shakespeare, *Twelfth Night*, 1. 1. 1–7.   [47] 'Music', in *Shelley: Poetical Works*, pp. 657–8.
[48] Letter to Thomas Love Peacock (23 March 1819), in *Letters of Percy Bysshe Shelley*, 2. 85.

In this poem violets are also melodious, having 'their breath [...] mixed with fresh odour, sent | From the turf, like the voice and the instrument' (*SPP*, p. 211), and it seems probable that Shelley is playfully exploiting the coincidence of the musical instrument known as the viola with 'viola', the Latin and Italian names for the violet.

Perfumery borrows the language of music—accords, notes, harmonies—to describe the successful blending of fragrance ingredients, and in older theories of smell, odour, like music, is understood as communicated through vibration. Like Bacon, Shelley understands the poetic conceit that the fragrance of a flower is its 'breath', a word commonly used at this time as a synonym for scent. The chemist Professor George Wilson observes how various poets 'place side by side with the utterance of speech and of music, the emission of fragrance'. Noting how 'The poets of all countries, [...] have delighted to call the scent of a flower its breath', he adds, 'breath is a sound, and, unless at the limit of faintness, an audible respiratory murmur.'[49] The breathing-out of scent and song necessarily reminds us of inspiration—the breathing-in of air or indeed others' quickening lyric words, reminds us also that 'air' can be a scented atmosphere and a synonym for a tune or song, and that influence itself is literally a 'flowing into', the influx of what, in *Prometheus Unbound*, Shelley calls 'the atmosphere of human thought' (1. 676; *SPP*, p. 156).

Traditionally, too, a poet's poems are his 'flowers'—*anthoi* in Greek—a collection of poems being an 'anthology'. Animated by the reader's voice, such eternal flowers are also a recollection where what seems ephemeral breathes again. In his essay 'A Defence of Poetry', Shelley details how reading the classical bucolic poets and their predecessors produces particular kinds of musical fragrance:

> Their poetry is intensely melodious; like the odour of the tuberose, it overcomes and sickens the spirit with excess of sweetness; whilst the poetry of the preceding age was as a meadow-gale of June which mingles the fragrance of all the flowers of the field, and adds a quickening and harmonizing spirit of its own which endows the sense with a power of sustaining its extreme delight. (*SPP*, p. 492)

We have encountered writers who conceive of scent as a mnemonic trigger that connects to an emotional memory, but Shelley suggests that reading and thus reactivating a poet's words releases his or her poetry as a distinct fragrance, which, breathed in or inhaled, has a specific emotional effect. Elsewhere in 'A Defence', Shelley uses the image of the fragrant violet to illustrate how the unique perfume of a poem is inextricable from the poet's original words, hence what he calls 'the vanity of translation' or the futility of trying to render verse into another language:

> [I]t were as wise to cast a violet into a crucible that you might discover the formal principle of its colour and odour, as seek to transfuse from one language to another the creations of a poet. The plant must spring again from its seed or it will bear no flower—and this is the burthen of the curse of Babel. (*SPP*, p. 484)

[49] Wilson, *Gateways*, p. 77.

And yet, accomplished translator that he was, Shelley arguably did make the plant 'spring again' just as, conversant with alchemical imagery, he must also have known that the violet in the crucible is one of the most notorious images of alchemical renewal. Walter Pater, in his essay on Sir Thomas Browne (1886), alludes to one of the most famous Renaissance alchemists, observing that 'there was a certain fantastic experiment, in which, as was alleged, Paracelsus had been lucky. For Browne and for others it became the crucial kind of agency in nature which, as they conceived it, was the proper function of science to reveal in larger operation.' Alluding to a request made to Browne by Dr Henry Power in 1648, Pater writes:

> What the enthusiastic young student expected from Browne, so high and noble a piece of chemistry, was the 're-individualling of an incinerated plant'—a violet, turning to freshness, and smelling sweet again, out of its ashes, under some genially fitted conditions of the chemic art. (*A*, pp. 151, 152)

'Insolent vaunt of Paracelsus, that he would restore the original rose or violet out of the ashes settling from its combustion', writes Thomas De Quincey.[50] Prior to his essay on Browne, Pater had already shown himself aware of the violet's regeneration in his Conclusion to *Studies in the History of the Renaissance* (1873), where 'the springing of violets from the grave' is one of 'ten thousand resulting combinations' of the 'elements' from which life is composed (*SR*, p. 118). Moreover, in 'The Child in the House' (1878), Pater's young protagonist Florian Deleal, confronted by the death of a playmate, finds 'what comforted him a little was the thought of the turning of the child's flesh to violets in the turf above him' (*IP*, p. 92).

In these references Pater is undoubtedly thinking of Shakespeare's *Hamlet* and Laertes's wish for the dead Ophelia cited earlier in this chapter—'And from her fair and unpolluted flesh | May violets spring', and beyond that the Greek myths of transformation which he alludes to in his essay 'The Myth of Demeter and Persephone' (1876), where he mentions 'The flowers in the grass which were once blooming youths, having both their natural colour and the colour of their poetry in them' (*GS*, p. 131). But I would suggest that Pater also has the colour of Shelley's poetry in him, and that his violets are the regenerated violets of Romanticism; for, as we shall see later in this chapter, there springs up a cult of the Romantic violet throughout the nineteenth century connected with the memory of both Shelley and Keats.

The violet was one of Shelley's favourite flowers.[51] He named his first daughter Ianthe ('violet-flower') after the heroine of his poem *Queen Mab* (1813), while 'Ione' meaning 'violet' is one of the Oceanides attending Prometheus in *Prometheus Unbound*. There are notable references in his letters and poems; for example, on 23 April 1819, he tells Peacock how the air at the ancient Italian city of Posidonia, the Greek name for Paestum, 'was scented with the sweet smell of violets of an extraordinary size & beauty'.[52] (Paestum was famous from antiquity for both its

---

[50] Thomas De Quincey, 'The Palimpsest' (1845), in *Suspiria de Profundis, Confessions of an English Opium-Eater and Other Writings*, ed. Barry Milligan (London: Penguin, 2003), p. 148.
[51] See Butter, *Shelley's Idols of the Cave*, p. 73.   [52] *Letters of Percy Bysshe Shelley*, 2. 79.

roses and its violets.) In 'Epipsychidion' Shelley describes the island paradise where he and his beloved might live and observes how:

> from the moss violets and jonquils peep,
> And dart their arrowy odour through the brain
> Till you might faint with that delicious pain.   (*SPP*, p. 385)

'The cemetery is an open space among the ruins covered in winter by violets and daisies. It might make one in love with death, to think that one should be buried in so sweet a place' (*SPP*, p. 309): so writes Shelley of the Protestant Cemetery in Rome, the resting place of his own infant son, William, but also the grave site of John Keats (whose words Shelley echoes here), and lastly, of course, of Shelley himself. In 'Adonais', the elegy he writes for Keats, the 'Frail Form' who represents Shelley himself and mourns over the deathbed, has his head 'bound [...] with faded violets, white, and pied, and blue' (*SPP*, p. 400). Joseph Severn, companion to the dying Keats, recorded that:

> At times during his last days he made me go to see the place where he was to be buried, and he expressed pleasure at my description of the locality of the Pyramid of Caius Cestius, about the grass and the many flowers, particularly the innumerable violets [...]. Violets were his favourite flowers, and he joyed to hear how they overspread the graves. He assured me 'that he already seemed to feel the flowers growing over him'.[53]

'And they do grow,' wrote Richard Monckton Milnes, Keats's first major biographer in 1848, 'even all the winter long—violets and daisies mingling with the fresh herbage' (see Plate 3).[54] Shelley and Keats are like the fair young men of Greek myth, with visitors to the cemetery seeing 'The flowers in the grass which were once blooming youths, having both their natural colour and the colour of their poetry in them.' Inevitably, literary pilgrims beat their way to what Thomas Hardy called 'the violet-sprinkled spot'.[55] Samantha Matthews remarks that 'the violets removed from Keats's grave in Rome and preserved in books were legion', while Joseph Severn had to instruct the custode of the cemetery to make continued resowings and plantings.[56] In 1856, Charles Eliot Norton, finding Keats's grave in a neglected state, arranged to have it reset and replanted with violets and myrtles, while around 1863, Alfred Austin, finding Shelley's resting place similarly neglected, cleaned the grave himself, planted pansies and violets, and left money with the

[53] William Sharp, *The Life and Letters of Joseph Severn* (London: Sampsom Low, Marston & Co., 1892), p. 93. Sharp says he follows the text of Severn's MS 'Recollections'; however, he undoubtedly embellished his text. See the terser, less lyrical version in 'My Tedious Life', in *Joseph Severn: Letters and Memoirs*, ed. F. Grant Scott (Aldershot and Burlington, VT: Ashgate, 2005), pp. 625–64 (p. 650). However, Sharp's version was undoubtedly influential in helping form the picture of Keats's last days.

[54] Richard Monckton Milnes, *The Life, Letters, and Literary Remains of John Keats* (London: Edward Moxon, 1848), p. 248.

[55] Thomas Hardy, 'At a House in Hampstead', in *The John Keats Memorial Volume*, issued by the Keats House Committee, Hampstead (London: John Lane, The Bodley Head, 1921), pp. 89–90; 90. Reprinted in *Late Lyrics and Earlier* (1923), and *The Complete Poems of Thomas Hardy*, ed. James Gibson (London and Basingstoke: Papermac, 1981), pp. 574–5.

[56] Samantha Matthews, *Poetical Remains: Poets' Graves, Bodies, and Books in the Nineteenth Century* (Oxford: Oxford University Press, 2004), p. 12; Joseph Severn, 'On the Vicissitudes of Keats's Fame', *Atlantic Monthly* 11.66 (April 1863), 401–7; 407.

custode 'for keeping the spot neat and flower-girt'.[57] Thanks to the good offices of these men, legion, too, are the poems that mention the flowers or violets on Keats's grave, with Shelley also receiving his share.[58] In 'Cor Cordium', a sonnet of 1873 that takes its title—'heart of hearts'—from words on Shelley's memorial stone, the artist Walter Crane concludes, 'But by thy grave to-day fresh violets bloom, | But on thy head imperishable bays.'[59] The Shelley critic John Addington Symonds pays homage with a sonnet of 1883 that opens:

> A bunch of violets plucked from Shelley's grave
> Or from that lowlier resting-place where lies
> The dust of Adonais 'neath blue skies, [...]

And he concludes:

> Not all the purple pomp of ancient Kings,
> Consuls acclaimed by hosts omnipotent, [...]
> Are worth one poet's song, one violet's scent.[60]

Ten years after writing this, Symonds, dying at Rome, would be interred near Shelley in the same cemetery.

Beneath the legend 'Cor Cordium', Shelley's gravestone is inscribed with words from Shakespeare's *The Tempest* that suggest transmutation:

> Nothing of him that doth fade
> But doth suffer a sea-change
> Into something rich and strange.[61]

Unlike Keats, Shelley was cremated, his body thus literally reduced to the ashes from which the alchemical violet grows and flowers again. Eleven years after Shelley's burial, Tennyson mourned the death of his friend, the poet and essayist Arthur Henry Hallam, who died in Vienna aged twenty-two. In his later elegy for Hallam, 'In Memoriam' (1850), Tennyson uses the image of the regenerate violet in conjunction with the figurative 'ashes' of the funeral service from the *Book of Common Prayer*. Anticipating the arrival of Hallam's body in England, the speaker declares:

> 'Tis well; 'tis something: we may stand
>   Where he in English earth is laid,
>   And from his ashes may be made
> The violet of his native land.[62]

---

[57] *Letters of Charles Eliot Norton*, ed. Sara Norton and M. A. De Wolfe Howe, 2 vols (Boston, MA, and New York: Houghton Mifflin Co., 1913), 1. 144 (note); *The Autobiography of Alfred Austin*, 2 vols (London: Macmillan, 1911), 1. 126.

[58] See, for example, Clinton Scotland, 'A Roman Twilight', Edith M. Thomas, 'On Severn's Last Sketch of Keats', and George Meason Whicher, 'The Grave of Keats', in *The John Keats Memorial Volume*, pp. 166, 183, 199.

[59] Walter Crane, *An Artist's Reminiscences* (London: Macmillan & Co., 1907), p. 152. Crane reports that he composed the sonnet while drawing Shelley's grave.

[60] 'A View of Rome with Violets in the Foreground' (26 December 1883), in *Letters and Papers of John Addington Symonds*, ed. Horatio F. Brown (London: John Murray, 1923), p. 269.

[61] Shakespeare, *The Tempest*, 1. 2. 403–5.

[62] 'In Memoriam' (Canto 18), in *Tennyson: A Selected Edition*, p. 362.

Steeped in the classics, Tennyson may also be recalling the lines from Persius' satire cited earlier in this chapter—'oh, now, out of those shades, out of the tomb and the oh-so-blessed cinders, will not violets spring?' However, the line 'The violet of his native land' suggests that he is also thinking of the violet-covered Roman Cemetery where Keats and Shelley are buried and emphasizing that, in contrast, Hallam's body, returned to his own country, will generate English violets. Later in Tennyson's elegy the regenerate violet recurs when, seeing the sights and sounds of another spring, the speaker finds:

> and in my breast
> Spring wakens too; and my regret
> Becomes an April violet,
> And buds and blossoms like the rest.[63]

Rekindled by the burgeoning season, the symbol for funerary mourning softens into the sweeter symbol of nostalgic regret. Shelley himself saw the violet as a symbol of regeneration. When he asks Emilia in 'Epipsychidion' if she is not 'A Solitude, a Refuge, a Delight? | [...] A cradle of young thoughts of wingless pleasure? | A violet-shrouded grave of Woe' (*SPP*, p. 375), the violets on the grave signify the rebirth and hope that come after loss.

And indeed the fragrant notes of Shelley's melodious violets are still audible in various late Victorian poems such as Edith Nesbit's 'Winter Violets'—'Your violets' voices breathed in unheard melodies' (although Keats is obviously present here as well); in Richard Wilton's 'Sweet Violets'—'Your odorous breath once more I feel | Like far off music o'er me steal'; while to Philip Bourke Marston, early violets are 'the trembling, rare | First note of Nature's prelude that leads on | The Spring'.[64]

Those fragrant notes are also present in a poem written at the very close of the Victorian period that brings together some of the key themes explored in this chapter. Katharine Bradley and Edith Cooper, the aunt and niece who wrote as Michael Field, were fervent admirers of Keats and Shelley, listing them among the poets they loved best in a Confessions Album of 1877.[65] They were members of the Shelley Society during its short existence in late 1880s to early 1890s, and had contributed to F. S. Ellis's *Shelley Concordance* (1892) by undertaking the analytic breakdown of 'The Sensitive-Plant', a poem immensely important to their own poetry.[66] Bradley declared in 1894 how Shelley's work gave 'infinite pleasure', and in 1900, how 'Almost all Shelley is within the enchanted pale.' In 1901, she

---

[63] 'In Memoriam' (Canto 115), in *Tennyson: A Selected Edition*, p. 463.

[64] Edith Nesbit, 'Winter Violets', in *Leaves of Life* (London and New York: Longmans, Green & Co., 1888), pp. 11–12; 12; Richard Wilton, 'Sweet Violets', in *Sungleams: Rondeaux and Sonnets* (London: Home Words, Publishing Office, 1882), p. 27; Philip Bourke Marston, 'Of Early Violets', in *The Collected Poems of Philip Bourke Marston*, ed. Louise Chandler Moulton (Boston, MA: Roberts Bros, 1892), p. 369.

[65] *Binary Star: Leaves from the Journal and Letters of Michael Field 1846–1914*, chosen and annotated by Ivor C. Treby (Bury St Edmunds: De Blackland Press, 2006), p. 84.

[66] A report by F. S. Ellis on *The Shelley Concordance* that mentions Michael Field's contribution can be found in *The Report of the Shelley Society for 1886–7* (London and Bungay: Printed by Richard Clay & Sons, 1887), pp. 11–12. Michael Field is listed as a Society member on p. 13 of the Original Prospectus for the Society reprinted at the back of this report.

honoured Keats as 'the Great Master'.[67] Years earlier, writing to Cooper from Rome in 1880, she had described visiting the Protestant Cemetery and laying flowers on the graves of Shelley and Keats. She enclosed in her letter mementoes—'cypress spines' for Shelley and 'violet leaves' for Keats, whose grave she called 'a violet garden'—and she instructed Cooper to 'paste one of the violet leaves carefully *into my Keats* with such inscription *as you like*'.[68]

Highly scent-sensitive, both women were exceedingly fond of flowers, which are mentioned frequently in their joint diary and are often the subject of their poems. They loved violets, relishing the scent of the white violets they grew in a cold-frame, with Bradley remarking that 'the soft, heated fragrance as we open the glass gives us joy'.[69] That same year, 1891, Cooper voiced her pleasure in 'a basketful of sugared violets' sent them as a Christmas present by her sister Amy—'a food for Gods, not men'. Bradley was delighted to be given 'scent of Rhine violets' as a Christmas present in December 1895, almost certainly Mülhens's 'Essence of Rhine Violets', which was widely advertised in the late 1890s and recommended as a suitable Christmas gift by lady columnists (see Figure 2.1).[70] On a more sombre note, when afflicted by the cancer that eventually killed her, Cooper was certain that the use of violet leaves and violet juice helped alleviate her symptoms.[71] Violets occupy a prominent position in the poetic work of both women. An early poem by Bradley about Leonardo's charming drawings of roses and violets in the Venetian Accademia celebrates the fact that, unlike regular spring flowers, the 'Flowers he chose should never fade'—his roses and violets are eternally regenerate, immortalized by art like the figures on Keats's Grecian Urn.[72] Edith Cooper's lyric 'Great violets in the weedy tangle' uses the image of violets visited by nectar-seeking bees as an analogy for youth's receptivity to sexual love.[73] After the women's conversion to Catholicism in 1907, violets also appear in their religious poems such as Cooper's 'A Gift of Sweetness' and Bradley's 'O Trinity, that art a Bank of Violets'.[74]

Two sonnets featuring violets stand out in *Wild Honey from Various Thyme*, a collection mainly authored by Katharine Bradley and published in 1908. Both

[67] Works and Days, Add MS 46782, fol. 143ʳ (25 December 1894); Add MS 46789 fol. 115ᵛ (early September 1900); Add MS 46790, fol. 11v (12 January 1901).

[68] Katharine Bradley, Letter of 10 September 1880 to Edith Cooper, in *The Fowl and the Pussycat: Love Letters of Michael Field 1876–1909*, ed. Sharon Bickle (Charlottesville, VA, and London: University of Virginia Press, 2008), p. 33.

[69] Works and Days, Add MS 46779, fol. 24ᵛ (22 March 1891).

[70] Works and Days, Add MS 46784, fol. 51ʳ (25 December 1895). See Mrs Fenwick-Miller's 'Ladies' Column', *Illustrated London News* (1 December 1894), 686; 'Filomena', 'Christmas Presents', *Illustrated London News* (10 December 1898), 884.

[71] Works and Days, Add MS 46802, fol. 163ʳ (1911). Violet leaves have a reputation as a herbal cancer cure, with some medical and scientific support. See Nelson Coon with Georgianne Giffen, *The Complete Book of Violets* (South Brunswick, NJ, New York, and London: A. S. Barnes & Co., and Yoseloff Ltd, 1977), p. 81.

[72] Michael Field, 'Drawing of Roses and Violets', in *Sight and Song* (London: Elkin Mathews and John Lane, 1892), p. 7.

[73] Michael Field, 'Great violets', in *Underneath the Bough* (London and New York: George Bell & Sons, 1893), pp. 120–2.

[74] Michael Field, 'A Gift of Sweetness', in *Poems of Adoration* (London and Edinburgh: Sands & Co., 1912), p. 108; 'O Trinity, that art a Bank of Violets', in *Mystic Trees* (London: Eveleigh Nash), p. 13.

these violet-themed sonnets are associated with the artist Charles de Sousy Ricketts (1866–1931), who, with his partner and fellow painter Charles Shannon (1863–1937), was a constant presence in the lives of both women from 1894. 'The Painters', as they were known, shared many of the women's interests, with Bradley in 1895 delightedly describing them as '*very* much like us [...] tingling with pleasure at sight of exquisite flowers or fruit'.[75] While the primary love of Bradley and Cooper was undoubtedly for each other, they also experienced strong love attachments to men—Cooper had a long-standing infatuation with the art critic and historian Bernard Berenson while Bradley appears to have nursed tender unreciprocated feelings for Charles Ricketts. In both cases the women seem to have treated their male love objects as muses who inspire their verse.[76]

Charles Ricketts had a particular fondness for violets. Cooper recorded in April 1898 that 'Ricketts wonders that we have not got violets everywhere on our table. He loves violets, and ground-ivy.'[77] In January 1912 she recorded him arriving at their Richmond home bearing 'masses of violets' to decorate the house and for them to wear.[78] Green violet leaves occur as a decorative device on the front cover of Ricketts and Shannon's Vale Press edition of Marlowe's *Hero and Leander* (1894), which they gave to Bradley and Cooper in May 1894, and Ricketts designed a border of violet flowers and leaves for the opening pages of the edition of Keats's poems produced by the Vale Press in 1898.[79]

Of Bradley's two Ricketts-inspired violet sonnets, the first, a Shakespearean sonnet 'Violets', dated 1 December 1900, was apparently sent to him with a bouquet of the flowers and ends with the lines 'Yea, learn how their nativity empowers—| Sprung from the blood of Ajax are these flowers.'[80] Although an extremely interesting poem, it does not include any reference to smell or fragrance, unlike the second sonnet, which bears the traces of the violet-infused memory trail we have been following. This poem is called 'A Violet Bank'—a title that at once conjures up Shakespearean references, especially Orsino's 'bank of violets' in *Twelfth Night*, but also perhaps Shelley's allusion to 'violet banks where sweet dreams brood' in 'The Triumph of Life' (*SPP*, p. 457):

> It was as if a violet bank
> Were breathing forth its purple, so profound
> And brimming was the beauty, and we drank
> In the discourse no meaning, though the sound
> Was musical; for if a flower should speak

---

[75] *Works and Days*, Add MS 46783, fol. 127ᵛ BL (8 August 1895).

[76] See Sarah Parker's recent treatment of the Michael Field–Berenson relationship in *The Lesbian Muse and Poetic Identity, 1889–1930* (London: Pickering & Chatto, 2013), pp. 51–70.

[77] *Works and Days*, Add MS 46787, fol. 26ʳ (21 April 1898).

[78] *Works and Days*, Add 46802, fol. 16ʳ (24 January 1912).

[79] *Works and Days*, Add MS 46782, fol. 45ʳ (22 May 1894). See the border for Keats's *Poems* in Maureen Watry, *The Vale Press: Charles Ricketts, a Publisher in Earnest* (London: The British Library, 2004), p. 146.

[80] 'Violets', in *Wild Honey from Various Thyme* (London: T. Fisher Unwin, 1908), p. 16. Some months before writing her poem, Bradley reports 'I have just read that violets are sprung from the blood of Ajax', without stating a source. See *Works and Days*, Add MS 46789, fol. 101ʳ (6 August 1900).

> At its full height and richness of perfume
> We could not listen, so on brow and cheek
> We rested by the very senses' doom.
> An instant, and the perilous charm was gone,
> The charm that was even as a prophecy
> Of the concentred youth, the happy years,
> With all the burthen of unladen tears,
> That sometimes, unaware, we find upon
> A face that very soon one feels must die.[81]

The sonnet was inspired by a conversation Bradley had with Ricketts on 19 December 1901, with the poem itself dated 20 December:

> Neither can I write what Ricketts said in the long, long talk before dinner. If a flower at its richest of perfume were to speak—one would not listen except to the odour, & it was as if a violet-bank were giving forth its purple—the beauty was so brimming so profound. The eyes bore tears as a burthen, as other people's eyes bear care; & the whole face was far too richly full & lighted, as one has sometimes seen dying faces.[82]

Watching Ricketts speak, Bradley is fascinated by the charm and beauty of his face and the musicality of his speech. Her heightened sensory pleasure, over-whelming the import of anything he actually says, is expressed through an elevated synaesthesia. While Orsino compares music to wafted violet fragrance, she compares Ricketts to a flower speaking its perfume, an image that recalls Shelley's melodious violets—'their breath [...] mixed with fresh odour, sent | From the turf, like the voice and the instrument'. In Bradley's sonnet the synaesthesia also involves colour in 'purple'—seemingly an intrinsic part of the smell and taste—in that the listeners 'drink' in the 'brimming' beauty of the youth's musical discourse, reminding us also that violets, long employed as a flavouring, were commonly used by the Greeks to infuse wine.

In her sonnet Bradley reworks the original incident, changing the 'I' to 'we' and transforming the thirty-five-year-old Ricketts (who would, in fact, outlive both Bradley and Cooper) into a younger figure. If the poem's complex synaesthesia conjures up Shelley, 'brimming' evokes Keats, inextricably connected with the poetic words 'brimming', 'brim', and 'o'erbrim'.[83] The shades of Keats and Shelley, cut off their prime, along with the fair and fated young men of classical myth, surely lurk behind the image of a youth whose fleeting charm seems to tempt an early death. The violets signifying the youthful charm that delights for a moment may also perhaps presage the violets of death, subliminally associated with Rome's Protestant Cemetery and, as Bradley described it in 1880, 'the grave of violet leaves where Adonais sleeps'.[84]

---

[81] Field, *Wild Honey from Various Thyme*, p. 30.

[82] Works and Days Add MS 46790, p. 171ʳ (*c.*19 December 1901).

[83] See Keats's 'Fill for me a brimming bowl', 'Ode to a Nightingale', and 'To Autumn', *PJK*, pp. 6, 526, 651. The relatively unusual word 'unladen' also occurs in 'Endymion', 3. 12 (*PJK*, p. 206), and Shelley's 'The Witch of Atlas', *l.* 592 (*SPP*, p. 364).

[84] Letter of 10 September 1880 to Edith Cooper, in *The Fowl and the Pussycat*, p. 33.

In representing the transience of this violet-scented moment, Bradley, perhaps unconsciously, plays on the characteristic of violet perfume mentioned earlier in this chapter, that the nose can smell ionone, the ketone responsible for violet odour, only for a short period of time before tiring, after which the fragrance disappears only to reappear sometime later. Bradley wittily has the violet effect disappear just after her sonnet's volta or turning point—'An instant, and the perilous charm was gone'—the sestet of her sonnet then enacting what might be described as a 'dying fall', a melancholy diminuendo, although, as suggested, there may be a hint of a return, a spectral whiff of violets in the premonition of death at the poem's end.

The pattern of violet fragrance's disappearance and reappearance might be thought of as a kind of forgetting followed by recollection. In the literary tradition, that pattern plays out across the generations as new experience of the fragrance constantly revives its memories and associations. Thus the scent of violets, intimately tied up with recollection, commemoration, and regeneration, pervades a literary trail that extends from Shakespeare and Bacon through Shelley, Keats, and their Victorian devotees, into a turn-of-the-century poetry still brimming with the perfume of the past.

—— *3* ——

Les Fleurs du Mâle

Algernon Swinburne and Walter Pater

Generally acknowledged as the founding father of British literary aestheticism, Swinburne's influential use of scented language and scented atmospheres in his poetry and prose can be seen as triggering an increased awareness of and attention to the pleasures and uses of perfume in those who followed after him, most notably his near contemporary Walter Pater. In this chapter I trace how Swinburne, and Pater after him, presented themselves as *olfactifs* and made a virtue of their scent sensitivities, using their receptiveness to fragrance as a way of savouring or appreciating the effect or impact of a literary author, school, or period. Swinburne's aestheticism is often understood as formed through his interaction with Charles Baudelaire's *Les Fleurs du mal* (1857, 1861), a volume also seen as responsible for inspiring the heavy scents associated with Swinburne's infamous *Poems and Ballads* (1866). Yet while Baudelaire and his perfumes, to a certain degree, helped shape Swinburne both as aesthete and *olfactif*, awareness of this has partly occluded his own distinctive artistic impulses and olfactory preferences. Swinburne's preferred scents may look closer to those that constitute conservative mid-Victorian taste but, as will be shown in this chapter, the signification he attaches to them is anything but conservative. Having indicated how scent permeates Pater's critical and creative work, I suggest that he adapted Swinburne's scented legacy into a somewhat more nuanced and studied appreciation of critical olfaction. In devising an alchemy that attempts to distil the fragrant essence of a literary experience, Pater not only alerted receptive readers to the 'perfume' of his texts but he also encouraged the development of a similar flair in aesthetic or decadent admirers that included Oscar Wilde and Arthur Symons.

SWINBURNE'S ART OF ODOURS

'Beauty is the beginning of all things, and the end of them is pleasure. [...] A beautiful soft line drawn is more than a life saved; and a pleasant perfume smelt is better than a soul redeemed': so writes Swinburne's Tebaldeo Tebaldei, narrator of a chronicle about Lucretia Borgia and the author of 'The Treatise of Noble Morals', a provocatively hyperbolic statement of aesthetic values.[1] A little earlier Tebaldei

---

[1] Algernon Charles Swinburne, *Lucretia Borgia: The Chronicle of Tebaldeo Tebaldei*, ed. Randolph Hughes (London: Golden Cockerell Press, 1942), p. 58; partially reprinted in *Algernon Charles Swinburne:*

has compared pleasure itself, explicitly the remembrance of the sexual love he has shared with Lucretia, with perfume:

> [A]s long as I endure I must always have some part of it; as if the pleasure clung about my soul and my body which were then clothed upon and coloured throughout with it; or as if, after a rose is dead and consumed, the scent of it should always abide within the senses of a man, visible and possible to smell and see. So it is with me and the pleasure of my love.[2]

Pleasure of this kind, far from being ephemeral, is like a perfume that lasts forever, and when Tebaldei justifies his statement about 'Beauty' in 'The Treatise of Noble Morals', he insists that spiritual experience cannot be separated from, indeed is dependent on, sensory experience:

> For all spiritual and lofty good comes to us only by perception and conception; which by their very nature are naturally of the senses. Therefore though we do much good and though we become very virtuous, notwithstanding, to take pleasure and give it again is better than all our good deeds.[3]

Swinburne was working on *Lucretia Borgia*, a narrative he never completed, at the very beginning of his literary career in 1860, and Tebaldei's views reflect those of his creator. After a conversation about Swinburne's poetic ideals in 1863, the Reverend William Sewell, a former early mentor, noted disapprovingly: 'He spoke of Poetry, of the duty and pleasure of creating beauty.'[4] The sentiments expressed by Tebaldei are indicative of many of the premises that underlie Swinburne's later poetry: his firm belief that body and spirit are inextricably intertwined and his commitment to beauty and pleasure as experienced through the senses. That physicality will become a characteristic of his poetry. As the poet and critic Arthur Symons would later comment, 'no English poet has ever presented bodily sensation with such curious and subtle intensity'.[5]

When in 1967, many years after Symons's observation, John D. Rosenberg pondered what he called the 'diffuseness' of Swinburne's poetic vision, he suggested that it threw the accent onto the other senses so that the poet is 'all tongue, and ear and touch'.[6] What is missing from this list is, of course, the nose, and smell—so

---

Major Poems and Selected Prose, ed. Jerome M. McGann and Charles L. Sligh (New Haven, CT: Yale University Press, 2004), p. 448. The high aestheticist creed cited here echoes the sentiment of Swinburne's hero Victor Hugo 'La beauté est parfaite, La beauté peut tout, La beauté est la seule chose qui n'existe pas à demi', as expressed his novel *Notre Dame de Paris* (1831), a sentiment that Swinburne cites at the end of his review 'Notes on Some Pictures of 1868' (1868), reprinted in his *Essays and Studies* (1875), p. 380.

[2] Swinburne, *Lucretia Borgia*, p. 46; not in McGann and Sligh.

[3] Swinburne, *Lucretia Borgia*, p. 58; McGann and Sligh, p. 448.

[4] Lionel James, *A Forgotten Genius: Sewell of St Columba's and Radley* (London: Faber & Faber, 1945), p. 230.

[5] Arthur Symons, 'Algernon Charles Swinburne', in *Figures of Several Centuries* (London: Constable & Co., 1916), p. 191.

[6] John D. Rosenberg, 'Swinburne', *Victorian Studies* 11 (1967), 131–52; 131. Arthur Symons touches on the issue of Swinburne's poetic vision in the essay cited in note 5. For another perspective, see ch. 5: '"Beneath the woman's and the water's kiss": Swinburne's Metamorphoses', in my *The Female Sublime from Milton to Swinburne*, pp. 178–221.

often regarded as the lowest of the lower senses that perhaps Rosenberg did not even think to mention it.[7] Yet Swinburne's olfactory powers were strikingly evident to other readers. The cosmopolitan writer Lafcadio Hearn, himself a lover of pleasing odours, wrote in one of the lectures given to his Japanese students:

> Swinburne has no equal in enthusiastic celebration of the beauties of sky and sea and wood, of light and clouds and waters, of sound and perfume and blossoming. Indeed, one of his particular characteristics, a characteristic very seldom found in English masterpieces, though common in the best French work, is his art for describing odours—the smell of morning and evening, scents of the seasons, scents also of life.[8]

Edward Sagarin, the American author of a book on perfumery published in 1945, includes Swinburne along with Robert Herrick, Shakespeare, Shelley, and Baudelaire as notable writers who allude to perfume in their works, declaring that: 'In Swinburne, just as there is the conscious effect of the poet to allow the reader to hear the music he is creating, so do his word images create smell sensations.'[9]

As we shall see in this and subsequent chapters, Swinburne's relish of fragrance triggers the expression and cultivation of olfactory sensitivity in the aesthetes and decadents who follow him. But even he is aware of the potential embarrassment attached to acknowledging smell in polite Victorian society: commenting on the draft of a poem by his friend Dante Gabriel Rossetti, he hesitates over a possible emendation, writing, 'I felt of course the patent objection to the word "smell"' (*TSL* 2. 73; 22 December 1869). Swinburne picks up the whiff of indelicacy from a word that imports an uncompromising physical immediacy or that savours too much of the body.

Yet even while he hesitates over the poetic use of the word 'smell', Swinburne nonetheless asserts immediately afterwards that 'I myself, like Baudelaire, am especially and extravagantly fond of that sense and susceptible to it'. Certainly his pride in his own sense of smell is evident, as can be seen in a later letter to Henry Arthur Bright, author of *A Year in a Lancashire Garden* (1879), a selection of personal gardening notes which includes a piece titled 'On Flowers and the Poets'. Bright had evidently sent Swinburne a copy of his book, which had delighted him, and his reply shows he had read it attentively. At one point Bright, alluding to Sir Francis Bacon's famous commendation of the scent of dying strawberry leaves in his essay 'Of Gardens', comments:

> Of other fruit I have nothing new to notice, unless it be to ask whether any one now living can smell the scent of dying Strawberry leaves? We all remember how Mrs. Gaskell in her delightful story gives Lady Ludlow the power, but now we all seem

---

[7] Although, *à propos* of Swinburne's early style, Rosenberg writes that 'he evokes the heady, Pre-Raphaelite scent of over-sweet violets' ('Swinburne', p. 132), a curious characterization, as this is not a scent one would normally associate with either the younger Swinburne or the Pre-Raphaelites in general.

[8] Lafcadio Hearn, 'Studies in Swinburne', in *Appreciations of Poetry*, ed. John Erskine (New York: Dodd, Mead & Co., 1916), p. 141.

[9] Edward Sagarin, *The Science and Art of Perfumery* (New York and London: McGraw Hill Book Company, 1945), p. 232.

to have lost it. Certainly my dying Strawberry leaves give me no sense of sweetness. Was it a mere fond and foolish fancy? or were the Strawberries of Elizabethan gardens different from those we are now growing? Bacon tells us that, next to the white double Violet and the Musk Rose, the sweetest perfume in the open air is 'Strawberry leaves dying, which yield a most excellent cordiale smell;' and I find in an old play by Sir John Suckling—

> 'Wholesome
> As dying leaves of Strawberries.'[10]

Swinburne, who admired Bacon and adored Gaskell—he included the latter in his list of a hundred greatest writers no longer living (*TSL* 5. 135; 24 January 1886)—rises to this olfactory challenge in his letter to Bright: 'My impression is that I *do* know quite well the soft slight odour of dying strawberry-leaves, distinct in its dim aroma from all others. But I have often been amazed at the *scentlessness* of many people who write about flowers' (*TSL* 4. 122; 6 January 1880).[11] As illustration of that scentlessness, Swinburne gives examples of two authors:

> One would think the whole race of writers were as noseless as Sir Wm. Davenant in one sense or Wordsworth in another—who, you remember, could never smell anything in his life but once, and then the momentary relish of a bed of stocks in blossom remained ever after in the poor man's memory like a passing gust of Paradise—never to be 'regained'.

Swinburne implicitly compares himself with two former Poet Laureates, the first instance tinged with a certain amount of black humour, as the Caroline poet William Davenant (1606–1668) had his nose severely disfigured by syphilis. Swinburne also shows his awareness of Wordsworth's anosmia or lack of smell, a surprising disability in a poet popularly associated with nature and with poems that hymn flowers such as the daisy and the daffodil.[12] Moreover, he follows this up with another literary reference: 'But I believe I have myself a bloodhound's—or Cassandra's—nose for all sweet smells—and alas! for all other than sweet.' For Swinburne, the 'bloodhound', a tracker dog with a phenomenally keen sense of smell, prompts a link with the doomed captive Trojan princess and prophetess Cassandra, who, in the play by Aeschylus, recoils at the smell of blood as she enters the palace of Agamemnon, King of Argos, scenting an odour undetectable to others that is a premonition of his death and her own.[13]

Like Cassandra, preternaturally sensitive to bad odours as well as pleasant ones—he was always relieved to escape 'the fog and filth of London' (*TSL* 3. 36; 22 June 1875)—Swinburne then asserts his superiority by relishing a delightful fragrance, the smell of tulips, that is imperceptible to many other people: 'Actually,

---

[10] Bright, *A Year in a Lancashire Garden*, pp. 98–9.

[11] Swinburne acknowledges Bacon's 'pre-eminence' in a related letter (*TSL* 5. 132; *c.*22 January 1888), but explains that the nature of his works requires specialized study.

[12] For a recent essay, see Boyson, 'Wordsworth's Anosmia'. The incident Swinburne refers to is mentioned in *The Life and Correspondence of Robert Southey*, ed. C. C. Southey (London: Longmans, 1849–50), p. 33.

[13] See Aeschylus, *Oresteia: Agamemnon, l.* 1309.

I have known people who could not smell or believe in the delightful scent of a tulip—which might be the very perfume of the sun!' Contrary to popular opinion, some varieties of tulips are scented, but here Swinburne is probably responding to another passage in Bright's book: 'The bed of Golden Prince Tulips is, however, doing better; this always seems to me a very handsome Tulip, and I sometimes fancy has a sweetness of scent beyond all other kinds—a something, which at times half reminds one of the odour of some Tea Rose.'[14] Whereas Swinburne had previously suggested that he, unlike Bright, possessed the rare ability to savour the 'cordiale smell' of dying strawberry leaves, here he tactfully suggests he shares with Bright an olfactory capacity denied to others.

There is other evidence that Swinburne was highly sensitive to odours—Clara Watts-Dunton, wife to Swinburne's long-term companion Walter Theodore Watts-Dunton, says that 'He never smoked and hated the very smell of tobacco', and he told John Addington Symonds that 'the very sight or smell' of a mushroom 'makes my gorge rise' (*UL*, 1. 266; 26 December 1872).[15] In his letter to Bright his presentation of himself as an *olfactif*, an individual with a refined sense of smell, carries in its discrimination of subtle pleasure the implication that he has what Shelley in 'A Defence of Poetry' calls 'the most refined organization', 'the most delicate sensibility and most enlarged imagination' belonging to the poet (*SPP*, p. 505).[16] What Swinburne does here, and what other aesthetes will do after him, is to rescue smell from its lowly position as a mode of perception and promote the appreciation of subtle odours and perfumes as a badge of refinement that sets one apart from ordinary citizens.

Swinburne had a number of English literary *olfactifs* to look to as precursors, including Shelley with whom he was often compared. Shelley was one of his poetic heroes, as was Walter Savage Landor, another *olfactif*, of whom Swinburne observed: 'His tender and ardent love of children, of animals, and of flowers, makes fragrant alike the pages of his writing and the records of his life.'[17] However, it is not these writers that are normally mentioned in regard to Swinburne's olfactory sensibility, and his comparison of his fondness for smell with that of Charles Baudelaire is, of course, indicative, as Baudelaire's poems are renowned for their appreciation of perfume and exotic odours. In an essay subsequently used to preface the 1868 edition of Baudelaire's works, Théophile Gautier singles out his friend as a notable poetic *olfactif*:

> In many a passage this preoccupation with aroma appears, surrounding with a subtle cloud all persons and things. In very few of the poets do we find this care. Generally they are content with putting light, colour, and music in their verses; but it is rare that

---

[14] See chapter 10: 'Perfume in Tulips', in Roy Genders, *Perfume in the Garden* (London: The Garden Book Club, 1954), pp. 88–92; Bright, *A Year in a Lancashire Garden*, p. 41.

[15] Clara Watts-Dunton, *The Home Life of Algernon Charles Swinburne* (London: A. M. Philpotts, 1922), p. 238.

[16] See also *SPP*, p. 507: 'a poet [...] is more delicately organized than other men, and sensible to pain and pleasure, both his own and that of others, in a degree unknown to them'.

[17] Swinburne, 'Landor', in *Miscellanies* (London: Chatto & Windus, 1886), p. 207.

they pour in that drop of pure essence with which Baudelaire's muse never failed to moisten the sponge or the cambric of his handkerchief.[18]

Swinburne, the author of the first English review of *Les Fleurs du mal*, was responsible for introducing French aesthetic thought into England, and saw himself, at least initially, as an English equivalent to Baudelaire.[19] In his review, published in the *Spectator* in September 1862, he describes *Les Fleurs du mal* as possessing 'a heavy heated temperature with dangerous hothouse scents in it', and notes that, for Baudelaire, 'perfection of sound and scent' are among those things 'that seem to have an infinite attraction for him'.[20] Among the poems Swinburne singles out for special mention are many that allude to perfume, including such famous examples as 'Parfum Exotique', 'La Chevelure', and 'Le Flacon'.[21]

Swinburne's own first and most notorious collection, *Poems and Ballads* (1866), a volume that emulates many aspects of Baudelaire's *Les Fleurs du mal*, is rich in reference to smell and perfume. Indeed, while olfactory allusion can be found throughout Swinburne's subsequent poetic volumes, it is nowhere as marked as in this, his debut collection. When Oscar Wilde infuses some of the incense of J. K. Huysmans's *A Rebours* (1884) into *The Picture of Dorian Gray* (1890, 1891) he follows Swinburne's earlier example of looking to France; for French aestheticism is an exotic perfume that, diffused through Swinburne, impregnates and spices up English letters. Indeed, responding to *Poems and Ballads*, the *London Review* (4 August 1866) showed the stock British horror of French manners and morals when it accused Swinburne of having 'drenched himself in the worst creations of Parisian literature'.[22]

Gautier wrote of Baudelaire:

> We shall astonish no one if we add that he preferred, to the simple perfume of the rose or violet, that of benzoin, amber, and even musk, so little appreciated in our days, and also the penetrating aroma of certain exotic flowers the perfume of which is too strong for our moderate climate.[23]

Baudelaire's preference for spicy or sultry fragrances such as tamarind, amber, benzoin, and incense is echoed by Swinburne's use of myrrh, frankincense, spikenard, cassia, sandalwood, and balm. As a member of a devout Anglo-Catholic family he may have been familiar with some of these materials in the form of church incense; certainly as an eighteen-year-old he had visited Catholic churches and been present at services when travelling in France and Germany. In comparison with Baudelaire's, Swinburne's perfumes tend to have a marked Biblical provenance, reminding us that although he had renounced religious belief while a student at Oxford, he retained an excellent knowledge of scripture. Undoubtedly

---

[18] Théophile Gautier, *Charles Baudelaire: His Life* [...] *with Selections from His Poems*, tr. Guy Thorne (London: Greening & Co., 1915), p. 39.

[19] Swinburne reviewed the revised expanded 1861 edition of Baudelaire's poems.

[20] Algernon Swinburne, 'Charles Baudelaire', in *Swinburne as Critic*, ed. Clyde K. Hyder (London: Routledge & Kegan Paul, 1972), p. 29.

[21] Ibid., pp. 29, 34.

[22] *London Review*, cited in *Swinburne: The Critical Heritage*, ed. Clyde K. Hyder (London: Routledge & Kegan Paul, 1970), p. 35.

[23] Gautier, *Charles Baudelaire*, p. 32.

borrowing from the fragrances that pervade the love poetry of the Song of Solomon, he uses perfume in *Poems and Ballads*, as Baudelaire does in *Les Fleurs du mal*, to intensify an erotic atmosphere and heighten sensual awareness. This is conspicuous in poems such as 'Laus Veneris' and 'The Masque of Queen Bersabe' that celebrate glamorous *femme fatales*. For example, in the procession of beautiful women that makes up 'The Masque', Queen Aholah tells us:

> My words were soft like dulcimers
> And the first sweet of grape-flowers
>   Made each side of my bosom sweet.
> My raiment was as tender fruit
> Whose rind smells sweet of spice-tree root,
>   Bruised balm-blossom and budded wheat.   (*Poems* 1. 228; *PBA*, p. 182)

Like Baudelaire, Swinburne delights in women's scented hair in poems such as 'Anactoria', 'Before Parting', 'Félise', 'Love and Sleep'. In 'La Chevelure', Baudelaire's speaker 'grows drunk with the mingling scents' of the woman's hair which smells of 'coconut-oil and musk and tar'.[24] In 'Laus Veneris', Swinburne's retelling of the Venus and Tannhäuser legend, the Christian knight Tannhäuser, who has given himself over to pleasure with Venus, reveals that:

> Her hair had smells of all the sunburnt south,
>
> Strange spice and flower, strange savour of crushed fruit,
> And perfume the swart kings tread underfoot
>   For pleasure when their minds wax amorous,
> Charred frankincense and grated sandal-root.   (*Poems* 1. 25; *PBA*, pp. 21–2)

'Savour', which can mean either 'smell' or 'taste', is a favourite word of Swinburne's and is frequently used by him to signify aroma just as it does in English translations of the Bible from Tyndale onwards.[25] However, perfume for both Baudelaire and Swinburne has an effect that goes beyond the mere gratification of the senses. Baudelaire's famous synaesthetic poem 'Correspondances' that famously describes perfume in terms of music—'There are perfumes fresh as children's flesh, sweet as oboes, green as fields'—lists complex perfumes—amber, musk, benzoin, and incense—which 'sing the ecstasies of the spirit and the senses'.[26] A synaesthetic poet like Baudelaire and Shelley, Swinburne is also, like both of them, deeply interested in the mingling of sense and spirit, something arguably encouraged by synaesthesia, which heightens the senses to a new level of perception. Swinburne's continuing preoccupation with what he calls 'the spirit in sense', a phrase he uses in variant forms throughout his poetry and prose, means that he is ever attentive to the deeper psychic effects of sensory experience.[27]

---

[24] Charles Baudelaire, *The Complete Verse*, intr. and tr. Francis Scarfe (London: Anvil Press Poetry, 1986), p. 84.

[25] See the OED entry for 'savour', item 2c.

[26] My translation. For the French text, see Baudelaire, *The Complete Verse*, p. 61.

[27] For 'spirit in sense', see, for example, *Tristram of Lyonesse*, in *Poems* 4. 32; 'Eros', *Poems* 5. 170; 'A Reminiscence', *Poems* 6. 229. For 'the spirit of sense', see Swinburne, *William Blake* (London: Chatto & Windus, 1868), p. 35; 'For the Feast of Giordano Bruno', *Poems* 3. 49; *Tristram of Lyonesse*, *Poems*

This can be seen in 'Laus Veneris', where the atmosphere of the Horsel, Venus' subterranean mountain palace, evokes Swinburne's characterization of *Les Fleurs du mal*: 'a heavy heated temperature with dangerous hothouse scents in it'.[28] Tannhäuser tells us, 'Inside the Horsel here the air is hot [...] | The scented dusty daylight burns the air' (*Poems* 1. 12; *PBA*, p. 10), and later he says:

> The scent and shadow shed around me make
> The very soul in all my senses ache;
>   The hot hard night is fed upon my breath,
> And sleep beholds me from afar awake.   (*Poems* 1. 14; *PBA*, p. 12)

Yet we can see that there is a difference between the relish of Baudelaire's speakers as they immerse themselves in the heady hypnotic perfumes of their lovers, and Swinburne's Tannhäuser, who has come to find the narcotic atmosphere, the 'fume of flowers and fires', of the Horsel cloying and oppressive. Love itself becomes a poison and a snare. Tannhäuser describes the signs that identify such destructive infatuation and, in doing so, uses imagery that links perfume and predators. Of 'bitter love', he says:

> sweet smells of lip and cheek,
> Like a sweet snake's breath made more poisonous
>
> With chewing of some perfumed deadly grass,
> Are shed all round his passage if he pass,
>   And their quenched savour leaves the whole soul weak,
> Sick with keen guessing whence the perfume was.
>
> As one who hidden in deep sedge and reeds
> Smells the rare scent made where a panther feeds,
>   And tracking ever slotwise the warm smell
> Is snapped upon by the sweet mouth and bleeds,[29]
>
> His head far down the hot sweet throat of her—
> So one tracks love, whose breath is deadlier,
>   And lo, one springe and you are fast in hell,
> Fast as the gin's grip of a wayfarer.   (*Poems* 1. 20; *PBA*, p. 17)

In describing the 'rare scent' of the panther, Swinburne follows classical precedent, for ancient Greek texts propose that the panther—*pórdalis* (masculine) or *párdalis* (feminine)—lured other animals by its sweet breath.[30] The perfume critic Susan

---

4. 95. For 'the spirit within the sense', see 'On the Cliffs', *Poems* 3. 315; 'A Nympholept', *Poems* 6. 127; 'Sunrise and Moonrise', *Poems* 6. 213. The phrase 'spirit of sense' occurs twice in Shakespeare's *Troilus and Cressida*, 1. 1. 55 and 3. 3. 101. Compare Swinburne's usages with Shelley, who, by contrast, isolates a kind of sense within the spirit. See his 'Epipsychidion' and Emilia's fragrance: 'The sweetness seems to satiate the faint wind; | And in the soul a wild odour is felt, | Beyond the sense' (*SPP*, p. 376).

[28] The Hörselberg or Venusberg is the mythical German mountain in which the pagan goddess Venus had her secret palace. In the medieval legend of Venus and Tannhäuser, the Christian knight Tannhäuser gives way to temptation and dwells with Venus in her palace as her lover.

[29] Swinburne's editor Kenneth Haynes explains: '"Slotwise" [...] for which the *OED* gives Swinburne as the first citation, is derived from "slot", the track of an animal' (*PBA*, p. 327).

[30] See Marcel Detienne, 'The Hunt and the Erotic', *Diogenes* 96 (1976), 110–31; 126–30, for an authoritative discussion of the ancient perception of 'the perfumed panther', which lures other animals

Irvine proposes that the Greeks appear to have confused the civet cat, an animal which produces a secretion used in perfume, with the panther 'when they described the latter as the perfumed panther'. Moreover, it seems 'The word for "panther" and "courtesan" in ancient Greece was the same',[31] a coincidence that Swinburne undoubtedly exploits, in that the symbols used for erotic infatuation—the scented snake and the perfumed panther—double for Tannhäuser's mistress, Venus, goddess of sexual love.[32]

The realm of Venus as described in *Poems and Ballads*, is a world of intense perfume, resinous, heavily spiced, and seemingly strengthened by animalic civet, but it seems to be one that Swinburne, like Tannhäuser, finds difficult to endure on a prolonged basis. We are reminded of the opening lines of 'Before Parting': 'A month or twain to live on honeycomb | Is pleasant; but one tires of scented time' (*Poems* 1. 184; *PBA*, p. 147). In 'Ave atque Vale', the elegy he wrote for Baudelaire, Swinburne also imagines the dead poet as a second Tannhäuser, 'A spirit sick with perfume and sweet night' (*Poems* 3. 56), who would like to escape the Horsel. In his unfinished, posthumously published novel *Lesbia Brandon*, Swinburne's eponymous heroine dies in a close-curtained room filled with 'the sweet strong smell of perfumes and drugs' where 'A funeral fragrance hung about all the air.'[33] Heavy perfumes are seen as stifling and deadening. It is notable too that elsewhere in Swinburne's poetry there is a marked absence of animalics—animal-derived scents such as musk and civet which add sensuality, depth, and staying power to perfume. Where these occur they are translations such as Francois Villon's 'sweet as civet', used in 'A Double Ballad of Good Counsel' (*Poems* 3. 137) or disparaging such as 'smells foul of mould or musk' from 'A Marching Song' (*Poems* 2. 155). In fact, as I shall argue, heavy animalic or narcotic scents are exceptional rather than typical of Swinburne's writing, which overwhelmingly reflects his preferred olfactory choices. These are explored in the next section of this chapter.

Swinburne's Scents

It is impossible to detail Swinburne's favourite smells without noting his passionate primary enthusiasm for the energizing scents of the sea and sea-breezes. (Interestingly, these are an inspiration in modern perfumery, which incorporates them within the

by its scent. A longer version of this essay can be found in ch. 2: 'The Perfumed Panther', in Detienne's *Dionysos Slain*, tr. Mireille Muellner and Leonard Muellner (Baltimore, MD, and London: Johns Hopkins University Press, 1979), pp. 20–52.

[31] Irvine, *Perfume: The Creation and Allure of Classic Fragrances*, p. 51. Detienne notes: 'This seduction through the olfactory sense must have born [*sic*] a close association between the panther and the image of the perfumed woman with a desirable body. For Aristophanes and his contemporaries, a courtesan is, in effect, a "panther" (*pórdalis*)' ('The Hunt and the Erotic', p. 129; *Dionysos Slain*, p. 39, with slight variation in translation).

[32] Swinburne will also use the panther image for a female lover in 'At a Month's End' in *Poems and Ballads* 2 (1878). There he bids farewell to the woman he addresses as 'my sleek black pantheress' and 'my queen of panthers' but finds that 'So to my soul in surer fashion | Your savage stamp and savour hangs; | The print and perfume of old passion, | The wild-beast mark of panther's fangs' (*Poems* 3. 32, 33).

[33] Swinburne, *Lesbia Brandon*, ed. Randolph Hughes (London: The Falcon Press, 1952), p. 158.

relatively new genre of marine, aquatic, and ozonic fragrances.) Born the son of a navy man (Captain, later Admiral, Charles Henry Swinburne), Swinburne spent his early years in the beautiful village of Bonchurch on the Isle of Wight, in 'East Dene', a house that looked out to the English Channel. 'As for the sea', he declared, 'its salt *must* have been in my blood before I was born' (*TSL* 3.12; 21 February 1875). As a boy, he loved to swim and play in the waves and to wander the nearby beaches and coastal paths, and the smell, sight, sound, and touch of the sea went deep. In *Lesbia Brandon* when young Herbert Seyton, a character based on Swinburne himself, is first described beholding the sea, we are told: 'All the colours and savours of the sea seemed to pass in at his eyes and mouth; all his nerves desired the divine touch of it, all his soul saluted it through the senses.'[34] Reflecting on William Blake's 'first daily communion with the sea', Swinburne, surely once more drawing on his own experience, speculates:

> [T]hat the sharp sweetness of the salted air was not without swift and pungent effect; that the hourly physical delight lavished upon every sense by all tunes and odours and changes and colours of the sea—the delight of every breath or sound or shadow or whisper passing upon it—may have served at first to satiate as well as to stimulate, before the pressure of enjoyment grew too intense and the sting of enjoyment too keen.[35]

In his own letters he frequently voices his pleasure in the scent of the sea or his desire to smell it: 'I am here safe and *so* well and fresh, thanks to the mere sight and smell of sea' (*TSL* 1. 308; 14 September 1868); 'I covet your sea, and *must* get a breath and taste of it somewhere this year' (*TSL* 3. 40; 7 July 1875).

As discussed in Chapter 1, most Victorian men did not wear perfume per se, but nonetheless incorporated scent into their toilettes in other ways in the form of perfumed soap and hair oil or in floral buttonholes. Clara Watts-Dunton notes with a touch of gentle satire the poet's fondness for a particular brand of scented soap:

> He had discovered—or a friend had discovered for him—a brand known as 'Samphire Soap,' which was extensively advertised by a quotation from 'King Lear':
>
> >   Half way down
> > Hangs one that gathers samphire, dreadful trade!
>
> This precious tablet smelt of the sea. Or was supposed to smell of the sea. A. C. S. believed implicitly that it was highly charged with the active principle of ozone. He sensed the wave in its odour, and the suds in his bath were refreshing to him as the foam of the ocean. Needless to say, 'Samphire' soap was a thing of which we never permitted ourselves to 'run short.' I still keep a cake of it as a souvenir of the happiest time of my life.[36]

Swinburne may have relished his soap because of its literary connection with *King Lear* and its ozonic smell of the sea, although if samphire was included in his soap, it was almost certainly marsh samphire (*Salicornia europaea*) and not rock samphire (*Crithmum maritimum*), a species that favours sea-cliffs and the type most likely alluded to by Shakespeare. Both these samphires are edible, salt-loving plants but

---

[34] Ibid., p. 7.   [35] Swinburne, *William Blake*, p. 34.
[36] Watts-Dunton, *Home Life*, p. 106.

are botanically unrelated, with rock samphire, in spite of its name, actually belonging to the carrot family. Marsh samphire, principally gathered from muddy estuaries, is high in sodium and had been used since medieval times to make soap and glass (hence its common name of 'glasswort'). The brand of soap favoured by Swinburne, identifiable by the quotation from *King Lear* (see Plate 4) was produced by J. C. and J. Field of Lambeth and introduced in 1884.[37] In the firm's advertisements, which appeared regularly throughout the mid to late 1880s in popular papers like the *Graphic*, the *Standard*, the *Era*, the *Daily News*, and the *Morning Post*, they declared that 'One Sixpenny Tablet contains the Hygienic Essentials of Twenty Sea-Baths', and asserted that their soap contained seaweed, iodine, glycerine, olive oil, palm oil, and eucalyptol. (Samphire is notably absent from this list of ingredients.) One of Field's adverts declared that 'The perfume has never been imitated or equalled in durability or delicacy of aroma.'[38]

It is unclear whether J. C. and J. Field knew of the poet's fondness for their product but throughout 1885 many of their adverts were headed with a quotation from Swinburne's poetic drama *Atalanta in Calydon* (1865)—'GREEN GIRDLES & CROWNS OF THE SEA GODS, COOL BLOSSOMS of WATER and FOAM' (see Figure 3.1). There is a faint though tantalizing possibility that he may have been happy to endorse their soap, although he would surely have balked at the misquotation, as the text should properly read: 'Cold girdles and crowns of the sea-gods, cool blossoms of water and foam!' (*l.* 2156; *Poems* 4. 328; *PBA*, p. 318). Even if he did not sanction the use of his drama, Swinburne's enthusiasm for samphire soap remained undiminished. William Black wrote in 1888 that

> a great poet of our own day, who is passionately fond of the sea, and is also an excellent swimmer, declares that, if you are pent up in town or country, you have only to use samphire soap in order to induce the impression that you have just come in from breasting the breakers off the rocks of Alderney or Sark.[39]

In 1890 he was generously bestowing it on his aunt Lady Mary Gordon, who thanks him for 'such a supply of that very pleasant soap' (*UL* 3. 13).

If Swinburne used any other scent at all, it seems to have been restricted to eau de cologne, which, being like all colognes lighter than either perfume or eau de toilette, was favoured by the Victorians for its 'refreshing' tonic quality and routinely used as a therapeutic restorative for faintness and general malaise. A blend of diluted alcohol, citrus oils, and herbal floral extracts such as lavender, rosemary,

---

[37] This company, originally candle-makers, began manufacturing soap in the 1840s. Item 4191 in the British Library Evanion Collection is a trade card for J. C. and J. Field (1885), which on one side carries three coloured advertisements for the firm's soap and candles. The largest and central image is for 'Samphire Soap' and represents a climber gathering rock samphire, with the lines from *King Lear*, mentioned by Clara Watts-Dunton, inscribed beneath in the bottom left-hand corner (see Plate 4).

[38] Advertisement for 'Samphire Soap', *Birmingham Daily Post* (2 June 1885).

[39] William Black, 'A Day's Stalking', *Longman's Magazine* 13 (December 1888), 179, cited in Terry Meyers's 'Supplementary Material to *The Uncollected Letters of Algernon Charles Swinburne*', in the online, freely accessible, Algernon Charles Swinburne Project based at Indiana University at http://swinburnearchive.indiana.edu/swinburne/.

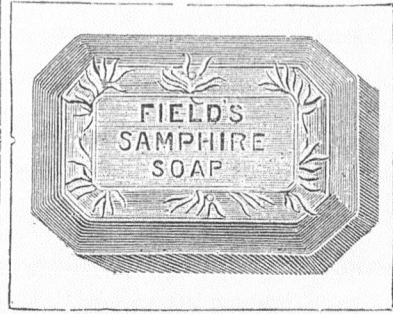
Figure 3.1 Advertisement for J. C. and J. Field's Samphire Soap, *Graphic* (27 July 1885), p. 71 (detail), N. 2288 b. 7 (vol. 32) (courtesy of The Bodleian Libraries, The University of Oxford)

and thyme, it was such an everyday resource that, as the perfumer Paul Jellinek explains, 'Using it, one did not feel that one was using perfume.'[40]

The history of the origins of eau de cologne is highly contested; even today, three brands—Farina, Roger et Gallet, and 4711—are seen as competing to be the authentic original eau de cologne, although Farina undoubtedly has the best claim. Eau de cologne is rumoured to have its origins in a general herbal toilet water, Aqua Mirabilis, created by an Italian barber, Gian Paolo Feminis (*c.*1660–1736), who moved to Cologne from his home in Crana, Val Vigezzo, Italy, in the late seventeenth century. He was later followed by a relative, the perfumer Giovanni Maria (aka Johann Maria or Jean Marie) Farina (1685–1766), who was brought up in Santa Maria Maggiore, also in Val Vigezzo, and moved to Cologne in 1706, having served an apprenticeship in commerce with an uncle based in Maastricht.[41] Whether directly inspired by Feminis or not, in 1709 Farina created a bergamot-based perfume which he called 'Cologne water' (Kölnisch Wasser) or eau de cologne, and which he described to his older brother Giovanni Battista as 'the scent of a spring morning in Italy, of mountain narcissus, orange blossom just after rain'.[42] That same year Giovanni Battista founded a business in Cologne selling luxury 'French goods' and the new perfume was sold at his shop in the city where it proved a huge commercial success. Giovanni Maria formally joined the business as a partner in 1714 and subsequently took German citizenship, becoming Johann Maria Farina, and in 1723 the business moved to the site opposite Gülichplatz, where it still flourishes.

After soldiers serving in Germany during the Seven Years' War took Farina's cologne home with them to Austria, France, and Russia, its fame spread throughout Europe, and it was embraced by royalty and famous names including those of Voltaire, Goethe, and Napoleon (see Plates 5 and 6). Because of the perfume's immense popularity, various relatives of the Farinas and other perfumers based in Cologne would later claim to be the originators of eau de cologne, requiring the direct descendants of Giovanni Maria to protect their product through legal challenges. In 1803 a Cologne perfumer, Wilhelm Mülhens, tried to assert a right to the Farina name for a perfume he had created in the late eighteenth century, but in 1881, after a lengthy legal battle, his heirs were forced to rebrand his cologne as 4711, named after the street number of Mülhens's house in Cologne. In 1806 Jean Marie Joseph Farina, a great-grand-nephew of Giovanni Maria Farina and the owner of a Paris-based perfumery business, created another eau de cologne to a new formula, marketed as Eau de Cologne Extra Vielle Jean Marie Farina. His business was later sold to the French company Roger et Gallet, who are the only other company allowed to use the Farina name on their product.[43]

---

[40] Paul Jellinek, *The Psychological Basis of Perfumery*, tr. and ed. J. Stephan Jellinek, 4th edn (London: Blackie Academic and Professional, 1997), p. 112.

[41] See Luigi Rossi, *Il Piemonte in Europa: 500 anni di emigrazione dalla Valle Vigezzo: La Famiglia Farina e L'Acqua di Colonia* (Novara: interlinea edizioni, 2009), pp. 70–9, for the most authoritative account of the relationship between di Feminis and Farina.

[42] Markus Eckstein, *Eau de Cologne: Farina's 300th Anniversary* (Cologne: J. P. Bachem Verlag, 2009), p. 4.

[43] See Tom Clark's 2009 interview with the present-day director, Johann Maria Farina, at http://www.basenotes.net/features/2726-20090617.

Visiting Cologne in July 1855, Swinburne, as a youth of eighteen, reports buying a bottle 'at the great huge shop here, Farina's', a shop still in existence and said to be the site of the world's oldest fragrance factory. Writing to his mother, he complains that 'Cologne is *awfully* dirty!' adding later that it 'wants all its eau-de-Cologne to counteract certain other perfumes which its streets emit'. The perfume, which he evidently liked, was one of Cologne's two redeeming features: 'I cannot say that I think it would be at all a nice city but for this *eau* and the Cathedral' (*TSL* 1. 2–3, 4; 18 July 1855). His perception of the notoriously smelly city shows that things hadn't changed much from 1828 when Coleridge penned his short poem 'Cologne', which opens:

> In Köhln, a town of monks and bones,
> And pavements fang'd with murderous stones,
> And rags, and hags, and hideous wenches;
> I counted two and seventy stenches,
> All well defined, and several stinks![44]

The crisp, bright, citrus zestiness and uplifting green floral and herbal notes of Farina's eau de cologne epitomize Swinburne's taste for fresh stimulating scents. Farina told his brother that his new perfume 'gives me great refreshment, strengthens my senses and imagination', and it appears to have done the same for Swinburne too, although not in ways its creator could have anticipated.[45] If, as Paul Jellinek remarks, eau de cologne's tonic qualities made it appear to be a non-perfume and, even, as he says, 'anti-erotic', the older Swinburne mischievously gives this respectable Victorian restorative a perverse application as a perfume that pleasurably rouses and sharpens the senses.[46] In an intimate letter to Richard Monckton Milnes, a correspondent who shared Swinburne's predilection for flagellation, he recounts boyhood floggings by a tutor at Eton who once:

> [L]et me saturate my face with eau-de-Cologne [...] counting on the pungency of the perfume and its power over the nerves, he meant to stimulate and excite the senses by that preliminary pleasure so as to inflict the acuter pain afterwards on their awakened and intensified susceptibility.

However, he notes gleefully:

> [T]he poor dear old beggar overreached himself, for the pleasure of smell is so excessive and intense with me that even if the smart of birching had been unmixed pain, I could have borne it all the better for that previous indulgence.

                                                        (*TSL* 1. 78; 10 February 1863)

By the same token, when Swinburne's Lesbia Brandon commits suicide, she does so by swallowing a mixture of opium and eau de cologne, a death by perfume that turns this stock item from a lady's toilette table into something altogether more decadent, although in reality it is extremely unlikely that eau de cologne would

---

[44] Samuel Taylor Coleridge, 'Cologne', in *Samuel Taylor Coleridge: Poems*, ed. John Beer (London and Melbourne: Everyman's Library, J. M. Dent, 1974), p. 348.
[45] Eckstein, *Eau de Cologne*, p. 4.   [46] Jellinek, *The Psychological Basis of Perfumery*, p. 121.

have fatal effects unless consumed in very large amounts.[47] Indeed, diluted and
sweetened with sugar, it was allegedly used as a medicinal cordial, stimulant, or
breath-freshener in the nineteenth century.[48] Certainly in August 1891, the poet
Edith Cooper, stricken with a severe sore throat while staying in Dresden, reports
using it as a gargle.[49]

When Swinburne tells Monckton Milnes about the flogging incident, he relates
how his sadistic tutor, aiming to stimulate the senses, would also 'prepare the
flogging-room (not with *corduroy* or *onion* but) with burnt scents; or choose a
sweet place out of doors with smell of firwood. *This* I call real delicate torment.' At
the end of the same letter he teases, 'Conceive trying it in a grove of budding
birch-trees scented all over with the green spring. Ah-h-h!' (*TSL* 1. 78)—the joke
being that the birch, a bound collection of birch twigs, is the instrument of cor-
poral punishment used to inflict flagellation—indeed the Latin name for birch,
Betula alba, is sometimes said to derive its name from the Latin verb *batuere*,
meaning 'to strike'.[50] Swinburne must have shared details of this same sadomasochistic incident with other of his confidants, because he sends Charles Augustus
Howell a sample from his erotic poem 'Dolores' and, presumably soliciting a
piece of flagellatory erotica in return, promises him more 'if you are amiable and
write me something as stimulating as the smell of firwoods' (*TSL* 1. 123; May/
June 1865). Interestingly, many kinds of fir tree have a citrus odour—the key note
of that stimulating scent, eau de cologne—while others smell of pine, a green
smell that, like the 'green' scent of spring which Swinburne mentions to Monckton
Milnes, is similarly tonic and enlivening.

The fresh, green, ozonic, or marine smells favoured by Swinburne, are not only
stimulants but have an astringent quality to them, a slight sting that evokes the
sting of the lash. The sting of perfume is also felt in *Lesbia Brandon* where Herbert
Seyton, embracing his sister, Lady Wariston, 'inhaled the hot fragrance of her face
and neck, and trembled with intense and tender delight. Her perfume thrilled and
stung him.'[51] Swinburne's Renaissance chronicler Tebaldeo Tebaldei writes of how
'bitter perfumes will sting and stab with excess of delight, burning inside nose and
mouth'.[52] At times, all the things that Swinburne relishes and savours—the wind,
the salt sea, beauty, love, joy, kisses, and even verses—sting, that is to say, rouse and
invigorate with a sharp pleasure that contains an element of pain, 'the pleasure that
winces and stings' as Swinburne puts it in 'Dolores' (*Poems* 1. 157; *PBA*, p. 125).[53]
Swinburne imagines the dead Baudelaire as sleeping 'Where stingless pleasure has

---

[47] Swinburne, *Lesbia Brandon*, p. 158.
[48] For the medicinal ingestion of eau de cologne, see Arnold J. Cooley, *The Toilet and Cosmetic Arts
in Ancient and Modern Times* (London: Robert Hardwicke, 1866), p. 565.
[49] Edith Cooper, British Library, Works and Days, Add MS 46779, fol. 88r. Cooper's eau de
cologne gargle did not do her much good. She complained that it 'increases the atrocious pain in my
throat', but then, unbeknown to her, she was suffering from the onset of scarlet fever.
[50] Incidentally, birch bark has been traditionally used to tan leathers, and birch-tar oil, a phenolic,
tarry-smelling substance, is used to produce the effect of leather notes in perfumes.
[51] Swinburne, *Lesbia Brandon*, p. 80.
[52] Swinburne, *Lucretia Borgia*, p. 58; McGann and Sligh, p. 448.
[53] See, for example, Swinburne, *Lesbia Brandon*, p. 148: 'things in verse […] hurt and sting like a cut'.

no foam or fang', that is, removed from the excitation of real pleasure (*Poems* 3. 51). Tannhäuser, trapped in the stifling, enervating atmosphere of the Horsel, recalls how ten years previously, beside:

> The blue curled eddies of the blowing Rhine,
> I felt the sharp wind shaking grass and vine
>   Touch my blood too, and sting me with delight
> Through all this waste and weary body of mine
>
> That never feels clean air [...].   (*Poems* 1. 19; *PBA*, pp. 16–17)

These clean, fresh and airy, often astringent scents that sting and enliven, for Swinburne, have an energetic libidinal charge that is missing from the heavier, narcotic, more animalic perfumes more usually associated with decadent sexuality. Although often unexpectedly carrying a sharp twang of something sexually strange or perversely piquant within them, Swinburne's favoured scents are not then the heavier perfumes associated with Baudelaire and decadence but the lighter ones favoured by polite mid-Victorian taste and conventionally associated with health and well-being. Although like Baudelaire, he eulogizes the smell of women's skin and hair, outside of a few well-known examples in poems such as 'Laus Veneris' these scents are often reminiscent of delicate floral odours. For example, in his early epistolary novel *A Year's Letters*, Redgie Harewood (another self-portrait) declares of his inamorata Clara Radworth: 'She has a throat like pearl-colour, with flower-colour over that; and a smell of blossom and honey in her hair. No one on earth is so infinitely good as she is. Her fingers leave a taste of violets on the lips.'[54] In *Lesbia Brandon*, when Herbert Seyton is enraptured by the fragrance of his sister's 'sweet-scented flesh', he declares, 'You smell of flowers in a hot sun.'[55]

Although he is famous for 'the raptures and roses of vice' and a femme fatale with a 'Red mouth like a venomous flower' ('Dolores', *Poems* 1. 156, 154; *PBA*, pp. 124, 122), Swinburne's blooms tend on the whole to have a more innocuous provenance. 'Ave atque Vale' (literally 'Hail and Farewell'), the elegy he wrote for Baudelaire, opens with the speaker asking the dead poet whether he would prefer a farewell offering of the more conventional 'rose or rue or laurel', 'quiet' or 'simple' wildflowers, or exotic 'fiery blossoms' (*Poems* 3. 50). The question is rhetorical with the speaker later acknowledging Baudelaire as 'the gardener of strange flowers' (52). Throughout his elegy Swinburne plays with the poetic convention whereby a poet's poems are his 'flowers', and towards the end of 'Ave atque Vale' Baudelaire is pictured as the creator of aberrant blooms, his own *Fleurs du mal*:

> Out of the mystic and the mournful garden
>   Where all day through thine hands in barren braid
>   Wove the sick flowers of secrecy and shade,

---

[54] Swinburne's *A Year's Letters* was first published in a censored form under the name of 'Mrs Horace Manners' in *The Tatler* in August–December 1877 and subsequently, also in censored form, as *Love's Cross-Currents* (London: Chatto & Windus, 1905). I use *A Year's Letters*, ed. F. J. Sypher (London: Peter Owen, 1976), p. 139.

[55] Swinburne, *Lesbia Brandon*, p. 80.

Green buds of sorrow and sin, and remnants grey,
    Sweet-smelling, pale with poison, sanguine-hearted,
    Passions that sprang from sleep and thoughts that started...   (*Poems* 3. 57)

Obviously these are metaphorical flowers but they take their character from exotic, sinister, toxic blooms. Yet anyone who studies Swinburne's poetry in any detail would realize his personal inclination towards the flowers he initially offered Baudelaire, the 'quiet sea-flower moulded by the sea, | Or simplest growth of meadow-sweet or sorrel, | Such as the summer-sleepy Dryads weave, |Waked up by snow-soft sudden rains at eve' (*Poems* 3. 50).

In her study of Baudelaire's literary influence, Patricia Clements observes how the flower imagery in 'Ave atque Vale' has a 'double character', with Swinburne associating Baudelaire 'with what might be described as artificial, over-complex, excessively paradoxical. His poem both begins and ends with an emphasized contrast between natural and Baudelairean fruits of the earth.'[56] By May 1867, when Swinburne reports starting 'Ave atque Vale' (*TSL* 1. 246; 22 May 1867), he had already published his first major collection and could be more self-assured about his poetic identity.[57] If, as I suspect, he is implicitly identifying with the simpler natural flowers while ceremoniously paying his last respects to a former idol, then he is also quietly putting some distance between himself and Baudelaire and, in so doing, making the poem into more of a 'farewell' ('Vale') than it is usually credited as being.

For when it comes to his own choice of flowers Swinburne shuns the exotic and artificial. He even disliked flowers being cut for ornamentation, preferring to see them growing in gardens or in the wild.[58] On holiday in Sidestrand, Norfolk, in 1883, he writes delightedly to his eldest sister of the garden of Mill House where he was staying: 'The whole place is fragrant with old-fashioned flowers, sweet-william and thyme and lavender and mignonette and splendid with great sun-flowers' (*TSL* 5. 35; 18 September 1883).[59] He had a fondness for particular flower perfumes but, in keeping with his predilection for airy fragrances, he relished the way floral scent combines or interacts with natural elements like the wind or sun.

In Swinburne, seasonal influences and natural elements enter into, enhance, release, or draw out the essences of herbs and flowers; the rose, for example, ubiquitous in his poems, being 'fulfilled to the roseleaf tips | With splendid summer and perfume and pride' ('The Triumph of Time', *Poems* 1. 43; *PBA*, p. 37). The smell of sun-warmed heather seems to have given him particular pleasure throughout

---

[56] Patricia Clements, *Baudelaire and the English Tradition* (Princeton, NJ: Princeton University Press, 1985), p. 56.

[57] Swinburne was under the impression that Baudelaire had died owing to an erroneous notice in the *Pall Mall Gazette* (16 April 1866). However, the ailing poet did not actually die till 31 August 1867. Swinburne subsequently published 'Ave atque Vale' in the *Fortnightly Review* in January 1868.

[58] Watts-Dunton, *Home Life*, p. 203. However, see the description of Swinburne's rapt admiration of a bouquet presented to him in Coulson Kernahan's *In Good Company: Some Personal Recollections* (London and New York: John Lane, The Bodley Head and John Lane Company, 1917), pp. 26–7.

[59] He commemorated this scene in his poem 'The Mill Garden', in the sequence *A Midsummer Holiday*. See *Poems* 6. 11–13.

his life. Describing the little marsh-flower, the sundew, in his early poem of that name—a plant that itself lacks fragrance—he notes how on a hot June day 'The deep scent of the heather burns | About it' (*Poems* 1. 186; *PBA*, p. 149), while in 'A Nympholept', a late poem, he writes 'I lean my head to the heather, and drink the sun | Whose flame-lit odour satiates the flowers' (*Poems* 6. 139). He similarly appreciated the flowers of wild gorse or 'whin'—'the sun's perfume fills their glorious gold | With perfume like the colour' ('To William Bell Scott', *Poems* 5. 232) and he noted how it complemented the effect of heather—'The heather kindles toward the light | The whin is frankincense and flame' ('The Tale of Balen', *Poems* 4. 157). In his poetic sequence 'A Dark Month' (Canto 31), he praises the 'Keen glad heart of heather, | Hot sweet heart of whin', which to the 'South-west wind' are 'Twin breaths in thy godlike breath close blended of wild spring's wildest of kin' (*Poems* 5. 366). Another similar natural bouquet brought about by 'hillside winds' is 'the marriage song of heather flower and broom' ('Thalassius', *Poems* 3. 300). In 'Relics', white laurustine or laurustinus (*Viburnum tinus*), a flower that grows along the West Undercliff of the Isle of Wight, is a bloom that recalls another of his loves—'This flower that smells of honey and the sea' (*Poems* 2. 26).

Swinburne adored the scent of may or hawthorn and, cherishing the may trees on Putney Heath as 'the honey of heaven, of the hives whence night feeds full on the springtide's breath' ('Hawthorn Tide', *Poems* 6. 290), devoted a series of poems to them.[60] Clara Watts-Dunton observed 'He never tired of talking of the beauty of these sweet-smelling bushes', and she describes a particular expedition she made with Swinburne to visit his favourite trees: 'When he got to one large hawthorn of divine loveliness he paused for a long time in front of it and drew in long deep breaths, as though he were inhaling the subtle emanation of the blossoms he so rapturously adored.'[61]

That 'subtle emanation', experienced in a natural setting, contrasts with the oppressive 'perfume of Indian lilies in a close bedroom' which Swinburne was convinced had poisoned him in the late summer of 1876 (*TSL* 3. 207; 17 October 1876), an experience which he claimed had left him 'prostrated for many wretched or unprofitable weeks' (*TSL* 3. 302; 20 March 1877). To John Nichol, a friend from his Oxford undergraduate days, he jokes that the episode 'solved the question I have heard debated (and denied by our old friend W. B. Scott, 16 or more years since, à propos of an incident in my first book, *The Queen Mother*) whether a man could actually be poisoned by perfumes'.[62] The experience also suggested to him another literary parallel: 'Hawthorne's story, of which you expressed such admiration to me once at Oxford in the years before the Flood, "Rappucini's [*sic*] Daughter"' (*TSL* 3. 211; 28 October 1876).

---

[60] Hawthorn scent, repellent to some, contains, according to the biologist D. Michael Stoddart, various amines suggestive of vaginal secretions, just as 'Flowers of berberry, henna, chestnut and lime have a strong semen-like odour.' See D. Michael Stoddart, *The Scented Ape: The Biology and Culture of Human Odour* (Cambridge: Cambridge University Press, 1990), p. 159.

[61] Watts-Dunton, *Home Life*, pp. 78, 81.

[62] Swinburne refers to his first published book containing the two dramas *The Queen-Mother* and *Rosamond* (1860).

Hawthorne's 'Rappaccini's Daughter' (1844) is the story of a nefarious Paduan scientist who has brought up his beautiful daughter to be immune to the poisonous perfumed flowers in his private garden. However, in tending these toxic blooms, she herself becomes poisonous to others.[63] As Swinburne would have known, Gautier had made a long comparison between Baudelaire and Hawthorne's story in his obituary notice of 1867: 'We never read *Les Fleurs du mal* by Baudelaire, without thinking of that tale by Hawthorne: it has those sombre and metallic colours, those verdigris blossoms and heady perfumes.'[64] To Swinburne in 1876, poisonous perfume may be fascinating as a literary or historical conceit but its actuality—the lilies' 'tropical prussic-acid perfume [which] left me half mad and half dead with sickness' (*TSL* 3. 210; 25 October 1876)—was alarming, a 'possibly romantic but certainly unpleasant experience' (*TSL* 3. 211). Rehearsed in letters to various friends and acquaintances, this episode is another, albeit oblique, declaration of the poet's sensitivity to fragrance, tinged here by a more conservative suspicion of intoxicating exotic floral scents.[65]

Thus, although Swinburne may have introduced into English letters a Baudelairean headiness of fragrance that later became associated with English literary decadence, such strong scents, unrepresentative of his own taste, are by no means typical in his poetry after the publication of *Poems and Ballads* in 1866 (and indeed a good few of the poems in that ground-breaking collection already signal his own preferences). Yet so pervasive is the association of Swinburne's early poetry with heavy scents that commentators insist on their continuing presence. In 1875 when the American critic E. C. Stedman reviewed Swinburne's achievement, his scent analogy (an application of the poem-as-flower metaphor) came a little too easily: 'The fruit may be, and here is, too luscious; the flower is often of an odor too intoxicating to endure. Yet what execution!'[66] This is somewhat surprising in view of the fact that Swinburne's most recent volume, *Songs before Sunrise* (1871), a volume Stedman goes on to praise, is decidedly unluscious, its somewhat austere poetic flowers being either dedicated to the Italian Risorgimento—'If a perfume be left, if a bloom, | Let it live till Italia be risen'—or expressive of humanity's continuing evolution, 'strong blossoms with perfume of manhood' (*Poems* 2. v, 78). Stedman himself concedes in his conclusion, 'If rank unwholesome flowers spring from too rich a soil, in the end a single fruitful blossoming will compensate us for the sterile *fleurs du mal* of youth.'[67] When after *Songs before Sunrise*, Swinburne does turn his attention to actual flowers, they are not intoxicating Baudelairean blooms. Indeed, 'Relics', Swinburne's best-known later flower poem first published in 1873 and

---

[63] See 'Rappaccini's Daughter', collected in in *Mosses from an Old Manse* (1846), and subsequently in Nathaniel Hawthorne, *Tales and Sketches* (New York and Cambridge: The Library of America, 1982), pp. 975–1005.

[64] Théóphile Gautier, 'Charles Baudelaire', *Le Moniteur*, 9 September 1867, reprinted in *Portraits contemporains* (Paris: Charpentier et Cie, 1874), p. 163.

[65] A more cynical but all too likely interpretation of this incident is that Swinburne suffered a severe bilious reaction as a result of one of the alcoholic episodes he was prone to at this time.

[66] E. C. Stedman, ch. 11 from his *Victorian Poets* (1875); extract in Hyder, ed., *Swinburne: The Critical Heritage*, p. 160.

[67] Stedman, in Hyder, ed., *The Critical Heritage*, p. 162.

then collected in *Poems and Ballads* 2 (1878), might well be seen as a response to the earlier 'Laus Veneris'.[68]

Like 'Laus Veneris', 'Relics' uses a version of the rhymed stanza that Edward FitzGerald made famous in his translation of Omar Khayyám's *Rubáiyát* (1859). However, 'Relics' employs a more complex version of this stanza so that all the poem's verses are interlinked by end-rhymes in an echoing chain (*aaba, bbcb, ccdc, dded*, etc.), a retrospective device that means each stanza recalls the one before. This formal structure seems well suited to a poem about memory activated by the sight and smell of flowers laden with past associations:

> This flower that smells of honey and the sea,
> White laurustine, seems in my hand to be
>   A white star made of memory long ago
> Lit in the heaven of dear times dead to me.
>
> A star out of the skies love used to know
> Here held in hand, a stray left yet to show
>   What flowers my heart was full of in the days
> That are long since gone down dead memory's flow.   (*Poems* 3. 26)

Although 'Laus Veneris' and 'Relics' are both poems that vividly use scent to tell a story, the former narrates a mythic legend suffused by heavy artificial perfume and the latter personal reminiscence triggered by natural floral fragrance—white laurustine and white acacia—scents that reflect Swinburne's actual tastes and offer autobiographical links to the Isle of Wight and Tuscany.[69] Without imposing an aesthetic value judgement, it is possible to see the revisionary form of the later poem, which sets a series of interlinked successive rhymes rippling throughout the poetic fabric, as subtly intimating that this is something which goes deeper in personal terms, an immersive experience that envelops and permeates the poet as speaker.[70] 'In all the roll of poets', wrote W. M. Rossetti in 1866, 'we certainly know none who has given such signal proof of his power to enter with re-creative, not imitative, sympathy into so many models of style and form, so diverse and so high; to search their recesses, and extract their essential aroma.'[71]

In 'Laus Veneris', Tannhäuser yearned to be released into the cleansing air outside the Horsel:

> Ah yet would God this flesh of mine might be
> Where air might wash and long leaves cover me,
>   Where tides of grass break into foam of flowers,
> Or where the wind's feet shine along the sea.   (*Poems* 1. 13; *PBA*, p. 11)

---

[68] 'Relics' was originally published as 'North and South' in the *Fortnightly Review* for May 1873.

[69] The white acacia Swinburne refers to is most likely the 'false acacia' or *Robinia pseudoacacia*, known in the United States as 'black locust', which can be found in many parts of the world including Tuscany and the UK. Its racemes of intensely fragrant white flowers are said to smell like orange blossom.

[70] For a longer reading of 'Relics' that notes the possible autobiographical elements in the poem, see my earlier short monograph, *Swinburne*, Writers and their Work Series (Tavistock: Northcote House, 2006), pp. 71–7.

[71] W. M. Rossetti, 'Swinburne's *Poems and Ballads*' (1866), in Hyder, ed., *Swinburne: The Critical Heritage*, p. 71.

After *Poems and Ballads* (1866), Swinburne arguably did leave the Baudelairean Venusberg for good; and with his personal tastes in scent now established, the remainder of this chapter examines how he uses these olfactory preferences to express his critical opinions in his prose from the 1860s onwards.

Swinburne and the Scent of Literature

Swinburne consistently employed olfactory language when considering and evaluating literary texts. He was certainly not the first person to do this. We have already seen in Chapter 2 how, setting an influential precedent, Shelley had famously said that the poetry of the Greek bucolic poets was 'like the odour of tuberose, it overcomes and sickens the spirit with excess of sweetness', and the use of a vocabulary expressive of malodour to express critical disapprobation has a long history that extends back to classical times. The Bible presents good deeds and right actions as incense pleasing to nostrils of God, while bad deeds and disobedience are a stench that offends him. Holy men and women, during their lives and even afterwards, give off the odour of sanctity. In common parlance, to be 'in good odour' or 'bad odour' is to be held in good or bad repute or regard. It is not surprising then to find Swinburne, an *olfactif* who identified perfume with pleasure, using a scented language to express his appreciation of the authors he valued.

Conversely, as his letters frequently show, when angered or disgusted, he would also use Rabelaisian terms of abuse connected with noisome or excremental smells to show his annoyance or disdain. This language, when unleashed on literary authors, might be suggested by their repellent subject matter, in itself often suggestive of bad smells. Such writers included the French novelist Émile Zola whom Swinburne abominated on the grounds of his grisly, often fetid, realism—'Zola's damnable dunghill of a book'—(*TSL* 4. 10; 8 June 1877)—and the historian and man of letters, Thomas Carlyle, whose 'perpetual copromania' revealed an obsession with faeces, sewers, and 'eternal cesspools' (*TSL* 4. 136; 20 April 1880). Carlyle had provoked matters by calling Swinburne 'a man standing up to his neck in a cesspool, and adding to its contents'.[72] In 1883 Swinburne, no stranger to scatology himself, would refer thus to the recently deceased Carlyle: 'The filthy and virulent Arch-Quack of Chelsea must, I do hope, have carried down his influence with himself into "the Eternal Cesspools" whereon his fancy loved to play—a noisy and noisome dung-fly, while his breath still infected the upper air' (*TSL* 5. 21; 15 May 1883). Carlyle's insult had been made public in a newspaper interview of 1874 given by Ralph Waldo Emerson, who had himself condemned Swinburne as a 'perfect leper and mere sodomite'.[73] Swinburne retaliated in a letter to the *New York Daily Tribune*, by calling Emerson 'a gap-toothed and hoary-headed ape [...] who now in his dotage spits and chatters from a dirtier perch of his own finding and fouling; Coryphaeus or choragus of

---

[72] Thomas Carlyle, cited by Ralph Waldo Emerson, in Hyder, ed., *Swinburne: The Critical Heritage*, p. 118.
[73] Emerson, in Hyder, ed., *Swinburne: The Critical Heritage*, p. 118.

his Bulgarian tribe of autocoprophagous baboons who make the filth they feed on' (*TSL* 2. 274; 30 January 1874).

Although not the focus of what follows, this preponderantly excremental language of denunciation offers a pointed contrast to the laudatory scented language Swinburne uses to express his approval. Dirt and excrement were antithetical to what Clara Watts-Dunton calls 'that passion for cleanliness which was part of his nature', and, as mentioned at the beginning of this chapter, Swinburne told Rossetti that he had 'a bloodhound's—or Cassandra's—nose for all sweet smells—and alas! for all other than sweet'.[74] To middle- and upper-class Victorians who had embraced an ethos of cleanliness and hygienic sanitation, the sight and smell of dirt and faeces were anathema, although Swinburne's own richly elaborate dialect of the sewer suggests an underlying fascination with what he claims to abhor. However, most of his olfactory invective—much of it too scatological for publication in its day—is necessarily confined to his private letters. While his critical prose does reveal instances of the writers he personally deemed to be 'in bad odour', his natural impulse erred more towards praise than blame; in 1866 he declared that he had 'never been able to see what should attract men to the profession of criticism but the noble pleasure of praising', and, correspondingly, in his published critical prose we find far more instances of 'good odour'.[75] Arguably he sets a descriptive trend for those aesthetic and decadent authors who come after him, who also come to evaluate other writers and artists by their scent, bouquet, or odorous atmosphere. In what follows I explore the various kinds of scented language used by Swinburne to express his approval for different kinds of writing, noting how it complements his scent preferences as discussed earlier in this chapter.

One of the earliest of Swinburne's scented evaluations occurs not in his own voice but in that of his alter ego, Redgie Harewood, in *A Year's Letters*, the novel he was writing in the early 1860s and which he submitted unsuccessfully to several publishers as early as 1863.[76] Here is Redgie writing about a love poem by a Jacobean ancestor who shares his name:

> I have rather a weakness for that pink and perfumed sort of poem that smells of dead spice and preserved leaves; it reads like opening an old jar of pot-pourri, with its stiff scented turns of verse and tags of gold embroidery gone tawny in the dust and rust. And in spite of all the old court-stuff about apples and roses and the rest, there is a kind of serious twang in it here and there, as if the man did care to mean something.[77]

The evocation of the scents of a bygone era to designate the style of an older literature that still holds charm is not very common in Swinburne's critical prose but certainly does occur elsewhere, as in his 1885 discussion of the essayist Charles Lamb (1775–1834), for whose writings he had the deepest affection:

---

[74] Watts-Dunton, *Home Life*, p. 123.
[75] Swinburne, 'Notes on Poems and Reviews' (1866), Appendix 1 in *PBA*, p. 415.
[76] F. J. Sypher, Introduction, in Swinburne, *A Year's Letters*, p. xxv.
[77] Swinburne, *A Year's Letters*, p. 116.

But for all who love him the charm of that companionship is alike indefinable and incomparable. It pervades his work as with an odour of sweet old-world flowers or spices long laid by among fine linens and rare brocades in some such old oaken or cedarn cabinet as his grandmother might have opened to rejoice the wondering senses of her boyish visitor at 'Blakesmoor.'[78]

In a similar vein he declares that some of Blake's 'earliest songs' 'have the scent and sound of Elizabethan times upon them', but he also uses synaesthesia to suggest that these same Blakeian lyrics were ahead of their own time, with a rich vitality lacking in other eighteenth-century poems: 'They have a fragrance of sound, a melody of colour, in a time when the best verses produced had merely the arid perfume of powder, the twang of dry wood and adjusted strings.'[79]

Some periods of literature are less attractive to him than others and just as the 'arid perfume of powder' characterizes the lifeless, contrived verses of Blake's contemporaries, so Swinburne describes the period verse he finds uncongenial as smelling of an unacceptably artificial perfumery. While Tudor and Stuart verse predating the Restoration (1660) is, for the most part, apparently exempt, being still compatible with modern taste, post-Restoration poetry, in his opinion, leaves much to be desired. In a review of *Lyra Elegantiarum* (1891), Frederick Locker-Lampson's anthology of 'social verse', Swinburne laments the lack of poetry from the time of Shakespeare, asserting that:

[T]he general tone of this poetry was more in accordance with the taste and the instinct of our own time than that of any social or fashionable verse from the Restoration to the Regency—at least. It is light and bright as spray in sunshine, but no less clean and sweet: neither stiff and fulsome with the starch and perfumery of courtly verse under the patronage of Charles I., nor gross and greasy with the reek of Whitefriars or Whitehall under the auspices of Charles II. And the best verse of Carew is impaired by the barber-like suggestion of 'powders to enrich your hair.'[80]

Swinburne also complains about the anthology's omission of simple late medieval religious lyrics in favour of what he calls 'Romanistic gush'—

If this sort of sanctified stuff is admissible, with its fetid fragrance of priestly perfumery and its rancid relish of ecstatic or spasmodic excitement, why and how do we find not one single example of the many lovely songs which English poetry owes to an older and purer and wholesomer form of piety?[81]

Conditioned by anti-Catholic sentiment, Swinburne's antipathy to the 'fetid fragrance of priestly perfumery' makes him react to the smell of incense he believes can detect in the 'effusion' of 'sickly Crashaw' (Richard Crashaw, *c*.1612–1649),

---

[78] Swinburne, 'Charles Lamb and George Wither' (1885), in *Miscellanies*, p. 194.
[79] Swinburne, *William Blake*, p. 9.
[80] Swinburne, 'Social Verse' (1891), in *Studies in Poetry and Prose* (London: Chatto & Windus, 1894), p. 92.
[81] Ibid., pp. 91–2.

a poet whose 'Catholic and apostolic erethism' makes him an exception to Swinburne's general sanction of pre-Restoration verse.[82]

Although specifically motivated by his dislike of fervent Romanism, that recoil from incense and the demand for 'purer and wholesomer' poetic expressions of piety nonetheless make for interesting comparison when we look back to Swinburne's famous 1862 review of Baudelaire, a writer whose poems are heavy with incense and are far from being pure and wholesome:

> The sound of his metres suggests colour and perfume. His perfect workmanship makes every subject admirable and respectable. Throughout the chief part of this book, he has chosen to dwell mainly upon sad and strange things—the weariness of pain and the bitterness of pleasure—the perverse happiness and wayward sorrows of exceptional people. It has the languid lurid beauty of close and threatening weather—a heavy heated temperature, with dangerous hothouse scents in it; thick shadow of cloud about it, and fire of molten light.[83]

The sultry, oppressively close, and scented atmosphere of the Baudelaire essay was perhaps helped by the fact that, according to Edmund Gosse, Swinburne wrote it in a Turkish bath in Paris.[84] It exhibits the kind of scented language that might be thought to typify Swinburne's prose, yet, outside of this review, examples of this sort of perfumed 'hothouse' atmosphere are rare. There is a hint of it in Swinburne's 1871 essay-review of his painter friend Simeon Solomon's illustrated prose poem 'A Vision of Love', an essay that also describes Solomon's designs. There Swinburne writes of a painting depicting 'two ministering maidens in the Temple of Venus': 'both have the languor and fruitful air of flowers in a sultry place'.[85]

---

[82] Ibid., p. 92. However, Swinburne's opinion of Crashaw fluctuated throughout his literary career. See John R. Roberts, *New Perspectives on the Life and Art of Richard Crashaw* (Columbia, MO: University of Missouri Press, 1990), p. 14.

[83] Swinburne, 'Charles Baudelaire', pp. 28–9. For example, both Baudelaire's 'Correspondances' and 'Le Parfum' feature incense.

[84] Edmund Gosse, 'Swinburne', in *Portraits and Sketches* (London: William Heinemann, 1912), p. 5. If Gosse's claim about the Parisian Turkish bath is correct, it is unclear precisely when Swinburne wrote his review, which treats Baudelaire's expanded 1861 edition of *Les Fleurs du mal*. It can't have been during his visit to Paris in early January 1861 as described in a letter to Pauline Trevelyan (*TSL* 1. 40; 19 January 1861), as Baudelaire's volume was not published until the first week in February 1861, and Swinburne had already left Paris for Menton. In February 1861 Swinburne left Menton for Venice via Genoa, Turin, and Milan. The next recorded trip by him to Paris is March 1863, after the Baudelaire review was published in the *Spectator* in September 1862. However, it is possible he subsequently made an unrecorded second trip to Paris, perhaps on his homeward journey from Italy in 1861, or travelling to and from Pau and Cauterets for a family holiday in April 1862. Alternatively he could have written the review in a Turkish bath in London, a city which, in the early 1860s, was much better provided with regard to these than Paris. In July 1893, Gosse also claimed that Swinburne wrote his elegy for Baudelaire in a Turkish bath—see Evan Charteris, *The Life and Letters of Sir Edmund Gosse* (London: W. Heinemann, 1931), p. 240—so he may have become confused as to which piece was written there. My warm thanks to Clive Simmonds for alerting me to this second source in Charteris, and for discussing with me this supposed incident and the dates of Swinburne's 1862 trip to the Pyrenees.

[85] Swinburne, 'Simeon Solomon: Notes on his "Vision of Love" and Other Studies', in *The Bonchurch Edition of the Complete Works of Algernon Charles Swinburne*, ed. Edmund Gosse and Thomas James Wise (London and New York: William Heinemann and Gabriel Wells, 1925–7), 15. 452. Swinburne's essay was originally published in the Oxford journal *The Dark Blue* (July 1871).

Interestingly this essay has a connection to Swinburne's 1862 review in that he alludes to Baudelaire in order to gloss what he sees as 'perverse nature' in Solomon's designs.[86] Significantly, Swinburne chose to reprint neither essay during his lifetime. In the case of the Solomon review this was due to the scandal attaching to the artist's name after his arrest for homosexual offences in 1873; in the case of the Baudelaire essay, Swinburne undoubtedly wanted to distance himself from a writer with whom he had been too closely identified. Yet his comments to William Sharp in 1901—'I never had really much in common with Baudelaire, though I retain all my early admiration for his genius at its best'—need not be seen as disingenuous (*TSL* 6. 153; 6 October 1901). When, after 1862, Swinburne writes about the authors he admires, he almost always does so using language that accents fresh, stimulating, natural scents suggestive of breeze-blown landscapes and sea-coasts, reflecting his passion for the airy moorlands, mountains, and coast of Northumberland, and the shorelines of the Isle of Wight, which, since boyhood, he had loved to explore on foot and horseback.

These natural ozonic scents are most noticeable in the critical essays Swinburne was writing in the 1860s and on into the 1870s, that is, both during and after the composition of *Poems and Ballads*. Swinburne's unpublished early essay 'Théophile' on the French Renaissance poet Théophile de Viau (1590–1626), an essay Gosse dates to 1862, makes for interesting contrast with its near contemporary, the Baudelaire essay. Throughout Swinburne establishes intimacy by referring to de Viau by his first name, and it seems that they have much in common, with Théophile intensely sensate like Swinburne and indeed another *olfactif*. Swinburne quotes him as remarking '"I love, too, all that especially touches on the senses— music, flowers, fine raiment, fine horses, good smells, good cheer."' Yet he emerges as a very different kind of personality from Baudelaire. '[T]here is a clear air of health', writes Swinburne, and Théophile lacks Baudelaire's morbid introspection, being 'robust and spontaneous and untroubled from within, with no respect for inward troubles'.[87] Swinburne relishes his early poetry, noting his 'many stanzas and some lyrics of the brightest and sweetest beauty, fragrant and radiant with youth and life. There is a light and breath about them as of sunny and dewy woodland, of blowing leaves and walking [*sic*] birds.'[88]

These scents are a notable feature of Swinburne's important study *William Blake*, which was published in 1868, though actually started in 1863 and completed in 1866. Although Swinburne's monograph opens with an epigraph from Baudelaire and he breaks off to lament Baudelaire's death in an extended footnote, the atmosphere he evokes for Blake's lyrical verse is both sea-fresh and greenly vernal. Here, for example, is Swinburne on Blake's earliest lyrical poems:

> There is in all these straying songs the freshness of clear wind and purity of blowing rain: here a perfume as of dew or grass against the sun, there a keener smell of sprinkled shingle and brine-bleached sand; some growth or breath everywhere of blade or

---

[86] Swinburne, 'Simeon Solomon', 15. 456.
[87] Swinburne, 'Théophile', in *Complete Works*, 13. 402.
[88] Ibid., 13. 403. It seems likely that 'walking' is an editorial mistranscription for 'waking'.

herb leaping into life under the green wet light of spring; some colour of shapely cloud or mound of moulded wave.[89]

When discussing Blake's *Songs of Experience* in relation to his *Songs of Innocence*, Swinburne makes an aromatic distinction between them in terms of intensity. The fragrance of each is undeniably natural but the *Songs of Experience*, which 'rise higher and dive deeper in mere words', have a more powerful fragrance, which gives us more of the essence of things and emotions:

> If the *Songs of Innocence* have the shape and smell of leaves or buds, these have in them the light and sound of fire or the sea. Entering upon them, a fresher savour and a larger breath strikes one upon the lips and forehead. [...] These give the distilled perfume and extracted blood of the veins in the rose-leaf, the sharp, liquid, intense spirit crushed out of the broken kernel in the fruit.[90]

Swinburne also greatly admired Blake's illustrated page designs for the *Songs*, observing that 'All the tremulous and tender splendour of spring is mixed into the written word and coloured draught; every page has the smell of April.'[91]

A word that occurs in the passages from 'Théophile' and *William Blake* is 'breath', and it recurs repeatedly in Swinburne's critical prose. As Swinburne is clearly aware, among the older historic meanings of the word 'breath' is 'a smell or odour' and also 'the air exhaled from anything, or impregnated with its exhalations, and retaining its characteristic odour'. In his writing 'breath' often retains these senses, being allied to the winds and breezes that carry scents and to the exhalations of flowers and foliage. In a wider sense, the respiratory associations of 'breath' also connect to Swinburne's notion of poetic inspiration, a breathing-in of creative influences whether these are natural or literary in origin, and there is also the corresponding intimation that when we read or breathe in inspiring authors, we also feel their breath upon us, as they 'breathe again' through their words. There's more than a hint of this in the passage from *William Blake*, which implies that we might feel Blake's spirit more intensely present in his *Songs of Experience* where 'a fresher savour and a larger breath strikes one upon the lips and forehead'. This is reinforced by other connotations of 'breath', which signify 'speech, articulate sound, or utterance' as, for example, the 'melodious breath' of D. G. Rossetti imagined by Swinburne in 'On an Old Roundel' (*Poems* 5. 174). Dead poets speak to us through their poetry, although we literally reanimate them by reading them aloud, breathing out their words, for the Latin *anima* means 'soul, spirit, life, air, breeze, breath'. In 'Anactoria', Swinburne's Sappho, punning on 'souls', speaks of how future generations will reanimate her and give her immortality by speaking or filling her poetic words 'with breath':

> For these shall give me of their souls, shall give
> Life, and the days and loves wherewith I live,
> Shall quicken me with loving, fill with breath,
> Save me and serve me, strive for me with death.   (*Poems* 1. 66; *PBA*, p. 55)

---

[89] Swinburne, *William Blake*, p. 134.   [90] Ibid., p. 116.   [91] Ibid., p. 113.

Supercharged words like 'breath' in Swinburne thus frequently have a synaesthetic reach, touching on more than one sense, but often with an additional spiritual dimension, an excellent illustration of 'spirit in sense'.[92] Reading a poet or author releases the characteristic fragrance of his words, a fragrance that doubles as his breath or spirit. The authors Swinburne likes and admires typically exhale or breathe out his favourite airy natural and elemental odours, and there is perhaps the intimation that, like Sappho's song in 'Anactoria', all inspired song blends with or beats time to the rhythms of the elemental song of nature.

Swinburne drew on his repertoire of favourite odours throughout 1867 when he wrote about a number of very different poets. In an introductory essay to a selection of Byron's poetry published early in the year, he felt that the 'tidal variety of experience and emotion' found in 'Don Juan', 'gives to the poem something of the breadth and freshness of the sea'.[93] Moreover, just as he had compared Blake's *Songs of Innocence* and *Experience* in terms of their varying odour, he wrote that the difference between Byron's 'Childe Harold' and 'Don Juan' was the difference between 'lake-water and sea-water': 'the one is fluent, yielding, invariable; the other has in it a life and pulse, a sting and a swell, which touch and excite the nerves like fire or like music'. In the stanzas of 'Don Juan' there is 'a delicious resistance, an elastic motion, which salt water has and fresh water has not. There is about them a wide wholesome air, full of vivid light and constant wind, which is only felt at sea.'[94] Although Swinburne admired Byron's poetry less than the verse of Shelley or Coleridge, it nonetheless recommended itself by the suggestion of a bracing maritime freshness: 'His love of wide and tempestuous waters fills his work throughout as with the broad breath of a sea-wind.'[95]

Some months after this in July, during the period he was working on 'Ave atque Vale', Swinburne published his review of his friend William Morris's epic romance 'The Life and Death of Jason'. Here he invokes the hothouse but only by way of a negative comparison. Explaining that Morris's romance was in the Chaucerian vein, he is keen to defend it against the charge of being an artificial construction or what he calls a 'hothouse daffodil' by emphasizing its unforced organic nature: 'Here is a poem sown of itself sprung from no alien seed, cast after no alien model; fresh as wind, bright as light, full of the spring and the sun.'[96] That naturalism is again to the fore when in October Swinburne reviews Matthew Arnold's poetry, and finds that his pastoral elegy, 'Thyrsis', written to commemorate Arthur Hugh Clough, has 'a grace ineffable, a sweet sound and savour of things past in the old beautiful use of the language of shepherds, of flocks and pipes; the spirit is none the less sad and sincere [...] because the verse remembers and retains a perfume

---

[92] Another example is 'sweet', a word Swinburne uses throughout *Poems and Ballads* (1866), which can refer to all five senses. 'Air' can signify both 'atmosphere' and 'tune', and, as a medium communicating sound, odour, and temperature, can also be made visible through light effects, as in 'bluest air', or 'silver air' ('August', *Poems* 1. 215, 216; *PBA*, p. 172).

[93] Swinburne, 'Byron', in *Essays and Studies*, p. 242. Byron was reviewed in the *Spectator* in March 1867.

[94] Swinburne, 'Byron', p. 243.   [95] Ibid., p. 274.

[96] Swinburne, 'Morris's "Life and Death of Jason"', in *Essays and Studies*, p. 117.

and an echo of Grecian flutes and flowers'; and he notes how 'the fragrance and freedom as of wide wings of winds in summer over meadow and moor, the freshness and expansion of the light and the lucid air, the spring and the stream as of flowing and welling water, enlarge the pleasure and power of the whole poem'.[97] The 'Grecian flutes and flowers' and 'wide wings of winds in summer over meadow' may also involve a reminiscence of 'A Defence of Poetry', and Shelley's praise of those Greek poets who, unlike their sickly sweet successors, were 'as a meadow-gale of June which mingles the fragrance of all the flowers of the field, and adds a quickening and harmonizing spirit of its own' (*SPP*, p. 492).

The image of the hothouse resurfaces once more when Swinburne concludes that Arnold's 'best work' 'refreshes with its cool full breath and serenity. On some men's nerves the temperature strikes somewhat cold; there are lungs that cannot breathe but in the air of a hothouse or a hospital.'[98] However, Swinburne makes it plain he is not of this number:

> His poetry is a pure temple, a white flower of marble, [...] unvexed within by fumes of shaken censers or intoning of hoarse choristers; large and clear and cool, with many chapels in it, full of quiet and music. [...] We do not always want to bathe our spirit in overflowing waters or flaming fires of imagination. [...] In each court or chapel there is a fresh fragrance of early mountain flowers which bring with them the wind and the sun and a sense of space and growth, all of them born in high places, washed and waved by upper airs and rains.[99]

Swinburne here pointedly spurns the Baudelairean 'hothouse' and the 'fumes of shaken censers' for the cool temperature of Arnold's 'pure temple' with its courts and chapels full of the 'fresh fragrance of early mountain flowers'. Furthermore, he earlier praises Arnold's 'English-coloured verse', noting approvingly that his 'field-flowers and hedgerow blossoms' are unmixed with 'foreign buds and alien bloom'.[100] English Arnold's verse might be, but in his vision of its scented landscape, Swinburne ultimately replaces the Oxfordshire of 'The Scholar Gipsy' and 'Thyrsis' with something closer to Northumberland, a cooler mountainous region where he himself feels physically and spiritually at home.

This preference for the fresher air of higher altitudes recurs later in his essay when he voices his disapproval of Arnold's tendency towards melancholy: 'We must all hope that the poet will keep to this clear air of the ancient heights, more natural and wholesome for the spirit than the lowlands of depression and dubiety where he has set before now a too frequent foot.' He deplores the 'sensible and stagnant influence of moist vapour from those marshes of the mind', reminding Arnold that 'Above those levels the sunnier fields and fresher uplands lie wide and warm.' When Swinburne exhorts Arnold to shake off negative moods, he sounds like he might be remembering his own Tannhäuser trapped in the stifling Horsel, even if the ostensible allusion is to Arnold's 'Growing Old': 'If a soul by nature high and clear [...] does ever feel itself "immured in the hot prison of the present", its fit work is not to

---

[97] Swinburne, 'Matthew Arnold's New Poems', in *Essays and Studies*, pp. 155–6.
[98] Ibid., p. 182.   [99] Ibid., pp. 182–3.   [100] Ibid., p. 156.

hug but break its chain; and only by its own will or weakness can it remain ill at ease in a thick and difficult air.'[101] (There is no mention of 'thick and difficult air' in Arnold's poem, something that seems more in keeping with 'Laus Veneris'.)

Such was Swinburne's enthusiasm for poetic fresh air scents that in a review of 1870 he even insists on finding them in the poems of his friend Dante Gabriel Rossetti, a writer whose verse, often seen as rarefied, was negatively described by Browning as '*scented* with poetry' and by Robert Buchanan as possessing an 'overpowering sickliness, as of too much civet'.[102] Swinburne had given Rossetti extensive feedback and advice on the manuscript drafts of his poems. Perhaps anticipating that Rossetti's complex, intricate, introspective verse, which predominantly treats love and sexuality, might be called both sensual and artificial, he asserts:

> There is a strength and breadth of style about these poems also which ennobles their sweetness and brightness, giving them a perfume that savours of no hotbed, but of hill-flowers that face the sea and the sunrise; a colour that grows in no greenhouse, but such as comes with morning upon the mountains.[103]

The word 'hotbed' is often used figuratively to mean the 'breeding ground' or 'cradle' of an unwelcome tendency. Here Swinburne uses it in its original horticultural sense, meaning 'a bed of earth, heated by fermenting manure, for raising or forcing plants'.[104] The 'hotbed' then is akin to the 'hothouse', an environment that artificially 'forces' growth out of season, an association reinforced by the synonym 'greenhouse' in the next line. As he did with Morris and Arnold, Swinburne claims his friend's poetry as natural, unforced, and wholesome. He laments the exclusion of an early religious lyric which he says has 'the colour and perfume in it of the choral air of the cathedral', but otherwise, Rossetti's 'Blessed Damozel' 'has the odour and colour of cloudless air' and his poetry is overwhelmingly seen as a natural, organic product characterized by its 'live bloom of perfect words, warm as breath and fine as flower-dust, which lies light as air upon the parting of lyric leaves that open into song'.[105]

Shakespeare is the poet whom Swinburne celebrates as epitomizing the vernal perfume of lyric poetry. In an essay of 1871 he writes of the playwright Thomas Decker:

> In Decker's best work we feel an air of the 'Winter's Tale' or 'Midsummer Night's Dream;' [...] Something of the April sweetness, the dew and breath of morning,

---

[101] Ibid., p. 161.

[102] Browning, Letter of 19 June 1870, in *Dearest Isa*, p. 336. Robert Buchanan originally published his article 'The Fleshly School of Poetry: Mr. D. G. Rossetti' under the name of 'Thomas Maitland' in the *Contemporary Review* (1871). See the reprinted essay in *Critical Essays on Dante Gabriel Rossetti*, ed. David Riede (New York: G. K. Hall & Co., 1992), p. 28. Buchanan subsequently published a longer, more damning version of his article as a pamphlet, *The Fleshly School of Poetry and Other Phenomena of the Day* (London: Strahan & Co., 1872), where the civet insult recurs on p. 38.

[103] Swinburne, 'The Poems of Dante Gabriel Rossetti', in *Essays and Studies*, p. 97.

[104] Although in 'hotbed' there is perhaps an additional connotative hint of the 'bed of illicit or riotous passion', something else that Swinburne is also keen to deny in Rossetti's verse, which for him properly emphasizes the inherent nobility of sexual love.

[105] Swinburne, 'The Poems of Dante Gabriel Rossetti', pp. 89, 83, 104.

which invests the pastoral and fairy world of the master, gives to the [...] pupil's work a not infrequent touch of delicate life and passionate grace.[106]

In the following year, when he turns his attention to another idol, Victor Hugo, it is a mark of the high esteem in which he holds this French writer that he compares his writing with the vernal fragrance of the lyric passages that relieve the darkness of Shakespeare's tragedies:

> With the one eternal exception of Shakespeare, what other poet has ever strewn the intervals of tragedy with blossoms of such breath and colour? The very verse seems a thing of flowerlike and childlike growth, the very body of the song a piece of living nature like any bud that bursts or young life that comes forth in spring.[107]

Spring-like odours and other favourite ambient scents will also infiltrate the various later essays that make up *A Study of Victor Hugo* (1886), as Swinburne marks his approval by imaginatively translating Hugo's texts into the landscapes he himself cherishes most.

One of those cherished landscapes, an originating source of Swinburne's approved scents, comes to the fore in his *A Note on Charlotte Brontë*, a short critical study of 1877. Although poetry is usually the focus of his scented evaluations, prose can elicit similar responses, and Emily Brontë's *Wuthering Heights*, a novel Swinburne loved, very obviously recommended itself through the wild northern moorland landscapes in which its action is set. In his study Swinburne breaks off from his discussion of Charlotte Brontë to eulogize her sister:

> Little need was there for the survivor to tell us in such earnest and tender words of memorial record how 'my sister Emily loved the moors': that love exhales, as a fresh wild odour from a bleak shrewd soil, from every storm-swept page of 'Wuthering Heights.' All the heart of the league-long billows of rolling and breathing and brightening heather is blown with the breath of it on our faces as we read; all the wind and all the sound and all the fragrance and freedom and gloom and glory of the high north moorland.[108]

Emily Brontë's love of the moors, and by implication her spirit as a writer who is inspired by them, is breathed out through the pages of her novel as a characteristic wind-blown 'fresh wild odour'. Moreover Swinburne, who revels in this fragrance, hints that he is Emily Brontë's ideal reader, fitted to this role by their shared love of moorland landscape, and by a recognition of sights and smells only he can fully appreciate:

> It is possible that to take full delight in Emily Bronte's book one must have something by natural inheritance of her instinct and something by earliest association of her love for the same special points of earth—the same lights and sounds and colours and odours and sights and shapes of the same fierce free landscape of tenantless and fruitless and fenceless moor.[109]

---

[106] Swinburne, 'John Ford', in *Essays and Studies*, p. 277.
[107] Swinburne, 'Victor Hugo: "L'Année Terrible"', in *Essays and Studies*, p. 26.
[108] Swinburne, *A Note on Charlotte Brontë* (London: Chatto & Windus, 1877), pp. 70–1.
[109] Ibid., pp. 75–6.

The wind-blown scents of this 'fierce free landscape' could hardly be further from the enclosed odours of the hothouse and the 'Half-faded fiery blossoms, pale with heat | And full of bitter summer' that Swinburne had suggested were Baudelaire's due in 'Ave atque Vale'.

The Scent of 'singing power'

Swinburne's scented evaluations tend to diminish as his literary career progresses although are still in evidence in his later works. A good instance is his essay on the seventeenth-century poet Robert Herrick, written as a preface for an 1891 collection of Herrick's verse edited by Alfred Pollard. This essay provides another example of Swinburne's sensitivity to the perfumes characteristic of a writer or period of literature but it also emphasizes his own antipathy to strong perfume and, in particular, animalic odours. Herrick's verse hails from an era more tolerant of strong smells. These included not only heady animalic perfumes like musk and civet, but also body odours. In these Herrick takes an unabashed pleasure, as can be seen in poems such as 'Upon Julia's Sweat'. This clearly was not to Swinburne's taste at all, his 'passionate desire for personal cleanliness' being, according to Clara Watts-Dunton, 'inconsistent with artistic Bohemia and its traditions'.[110] Consequently, he makes his displeasure evident:

> The sturdy student [...] will probably find himself before long so nauseated by the incessant inhalation of spices and flowers, condiments and kisses, that if a musk-rat had run over the page, it could hardly be less endurable to the physical than it is to the spiritual stomach. [...] It was doubtless in order to relieve [the saccharine monotony of his work that Herrick] thought fit to intersperse these interminable droppings of natural or artificial perfume with others of the rankest and most intolerable odour.[111]

In point of fact, a poem like 'Upon Julia's Sweat', included in Pollard's edition, proposes that the perspiration of the beloved woman smells like flower fragrance— 'Would ye oil of blossoms get? | Take it from my Julia's sweat'.[112] This perception is so not very different from the observations of Swinburne's novelistic heroes who declare that the women they love 'smell like flowers in a hot sun' or have 'fingers that leave a taste of violets on the lips'. In all three cases the suggestion is that these women naturally smell like flowers. Yet the crucial difference is that Swinburne leaves out the physiology; for him, the woman simply and naturally emanates her delicate fragrance like a flower, and, although an increase in warmth no doubt

---

[110] Watts-Dunton, *Home Life*, p. 120.

[111] Swinburne, Preface to Robert Herrick, *The Hesperides and Noble Numbers*, ed. Alfred Pollard, The Muses' Library, 2 vols (London: Lawrence & Bullen, 1891), 1. xii. It is the musk deer that is the acknowledged source of the musk used in perfumery, and not the muskrat, a semi-aquatic rodent native to North America, which has a musky smell. However, from Swinburne's perspective, a musk deer could hardly 'run across the page'. That said, in 1945 Edward Sagarin, discussed the contemporary North American experimental use of muskrat oil or 'Musc Zibata'. See his *The Science and Art of Perfumery*, pp. 56, 63–6.

[112] Herrick, *The Hesperides and Noble Numbers*, 2. 54. Herrick could also be understood as implying that the sweat of a beloved woman is as delicious as flower fragrance.

produces 'the hot fragrance of her face and neck', he is too much a Victorian gentleman to want to think of her doing anything as coarse as 'sweat'.

As with women so with flowers and poetry—Swinburne suggests that fragrance, the indefinable quality that enhances and completes a flower, cannot be anatomized or explained. As he observed in relation to Wordsworth's best poetry in 1884, 'Analysis may be able to explain how the colours of this flower of poetry are created and combined, but never by what process its odour is produced.'[113] By contrast, in Swinburne's study of 1889, the verses of the Jacobean poet and playwright Ben Jonson lack this quintessential perfume of poetry:

> [T]he flowers of his growing have every quality but one which belongs to the rarest and finest among flowers: they have colour, form, variety, fertility, vigour: the one thing they want is fragrance. Once or twice only in all his indefatigable career of toil and triumph did he achieve what was easily and habitually accomplished by men otherwise unworthy to be named in the same day with him; by men who would have avowed themselves unworthy to unloose the latchets of his shoes. That singing power which answers in verse to the odour of a blossom, to the colouring of a picture, to the flavour of a fruit,—that quality without which they may be good, commendable, admirable, but cannot be delightful,—was not, it should seem, a natural gift of this great writer's.[114]

What Swinburne was looking for in the writers he read was that indefinable perfume, 'That singing power which answers in verse to the odour of a blossom', and Jonson's poetry, although competent, fails when read to exhale the inspired breath of song and the fragrance of the true poet's spirit, or what Walter Pater in the second part of this chapter will call 'soul perfume', the intimate presence and influence of an author as diffused through his or her style.

Although Swinburne nearly always chose to represent this fragrance as the natural airy scent of flowers and leaves that breathes from the page, in 'Thalassius', his poetic autobiography from *Songs of the Springtides* (1880), he uses the image of the transient flower distilled into liquid perfume as an analogy for the way in which the inspired soul of the poet might live on in his song after death. Just as those who leave legacies of good deeds and words live on as inspiration in the minds of later generations, and the sweet soul of the flower lives on transformed into a much stronger perfume, so too might the poet's soul endure in his 'loving light of song and love' to transform the lives of others:

> As such men dying outlive themselves in man,
> Outlive themselves for ever; if the heat
> Outburn the heart that kindled it, the sweet
> Outlast the flower whose soul it was, and flit
> Forth of the body of it
> Into some new shape of a strange perfume
> More potent than its light live spirit of bloom,
> How shall not something of that soul relive [...]?   (*Poems* 3. 299–300)[115]

---

[113] Swinburne, 'Wordsworth and Byron', in *Miscellanies*, p. 127.
[114] Swinburne, *A Study of Ben Jonson* (London: Chatto & Windus, 1889), p. 4.
[115] Swinburne is almost certainly recalling Shakespeare's image of flowers preserved as perfume in his Sonnet No. 5.

After Swinburne's death, his biographer Edmund Gosse provided a short critical introduction to a selection of his verse included in Thomas Humphry Ward's multi-volume anthology *The English Poets*. Here, as elsewhere, Gosse writes about Swinburne with an admiration tainted by an underlying envious resentment:

> But the paradox is that Swinburne, soaked as he was in the wisdom of the ages, responsive like an Æolian harp to every breath of the wind of past poetry, is one of the most definitely original of all writers. He is *himself* to a fault, to our positive impatience and annoyance; he has a quality of style, a sort of perfume, which is so exclusively his own that it vexes us when or where it ceases to please us. Swinburne was a master of every artifice of imitation, and yet—except where he is intentionally a parodist—he is instantly recognizable under all disguises. He floods whatever he touches with his own pungent musk.[116]

Gosse, absorbing Swinburne's own pervasive metaphors, refers to him as 'responsive [...] to every breath of the wind of past poetry', and having 'a sort of perfume'. But Swinburne would have loathed that animalic characterization of himself as 'flood[ing] whatever he touches with his own pungent musk', a description that not only suggests a lingering memory of him as a Baudelairean decadent, but also aggressively registers Gosse's irritation at Swinburne's dominance, for the male musk deer uses its scent to mark its territory.

No doubt Swinburne would have preferred a description of his poetry or his 'singing power' as 'the broad breath of a sea-wind' or 'a fresh wild odour from a bleak shrewd soil', a clean, sharp, and enlivening fragrance to be cherished by his readers after the pattern he envisaged in his elegy 'In Memory of Barry Cornwall'; for it is his readers who, by giving their breath to his poetry, perpetuate both its music and its inimitable perfume:

> Time takes them home that we loved, fair names and famous,
>   To the soft long sleep, to the broad sweet bosom of death;
> But the flower of their souls he shall take not away to shame us,
>   Nor the lips lack song for ever that now lack breath.
> For with us shall the music and perfume that die not dwell,
> Though the dead to our dead bid welcome, and we farewell.   (*Poems* 3. 71)[117]

PATERIAN FLAIR

> Flair, from the Old French, *flair*, odour, derived in turn from the Vulgar Latin *flagrare*, to emit an odour. Originally used to mean an odour, in the nineteenth century, influenced by the French *flairer*, to smell, to detect, it came to mean instinctive discernment.[118]

[116] Edmund Gosse, 'Algernon Charles Swinburne (1837–1909)', in *The English Poets: 1880–1918*, vol. 5: *Browning to Rupert Brooke*, ed. Thomas Humphry Ward (London: Macmillan & Co., 1918), pp. 368–75; 371. See my comments on Gosse's underlying resentment of Swinburne in Maxwell, *Swinburne*, pp. 5–6.

[117] 'Barry Cornwall' is the pseudonym of the poet Bryan Waller Procter (1787–1874). He and his wife were good friends of Swinburne. Swinburne's poem bears the subscription 4 October 1874, although Procter's date of death is usually stated as 5 October 1874.

[118] Constance Classen, *Words of Sense: Exploring the Senses in History and Across Cultures* (London and New York: Routledge, 1993), pp. 65–6.

'Flair', glossed by the cultural historian Constance Classen as one of her 'words of sense', suggests a natural progression from olfactory acuity to the 'instinctive discernment' of the aesthete, something also suggested by the anecdote about Pater related by the Oxford Fellow and classical scholar Robert Raper. Asked by Raper 'if he would care to come to see our Trinity Chapel', Pater replied '"No, but I should like to smell it if I might," remembering the aroma of the cedar wood).'[119] Gerald Monsman's comment, 'This droll rejoinder reflected more than a bit of that "preciosity" which came to caricature his brand of aestheticism', implicitly reads Pater's smell sensitivity as a marker of a certain kind of aesthetic sensibility. Monsman is understandably uneasy with the caricature, the popular 'Victorian view of what Pater's work was about: an "impressionism" devoted to intensities and subtleties of sensuous colors, fragrances, and forms—and a dangerous enthusiasm for the separation of art and morality' (*ME*, p. vii). However, that should not discourage a more considered examination of the sensuous element, and in particular fragrance, in his writing.

In fact modern critics have explored in some detail nearly all of the senses as represented in Pater's œuvre. Vision unsurprisingly dominates because of his commitment to the visual arts, but more recently hearing (especially in relation to music), touch, and even taste have received attention.[120] Smell, historically the most maligned of the senses, is the one so far unexplored in Pater's work in spite of the fact that it was evidently important to him. What follows is an attempt to rectify that omission starting with an account of Pater's own smell preferences and leading into a discussion of the way it informs his writing and its significance for him. My focus here is specifically on perfume, that is to say scent cultivated or relished for pleasure's sake.

As shown in Raper's anecdote, Pater presents himself as an *olfactif*, an individual with a refined sense of smell. Using Jim Drobnick's recent coinage, one might also call Pater a '*flaireur*', someone 'for whom smell is a pre-eminent aspect of being in the world'. Drobnick writes: 'For the *flaireur*, "smelling well" connotes not only the acts of relishing fragrances and presenting oneself in a pleasingly scented manner, but, more significantly, serves as an olfactory model upon which one's core

---

[119] Robert Raper, letter of July 1915 to Edmund Gosse, cited in Monsman's commentary in *GL*, p. 145, and Monsman's Introduction to *ME*, p. vii.

[120] Many critics discuss Pater's visuality but Paul Barolsky's *Walter Pater's Renaissance* (University Park, PA, and London: Pennsylvania University Press, 1987) and Østermark-Johansen's *Walter Pater and the Language of Sculpture* are notable. My *Second Sight* discusses the more rarely mentioned topic of Pater's visionariness. See also Jerome Bump, 'Seeing and Hearing in *Marius the Epicurean*', *Nineteenth-Century Fiction* 37 (1982), 188–206. For hearing, see Angela Leighton, 'Pater's Music', *Journal of Pre-Raphaelite Studies* 14 (2005), 67–79; Andrew Eastham, 'Walter Pater's Acoustic Space: "The School of Giorgione", Dionysian *Anders-streben*, and the Politics of Soundscape', in *The Arts in Victorian Literature*, guest ed. Stefano Evangelista and Catherine Maxwell, *The Yearbook of English Studies* 40.1 and 40.2 (2010), 197–216; and Elicia Clements, 'Pater's Musical Imagination: The Aural Architecture of "The School of Giorgione" and *Marius the Epicurean*', in *Victorian Aesthetic Conditions: Walter Pater across the Arts*, ed. Elicia Clements and Lesley J. Higgins (Basingstoke: Palgrave Macmillan, 2010), pp. 152–66. For touch, see also Østermark-Johansen, *Walter Pater and the Language of Sculpture*. For taste, see Matthew Kaiser, 'Pater's Mouth', *Victorian Literature and Culture* 39 (2011), 1–18.

identity is constructed.'[121] Undoubtedly influenced by Baudelaire and Swinburne, Pater's flair or scent sensitivity is a badge of honour that signals his sensibility and aesthetic credentials; yet, more than an mark of mere affiliation, it is an integral part of his identity as a literary artist, his early awareness and responsiveness to scent figuring in the semi-autobiographical story 'The Child in the House' (1878) as part of that 'brain building by which we are, each of us, what we are [...] inward and outward being woven through and through each other into one inextricable texture' (*IP*, p. 84).

Pater's genuine interest and pleasure in scent can be gleaned from a number of sources. I have not been able to find any evidence that he used perfume himself, but such use would have been less common among the older generation of male aesthetes as opposed to the younger decadent bohemians like Wilde and Symons whose perfume tastes are better documented. Yet he evidently enjoyed scented atmospheres, and these, as we will see in this chapter, come to pervade his writing in various significant ways. William Sharp noted the seasonal flowers—wallflowers, lavender, chrysanthemums, or winter aconites, all of which are fragrant—that Pater always kept in his college rooms, whilst F. W. Bussell remarked on the annually renewed bowl of dried rose leaves, made to a 'special receipt', that served as potpourri.[122] Thomas Wright records that Pater commented of a 'favourite flower, the common white pink [...], "Its fragrance is the breath of Euterpe." '[123] Sharp recalls walking with Pater in Oxford—'He was singularly observant of certain natural objects, aspects, and conditions, more especially of the movement of light in grass and among leaves, of all fragrances, of flowing water'—and records a particular conversation about flower scent:

> How well I remember one evening in the meadows by the Cherwell! It was a still, golden sunset. Already the dew had begun to fall, and the air was heavy with the almost too poignant fragrance of the meadowsweet. I had made a remark about the way some people were haunted by dream-fragrances, and instanced queen-of-the-meadow, as we call it in Scotland, in my own case. Pater replied that certain flowers affected his own imagination so keenly that he could not smell them with pleasure: and that while the white jonquil, the gardenia, and the syringa actually gave him pain, the meadowsweet gave him a sudden fugitive sense of distant pastures, and twilit eves, and remote scattered hamlets.[124]

The heavy flower scents mentioned by Pater as giving him pain—the white jonquil (*Narcissus jonquilla*), the gardenia, and the syringa (lilac)—in common with other strongly perfumed white flowers contain indole, an organic compound 'reminiscent

---

[121] Jim Drobnick, 'Preface: Flaireurs', in *The Smell Culture Reader*, ed. Jim Drobnick (Oxford and New York: Berg, 2006), pp. 163, 164. See also Jim Drobnick 'Toposmia: Art, Scent and Interrogations of Spatiality', *Angelaki* 7.1 (April 2002), 31–46; 34.

[122] William Sharp, 'Some Personal Reminiscences of Walter Pater', *Atlantic Monthly* 74 (December 1894), 801–14; 806. (Reprinted in *Walter Pater: A Life Remembered*, ed. R. M. Seiler (Calgary, AB: University of Calgary Press, 1987), pp. 78–98.) Bussell, cited in *Walter Pater: The Critical Heritage*, ed. R. M. Seiler (London: Routledge & Kegan Paul, 1980), p. 285.

[123] Thomas Wright, *The Life of Walter Pater*, 2 vols (London: Everett & Co., 1902), 2. 62. Euterpe is the muse of lyric poetry whose name means 'giver of delight'. Most pinks are clove-scented.

[124] Sharp, 'Some Personal Reminiscences', pp. 807, 809–10.

of decay and faeces', that gives such blooms a 'putrid-sweet, sultry-intoxicating nuance'.[125] Meadowsweet, a perennial wildflower with feathery tufts of delicate, creamy-white flowers that have a sweet, honey-like aroma, represents the antithesis of these richly scented blooms, a contrast also reflected in the title of the verse collection *Tuberose and Meadowsweet* (1885) produced by Pater's friend, the young poet Mark André Raffalovich. Pater here reflects a more conservative mid-Victorian preference for light floral fragrances as opposed to the heavier scented, indolic 'sultry-intoxicating' flowers that will be associated with Victorian decadence and epitomized in the Wildean cult of the lily. Similar disquiet about a certain kind of floral fragrance is expressed in *Gaston de Latour* (1888, 1896) when Pater refers to 'the sickliness of all spring flowers since the days of Proserpine' (*GL*, p. 26), or in 'The Myth of Demeter and Persephone' (1876) to the 'heavy and narcotic aroma of spring flowers', doubtless recalling that 'narcissus', from the Greek *narkē* or numbness, is so named for its 'narcotic' fragrance (*GS*, p. 116).

Instances of Pater's flair for delicate floral scents also emerge in his essays 'A Study of Dionysus' (1876) and 'The Bacchanals of Euripides' (1889), where he notes 'the scented air of the vineyards (for the vine-blossom has an exquisite perfume)' and 'the little mezereon-plant of English gardens, with its pale-purple, wine-scented flowers upon the leafless twigs in February' (*GS*, pp. 62, 26). In the unfinished imaginary portrait 'An English Poet', his protagonist takes pleasure in a honey-suckle, 'an exotic from France, the colour of its flower ripening from a peerless white to brown gold, with a whole round of fragrant changes in the spirit of the tiny thing still fragrant in death' (*IP*, p. 105).[126] The poet's later declaration about the authenticity of fragrant writing reflects Pater's own carefully cultivated know-ledge and intimate awareness of scent: 'for if your words regarding it are to be fragrant, [...] you must have been for a time in slavish possession of the flower' (*IP*, p. 111). In another imaginary portrait, 'Emerald Uthwart' (1892), Pater, describing Emerald's undergraduate years, records botanical scents that show his own 'slavish possession of the flower', for example, the snake's-head fritillaries indigenous to Oxford—'does the reader know them? That strange remnant just here of a richer extinct flora—dry flowers, though with a drop of dubious honey in each'—and he observes how 'On summer nights the scent of the hay, the wild-flowers, comes across the narrow fringe of the town to right and left; seems to come from beyond the Oxford meadows' (*IP*, pp. 260, 259).[127]

Elsewhere, showing interest in a fellow *flaireur*, Pater reproduces remarks by the seventeenth-century antiquarian and 'industrious local naturalist' Sir Thomas

---

[125] Jellinek, *The Psychological Basis of Perfumery*, p. 42.

[126] Originally published as Walter Pater, 'Imaginary Portraits 2: An English Poet', ed. May Ottley, *Fortnightly Review* 129 (April 1931), 433–48. Pater's 'English' poet, raised in Cumberland, is actually of Anglo-Norman parentage, combining English and French influences. His Baudelairean taste for 'exotic' French flowers, along with his yearning 'for that warmer soil', is counterbalanced by his later appreciation of a perfumed strain of exoticism in English literature.

[127] 'Emerald Uthwart' was first collected in *MS* (1895). Roy Genders notes that the snake's-head fritillary (*Fritillaria meleagris*) 'has a soft mossy fragrance which is more pronounced in the white forms'. See his *The Scented Wild Flowers of Britain* (London: Collins, 1971), p. 209. For me, it has a faintly unpleasant dirty smell, which may have provoked Pater's use of the phrase 'dubious honey'.

Browne on sweet-smelling insects; a beetle supposed to smell of nutmeg and cinnamon that Browne said actually ' "smelt like roses, santalum [sandalwood] and ambergris" ', and ' "a small bee-like fly of an excellent fragrant odour, which I have often found at the bottom of tulips" '. Curious, Pater asks, 'Is this within the experience of modern entomologists?' (*A*, pp. 139, 140). His own preference may be for light, airy odours over the 'sickly perfumes' such as those Phædra vainly employs to entice Hippolytus in 'Hippolytus Veiled' (1889) (*IP*, p. 233), but he is more catholic in his tastes than this may suggest, at other times relishing incense or imagining the 'fragrant odour' of burnt herbs (juniper and lad's-love) offered to Aphrodite of Sicyon (*GS*, p. 249). Unlike his contemporaries, Swinburne and Symonds, he seems not to have had the marked aversion to animalic musk characteristic of a time when animal-derived scents such as musk, civet, ambergris, and castoreum, popular in the eighteenth century and earlier, were not openly appreciated.

Animalic musk has a particularly penetrating and tenacious odour that in perfume produces a sweet, sometimes sweaty note. Aware of its use in earlier eras, Pater uses it to signify artificiality, as in his imaginary portrait 'Duke Carl of Rosenmold' (1887), set in early eighteenth-century Germany. The young Duke Carl, hoping to bring about a German cultural and artistic enlightenment, looks to France and the court of the 'Sun King', Louis XIV, for inspiration. Louis was 'known as the "sweetest smelling" monarch in French history', and his passion for 'strong scents (ambergris, musk, heavy floral odors)', for Pater, becomes identified with his cultural legacy and what Richard Stamelman calls 'the excessive artificiality of [Louis's] reign' (1643–1715).[128] Without leaving home, Duke Carl imports Louis's aesthetic and intellectual legacy:

> its more portable flowers came to order in abundance. That the roses, so to put it, were but excellent artificial flowers, redolent only of musk, neither disproved for Carl the validity of his ideal nor for our minds the vocation of Carl himself in these matters. [...] It was but himself truly, after all, that he had found, so fresh and real, among those artificial roses. (*IP*, p. 198)

For Pater, though, artificiality is no crime and he is hardly censorious; the flowers of seventeenth-century rococo culture may seem less than authentic but the imaginative enthusiasm of Carl bestows on them the vitality they lack. Similarly, in the classical culture of *Marius the Epicurean* (1885) artificiality is no weakness when it characterizes the collection of Apuleius' carefully wrought pronouncements— '*Florida* or *Flowers*'—'elaborate, carved *ivories* of speech, drawn at length, out of the rich treasury of his memory and as with a fine savour of musk about them' (*ME*, p. 215).

Olfactory impressions, seemingly from Pater's own early life, occur in both 'The Child in the House' and 'Emerald Uthwart', although it is possible his scented memories may have been mediated by another semi-autobiographical tale, 'The History of a Child' (1836), by the Romantic poet Letitia Landon, which he could

---

[128] Stamelman, *Perfume*, pp. 58, 62.

conceivably have read as a boy. The remembered girlhood of Landon's narrator is more melancholy and solitary than the boyhood of Pater's Florian Deleal, and, although scent does not permeate her story so thoroughly as it does Pater's, it nonetheless signals her sensory acuity and openness to natural influences. Absorbed by her impressionable mind, scent pervades or triggers powerful memories. Recollecting in adulthood, 'the sweet languor of the pale primrose' and 'the purple arabia of the breathing violet', she declares 'those fair fresh banks rose distinct on my mind's eye. They colour the atmosphere with themselves, their breath rises on the yet perfumed air, and I think with painful pleasure of all that once surrounded them.'[129] Devouring the stories of the Arabian Nights for the first time, she recalls 'How delicious was the odour of the Russia leather in which they were bound', and she reminisces how the porch of the house belonging to her one childhood friend 'was enlivened by that rare and odiferous shrub, the yellow musk rose', which, at evening, 'filled the whole air with its peculiar and aromatic fragrance'.[130]

As well as being a *flaireur*, Pater is also, like Landon, an aromancer, a story-teller who conjures the past through scent, and his Florian Deleal recalls 'the very scent upon the air' of his childhood home (*IP*, p. 83), the 'perfumed juice of [...] fallen fruit' (p. 84), the 'empty scent bottles still sweet' found in the attic (p. 84), the fragrance of 'the little white flowers of the lime-tree' and the 'red flowers' of the hawthorn (pp. 86, 91), sunshine pervaded by 'the perfume of the garden' (p. 93), and the 'languid scent' of ointment put on a burn (p. 93). These vivid sense impressions contribute to what he calls 'the gradual expansion of the soul' (p. 84). This intimate alliance between sense and spirit at times approaches synaes-thesia, something that tinges the description of the garden in Emerald's childhood home, where floral musk, like that breathed by Landon's musk rose, pervades the atmosphere:

> How they shook their musk from them!—those gardens [...]. Brothers and sisters, all alike were gardeners, methodically intimate with their flowers. You need words com-pact rather of perfume than of colour to describe them, in nice annual order; terms for perfume, as immediate and definite as red, purple, and yellow. Flowers there were which seemed to yield their sweetest in the faint sea-salt, when the loosening wind was strong from the south-west; [...] Others consorted most freely with the wall-fruit, or seemed made for *pot-pourri* to sweeten the old black mahogany furniture. The sweet-pea stacks loved the broad path through the kitchen garden; the old-fashioned garden azalea was the making of a nosegay, with its honey which clung to one's finger. There were flowers all the sweeter for a battle with the rain; a flower like aromatic medicine; another like summer lingering into winter; it ripened as fruit does; and another was like August, his own birthday time, dropped into March.   (*IP*, pp. 240–1)[131]

This amalgamation of smell with taste reminds us that taste is in fact ninety per cent smell—pinch your nose while eating and you will be unable to taste much

---

[129] 'The History of a Child', in *Letitia Elizabeth Landon*, pp. 154–5.
[130] Ibid., pp. 155, 157.
[131] A number of flowers—musk roses, musk mallows, muscari (musk hyacinth), mimulus—emit a sweet floral version of musk to attract pollinating insects.

beyond the sensations of sweet, sour, salt, and bitter.[132] Smell is vital to the relish of flavour we call 'savouring'. Diane Ackerman writes: 'If we have a mouthful of something delicious which we want to savor and contemplate, we exhale; this drives the air in our mouths across our olfactory receptors, so we can smell it better.'[133] Smell thus determines flavour and, as Classen remarks, the word 'flavour', now used almost exclusively for taste sensations, 'Originally [...] meant a smell', a meaning still found in the nineteenth century.[134] Pater, ever attentive to the 'historic sense', to what in his essay on 'Style', he calls 'the finer edge of words still in use' (*A*, p. 16), would have been aware of this and the way in which language used to describe the one sense often does duty for the other.

A case in point is the favourite Paterian term 'savour', claimed by Matthew Kaiser in his fine essay 'Pater's Mouth' as a word denoting 'taste', but which often means 'smell'—as it frequently does in Swinburne and as it almost exclusively does in the Authorized Version of the Bible, both powerful influences on Pater.[135] While he undoubtedly uses 'savour' to refer to a pleasurable relish of the mouth, Pater also uses it to indicate fragrance, as in his earliest essay 'Diaphaneitè'. There, describing the diaphanous ideal nature, he writes, 'the presence of this nature is felt like a sweet aroma in early manhood. Afterwards, as the adulterated atmosphere of the world assimilates us to itself, the savour of it faints away' (*IP*, p. 82; *SR*, p. 139).[136] In this instance Pater is almost certainly recalling various New Testament formulations in which Christ, the godly, and their gifts are described as a sweet 'savour', but also, perhaps, 'the odour of sanctity', that mysterious aura of beautiful perfume said to emanate from saints and mystics.[137] He may hint too at that 'natural fragrance of the skin' that the Greek poet Straton of Sardis attributes only to boys (Epigram 7) in the *Mousa Paidikē* or *Musa Puerilis* ('Boyish Muse'), the collection of homoerotic lyrics and epigrams that forms the twelfth book of the Greek Anthology. Possibly literal in origin but quickly shading into figurative meaning, the 'sweet aroma' of Pater's 'Diaphaneitè' suggests how his fondness for the scented atmospheres remembered in 'The Child in the House' and 'Emerald Uthwart' might inform the many other atmospheres found elsewhere in his critical prose.

Those 'atmospheres'—Pater uses the word repeatedly—are the emotional, intellectual, or spiritual ambiences or influences created or emanated by specific periods of culture, schools, individuals, or works of art, and are often scented. In this, he was most obviously influenced by Swinburne's earlier prose—the Baudelaire review as well as *William Blake* and the critical essays that reject

---

[132] Burr, *The Emperor of Scent*, p. 57.

[133] Diane Ackerman, *A Natural History of the Senses* (London: Chapmans, 1990), p. 13.

[134] Classen, *Words of Sense*, p. 66.

[135] Kaiser, 'Pater's Mouth', pp. 3, 4. Other Paterian words that have an odorous dimension are 'racy', used of the aroma as well as the taste of wine (*OED* item 1a), and 'relish', an alteration of Middle English *reles*, a scent or aftertaste.

[136] 'Diaphaneitè', read aloud as a paper in 1864, was first published in *MS* (1895).

[137] See 2 Corinthians 2:14; Philippians 4:18; Ephesians 5:2.

the 'hothouse' and espouse 'fresh', 'sweet', airy fragrances.[138] However, there is a much stronger awareness in Pater of literary eras or periods as unified by scent and giving off a distinctive fragrance. The most obvious of Pater's scented atmospheres is the Renaissance itself, which is invariably 'sweet'. Moreover, many of the representative figures who feature in Pater's *Studies in the History of the Renaissance* (1873)—Luca della Robbia, Michelangelo, Pico della Mirandola, Joachim du Bellay—are associated, however briefly, with 'sweetness.' Kaiser notes that in Pater 'the Renaissance tastes sweet. Pater's frequent use of "sweetness," "sweet," "sweeten," and "sweetly" is no stylistic quirk'; yet while many of these usages refer to taste, some of them indicate smell, something that Kaiser glosses over when he casually absorbs scent into his argument: 'In all things sweet, in their *perfumes* and juices, [Pater] tastes the Renaissance' (my emphasis).[139] For Pater also smells the Renaissance and indeed the first and leading characterization of its pervasive sweetness comes in the Preface to *Studies*, where the image is of sweet-smelling grass or flowers. Describing its long reach, its enduring influence, Pater writes of 'the Renaissance thus putting forth in France an aftermath, a wonderful later growth, the products which have to the full the subtle and delicate sweetness which belong to a refined and comely decadence' (*SR*, p. 5).[140]

Flowers and blossoms with their implicit fragrance recur throughout *The Renaissance*; in Leonardo, for instance, who finds nothing 'poisonous in the exotic flowers of sentiment that grew' in Quattrocento Florence, and later 'Out of the secret places of a unique temperament [...] brought strange blossoms and fruit hitherto unknown' (*SR*, p. 66). Such passages recall the 'strange flowers, and curious odours' as among the things to be sought out by the aspiring aesthetic critic, mentioned in 'Poems by William Morris' (1868), subsequently revised as part of the Conclusion to *Studies*.[141] They are clearly influenced by Baudelaire's exotically perfumed *Les Fleurs du mal*, and by Swinburne's 'Ave atque Vale' (published January 1868), which calls the French poet 'a gardener of strange flowers' (*Poems* 3. 52), and includes several references to fruit. (Baudelaire was a source that Pater, perhaps anxious to play down the controversial aspects of *Studies*, was later at pains to disguise, changing the 'flowers' of the Conclusion to 'colours' after 1873, presumably to obscure the link.) The opening of the Morris review, afterwards 'Æsthetic Poetry' (1889), uses an image similar to that of the 'aftermath', remarking how verse such as Morris's, evoking 'the poetry of a past age', is 'Like some strange second flowering after date.'[142] Moreover, for Pater, Provençal poetry, imitated by Morris

---

[138] That said, some of Pater's literary and cultural scented atmospheres possibly influenced Swinburne's own later essays, such as his 1891 review of *Lyra Elegantiarum*. Pater's essay on 'Charles Lamb' (1878) precedes Swinburne's essay on Lamb of 1885.

[139] Kaiser, 'Pater's Mouth', p. 8.

[140] An 'aftermath' is the new growth after a field or meadow has been cut or mown. Pater teasingly uses this naturalistic agrestic image to describe a decadence, albeit 'a refined and comely one'.

[141] Walter Pater, 'Poems by William Morris', *Westminster Review* 34 (October 1868), 300–12; 311. See also *SR*, p. 120.

[142] Pater, 'Poems by William Morris', p. 300. See also Pater, 'Æsthetic Poetry', in *Appreciations with an Essay on Style* (London: Macmillan, 1889), p. 213. Pater dropped 'Æsthetic Poetry' from subsequent editions of *Appreciations*.

in his first verse collection, has something of a Baudelairean 'extravagance': 'Here, under this strange complex of conditions, as in some medicated air, exotic flowers of sentiment expand, among people of a remote and unaccustomed beauty.'[143]

Yet not all Paterian symbolic flowers are Baudelairean in origin. The sweetness of the Renaissance, Pater tells us, begins 'when the rude strength of the middle age turns to sweetness; and the taste for sweetness becomes the seed of the classical revival in it' (*SR*, pp. 9–10). Those regenerated classical blooms include Pater's depictions of 'flowerlike' young men (evoking texts such as Epigram 256 in the *Mousa Paidikē*) and metamorphic myths of fair boys transformed into flowers, as touched on in his retelling of the Hyacinthus story in 'Apollo in Picardy' (1893) and alluded to in 'The Myth of Demeter and Persephone': 'the flowers in the grass, which were once blooming youths, having both their natural colour and the colour of their poetry in them' (*GS*, p. 131). Pico della Mirandola, prematurely dead 'like the field flowers [...] withered by the scorching sun' in 'the time of the lilies' but famously still 'alive in the grave' with his 'qualities still active' (*SR*, pp. 25, 28) might be considered the Renaissance cultivar of one such classical bloom. Classical sweetness is transfused not only through such revitalized stock but also through texts and artefacts that transmit the purified atmosphere of Hellenic times, 'That delicate air, "nimbly and sweetly recommending itself to the senses"', as Pater imagines it in 'Winckelmann' (*SR*, p. 103), while in *Marius the Epicurean* he attributes similar qualities to the 'pure air' of the Italian countryside in the second century (*ME*, pp. 9, 24).

The beneficent sweetness of Pater's Renaissance also owes something to Matthew Arnold's description of culture as 'sweetness and light', in *Culture and Anarchy* (1868) and to one of Swinburne's favourite adjectives, 'sweet', sources briefly noted by Kaiser who interprets them as gustatory.[144] Arnold's chapter 'Sweetness and Light' formed part of his concluding lecture as Oxford's Professor of Poetry in May 1867, published two months later in the *Cornhill*. Arnold's 'sweetness' may have originally been associated with the taste of honey—it is an allusion to the story of the Bee and the Spider in Jonathan Swift's *Battle of the Books*—but in his use it subtly volatilizes, becoming vaporous and odorous, as when he states that culture's aim is 'to make all men live in an atmosphere of sweetness and light', or when he states that the great men of culture like Lessing and Herder are those who 'worked powerfully to diffuse sweetness and light'.[145] Kaiser declares Swinburne's 'sweet' a symptom of his 'notoriously fetishistic orality', but he might just as easily read it as a symptom of olfactory pleasure.[146] Rebuked for his overuse of this word, Swinburne nonetheless often employs it strategically to challenge his culture's perception of what is 'sweet'.[147] His most conspicuous use of 'sweet' in *Poems and*

---

[143] Pater, 'Poems by William Morris', p. 302; 'Æsthetic Poetry', p. 217.

[144] Kaiser, 'Pater's Mouth', p. 8.

[145] Matthew Arnold, *Culture and Anarchy*, ed. J. Dover Wilson (Cambridge: Cambridge University Press, 1960), pp. 54, 70, 71.

[146] Kaiser, 'Pater's Mouth', p. 8.

[147] Reviewing *Poems and Ballads* and *Chastelard* (1865) for the *Examiner* (22 September 1886), Henry Morley wrote: 'Of "sweet"—"sweet"—"sweet", he has the iteration of a canary bird. There are "sweets" enough in these two little volumes to set up a wholesale grocer for his life-time.' See Hyder, ed., *Swinburne: The Critical Heritage*, p. 44.

Ballads (1866) is in one of his most notorious poems, 'The Leper', where it is compulsively repeated, as the speaker's insistence on the 'sweetness' of his dead mistress, spoken over her decaying corpse, ironically engages and teases olfactory expectation as it does other assumptions about the nature of love.

It is fitting that these different kinds of sweetness, classical and contemporary, act on Pater as an influence, because in his own work scent and sweetness act as figures for influence. They can act as effective figures precisely because, for him, at a physical level scent and sweetness are aromatherapeutic, altering or conditioning mood, or spiritual, and intellectual states. He must have been taken by Michel de Montaigne's remarks in his essay 'On Smells', for he reproduces them in *Gaston de Latour* when Montaigne, in conversation with Gaston, remarks, 'Of scents, the simple and the natural seem to me the most pleasing, and I have often observed that they cause an alteration in me, and work upon my spirits according to their virtues' (*GL*, p. 57).[148] Gaston himself, accustomed to climb the tower of Jean de Beauce to seek out a view of 'large, quiet, country spaces', was 'become well aware of the power of those familiar influences in restoring equanimity as he might have used a medicine or wine', his cares dropping away as he ascends and 'the flight of birds, the scent of the field swept by him' (*GL*, p. 21).

Pater frequently notes the tonic effects of pure, good, or rural air, which even in its purity seems to have an understated or implicit fragrance. Adjectives like 'delicate', a word that has a long history of being applied to smell (see *OED* item I.1.a), or 'fresh', a favourite word of both Swinburne and Pater (and a word frequently used in perfumery), seem to carry more than a trace of the vivifying and cleansing exhalations of plants and trees, as in the park-like enclosure around the Temple of Aesculapius in *Marius* where 'All the objects of the country were there at their freshest. [...] and that freshness seemed to have something moral in its influence, as if it acted upon the body and the merely bodily powers of apprehension, through the intelligence' (*ME*, p. 28). In 'Hippolytus Veiled', the goddess Artemis, settled in Eleusis, has her aggression tamed 'thanks to some kindly local influence (by grace, say, of its delicate air)' (*IP*, p. 226). The young English poet, a visitor to the Normandy coast, enjoying the 'smooth winds from the sea, [...] seemed to appreciate the material elements [...] of their balm and salt, coaxing him into a sort of renewed life' (*IP*, p. 112). Some kinds of air, however, are perhaps not so unequivocally pure. Gaston, 'yielding himself' to the 'influence' of Ronsard's clerical study, finds 'An exotic embalming air, escaped from some old Greek or Roman pleasure-place, had turned the poet's workroom into a strange kind of sanctuary' (*GL*, p. 35). In 'Apollo in Picardy', as Prior St-Jean readies himself to recommence work on his manuscript, Apollyon's uncanny intellectual influence is presaged or partnered by the untimely fragrance of spring flowers blooming in midwinter: 'the great glazed windows remain open; admit [...] what seems like a stream of flowery odors, the entire moonlit scene, with the thorn bushes on the vale-side prematurely bursting into blossom' (*IP*, p. 286).

---

[148] See Monsman's excellent notes (*GL*, p. 169). Cf. Pater's citation of Browne's belief 'in the operation "of the air and genius of gardens upon human spirits, towards virtue and sanctity"' and his hatred of gardens that ' "smell more of paint than of flowers and verdure"' (*A*, pp. 140, 141).

Influence, literally 'a flowing into', is a matter of atmosphere, something almost imperceptible 'in the air'; taken for granted, it nonetheless surrounds one and supports one's very existence. Breathed in and savoured, atmosphere may prove to be 'inspiring', filling one with breath. Indeed, as we have seen with Swinburne, 'breath' originally meant a smell or odour, and when used by Pater often retains this sense for him, as in 'the evening breath of the honeysuckle' (*GL*, p. 39) or 'the breath of the sea and sand' enjoyed by his young English poet (*IP*, p. 112). On their arrival at the Grange in Picardy in winter, Prior St-Jean and Hyacinth find that 'From the very first, the atmosphere, the light, the influence of things seemed different from what they knew [...]. Was there the breath of surviving summer blossom on the air?' (*IP*, p. 275). Sebastian van Storck, who 'liked to breathe, so nearly, the sea and its influences', seems ineluctably drawn to surrender his life to its waters in an act of heroism that helps him achieve his desired goal of 'self-effacement' (*IP*, pp. 152, 164). Duke Carl of Rosenmold finds 'After unclean streets, the country air was a perfume by contrast, or actually scented with pinewoods. One seemed to breathe with it fancies of the woods, the hills, and water—of a sort of souls in the landscape, but cheerful and genial now, happy souls' (*IP*, p. 206). In 'Denys l'Auxerrois', set in the medieval French town of Auxerre, Denys, a possible Dionysian god in exile, endures three phases of being, each with a different transformative effect on those around him. Entering the second, more sophisticated phase that will trigger 'a kind of degeneration' in his community, Denys returns to Auxerre after a trip to the south, bringing back, among other things Eastern, 'incense' and—a Baudelairean touch—the 'seeds of marvellous new flowers' (*IP*, p. 179).[149] If, towards the end of this phase, his influence seems malign, it works to better effect when, in his more austere third phase, he enters the monastery. Here, bereft of skills, 'he could but compound sweet incense for the sanctuary', yet, like that incense, alters the very atmosphere: 'again by merely visible presence, he made himself felt' (*IP*, p. 182). Defining 'unconsciously a manner, alike of feeling and expression', his influence is breathed in, inspiring anew the arts and handicrafts around him (*IP*, p. 183).

Sensitive to 'those who experience most directly the influences of things which touch thought through the senses' (*GS*, p. 57), and presumably counting himself among them, Pater provides in *Marius the Epicurean* a Platonically derived theory that explains how atmospheric influences, whether derived from places or persons, might work. Early on the young Marius stays at the Temple of Aesculapius for the sake of his health where he is 'alive to the singular purity of the air' (*ME*, p. 24). Ostensibly describing the boy's susceptibility to visual impressions, the narrator gives us a 'theory of influence' that seems to privilege vision but on closer examination seems equally dependent on smell. Marius, we are told:

[A]fterwards found in Plato's *Phædrus*, the theory of the ἀπορρόη τοῦ καλλοῦς [effluence of beauty], which supposes men's spirits to be susceptible to certain influences, diffused, like streams or current, by fair things or persons visibly present—green fields

---

[149] In *Greek Studies* Pater writes of how 'the flowers, the incense of the East, have attached themselves deeply to [Dionysus]', and of his 'long vesture [...] fragrant with Eastern odours' (*GS*, pp. 62, 49).

and children's faces, for instance—into the air around them; and which, with certain natures, are like potent material essences, conforming the seer to themselves as by some cunning physical necessity.   (*ME*, p. 25)

The 'essence' of beauty 'diffused [...] into the air' seems like the kind of spiritual scent or perfume aura we find in 'Diaphaneitè'. This 'effluence of beauty', which for the impressionable aesthetic perceiver constitutes 'influence', is here experienced as an immediate physical encounter but elsewhere Pater indicates that there is a form of influential encounter that still has something of physical immediacy, which can be accessed through reading.

Reading opens one to other forms of influence; as mentioned earlier in this chapter in relation to Swinburne, when inspired by the texts of the past, one 'breathes in' and savours the words of others, finding that the best authors have a characteristic fragrance. Throwing himself into reading, Pater's young English poet finds that a 'good book would be like an actual place visited', governed by 'a special recognised influence, a certain controlling atmosphere, always to be experienced there, when one had a will to turn the key' (*IP*, p. 107). That atmosphere is scented, for we learn that the young man, raised in an uncongenial climate and, possessed by a 'sensuous longing for that warmer soil out of which exotic flowers [...] would naturally grow, [...] found the exotic full-blown at last in books of prose and poetry' (*IP*, p. 107).

Pater builds on what seems more implicit and intuitive in Swinburne to formalize that idea of a writer's characteristic fragrance. In his essay on 'Style' (1888) he discusses those influential authors who have a 'soul perfume'. He contrasts what he calls 'mind' and 'soul' in style, the latter experienced as a kind of intimate personal contact or spiritual presence informing the text, which is intuited and cannot be isolated in or attributed to individual textual characteristics. Both 'mind' and 'soul' have distinct imperatives—soul seeking 'unity of *atmosphere*' and mind 'unity of design'; 'soul securing colour (or *perfume*, might we say?) as mind secures form, the latter being essentially finite, the former vague or infinite, as the *influence* of a person is practically infinite' (*A*, pp. 26–7; my emphasis). And in conclusion Pater identifies mind as 'reasonable structure', and 'soul' as 'colour and mystic *perfume*' (*A*, p. 38; my emphasis). The influence of 'soul' is infinite because it cannot be contained by any specific form and moves beyond it, like perfume that expands and diffuses in the air; 'soul', the mysterious spiritual essence of a person, is experienced as a perfume aura diffused through style with an afterlife or presence outside the text.

Textual or aesthetic influence-as-perfume is hinted at elsewhere in Pater in his constant reference to the 'essence' of writers and artists. As I have shown in other works, this derives from his use of an alchemical imagery to describe the creative process or the means by which the critic distils and extracts the essence or 'virtue' of the artist or writer he analyses (*SR*, p. 4).[150] The goal of the alchemical process, the elixir or philosopher's stone that confers immortality, is brought about through

---

[150] Maxwell, *Second Sight*, pp. 82–90; see also my 'Shelley's Alchemy, Pater's Transformations', in *Legacies of Romanticism: Literature, Culture, Aesthetics*, Routledge Studies in Romanticism, ed. Carmen Casaliggi and Paul March Russell (London: Routledge, 2012), pp. 85–100.

the *coniunctio* or *coincidentia oppositorum*, the alchemical marriage or bringing together and combining of opposite elements. In Pater we also see this obsession with the reconciliation or union of opposites, when he defines the essence of subjects such as Michelangelo and Leonardo through combinations such as 'sweetness and strength', 'beauty and terror', or 'curiosity and the desire for beauty' (*SR*, pp. 40, 59, 62), or when he characterizes Romanticism as 'the union of strangeness and beauty' (*A*, p. 247).

Alchemy is not only the forerunner of modern chemistry but it shares its techniques and processes such as distillation, and its equipment with perfumery—with words like 'alembic' used in perfume manufacture to refer to the vessel for distillation; indeed, early alchemists were also often perfumers, while perfume, another kind of precious essence, is itself an 'alchemical marriage' of opposites. A liquid that contains within it the traces of once-material things, it also volatilizes as a vapour; it hovers on the borders between the physical and non-physical; it is a presence and an absence, a plenitude and a loss. More prosaically it combines animal and vegetable extracts, and—in modern perfumery—natural extracts and synthetic molecules. Beautiful fragrances contain not only pleasant-smelling substances but unpleasant ones too, such as some animalic extracts (musk, civet, castoreum), or indole, that smell of decay found in certain flowers, which nonetheless helps give them (and manufactured perfume) character, a rich and complex bouquet. Perfume is a physical substance worn on the body, which can speak to the body of physical desire and pleasure, but it transforms the odour of corporeality into something elevated and refined. It can lift the mind to higher things and cross into the realm of the spirit, and once volatilized, it is an aura that influences mood and emotion and can indicate personality, intelligence, and soul.

For Pater, the Renaissance, itself a combination of different impulses and influences, has a 'unity of [...] spirit which gives unity to all [its various] products' (*SR*, p. 6) and, as we have seen in this chapter, its own perfume, perceptible in the 'early sweetness, a languid excess of sweetness' he finds in the thirteenth-century French story of Aucassin and Nicolette, where the evocation of natural fragrances blends into a period or genre fragrance (*Ren*, p. 12). Charmed by the 'faint Eastern delicacy' of details that include 'the full-blown roses' and 'the odour of plucked grass and flowers', he notes that 'all through [the story] one feels the influence of that faint air of overwrought delicacy, almost of wantonness, which was so strong a characteristic of the poetry of the Troubadours' (*SR*, p. 14). Indeed, when Pater specifies the essence of writers, texts, genres, and periods of artistic and literary endeavour, there is often the sense that this essence is also a perfume. Sometimes this is explicit as when, in 'Art Notes in North Italy', he refers to St Jerome as 'author of the fragrant Vulgate version of the Scriptures' (*MS*, pp. 105–6), or says that Whetstone's retelling of Shakespeare's *Measure for Measure* has 'the fragrance of that admirable age of literature about it' (*A*, p. 172); or that Charles Lamb's collection of Tudor dramatic verse has 'the choicest savour and perfume of Elizabethan poetry', with Lamb's own notes 'the very quintessence of criticism' (*A*, p. 111). For Pater, Lamb himself is so faithful to older literature that 'in what he says casually there comes an aroma of old English' (*A*, p. 113). Sometimes the perfume is less immediately obvious, as when Pater writes that the works of Greek sculptors 'came to be like some subtle extract or essence' (*SR*, p. 37); although 'extract' is suggestive of fragrance or aroma, an impression intensified by immediate reference to the diffusion of the sculptures' abstract purity and universality 'which has carried their influence far beyond the age which produced them' (*SR*, p. 38).

Figures of alchemical extraction underlie the opening of 'Poems by William Morris' and 'Æsthetic Poetry'. Jonathan Freedman notes how '"aesthetic poetry" is described in the language of alchemy, "sublimat[ing]" and "extract[ing]" elements from the real and artificial alike'.[151] Both essays subsequently use images of exotic flowers and scented atmospheres to describe Provençal poetry and Morris's imitation of it, making this a perfumer's alchemy. Similar effects permeate 'The School of Giorgione' (1877), included in the third edition of *The Renaissance* (1888), and one of Pater's essays most evidently infiltrated with alchemical imagery, with recurrent references to 'gold' and 'essence'. It is also rich in images of air, a conductor, as Andrew Eastham has recently pointed out, of sound, but also, I would suggest, of perfume.[152] Giorgione's paintings are experienced as perfume; the artist having made his works portable 'so that people may move them readily', the paintings 'coming like an animated presence, into one's cabinet, to enrich the air as with some choice aroma' (*SR*, p. 128). Giorgione's formal capture of the dramatic instant in his genre paintings is a kind of alchemical 'condensation', the paintings being like 'some consummate extract or quintessence of life'; they are thus an alchemical distillate that could also be a perfume.[153] The distillate/perfume analogy is even stronger in Pater's original version of this passage in which the 'ideal instants' of the paintings are 'phases of subject in themselves *already volatilised almost to the vanishing point*, exquisite pauses [...] which are like an extract, *or elixir*, or consummate fifth part of life'.[154] A subsequent paragraph, also omitted from *The Renaissance*, concludes: 'Well! in the school of Giorgione you drink water, *perfume*, music, lie in receptive humour thus for ever, and the satisfying moment is assured.'[155] Like writers and artists, readers and critics of literature and artworks are perfumers-cum-alchemists who distil and extract the scent, the essence of style, as does Pater's English poet, who in reading requires:

[T]he genius of refinement; and this not as the new subject of writing, of its more obvious and immediate presentations, but by a subtler operation from the style, the *ether-like* manner of the thing. So written language came to be form and colour as well

---

[151] Jonathan Freedman, *Professions of Taste: Henry James, British Aestheticism, and Commodity Culture* (Stanford, CA: Stanford University Press, 1990), p. 5.

[152] Eastham, 'Walter Pater's Acoustic Space', p. 206.

[153] Compare Gaudenzio Ferrari's *Our Lady of the Fruit-garden* at Vercelli, a painting that, for Pater, evokes the garden scents of the north Italian town where it is located, and afterwards leaves its 'savour' in the visitor's memory (*MS*, p. 95).

[154] Walter Pater, 'The School of Giorgione', *Fortnightly Review* 22 (October 1877), 526–38; 536; my emphasis.

[155] Pater, 'The School of Giorgione', p. 536; my emphasis. See also Donald Hill's 'Textual Notes' in *Ren*, pp. 241, 242. The phrase 'fifth part of life' is a synonym for 'quintessence', itself a term widely used in alchemy for the arcane 'fifth essence' that characterizes a thing or substance and which can supposedly be extracted by distillation or other procedures.

as sound to him, *exotic perfume* almost. Having nothing else to live on, he *extracted* all they could yield from words, and his sense of them came to be curiously cultivated at all points. (*IP*, p. 110; my emphasis)

Aftermath: Critical Olfaction

The immediate effects of Paterian influence-as-perfume can be seen in the work of Wilde, one of Pater's most devoted readers. In *The Picture of Dorian Gray*, the actual perfumes of the garden and studio that form the heady atmosphere in which Dorian will fall under Lord Henry's seductive influence presage more figurative uses. Lord Henry wonders if one might 'convey one's temperament into another as though it were a subtle fluid or a strange perfume', while the malefic pseudo-*A Rebours* with which he corrupts Dorian is 'a poisonous book. The heavy odour of incense seemed to cling about its pages and to trouble the brain' (*DG*, pp. 34, 104). But that book, 'bound in yellow paper', indeed referred to as 'the yellow book', its colour signalling its dubious French provenance, recalls Pater's two influential scented yellow books: the 'golden book' of Apuleius enjoyed by Marius and Flavian, 'perfumed with oil of sandalwood' with its 'handsome yellow wrapper' (*ME*, p. 39) and, with its 'yellow edges', Ronsard's *Odes* beloved by Gaston, which carries 'the perfume of the place where it had lain—sweet but with something of the sickliness of all spring flowers since the days of Proserpine' (*GL*, p. 26).[156] Moreover, the Roman belief that 'all the maladies of the soul might be reached through the subtle gateways of the body' (*ME*, p. 22) finds a more epigrammatic expression in Lord Henry's axiom that '"Nothing can cure the soul but the senses, just as nothing can cure the senses but the soul"' (*DG*, p. 21). Admitting, as well he might, that Pater had his imitators, Wilde, reviewing *Appreciations* in 1890, observed, 'in art so fine as his there is something that, in its essence, is inimitable'.[157] True though that may be, other of Pater's readers and reviewers were quick to savour that inimitable essence.

Olfactory images are not uncommon in Victorian literary criticism. Disapprobation is often expressed by reference to unpleasant, disgusting, or loathsome smells relating to dirt and disease. Such comparisons may draw on a morally inflected Biblical language or they may have associations either with older miasmic theories of contamination or the newer Victorian ethos of moral hygiene. Images of fragrance can be either positive or negative, reflecting the predilections of the critic who may well approve some kinds of scent but not others. A conservative British prejudice against strong-smelling exotic perfume and against men's use of fragrance of any kind seeps into the language of critical evaluation from the mid to the end of the Victorian era. We saw earlier in this chapter how on the publication of *Poems and*

---

[156] *DG*, pp. 102, 103. French novels, frequently regarded as risqué by Victorian readers, were often bound in yellow paper. This association was later exploited by the leading journal the *Yellow Book*, which was linked with aestheticism and decadence, and published by Elkin Mathews and John Lane from 1894 to 1897.

[157] Oscar Wilde, Review of Pater's *Appreciations*, 22 March 1890, in *Walter Pater: The Critical Heritage*, p. 236.

Ballads, Swinburne was accused of having 'drenched himself in the worst creations of Parisian literature'. Frederic Harrison satirically portrayed Matthew Arnold's version of Culture as remote and rarefied, sitting 'high aloft with a pouncet-box [perfume-box] to spare her senses aught unpleasant', and Arnold's sermonizing to a '*petit-maître* [dandy] preacher passing his white hands through his perfumed curls, and simpering thus about the fringes of a stole'.[158]

Attesting to the perfume of his prose, Pater's readers and critics respond to him in kind, starting with Swinburne, who, asked by Rossetti if he could detect his own influence on Pater's writing, cheerfully acknowledged 'a little spice of my style as you say' (*TSL* 2. 58; 28 November 1869). Writing to Swinburne on the publication of *Studies in the History of the Renaissance* in 1873, John Addington Symonds gushes, 'What a wonderfully finished piece of artistic work in criticism Pater has given us! The style has an indefinable perfume & charm' (*LJAS* 2. 276; 4 March 1873).[159] But to his close friend, Henry Dakyns, he confided his reaction to Pater's style in a less complimentary metaphor that mutates synaesthetically from music to fragrance: 'There is a kind of Death clinging to the man, wh makes his Music (but heavens! how sweet that is!) a little faint & sickly' (*LJAS* 2. 273; after 20 February 1873). In his published and somewhat guarded review of *Studies* in *The Academy*, Symonds prudently reined in such criticism, referring only to the 'peculiar flavour' of the volume.[160] He told his sister, Charlotte Symonds Green: 'I am pleased to hear Pater liked my review. I thought he might think it aigre-doux [bitter sweet]' (*LJAS* 2. 279; 24 March 1873). Olfactory images often morph into taste metaphors. Symonds would later complain to Horatio Brown that a bout of influenza made it hard to concentrate on a difficult book: 'I tried Pater's "Appreciations" to-day, and found myself wandering about among the precious sentences, just as though I had lost myself in a sugar-cane plantation—the worse for being sweet' (*LJAS* 3. 440; 19 January 1890).

However, when Symonds complained about Pater's style to Henry Sidgwick, he reached again for an olfactory metaphor, namely civet, revealing a conservative Victorian aversion to animalics: '"Marius" I have not read. I suppose I must. But I shrink from approaching Pater's style, which has a peculiarly disagreeable effect upon my nerves—like the presence of a civet cat' (*LJAS* 3. 43; 5 April 1885).[161] Symonds, a consumptive with severe respiratory problems, was obliged to live in the Swiss Alps, an atmosphere he associated with a bracing healthiness and one therefore unsuitable for reading a decadent perfumed style that requires an altogether different kind of ambience. Hence his comment to the poet Mary Robinson:

> Mr Pater's 'Marius' will of course be read by me—I hope in a gondola. My brain is so badly made that I cannot bear the sustained monotonous refinement in his style. To that exquisite instrument of expression I daresay that I shall do justice in the languor & the

---

[158] Frederic Harrison, 'Culture: A Dialogue', *Fortnightly Review* 2 (November 1867), 603–14; 610, 611.

[159] Barring the letter to his sister, extracts from Symonds's *Letters* can also be found in Seiler, ed., *Walter Pater: The Critical Heritage*, pp. 55, 228, 124.

[160] John Addington Symonds, *Academy* (15 March 1873), in *Walter Pater: The Critical Heritage*, p. 58.

[161] Diluted, civet smells sweet and feline, a touch of cat's urine with honey. In its raw state or in a paste, it smells more faecal, with some commentators remarking on its resemblance to the odour of vomit.

largeness of the lagoons—better than I can in this larger air of the mountains, where everything is jagged & up & down & horribly *natural.*   (*LJAS* 3. 41–2; 30 March 1885)

Others, besides Symonds, reach for smell (and occasionally taste) imagery when assessing Pater. Havelock Ellis was clearly alert to Pater's alchemical and perfume imagery. As befitting someone who would make an extensive study of smell, he claims in a critical essay of 1885 that, for Pater:

> [T]here is nothing so good in the world as the soft, spiritual aroma—telling, as nothing else tells, of the very quintessence of the Renaissance itself—that exhales from Della Robbia ware, or the long-lost impossible Platonism of Mirandola, or certain subtle and evanescent aspects of Botticelli's art. To find how the flavour of these things may be most exquisitely tasted, there is nothing so well worth seeking as that.[162]

But, discussing Pater's treatment of his objects of criticism, he finds an inappropriate kind of self-indulgence:

> [T]hey are, as it were, plants from each of which he wishes to abstract its own peculiar alkaloid or volatile oil [...] This was an ingenious or almost scientific theory of criticism, and had not Mr Pater seemed to swoon by the way over the subtle perfumes he had evoked, he might, one thinks, have gone far.[163]

For Ellis, it seems to be a matter of degree. Pater's feminine 'swooning' is a step too far, the aesthetic critic overwhelmed by the very atmosphere he conjures and unable to remain objective. In contrast, Pater's decadent supporters embraced the language of fragrance more enthusiastically. Arthur Symons, in the original version of his essay on 'The Decadent Movement in Literature' (1893), an essay almost exclusively focused on contemporary French literature, called Pater's 'the most beautiful English prose which is now being written', while nonetheless observing 'how far away from classic ideals of style is this style in which words have their color, their music, their perfume'.[164] Symons, a future translator of *Les Fleurs du mal*, also imports a quasi-Baudelairean exoticism when in 1887 he declares of *Studies* 'an almost oppressive quiet, a quiet which seems to exhale an atmosphere heavy with tropical flowers, broods over these pages'.[165]

Pater's supporters also find fragrance in other of his works. The Irish writer George Moore, who, while living in Paris, had immersed himself in French literature, instinctively made use of a scent analogy when he wrote in his *Confessions of a Young Man* (1886) of the impact *Marius* made on him:

> [T]his book was the first in English prose I had come across that procured for me any genuine pleasure in the language itself, in the combination of words for silver or gold

---

[162] Havelock Ellis, 'The Present Position of English Criticism' (1885), in *Walter Pater: The Critical Heritage*, p. 110.

[163] Ibid.

[164] Arthur Symons, 'The Decadent Movement in Literature', *Harper's New Monthly Magazine* 87 (November 1893), 858–67; 866. See also Seiler, ed., *Walter Pater: The Critical Heritage*, p. 269.

[165] Arthur Symons, Review of *Imaginary Portraits* (1887), in *Walter Pater: The Critical Heritage*, p. 177. For Symons's translation of Baudelaire, see Charles Baudelaire, *Les Fleurs du mal*, tr. Arthur Symons (London: The Casanova Society, 1925).

chime, and unconventional cadence, and for all those lurking half-meanings, and that evanescent suggestion, like the odour of dead roses, that words retain to the last of other times and elder usage.[166]

Richard Le Gallienne, appraising *Marius* in his obituary notice for Pater, feels compelled to defend the novel's and, by implication, its author's, masculinity: 'despite Mr Pater's detractors, it is, in the best sense of the word, a manly book. [...] and for sheer beauty, glamour, fragrance—that mysterious beauty as of incense which clings about every word Mr Pater wrote—where in English literature is there a book like it?'[167] (For 'Mr Pater's detractors' that attribution of manliness must have sat rather awkwardly with the incense.) Although unimpressed by their factual content, the archaeologist L. R. Farnell enjoyed the 'faint fragrance' of Pater's lectures on Greek sculpture which he heard as an Oxford undergraduate and which seem to have acted as an influence as he 'resolved to go further afield in this line'.[168] Similarly, whether expressing praise or reservations, Symonds, Ellis, Symons, and Le Gallienne, like Wilde, influenced by the 'exotic perfume' of Pater's prose, would all go further afield in the line of *flairerie*. Indeed, Symonds and, more briefly, Ellis appear in Chapter 4, in which *flairerie* assumes a cosmopolitan flavour, and takes in the specific scents of foreign literatures, climes, and cultures, as well as the bodies to be discovered within them.

---

[166] George Moore, extract from *Confessions of a Young Man* (1888), in *Walter Pater: The Critical Heritage*, p. 153.
[167] Richard Le Gallienne, Obituary Notice (August 1894), in *Walter Pater: The Critical Heritage*, p. 283.
[168] L. R. Farnell, cited in Østermark-Johansen, *Walter Pater and the Language of Sculpture*, p. 216.

4

Scent, the Body, and the Cosmopolitan
Flaireur
John Addington Symonds and Lafcadio Hearn

The literary critic Hans J. Rindisbacher calls body odour 'the indispensable Other of the perfume and fragrance industry, despised and feared at the same time; to be eradicated, yet its *raison d'être*'.[1] But body odour is far from being the antithesis of perfume. When it comes to the olfactory spectrum, perfumers are a good deal more tolerant than most people, often intrigued by smells that many would find objectionable or repellent. Moreover, they know that many perfumes, even the most apparently fragrant ones, incorporate elements of those despised corporeal odours in order to add depth and complexity. The contemporary perfumer Kilian Hennessy is quoted as saying

> I know every scent there is. [...] I know how to create them. Animalic notes have always been around, have always been at the disposal of the perfumer. The scents of decay, of death, they do not repulse me. [...] The only thing that sickens me are tacky perfumes. I am repulsed only by what is poorly made.[2]

The great Jacques Guerlain (1864–1963) famously remarked that his perfumes 'should smell like the underside of my mistress', while Germaine Cellier, creator of Fracas and Bandit, was reported to demand the underwear of models after they had stepped off the catwalk in order to capture the bouquet of youthful female sexuality.[3] *A propos* of Shocking (1937), designed by Jean Carles for Elsa Schiaparelli and claimed as 'the first sex perfume', Denyse Beaulieu attests that it 'does reek of *gousset*, the small triangle of fabric sewn into the *petite culotte*'.[4] Detailing modern perfumistas' enthusiasm for 'skank' fragrances that contain 'dirty' notes, she proposes that 'overcoming our aversion to stink through its incorporation into beautiful compositions could be a way of not renouncing our more primal desires; of drawing

---

[1] Rindisbacher, *The Smell of Books*, p. 189.

[2] Kilian Hennessy, interviewed by Derek McCormack for *National Post* (8 March 2008) and posted on http://hisnherperfumes.blogspot.co.uk/2008/06/all-in-stink-about-perfume.html.

[3] Herman, *Scent and Subversion*, pp. 136, 79. Susan Irvine, *The Perfume Guide* (London: Haldane Mason, 2000), p. 114. See also Hannah Betts, 'Let us Spray', *Guardian* (6 December 2008), https://www.theguardian.com/lifeandstyle/2008/dec/06/perfume-ingredients.

[4] Beaulieu, *The Perfume Lover*, p. 164.

the pleasures that Western civilization considers base, and that our education leads us to reject, into the life of the mind'.[5]

As detailed in Chapter 1, personal hygiene became *de rigueur* during the Victorian era as the middle and upper class adopted daily bathing and the respectable aspirant lower classes emulated them with more frequent ablutions as far as was possible. In polite society it would certainly be unacceptable to smell unwashed. However, it seems safe to assume that even well-to-do Victorians were more tolerant of certain body odours than we are. Hair, though kept clean from dust and grime by much combing and brushing, was washed far less frequently, making it likely to smell of those natural scalp oils nowadays obliterated by daily shampooing. Women's formal dresses might be 'sponged down' and dress-shields protecting clothes from perspiration regularly replaced, but most gowns could not be laundered. Eau de cologne, toilet water, violet powder, and medicated soap might do duty for deodorant but were unlikely to meet modern standards of effectiveness. Julia Twiss comments, 'By the end of the nineteenth century it was still possible to speak of *bouquet de corsage*, the attractive smell of perspiration in the ballroom. By the 1930s this had become BO.'[6]

Certainly during the Victorian era there is an appreciation for the natural fragrance of the flesh. Alain Corbin cites a French commentator of 1846 who declares that 'the tender odor of marjoram that the virgin exhales is sweeter, more intoxicating than all the perfumes of Arabia'.[7] Virginity, however, may not have been a prerequisite for this intoxicating odour. Some courtesans were famed for their natural scent, including Sweet Nelly Fowler, a popular *fille de joie* in London during the 1860s, of whom it was said 'This beautiful girl had a natural perfume, so delicate, so universally admitted, that love-sick swains paid large sums for the privilege of having their handkerchiefs placed under the Goddess's pillow, and sweet Nelly pervaded—in the spirit, if not in the flesh—half the clubs and drawing-rooms of London.'[8]

But less exotic variants of female scent were also valued. In his erotic memoirs published in 1888, the author known as 'Walter' records how, as a sexually curious adolescent schoolboy, he became aware of women's natural perfume when he persuaded a servant to show him her neck and breast:

> I threw my arms round her, buried my face in her neck and kissed it. 'I like the smell of your breast and flesh', said I. She was a biggish woman, and I dare say I smelt breasts and armpits together; but whatever the compound, it was delicious to me, it seemed to enervate me. The same woman, when I kissed her on the sly afterwards, let me put my nose down her neck to smell her.[9]

[5] Ibid., p. 162.

[6] Julia Twiss, *Bathing: The Body and Community Care* (London and New York: Routledge, 2000), p. 41.

[7] A. Debay, *Les Parfums et les fleurs, leur histoire et leurs diverses influences sur l'économie humaine* (Paris: Moquet, Libraire-Éditeur, 1846), p. 49, cited in Corbin, *The Foul and Fragrant*, p. 183.

[8] [Donald Shaw], *London in the Sixties (with a Few Digressions) by One of the Old Brigade* (London: Everett & Co., 1908), p. 34.

[9] 'Walter', *My Secret Life*, Wordsworth Erotic Classics, 2 vols (Ware: Wordsworth, 1995), 1. 37.

Walter then interrogates his mother about this scent:

'What makes ladies smell so nice?' said I to my mother one day. My mother put down her work and laughed to herself. 'I don't know that they smell nice.' 'Yes, they do, and particularly when they have low dresses on.' 'Ladies', said mother, 'use patchouli and other perfumes.' I supposed so, but felt convinced from mother's manner, that I had asked a question which embarrassed her.

I used to lean over the backs of the chairs of ladies, get my face as near to their necks as I could, quietly inhale their odours, and talk all the time. Not every woman smelt nice to me, and when they did, it was not patchouli, for I got patchouli, which I liked, and perfumed myself with it. This delicate sense of smell of a woman I have had throughout life, it was ravishing to me afterwards, when I embraced the naked body of a fresh, healthy young woman.[10]

In 'La Fleur du Jardin d'ici bas', the decadent poet Theodore Wratislaw hymns as a 'perfume headier than wine', the 'Odour of women faintly wrought | In folds of silken bodices', specifically distinguishing this scent from cosmetic fragrance:

> Nor musk nor heliotrope it is,
> Nor scent of violet-powder caught
> Within the soft skin's crevices.[11]

Interestingly, Susan Irvine writes of the modern perfume Trésor (1990), designed for Lancôme by Sophia Grojsman, that it 'is built around an accord she code-named "cleavage", and it smells, she says, like a young woman's décolleté'.[12] Perhaps this is also the source of the 'fresh young fragrance' emanated by the frivolous Undine in Edith Wharton's *The Custom of the Country* (1913), a novel set in the earliest years of the twentieth century.[13]

Walter, as one might guess, is also a fan of women's more intimate sexual odour, though it is clear that he preferred the smell of 'nice women'—presumably women with the means to practise better hygiene:

I revelled as said in the smell of a nice woman; with the poor cheap women I had for some time had, their smell offended me, I avoided kissing them even, why I can't say. With Mary this delight returned, her aroma overpowered me, and added to my voluptuous delight in her embraces. On every possible opportunity I used to lift her petticoats, and smell her flesh, it intoxicated me, and instantly made me wild with lewdness.[14]

Not all men were so enthusiastic. The twenty-one-year-old Dante Gabriel Rossetti, writing home to his brother William from Paris in 1849, was evidently disgusted by a performance of the can-can, a dance whose eroticism relied on the dancers high-kicking while not wearing underwear and described by the *Pall Mall Gazette*

---

[10] Ibid., 1. 37.   [11] Theodore Wratislaw, 'La Fleur du Jardin d'ici bas', in *Orchids*, p. 8.
[12] Irvine, *The Perfume Guide*, p. 40.
[13] In the novel Ralph Marvell wistfully craves his absent wife's letters: 'Sometimes the mere act of holding the blue or mauve sheet and breathing its scent was like holding his wife's hand and being enveloped in her fresh young fragrance.' See Edith Wharton, *The Custom of the Country*, ed. Stephen Orgel (Oxford: Oxford University Press, 2008), p. 193.
[14] 'Walter', *My Secret Life*, 1. 421.

in 1868 as a spectacle 'no women should witness and no man applaud'.[15] Concluding a private sonnet on this 'toothsome feast | Of blackguardism and whoresflesh and bald row', Rossetti wrote:

> For me,
> I confess, William, and avow to thee,
>   (Soft in thine ear!) that such sweet female whims
>   As nasty backsides out and wriggled limbs
> Are not a passion of mine naturally;
>   Nor bitch-squeaks, nor the smell of heated quims.[16]

Admittedly Rossetti was also repelled by the ugliness of the dancers, who did not fall into his category of 'nice women'. A lover praising his beloved might be expected to be more rapturous, as was the case with the Reverend Charles Kingsley whose intimacy with his fiancée Fanny Grenfell exceeded the boundaries thought proper for unmarried couples at this time: 'my hands are perfumed with her precious limbs, and I cannot wash off the scent, and every moment the thought comes across me of the mysterious recesses of beauty where my hands have been wandering'.[17] Havelock Ellis also thought that romantic attachment made a difference. Writing on the role of smell in sexual selection in his *Studies in the Psychology of Sex* (1905), and having cited a male correspondent who remarked '"I dislike the smell of a woman's vagina"', he comments 'While the last statement seems to express the feelings of many if not most men, it may be proper to add that there seems no natural reason why the vulvar odor of a clean and healthy woman should be other than agreeable to a normal man who is her lover.'[18]

Scent—especially the scents of male and female bodies—plays an important role in the work of the two late nineteenth-century writers who occupy the rest of this chapter. The first of these, a friend of Havelock Ellis and a collaborator with him, is the classicist, literary critic, and historian, John Addington Symonds (1840–1893); the second is the journalist, critic, and travel writer, Lafcadio Hearn (1850–1904). Both these writers have strong links with aestheticism that have often been overshadowed by other aspects of their work that have gained more critical attention. For example, although he maintained a keen interest in the Pre-Raphaelites and other aesthetic writers, Hearn, who left Britain at the age of nineteen, is more usually considered in relation to the places he visited and wrote about—the United States, the French West Indies, and Japan—and his links with British aestheticism are rarely considered. John Addington Symonds is best known today as a key nineteenth-century apologist for homosexuality. His poor health kept him out of Britain for much of his writing career, with the consequence that that he tends not to be seen in context with his aesthetic peers, while

---

[15] *Pall Mall Gazette* (Friday, 27 March 1868), 11b.

[16] Letter of 8 October 1849, in *The Correspondence of Dante Gabriel Rossetti*, ed. William Fredeman, 10 vols (Woodbridge and Rochester, NY: D. S. Brewer, 2002–15), 1: *The Formative Years 1835–1854*, pp. 114–15.

[17] Susan Chitty, *The Beast and the Monk: A Life of Charles Kingsley* (London: Hodder & Stoughton, 1975), p. 82. Kingsley married Fanny in January 1844.

[18] Ellis, *Studies in the Psychology of Sex: Sexual Selection in Man*, p. 85.

his ambivalence about various of those peers—Rossetti, Swinburne, Pater, Wilde, and Vernon Lee—also helped set him apart. Yet this should not obscure the fact that Symonds's own writing manifests many aesthetic traits.

Symonds and Hearn, both of them committed travellers, can be considered cosmopolitan aesthetes and *flaireurs*, sampling a range of climates, cultures, and geographical locales, with scent a key element in their appreciation of places and the bodies they encountered there. However, their cosmopolitanism should not be considered only in relation to physical locales but also in relation to the literatures of different countries, both past and present, which they enthusiastically consumed. My analysis starts with Symonds, whose cosmopolitanism is evident in his exploration of odorous bodies as read through contemporary German sexology, classical Greek culture, and the work of one of America's leading nineteenth-century poets.

JOHN ADDINGTON SYMONDS: INHALING THE ODOUR OF THE TEXT

In his essay 'A Problem in Modern Ethics: Being an Enquiry into the Phenomenon of Sexual Inversion', privately printed in 1891, John Addington Symonds specifies antipathy to the odour of the female body as a symptom of the 'Urning', a term coined by the sexologist Karl Heinrich Ulrichs to denote the male homosexual. Discussing the research of another influential German sexologist, Richard von Krafft-Ebing, Symonds states in a footnote 'the physical repugnance of true Urnings for women may be illustrated by passages from three of Krafft-Ebing's cases'. In the translated passages he cites, homosexual men express how they are repelled by women's natural odour, with the last witness specifically decrying the feminine *bouquet de corsage*: '"*I loathe the odour which the so-called fair sex exhales when heated by the dance.*"' Symonds summarizes: 'The disgust inspired in these three Urnings by the smell of the female is highly significant, since we know that the sense of smell acts powerfully upon the sexual appetite of normal individuals.' And he concludes, 'It may be remarked that in all the instances of pronounced Urnings, sexual congress with women seems to have been followed with disgust, nervous exhaustion, and the sense of an unnatural act performed without pleasure. This is true even of those who have brought themselves to marriage.'[19]

There is manifestly a degree of identification here as Symonds, himself a married man and the loving father of four daughters, was himself unmoved by sexual intercourse with his wife, whom he nonetheless cherished as his domestic companion. As he recorded in his confidential *Memoirs*, his wedding night was a disaster as his sexual inexperience meant that he was unable to consummate the marriage. He also 'discovered that the physical contact of a woman, though it did not actually disgust me, left me very cold'.[20] Symonds himself appears as Case XVIII in *Sexual*

---

[19] J. A. Symonds, *John Addington Symonds (1840–1893) and Homosexuality: A Critical Edition of Sources*, ed. Sean Brady (London and Basingstoke: Palgrave Macmillan, 2012), p. 158.
[20] J. A. Symonds, *The Memoirs of John Addington Symonds*, ed. Phyllis Grosskurth (New York: Random House, 1984), p. 157.

Inversion (1897), co-authored by himself and Havelock Ellis, where we are told that 'In early childhood, and up to the age of 13 he had frequent opportunities of closely inspecting the sexual organs of girls, his playfellows. These roused no sexual excitement. On the contrary the smell of the female parts affected him disagreeably.'[21] Again in his *Memoirs*, he mentions how as a child he 'was unfortunate enough to be thrown into the society of a coarse girl' who got him to touch her sexual organs: 'It neither attracted nor repelled me, nor did they rouse my curiosity, only they displeased my sense of smell.'[22]

In his study of smell in sexual selection, Havelock Ellis claimed that among sexual inverts 'olfactory attractions are often specially marked', and 'That the body odor of men may in a large number of cases be highly agreeable and sexually attractive is shown by the testimony of male sexual inverts. There is abundant evidence to this effect.'[23] In 1868, the married Symonds, still struggling with his sexuality, developed an intense romantic passion for a handsome sixth-former at Clifton College named Norman Moor, who was preparing to go to university. Their physical relationship did not go beyond kisses and embraces, although just before Norman departed for Oxford, Symonds confided to his diary (28 January 1870) a lengthy lyrical appreciation of his lover's naked body, which included 'the scent of his sweet flesh and breathing mouth', and 'the open, passionate full-perfumed mouth, the chalice of soul-nourishing dew'. He further rhapsodized: 'Ah, but the fragrance of his body! Who hath spoken of that scent undefinable, which only love can seize, and which makes love wild mad and suicidal?'[24]

Symonds's romantic passion was undoubtedly fed by classical Greek and Latin sources detailing the romantic feeling of men for adolescent boys (*paiderastia*) that underpins the ancient Greek system of educational mentorship. Indeed, Symonds would, in an interesting—surely olfactory?—metaphor, describe the ancient 'popular

---

[21] For Case XVIII, see Havelock Ellis and J. A. Symonds, *Sexual Inversion: A Critical Edition, Havelock Ellis and John Addington Symonds (1897)*, ed. Ivan Crozier (Basingstoke and New York: Palgrave Macmillan, 2008), pp. 142–7; 143. Published after Symonds's death, the first edition of *Sexual Inversion*, bearing the names of both authors, had appeared in German in 1896 and contains some additional content that was subsequently cut by Ellis from the first English edition that appeared the following year. That edition, the co-authored *Studies in the Psychology of Sex: Sexual Inversion* (London: Wilson & Macmillan, 1897), was almost entirely bought up and destroyed by Symonds's literary executor Horatio Brown. A second English edition, also 1897, dropped Symonds's name and the text was amended to appease Brown and Symonds's widow. It was banned in Britain in 1898 as an obscene publication. Ellis subsequently shifted publication of his sexological works to the United States where a new edition of *Sexual Inversion* was published in 1901. Case XVIII would become Case XXV in the *Studies in the Psychology of Sex: Sexual Inversion* (Philadelphia, PA: F. A. Davis Company, Publishers, 1901), pp. 85–90, a text that bears Ellis's name alone. The text of Case XVIII, reprinted from the first English edition along with translations of the portions deleted or amended from the original German text, can also be found in John Addington Symonds, *Soldier Love and Related Matter*, tr. and ed. Andrew Dakyns (Eastbourne: Andrew Dakyns, 2007), pp. 43–7. (This publication also contains a translation of Symonds's essay on 'Soldier Love', originally an appendix to chapter 4 of the German edition.) The version of Case XVIII (labelled as Case XVII), reprinted in Phyllis Grosskurth's edition of Symonds's *Memoirs*, is abbreviated, but a similarly worded comment about 'female parts' occurs on p. 284.

[22] Symonds, *Memoirs*, p. 62.   [23] Ellis, *Studies in the Psychology of Sex: Man*, pp. 75, 89.

[24] Symonds, *Memoirs*, pp. 209, 210.

imagination as impregnated by notions of Greek love' and the Greek and Latin classics as 'a literature impregnated with paiderastia'.[25] In *Studies of the Greek Poets* (1873) he had written 'the literature of the Greeks has for the last three centuries formed the basis of our education; their thoughts and sentiments, enclosed like precious perfumes in sealed vases, spread themselves abroad and steep the soul in honey-sweet aromas'.[26]

Classical Greek poetry typically pictures desirable adolescent males as flowers and blossoms, a form of tribute that in the European lyrical tradition dates principally from the Middle Ages and is more usually associated with women and maidens. In *Studies of the Greek Poets* Symonds himself praises Meleager for his 'Most exquisite' couplets that 'compare the boys of Tyre to a bouquet culled by Love for Aphrodite'.[27] Early on in his courtship of Norman (7 February 1869), agonizing over his feelings for the boy in his diary, he quotes Pindar (Fragment 123. 8), asking 'Why was I born for this—to be perpetually seeking 'τῶν παίδων νεόγυιον ἄνθος' [the fresh flower of boys]?' On 13 February, he sends Norman violets, accompanied by two lines of poetry in Greek that, translated, mean 'The first-fruits of spring have I sent, a most fragrant garland of violets, to you who are even more fragrant than they.'[28] Violets are also associated with Norman in the long diary entry that precedes his departure for university where Symonds laments that 'into Oxford rooms and walks and gardens, he will carry his perfume (as of some white violet) for other men'.[29]

The smell of the body, especially the male body, associated with the scent of flowers and plants is also a striking feature of the verse of the American poet, Walt Whitman, which Symonds deeply admired and had discovered for the first time in 1865.[30] In his later study of Whitman, Symonds would write: 'By subtle associations, he connects the life of nature, in dewy forests and night-winds, in scents of fruits and pungent plants, in crushed herbs, and the rustling of rain-drenched foliage against our faces, with impressions of the sexual imagination.'[31] It is not hard to see that, to Symonds, still coming to terms with his sexual desires, Whitman's belief in the holiness of the heart's affections and the sanctity of the body must have been an immense reassurance. In 'Song of Myself' from *Leaves of Grass* (1855), Whitman had announced:

> I believe in the flesh and the appetites;
> Seeing, hearing, feeling, are miracles, and each part and tag of me is a miracle.

> Divine am I inside and out, and I make holy whatever I touch or am touched from;
> The scent of these armpits is aroma finer than prayer,
> This head is more than churches or bibles or creeds.[32]

---

[25] Symonds, 'A Problem in Greek Ethics', in Ellis and Symonds, *Sexual Inversion*, ed. Crozier, p. 239; 'A Problem in Modern Ethics', in *John Addington Symonds (1840–1893) and Homosexuality*, p. 207.

[26] Symonds, *Studies of the Greek Poets*, 1. 422.   [27] Ibid., 1. 378.

[28] Symonds, *Memoirs*, pp. 196, 197.   [29] Ibid., p. 211.

[30] See Phyllis Grosskurth, *John Addington Symonds: A Biography* (London: Longmans, Green & Co., Ltd, 1964), p. 118.

[31] Symonds, *A Study of Walt Whitman* (London: John C. Nimmo, 1893), p. 63.

[32] Walt Whitman, 'Song of Myself' (*ll.* 522–6), in *Complete Poetry and Collected Prose*, ed. Justin Kaplan (New York: Literary Classics of the United States, 1982), pp. 27–88; 51.

Whitman himself is recorded as having a pleasant personal aroma. In his study of smell, Symonds's friend, Havelock Ellis, observed, 'The agreeable odor of Walt Whitman has been remarked by Kennedy and others', and in his introduction to his own study of Whitman (1893), Symonds noted the comments of those who knew him and interpreted that fragrance as a moral or spiritual emanation, faintly reminiscent of the odour of sanctity:

> Indeed, an exquisite aroma of cleanliness has always been one of the special features of the man; it has always belonged to his clothes, his breath, his whole body, his eating and drinking, his conversation, and no one could know him for an hour without seeing that it penetrated his mind and life.
>
> I marked [...] the simplicity and purity of his dress cheap and plain, but spotless, from snowy falling collar to burnished boot, and exhaling faint fragrance; the whole form surrounded with manliness as with a nimbus, and breathing, in its perfect health and vigour, the august charm of the strong.[33]

Symonds was fascinated by the homoerotic poems Whitman included in his 'Calamus' sequence in the third edition of *Leaves of Grass* (1860). *Calamus acorus*, known as 'sweet flag' or 'calamus', often incorrectly identified as a rush or sedge, is a wetland plant with long, thin, scented spiky leaves and a scented rhizome. The leaves, which release their perfume when bruised, have for this reason often been used for strewing, and essential oil from the plant is used in perfumery. In 'Scented Herbage of my Breast', the prefatory poem of 'Calamus', Whitman imagines his lyrical sentiments as 'slender leaves! O blossoms of my blood' that will grow out of his heart into the world to infuse it with his message long after he himself is dead. That message can be understood to be an affirmation of homoerotic comradeship and affection legible to the cognoscenti: 'O I do not know whether many, passing by, will discover you, or inhale your faint odor—but I believe a few will.'[34] Symonds enthusiastically did inhale that 'faint odor', commenting in his monograph on Whitman:

> The first thing that strikes us is the mystic emblem he has chosen for masculine love. That is the water-plant, or scented rush, called 'Calamus,' which springs in wild places, 'in paths untrodden, in the growth by margins of pond-waters.' He has chosen these 'emblematic and capricious blades' because of their shyness, their aromatic perfume, their aloofness from the patent life of the world. He calls them 'sweet leaves, pink-tinged roots, timid leaves,' 'scented herbage of my breast.'[35]

Writing his first fan letter to Whitman on 7 October 1871, Symonds sent him one of his own poems, 'Love and Death: A Symphony', remarking that 'it is of course

---

[33] Ellis, *Studies in the Psychology of Sex: Man*, p. 62. Anonymized sources cited by Symonds in his Introduction to *A Study of Walt Whitman*, pp. xvii, xx.

[34] Walt Whitman, 'Scented Herbage of my Breast', in *Complete Poetry and Collected Prose*, p. 269.

[35] Symonds, *A Study of Walt Whitman*, p. 77. This passage also occurs in the earlier 'A Problem in Modern Ethics' (1891), in a warm appreciation of the treatment of male comradeship in Whitman's *Leaves of Grass*. See *John Addington Symonds (1840–1893) and Homosexuality*, pp. 184–202; 197–8.

implicit already in your Calamus, especially in "Scented herbage of my breast"' (*LJAS*, 2. 167).[36] Perhaps unsurprisingly, in his *Studies of the Greek Poets*, Symonds also claimed that 'Walt Whitman is more truly Greek than any other man of modern times', making his meaning more explicit in later remarks such as 'the celebration of comradeship by Walt Whitman in *Calamus* [...] rings curiously like the Doric celebration of παιδεραστία'.[37]

In view of his preference for natural body odours, it seems very unlikely that Symonds wore perfume himself. His case study proclaims him 'never feminine in dress or habit', and he seems to have been uneasy about more flamboyant, effeminate styles of homosexual self-presentation.[38] In the essay on 'Soldier Love' he contributed to the German edition of *Sexual Inversion* he refers with some horror to 'the inexplicable craving of womanish and enfeebled natures, who, insofar as they are able, ape and parade the characteristics and habits of women'.[39] Although his poor health prevented him from vigorous physical pursuits, he identified as a virile man—'only non-masculine in his indifference to sport'—who was 'a great smoker, and has at times drunk much'.[40] He was attracted to robust young men of a lower rank, most often soldiers, sailors, and peasants; in his annual trips to Venice from his Swiss home in Davos, he specifically sought out working-class men like gondoliers and porters. In 'Soldier Love', he quotes two of his own translations of epigrams from the Greek Anthology that celebrate 'the love of enthusiastic natures for real men'. The first of these praises:

> a lad whose face and hand
> Are rough with dust or circus sand;
> Whose ruddy flesh exhales the scent
> Of health without embellishment
> Sweet to my taste is such a youth
> Whose charm has all the charms of truth.
> Leave paints and perfumes, rouge and curls
> To lazy, lewd Corinthian girls.

The second eulogizes Euphorion, the winner of a boxing-match, whose bruised face is kissed passionately by his lover: 'More fragrant than frankincense, I swear | Was the fierce chrism of blood that thence did ooze.'[41]

---

[36] 'Love and Death: A Symphony' was published in Symonds's *Many Moods: A Volume of Verse* (London: Smith, Elder & Co., 1878), pp. 159–69.

[37] Symonds, *Studies of the Greek Poets*, 1. 422. The comment about Whitman occurs in the privately printed version of 'A Problem in Greek Ethics' (1883), see *John Addington Symonds (1840–1893) and Homosexuality*, pp. 39–122; 115. Symonds deleted the section in which this comment appears when the essay was subsequently published in a revised form in 1897 along with *Sexual Inversion*. See Ellis and Symonds, *Sexual Inversion*, ed. Crozier, pp. 227–95.

[38] Ellis, Case XVII, in Ellis and Symonds, *Sexual Inversion*, ed. Crozier, p. 146.

[39] Symonds, *Soldier Love*, p. 15.

[40] Ellis, Case XVII, in Ellis and Symonds, *Sexual Inversion*, ed. Crozier, p. 146.

[41] Symonds, 'Soldier Love', p. 15. These epigrams are also cited in reverse order in 'A Problem in Greek Ethics', published with *Sexual Inversion* (1897). See Ellis and Symonds, *Sexual Inversion*,

This firm preference for male body scents over the artifice of perfume is a hallmark of the 'manly man' who loves other men, as distinct from the effeminate gay man, a type from which Symonds was anxious to dissociate himself.[42] In 'A Problem in Modern Ethics' he is keen to disabuse his readers of:

> [T]he common belief that all subjects of inverted instincts carry their lusts written in their faces; that they are pale, languid, scented, effeminate, painted, timid, oblique in expression. [...] A certain class of such people are undoubtedly feminine [...] The majority differ in no detail of their outward appearance, their physique, or their dress from normal men.[43]

In 'A Problem in Greek Ethics', he writes concerning the homoerotic verse of the Greek Anthology, 'Μαλακία [effeminacy] is the real condemnation of this poetry, rather than brutality or coarseness.'[44] Although in this essay he traces the degeneration of Greek *paiderastia* as it moved away from the ideal of martial manly comradeship towards a more debased form of sensual attraction, he comments 'the fact remains that, till the last, Greek paiderastia among *the better sort of men* (the καλοκαγαθοί) implied no effeminacy'.[45] Nonetheless, temptations might lead impressionable Greek youths into more decadent and effeminate behaviour, and he stipulates that 'The shops of the barbers, surgeons, perfumers, and flower-sellers had an evil notoriety, and lads who frequented these resorts rendered themselves base.'[46] Symonds also read the Ἔρωτες [Loves], a dialogue on 'erotic passion' attributed to Lucian that compared the love of women and the love of boys, as a cynical and debased treatment of the subject, remarking disapprovingly: 'We have exchanged the company of Plato, Xenophon, or Æschines for that of a Juvenalian *Græculus*, a delicate æsthetic voluptuary. Every epithet smells of musk and every phrase is a provocative.'[47]

Symonds's allusion to musk, that penetrating aromatic animalic substance used in perfumery and frequently associated with sensuality, puts him in the company of those conservative Victorians who found its scent unseemly and objectionable. The term 'æsthetic voluptuary' suggests that he is also drawing an unfavourable comparison with the literary aestheticism of his own day and its emphasis on rarefied pleasures and sensations. (He would use another animalic allusion with a similar application when he complained that Pater's refined aesthetic style had 'a peculiarly disagreeable effect upon my nerves—like the presence of a civet cat'

---

ed. Crozier, p. 262. In the earlier 1883 version, Symonds does not supply translations of these epigrams but, in a footnote (*John Addington Symonds (1840–1893) and Homosexuality*, p. 79), refers to their sources as nos 123 and 192 in the *Mousa Paidikē*, the twelfth book of the Greek Anthology.

[42] Symonds's preference for straightforward manly types seems to have evolved, as earlier he was capable of forming a sudden crush on a Mr Grey, encountered at Falmouth in December 1872, whom he described as 'like a woman dressed in male clothes on the stage' and 'this man-woman, so strong & sweet & magnetic' (*LJAS* 2. 251–2).

[43] Symonds, 'A Problem in Modern Ethics', p. 134.

[44] Symonds, 'A Problem in Greek Ethics', in Ellis and Symonds, *Sexual Inversion*, ed. Crozier, p. 282.

[45] Ibid., p. 262.   [46] Ibid., p. 268.

[47] Ibid., p. 280. *Græculus* is a dismissive term used by the Roman writer Juvenal in his third Satire (3. 77–8), meaning 'little Greek' or 'Greekling': 'The hungry little Greek knows all.'

(*LJAS* 3. 43; 5 April 1885).) Moreover, the words 'scented' and 'perfumed' would appear as pejorative terms in his response to the 1890 *Lippincott's Magazine* version of *Dorian Gray* sent him by the author. Pronouncing Wilde's 'novelette' 'unwholesome in tone, but artistically and psychologically interesting', he nonetheless declared to Horatio Brown, 'I resent the unhealthy, scented, mystic, congested touch which a man of this sort has on moral problems.' In a second letter written the same day to Edmund Gosse, he professed his dislike of 'the morbid & perfumed manner of treating such psychological subjects' (*LJAS* 3. 477, 478; 22 July 1890). Here Symonds resists a style of homosexuality that he finds decadent and unmanly in contrast to his own presentation of a virile sexual exchange between men.

Symonds's antipathy to scented effeminacy and his preference for the perfume of manly flesh might suggest that he was not particularly sensitive to fragrance but nothing could be further from the truth. The following section demonstrates his olfactory acuity and his lifelong pleasure and interest in natural scent, a pleasure nurtured by his extensive travels in continental Europe. Having established his particular tastes, their expression in his writing, and the importance of fragrance to him, the subsequent section 'Symonds's "scented herbage" and the Perfume of the Flesh' circles back to the question of bodies and their odours to show how his scent preferences informed his sexual pleasure.

Symonds as Cosmopolitan *Flaireur*

Although he may have shunned manufactured perfume, Symonds portrayed himself as highly responsive to the scents of nature, in this perhaps emulating the olfactory sensitivity of his idol Walt Whitman. Regarding Whitman's unusually developed sense of smell, Norman Foerster, an early twentieth-century critic, writes:

> He could detect fragrance in wellnigh everything. [...] He discerned countless odors: those of grass, moist air, milk, willows, matted leaves, swamps, green leaves and dry leaves, hair, birch-barks, sea-rocks, shore mud. 'There is a scent to everything', he wrote in his diary, 'even the snow, if you can detect it—no two places, hardly any two hours, anywhere exactly alike. How different the odor of noon from midnight, or winter from summer, or a windy spell from a still one.' Keenness of scent can hardly go farther, in man at least.[48]

Symonds displays his own acute sensitivity to natural fragrance in a letter of 1884 to the artist and garden writer Eleanor Vere Boyle (1825–1916), where he responds to a passage in her recently published book *Days and Hours in a Garden* (1884). Boyle had suggested 'It is a favourite idea, too obscure to be a doctrine or even a theory, that the sweet smells of flowers and aromatic leaves and all kinds of green things, have a certain virtue for different conditions of health.' And she goes on to propose aromatherapeutic properties for the scents of plants as they are encoun-tered in their garden habitat, including the following among her examples: 'To smell wild Thyme, will renew the spirits and vital energy in long walks under an

---

[48] Norman Foerster, 'Whitman as a Poet of Nature', *PMLA* 31.4 (1916), 736–58; 755.

August sun. The pure, almost pungent scent of Tea Rose Maréchal Niel, is sometimes invigorating in any lowness of mind or body. Sweet Briar promotes cheerfulness.' But she also observes: 'The subject is full of indistinctness, since that which is life to one may be death to many. I have known an instance of even white Sweet Peas and white Pink being unendurable.'[49]

Being consumptive and thus sensitive to temperature, climate, and atmosphere, Symonds evidently found this discussion of 'healthful Flower-scents' relevant to his own condition.[50] To Boyle he wrote:

> The passage on scents struck me much. I am very much affected by flower scents. Mignonette makes me positively ill with a peculiar contraction of the internal muscles. The scent wh[ich] I find most 'cordial' is that of the Trifolium Alpinum [Alpine clover]. I revel in that, especially when it has dried upon a sunny slope. I can smell the perfume of dried wild strawberry leaves, & seek places often here where it is exhaled under pines.   (*LJAS* 2. 957; 31 October 1884)

Forced to live in an alpine environment for the sake of his health, Symonds came to cherish the salutary scents of its flora. Indeed, he even claimed that the very memory of such scents could be restorative: 'When our life is most commonplace, when we are ill or weary in city streets, we can remember the clouds upon the mountains we have seen, the sound of innumerable waterfalls, and the scent of countless flowers.'[51] However, his letter is more than just the elaboration of natural scents he found injurious or beneficial, for his use of the word 'cordial' alludes to Francis Bacon's famous essay 'Of Gardens' and he explicitly mentions that elusive odour mentioned there and prized as a badge of honour by the English *olfactif*— 'strawberry-leaves dying, which [yield] a most excellent cordial smell'.[52] One of the interesting aspects of Symonds's statement is the way that his preferred 'cordial' scents—Alpine clover and dried strawberry leaves, plants found in his Swiss mountain home—are tangled up with literary allusion, a characteristic that we will see elsewhere in his travel writing where description of natural perfume can be understood to be permeated by the scents of other literary texts. Moreover, Symonds's letter, far from being a simple statement of physical susceptibilities, clearly manifests the credentials of the aesthete. Indeed, the sentiment of the entire passage sounds uncharacteristic of the hearty manly-man persona that Symonds liked (latterly) to adopt and more like an indication of the aesthete's exquisitely nuanced sensibility.

That aesthetic self, an integral part of Symonds's identity, emerges in the specific guise of the cosmopolitan *flaireur*, the sophisticated citizen of the world who relishes the fragrance of travel. It is immediately apparent in Symonds's sole meeting with the older Swinburne at a dinner party of Benjamin Jowett's in October 1872, in which an aesthetic cosmopolitan love of scent swiftly secures mutual recognition and bonding. Robert Raper, having introduced the two at Symonds's request,

---

[49] Boyle, *Days and Hours in a Garden*, pp. 107, 108.   [50] Ibid., p. 109.
[51] Symonds, 'The Love of the Alps', in *Sketches in Italy and Greece* (London: Smith, Elder, & Co., 1874), p. 303.
[52] See my discussion of Bacon's 'Of Gardens' in Chapter 1. Boyle does not refer explicitly to this 'cordial smell'.

reported to Edmund Gosse: 'They talked across me, and at once plunged into an animated conversation concerning the prevailing perfumes of flowers in various pleasure resorts in Italy.'[53] It is probable that in what Raper calls 'Their enthusiasm for these fascinating fragrances' the pair also discussed their shared admiration for Whitman. In a poem in his recently published *Songs before Sunrise* (1871), Swinburne had petitioned Whitman to 'Send us a song [...] | Sweet-smelling of pine-leaves and grasses', and Symonds mentions Whitman in a letter he sent Swinburne along with some of his own poems shortly after this meeting (*LJAS* 2. 249–50; 8 December 1872).[54]

Symonds and his wife, Catherine, were passionately fond of flowers—he described them both as 'flower lovers' in his letter to Eleanor Vere Boyle. Catherine Symonds created an 'enchanted garden' around Am Hof, their house at Davos, and although the intense winter cold meant that blooms flourished outside only in the warmer months, the house itself brimmed with plants and imported cut flowers.[55] 'Our rooms are filled now with roses and tuberoses from Cannes, violets and chrysanthemums from Sidbury', writes Symonds on 31 December 1882 (*LJAS* 2. 796). As this shows, his tastes include flowers other than those more generally admired for their intoxicating fragrance. An early sonnet praising chrysanthemums as 'Purer of scent than honeyed heliotrope' shows affection for a flower whose scent puts it among those classed as 'nose-twisters' by Louise Beebe Wilder, a group that takes its name from the Latin words that give us 'nasturtium' (*nasus*, 'nose' and *tortus*, 'twisted') and includes 'Marigold, Calendula, Tansy and others of a like bitter pungence'.[56] These flowers retained their charms for Symonds: in a letter of 18 November 1881 he declares himself to be 'writing in a hurly-burly of chrysanthemums', and remarks 'These flowers have always had for me a most peculiar attraction, coming as they do in the deadest season of the year—so pure themselves, so pungent without any perfume, so coloured, and so exquisite in form' (*LJAS* 2. 709). By 'perfume', Symonds here seems to mean 'sweet fragrance'.

[53] Robert Raper, letter of July 1915 to Edmund Gosse, cited in Walter Pater, *GL*, p. 145. Phyllis Grosskurth in 'Swinburne and Symonds: An Uneasy Literary Relationship', *Review of English Studies* 14.55 (1963), 257–68, not unreasonably assumes that Swinburne and Symonds must have met when they were both undergraduates at Balliol. However, Raper explicitly states that Symonds asked him to introduce him to Swinburne 'whom he had never met'. Although the two writers corresponded after this meeting, they do not appear to have met again. Symonds does not mention flower fragrance in his account of the meeting to Henry Sidgwick where he nonetheless says he 'talked to Swinburne the whole evening' (*LJAS* 2. 246; 25 October 1872).

[54] 'To Walt Whitman in America', in *Poems* 2. 120. Earlier, comparing Whitman with Blake, Swinburne had written 'his work is generally more frank and fresh, smelling of sweeter air' (*William Blake*, p. 303). Swinburne's initial admiration for Whitman would wane, eventually resulting in the aggressive article 'Whitmania', published in the *Fortnightly Review* in 1887, which elicited a somewhat lukewarm defence from Symonds, anxious not to offend Swinburne. See Grosskurth, 'Swinburne and Symonds', pp. 262–4.

[55] Margaret Symonds (Mrs W. V. Vaughan), *Out of the Past, with an Account of Janet Catherine Symonds by Mrs Walter Leaf* (London: John Murray, 1925), p. 302.

[56] Symonds, 'To Chrysanthemums', in 'Juvenilia', in *Vagabunduli Libellus* (London: Kegan Paul, Trench, & Co., 1884), p. 149; Louise Beebe Wilder, *The Fragrant Path: A Book about Sweet Scented Flowers and Leaves* (New York: Macmillan Co., 1931), p. 101. Acknowledging that 'persons of hyper-sensitive nasal organs may turn from' such plants, Wilder admits 'personally I am very fond of the Nose-twisters' (p. 101).

Margaret Symonds wrote of her parents that 'They both of them possessed an almost abnormal love for natural things; chiefly for flowers, and this they passed on to us.'[57] Catherine Symonds was known to declare that she preferred flowers to people, while her husband informed the widow of the poet Arthur Hugh Clough: 'Flowers *are* next to persons in the way they excite our love, attract us, repel us at times, and not unfrequently bore: I mean that different flowers, like different people, have these various effects' (*LJAS* 1. 801; 31 March 1868).[58] Yet if he saw flowers as 'next to persons', he also viewed them, or the landscapes that nurtured them, as 'poems', inseparable from the literary texts and contexts of the past that enriched their cultural meaning and history. He wrote to Edmund Gosse from Monte Generoso overlooking the Lombard plains:

> The meadows are one drift of white lilies & narcissus & asphodel, wanting only Proserpine or the figure of Dante's Matilda to make them poems. Indeed, they are poems with that unchanging background of history & romance & art and human life—the plain, against whose violet breadth they quiver to the little winds.
>
> (*LJAS* 2. 551; 9 June 1878)[59]

Symonds's letters, poems, and travel essays are full of references to flowers, trees, and plants. In the essays in particular, the litanies of flowers, often rich in association, are an integral part of the scenic descriptions that regularly punctuate the text. Not all of Symonds's readers appreciated this aspect of his writing. His daughter Margaret Symonds writes:

> Many of the reviewers of my Father's books [...] disliked descriptions of flowers: 'We cannot *bear* the mesembrianthemum!' one of them once exclaimed (in the *Athenæum*, I think), with a wail of heart-wrung bitterness; and no one was fonder than quoting this cry of distress than my Father himself.[60]

The querulous reviewer is actually Edmund Gosse, who though discussing the second volume (1876) of *Studies of the Greek Poets*, apparently alludes to 'Syracuse and Girgenti' in *Sketches in Italy and Greece* (1874), where Symonds writes 'There is even one spot planted with magenta-coloured mesembrianthemums of dazzling brightness; and the air is loaded with the drowsy perfume of lemon-blossoms.'[61] This pairing of scent and colour is characteristic of Symonds's descriptive style; a little later in the same essay the two sensations even seem to combine: 'As the sunlight faded, Venus shone forth in a luminous sky, and the deep yellows and

---

[57] Symonds, *Out of the Past*, p. 165.

[58] Catherine Symonds, cited by Mrs Walter Leaf, in Symonds, *Out of the Past*, p. 299.

[59] As was his habit, Symonds incorporated a very similar passage into his essay 'Lombard Vignettes', first published in the *Cornhill Magazine*, that same June in 1878, and then in his *Sketches and Studies in Italy* (London: Smith, Elder, & Co., 1879), p. 373.

[60] Symonds, *Out of the Past*, p. 131.

[61] Many thanks to Amber Regis for identifying Edmund Gosse as the reviewer. Gosse reviews volume 2 of *Studies of the Greek Poets* (1876), not in the *Athenæum*, but in the *Examiner* (24 June 1876), p. 713. The word 'mesembrianthemum' (or 'mesembryanthemum') does not occur in either the 1873 or 1876 volumes of *Greek Poets*, but is an allusion to what Gosse calls the 'over-sweet luxuriance of [Symonds's] Italian volumes'. See Symonds, 'Syracuse and Girgenti', in *Sketches in Italy and Greece*, p. 185.

purples overhead seemed to mingle with the heavy scent of orange-flowers from scarcely visible groves by the roadside.'[62]

Although Symonds claimed to reject the rich and intricate patterning of aesthetic and decadent texts, preferring a 'fresh & unaffected style' to 'Pater's or Swinburne's affectations' (*LJAS* 2. 832; 15 July 1883), it seems incontrovertible that he adapted the impressionistic prose of these writers to his own devices. Symonds's early biographer, Van Wyck Brooks, comments 'No one, I daresay, could have been so acutely annoyed by Pater's style who was not himself on the perilous edge of preciosity.'[63] Aesthetic and decadent literary texts often feature sonorous lists that suggestively heap up the names and attributes of beautiful and exotic objects to transport, dazzle, and ravish the sympathetic reader's imagination. Symonds may have recoiled from the close, elaborate, decadent interiors of a novel like *Dorian Gray*, but his travel essays use natural settings to showcase a cosmopolitan aestheticism through carefully constructed impressionistic catalogues of plants and flowers that, as mentioned, typically bring floral scent and colour into striking atmospheric combinations, often with sound effects adding to the general ambience. The words 'mingle' or 'mingled' frequently occur when detailing these different sense impressions, for in Symonds's rich sensorium one sensation is enhanced or helped out—actually or in fancy—by others.

Such passages undoubtedly rely on the vivid personal evocation of places visited, but they also have more than a touch of artifice, even a studiedly literary flavour that recalls other writers. Consider the following lush description taken from 'The Cornice', the opening essay of *Sketches in Italy and Greece* (1874), which depicts the area around Menton, the French Riviera town on the Franco-Italian border:

> We do not often scale these altitudes, but keep along the terraced glades by the side of olive-shaded streams. The violets, instead of peeping shyly from hedgerows, fall in ripples and cascades over mossy walls among maidenhair and spleenworts. They are very sweet, and the sound of trickling water seems to mingle with their fragrance in a most delicious harmony. Sound, smell, and hue make up one chord, the sense of which is pure and perfect peace. The country-people are kind, letting us pass everywhere, so that we make our way along their aqueducts and through their gardens, under laden lemon-boughs, the pale fruit dangling at our ears, and swinging showers of scented dew upon us as we pass. [...] The narcissus sends its arrowy fragrance through the air, while, far and wide, red anemones burn like fire, with interchange of blue and lilac buds, white arums, orchises, and pink gladiolus. Wandering there, and seeing the pale flowers, stars white and pink and odorous, we dream of Olivet, or the grave Garden of the Agony, and the trees seem always whispering of sacred things.

If Symonds's synaesthetic treatment of scent seems to echo Shelley's melodious fragrant violets, this is no coincidence. He knew Shelley's poetry intimately from boyhood and would contribute the volume on him (1878) to Macmillan's English

---

[62] Symonds, 'Syracuse and Girgenti', in *Sketches in Italy and Greece*, p. 188.
[63] Van Wyck Brooks, *John Addington Symonds: A Biographical Study* (London: Grant Richards, 1914), pp. 91–2.

Men of Letters Series.[64] In this passage he borrows from 'Epipsychidion' the unusual epithet 'arrowy', used by Shelley for violet fragrance but here deployed to describe the scent of the narcissus. Small wonder then, that, concluding this passage, he acknowledges: 'This shore would stand for Shelley's "Island of Epipsychidion".'[65] Scent and poetry, being expressive exhalations, are for Symonds inextricably connected and, as we saw in Chapter 2, he joins them in a poem of 1883 that commemorates Shelley and Keats: 'Not all the purple pomp of ancient kings | Consuls acclaimed by hosts omnipotent | [...] Are worth one poet's song, one violet's scent.'[66]

In Symonds's essays of travel, natural scent can be understood as the essence of a place—perhaps, as in Shelley's 'Sensitive-Plant', an inaudible perfumed song—breathed out by native plants to form an atmosphere, which it is the poet or writer's job to capture in words. In warm exotic climes a favourite and characteristic fragrance is the heavy scent of lemon and orange blossom: 'The air swoons with the scent of lemon-groves' ('The Cornice'); 'the air is loaded with the drowsy perfume of lemon-blossoms' ('Syracuse and Girgenti'); 'The roads are sweet with scent of acacia and orange flowers' ('Amalfi, Pæstum, Capri').[67] This perfumed essence possibly contains notes of a specifically Shelleyan song, indeed another reminiscence of 'Epipsychidion': 'The light clear element which the isle wears | Is heavy with the scent of lemon-flowers' (*SPP*, pp. 384–5). However, atmospheric perfume is often a bouquet compounded of many mingled odours, as in the following passage that describes the great pine forest near Ravenna:

> The air is sweet with aromatic scents: the resin of the pine and juniper, the mayflowers and acacia-blossoms, the violets that spring by thousands in the moss, the wild roses and faint honeysuckles which throw fragrant arms from bough to bough of ash or maple, join to make one most delicious perfume.[68]

Describing the native brushwood (*macchia* in Italian, *maquis* in French) of Ajaccio on Corsica, Symonds explains how its blossoming thickets of box, ilex, lentisk, arbutus, and laurustinus produce another characteristic bouquet:

> It is, indeed, the native growth of the island; for wherever a piece of ground is left untilled, the macchi [*sic*] grow up, and the scent of their multitudinous aromatic blossoms is so

[64] Symonds's father had been 'one of the first to admire Shelley', and Wyck Brooks comments of Symonds that 'Shelley had been from earliest childhood one of the men to whose writing he had submitted himself with "slow, dumb, inhibition"' (*John Addington Symonds*, pp. 7, 119). See also J. A. Symonds, *Shelley* (1878) , which contains an extensive quotation from the relevant section of 'Epipsychidion' on pp. 139–41. Symonds's *Shelley* is rather pedestrian and does not rank among his best works, but 'Epipsychidion' clearly had a powerful effect on him: 'the description of this visionary isle, and of the life to be led there [...] is the most beautiful that has been written this century in the rhymed heroic metre' (p. 139).

[65] Symonds, 'The Cornice', in *Sketches in Italy and Greece*, pp. 4–5, 5–6. The essay was originally published as 'On the Cornice' in the *Cornhill Magazine* in November 1866. The Cornice or *La Grande Corniche* is a scenic road on a ledge running east from Nice to Menton.

[66] 'A View of Rome with Violets in the Foreground', p. 269.

[67] Symonds, *Sketches in Italy and Greece*, pp. 10, 185; *Sketches and Studies in Italy*, p. 26.

[68] Symonds, 'Ravenna', in *Sketches in Italy and Greece*, p. 256. First published as 'Ravenna and the Pine Forest' in the *Cornhill Magazine*, March 1867.

strong that it may be smelt miles out at sea. Napoleon, at St Helena, referred to this fragrance when he said that he should know Corsica blindfold by the smell of its soil.[69]

Underlying all such descriptions of atmospheric bouquets is the influential memory of Symonds's private Eden, the garden of Clifton Hill House, his beloved family home at Bristol, which he was forced to give up in 1880 when he had to move to Davos for the sake of his health. His first encounter with the garden as a boy in the summer of 1851 left a lasting impression, which he recalled as an adolescent in a letter of 15 May 1857 (*LJAS* 1. 108), and much later in his *Memoirs*, begun in 1889. Recollecting in those *Memoirs* that early encounter pervaded by the 'mingled perfume of musk and rose', Symonds explains how the scent of musk still remains a potent mnemonic trigger for him (the musk of the Clifton garden being the floral variety produced by mallow, mimulus, and the musk rose to attract pollinating insects):

On that eventful morning, the air hung heavy with a scent of hidden musk. The broad flowerbeds upon the terrace were a tangle of old fashioned herbs in bloom—mulberry-coloured scabious, love-in-idleness, love-in-a-mist, love-lies-a-bleeding, corncockles, devil-in-the-bush, hollyhocks, carnations, creeping-jenny, damask and cabbage and York-and-Lancaster roses. The mingled perfume of musk and rose pervades my memory when I think of that day; and when I come by accident upon the scent of musk in distant places, I am transported to the fairyland of boyhood. The throat-notes of thrush and blackbird, the music of tinkling fountains, the drowsy rhythm of hammers struck on timber in the city dockyards, blend in my recollection with pure strong slumberous summer sunlight and rich odours.[70]

Symonds's evocation of the 'mingled perfume of musk and rose' is characteristic-ally accompanied by quasi-synaesthetic mingled impressions of light and sound. Synaesthesia, even of the imagined associative kind, may recapture a time in infancy, possibly even early childhood, when the senses and the information they relayed were less distinct; remnants or submerged memories of this 'mingling' may linger into childhood and even adulthood where they might be reactivated.[71]

---

[69] Symonds, 'Ajaccio', in *Sketches in Italy and Greece*, p. 25. First published in the *Cornhill Magazine*, October 1868. Lentisk (*Pistacia lentiscus*) is an evergreen shrub or small tree cultivated for its aromatic resin known as 'mastic', which is used as a flavouring, in medicine, and in perfumery. Mastic is an important note in the modern perfume Corsica Furiosa by Marc-Antoine Corticchiato for Parfum d'Empire (2014).

[70] Symonds, *Memoirs*, p. 70. Although there can be no question of influence, Symonds's description resembles the passage from Pater's 'Emerald Uthwart' with its floral musk and synaesthesia, cited in Chapter 3. Pater's story was first published in *The New Review* in 1892. Symonds's passage also occurs in the excerpt provided in *John Addington Symonds: A Biography*, compiled from his Papers and Correspondence by Horatio Brown, 2nd edn (London: Smith, Elder, & Co., 1908), p. 28. I have replaced Grosskurth's unlikely 'scabrius' with 'scabious' (as in Brown's text).

[71] John Harrison writes concerning what is known as 'the neonatal synaesthesia hypothesis': 'One possibility then is that we all of us have a *forme fruste* of synaesthesia and are not qualitatively different from [genuine] synaesthetes but merely qualitatively so.' See his *Synaesthesia: The Strangest Thing* (Oxford: Oxford University Press, 2001), pp. 220 and 19. Shelley, of course, posits an originary 'antenatal' synaesthesia.

Shelley himself in 'Epipsychidion' hints that the intense synaesthetic response to the beauty of the paradisal isle springs from an earlier perceptive self buried within:

> And every motion, odour, beam, and tone,
> With that deep music is in unison:
> Which is a soul within the soul—they seem
> Like echoes of an antenatal dream.　　(*SPP*, p. 385)

Symonds's mingling of sense impressions may tap into a remembered or imagined originary synaesthesia, though it could also be another reminiscence of Shelley's synaesthesia. Either way it certainly seems to summon up the blissful state of contemplative harmony that Shelley alludes to in 'Epipsychidion'. We see this in the close of Symonds's essay on 'Perugia', where he imagines himself:

> [I]n the Close of Salisbury on a perfumed summer afternoon. The drowsy scent of lime-flowers and mignonette, the cawing of elm-cradled rooks, the hum of bees above, the velvet touch of smooth-shorn grass, and the breathless shadow of motionless green boughs made up one potent and absorbing mood of the charmed senses.[72]

In a later essay, 'Lombard Vignettes' (1878), he pictures himself on a mountain overlooking the Lombard plains and enjoying the meditative silence of the dusk, adding:

> Yet I must rise and go—passing through meadows, where white lilies sleep in silvery drifts, and asphodel is pale with spires of faintest rose, and narcissus dreams of his own beauty, loading the air with fragrance sweet as some love-music of Mozart.[73]

In such descriptions Symonds may be reaching back not only to childhood Eden but to a fantasized original wellspring of creativity, a synaesthetic Hellenic island paradise, made after the likeness of Shelley's ' "Island of Epipsychidion" ', where place and poetry were in perfect harmony, the one breathing into the other. Such a place is Lesbos, home to Sappho and her fellow lyric poets. Intriguingly Symonds, allowing the 'Lesbian ladies' a license that he would be reluctant to concede to Greek men, here portrays them uncritically as aesthetic voluptuaries, revelling in the mingled sensory pleasures of their 'luxurious land':

> Unrestrained by public opinion, and passionate for the beautiful, they cultivated their senses and emotions, and developed their wildest passions. All the luxuries and elegances of life which that climate and the rich valleys of Lesbos could afford, were at their disposal; exquisite gardens, in which the rose and hyacinth spread perfume; river-beds ablaze with the oleander and wild pomegranate; olive-groves and fountains, where the cyclamen and violet flowered with feathery maiden-hair; pine-tree-shadowed coves, where they might bathe in the calm of a tideless sea; fruits such as only the southern sun and sea-wind can mature; marble cliffs, starred with jonquil and anemone in spring, aromatic with myrtle and lentisk and samphire and wild rosemary through

---

[72] Symonds, 'Perugia', in *Sketches in Italy and Greece*, p. 93. The essay was inspired by a journey undertaken in 1873–4, just before *Sketches* was published in 1874, and appears in that volume for the first time.

[73] Symonds, 'On a Mountain' from 'Lombard Vignettes', in *Sketches and Studies in Italy*, p. 373.

all the months; nightingales that sang in May; temples dim with dusky gold and bright with ivory; statues and frescoes of heroic forms. In such scenes as these the Lesbian poets lived, and thought of Love. When we read their poems, we seem to have the perfumes, colours, sounds, and lights of that luxurious land distilled in verse.[74]

Evidently perfume was among 'the luxuries and elegances' provided by Lesbos— not just the scent of its 'exquisite gardens' but also the liquid fragrance made from flowers and other natural ingredients. Sappho herself writes of a lover anointing herself with 'perfumed oil' in a fragment that, as Michael Shanks points out, makes associations between 'flowers, love lyric and perfume' (Fragment 94).[75] Symonds was tentative about associating ancient Greek men with actual perfume—a boy might remind one of flowers but should smell not of artificial perfume but his own sweat; however, he apparently had no such anxiety with respect to the Lesbian women who freely enjoy fragrance which, mingled with other sensory influences, is 'distilled' into their verse. That distillate is best found in Sappho herself, history's most famous women poet, not only the genius loci of the island but the purveyor of the very essence of lyricism: 'Of all the poets of the world, of all the illustrious artists of all literatures, Sappho is the one whose every word has a peculiar and unmistakable perfume, a seal of absolute perfection and inimitable grace.'[76] In Symonds's imaginative travelogue, Lesbos is, like Shelley's island, an idyllic place of love—here same-sex love—where readers can recover the fragrance of Greek literature, those 'thoughts and sentiments' that 'enclosed like precious perfumes in sealed vases, spread themselves abroad and steep the soul in honey-sweet aromas'.

Symonds's 'scented herbage' and the Perfume of the Flesh

If the Lesbian women were allowed more latitude in using and enjoying perfume, for Symonds, the beautiful male body, ancient or modern, had its own bouquet reminiscent of the scents of nature just as, contrariwise, Whitman associated 'the life of nature [...] in scents of fruits and pungent plants, in crushed herbs [...] with impressions of the sexual imagination'. To discover the savour of that bouquet, we turn again to Symonds's recorded scent preferences, and in doing so find there is one particular fragrance element that is consistently liked from its appearance in childhood through into late adulthood. One of his earliest scent memories derives not from flower fragrance but from aromatic seeds. In his *Memoirs* he recalls the house of his redoubtable grandmother Sykes in Cornwall Crescent, Bristol, where 'the perfume of potpourri in a blue Chinese bowl and of Tonquin beans exhaling

---

[74] Symonds, *Studies of the Greek Poets*, 1. 128–9. Symonds does see Lesbos as ultimately succumbing to decadence and 'corruption' through an overemphasis on 'sensuality' and the 'voluptuous charms of the flesh' (pp. 127–8), but, in the long passage cited, he unequivocally celebrates the 'the flower-time of the Æolians, their brief and brilliant spring' (p. 127). For a discussion of Lesbos and decadence, see Stefano Evangelista, *British Aestheticism and the Greeks* (Basingstoke and New York: Palgrave Macmillan, 2009), pp. 104–5.

[75] Michael Shanks, *Art and the Early Greek State* (Cambridge: Cambridge University Press, 2004), p. 89. See also *If Not, Winter*, p. 187.

[76] Symonds, *Studies of the Greek Poets*, 1. 129–30.

from drawers and workbasket gave distinction to the rooms'.[77] Now more usually called tonka beans, tonquin beans are described by Piesse's *Art of Perfumery* as 'exceedingly fragrant, having an intense odour of newly made hay'. Piesse also specifies that 'They are often, [...] to be seen in hosiers' shops, where they are sold for placing in drawers with linen', a practice apparently adopted by Symonds's grandmother.[78] The beans are the fruit of *Dipteryx odorata*, a flowering tree commonly known as cumaru (*coumarou* in French), native to Central and South America.[79] When dried out, each fruit's wrinkled black casing gives way to reveal a long, almond-shaped, shiny brown bean.

Tonka beans used to be a key material in perfumery, as they possess an extractible crystalline substance known as 'coumarin' that has a sweet vanilla-like and hay-like aroma. Tincture of tonka beans, obtained by infusing the beans in spirit, was a key ingredient in making the agrestic perfumes that were immensely popular in the nineteenth century such as New Mown Hay (Foin Coupé) or Bouquet du Champ (Field Bouquet), of which Piesse writes: 'the great resemblance of which to the odour of the hay-field, renders it a favourite to the lovers of the pastoral'.[80] However, as mentioned in Chapter 1, naturally extracted coumarin is costly and the discovery of synthetic coumarin in 1868 by William Perkin led to the first fragrance containing a synthetic odorant, Houbigant's Fougère Royale (1882). 'Fougère' or 'fern' perfumes are archetypal masculine fragrances that are built on an 'accord' (a specific combination of fragrance notes) that in a classic fougère consists of a lavender top-note with coumarin and oakmoss base notes.

Coumarin is also present in other plants like 'sweet vernal grass' (*Anthoxanthum odoratum*), a common perennial of summer-flowering grasslands and meadows, which is aromatic when dried. Piesse states that 'The odour of hay is due to the vernal grass it contains', although hay may be composed of many cut and dried grasses, herbs, and wildflowers.[81] Woodruff (*Galium odoratum*), a wild plant that grows in woodland or damp shady spots and was mentioned by Margaret Symonds as particularly liked by her father, is another herbaceous plant that, when dried, owes its strong sweet smell to coumarin.[82] Coumarin is sometimes described as having a tobacco-like smell and indeed was often added to tobacco products. Symonds was a heavy smoker who seems to have been pleased by coumaric fragrances such as tonka beans and hay, writing nostalgically to Edmund Gosse from Davos on 27 July 1878 that 'no poetry is sweeter than an English summer smothered deep in flowers & hay & heavy lime-laden air' (*LJAS* 2. 565).

Yet hay was no less an important element in Alpine life. As Symonds continues in his letter to Gosse: 'We have hay making all over our valley today.' His biographer Phyllis Grosskurth writes that, when invited by his Davos neighbours, 'he rolled

---

[77] Symonds, *Memoirs*, pp. 42–3.

[78] Piesse, *Art of Perfumery* (1855), p. 78. The subsequent comment is taken from the extended entry in the 4th edn (1879), p. 210.

[79] The word *coumarou* can also signify the beans themselves.

[80] Piesse, *Art of Perfumery* (1855), p. 80.

[81] Piesse, *Art of Perfumery*, 3rd edn (1862), p. 210.   [82] Symonds, *Out of the Past*, p. 286.

Figure 4.1 Photograph of John Addington Symonds with hay-making Swiss peasants at Davos (courtesy of Bristol Special Collections)

up his sleeves and helped them with the haymaking', and a photograph shows him lying beside a small pile of hay, with Swiss peasants and children standing around him (Figure 4.1). The illustrated second edition of the collection *Our Life in the Swiss Highlands* (1907) reproduces his pencil sketch of haymaking in the Davos valley (Figure 4.2).[83] In her memoir of her father, Margaret Symonds explains how the house constructed for the Symonds family at Davos and completed in 1882

> was called Am Hof because it was built in a big meadow of that name. It was the first house built in that broad hayfield—a pleasant sunny place, full of field flowers which rendered up a splendid crop of hay in summer. In early days all the rare Alpine flowers grew in the meadow.[84]

In 'Hay Hauling on the Alpine Snow', one of the essays she contributed to *Our Life in the Swiss Highlands* (first published in 1892), Margaret Symonds describes the special properties of Alpine hay mown from the higher pastures, which 'has a

---

[83] John Addington Symonds and Margaret Symonds, *Our Life in the Swiss Highlands* (London and Edinburgh: Adam & Charles Black, 1907), p. ix. The first edition (same publisher) was published in 1892 but I use throughout the second edition, which includes Margaret Symonds's Preface written after her father's death. The sketch is titled 'The Davos Valley and Hay-Making in the Summer of 1877', but Symonds was not in Davos in 1877 to see the hay harvest of June–July, so it is more likely to be 1878 or later.

[84] Symonds, *Out of the Past*, p. 189.

Figure 4.2 John Addington Symonds, pencil sketch of Swiss haymaking, in J. A. Symonds and M. Symonds, *Our Life in the Swiss Highlands*, 2nd edn (1907), p. ix. (Photo: Daichi Ishikawa, Author's collection)

peculiar and very refined quality. It is chiefly composed of strong herbs, such as arnica and gentian, and is greatly prized by the peasants.'[85] Such hay would almost certainly contain coumarin-rich Alpine sweet grass (*Hierochloe alpina*) and the Alpine clover that Symonds loved for its 'cordial' scent, which the botanist Somerville Hastings specifies as 'very common in the meadows and pastures in the central Alps'. Calling this plant 'the most beautiful and sweetly scented of all the clover tribe', Hastings remarks of its flowers 'The Alpine breezes are often filled with their delicate fragrance.'[86] In her essay Margaret Symonds explains how Alpine hay is stored in barns high in the mountains till it is needed, when it is raked into bundles and sledged down to the villages below (see Plate 7). She relates her own expedition up to the barns where 'a wealth of withered flowers and grasses lay within in heaps upon the floors. The pent-up scent of all these summer flowers rushed out upon the winter air, and burdened it with aromatic fragrance.'[87]

'"Good hay, sweet hay, hath no fellow"', declares Bottom in Shakespeare's *A Midsummer Night's Dream*, a sentiment quoted by Piesse with regard to the bouquet perfume New Mown Hay. He adds in endorsement 'true the fragrance of hay is one of the most grateful to our senses, and it is natural there should be a demand for a perfume of this odour'.[88] Extracted from dried Alpine sweet grass, hay absolute is described by the artisan perfumer Alec Lawless as 'warm, sweet, rich, green' and 'Perhaps a contender for a happy smell.'[89] For Symonds, too, the smell of hay acquires idyllic associations. He reports an incident from the autumn of 1877 just after the Symonds family had arrived in Davos and he and his wife had finally abandoned sexual relations. A young Tyrolese pedlar, 'a handsome fellow with a bold bright gaze and the loose free lounge of a born mountaineer' passed by the terrace of the hotel where he was sitting and 'stopped at no great distance to obey a natural call': 'Desire for the *Bursch* [youth] shot through me with a sudden stab. I followed him with my eyes until he passed behind a haystall; and I thought—if only I could follow him, and catch him there, and pass the afternoon with him upon the sweet new hay!'[90]

Coumarin, which gives hay its distinctive aroma, has sometimes been associated with certain body odours. The biologist D. Michael Stoddart suggests that it is reminiscent of human axillary odour (armpit sweat).[91] Havelock Ellis, in his psychological study of smell, concurs, while adding other suggestions:

> The odor of the leguminous fenugreek, a botanical friend considers, closely approaches the odor given off in some cases by the armpit in women. It is noteworthy that fenugreek

[85] Margaret Symonds, 'Hay Hauling on the Alpine Snow', in *Our Life in the Swiss Highlands*, p. 187.

[86] Somerville Hastings, *Summer Flowers of the High Alps* (London and New York: J. M. Dent & Sons and E. P. Dutton, 1910), p. 22, with a coloured illustration facing on p. 23. Like most clovers, Alpine clover contains coumarin.

[87] Symonds, 'Hay Hauling on the Alpine Snow', p. 189.

[88] Shakespeare, *A Midsummer Night's Dream*, 4. 1. 31; Piesse, *Art of Perfumery*, 3rd edn (1862), p. 210.

[89] Alec Lawless, *Artisan Perfumery or Being Led by the Nose* (Stroud: Baronia Souk, 2009), p. 81. Although hay absolute is used infrequently in modern perfumery because of the availability of much cheaper synthetic coumarin, it is found a few fragrances such as Chergui by Christopher Sheldrake for Serge Lutens (2005).

[90] Symonds, *Memoirs*, p. 261.   [91] Stoddart, *The Scented Ape*, pp. 158–9.

contains cumarine, which imparts its fragrance to new-mown hay and to various flowers of somewhat similar odor. On some persons these have a sexually exciting effect, and it is of considerable interest to observe that they recall to many the odor of semen. [...] Another correspondent, this time a man, tells me that he has noted the resemblance of the odor of semen to that of crushed grasses.[92]

Such attributions are highly subjective, but it is worth pausing over a statement used by Ellis to support his proposal that 'the body odor of men' may be 'a sexual attraction to the male invert'. Having first referenced a relevant discussion of smell and male inverts in Mark André Raffalovich's recently published *Uranisme et Unisexualité* (1896), Ellis then cites a long extract from a source of his own, calling it 'a communication which has reached me recently concerning the attractiveness of the odor of peasants':

> One predominant attraction of these men is that they are pure and clean; their bodies in a state of healthy normal function. Then they possess, if they are temperate, what the Greek poet Straton called the φυδικὴ χρωτὸς (a quality which, according to this authority, is never found in women). This 'natural fair perfume of the flesh' is a peculiar attribute of young men who live in the open air and deal with natural objects. Even their perspiration has an odor very different from that of girls in ball-rooms: more refined, ethereal, pervasive, delicate, and difficult to seize. When they have handled hay—in the time of hay-harvest, or in winter, when they bring hay down from mountain huts—the youthful peasants carry about them the smell of 'a field the Lord hath blessed'. Their bodies and their clothes exhale an indescribable fragrance of purity and sex combined. Every gland of the robust frame seems to have accumulated scent from herbs and grasses, which slowly exude from the cool, fresh skin of the lad. You do not perceive it in a room. You must take the young man's hands and bury your face in them, or be covered with him under the same blanket in one bed, to feel this aroma. No sensual impression on the nerves is more poignantly impregnated with spiritual poetry—the poetry of adolescence and early hours upon the hills, and labor cheerfully accomplished, and the harvest of God's gifts to man brought home by human industry. It is worth mentioning that Aristophanes, in his description of the perfect Athenian Ephebus, dwells upon his being redolent of natural perfumes.[93]

There are good reasons for thinking Symonds the author of this passage— the reference to the mountain locale, the recondite classical citations, and the admiring references to the virile peasant physique such as we find in some of his essays in *Our Life in the Swiss Highlands*.[94] Moreover, the remark about the odour of young men's perspiration being superior to that of 'girls in ball-rooms' recalls his essay 'A Problem in Modern Ethics' where he cited one of Krafft-Ebing's subjects who complained "*I loathe the odour which the so-called fair sex exhales when heated by the*

---

[92] Ellis, *Studies in the Psychology of Sex: Sexual Selection in Man*, pp. 105–6. It should be noted that 'fenugreek' is derived from the Latin botanical name, *Trigonella foenum graecum*, the last two words meaning 'Greek hay'.

[93] Ellis, *Studies in the Psychology of Sex: Sexual Selection in Man*, pp. 89–90. Ellis references Raffalovich's *Uranisme et Unisexualité* (Paris: Storck, Lyons and Masson, 1896), p. 126.

[94] Symonds, 'Swiss Athletic Sports', in *Our Life in the Swiss Highlands*, pp. 177–8; 'A Page of My Life', in *Our Life in the Swiss Highlands*, p. 222.

dance.'" Unsurprisingly, Ellis's 'communication' turns out to be virtually identical to a passage in Symonds's essay 'Soldier Love and Related Matter', included in the 1896 German edition of *Sexual Inversion* but omitted from the English edition of 1897 and all subsequent editions in English. Symonds's original English typescript being lost, this brief essay existed only in German till it was translated by Andrew Dakyns in 2007, but the more elegantly worded extract Ellis quotes is likely to be Symonds's original text.[95] Obliged to delete Symonds's name and contribution from the English editions of *Sexual Inversion*, Ellis evidently decided to reuse some of that material in an anonymized form in his study of smell.[96]

What is remarkable about this passage, and indeed is true of other passages in his letters and *Memoirs* where Symonds describes the fragrance of male lovers, is that something one might expect to be earthily corporeal is in fact spiritualized. Here the young peasant men seem permeated by the aroma of the hay they work with—a kind of natural fougère—so that they embody the purity and freshness of the landscape they work in. Released through sensual physical contact, the scent—'refined', 'ethereal', 'delicate', 'difficult to seize'—conjures up a spiritual impression of 'the poetry of adolescence and early hours upon the hills'. There is an absence here of the kind of animalic musky notes, which one might expect to find in a sexually attractive odour, or perhaps those musky notes are experienced or interpreted as something altogether more elevated. Moreover, in eschewing more obvious animalic odours, Symonds rewrites the fragrance of the flesh as a light fresh scent consonant with the delicate airy fragrances thought most desirable by most conservative Victorians. Coumaric natural fragrances—hay, clover, tobacco—may be pleasurable because they carry a hint of sex but, for Symonds, the sexual

---

[95] Symonds, *Soldier Love*, p. 10. The essay was originally an appendix to chapter 4 of the German edition of *Sexual Inversion* (1896). There are a few small differences, one being that the final allusion to Aristophanes occurs in a footnote in *Soldier Love* (p. 16, note 1). The quotation from Straton 'φυδικὴ χρωτὸς', which Symonds translates as 'natural fair perfume of the flesh', is the slightly longer 'φυδικὴ χρωτὸς εὐπνοιή' in *Soldier Love*, and is a quotation from Epigram 7, in the *Mousa Paidikē*, the twelfth book of the Greek Anthology. Iwan Bloch, a German sexologist, included the very similar passage from 'Soldier Love' in his *Die sexuelle Osphresiologie*, an influential study of smell and sexuality, which he published under the name of Albert Hagen in 1901. This book was translated and published under Bloch's name as *Odoratus Sexualis: A Scientific and Literary Study of Sexual Scents and Erotic Perfumes* by the American Anthropological Society in 1933 (translator unspecified), with various reprints since then. I use Iwan Bloch, *Odoratus Sexualis: A Scientific and Literary Study of Sexual Scents and Erotic Perfumes* (North Hollywood, CA: Brandon House, 1967), where the translated passage from Symonds's 'Soldier Love' occurs on pp. 122–3. Bloch does not specify the source, merely noting 'John Addington Symonds has made noteworthy studies concerning the role of erotic odors among male homosexuals' (p. 122). 'Soldier Love' is not listed separately in Bloch's sketchy Bibliography, although Symonds's name appears with Ellis's for *Sexual Inversion*, which Bloch would have read in the original German edition that contains Symonds's essay. There are a few small differences between the translation by Dakyns and the one produced by Bloch's translator.

[96] Ellis prefaces Symonds's appreciation of the fragrant young peasants by quoting from a letter previously cited in a footnote in Symonds's *Soldier Love* glossing 'the impression which peasants make on certain natures'. The author of this letter, an Italian marquis, relates savouring his lover's *fascia*, or girdle of netted silk', worn next to his skin: 'I buried my face in it, and was half inebriated by its exquisite aroma of young manhood and fresh hay.' See Ellis, *Studies in the Psychology of Sex: Sexual Selection in Man*, p. 89, and compare Symonds, *Soldier Love*, p. 16, note 2. The respective translations of this Italian letter, while not identical, are clearly versions of the same text.

scent itself sublimes into an etherealized poetic essence, a naturalized odour, if not of sanctity, then certainly of virtue.

The fragrant young peasant recalls the ideal *ephebe* or Greek youth preparing for citizenship, who exudes the 'natural fair perfume of the flesh'. In his *Memoirs* and essays Symonds drew comparisons between the young Swiss peasant men he met and the Greeks—his friend Christian Buol, for example, whom he described as 'an ancient Greek of the Homeric age, perfect in σωφροσύνη [temperance] and unassuming power'.[97] Moreover, the 'fragrance of purity' emitted by the peasant is not unlike Whitman's own 'exquisite aroma of cleanliness'. Certainly the democratic camaraderie Symonds saw among the Swiss also reminded him of Whitman, a party he attended at Buol's house seeming 'like a scene out of one of Whitman's poems'.[98] Thus the fragrance of the young Swiss men, a 'sensual impression [...] poignantly impregnated with spiritual poetry', is at once ancient and modern, reminiscent of both the fragrance of classical literature 'impregnated with paiderastia' and the 'faint odor' of Whitman's *Calamus*, itself a version of paiderastia. Indeed, what is this hay-like fragrance if not Symonds's own odorous 'leaves of grass', a scent that captures the essence of his idealized homoeroticism?

Thus, although Symonds manifests a clear and consistent liking for a range of aromas linked by their coumaric, hay-like smell, a smell definitively captured in his Swiss mountain-home environment and the bodies of young Swiss men, that fragrance is saturated with the literary and textual associations of his cosmopolitan reading in history, sexology, and poetry, as documented in the opening section of this chapter. Moreover, this final rich concentrate of odour, influence, and allusion validates our previous findings that Symonds's observations as cosmopolitan *flaireur* are mediated through antecedent literary and cultural texts and through influential literary modes of perception like Shelleyan synaesthesia. For Symonds, it is indeed the 'thoughts and sentiments', not merely of Greek literature but of a whole variety of texts, that 'spread themselves abroad', steeping his soul in many 'sweet aromas'.[99]

---

[97] Symonds, *Memoirs*, p. 263. Symonds makes comparisons between Swiss youth and classical sculptural types in *Our Life in the Swiss Highlands*, pp. 176, 177. He would found 'a gymnasium for the young men of Davos', 'A Page of My Life', p. 216. Symonds was also anxious to acquire a photograph of 'The Mower', a naturalistic and arguably homoerotic sculpture of a muscular, shirtless labourer posed with a scythe, by the young British sculptor Hamo Thornycroft, also known for his classical male nudes. See *LJAS* 2. 926 (6 July 1884); 954 (11 October 1884); 956–7 (23 October 1884); 961 (8 November 1884). Symonds mentioned to Edmund Gosse, the intimate friend and possibly lover of Thornycroft, that he had contemplated buying the statue (*LJAS* 3. 466; 13 June 1890). Symonds praises 'The Mower' in the conclusion of his essay 'Democratic Art with Special Reference to Walt Whitman', in his *Essays Speculative and Suggestive*, 2. 77, an essay in which he also mentions, apropos of the 'characteristic beauty' of 'diurnal service', 'the superb poise of the mower as he swings his scythe' (p. 44). See also Michael Hatt, 'Near and Far: Homoeroticism, Labour and Hamo Thornycroft's Mower', *Art History* 26 (2003), 26–55.

[98] Symonds, *Memoirs*, p. 263.

[99] This passage from Symonds's *Studies of the Greek Poets*, 1. 422, seems itself to be a partial remembrance of the opening lines of Thomas Moore's translation of an ode by Anacreon (Ode 48) in his *Odes of Anacreon, Translated into English Verse, with Notes* (London: John Stockdale, 1800): 'When my thirsty soul I steep | Every sorrow's lull'd to sleep' (p. 171). Symonds was clearly familiar with Moore's translations and in *Studies of the Greek Poets* cites a translation by him of a poem attributed to Antipater in praise of Anacreon (1. 362).

LAFCADIO HEARN AND THE PERFUMED
BREEZE OF BEAUTY

If, as cosmopolitan *flaireur*, John Addington Symonds finds his perfect scent in the bodies of young Swiss peasant men, then his ideal heterosexual counterpart is the essayist and critic Lafcadio Hearn, lover of perfume and travel, and haunted by the scent of women. Hearn's early article 'Spring Fever Fancies' touches on two of these passions in its opening sentence: 'Together with the languor and dreaminess begotten by the spring's fragrance and its tepid winds, there comes to many, year after year, in whatever climate or country, but especially perhaps in our own, that vague longing for other lands and strange places—that thirst for the solitude of unfamiliar lands.'[100]

Hearn, perhaps the ultimate cosmopolitan aesthete, is well placed to explore what he also calls 'this vague and undefinable longing for far-way lands'.[101] Of Anglo-Irish and Greek parentage, raised in Dublin, educated in Durham, he left England, aged nineteen, never to return, arriving in America in 1869 where he worked as a journalist for some eighteen years. 'Spring Fever Fancies' was written for the New Orleans *Daily City Item* in 1879. Although he had moved from Cincinnati to Louisiana in 1877, he was already prey to the longing for exploration he describes as afflicting many 'especially perhaps in our own country'. From 1887 this would impel him to spend two years in the French West Indies and then, in 1890, to undertake a trip to Japan where he would finally settle. However, in this early article, Hearn's aching wanderlust is triggered not just by the advent of the spring but specifically a sensory cue—'the spring comes with its burst of roses, its magical perfumes, its genial warmth'—and it is this vernal fragrance that seemingly helps release what he calls 'the long pent-up vapors of fancy'.[102]

Hearn's many essays, articles, and stories attest his vibrant interest in the different places and cultures he inhabited. Severely myopic and blind in one eye from an accident incurred as a schoolboy, he was nonetheless a passionate lover of beauty. His strong aesthetic sensibility was partly stimulated by a love of literature and art, especially the visually voracious short stories of Théophile Gautier, which he translated brilliantly for newspaper serialization and eventually published as the collection *One of Cleopatra's Nights and Other Fantastic Romances* (1882). Other French writers translated by him included Flaubert, de Maupassant, Daudet, and Pierre Loti. Loti in particular was a lasting inspiration: 'No other literary man living sees and hears and smells and thrills so finely as he.'[103] Hearn was also widely read in English literature and especially loved the poetry of Swinburne and Rossetti.[104]

---

[100] Lafcadio Hearn, 'Spring Fever Fancies', *Item* (16 March 1879), in *Editorials by Lafcadio Hearn*, ed. Charles Woodson Hutson (Boston, MA, New York, and Cambridge: Houghton Mifflin Co. and The Riverside Press, 1926), p. 43.

[101] Ibid., p. 45.   [102] Ibid., p. 44.

[103] Hearn, *The Japanese Letters of Lafcadio Hearn*, ed. Elizabeth Bisland (Boston, MA, and New York: Houghton Mifflin Co., 1910), p. xliii.

[104] See, for example, *Books and Habits from the Lectures of Lafcadio Hearn*, ed. John Erskine (New York: Dodd, Mead & Co., 1921) and *Pre-Raphaelite and Other Poets: Lectures by Lafcadio Hearn*, ed. John Erskine (New York: Dodd, Mead & Co., 1922).

He was an admirer of Symonds, acknowledging his monumental *Renaissance in Italy* as 'a work of great special value', but singling out *Studies of the Greek Poets* and *Sketches and Studies in Italy and Greece* for special praise.[105] British aestheticism's cult of beauty also made a strong impression on him, as can be seen in an article he wrote in 1882 for the New Orleans newspaper, the *Times-Democrat*, defending the philosophy of Oscar Wilde who at that time was on his lecture tour of America. Here, using a simile akin to that in his earlier article about the attraction of unfamiliar lands, Hearn portrays the influence of aesthetic beauty as a fragrant enlivening breeze:

> The influence of beauty purifies and moralizes; it is an ethical force sweet as the presence of a woman at whose advent rough men curb their tongues and doff their hats; there is a holiness in it as of Omnipotence. He who exhorts us to love beauty exhorts us to happiness and joy, to pulchritude of soul and nobility of heart, to the divinely gentle philosophy that sweetens life and brings something of Paradise into the world, like a breeze laden with strange perfumes from some far-off land.[106]

Hearn's imagery suggests the kinship between the lure of aestheticism and the magic of distant lands, both of which are pictured as arousing the imagination as though by a tantalizing perfumed breeze. However, in this second article, the influence of beauty is also compared to the morally uplifting presence of a woman whose appearance civilizes the behaviour of 'rough men'. Her presence is 'sweet' in that it exerts a benign influence but, as we shall see in the next section, Hearn habitually regards women as both morally and actually fragrant, so that the link between women's sweet influence and the beneficent perfumed breeze is far from coincidental.

Like the perfumed breeze preparing the mind with hints of things to come, olfaction helps out the visual faculty. Hearn's impaired sight was aided, even partly compensated, by his powerful sense of smell, which permeates various of his compositions, invigorating his observations, which are those not just of a journalistic *flâneur* but of a *flaireur*, someone who loves to detect things, to scent them out,

---

[105] Hearn, 'Pessimists and their Kindred', in *Complete Lectures on Poets by Lafcadio Hearn*, ed. Ryuji Tanabé, Teisaburo Ochiai, and Ichiro Nishizaki (Tokyo: The Hokuseido Press, 1934), pp. 276–7. Although Hearn rated Symonds as a translator, declaring 'Some of his translations from the Greek Anthology are really the best of their kind' (p. 277), he disliked his original poetry, which he found pessimistic and 'dismal'. In a letter of 14 June 1893 he also confessed his disappointment in Symonds's essay on colour 'In the Key of Blue' to Basil Chamberlain, 'Though I reverence almost religiously the man who could have written that blazing splendid chapter on Sappho in the "Studies of the Greek Poets".' See *Japanese Letters*, p. 112.

[106] Hearn, 'The Apostle of Aestheticism', *Times-Democrat* (16 April 1882), in *Literary Essays by Lafcadio Hearn*, ed. Ichiro Nishizaki (Tokyo: The Hokuseido Press, 1939), p. 122. Hearn also wrote a rather less sympathetic article, 'Oscar Wilde as Fashion Designer', *Times-Democrat* (14 May 1882), in *Literary Essays*, pp. 123–6. In June 1882 Wilde briefly visited New Orleans to lecture and met several times with a friend of Hearn's, the novelist George Washington Cable. It is possible that Hearn may have heard Wilde lecture and likely that Cable would have discussed his visitor with Hearn. See William W. Rogers, Robert David Ward, and Dorothy McLeod MacInerney, 'Oscar Wilde Lectures in New Orleans and Across the South in 1882', *Southern Studies* 11.3–4 (Fall–Winter 2004), 31–65, and, in particular, 45–6, 48. Wilde's request that Cable take him to see a voodoo ritual in New Orleans is particularly interesting as Hearn was knowledgeable about such matters.

and discern them. In her memoir of Hearn, his second wife Setsuko Koizumi recalled that 'he had a very sensitive nose for odors'.[107] As Elizabeth Bisland, his biographer and the editor of his letters, observed, 'There are constant records in his writings of odours and perfumes. Of smells of flowers and herbs, smells of fruits, smells of flesh, of races, of incense, of old books, of all the thousand intimations seized upon by keen and delicate olfactories.'[108] In 1924 the American writer and philanthropist Edward Larocque Tinker wrote a valuable short article on Hearn's 'abnormally keen' 'olfactory sense', which noted how he was 'deeply concerned with the subtle variations of odor which were constantly assailing his supersensitive nostrils'.[109] Tinker's article does not attempt a survey of Hearn's olfactory references in his writings and indeed concludes by suggesting 'a new interest for readers of Hearn—that of tracing the tremendous influence that his supersensitive nose exercised over his literary output'. My own discussion of Hearn and scent does not aim at any kind of comprehensive overview but instead restricts itself to commenting on a number of salient instances, mainly from his time in America and especially the period he spent in New Orleans where the links between perfume, place, and femininity are particularly strong.

However, before he settled in New Orleans, Hearn's olfactory sensibilities were undoubtedly honed and tested by certain aspects of his work in Cincinnati as an investigative journalist. While his later writing tends to show his sense of smell as piqued by pleasant or curious odours, these were not to the fore during what is known as his 'period of the gruesome' when he was exploring the seamier side of the city. Thus we find him exercising his gifts in an eye-watering account of the 'ghoulish aroma' he experienced when visiting a fertilizer factory near the railway stop of Gilead. Wittily titled 'Balm of Gilead: An Afternoon at the Stink Factory: What Becomes of our Dead Animals', this article of October 1875 relates how the smells generated by decaying animal remains emanating from the Cincinnati Fertilizer Manufacturing Company could be detected two and a half miles away and on occasion had 'offended the nostrils of people living four miles distant'.[110] Hearn's report is an object lesson in preparing the mind for sights to come as, journeying on foot towards the factory, he describes how:

> [T]he nose is continually assailed by new varieties of stench. First a faint odour, like that of very ancient shoe leather, then a smell as of decaying cats, mingling with the

---

[107] Setsuko Koizumi (Mrs Hearn), *Reminiscences of Lafcadio Hearn*, tr. Paul Kiyoshi Hisada and Frederick Johnson (Boston, MA, and New York: Houghton Mifflin Co., 1918), p. 42.

[108] Elizabeth Bisland, Preface, in *Japanese Letters*, p. xxxvii.

[109] Edward Larocque Tinker, 'Lafcadio Hearn and the Sense of Smell', *The Bookman* (January 1924), 519–27; 520. (US edition of *The Bookman*, published in New York.) Most of this article is reproduced in a different form in Tinker's *Lafcadio Hearn's American Days* (New York: Dodd Mead, 1924), pp. 229–37. There are small pieces of information that appear in only one or the other source.

[110] Hearn, 'Balm of Gilead: An Afternoon at the Stink Factory: What Becomes of our Dead Animals', *Cincinnati Commercial* (3 October 1875), in *Period of the Gruesome: Selected Cincinnati Journalism of Lafcadio Hearn*, ed. Jon Christopher Hughes (London and New York: University Press of America, 1990), p. 208. Hearn wryly notes how the factory is located near 'a rail-road station called "Gilead," so christened doubtless, by some railroad official with a fine sense of irony'—balm of Gilead being, of course, a healing balsam mentioned in the Bible.

first smell; then a smell resembling that of rotten hides mingling with the two previous smells; and so on as you near the great focus of simon-pure stench itself, by which time the odors have become so multitudinous, so overpowering and so mingled together that the nostrils are numbed beyond the power of further analysis.[111]

After a detailed inventory of the gory sights of animal carcasses and entrails and the means of processing them, he observes that 'A large soap factory is connected with the other establishment, and it is curious to note what fine looking soaps— even mottled castile almost resembling red marble—can be manufactured from the products of the Stink Factory.'[112] According to Hearn, the factory is estimated to produce 60,000 pounds of soap a week, a figure that suggests that this establishment belonged to William Proctor and James Gamble, a candle-maker and a soap-maker who had started a joint business in 1837 that would eventually grow into the world's largest consumer goods company. Cincinnati was known for its meatpacking houses, the key source of the fats used in Proctor and Gamble's soap and candles, although here Hearn indicates that the Fertilizer Company is also a supplier. The 'mottled castile almost resembling red marble' certainly sounds like Proctor and Gamble's 'Mottled German Soap', described as 'a hard, white soap with visible red mottling or marbling'. Used as a laundry product, its red veining was caused by 'red oil' or oleic acid derived from pig fat.[113] Concluding his article Hearn is evidently intrigued by the dubious origins of the soap, but notes that 'The tallow, grease and lard obtained from the carcasses is however, as clean and wholesome to touch, taste, and smell as any other; and after a careful examination, any wonder as to the quality of the soap ceases.'[114] His perception that these 'fine looking soaps' derive from putrid and repellent matter mirrors, in a more exaggerated form, the irony that many perfumes owe their delightful fragrance to the careful use of small amounts of unpleasant smelling odorants, often animalic in origin.

Hearn's interest in disconcerting and disagreeable odours continued when he relocated to New Orleans in 1877, where he vividly recorded how, in the prolonged periods of damp weather, a 'mouldy, musty smell pervades the atmosphere', and remarked on the musky smell 'emanating from ancient buildings,—nauseous, heavy, unutterable; the odors of the droppings of innumerable bats'.[115] That smell was also described by him as containing 'suggestions of many odours—decaying shoe-leather, miscarried eggs, and dead cats—and yet is unlike any of these. It is an original and astonishing odour which inspires fantastic dreams of death and dissolution.'[116] However, New Orleans was predominantly for him 'this land of

---

[111] Hearn, 'Balm of Gilead', *Period of the Gruesome*, p. 209.   [112] Ibid., p. 214.
[113] Juliann Sivulka, *Stronger than Dirt: A Cultural History of Advertising Personal Hygiene in America, 1875 to 1940* (New York: Humanity Books, 2001), p. 51.
[114] Hearn, 'Balm of Gilead', *Period of the Gruesome*, p. 214.
[115] Hearn, 'New Orleans in Wet Weather' (22 December 1877), in *Inventing New Orleans: Writings of Lafcadio Hearn*, ed. S. Frederick Starr (Jackson, MI: University Press of Mississippi, 2001), p. 39; letter to H. E. Krehbiel, cited in Tinker, 'Lafcadio Hearn and the Sense of Smell', p. 520.
[116] Hearn, Editorial, *Item* (22 May 1880), cited in Tinker's book, *Lafcadio Hearn's American Days*, p. 231, and article, 'Lafcadio Hearn and the Sense of Smell', p. 522, and also in *Inventing New Orleans*, p. 181, my text here.

perfume and of dreams'.[117] Indeed, according to his friend Edward Henderson, the lure of its perfume was one of the factors that tempted him to leave during the time he was working on the *Cincinnati Commercial*:

> One morning, after the usual hard work of an unusually nasty winter night in Cincinnati, in a leisure hour of conversation, he heard an associate on the paper describe a scene in a Gulf State. It was something about a grand old mansion of an antebellum cotton prince, with its great white columns, its beautiful private drive down to the public road, whitewashed negro-quarters stretching away in the background, in the distance some cypress and live-oaks and Spanish moss, and close by a grove of magnolias with their delightful odors and the melody of mocking birds in the early sunlight. Hearn took in every word of this, though he had little to say at the time, with great keenness of interest, as shown by the dilation of his nostrils. It was as though he could see and hear and smell the delights of the scene. Not long after this, on leaving Cincinnati for New Orleans he remarked: [...] 'I had to go sooner or later, but it was your description of the sunlight and melodies and fragrance and all the delights with which the South appeals to the senses that determined me.'[118]

In a later article about the romance travelling by riverboat, Hearn wrote:

> We sail out of Northern frosts into Southern lukewarmness, into the luxuriant and somnolent smell of magnolias and lemon blossoms;—the sugar-country exhales its incense of welcome. And the giant crescent of lights, the steam-song of joyous boats, the world of chimneys, the forests of spars, the burst of morning glory over New Orleans, viewed from the deck of a pilot-house. . . .
>
>   These may never be wholly forgotten; after the lapse of fifty years in some dusty and dreary inland city, an odor, an echo, a printed name may resurrect their recollection, fresh as one of those Gulf winds that leave sweet odors after them, like coquettish women, like Talmudic angels.[119]

Here Hearn, in a retrospective rather than anticipatory mood, compares the unforgettable memories of approaching a cherished place—New Orleans—with odorous breezes that in turn evoke the perfumed wake left by women and by angels.

New Orleans and *Odor di Femina*

That first scent of the city was a herald of things to come, for arriving in New Orleans in November 1877, Hearn was immediately struck by the lush gardens—

---

[117] Letter to H. E. Krehbiel (1878), in *Life and Letters of Lafcadio Hearn*, ed. Elizabeth Bisland, 2 vols (London, Boston, MA, and New York: Archibald Constable & Co., and Houghton, Mifflin & Co., 1907), 1. 194.

[118] George M. Gould, *Concerning Lafcadio Hearn*, with a Bibliography by Laura Stedman (London and Leipzig: T. Fisher Unwin, 1908), pp. 50–1. I have chosen to use the version ascribed by Gould to Edward Henderson, but Bisland provides a very similar account with some slight variations in the text in her *Life and Letters*, 1. 65–6, where it is ascribed to Joseph Tunison.

[119] Hearn, 'A River Reverie', *Times-Democrat* (2 May 1882), in *Fantastics and Other Fancies*, ed. Charles Woodward Hutson (Boston, MA, and New York: Houghton Mifflin, 1914), pp. 194–5. See also *Lafcadio Hearn: American Writings*, ed. Christopher Benfey, The Library of America (New York: Literary Classics of the United States, Inc., 2009), p. 723.

Orange and fig trees; bananas and palms; magnolias and myrtles, cypresses and cedars; and flowers of so rich a hue, so sweet, so fragrant that they vary the varied green with a thousand tints, and make the air odorous with drowsy perfume [...] And you can walk through this paradise hour after hour, mile after mile; and the air only becomes yet more fragrant and the orange trees more heavily freighted with golden fruit.[120]

Ten days later he recorded the beauty of the women of the city and their graceful management of their long dresses, which 'make the air odorous as they pass, by the exquisite perfume of the South, the breath of orange flowers'.[121]

Significantly for Hearn the city's beautiful women seem to exude the very essence of the 'South'. As Helen Taylor has pointed out, late nineteenth-century New Orleans, 'a city of unique racial mixture', bucked 'the American discursive trend to masculinize cities as sites of power, capital, and labour', being 'often compared to Paris—specifically in relation to a metaphoric femininity, with both seen as sites of romance, glamour and sexualized street life, particularly prostitution'.[122] 'New Orleans has long been celebrated for the beauty of her women', writes Hearn, 'and most deservedly so, I think.'[123] Feminized and eroticized, New Orleans as the South appears in another letter sent soon after his arrival in the city where he writes of his experience of 'the paradise of the South [...] deserted, and half in ruins': 'it was like young death,—a dead bride crowned with orange flowers,—a dead face that asked for a kiss. I cannot say how fair and rich and beautiful this dead South is. It has fascinated me.'[124]

Like Edgar Allan Poe, Théophile Gautier, and other nineteenth-century writers, Hearn was fascinated by the 'poetic' image of a beautiful dead woman, an image that recurs in 'All in White', one of the short stories he published in the New Orleans *Item*.[125] In this tale, place, perfume, and femininity come together once more when the narrator, on a fleeting visit to Havana, sees through a window, laid out on a bed, a beautiful dead girl all in white, 'one white tropical flower in her black hair, shining like a star. I do not know what it was; but its perfume came to me through the window, sweet and strange'.[126] Here death helps intensify the otherworldliness, the entrancing alterity of women.

That alterity is also reflected in Hearn's notion of woman's moral nature, for he undoubtedly embraced the romantic and chivalric conception of women as distinct from men by virtue of their innate goodness. The narrator of his early short

---

[120] Hearn, 'At the Gate of the Tropics' (19 November 1877), in *Occidental Gleanings: Sketches and Essays*, ed. Albert Mordell, 2 vols (London: W. Heinemann, 1925), 1. 168–9, and *Inventing New Orleans*, p. 8.

[121] Hearn, 'The City of the South' (29 November 1877), in *Inventing New Orleans*, p. 15.

[122] Helen Taylor, '"The perfume of the past": Kate Chopin and Post-Colonial New Orleans', in *The Cambridge Companion to Kate Chopin*, ed. Janet Beer (Cambridge: Cambridge University Press, 2008), p. 148.

[123] Hearn, 'The City of the South', p. 18.

[124] Hearn, *Letters from the Raven: Being the Correspondence of Lafcadio Hearn with Henry Watkin*, ed. Milton Bronner (New York: Brentano's, 1907), pp. 42–3.

[125] In 'The Philosophy of Composition' (1846) Edgar Allan Poe famously writes 'The death of a beautiful woman is, unquestionably, the most poetical topic in the world.' See Poe, *Essays and Reviews* (New York: Literary Classics of the United States, 1984), p. 19.

[126] Hearn, 'All in White', *Item* (14 September 1879), in *Fantastics*, p. 30.

story, 'Fantasy of a Fan' (1874), declares: 'There can be no doubt, to my mind that women have something of the nature of rare and precious flowers.'[127] This chivalry also expresses itself in a letter to 'an unnamed lady' (actually Mrs Ellen Ricker Freeman) with regard to his feeling for scented flowers:

> Still, flowers and me have so little in common, that much as I love them, I feel I ought not to be near them,—just as one who loves a woman so passionately that his dearest wish is to kiss her footprints. [...] Of course this is an extravagant simile; but the nature of a man is so coarse and rude compared with the fragrance and beauty of the flowers, that he feels in a purer atmosphere when they are breathing perfume about him. Flowers do seem to me like ghosts of maidens, like 'that maid whom Gwydion made by glamour out of flowers'.[128]

Gwydion is a medieval mythical Welsh magician who makes Blodeuwedd, a beautiful maiden, out of flowers, and the line Hearn quotes is from Tennyson's 'Enid' from the *Idylls of the King* (1859), later 'The Marriage of Geraint', and was evidently a favourite as he cites it on a number of other occasions.

Comparing women with flowers is hardly unusual in the nineteenth century, although Hearn gives such comparisons special emphasis when it comes to the notion of scent, writing later in the same letter, 'And talking of little roses, luxurious roses, I like them because of the fancies they evoke; their leaves and odor seem of kinship to the lips and the breath of a fair woman.'[129] For Hearn, women, like flowers, also induce a 'purer atmosphere when they are breathing perfume about him'. In his esoteric story 'Karma', originally published in *Lippincott's Magazine* in May 1890, the ideal beloved woman—'one of those marvelously specialized human-flowers that bloom only in the higher zones of aspirational being'—is 'a perfumed chalice-blossom stored with all the sweetness of humanity'.[130]

Hearn's sense of the fragrant atmosphere emanated by femininity is somewhat unusually communicated by his particular use of the phrase 'odor di femina', which occurs several times in his work. Ordinarily used with a mocking or pejorative application, 'odor di femina' is a phrase made famous by Mozart's rake Don Giovanni who, when his wife, Donna Elvira, appears at the stage rear (Act 1, sc. 4), tells his servant Leporello, 'Be quiet! I think I smell the odour of woman.' It was later taken up in a crudely misogynistic way by the French writer Jules Barbey

---

[127] Hearn, 'Fantasy of a Fan', *Ye Giglampz* 6 (26 July 1874), 2–3; 2, in *Ye Giglampz: A Weekly Illustrated Journal devoted to Art, Literature and Satire, ed. Lafcadio Hearn and Henry Farny*, ed. Jon Christopher Hughes (Cincinnati, OH: Crossroads Books with the Public Library of Cincinnati and Hamilton County, 1983).

[128] Hearn, 'Letters to a Lady', in *Letters from the Raven*, pp. 113–51; 148–9. Individual letters are undated but are said in the Preface (p. 113), to be written in 1876. It is interesting to compare the tale of Gwydion and Blodeuwedd, a legend of fragrant femininity transcribed into Middle Welsh from oral tradition in the eleventh century, with Hearn's later retelling of a story from the Mahābhārata in which Viswakarman is instructed by Brahma to create from various precious ingredients, such as 'all perfume of flowers', a surpassingly beautiful woman bewitching to every sense, including 'the sense of odors': 'All blossom beauty tempted in her bosom; all perfume lingered in her breath.' See Lafcadio Hearn, 'The Making of Tilottama', in *Stray Leaves from Strange Literature* (Boston, MA: James R. Osgood & Co., 1884), pp. 49–60; 56.

[129] Hearn, 'Letters to a Lady', p. 150.

[130] Hearn, 'Karma', in *Karma and Other Stories* (New York: Boni and Liveright, 1918), p. 15.

d'Aurevilly, when writing about 'bluestockings', to indicate the inferior quality of women's art: 'Study their works and open them at random! At the tenth line, and without knowing by whom they are, you are warned; you smell woman! *Odor di femina*.'[131] In assessing women's work Barbey claims to be overpowered by a pervasive female odour—presumably not dissimilar to T. S. Eliot's 'hearty female stench'—a smell that suggests women cannot transcend their biological sex and its limitations.

For Hearn, the phrase 'odor di femina' does not have these negative connotations. He was most likely influenced by its positive use by his idol Théophile Gautier who, in his introduction to Balzac's collected works, observes: 'There is in his work an odour of women: *odor di femina*; when one entered one heard behind the doors that shut on the secret staircase the rustle of silk and the creaking of shoes.'[132] As a cosmopolitan aesthetic reader and, specifically, a lover and translator of French literature, Hearn finds 'odor di femina' characteristic not of women's writing but of modern French literature in general. In his article 'The Sexual Idea in French Literature' (1881), he writes:

> If this literature be the most dainty and beautiful in the world, the most artistic in conception and execution [...] it is owing in no small degree to the fact that all of such art [...] is influenced by a sexual idea little comprehended by those not of the Latin race. *L'éternal féminin* appears in the idea of a novel as well in the shapeliness of a bronze; the *odor di femina* impregnates everything produced by the magic of Paris. The idea of a love, not spiritual or vague, but love as warmly material [...], is there omnipresent as an atmosphere, tinting all it touches and penetrates. [...] in a fine French romance, passion is [...] the beginning and end of all; and the least drop of that flavor has the intoxicating sweetness of Persian rose-essence.[133]

Modern French literature, like most of the romantic places Hearn eulogized, has a feminine soul. His celebratory notion of literary 'odor di femina' has no suggestion of rank corporeality. He also uses the phrase in an 1880 editorial 'Women's Influence', about the power of women to effect moral change. Here he declares 'There is something good in all women. Men may become morally depraved; but

---

[131] Mozart's *Don Giovanni* with a libretto by Lorenzo da Ponte was composed and first performed in 1787. See also Jules-Amédée Barbey d'Aurevilly, *Les Bas-bleus* (Paris: Société Générale de Librarie Catholique, 1878), p. xxii, and Elaine Marks, '1929 "Odor di Femina" [*Sic*]' in *A New History of French Literature*, ed. Denis Hollier (Cambridge, MA: Harvard University Press, 1994), p. 889. As Marks points out, in the original Italian the phrase is properly *odor di femmina*.

[132] Théophile Gautier, 'Honoré de Balzac', in *Œuvres complètes de H. de Balzac*, 20 vols (Paris: A. Houssiaux, 1855), 1. 13: 'Il y a dans son œuvre comme une odeur de femme: *odor di femina* quand on y entre, on entend, derrière les portes qui se referment, sur les marches de l'escalier dérobé, des frou-frou de soie et des craquements de bottines.' Gautier extended this essay into a book, *Honoré de Balzac* (Paris: Poulet Malassis et de Broise, 1859), where the phrase occurs on p. 149. Marks does not mention Gautier's usage in '1929 "Odor di Femina" [*Sic*]'. I use Arthur Symons's translation of Gautier's sentence, cited in his essay 'Charles Conder', in *The Memoirs of Arthur Symons: Life and Art in the 1890s*, ed. Karl Beckson (University Park, PA, and London: Pennsylvania State University Press, 1977), p. 184, but see also 'Honoré de Bazac', in *The Works of Théophile Gautier*, tr. and ed. F. C. de Sumichrast, 24 vols (London: G. G. Harrap, 1900), 6: *Portraits of the Day*, p. 117.

[133] Hearn, 'The Sexual Idea in French Literature', *Item* (17 June 1881), in *Editorials*, pp. 142–3, 144.

there is something always good in the heart of the worst of women. Men may become wholly indifferent to ethical ideas; women never. Goodness is a part of their being.' This claim is buttressed by an example drawn from recent French politics when women prompted officials to resign in protest about punitive government decrees against religious orders. 'There was an *odor di femina* about those resignations', writes Hearn approvingly, ending his article with the assertion that 'the religious orders may regain more than they have lost. If they do, there will be an *odor di femina* in the transformation.'[134] My purpose here is not to unpick Hearn's evident sentimental essentialism but merely to highlight his use of the phrase as indicating women's beneficent influence, an essence of moral femininity that emanates like a perfume.

I write 'like a perfume' but Hearn actually did impute a natural fragrant odour to women. In 1880 he wrote a short article 'The Physiology of Smells', reviewing the physiological theories of the German hygienist Dr Gustav Jäger or Jaeger (1832–1917), now chiefly known for advocating the 'sanitary' wearing of animal fibres, especially wool, next to the skin, a hygienic system that inspired the Jaeger clothing brand. However, in his own day Jäger was also famous for his book *Die Entdeckung der Seele* (1878), or *The Discovery of the Soul*, which, according to Hearn, propounded that 'the soul is in the nose' and that different human emotions cause the body to give off different human odours as 'emanations of the soul'.[135] It is unclear whether Hearn had read Jäger's theories himself, as *Die Entdeckung der Seele* had not been translated into English or French (and indeed remains untranslated). It should be said, however, that Jäger is writing about what he specifically calls 'the animal soul', 'a distinct chemical substance' made up of odiferous volatile substances 'subject to the changes of matter' given off by animal bodies.[136] Certain recent commentators have seen his theories, eccentric though some of them may seem, as anticipating modern scientific ideas about pheromones.

In his article Hearn agrees with Jäger that emotions may be reflected in the odours given off by the human body but attributes this solely to health and physical well-being:

[S]ickness is apt to produce nasty exhalations and health a fresh odor by no means unpleasant—what has been called by French writers 'the perfume of youth.' Little animals, young doves, puppies—all little creatures just newly entering upon life

---

[134] Hearn, 'Woman's Influence', *Item* (12 December 1880), in *Editorials*, pp. 116, 115, 117.

[135] Hearn, 'The Physiology of Smells', *Item* (3 January 1880), page number not indicated. Warm thanks to Philip Bullock for supplying me with a PDF copy of the original newspaper article.

[136] Gustav Jäger's extensive body of writing exists only piecemeal in English translation. However, see 'The Animal Soul', in *Problems of Nature: Researches and Discoveries by Gustav Jaeger, Selected from his Published Writings*, tr. and ed. Henry G. Schlicter (London, Edinburgh, and Oxford: William & Norgate, 1897), pp. 58–61; 60–1. See also *Dr Jaeger's Health-Culture*, tr. and ed. by Lewis R. S. Tomalin, rev. and greatly enlarged edn (London: Waterlow & Sons Ltd, 1887), p. 13, which discusses how emotions can be given off as bodily essences that can be smelt. Jäger's ideas about smell are discussed throughout Iwan Bloch, *Odoratus Sexualis: A Scientific and Literary Study of Sexual Scents and Erotic Perfumes* (New York: American Anthropological Society, 1933), and are mentioned briefly in Amber Marks, *Headspace: Sniffer Dogs, Spy Bees and One Woman's Adventures in Surveillance Society* (London: Virgin Books, 2009), pp. 293–7.

have a pleasant odor. There is a fresh, pleasant smell about cleanly young children; and the hair of a girl has a natural perfume, sweeter than all the cosmetic odors Fashion drowns it with,—what some Latin writers have dared to call 'the perfume of women'.[137]

Here 'odor di femina' is the 'natural perfume' of woman, sweeter than artificial 'cosmetic odors'. Hearn is undoubtedly also thinking back to 'Fantasy of a Fan', the short story he wrote in 1874, which also treats this issue of a woman's natural and 'subtly delicate perfume'. In this vignette, Jack finds a Japanese fan in his friend's room that he wagers must be a present 'because the perfume of a pretty woman lingers on it'.[138] It was not uncommon in the nineteenth century and earlier to perfume women's fans, but Jack's friend, the narrator, confirms that the scent in question is not cosmetic.[139] Snatching back the fan, he confides to the reader that Jack was correct in that 'a faintly exquisite odor [...] had betrayed the romance of the fan', and his admission prompts a nostalgic reverie about that scent and an implicit plea for corroboration by his (male) reader:

> And if you have ever laid your head on Somebody's—shoulder, and felt Somebody's perfumed breath upon your face, like a summer wind laden with the scent of newly-mown hay, and ever played with anybody's sweetly odorous hair, and ever followed Somebody unobserved along the street when she leaves the air behind her fragrant with a perfume, you really begin to fancy her a realization of that idyllic maid —'Whom Gwydion made by glamour out of flowers.'[140]

Fending off explanations by his imagined interlocutor, he insists the perfume is a natural female fragrance: 'Don't tell me it's musk, or otto-of roses, or night-blooming-cereus, or jockey-club; because I won't believe you. No: it is the maiden herself, not her softly-rustling robes of silk, that exudeth perfume.'[141] Emphatic about the natural origin of this perfume—'I believe it has ever been so with the maidens of

---

[137] Hearn, 'The Physiology of Smells'. This editorial is reproduced in *The New Radiance and Other Scientific Sketches by Lafcadio Hearn*, ed. Tchiro Nishizaki (Tokyo: The Hokuseido Press, 1939), pp. 83–4; 84. However, the punctuation of the last sentence cited has been garbled. It is correctly cited in Tinker's 'Lafcadio Hearn and the Sense of Smell' (p. 524), although Tinker incorrectly attributes Hearn's comments to Jäger.

[138] Hearn, 'Fantasy of a Fan', *Ye Giglampz*, p. 2.

[139] For perfumed fans, see the illustrated exhibition catalogue *Fanning the Senses, 13 March 2007–1 July 2007*, preface by H. E. Alexander (London: The Fan Museum, 2007).

[140] Hearn, 'Fantasy of a Fan', *Ye Giglampz*, pp. 2, 3.

[141] Musk, otto of roses, and jockey-club are all perfumes widely available in nineteenth-century Britain and America. The more exotic-sounding 'night-blooming cereus' refers to a cactus found in the warmer southern American states, which produces, late at night, highly fragrant, vanilla-smelling white flowers that last only for a few hours. According to David G. Williams, there was a nineteenth-century 'cactus flower' perfume that imitated the scent of 'night-blooming cereus'. See his *Perfumes of Yesterday*, pp. 268–9. The formula for 'night-blooming cereus' perfume includes tincture of benzoin (for the vanillic notes), tonka bean tincture, civet, rose, and jasmine. Williams writes that 'The Night-Blooming Cereus formula dates back to the end of the nineteenth century' (p. 269), but for Hearn to list it as a perfume, it must have been in existence by 1874, the date of his article. Septimus Piesse in his *Art of Perfumery*, 2nd edn (1856) mentions night-blooming cereus as a nocturnally odoriferous flower (pp. 20, 21) but does not mention an artificial perfume based on it in this or in subsequent editions.

high degree and high blood'—the narrator then romantically imagines groups of women from antiquity—Egyptians, Thebans, Assyrians, and others—concluding with the assertion that 'all shook just such a perfume from their garments as to-day perfumes my fan'.[142]

Hearn had wanted to call this story, written while he was still in Cincinnati, 'The Smell of a Woman'. But Henry Farny, his co-editor of the short-lived *Giglampz* journal, balked at this. He thought the tale was disgusting and that it 'smacked too much of Mademoiselle de Maupun [*sic*]', Théophile Gautier's risqué novel of 1835. However, he finally consented to publication after a minor emendation and change of title.[143] 'Fantasy of a Fan', Hearn's own early discourse on 'odor di femina', obviously informs his 1880 response to Jäger, as does a piece he had written two years previously for the New Orleans *Item* in 1878. Titled 'An Odorous Subject', this article tentatively speculates that the sense of smell might be 'developed to a greater pitch of usefulness', enabling physicians to diagnose ailments and 'romanticism' to:

> [R]ejoice in the discovery that youth and beauty in women is marked by a perfume like that of the garments of the Sulamitess—'a smell as of Lebanon,' a perfume like that of the ideal maid 'whom Gwydion made by glamour out of flowers.' Indeed there are romanticists of this present era who claim as much; poets who aver that the presence of a beautiful woman is sweet to the sense as the passage of those Rabbinical angels who left rich perfumes as memories of their visits in the dwellings of the faithful.[144]

Hearn corroborates his last assertion by extended reference to Baudelaire's poetry about perfume and the scent of women's hair, as well as incorporating a brief allusion to Swinburne. Thus he shows his awareness of two major literary precursors who evidently prided themselves on their olfactory powers. ('Baudelaire', he remarks, 'had an abnormally delicate sense of smell.') As Tinker points out, Hearn's article contains 'implied admission of his own supersensitiveness of smell'.[145]

The Scent of the Shulamite and the Fragrance of Youth

In 1881, following both 'An Odorous Subject' and his Jäger review, Hearn published a revised, more sophisticated version of 'Fantasy of a Fan', which bears identifiable marks of its relocation to New Orleans. In this short impressionistic tale called 'The Tale of a Fan', the narrator, having picked up 'a little Japanese fan' in the

---

[142] Hearn, 'Fantasy of a Fan', *Ye Giglampz*, p. 3.

[143] Jon Christopher Hughes, Introduction, in *Ye Giglampz: A Weekly Illustrated Journal*, p. 15.

[144] Hearn, 'An Odorous Subject', *Item* (12 August 1878), 1. Warm thanks to Philip Bullock for supplying me with a PDF of the original article. The article is cited in Tinker, 'Lafcadio Hearn and the Sense of Smell', p. 523, but with altered punctuation and 'Salamites' a misprint for 'Sulamitess'. The Sulamitess or Shulamitess refers to the Shulamite, the female protagonist of the Biblical Song of Solomon, a text much loved by Hearn (*Life and Letters*, 1. 227). Hearn uses the term 'Sulamitess' in another essay, 'Fair Women and Dark Women', *Item* (25 August 1878), in *Editorials*, p. 37.

[145] Tinker, 'Lafcadio Hearn and the Sense of Smell', p. 523.

New Orleans streetcar, muses on its owner. Having first admired the painted design, he comments:

> But the fairy colors were less strongly suggestive than something impalpable, invisible, indescribable, yet voluptuously enchanting which clung to the fan spirit-wise, a tender little scent,—a mischievous perfume,—a titillating, tantalizing aroma,—an odor inspirational as of the sacred gums whose incense intoxicates the priest of oracles. Did you ever lay your hand upon a pillow covered with the living supple silk of a woman's hair? Well, the intoxicating odor of that hair is something not to be forgotten.[146]

As in 'Fantasy of a Fan', the narrator makes it clear he is talking not about applied perfume but the actual perfume of women; however, in this story he is a connoisseur who discriminates between the scents produced by different kinds of women:

> There are blond and brunette odors; [...] There is a sharp, tart, invigorating penetrating, tropical sweetness in brunette perfumes; blond odors are either faint as those of a Chinese yellow rose, or fiercely ravishing as that the white Jessamine so bewitching for the moment, but which few can endure all night in the sleeping-room, making the heart of the sleeper faint.[147]

The narrator's views on the links between hair colour and body scent may sound far-fetched, but were not unusual in the nineteenth century. We know that Hearn had read J. K. Huysmans's prose poem 'Le Gousset' [The Arm-pit] from his *Croquis Parisiens* (1880), which he describes to Henry Krehbiel in 1881 as 'a terrible essay on the odors which emanate from a woman's armpits, the differences of the emanation being studied from the standpoint of character and passionate possibility'.[148] Huysmans's 'essay' does dilate on the relationship between axillary odour and hair colour, such odour being 'Bold, and at times tiring in a girl with brown or black hair, sharp and fierce in a red-head, [...] elusive yet heady in the case of the blonde, like certain sweet wines.'[149] However, Hearn's treatment of 'the perfume of women' is far more lyrical; what is more, 'The Tale of a Fan' precedes by five years the most famous work on the topic, Augustin Galopin's *Le Parfum de la femme et le sens olfactif dans l'amour*, published in 1886. In the words of Iwan Bloch, 'Galopin believes that the general *parfum de la femme* pervades the hair in a concentrated area. This is the bouquet of the body which renders superfluous any other perfume.' Bloch summarizes Galopin's findings thus:

> Blondes with ash-blonde hair are wont to exude a very delicate amber odor. Sometimes women with chestnut brown hair have this odor, but more often they have a sort of violet odor which appears to be connected with the secretions of the sebaceous glands.

---

[146] Hearn, 'The Tale of a Fan', *Item* (1 July 1881), in *Fantastics*, pp. 166–7.   [147] Ibid., p. 168.
[148] Hearn, Letter of 1881 to H. E. Krehbiel, in *Lafcadio Hearn: American Writings*, p. 794. This and other parts of this same letter are omitted, presumably censored on account of their sexual nature, by Elizabeth Bisland in her *Life and Letters*, 1. 225–9.
[149] J. K. Huysmans, 'The Arm-pit', in *Parisian Sketches: A Translation of Croquis Parisiens*, tr. Richard Griffiths (London: The Fortune Press, 1962), pp. 64–6; 66. Havelock Ellis translates a substantial piece of Huysmans's prose poem in his *Studies in the Psychology of Sex: Sexual Selection in Man* (p. 81).

Brunettes not infrequently have an odor of ebony wood which, during their periods, combines with a light but not unpleasant musk odor.[150]

Such views were still prevalent in the twentieth century. One of Colette's characters sprays herself liberally with perfume because she 'is always scared that people will say I smell like a redhead'.[151] The theory, according to the chemist Paul Jellinek, writing in 1951, is that 'a specific hair color is usually associated with a certain appearance of the skin and with certain activity patterns of its organs, and therefore with a specific type of personal odor', later defined as 'the individual odor of the clean unclad body from some distance'. Less romantic than Hearn or even Galopin, Jellinek goes on to specify blonde-type odours as 'sour-cheesy', redheads as 'pungent-burnt', and brunettes as 'sweetish-rancid'.[152] These types have also been used prescriptively, with certain fragrances specified as suiting particular hair colours, with Jellinek suggesting 'fresh' perfumes for blondes, 'exalting' perfumes for redheads, and 'sultry' perfumes for brunettes.[153] Indeed, in 1925, Jean Patou had released a trio of fragrances—Amour Amour for blondes, Que Sais-Je? for brunettes, and Adieu Sagesse for redheads—each supposedly reflecting a different stage of love, while in 1940 Dana had released Platine (or Platinum) 'for the precious blonde'.[154] Although this hair-colour scent typology is now rarely invoked, it may very occasionally persist in advice offered to would-be perfume purchasers.[155]

In 'The Tale of a Fan', Hearn's narrator, evidently an expert on the perfumes of women with his own range of associations, opines that:

[T]he odor of the fan was not a blond odor:—it was sharply sweet as new mown hay in autumn, keenly pleasant as a clear breeze blowing over sea foam:—what were frankincense and spikenard and cinnamon and all the odors of the merchant compared with it?—what could have been compared with it, indeed, save the smell of the garments of the young Shulamitess or the whispering robes of the Queen of Sheba? And these were brunettes.[156]

The Shulamitess, better known as the Shulamite, is the female protagonist of the Biblical Song of Solomon, who refers to herself as 'black' (S. of S. 1:6) because she has had to work in the sun. The Queen of Sheba, another Biblical figure who visits King Solomon to test his wisdom, is often assumed to be Ethiopian and thus also

---

[150] Augustin Galopin, *Le Parfum de la femme et le sens olfactif dans l'amour* (Paris: Saint-Germain, 1886), pp. 138–41; Bloch, *Odoratus Sexualis*, pp. 61, 53. Bloch uses 'amber', meaning 'ambergris' for Galopin's 'l'ambre gris' (*Le Parfum*, p. 139).

[151] Colette, *Claudine s'en va* (Paris: Société d'Éditions littéraires et artistiques, Librairie Paul Ollendorff, 1903). Marthe declares, 'j'ai toujours peur qu'on dise que je sens la rousse!' (p. 216).

[152] Jellinek, *The Psychological Basis of Perfumery*, p. 29. The first German edition dates to 1951.

[153] Jellinek, ch. 14: 'Odor Effects Diagram and Personal Perfume', in *The Psychological Basis of Perfumery*, pp. 114–25; 115.

[154] Herman, *Scent and Subversion*, pp. 43, 78.

[155] See, for example, John Oakes, *The Perfume Zodiac* (London: Prion, 2000), which, in addition to listing perfumes suitable for different star signs, also suggests, though in a far from dogmatic way, perfumes suitable for 'Fair' and 'Dark' complexions. Most modern perfume guide writers reject this idea and insist that perfume selection should be a matter of choice. See Irvine, *The Perfume Guide*, p. 9.

[156] Hearn, 'The Tale of a Fan', p. 169.

dark-skinned. According to Tinker, Hearn claimed that he was also able to distinguish the nuances of mixed-race identity by smell:

> He often declared that by the sense of smell alone he could immediately tell the difference between octoroons, quintroons, quadroons, mulattoes, and pure blooded Africans. As if this were not sufficiently remarkable, he would continue by saying that blind-folded he could tell the difference between a blonde and a brunette.[157]

Such language fills the modern reader with unease, as many older discourses on race and smell are firmly racist, attributing unpleasant odours to people of colour.[158] However, Hearn did not ascribe negative or denigratory value to his olfactory detections. During his time in Cincinnati, he had been married briefly (and illegally, according to the miscegenation laws of the day) to Alethea ('Mattie') Foley, an ex-slave—a marriage that cost him his job at the *Cincinnati Daily Enquirer*. Possibly emulating Baudelaire whom he noted as having 'a great passion for describing the charms of Malabaresses, and Hindoo girls, and dark Venuses belonging to the notably odorous races', Hearn was evidently attracted to black and mixed-race women, enjoyed their company, and liked their scent.[159] In New Orleans he spent comparatively little time with Caucasians, and though normally shy and retiring, seems to have come out of his shell when socializing with people from other racial groups. To his friend Henry Krehbiel he wrote in 1880: 'I seldom hear the English tongue except when I enter the office for a few brief hours every day. I eat and drink and sleep with members of the other races you detest like the son of Odin you are.'[160] On at least one occasion he was an enthusiastic attender at one of the New Orleans 'quadroon balls'. These dances were organized for handsome mixed-race women of colour (so-called 'quadroons' and 'octoroons') who were seeking wealthy white male protectors (although they were legally disbarred from marrying such men). Hearn reportedly threw himself into the party atmosphere and enjoyed himself so much that he refused to go home with his male companion at 3.00 a.m.[161]

New Orleans was famous for the beautiful Creole prostitutes of colour who worked in its brothels, and Hearn regularly spent time in what Tinker calls 'the patchouli-scented interiors of these places'.[162] Refreshingly, this seems to have done nothing to diminish his belief in women's superior moral nature. While his views on women were not especially progressive, he thought none the less of those from whom he bought sex and seems to have treated his Cyprian partners with some gallantry, often idealizing them, and occasionally falling in love with them. The appreciative remarks about the Shulamitess and Queen of Sheba in 'The Tale

---

[157] Tinker, 'Lafcadio Hearn and the Sense of Smell', p. 522.

[158] See, for example, ch. 3: 'Odorous Others: Race and Smell' in Reinarz, *Past Scents*, pp. 85–112.

[159] Hearn, 'An Odorous Subject', p. 1. 'Malabaresses' are presumably female inhabitants of India's Malabar Coast.

[160] Cited in Jonathan Cott, *Wandering Ghost: The Odyssey of Lafcadio Hearn* (Tokyo, New York, and London: Kodansha International, 1992), p. 180. Cott points out that Elizabeth Bisland, Hearn's biographer, altered 'sleep' to 'converse' in her *Life and Letters*, 1. 217.

[161] Tinker, *Lafcadio Hearn's American Days*, p. 94.   [162] Ibid., p. 214.

Plate 1. Grossmith fragrances in their original packaging with names to evoke exotic travel: Hasu-No-Hana (1888), Phūl-Nānā (1891), and Shem-el-Nessim (1906), © Grossmith, London

Plate 2. Violet (*Viola odorata*). Alamy Stock Photo

Plate 3. Keats's Grave with Violets, Non-Catholic Cemetery (formerly known as the 'Protestant Cemetery'), Rome. Photo S. Manicone, © Keats-Shelley House, 2011

Plate 4. Central panel of trade card of J. C. and J. Field (*c.*1885) depicting Samphire Soap with a quotation from Shakespeare's *King Lear*, © The British Library Board

Plate 5. Farina classic elongated eau-de-Cologne bottles—eighteenth century to the present day, © Johann Maria Farina, Cologne

Plate 6. Farina nineteenth-century eau-de-Cologne bottle, © Johann Maria Farina, Cologne

Plate 7. *Hay Hauling on the Alpine Snow*, painting by J. Hardwicke Lewis, in J. A. Symonds and M. Symonds, *Our Life in the Swiss Highlands*, 2nd edn (1907), p. 188. Photo: Daichi Ishikawa

Plate 8. Tuberose (*Polianthes tuberosa*), © judywhite/GardenPhotos.com

Plate 9. Tuberose (*Polianthes tuberosa*). Photo: Catherine Maxwell

Plate 10. Common Myrtle (*Myrtus communis*), flowering twig. Alamy Stock Photo

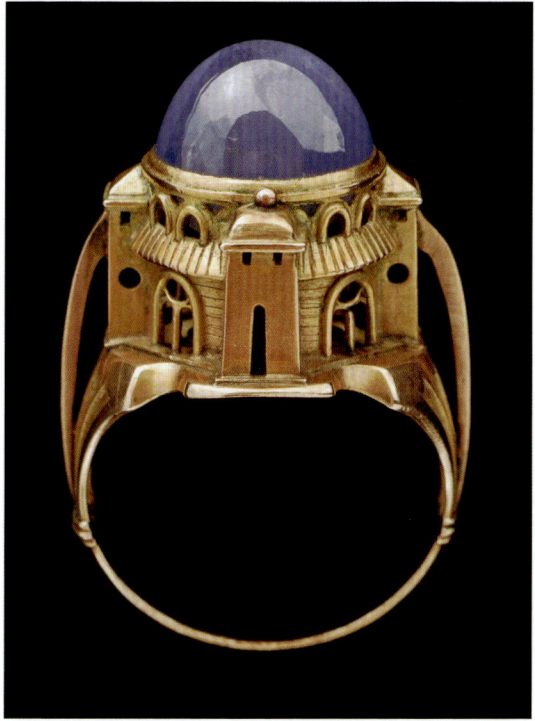

Plate 11. The Sabbatai Ring designed by Charles Ricketts for Katharine Bradley (1904). Intended to appeal to the senses, its bezel was to be smeared with ambergris, © The Fitzwilliam Museum, Cambridge

Plate 12. Lawrence Alma-Tadema, *The Roses of Heliogabalus* (1888), Oil on canvas, 132.7 × 214.4 cm, Pérez Simón Collection, Mexico, © Studio Sébert Photographes

Plate 13. 'Grand Mogul' Rose, from William Paul, *The Rose Garden in Two Divisions* (10th edn, 1903), © The British Library Board

of a Fan' hint at Hearn's admiration for darker women, an admiration he had also expressed somewhat discreetly in his 1878 article 'Fair Women and Dark Women':

> All the most famous canticles of love have been devoted to the darker type of beauty— the ebon hair and velvet eye and olive tint of the brunette—that tender brown tint which suggests the color-tone of ancient marbles, mellowed by time. The greatest of love songs is Solomon's song of the Sulamitess—or the song of songs; and the Sulamitess was a brunette. 'I am black but beautiful, O ye daughters of Jerusalem, as the tents of Kedar—or as the curtains of Solomon.'[163]

More explicitly, in a later letter to Basil Chamberlain of 1894, Hearn declared that he found white skin 'the *least* beautiful' of human skins and commented that 'Beauty there is in the North, of its kind. But it is surely not comparable with the wonderful beauty of colour in other races.'[164] With these references in mind, it is more than likely that the owner of the Japanese fan is herself a light-skinned woman of colour. Hearn's narrator uses smell to help project her image, and the story concludes with him asking, like a more romantic Sherlock Holmes, 'Young, slenderly graceful, with dark eyes and hair, skin probably a Spanish olive!—did such an one lose a little Japanese fan in car No. ------ of the C. C. R. R. during the slumberous heat of Wednesday morning?'[165] Indeed, Hearn, with his 'supersensitive nostrils', would have been contemptuous of Holmes and his belief that there were only 'seventy-five perfumes, which it is necessary that a criminal expert should be able to distinguish from each other'.[166]

Edward Larocque Tinker tells us of the rumour that Hearn 'had written and had privately printed a book entitled "The Perfume of Women" [...] of which not more than thirty copies were made', with one source claiming that Hearn had penned this treatise for a large New York perfume manufacturer. However, no copy has ever been found.[167] Later in his life, after he had relocated to Japan, Hearn did, however, write a short essay 'Parfum de Jeunesse', which appeared for the first time in *Exotics and Retrospectives* (1898). It opens with a reminiscence of a friend who could always find his girlfriend's cloak in the dark 'because it had the smell of sweet new milk'.[168] Meditating on this perfume of youth, Hearn writes that it:

> [I]s not uncommon, though I fancy that it belongs to Northern rather than to Southern races. It signifies perfect health and splendid vigor. But there are other and

---

[163] Hearn, 'Fair Women and Dark Women', p. 37.

[164] Hearn, Letter to Basil Chamberlain of 6 March 1894, in *Japanese Letters*, pp. 270, 272. Being half Greek, Hearn was himself olive-skinned, becoming deeply tanned in hot climates. His one memory of the Greek mother from whom he was separated as a child was of her 'dark, brown and beautiful face, with large brown eyes'. He nonetheless identified with her and not his Anglo-Irish father. See Paul Murray, *A Fantastic Journey: The Life and Literature of Lafcadio Hearn* (Folkestone: Japan Library, 1993), pp. 211, 214, 228.

[165] Hearn, 'The Tale of a Fan', p. 169. 'C. C. R. R.' stands for 'Crescent City Railroad'. New Orleans is known as the 'Crescent City' because, in the nineteenth century, it took the shape of a crescent along a bend of the Mississippi River.

[166] Arthur Conan Doyle, 'The Hound of the Baskervilles' (1902), in *The Complete Adventures of Sherlock Holmes* (Harmondsworth: Penguin, 1981), p. 765.

[167] Tinker, 'Lafcadio Hearn and the Sense of Smell', p. 526.

[168] Hearn, 'Parfum de Jeunesse', in *Exotics and Retrospectives* (Boston: Little, Brown, & Co., 1914), p. 221.

more delicate varieties of the attraction. Sometimes it may cause you to think of precious gums or spices from the uttermost tropics; sometimes it is a thin, thin sweetness,
like a ghost of musk. It is not personal (though physical personality certainly has an
odor): it is the fragrance of a season, of the springtime of life. But even as the fragrance
of spring, though everywhere a passing delight, varies with country and climate, so
varies the fragrance of youth.

Whether it be of one sex more than of another were difficult to say. We notice it
chiefly in girls and in children with long hair, probably because it dwells especially in
the hair. But it is always independent of artifice as the sweetness of the wild violet is.[169]

Here, initially at least, 'parfum de jeunesse' is a scent predominantly associated for
Hearn with girls or young women, just as for Symonds it was exclusively identified
with young men. Symonds linked it with the early summer harvest, while with
Hearn we return to the scent of spring, a smell that in earlier writings he had connected with both aesthetic beauty and wanderlust. Yet he also stipulates that the
'fragrance of youth' is subject to racial or geographical variations just as spring
smells differently in different countries, a judgement that he was well equipped to
make, having by this stage in his life lived on three different continents.

In 'Parfum de Jeunesse' Hearn looks back to his earlier article of 1880, 'The
Physiology of Smells', where he had touched on

what has been called by French writers "the perfume of youth". Little animals, young
doves, puppies —all little creatures just newly entering upon life have a pleasant odor.
There is a fresh, pleasant smell about cleanly young children; and the hair of a girl has
a natural perfume, sweeter than all the cosmetic odors Fashion drowns it with.

Nine months after this early article, in 'The Flower-Sellers', a short sketch of the
elderly women who market their 'bright blossoms' on the streets of New Orleans,
Hearn had declared, 'Evanescent as the beauty of Woman are the colors of the
flowers;—volatile their drowsy-sweet odors as the perfume of youth.'[170] A short
story, 'Torn Letters', that appeared in the *Times-Democrat* four years later, enlarged
on this theme poetically:

The wind lifts her long loose hair across my face,—as inviting me to inhale its perfume.
Exquisite and indescribable perfume of youth! what flower-ghost prisoned in crystal
owneth so delicate a magic as thou? Unnumbered the songs which celebrated the breath
of blossoms, the scent of gardens,—yet what blossom-scent, what flower-witchery
might charm the sense like the odour of a woman's hair, the natural perfume of the
beauty, the fresh and delicious fragrance of youth.[171]

Hearn was also aware of the legendary tradition that ascribed therapeutic or rejuvenating powers to the 'parfum de jeunesse', for in his novel *Chita* (1888), in an
apostrophe to the sea, he exclaims:

---

[169] Hearn, 'Parfum de Jeunesse', pp. 221–2.
[170] Hearn, 'The Flower-Sellers', *Item* (1 September 1880), in *The New Orleans of Lafcadio Hearn:
Illustrated Sketches from the Daily City Item*, ed. Delia LaBarre (Baton Rouge, LA: Louisiana State
University Press, 2007), p. 82.
[171] Hearn, 'Torn Letters', *Times-Democrat* (14 September 1884), in *Miscellanies*, ed. Albert
Mordell, 2 vols (London: William Heinemann, 1924), 2: *An American Miscellany*, p. 63.

Still is thy quickening breath an elixir unto them that flee to thee for life,—like the breath of young girls, like the breath of children, prescribed for the senescent by magicians of old,—prescribed unto weazened elders in the books of Wizards.[172]

In fact this therapeutic use of the 'parfum de jeunesse' is part of the practice known as 'Shunamitism', named after a famous instance in the Bible (1 Kings 1:1) in which the elderly and infirm King David is prescribed as a bedfellow a fair young virgin from Shunem named Abishag—not to have intercourse with him, but to warm and revitalize him. Iwan Bloch devotes an appendix to 'Shunammitism' [*sic*] in his *Odoratus Sexualis*, in which he cites a variety of sources including Marsilio Ficino and Francis Bacon, and where he states that 'the quintessence of Shunammitism is the attribution of a healing and life-prolonging power to the corporeal scents of young, healthy and chaste persons'. However, he concludes

> Modern science has not yet discovered a single fact to prove that the odors or exhalations of young people can rejuvenate or extend the lives of old and wasted persons. [...] At best Shunammitism is a sort of suggestion-therapy, but it is quite unlikely that the exhalations of young persons as such exercise any positive effect.[173]

However, in his essay Hearn steers clear of such prescriptions and, while he does attribute a rejuvenating power to 'parfum de jeunesse', this lies in rather its ability to rekindle or revivify not merely personal memory but the ghosts of ancestral memory:

> [O]dor of blossom and odor of youth alike have now become for us excitants of the higher emotional life, of vague but voluminous and supremely delicate aesthetic feeling.
> Like the feeling awakened by beauty, the pleasure of odor is a pleasure of remembrance, is the magical appeal of a sensation to countless memories of countless lives. And even as the scent of a blossom evokes the ghosts of feelings experienced in millions of millions of unrecorded springs, so the fragrance of youth bestirs within us the spectral survival of sensations associated with every vernal cycle of all the human existence that has vanished behind us.[174]

Moreover, in concluding his essay, Hearn introduces a new association:

> And this fragrance of fresh being likewise makes invocation to ideal sentiment, to parental scarcely less than to amorous tenderness, because conjoined through immeasurable time with the charm and the beauty of childhood. Out of night and death is summoned by its necromancy more than a shadowy thrill from the rapture of perished passion, more than a phantom-reflex from the delight of countless bridals; even something also of the ecstasy of pressing lips of caress to the silky head of the first-born, faint refluence from the forgotten joy of myriad millions of buried mothers.[175]

---

[172] Hearn, *Chita*, in *Lafcadio Hearn: American Writings*, p. 133. *Chita* first appeared in *Harper's New Monthly Magazine* in April 1888.

[173] Bloch, *Odoratus Sexualis*, pp. 187, 205.

[174] Hearn, 'Parfum de Jeunesse', pp. 223–4. Hearn had shown a much earlier interest in ancestral memory in 'Hereditary Memories', *Item* (22 July 1880), in *Fantastics*, pp. 60–5.

[175] Hearn, 'Parfum de Jeunesse', p. 224.

By the time he wrote this essay he had himself become a father to two sons (born respectively in 1893 and 1897), an experience that makes him aware of how the 'fragrance of fresh being' appeals to 'parental scarcely less than to amorous tenderness'. After first arriving in Japan, Hearn had continued to frequent brothels, but his marriage in 1891 and his transformation from sexual adventurer to respectable husband and devoted father meant that the domestic arena and the bodies of children took precedence over the bodies of *filles de joie*. That respectability infiltrates the lectures that he gave as an academic teaching English literature, where a protective paternalism towards his young male Japanese students makes him treat sexual topics with a certain tact and reticence. Although the topic of 'parfum de jeunesse' surfaces in his lecture on Swinburne, he explains it obliquely by allusion to a child rather than to women, the proper focus of Swinburne's poetry:

> What the French call the *parfum de jeunesse* or odour of youth, the pleasant smell of young bodies, the perfume that we notice, for example, in the hair of a healthy child, is something which English writers very seldom venture to treat of; but Swinburne has treated it quite as delicately at times as a French poet could do, though sometimes a little extravagantly.[176]

Odorous and Odourless: Savouring Japan

'The first charm of Japan is as intangible and volatile as a perfume', remarked Hearn in 'My First Day', an article recording his early impressions of the country.[177] Yet although his sense of smell seems to have remained acute throughout his life, his comments on body scents noticeably diminish during his residence in Japan. This may be because most East Asians, including Japanese people, belong to a genetic group that has fewer apocrine sweat glands, making them less prone to body odours. Moreover, as was frequently observed by nineteenth-century visitors, compared to their Western counterparts even the humblest Japanese citizens maintained high levels of personal hygiene, bathing on a daily basis in hot water amply supplied by the country's many thermal springs. In 1891 Sir Edwin Arnold, an author much admired by Hearn, commented in his essay 'Japanese People':

> [M]ark well how the people frequent the *furo-do* [bath; or the way or practice of bathing]; they are the greatest lovers of 'the tub' in the world, and indubitably the cleanliest of all known people. A Japanese crowd has no odour whatever, and your *jinricksha*-man [rickshaw man] perspires profusely without the smallest offence to the nicest sense of his fare close behind.[178]

---

[176] Hearn, 'Studies in Swinburne', in *Pre-Raphaelite and Other Poets*, p. 140.

[177] Hearn, 'My First Day', in *Glimpses of Unfamiliar Japan*, 2 vols (London: Osgood McIlvaine & Co., 1894), 1.1.

[178] Sir Edwin Arnold, 'Japanese People', in *Japonica* (London: James R. Osgood, McIlvaine & Co., 1891), p. 52. In 1883 in a letter to W. D. O'Connor, Hearn asked, regarding Edwin Arnold's *The Light of Asia* (1879), his popular narrative poem about the Buddha, 'Have you seen the exquisite new edition of Arnold's "Light of Asia"? It has enchanted me,—perfumed my mind as with the incense of a strangely new and beautiful worship.' See *Life and Letters*, 1. 291. My thanks to Daichi Ishikawa for his explanation of the obsolete phrase *furo-do*.

Hearn's friend, Basil Chamberlain, Professor of Japanese and Philology at Tokyo University, had written similarly in an entry on 'Bathing' in his *Things Japanese* the previous year:

> Some Europeans have tried to pick holes in the Japanese system, saying that the bathers put on their dirty clothes when they have dried themselves. True, the Japanese of the old school have nothing so perfect as our system of daily renovated linen. But as the bodies even of the men of the lowest class are washed and scrubbed daily, it is hardly to be supposed that their garments, though perhaps dusty outside, can be very dirty within. A Japanese crowd is the sweetest in the world. The charm of the Japanese system of hot bathing is proved by the fact that almost all the foreigners resident in the country abandon their cold tubs in its favour.[179]

Arnold reiterated the 'sweetness of the Japanese' in his *Seas and Lands* (1891), adding his own perception: 'a Japanese crowd is the sweetest and least objectionable in the world; indeed, the natural odour of the people is not unlike that of the leaf of the lemon-geranium'.[180]

Hearn alluded to both Chamberlain and Arnold in his essay 'The Genius of Japanese Civilization':

> Professor Chamberlain has well said, 'a Japanese crowd is the sweetest in the world'. Your Japanese tramp takes his hot bath daily, if he has a fraction of a cent to pay for it, or his cold bath, if he has not. In his little bundle there are combs, toothpicks, razors, toothbrushes. He never allows himself in any way to become unpleasant.[181]

In a footnote in the same essay he also defended Arnold's analogy:

> Critics have tried to make fun of Sir Edwin Arnold's remark that a Japanese crowd smells like a geranium-flower. Yet the simile is exact! The perfume called *jako* [musk], when sparingly used, might easily be taken for the odor of a musk-geranium. In almost any Japanese assembly including women a slight perfume of *jako* is discernible; for the robes worn have been laid in drawers containing a few grains of *jako*. Except for this delicate scent, a Japanese crowd is absolutely odorless.[182]

Interestingly, while defending Arnold, Hearn alters his analogy from 'the leaf of the lemon-geranium' to 'geranium-flower' and then 'the odor of a musk-geranium'. The scented geranium (*Pelargonium*, from the family *Geraniaceae*), a half-hardy or tender plant grown for the fragrance of its leaves rather than its flowers, was popular with the Victorians, who used its aromatic foliage to perfume rooms. There are many varieties with different kinds of scent such as lemon, rose, apple,

---

[179] Basil Hall Chamberlain, 'Bathing', in *Things Japanese* (London: Kegan Paul, Trench, Trübner & Co., Ltd, 1890), p. 44.

[180] Sir Edwin Arnold, ch. 30: 'The Japanese Shampooer' (10 June 1890), in *Seas and Lands: Reprinted by Permission of the Proprietors of the 'Daily Telegraph' from Letters Published under the Title 'By Sea and Land' in that Journal* (London: Longman & Co., 1891), p. 406.

[181] Hearn, 'The Genius of Japanese Civilization', in *Kokoro: Hints and Echoes of Japanese Inner Life* (London: Gay & Bird, 1895), pp. 30–1.

[182] Ibid., p. 31.

orange, peach, peppermint, pine, and eucalyptus.[183] Musk geranium (*Geranium macrorrhizum*) also comes from the same general family *Geraniaceae*, but like most true geraniums is a hardy perennial plant. Its leaves have a warm, musk-like fragrance, and have been used in perfumery and potpourri. Hearn thus switches plants, changing the smell of the Japanese crowd that Arnold identifies as lemon to that of musk, a very different aroma and one not emitted by the actual bodies of Japanese people but by their clothes. For Hearn also transumes herbaceous musk into *jako*, the animalic musk grains used to scent Japanese women's robes.

Arnold does mention *jako* as an applied perfume in another essay, 'A Delicate Entertainment', in his collection *East and West* (1896), where he briefly alludes to 'musk or "jako"—of which the ladies of Dai Nippon are very fond. Some of them have the custom of sewing a tiny bag of musk-dust inside a velvet fillet, and fastening it under their sleeve upon the upper arm.'[184] In one of his literary lectures, Hearn writes

> 'Musk' is a perfume used by English as well as Japanese ladies, but there is no perfume which must be used with more discretion, carefulness. If you use ever so little too much, the effect is not pleasant. But if you use exactly the proper quantity, and no more, there is no perfume which is more lovely.[185]

Thus, for Hearn, the delicate perfume of musk discreetly applied is the scent of the Japanese crowd, which might otherwise appear to be 'odorless'. This is very different in kind from his earlier olfactory typologies based on hair and skin colour.

Lest Japanese culture might also be thought odourless, Arnold points out in 'A Delicate Entertainment', that olfactory connoisseurship was taken very seriously in nineteenth-century Japan. Having bewailed the 'deplorable' neglect of 'sweet odours' in England, he asserts:

> They do not so disregard the nose in Japan, or neglect the delicious kingdom of sensations of which it is the well-provided and happy channel. Less fortunate than we are in the variety and delicacy of manufactured perfumes, they appreciate intensely those which they possess, and give lovely and appropriate names to distinguish one odour from the other.

He then proceeds to explain that 'For the most part, Japanese perfumes are prepared not in the liquid form, as with us, but in powder or solid shape, necessitating the use of incense-burners to develop the aroma of each.'[186] The remainder of this short essay principally explores (although Arnold does not use the term) *kōdō*, or

---

[183] Since the early nineteenth century, certain rose-scented varieties (*Pelargonium graveolens*, *Pelargonium capitatum*) have been used to provide rose-geranium oil for the perfume industry, an oil often seen as a cheap alternative to authentic rose oil, which is extremely expensive.

[184] Sir Edwin Arnold, 'A Delicate Entertainment', in *East and West: Being Reprinted from the 'Daily Telegraph' and Other Sources* (London: Longmans, Green, & Co., 1896), p. 372.

[185] Hearn writes about musk in his lecture 'On Love in English Poetry' in relation to Coventry Patmore's line 'Showy as damask-rose and shy as musk' without seeming to realize that by 'musk' Patmore means the 'musk rose'. See Hearn, ch. 1: 'On Love in English Poetry', in *Appreciations of Poetry*, p. 22.

[186] Arnold, 'A Delicate Entertainment', p. 372.

the art of appreciating Japanese incense, with special attention paid to the institution of 'the incense party' where invited guests play an elaborate formal game in which they have to distinguish one kind of incense from another. This game is also the main focus of 'Incense', a much lengthier and far more detailed essay by Hearn included in his collection *In Ghostly Japan* (1899) and still cited today in discussions of Japanese incense.[187]

Developing an initial observation that 'It is almost ubiquitous,—this perfume of incense. It makes one element of the faint but complex and never to be forgotten odor of the Far East', Hearn sketches a very brief history of the history of aromatics in Japan, conceding that because of the extensive body of data, 'The merest outline is terrifying!' What follows, he writes, are 'a few notes about the religious, the luxurious, and the ghostly uses of incense'.[188] When he comes to the central section devoted to the incense-party or *kō-kwai*, Hearn notes that guests invited to such parties:

> [A]ll attend the same in as *odorless* a condition as possible: a lady, for instance, must not use hair-oil, or put on any dress that has been kept in a perfumed chest-of-drawers. Furthermore, the guest should prepare for the contest by taking a prolonged hot bath, and should eat only the lightest and least odorous kind of food before going to the rendezvous.[189]

The unperfumed body is, of course, a necessary precondition for a successful incense game, but in general Hearn's perception of perfume in Japanese culture marks a shift from the scents of the body, whether these are natural or applied, to an appreciation of ambient or atmospheric smells. These include not only the 'ubiquitous' fragrance of incense but also 'rice-fields, and cedar groves', and 'the divine Sea', as well as less pleasant emanations such as those given off by malodorous beetles, the preparation of 'daikon', and the 'atrocious smells' of the 'cuttlefish industry'.[190] It is these smells that replace what in in a short story of 1881 Hearn had referred to as 'the odor of a woman's hair, the incense of a woman's youth'.[191]

While he always loved what he called 'the fragrance of words, [...] the perfume of syllables in blossom', it is Hearn's earlier passions for women, beauty, exotic feminized places, and French and English Romantic and aesthetic literature that are impregnated with the scent he calls 'odor di femina' and its predominantly feminine counterpart 'parfum de jeunesse'. Just as John Addington Symonds's love of the natural perfume of the youthful male body brought together his academic and literary interests and his appetite for travel, so too do these particular fragrances mark for Hearn the special provenance of the cosmopolitan aesthete as *flaireur*.[192]

---

[187] See, for example, Kiyoko Morita, *The Book of Incense* (Tokyo: Kodansha International Ltd, 1992), p. 132. Another useful book, although it does not mention Hearn, is David Pybus, *Kodo: The Way of Incense* (Boston, MA: Turtle Publishing, 2001.)

[188] Hearn, 'Incense', in *In Ghostly Japan* (Boston, MA: Little, Brown, & Co., 1899), pp. 19–45; 20, 25.

[189] Hearn, 'Incense', p. 40.

[190] *Japanese Letters*, pp. 146, 161, 266, 417. Daikon is a root vegetable that Hearn says he enjoys, although he dislikes its smell while it is being cooked.

[191] Hearn, 'El Vómito', *Item* (21 March 1881), in *Fantastics*, p. 139.

[192] Letter to Basil Chamberlain (5 June 1893), in *Japanese Letters*, pp. 106, 107.

5

Carnal Flowers, Charnel Flowers
Tuberose in Late Victorian Poetry

An orchid-collector purchases at auction a selection of plants belonging to a fellow collector found dead in a mangrove swamp, his body apparently sucked dry by leeches. Among the plants purchased is an unidentifiable rhizome that, once planted in his hothouse, quickly produces shoots and leaves. Entering his glass-house the collector realizes his plant has flowered by 'a new odour in the air, a rich, intensely sweet scent, that overpowered every other', but on admiring the blooms that are the source of this scent, begins to find it 'insufferable', feels faint, and passes out. In the nick of time his housekeeper cousin, a woman suspicious of the strange and exotic, finds him in the hothouse where the orchid has begun to feed on him with its leech-like suckers. Resisting the faintness caused by the scent and having managed to drag him outside, she kills the predatory orchid by exposing it to the cold air, thus saving her cousin.

H. G. Wells's 'The Flowering of the Strange Orchid' of 1894, makes use of key decadent tropes and figures—the foreign invader, the 'strange flower', the dangerous artificial hothouse atmosphere, a poisonous perfume that overwhelms the senses. The story is a tongue-in-cheek cautionary tale about the dangers of a vampirical decadence, whose orchidaceous excesses can nonetheless be quickly quelled by the application of a brisk and breezy common sense. However, we might notice that the collector, recovered from his ordeal, seems curiously energized by it, appearing 'bright and garrulous [...] in the glory of his strange adventure'.[1]

One of the iconic flowers of decadence, the orchid's out-of-the-ordinary, even peculiar, appearance reliably puts it in the category of 'strange flowers' that Walter Pater suggests should be sought out by the aspiring aesthete along with 'strange dyes' and 'curious odours' (*SR*, p. 120). Unsurprisingly then, orchids appear to greatest effect in *fin-de-siècle* texts where they are associated with monstrosity, perversity, and sin. Oscar Wilde's Lord Henry Wotton cuts for his buttonhole an orchid, which he says is 'a marvellous spotted thing, as effective as the seven deadly sins', while Dorian Gray is another man who mysteriously faints among the orchids in his own hothouse, although not, it should be said, on account of their overwhelming perfume (*DG*, p. 165).

Rare, exotic, high-maintenance foreign beauties requiring a carefully controlled artificial environment at some considerable expense, orchids tick all the boxes

---

[1] H. G. Wells, 'The Flowering of the Strange Orchid', in *The Stolen Bacillus and Other Incidents* (London: Macmillan & Co., 1904), pp. 17–35; 30, 35.

when it comes to decadent credentials. These include the flowers' none-too-subtle, uncanny evocation of human sexuality. 'Orchid' derives from the Greek *orchis*, meaning testicle, which the tuber of the plant was thought to resemble, although most viewers find the flowers vulval in appearance. Moreover, the vanilla orchid, whose fruit produces the sweet essence used in perfume and cookery, takes its name from the diminutive of the Spanish *vaina*, meaning 'pod' or 'sheath', itself derived from the Latin word 'vagina'. Orchids thus have the characteristics of what we might call a 'carnal flower', a flower whose nature inevitably causes one to think of sex and sensuality.

Although the orchid nicely introduces us to the notion of dangerous intoxicating perfume and sensual pleasure, it is not the carnal flower I intend to explore in this chapter. That distinction falls to the tuberose (*Polianthes tuberosa*), the inspiration for the contemporary fragrance Carnal Flower created by the perfumer Dominique Ropion for the niche perfume house Frédéric Malle. Carnal Flower contains more tuberose oil than any other contemporary perfume currently available, a fact reflected in its price at £150 for a 50 ml bottle, as good-quality tuberose absolute, at £5,500–10,000 per kilo, is one of the most valuable substances in the world. Although tuberose does not have the immediate visual impact and graphic sexual suggestiveness of orchids, it is the carnal flower par excellence because of its fragrance, being called by the perfumer Roja Dove 'the harlot of perfumery'.[2]

In spite of the seeming connection, the tuberose is not related to the rose, its name deriving from its tuberous root. Its flower sprays of white blossoms, sometimes tipped with pale pink in the bud, look innocent enough but emit a complex sweet fragrance often described as heady and narcotic and composed of several hundred different molecules with different scent properties (see Plates 8 and 9). The artisan perfumer Alec Lawless describes tuberose as 'Sweet, heavy, floral and balsamic, with a slightly green, honey back note. Has been described as a "well stocked garden at eventide".'[3] Lawless apparently alludes to Piesse's *Art of Perfumery* (1855), which says the scent is 'a nosegay in itself, and reminds one of a well-stocked flower-garden at evening close', and declares 'And oh, what a fragrance breathes from it! what a bouquet, snatching perfume from every flower with superb eclecticism!'[4] Among that bouquet initial notes may strike one as camphoraceous, a medicinal scent of wintergreen or Vicks VapoRub induced by methyl salicylate, a natural compound found in the flower. Also present is eugenol, a spicy isolate of clove oil, more usually associated with carnations. And then there is a strange rubber note. The bio-physicist and perfume critic Luca Turin describes tuberose absolute as 'black rubber flower', observing: 'This is a natural oil, a complex mixture. This one's smell evolves. The rubber is kinky, dusted with talcum. Then an almost meaty blood-like smell reminiscent of carnations, and finally a "white flower" […] Decorous but unquestionably poisonous.'[5]

---

[2] Dove, *The Essence of Perfume*, p. 59.
[3] Lawless, *Artisan Perfumery or Being Led by the Nose*, p. 75.
[4] Piesse, *Art of Perfumery* (1855), p. 80. The comment starting 'And oh' appears for the first time in the *Art of Perfumery*, 4th edn (1879), p. 213.
[5] Luca Turin, cited in Burr, *The Emperor of Scent*, p. 18.

Indeed, in common with other sensual white flowers, tuberose has an underlying animalic character, with fragrance notes that hint at the body and sex. Such white flower scents, including tuberose, are often described as indolic, as they contain indole, an inky or tarry-smelling molecule, also found in faeces and rotting corpses, that gives flowers like lilies, ylang ylang, orange blossom, lilac, and gardenia a putrid-sweet, sultry, intoxicating note. According to the perfume critic Denyse Beaulieu, 'tuberose is the white flower that contains the greatest quantity and variety of lactones', fatty or buttery-smelling molecules with 'coconut, hay and peach facets', which are also produced by the human scalp. Tuberose scent also contains a trace of skatol, a natural isolate found in animalic civet, and butyric acid, found in cheese and foot odour. This complex bouquet helps tuberose flowers achieve pollination. Beaulieu comments:

> Tuberose and her sisters jasmine, orange blossom, gardenia, honeysuckle are the vamps of the floral world, pallid creatures whose hypnotic, diffusive scents are potions for attracting nocturnal pollinating insects [...] Stick your nose in them. Go past the pretty. Zero in on the weird. Butter, Camembert, mushrooms, horse manure, bad breath, dirty feet, blood, meat, shit... Despite their tiny size and pristine petals, white flowers bellow Nature's obscene secret through their outsized fragrance: flowers are sexual organs. And if those organs have ended up grafted David Cronenberg-style onto our skin, it is precisely *because* they also smell like the human body in all its extreme states, whether pleasure or death.[6]

As Beaulieu intimates, tuberose is a flower whose scent is stronger at night to attract pollinators, specifically moths. In India and Malaya, tuberose is called 'mistress of the night', another detail that hints at its after-hours harlotry. In darkness the white blossoms of the flower also have a luminescence that helps them attract insects. In his oriental poetic romance *Lalla Rookh* (1817), Thomas Moore writes of:

> The tube-rose, with her silvery light,
>   That in the Gardens of MALAY
> Is call'd the Mistress of the Night,
> So like a bride, scented and bright,
>   She comes out when the sun's away.[7]

Although Moore's bridal imagery suggests something more virtuous, the vigorous night-life of the flower leads the twentieth-century perfumer, William A. Poucher, to explain:

> The tuberose has for years been regarded as the symbol of voluptuousness, and the reasons for this may be traced to the beliefs of some of the older writers who generally considered the perfume to be slightly intoxicating. For instance, one writer recommends good girls not to breathe the odour of the tuberose on a fine evening, because its subtle perfume throws one into a voluptuous intoxication from which one does not easily become liberated.[8]

---

[6] Beaulieu, *The Perfume Lover*, pp. 128, 125–6.

[7] Moore, *Lalla Rookh: An Oriental Romance*, pp. 311–12.

[8] William A. Poucher, *Perfumes, Cosmetics and Soaps with Especial Reference to Synthetics*, 2 vols (London: Chapman & Hall, 1925–6), 2. 161.

John Ingram, the Victorian author of a book on the symbolism of flowers, concurs, writing that the flower's 'white blossom exhales the most exquisite perfume—a perfume, however, it is alleged, so powerful, that to enjoy it without danger it is necessary to keep at some distance from the plant'.[9]

Contrary to popular belief, there is no one stable set of significations for the Victorian language of flowers, which varies considerably from authority to authority. However, tuberose is something of an exception, proving remarkably consistent across different flower dictionaries, where it reliably translates as 'dangerous pleasures' or, as Poucher specifies, 'voluptuousness'.[10] I would suggest that this rare consistency arises from consensus on the strong sensual scent of the tuberose. Moreover, adding to its dangerous reputation, various commentators have noted the flower's ability to stage an uncanny light display. In her 1879 book on flower lore, Miss Carruthers explains that in addition to its luminosity, 'The tuberose has been observed, in a sultry evening after thunder, when the air was highly charged with electric fluid, to dart small sparks or scintillations of lurid flame from such of its flowers as are fading.'[11] Such effects had also been noticed by a number of Victorian poets like the Spasmodic Philip James Bailey, who mentions 'The fragrant tuberose scintillating light' in 'A Spiritual Legend' (1855), while in 'The Garden of Proserpine' (1869) Dora Greenwell observes how 'the tuberose | In its swift fading glows | And lights within its heart a funeral pyre'.[12]

Like jasmine, tuberose is too delicate to be subjected to the regular extraction processes of steam distillation, one of the factors that make tuberose absolute so extremely expensive. Although nowadays almost exclusively produced by solvent extraction, it was formerly obtained through the process known as 'enfleurage' in which the flowers are covered in a thin layer of highly refined, odourless fat, which they imbue with their odour. The resulting 'pomade' is melted, washed with alcohol, and the alcohol heated and evaporated, leaving the rich, full-bodied absolute. Tuberose flowers have the unusual quality of producing essential oil for up to seventy-two hours after they are picked, which makes them ideal for enfleurage. Reminding us of the tuberose's night-time blandishments, its 'marked exhalation of odour after sundown', Piesse's *Art of Perfumery* observes that 'The *enfleurage* laboratory is always kept dark, an artificial inducement [...] for the blossoms to "work hard".'[13] This is an extended afterlife that is also a slow death. Beaulieu remarks of the languorous demise of culled white flowers 'They are *dying*, not fading', citing her fellow perfume critic Octavian Coifan: '"The white flower is a flower that decomposes in sheer beauty!"'[14]

[9] John Ingram, *Flora Symbolica or the Language and Sentiment of Flowers* (London and New York: Frederick Warne & Co., 1870), p. 134.

[10] Ed Madden, 'Say it with Flowers: The Poetry of Marc-André Raffalovich', *College Literature* 24 (1997), 15. See also Madden's source—Beverly Seaton, *The Language of Flowers: A History* (Charlottesville, VA: University Press of Virginia, 1995), pp. 196–7.

[11] Miss Carruthers, *Flower Lore: The Teaching of Flowers, Historical, Legendary, Poetical and Symbolical* (Belfast: McCaw, Stevenson & Orr, 1879), p. 106.

[12] Philip James Bailey, 'A Spiritual Legend', in *The Mystic and Other Poems* (London: Chapman & Hall, 1855), p. 88; Dora Greenwell, 'The Garden of Proserpine', in *Carmina Crucis* (London: Bell & Daldy, 1869), p. 1.

[13] Piesse, *Art of Perfumery*, 4th edn (1879), p. 214.

[14] Beaulieu, *The Perfume Lover*, p. 129.

The prolonged fragrant expiration of tuberose is not its only link with death, for if it is a carnal flower it is also a charnel flower. Originally found in Mexico, it was cultivated by the Aztecs who called it 'bone-flower' (*omixochitl*) on account of its white blossoms.[15] According to Beaulieu, it was one of the white flowers used in Aztec sacrificial rituals, its scent blending 'with the stench of [the] sacrificial victim's blood—there is a bit of a blood note in the tuberose, and that hint of blood is, again, a bond between death and life, human sacrifice and female fertility'.[16] Like other indolic white flowers, tuberose has been also used as a funeral flower, its strong scent helping camouflage but also blending with the smell of human decay, an association possibly responsible for a not uncommon ambivalence or queasiness about white flower scents.

Something of that ambivalence can be found in the Romantic poet Percy Shelley, author of some of the most influential literary references to tuberose. In 'The Sensitive-Plant', he celebrates 'The jessamine faint, and the sweet tuberose, | The sweetest flower for scent that blows' (*SPP*, p. 211), while in 'The Woodman and the Nightingale', the nightingale's song is able to 'Satiate the hungry dark with melody | [...] as a tuberose | Peoples some Indian dell with scents which lie | Like clouds above the flower from which they rose'.[17] However, when referring to the classical bucolic poets in his 'A Defence of Poetry' (1821), Shelley finds:

> Their poetry is intensely melodious; like the odour of the tuberose, it overcomes and sickens the spirit with excess of sweetness; whilst the poetry of the preceding age was as a meadow-gale of June which mingles the fragrance of all the flowers of the field, and adds a quickening and harmonizing spirit of its own which endows the sense with a power of sustaining its extreme delight.   (*SPP*, p. 492)

John Addington Symonds endorses this assessment in his *Studies of the Greek Poets* (1873):

> Over the waning day of Greek poetry Theocritus, Bion, and Moschus cast the sunset hues of their excessive beauty. Genuine and exquisite is their inspiration; pure, sincere, and true is their execution. Yet we agree with Shelley, who compares their perfume to 'the odour of the tuberose, which overcomes and sickens the spirit with excess of sweetness'.[18]

Picking up on that note of cloying sweetness, Symonds goes on to draw out a more explicit comparison with decay in contemporary literary decadence:

> In the same way the erotic epigrammatists, though many of them genuine poets, especially the exquisite Meleager of Gadara, in the very perfection of their peculiar quality of genius offer an unmistakable sign of decay. It is the fashion among a certain class of modern critics to rave about the art of Decadence, to praise the hectic hues of consumption and even the strange livors of corruption, more than the roses and the

---

[15] Emily W. Emmart Trueblood, '"Omixochitl": The Tuberose (*Polianthes tuberosa*)', *Economic Botany* 27 (1973), 157–73.

[16] Beaulieu, *The Perfume Lover*, p. 130.

[17] Shelley, 'The Woodman and the Nightingale', in *Shelley: Poetical Works*, p. 562.

[18] Symonds, *Studies of the Greek Poets*, 1. 33.

lilies of health. Let them peruse the epigrams of Meleager and of Straton. Of beauty in decay sufficient splendours may be found there.[19]

The phrase 'livors of corruption' references the Latin term 'livor mortis', alluding to the lividity, or purplish red discoloration of the skin that can set in after death. Shelley's sickly tuberose seems inevitably to lead Symonds to thoughts of decadent death and decay, perhaps something not surprising in a writer whose own favourite scent was the airy fragrance of cut grass and hay, closer to the June 'meadow-gale' or breeze that Shelley himself seems to prefer.

Yet Walter Pater, whose own perfume tastes tend mainly towards light florals, calls upon the tuberose to represent an exotic style of writing that can be accomplished within one's native English. In his unfinished imaginary portrait, 'An English Poet', Pater's Anglo-French protagonist, out of sympathy with Cumberland, and filled with a Baudelairean 'sensuous longing for that warmer soil out of which exotic flowers [...] would naturally grow', nonetheless finds sanctuary in a species of literary English:

> [T]he English tongue had revealed itself to him as a living spirit of mysterious strength and sweetness and he had elected to be an artist in that. [...] the boy required from words, and not in vain, in books, the picture, the tuberose, the marble face, the fading light on ancient cities, all that was not actually there for ear and eye, above all the genius of refinement; and this not as the new subject of writing, its more obvious and immediate presentations, but by a subtler operation from the style, the ether-like manner of the thing. So written language came to be form and colour as well as sound to him, exotic perfume almost.   (*IP*, pp. 107, 110)

Here the exotic or 'strange flower', the tuberose, again represents a highly refined, nuanced, or rarefied style, such an exquisite style as characterizes Pater's own aesthetic prose, imitated by his decadent successors.

One of those decadent successors is the poet Mark André Raffalovich (1864–1934), a Russian Jewish émigré, whose wealthy, cultured family moved from Odessa to Paris in 1863 where Marie, his brilliant multilingual mother, became a noted *salonnière*. In 1882 the eighteen-year-old Raffalovich, accompanied by his former governess, settled in London where he began writing poetry, fiction, and drama in English. His first collection of poetry, *Cyril and Lionel*, was published in 1884, his second, *Tuberose and Meadowsweet*, in 1885. *Tuberose and Meadowsweet* is best known not for its content, but for a somewhat feline notice by Oscar Wilde, who reviewed it anonymously for the *Pall Mall Gazette* of 27 March 1885.

Wilde undoubtedly realized that *Tuberose and Meadowsweet*, a volume that explores love through a series of poems featuring different flowers, is a collection of homoerotic verse. The language of his review specifically evokes a decadent register:

> This is really a remarkable little volume, and contains many strange and beautiful poems. To say of these poems that they are unhealthy, and bring with them the heavy odours of the hothouse, is to point out neither their defect, nor their merit, but their quality merely. And, though Mr. Raffalovich is not a wonderful poet, still he is

---

[19] Ibid.

a subtle artist in poetry. Indeed, in his way he is a boyish master of curious music, and of fantastic rhyme.[20]

The word 'odours' suggests Pater's Conclusion, while words like 'strange', 'curious', and 'subtle' have strong associations with his essay 'Leonardo da Vinci' (1869) that hints at the painter's homosexuality.[21] (As Wilde probably knew, Raffalovich and Pater were friends.[22]) Wilde's review also echoes Swinburne's 1862 review of Baudelaire's *Les Fleurs du mal*, a volume described as possessing 'a heavy heated temperature with dangerous hothouse scents in it'.[23] Raffalovich had prefaced his volume with an unattributed epigraph taken from Swinburne's poem 'Relics' (1873) and the collection has in places a marked Swinburnian register.[24]

Wilde apparently outs Raffalovich as a decadent poet but almost immediately undercuts the gesture by questioning his basic credentials. *Tuberose and Meadowsweet* is named after one of the principal poems in the collection in which the word 'tuberose' is continually repeated: 'Of tuberose, O love, of tuberose, | I sing of tuberose, of tuberose!'[25] Referring to the title and doubtless aware of its author's foreign origins, Wilde teasingly charged Raffalovich with failing to pronounce the word 'tuberose' correctly, claiming (falsely as it happens), it should be stressed as a disyllable not a trisyllable, and adding 'though he cannot pronounce "tuberose" aright, at least he can sing of it exquisitely'.[26] This claim sparked a sparring match in the *Pall Mall Gazette* with both parties citing Shelley in their defence.[27] Regardless of the rights of the matter, Wilde set himself up as a gatekeeper, making the exotic word 'tuberose' a decadent poetic shibboleth. Mispronunciation suggests one's ineligibility as a true English poet, inheritor of Shelley, and rightful claimant to the contemporary poetic scene. In spite of this tussle, Wilde and Raffalovich remained on more or less cordial terms until the 1890s when their relations rapidly degenerated.[28]

Ed Madden, one of few critics to discuss Raffalovich's verse, suggests that he 'turned to the Victorian "language of flowers"—a language of romance and courtship codified in the floral dictionaries and gilt-bound gift-books of the period—and he used this

---

[20] Oscar Wilde, 'A Bevy of Poets', in *The Complete Works of Oscar Wilde*, 6. 46.

[21] Pater, 'Leonardo da Vinci', in *SR*, pp. 56–72. The word 'strange' occurs twenty-two times in this essay, 'curious' and 'curiosity' sixteen times, and 'subtle' and its variants seven times.

[22] Their relationship dates from when Pater interviewed the young Raffalovich for entry to Brasenose, Oxford, although poor health prevented him from attending university. See Brocard Sewell, *Footnote to the Nineties: A Memoir of John Gray and André Raffalovich* (London: Cecil and Amelia Woolf, 1968), p. 25.

[23] Swinburne, 'Charles Baudelaire', p. 29.

[24] For 'Relics', see Swinburne, *Poems*, 3. 28. Raffalovich sent Swinburne a presentation copy of *Tuberose and Meadowsweet* that was sold at Christie's in New York in 1992 for $2,420.

[25] Mark André Raffalovich, *Tuberose and Meadowsweet* (London: David Brogue, 1885), pp. 37–43; 39. See the Appendix to this book for the entire poem.

[26] Wilde, 'A Bevy of Poets', 6. 46.

[27] For Raffalovich's reply and Wilde's subsequent response, see the Commentary in *The Complete Works of Oscar Wilde*, 6. 249–51.

[28] Although Raffalovich was already disenchanted with Wilde, the final break came in 1892 when he 'rescued' the young poet John Gray from Wilde's affections and started a lifelong, devoted, chaste attachment to him. See Jerusha Hull McCormack, *John Gray: Poet, Dandy, Priest* (Hanover, NH, and London: Brandeis University Press, 1991), pp. 46–8, 148–9.

sentimental, heterosexual, and usually feminized language to portray homosexual love'.[29] Madden's legitimate claim that Raffalovich '*queers* the language of flowers—both making it strange and (homo) sexualizing it' nonetheless ignores the fact that prior to 1885 a number of Victorian women poets—such as Michael Field and A. Mary F. Robinson—had used floral poetry as a device to convey love between women and that there are classical traditions of figuring both lesbian and male homosexual love via floral emblems that reach back to 'violet-crowned' Sappho and the homoerotic verse of the Greek Anthology.[30] Indeed, as mentioned in Chapter 2, 'anthology' means a collection or garland of flowers—a poet's poems being traditionally his 'flowers'—*anthoi* in Greek—an association punningly made by Swinburne in the poetic quotation Raffalovich uses for the epigraph to his book: 'Such words of message have dead flowers to say [...] | Before I throw them and these words away.'

Lest we should think his floral imagery merely a convenient veil, it should be pointed out that Raffalovich adored flowers, and one commentator observes that 'ladies envied his exquisite disposition of [them]'.[31] In later life he was apparently 'a stickler for correct botanical names', and cherished his Edinburgh garden 'which was always kept in meticulous order, and gay with flowers according to the season'.[32] Commenting on the soirées and dinner parties he held at this time, Margaret Sackville, one of his visitors, wrote: 'Every week small exquisite blossoms were grouped together in impermanent masterpieces. He possessed the genius the flower painter so often lacks: that is to say, he really *did* make flower *pictures!*'[33] However, by this date, his moral outlook had changed, and another visitor, Janet Grierson, noted his efforts to redefine his tastes as befitting those of an older respectable man of the church. She recalls his displeasure when a guest picked one of his roses to present to her sister:

[F]or his roses were sacred; of a certain *parti pris* he had for the simple and the healthy, though it was obviously an attitude and part of his revolt against what had once been his tastes. I remember he once advised me with great seriousness what scent to use, and stipulated that it must never be an artificial scent, but a flower perfume.[34]

Of course all manufactured perfume, however apparently natural, is always an artificial affair; moreover, as we have seen earlier in this chapter, some flowers and flower scents have a complex, decidedly 'unwholesome' aura, as indeed Grierson suggests when she observes the efforts of the older Raffalovich to champion the rose over less 'simple', stranger flowers.

Tuberose and Meadowsweet does include some of those simpler flowers—cranesbill, nettle, love-in-a-mist, ivy, anemone, meadowsweet itself—but the volume's title

[29] Madden, 'Say it with Flowers', p. 11.   [30] Ibid., p. 13.

[31] Walter Shewring, 'Two Friends', in *Two Friends: John Gray and André Raffalovich: Essays Biographical and Critical*, ed. Brocard Sewell (Aylesford: St Albert's Press, 1963), p. 149.

[32] Peter F. Anson, 'Random Reminiscences of John Gray and André Raffalovich', in *Two Friends*, p. 137.

[33] Margaret Sackville, 'At Whitehouse Terrace', in *Two Friends*, p. 143.

[34] Cited in Brocard Sewell, 'John Gray and André Sebastian Raffalovich: A Biographical Outline', in *Two Friends*, pp. 35–6.

suggests a union or marriage between the exotic and the simple, and perhaps also between urban sophistication and pastoral innocence. Moreover, the perfume of flowers is all-important, as borne out by the title poem in which the speaker celebrates his love for his beloved by evoking two contrasting flowers and their scents, the narcotic tuberose 'Whose scent in living pulses seems to beat: | Magnetic ardour, drowsy scent of love' and the meadowsweet 'most mystical and fresh, | Whose breath can thrill us with a breath most sweet'.[35] In her book on plant aromatics Jennifer Peace Rhind lists meadowsweet, a wildflower, among those plants that produce the typical agrestic odours of the meadow or hayfield, noting that its 'clusters of creamy flowers' have a 'sweet, honey-floral odour'.[36] In common with other agrestic plants, meadowsweet also contains coumarin, an organic chemical compound with the scent of hay and cut grass—a fresh out-of-doors fragrance. The speaker associates the scent of meadowsweet with 'my passion's purity, | O distant echo, faintness rapt and fresh, | That means my soul to thee, and thine to me' (p. 37). However, lest this look like a straightforward contrast between sexual and spiritual passion, the speaker complicates matters by telling us that meadowsweet is also reminiscent of the touch of 'warm seraphic flesh' (p. 39), an image that somewhat curiously blends the physical and the spiritual. Meadowsweet thus represents the idealized grace and delicacy of the beloved's body: 'Slender and sweet, like honey, like thy hair, | O like my words to thee, like meadowsweet, | Stainless and tender, tall and fair' (p. 39). However, it is the exotic sensuality of tuberose that proves the dominant perfume, taking over from and overwhelming the lighter, more innocent fragrance of meadowsweet. Asking archly 'It may be summer in the woods to-day, | Or winter with the trees, or spring, who knows?' (p. 39), the speaker shifts from the external world of natural beauty to the enclosed realm of the bedroom where seasons or even the time of day are no longer important: 'Behind the soft green curtains half undone, | The fluttering paleness, is it morn or eve, | To-day that ends, to-morrow that's begun?' (p. 40).

In the next stanza we enter the darkened space of that room which is suffused by the erotic perfume of tuberose. Without recourse to more explicit language, the strong carnal presence of the scent seems to signify 'voluptuousness', a sexual pleasure that erases thoughts of anything beyond the moment:

> Here in the vague and close confined room
> All senses are as one acutely blent,
> When speechless, touching not, in silent gloom
> We yearn and languish with a single scent,
> Relentlessly and subtly odorous.
> Here in the vague and close confined room
> And of Lethean pleasures redolent,
> The strong inevitable tuberose

---

[35] Raffalovich, *Tuberose and Meadowsweet*, pp. 37, 39. Subsequent references given in the text.

[36] Jennifer Peace Rhind, *Fragrance and Wellbeing: Plant Aromatics and their Influence on the Psyche* (London and Philadelphia, PA: Singing Dragon, 2014), p. 282. Peace Rhind, a chartered biologist and aromatherapist, also remarks 'some say it is reminiscent of almonds, but this smell comes from its leaves' (p. 282). The almond smell may come from heliotropin, another chemical constituent.

Surrounds irradiating to a tomb,
Where half-unconsciousness is well content.
Here in the vague and close confined room
All senses are as one acutely blent.   (pp. 40–1)

This interlude, a typical Swinburnian interspace between life and death, has both an overcharged awareness and an enervated lassitude. Indeed, the oppressive scented atmosphere and synaesthetic merging of the senses—'All senses are as one acutely blent'—recall Swinburne's Christian knight, Tannhäuser, in 'Laus Veneris', languishing in the enclosure of the Horsel, Venus' subterranean pleasure-palace.

Raffalovich's speaker describes the tuberose as 'of Lethean pleasures redolent'. Lethe is the river of forgetfulness in the Underworld that the dead must drink from in order to forget their earthly lives. Are Lethean pleasures 'forgotten', or even 'deadly' or 'dangerous pleasures' that, revived by this tuberose-perfumed idyll, can be once more enjoyed, or are they pleasures that require a narcotized obliviousness of the quotidian world? Such short-lived oblivion—the dying to one's everyday life, the temporary dissolve of consciousness and identity along with ecstatic release—is a symbolic form of death. But the fleshly tuberose, manifesting its funereal character, decomposing in sheer beauty, and irradiating its scent and its faint phosphorescent light in the dim tomblike confines of the chamber, also rouses thoughts of death proper, which continue into the next stanza:

If this be death, then we are dead indeed!
O do not stir lest we find life again:
What should we have of life? There is no need
For us to fill the hollow hours in vain
Or lengthen out the sobbing of our breath.
If this be death, then we are dead indeed,
Or waiting for the whole of life to wane,
After the last sigh, love, the first kiss, death!
I think that on some battlefield we bleed,
And I would live once more to be so slain.
If this be death, then we are dead indeed.
O do not stir lest we find life again!   (p. 41)

Life outside the chamber, where the lovers are compelled to disguise their passionate feelings for each other, might well seem like 'hollow hours' and a prolonged torture, to which sexual consummation, figured as a kind of *liebestod*, seems entirely preferable. The date of Raffalovich's collection, published in the spring of 1885, reminds us that the August of that year would see the passing of the infamous Labouchère Amendment that criminalized sexual activity between consenting men in private, making it a dangerous pleasure indeed.

In the ensuing final stanzas of the poem, the speaker, now apparently at a distance from his lover and recalling their mutual passion, impresses on us the need for secrecy, addressing his lover as the

flower, whose name I may not tell
Save unto one alone who is not here,

> But who perhaps like me remembers well
> One flower, one scent, one hour and one called dear.　(pp. 41–2)

To this unnamed absent lover, he announces how the fragrance of the tuberose has become the essence of their secret love:

> For this perfume since then a grave profound,
> Wherein is laid of life the perfect whole,
> Has undivided from desire been wound
> About the inmost longings of my soul.
> And when I sicken of my living now
> This wizard flower brings back again thy breath,
> Touches my mouth and hands: how far art thou?
> For I do feel thee like delight or death,
> Thy shoulders and thy arms, thy shadowed hair,
> Thy speechless lips and thy unaltered stare.
> Of tuberose, desirous tuberose,
> Of tuberose I sing, of tuberose,
> Of tuberose I sing and meadowsweet.　(p. 42)

The scent in its carnal–charnel nature is a grave that buries but also commemorates and protects the precious perfect life of the speaker's concealed desire. However, it also has the power to resurrect it, with an intense evocation of the beloved's fleshly presence. That evocation is infused with the reminiscence of another same-sex love as Raffalovich echoes the accents of Swinburne's Sappho hymning Anactoria:

> Ah sweeter than all sleep or summer air
> The fallen fillets fragrant from thine hair!
> Yea, though their alien kisses do me wrong,
> Sweeter thy lips than mine with all their song;
> Thy shoulders whiter than a fleece of white.　(*Poems* 1. 61; *PBA*, p. 50)

That Swinburnian echo helps press home the message that Raffalovich's poem is not a song of heterosexual love.

Yet lesbianism, unlike male homosexuality, was ignored by the Labouchère Amendment, in which 'dangerous pleasures' became specifically criminal pleasures. Raffalovich would go on to become a writer on sexual inversion, the author of a substantial book on the topic, *Uranisme et Unisexualité* (1896), and numerous articles contributed from 1894 onwards to the French review *Archives d'Anthropologie Criminelle*. Influenced by his growing religious feeling—he would become a Catholic in 1896—these later writings advocated a chaste non-physical love between men. (A later anti-decadent sonnet in praise of simpler wholesome flowers marks his turn away from the exotic blooms of his youth that represented sensual love, now denigrated as 'Voluptuous, tawdry, evil, tuberoses, | Orchids uncouth, foxglove or aconite'.[37]) Nonetheless, even though Raffalovich's later writings promoted chaste male homosexuality, they still had to be published in France as they would have

---

[37] Mark André Raffalovich, 'The Green Carnation', in *The Thread and the Path* (London: David Nutt, 1895), p. 67.

been condemned, if not criminally prosecuted, in Britain. At least one bookseller would have criminal charges brought against him for stocking Havelock Ellis's book *Sexual Inversion* when it was published in 1897.

We shall return later in this chapter to the dangerous and even criminal pleasures of the carnal flower. In the meantime we move on three years to the short sonnet sequence 'Tuberoses' by the poet Mary Robinson, from her collection *Songs, Ballads, and a Garden Play* of 1888. Robinson, who for seven years had been the lover of Violet Paget (better known as Vernon Lee), shocked her partner and her family by becoming engaged in August 1887 to the orientalist James Darmesteter, whom she had met on just three occasions. The union seems to have been by mutual consent a *mariage blanc* but was evidently a happy companionable affair. We don't know exactly what prompted Robinson's sudden decision. She may have craved her independence, away from her protective parents, and there is a hint that she may have intended Vernon Lee to live with her and her new husband in Paris.[38] If this was the case, Lee was having none of it. After a temporary breakdown, she found solace in a new partner, the painter Kit Anstruther-Thomson. Following Robinson's marriage in March 1888 the two women continued to correspond and to see each other occasionally but relations between them were never the same.

Songs, Ballads, and a Garden Play is dedicated to Robinson's sister, the novelist Mabel Robinson. In her dedicatory preface dated 27 February 1888, written just before her marriage, Robinson recalls a conversation about the 'Garden Play' of the title at the Robinsons' out-of-town house in Surrey, 'one happy afternoon, more than a year ago, when Vernon and you and I walked up and down the sunny Epsom garden and laid a deep plan for the acting of that trifle'.[39] She then concludes: 'The only real things, you know, are the things that never happen; and so it will always seem to me that the Play belongs to you and Vernon and the Epsom garden.' This preface has an important thematic link with Robinson's 'Tuberoses' whose final sonnet announces:

> But fashion'd in the mirage of a dream,
>   Having nor life nor sense, a bubble of nought,
> The enchanted City of the Things that seem
>   Keeps till the end of time the eternal Thought.[40]

There is a distinct sense of melancholy and loss that pervades both the preface and the poem; indeed the volume has as its frontispiece plate a reproduction of Dürer's *Melencolia*. The preface seems addressed as much to Lee as it is to Mabel and it is possible that the thematically linked poem 'Tuberoses' may be a reflection on the end of their relationship, as it is an elegy to 'things that perish, | Memory,

---

[38] See Sally Newman, 'The Archival Traces of Desire: Vernon Lee's Failed Sexuality and the Interpretation of Letters in Lesbian History', *Journal of the History of Sexuality* 14 (2005), 71.

[39] A. Mary F. Robinson, *Songs, Ballads, and a Garden Play* (London: T. Fisher Unwin, 1888), p. 6.

[40] A. Mary F. Robinson, 'Tuberoses', *Songs, Ballads, and a Garden Play*, pp. 22–4; 24. See the Appendix to this book for the entire poem.

roses, love we feel and cherish'.[41] The following reading is not primarily biographical, although, according to the garden historian Roy Genders, during the Victorian period tuberose bulbs were brought into Britain from Italy, Lee's adopted homeland, possibly suggesting her identity with this exotic import.[42]

'Tuberoses' is an extremely conflicted poem. Its final sonnet is an apparent celebration of the enduring imaginative ideal over the transient real, the city of fancy over the manmade city that will crumble and decay, evoking Théophile Gautier's aesthetic manifesto poem 'L'Art', which proclaims that 'the sculpted bust survives the city'.[43] Yet the poem's melancholy is more in line with Keats's 'Ode on a Grecian Urn', whose speaker's deliberately over-fervent praise of art's longevity is undercut by his palpable attraction to 'breathing human passion' (*PJK*, p. 535). Robinson's conclusion proposes that art, aesthetic meditation, and aesthetic imaginings inevitably arise out of our need to deal with death, change, and decay, but also suggests that art is a deceptive illusion, 'having nor life nor sense, a bubble of nought', holding out the lure of permanence, while depriving us of more immediate joys and sorrows.

The conflicted emotion of the conclusion also affects the flower that gives its name to this poem. The opening of Sonnet 1 tells us the tuberose is the gift of the poem's addressee whom we assume is the speaker's lover: 'The Tuberose you left me yesterday | Leans yellowing in the glass we set it in'. Although the first and most subsequent printings of this poem give us 'glass', the version published in Robinson's *Collected Poems* of 1902 gives 'grass', suggesting that the couple planted a flowering tuberose in the speaker's garden. 'Glass' is the more likely reading, but the second one, 'grass', is interesting because it suggests the lover's intention that the flower continue living and blooming as an enduring symbol of their romance. (Indeed, later the speaker will refer to 'the flower we lov'd so long' suggesting that the tuberose is part of the couple's shared romantic history.) Tuberoses are not native to Britain but it is perfectly possible to grow them as garden flowers if they are planted out when the weather is warmer, and they were regularly grown in borders throughout the second half of the nineteenth century. Whether cut or growing, the carnal tuberose and its sensual scent should, as we have seen earlier in this chapter, represent voluptuousness, something the lover may have wanted to signify in giving this flower to the speaker.

However, if the tuberose formerly represented erotic passion to the speaker, she indicates that such passion is now sadly depleted. A cut tuberose spray should remain powerfully fragrant for several days but the speaker suggests the vitality and perfume of the flower are dependent on the presence of her lover, now 'gone away' but addressed as 'my dear'. This tuberose has become a funereal flower but does it

---

[41] Robinson did send Lee a presentation copy inscribed 'Vernon, with Molly's love. June 29th 88. Epsom Common', now in the Norman Colbeck Collection, University of British Columbia Library. See Bose and Tiessen, eds., *A Bookman's Catalogue*, 1. 235.

[42] Roy Genders, *Bulbs: A Complete Handbook of Bulbs, Corms and Tubers* (London: Robert Hale & Co., 1973), p. 472.

[43] Théophile Gautier, 'L'Art', 'Tout passe.—L'art robuste | Seul a l'éternité. | Le buste | Survit à la cité.' For a dual-language text, see Théophile Gautier, *Selected Lyrics*, tr. Norman A. Shapiro (New Haven, CT, and London: Yale University Press, 2011), pp. 262–7; 264–5.

represent the speaker herself or her feelings for the absent lover? Does she feel abandoned or bereft or resentful at her lover's absence? Is she pining or does she find that her feelings ebb and diminish once her lover is out of sight? And what about that extraordinary second quatrain in which the fast-fading fragrance of the flower is compared to the misgivings following a short-lived episode of guilty passion? Why does the speaker choose such an analogy? Is she thinking about an experience with the absent lover or with another? There is also an awkwardness in the wording: the 'faint' fragrance of the dying flower is also 'poisoned at the source', although a 'poisoned' fragrance suggests something stronger than a faint odour. And what is this 'source'? Is it the speaker's heart or feelings? Moreover, the lingering guilty 'passion' of the analogy is mismatched, being not 'faint' at all but finding instead 'its sweetness heavy with remorse'.

In the third quatrain of Sonnet 1 the speaker casually merges the specificity of the fading tuberose into generalized 'dying roses', although the tuberose is botanically unrelated to the rose and bears it no physical resemblance. One could interpret this as an act of aggression as well as repression, reinforced by the speaker's suggestion that she 'shut' the 'dying flowers' 'in weighty tomes where none will look'—as if, ashamed of her feelings, she wishes to hide away and forget the emblem of her former love. This suggested concealment is to be accompanied by an amnesia so profound that she will later 'wonder when the unfrequent page uncloses | Who shut the wither'd blossoms in the book?' Robinson may be partly remembering the image of woman as a 'rose shut in a book', used by D. G. Rossetti in his dramatic monologue, 'Jenny', to describe how the prostitute is cut off from other untainted women. Jenny is compared to a flower pressed in a pornographic book in which 'pure women may not look', and thus forgoes the sympathy they would otherwise surely have for her 'crushed' state.[44] Here the speaker implies she will press the dying flower not in an erotic book but in a 'weighty tome'—surely a dry or boring book that she will rarely want to consult.

Sonnet 2 opens with a remembrance of the couple's shared admiration for the tuberose when it was growing 'Alive and white', a vigorous 'spike of waxy bloom' rather than a 'Poor spike of withering sweetness'. This shared memory of the blooming tuberose—not, it seems, the same blossom as the withered cut flower—recalls an earlier time when the couple's own relationship was 'Alive', and thus helps explain the plural 'tuberoses' of the title. Even so, this memory is bound up with the view that the tuberose 'grows and grows | Until at length it blooms itself to death'. The tuberose, whether cut or cultivated, will eventually die. Again strategically shifting us away from the particularity of the withered tuberose and the fading relationship, this sonnet embraces the larger theme that 'everything passes' and adopts a more generalized perspective as it considers how transient experiences or precious memories of them can be preserved. Here the image of the pressed flower in a book is converted into the idea of a commemorative poem in a book as, in a wittily self-reflexive manoeuvre, the emblematic flower

---

[44] Dante Gabriel Rossetti, 'Jenny', in *The Collected Works of Dante Gabriel Rossetti* (London: Ellis, 1911), p. 40.

becomes the poetic flower, the speaker's poem or *anthos*. The commemorative poem, unlike the pressed flower, is not hidden away, but the speaker signals that there is nonetheless a violence in transforming lived experience into art, that the poetic image can be created only at the expense of the real, by killing or crushing the living referent:

> Everything dies that lives—everything dies;
>   How shall we keep the flower we lov'd so long?
> O press to death the transient thing we prize,
>   Crush it, and shut the elixir in a song.

As mentioned, tuberose oil was not extracted from the flower by expression but by enfleurage, a gentle death in which the flower gradually yields up its fragrance. Nor is expression, a technique reserved for citrus oils, used for other flowers, which are instead processed by steam distillation. This may sound rather pedantic but the speaker is evidently employing a reference to perfumery-cum-alchemy—perfumery, of course, having its origins in alchemy, with both processes focused on capturing the definitive essence of a thing rather than the thing itself. Both processes also are analogous with aesthetic transformation; the young Yeats, for example, resolutely anti-material and fascinated by alchemy, in 1898 describes the new decadent arts as 'filling our thoughts with the essences of things, and not with things'.[45] In alchemy the *elixir vitae*, elixir of life, prolongs or revives life rather than taking it away, just as perfume or *extrait* preserves and enhances the fragrance of flowers long dead. Robinson's sonnet is clearly in dialogue with Shakespeare's Sonnet No. 5, which uses the image of perfume extending the life of transient summer flowers to encourage the fair youth to eternalize his beauty through having fair children of his own. Shakespeare's sonnet concludes by insisting that 'flow'rs distilled, though they with winter meet | Leese but their show; their substance still lives sweet'.[46] And there is the strong suggestion that the condensed and concentrated space of the sonnet is also the container of 'beauty', its essence, or sweetness. However, Robinson's speaker suggests that the commemorative song is a poor substitute for actual experience or beauty, that art seems sterile and lifeless in comparison, its one superiority over life being its longevity:

> A song is neither live nor sweet nor white.
>   It hath no heavenly blossom tall and pure,
> No fragrance can it breathe for our delight,
>   It grows not, neither lives; it may endure.

This speaker refuses to acknowledge the reviving powers implied by her own use of the word 'elixir', and her insistence that the poem is but a dry husk of an experience and cannot replace the beauty of the living flower—an act of poetic self-contempt—may be her way of finally acknowledging the true loss of the dying tuberose, a bereavement that cannot be compensated by art.

---

[45] Yeats, 'The Autumn of the Body', p. 193.
[46] Sonnet 5 in *Shakespeare's Sonnets*, ed. Stephen Booth (New Haven, CT, and London: Yale University Press, 2000), pp. 7–8.

While we know that memory is powerfully activated by smell, the question of whether a smell can be conjured up by a memory or prompted, say, by a poem or artwork, is more debatable, though many perfumers, wine tasters, and chefs claim the ability of olfactory recall. However, though for most subjects a poem or painting may not be able to conjure up an actual smell, it can certainly evoke vivid feelings and images associated with that smell or with an analogous smell sensation. Poems about smell and other sensory experiences clearly speak to emotions deep-rooted in our corporeal existence. There is, of course, a paradox or irony at work in Robinson's poem, which depends on our awareness of what fragrance is and what it might signify, only then to deny the very evocative power on which it calls. In the final lines of Sonnet 2 the tuberose is bade farewell and banished, its place to be taken by the enduring poetic dream or thought, but for the reader of Robinson's poem the flower has always been such a dream or thought, permanently arrested in its long demise.

From the melancholy funereal tuberose of Robinson's sonnets we pass to our final poem from Theodore Wratislaw's collection *Orchids* (1896). Wratislaw, whose other poems in both this and an earlier collection, *Caprices* (1893), reveal a keen interest in perfumes such as frangipani, opoponax, and white lilies, finds himself unable to resist the blandishments of the tuberose. As in 'Tuberose and Meadowsweet' and 'Tuberoses', where the flower emblematizes a sexual or romantic relationship, associations with both sex and death are in play. Wratislaw intensifies these associations through the figure of the femme fatale, an alluring *fleur du mal*, to produce an archetypal decadent poem. Like various modern tuberose perfumes that capitalize on the sensational impact or attack of the flower, Wratislaw's poem is a deliberate provocation:

> Cool flower! that to my heated lips
> Hast clung through half an amorous hour,
> I love thee and thy honey drips!
> White, languid, heady-scented flower!
>
> My mistress plucked thee from the lulled
> Heat of her odorous alcove.
> I know the smooth white hands that culled
> Thy stem, white messenger of love!
>
> But ah! what missive comes with thee,
> My tender bloom, my welcome guest?
> In secret dost thou bear to me
> The languid fragrance of her breast?
>
> Haply among thy honeyed whirls
> A fervent kiss alone abides:
> And yet in these enchanted curls
> Perchance some traitor poison hides.
>
> Dear poison, send thy deadliest breath
> Subtly about me as I lie,
> That none may part from me in death
> The murderous flower by whom I die![47]

---

[47] Theodore Wratislaw, 'Tuberose', in *Orchids*, p. 30.

The speaker has been sent a spray of tuberose by his mistress, which he smells and kisses as he fantasizes about the giver and the possible implications of her gift. The flower is also a fetish, a synecdoche for the absent mistress, and redolent of certain characteristics that the speaker ascribes or wants to ascribe to her. Although the exotic flower, like the mistress, requires the luxury of warmth in which to flourish, like her, the flower itself is 'Cool', seemingly calculating in its efforts to make its recipient 'heated'. Its 'whiteness' echoes her 'smooth white hands' that have clearly little more to do than cull flowers and please lovers, the 'languid' blossom hinting at her own cultivated lassitude. The speaker declares that she has plucked the flower spray from a tuberose by her bedside; the word 'alcove' has a Baudelairean provenance, signifying a recess for a bed, the flower bringing with it, like an invitation, this suggestion of the heated, scented boudoir and its erotic pleasures, along with the risqué hint at a bodily recess.[48] Asking 'But ah! what missive comes with thee [...]?' the speaker teases us with an allusion to the sentimental language of flowers as conventionally encoded in the lover's proffered posy or bouquet, but the sensuous aspects of tuberose are so evident in its fragrance that it requires no decryption: the skin notes in the fragrance of the flower evoke his mistress's own body scent, 'The languid fragrance of her breast'. As mentioned in Chapter 4, in 'La Fleur du Jardin d'ici bas', Wratislaw hymns the 'Odour of women faintly wrought | In folds of silken bodices' as a 'perfume headier than wine'.[49] In the nineteenth century the phrase 'bouquet de corsage' could refer not merely to the fragrance of flowers worn in a woman's bodice, but to the smell of her perspiring skin as savoured by her partner on the dance floor.[50]

Burying his lips in the 'honeyed whirls' of the florets the speaker hopes to find the kiss that his mistress bestowed on the spray before she sent it to him, but he also fantasizes that the flowers' curled petals hold the less innocuous gift of 'poison'. Yet this idea of poison seems to arouse rather dismay him. Apostrophized in the final stanza, 'Dear poison' is a sadomasochistic aphrodisiac imagined as conferring a blissful death. It is the essence of the 'murderous flower by whom I die', the dangerous pleasures of the vampish woman as tuberose, because to succumb to her narcotic and deadly spell is at least to suffer no parting from her.

The notion of a poisonous perfume has a long history that predates Wratislaw. In the Renaissance, when perfume was used to scent leather and fabric rather than directly applied to the body, Catherine de' Medici is supposed to have dispatched her daughter's future mother-in-law, Jeanne de Navarre, with the gift of poisoned

---

[48] See, for instance, 'Le Revenant', in the dual-language text Baudelaire, *The Complete Verse*,. 143.

[49] Wratislaw, 'La Fleur du Jardin d'ici bas', p. 8.

[50] See the comment of an elderly lady surprised by the advent of modern deodorants: 'when I went to balls, the gentlemen used to *like* what we called a "bouquet de corsage"'. Cited in Alison Adburgham, *Shops and Shopping 1800–1914: Where, and in What Manner the Well-dressed Englishwoman Bought her Clothes*, 2nd edn (London: George Allen & Unwin, 1981), p. 262.

gloves.[51] Nathaniel Hawthorne's gothic short story 'Rappaccini's Daughter' (1844) features a young woman who becomes as poisonous as the dangerously perfumed flowers she tends. In the nineteenth century there were debates about the possibly dangerous, even fatal effects of flower fragrance. In 1843 the periodical *The Garden and Practical Florist* cited the speculations of Dr Ingenhousz, concerning poisonous exhalations from flowers, who opined that 'a person shut up in a small and close room, containing a large quantity of the most fragrant flowers, might lose his life by this most treacherous of all poisons'.[52] As mentioned in Chapter 3, Swinburne was convinced that he had been poisoned by the perfume of some Indian lilies left overnight in his bedroom, an experience that he believed had left him 'prostrated for many wretched or unprofitable weeks' (*TSL* 3. 302; 20 March 1877).

Tuberose absolute diluted as an essence was widely used in bouquet perfumes throughout the nineteenth century, and, more specifically, bottled soliflore tuberose perfume was certainly available. However, it may not have had the impact of the actual flower, or at least not for long, because, as Piesse's perfume manual points out, 'essence of tuberose [...] is exceedingly volatile, and, if sold in its pure state, quickly flies off the handkerchief', and he advises the use of fixatives such as storax or vanilla to delay its volatility.[53] Tuberose perfume would really come into its own in the twentieth century when additional use of synthetics and more complex design gave the fragrance more force and staying power. What is interesting, however, is that the associations with the floral fragrance that I have been exploring through these poems—sexuality, death, criminality, poison—uncannily anticipate the great tuberose perfumes of the twentieth century which exploit the sensational aspects of the flower. The poems, if you like, suggest ways of reading and responding to tuberose scent that are later encapsulated in perfumes, starting with the violent disturbance of Germaine Cellier's Fracas for Robert Piguet (1948), the mother of all famous tuberose fragrances. Fracas gives birth to Edouard Fléchier's Poison for Christian Dior (1985), Christopher Sheldrake's Tubéreuse Criminelle for Serge Lutens (1998), Dominic Ropion's Carnal Flower for Frédéric Malle (2005), and Calice Becker's Beyond Love for By Kilian (2007). Tessa Williams comments that Tubéreuse Criminelle 'is said to have been inspired by a murder that took place in a room full of tuberose', a decadent detail worthy of Wratislaw, while in her perfume guide Susan Irvine cites an article in French *Vogue* for 1997 with regard to Fracas: 'This white flower is a torrid poison which acts seductively on men. It is an agony, an olfactory rape.'[54] Beyond Love, or Beyond Love, Prohibited, to give

---

[51] For an informed commentary on the apocryphal poisoning of Jeanne de Navarre (dramatized by Christopher Marlowe in his play *The Massacre at Paris* (1594)), see Evelyn Welch 'Scented Buttons and Perfumed Gloves: Smelling Things in Renaissance Italy', in *Ornamentalism*, ed. Bella Mirabella (Ann Arbor, MI: University of Michigan Press, 2011), p. 27.

[52] Cited in Tom Carter, *The Victorian Gardener* (London: Bell & Hyman, 1984), p. 106. 'Dr Ingenhousz' is the Dutch physiologist, biologist, and chemist Jan Ingenhousz (1730–1799), who discovered photosynthesis and the cellular respiration of plants.

[53] Piesse, *Art of Perfumery* (1855), pp. 80–1.

[54] Tessa Williams, *Cult Perfumes: The World's Most Exclusive Perfumes* (London and New York: Merrell, 2013), p. 173; Irvine, *The Perfume Guide*, p. 59.

it its full name, features in By Kilian's 'L'Oeuvre Noire' range, the perfumes, in their iconic black packaging, pitched to suggest an edgy S&M vibe. *A propos* of Dior's Poison, Irvine comments that 'Scent has always been sold as bottled sex, but it has to be forbidden sex to be truly alluring', a sentiment that in different ways pervades and enhances the appeal of the poems by Raffalovich and Wratislaw.[55] The concept or 'story' that lies behind most modern fragrance is, for tuberose perfume, already there in the poetry of Victorian decadence, adding piquancy to the saying of the contemporary perfumer Jean-Claude Ellena: 'Smell is a word, perfume is literature.'[56]

[55] Irvine, *The Perfume Guide*, p. 124.   [56] Ellena, *The Diary of a Nose*, p. iii (epigraph).

6

Michael Field's Fragrant Imagination

Perfume was a constant presence in the lives of Katharine Bradley and Edith Cooper, an expression of their personalities and their love for each other. Writing to the twenty-year-old Edith in September 1882, Katharine Bradley signs off, 'And so my sweet Sea Lavendar [sic], Farewell. Thou are not a savour to me like the saints; but a *fragrance*. Some are born so. I think of you more as scent than colour.'[1] And in March 1914, four months after Cooper's death from cancer, she notes sadly that 'The fragrance of Henry seems fainter in Paragon.'[2]

Establishing the importance of perfume to both women, this chapter examines its key role in the poetry produced by Katharine Bradley up to and including her finest volume *Wild Honey from Various Thyme* (1908), with reference to the influential and complementary diary entries produced by Edith Cooper and Bradley herself. Love is the emotion that most often inspires Bradley's poems, and her use of perfume in her poetry is shown as inextricable from the way that she expresses love and affection for those dearest to her. Moreover, fragrance is closely identified with poetic creativity itself, and this chapter ends with a focus on one particular flower cherished by Michael Field, showing how its fragrance, combined with some other distinctive notes, could be said to represent a signature scent for the Fieldian imagination.

Both Bradley and Cooper seem to have been remarkably sensitive to fragrance and both loved flowers. Their friend, the artist Charles Ricketts, remarked of Edith Cooper that 'Her passion for flowers was without comparison greater than that of any person I have met.'[3] Cooper writes beautifully about flowers in the women's shared diary where her sensitivity to colour and texture is matched by her appreciation of fragrance. Finding the 'most delicate primroses' in March 1894, she recorded that 'we smell the breath of their softness'.[4] The following year she enjoys 'a great sheaf of chrysanthemums, filling the air with the cordiality of their scent, & the eyes with the confluence of their splendid hues dreaming as one dreams of colour'.[5] She also takes pleasure in other vegetal scents, noting, for example, how bracken is 'full of that intimate, vigorous odour that seems to come from the

---

[1] Field, *The Fowl and the Pussycat*, p. 93.
[2] Works and Days, Add MS 46804A, fol. 21ʳ (21 March 1914).
[3] Charles Ricketts, 'Michael Field', in *Letters from Charles Ricketts to 'Michael Field' (1903–1913)*, ed. J. G. Paul Delaney (Edinburgh: The Tregara Press, 1981), pp. 1–8; 7.
[4] Works and Days, Add MS 46782, fol. 19ʳ (22 March 1894).
[5] Works and Days, Add MS 46784, fol. 23ʳ⁻ᵛ (21 November 1895).

very body of the earth'.[6] Gathering hops with Bradley and her sister Amy in September 1890, she writes: 'We picked for ½ an hour. The scent is stimulating, with a wonderful richness under the bitter suggestion with wh: it meets you. We plunged our hands into the pale harvest, as soft as curds—delicious and astringent.'[7]

Katharine Bradley also relishes the nuances of plant aroma, as seen in her short lyric about the nymph Daphne who escaped Apollo's advances by being changed into a laurel tree. The poem, Bradley later notes, was 'Written in full perfume of the daphne—the deep pink daphne with its honey, and the laurel-spurge with its emphatic, arresting perfume.'[8] In this witty revisionist lyric, Daphne, regretting her rejection of Apollo, solicits him through her lovely fragrance:

> She fled from love, her suit was granted,
> Daphne was changed into a laurel-tree.
> But after, with so keen a zest she panted
> To yield her sweets, and, in despair,
> Cast such engrossing odours through the air,
> Apollo, breathing them, had all he wanted.

As we shall see throughout this chapter, perfume—not only a seduction and delight but also the essence of a thing or person—recurs repeatedly in Bradley's verse. A more prolific poet than Cooper and the author of many of the best poems that appear under the name 'Michael Field', she is also responsible for the preponderance of 'scented verse'. Although not one of her more polished compositions, the unpublished poem 'On opening a box of flowers from the Riviera', from December 1894, is a lively occasional piece that celebrates her intense sensory pleasure in the fragrance, colour, and texture of flowers sent from Italy. Following a first line that doubles as an aside—'From Bordighera: I am glad'—the poem continues:

> Open! What fragrance meets the nose—
> Spices and pepper in a dose,
> Overcome by the heaps of rose;
>
> Eucalyptus, in silky sheen
> Of flowers and scimitar leaf, between
> Wedges of violets; acacia-green
>
> Of saffron-feather, and, under these,
> Stuffed in as ballast, what you please,
> Rainy-scarlet anemones;

---

[6] Works and Days, Add MS 46782, fol. 84ᵛ (6 July 1894).

[7] Works and Days, Add MS 46778, fol. 114ʳ (13 September 1890).

[8] The poem, 'Apollo's Triumph' (dated 29 April 1894), appears in various draft forms in Works and Days, Add MS 46782, fols 38v–39ʳ, with an entry on fol. 39ʳ about the daphne scent. For Bradley's note on the poem as cited, see typescript MS, Bodleian Library, Oxford, MS Eng. poet. d. 65, fol. 10. The poem was published in the American edition of Michael Field, *Underneath the Bough* (Portland, ME: Thomas B. Mosher, 1898), p. 79.

And in the corners what treasure-trove—
Anthers and pollen, silver-mauve,
With bloody spots of carnation-clove.

Again the aroma! Crush the pad
Of fern on the flowers; they drive me mad![9]

The intoxication of scent produces something akin to pagan rapture or maenadic madness. Bradley and Cooper, passionate about ancient Greek myth and religion, loved to imagine themselves as Dionysus' entranced female followers, but also saw themselves as worshippers of Aphrodite, goddess of love.

Bradley's 'An Invitation', from *Underneath the Bough* (1893), features an aromatic plant that becomes an emblem of the couple's love. Written in January 1891, the poem imagines the poets' study at Durdans, their Reigate home, where they would move in the March. Enticing the 'Lady' (Cooper) with a description of this room and images of their shared life together, the speaker (Bradley) tells her:

There are myrtles in a row;
Lady, when the flower's in blow,
Kisses passing to and fro,
    From our smelling
Think, what lovely dreams will grow![10]

This, the last poem in the collection's 'Third Book of Songs', acts as prelude to 'Our myrtle is in flower', the opening poem of 'The Fourth Book of Songs', composed 7 August 1891. The all-important myrtle of both poems has its basis in reality, as borne out when the artists Charles Ricketts and Charles Shannon first visited the two women in May 1894. Cooper recorded that 'they compare the actual study with the study as described in <u>Underneath the Bough</u>. "You have real myrtles" exclaims Ricketts—"Shannon, you see the myrtles."'[11] As predicted in 'An Invitation', the shared smelling of myrtle inspires the lovelier, more potent dream of the later poem:

Our myrtle is in flower;
    Behold Love's power!
The glorious stamens' crowded force unfurled,
    Cirque beyond cirque
At breathing, bee-like, and harmonious work:
The rose-patched petals backward curled,
    Falling away
To let fecundity have perfect play.

    O flower, dear to the eyes
        Of Aphrodite, rise
As she at once to bare, audacious bliss;
    And bid us near

[9] 'On opening a box of flowers from the Riviera', transcribed from Bodleian typescript, MS Eng. poet. d. 65, fol. 40. Some slight variations from the original composition found in Works and Days, Add MS 46782, fol. 142ʳ (21 December 1894).
[10] Field, *Underneath the Bough* (1893), p. 80.
[11] Works and Days, Add MS 46782, fol. 45ᵛ (22 May 1894).

> Your prodigal, delicious hemisphere,
> Where thousand kisses breed the kiss
> That fills the room
> With languor of an acid, dark perfume![12]

In the women's diary the poem follows an entry by Cooper dated 29 July: 'The first bloom on our myrtles—a perfect little hemisphere of stamens, close, white, with an acid fragrance. And the tiny curled petals, blotted with crimson beneath, fall away before the expansive freedom of love.'[13] Central to the poem is the praise of myrtle (*Myrtus communis*), an evergreen shrub with sweetly scented white blossoms and aromatic leaves, sacred to Aphrodite (see Plate 10). In his poem, the *Fasti*, the Roman poet Ovid describes Venus-Aphrodite shielding her nakedness with myrtle, but Bradley's goddess glories in her 'bare, audacious bliss'.[14] (Four years previously Bradley had been rather disapproving of Botticelli's depiction of a 'shy, recoiling girl-form' in *The Birth of Venus*, intimating her preference for 'the Greek Venus, joyous & unabashed'.[15])

Geoffrey Grigson writes that 'For the Greeks, in a frank way, these scented leaves and stems indicated love, and its pleasures, in mutuality.'[16] It has also been said that the myrtle was dedicated to Aphrodite because the shape of its leaves resembles the female pudenda; indeed, the ancient Greek word for myrtle (*murtos*) can signify 'pudenda', thus helping confirm the plant's reputation as aphrodisiac.[17] Bradley, a competent Greek scholar, may have been aware of this possible connotation, although the poem has its own intense erotic charge without it. Indeed, here it is the flower—its five white petals surrounding a half sphere of multiple radiating stamens—that captures the speakers' gaze and, by implication, becomes the symbol of their love and an invitation to further intimacy.

Open to the pollinating activity of the bee, the fertilized flowers eventually result in the blackish-blue myrtle berries, considered an aphrodisiac in Roman times, and still used in Mediterranean cooking and mirto liqueur. (Bradley will refer to explicitly to 'The myrtle berry's black' in her unpublished sonnet 'Bits of Things' and 'Thy myrtle with its Erebus-black fruit' in her sonnet 'To the Winter Aphrodite'.)[18] The berries taste rather like juniper and rosemary with an initial aroma of pine, and when fresh and soft give a fleeting sweetness followed by a bitter tannic aftertaste. Although in her diary entry Cooper refers to the scent of the white myrtle flowers as 'acid', Bradley's addition of the word 'dark' makes one think of the

---

[12] Field, *Underneath the Bough* (1893), p. 87.

[13] Works and Days, Add MS 46782, fol. 61ʳ (29 July 1891). The poem is on fol. 61ᵛ.

[14] Ovid, *Fasti*, 4. 141–4.

[15] Works and Days, Add MS 46778, fol. 64ᵛ (Summer 1890).

[16] Geoffrey Grigson, *The Goddess of Love: The Birth, Triumph, Death and Return of Aphrodite* (London: Constable, 1976), p. 195.

[17] Malcolm Stuart, *Encyclopedia of Herbs and Herbalism* (London: Orbis Publishing, 1979), p. 27; Jeremy Tanner, *The Invention of Art History in Ancient Greece: Religion, Society and Artistic Rationalisation* (Cambridge: Cambridge University Press, 2006), p. 48.

[18] 'Bits of Things', composed January 1895, first published in Michael Field, *Music and Silence: The Gamut of Michael Field*, ed. Ivor C. Treby (Bury St Edmunds: De Blackland Press, 2000), p. 102; 'To the Winter Aphrodite' (composed 1901), in Field, *Wild Honey*, p. 23.

black myrtle berries. The scent of myrtle flowers is sweetly spicy and the leaves have an aroma of orange and eucalyptus with a hint of nutmeg, so it could conceivably be the fragrance of the berries that is alluded to in the 'acid, dark perfume' of the poem's final line.[19] The 'delicious hemisphere' of the flower, whose alluring scent represents a 'thousand kisses' to its admirers and the pollinating bee, metamorphoses or is 'bred' into the aromatic berry whose 'kiss' or scent 'fills the room | With languor of an acid, dark perfume!' Yet also implied by the natural rhythm of that sequence is a possible languorous human kiss and love scene. Another reading might be that the flower's fragrant kisses directly prelude and provoke the more sensual scent of human intimacy. Either way there is a shift in the poem from the garden outside to the scented 'languor' of the room inside, and from the flower's inviting receptivity to the bee through to consummation or ripeness.

Bradley may have been aware of the popular etymology that connects the ancient Greek words for myrtle (*murtos*) and perfume or scented oil (*muron*), a link that might suggest that the scent of Aphrodite's plant with its arousing properties is an archetypal perfume that plays an essential role in human experience.[20] Moreover, in the poem, the subtle parallels between myrtle and the love shared by the speakers also imply that the 'perfume' or 'essence' of their love is distilled from the authentic flower or fruit of Aphrodite. In October 1904, in a little two-line poem addressed 'To Michael from Field', Cooper would write to Bradley: 'You shall find the lover's wreath of myrtle | Deathless as the poet's wreath of bay.'[21] Recognizing that in antiquity 'The myrtle was the symbol of lovers and their poets', both women claim it as the symbol of lovers who *are* poets and who understand love as central to their poetry.[22]

'AND ALL THEIR PERFUME I WOULD GIVE TO THEE'

Given this association of natural fragrance with the expression of love, it is not surprising that scented flowers were a gift often given by one woman to the other—predominantly by Bradley to Cooper. Confined to home with influenza on 23 February 1893, Cooper receives a box of flowers—snowdrops, violets, lilies of the valley, mignonette—from her partner away in town visiting the theatre:

> I shall never forget them as a symbol of my own Love's love. I am proud of my flowers—women do not have such gifts—except from men—because they have not

[19] Piesse's *Art of Perfumery* (1855) states: 'Myrtle-flower water is sold in France under the name of eau d'ange' and that 'A very fragrant otto may be procured by distilling both flowers and leaves of the common myrtle' (pp. 54, 53). Subsequent editions mention distilling the leaves only.

[20] See Pierre Chantraine, *Dictionnaire étymologique de la langue grecque: Histoire des mots* (Paris: Librarie Klincksiek, 2009), p. 696. A link with myrrh (*murra*) is also suggested.

[21] Dated 27 October 1904 and included as an MS illustration in Ivor C. Treby, ed., *The Michael Field Catalogue: A Book of Lists* (Bury St Edmunds: De Blackland Press, 1998), p. 125. Cooper possibly recalls James Thomson's 'The Lover's Myrtle and the Poet's Bay', from 'Summer', *l.* 1513. See Thomson's *The Seasons*, ed. James Sambrook (Oxford: Clarendon Press, 1981), p. 128.

[22] Wihelmina Feemster Jashemski and Frederick G. Meyer, eds., *The Natural History of Pompeii* (Cambridge: Cambridge University Press, 2002), p. 130.

learnt through the centuries to give their love lavishly in signs & lavish tokens—they give their hearts, their lips, themselves, but nothing impersonal which they endow with ardour. But my flowers dilate my life as I breathe them, gaze at them, set them in the bowl.[23]

The breathed-in fragrance of flowers is a loving, sustaining communication sent from lover to beloved, as Bradley acknowledges when, on 8 February 1897, she records sending roses 'to my Love':

> It is my purest pleasure. To choose them, to direct them, to spend on them—to impoverish for their sake! And to dream the imagined opening. Besides, they are what my love is like—a synonym for the universal equivalent, Eros, equivalent to Aphrodite. And they just smell sweet & the secret of their passion is smothered away in the heart of the beloved.[24]

Imagining the roses lovingly clasped to her beloved's heart, Bradley implies their inhaled sweetness is eloquent, synonymous with 'the secret of their passion', just as the rose itself is not merely an icon for amorous love, but a literal synonym or anagram that spells 'eros'.

However, Cooper also made her own gifts of fragrant flowers. Celebrating Bradley's birthday in 1895, she declared 'The study bridal with heaps of flowers—stephanotis (it has the very odour of my soul—I shall give heaps of it to my Love next year) & roses & chrysanthemum & asparagus fern.'[25] And in 1897 when the couple were staying in Oxford, to cheer Bradley while she was mourning the loss of her brother-in-law, Cooper made her 'a little shrine' consisting of Muscat grapes, 'rubied pears', her favourite Marie Van Houtte roses, tuberose, and a volume of Matthew Arnold's poems, so that Bradley exclaimed 'thus I have flowers, fruit, & literature in fragrance—& all breathing of Hennie's heart'.[26] Cooper also seems to have been the chief purchaser of bottled perfume which she gave to Bradley as presents: a 'White Rose' scent in Christmas 1894, 'scent from Legrand—Muguet des Bois & Rose Blanche', for Christmas 1897, and for Christmas 1898 what Bradley simply referred to as 'some exquisite scent'.[27] For Bradley's birthday in 1904, she gave her 'A blue case from [the London perfumer] Piesse & Lubin containing Holy Basil | Bergamotte | Civit [*sic*], A bottle of Sweet Briar & a box of Frangipanni

---

[23] Works and Days, Add MS 46781, fol. 18ʳ (23 February 1893).

[24] Works and Days, Add MS 46786, fol. 12ᵛ (8 February 1897).

[25] Works and Days, Add MS 46784, fol. 6ʳ (26 October 1895).

[26] Works and Days, Add MS 46786, fol. 117ᵛ. In July 1895 Bradley had commented that 'Marie Van Hutte [*sic*] continues my Rose' (Works and Days, Add MS 46785, fol. 124ᵛ).

[27] Works and Days, Add MS 46782, fol. 142ᵛ (Christmas 1894); Add MS 46786, fol. 160ᵛ (Christmas 1897); MS 46787, fol. 134ᵛ (Christmas 1898). Legrand is the Parisian perfume house of Oriza L. Legrand, founded in 1720 and recently relaunched in 2012. During the nineteenth century it won many medals for its perfumes. The *Chemist and Druggist* for 6 November 1897 (Advertising Section, p. xxvii) includes an advertisement for the 'Oriza-Perfumery of L. Legrand', specified as 'Sold by all Perfumers, Druggists, etc.') Legrand perfume is listed in the 1898 Army and Navy Stores catalogue (British Library), but was stocked by other British stores during the late 1890s, for example, Messrs Henry Hodder & Co., of Broad Street, Bristol, mentioned in the article 'A Bristol Lady's Letter', *Bristol Mercury* (17 December 1898), Issue 15789, p. 6.

Incense.'[28] In 1906 her birthday gifts to Bradley included 'Eastern scent', just possibly Grossmith's Shem-el-Nessim released that same year, the bottle and advertisements bearing the legend 'The Scent of Araby'.[29]

Unsurprisingly, because of their shared passion for perfume Bradley and Cooper use the language of fragrance to express their loving unity. On Queen Victoria's Diamond Jubilee Day (Tuesday, 22 June 1897), having decked the house with Idéal roses, Cooper writes 'We are each to each more perfectly necessary & fragrantly close & happy.'[30] Moreover, for Cooper, Bradley's letters themselves are synonymous with scented flowers, redolent of the spiritual ambience or ideal atmosphere of the things and places she describes: 'Your letters, like a crushed rose, give me a little of the rapturous fragrance of Italy.'[31] Better still, Cooper finds in them the essence of Bradley herself: 'You know that your Pretty always appreciates your fine thoughts, and treasures them as the windfalls from your rich brain or as rose-leaves from the rose of your imagination.'[32]

In her turn Bradley distilled some of the essence of her beloved into verse, as can be seen in the short lyric 'There are hours my soul believes', prompted by Cooper's gift of 'a pot of sweet-scented golden tulips'.

> There are hours my soul believes
> All her bliss is in your eyes,
> Then in slumber you dissuade:
> Or, it is the mouth I prize,
> Till, in starry dark, the voice
> Half obliterates my choice.
> Wholly is your sweetness blent
> With your beauty, as the scent
> Of the golden tulip lies
> Golden in the verdant leaves.[33]

The fragrant essence of the beloved is also implicit in the condensed sweetness of the short lyric 'Sweet-Briar in Rose':

> So sweet, all sweet—the body as the shyer
> Sweet senses, and the Spirit sweet as those:
> For me the fragrance of a whole sweet-briar
> Beside the rose![34]

Here Bradley dilates on the scent of the sweetbriar or eglantine rose (*Rosa rubiginosa*), for it is not only the flower of this plant that is fragrant but also the leaves, which, according to Roy Genders, 'release an aromatic fruity smell like ripe apples when

---

[28] *Works and Days*, Add MS 46793, fol. 163ʳ–ᵛ (27 October 1904).

[29] *Works and Days*, Add MS 46795, fol. 193ᵛ (27 October 1906).

[30] *Works and Days*, Add MS 46786, fol. 74ᵛ (22 June 1897). 'L'Idéal' is a metallic red, yellow-tinted rose, introduced by Nabonnard in 1887.

[31] Cooper to Bradley (September 1880), in *The Fowl and the Pussycat*, p. 36.

[32] Ibid., p. 37.

[33] 'There are hours my soul believes' (composed 20 January 1899), in Field, *Music and Silence*, p. 115.

[34] 'Sweet-Briar in Rose', in *Wild Honey*, p. 174; *Works and Days*, Add MS 46782, fol. 71ʳ (composed 6 July 1894).

pressed, or even without bruising when the sun shines upon them'.[35] The fragrance of the whole plant as opposed to the flower alone is like the composite sweetness of the beloved's body and soul considered as one.

For Christmas 1900, Cooper, who had received from her partner a little green silk book titled 'Onycha', commented: 'In this she is going to write all the perfect poems she has written to me.' Bradley added: 'In it I have only written the lyrics I dare write beneath Sappho's eye.'[36] Cooper explained the title: 'It is to be called Onycha—for in reading of the Incence [sic] commanded for the Tabanacle [sic] by God we came this morning on two perfumes that are henceforth to be our name-sakes—onycha & stacte.'[37] The couple revelled in nicknames and pet names for themselves and their friends and Cooper here becomes 'Onycha', an Old Testament ingredient for the holy incense used in Mosaic ritual (Exod. 30:34–8). It is supposedly derived from the operculum or door membrane of a shell-like mollusc found in the Red Sea, a powerful aromatic fixative still used today by Japanese incense makers and in India and the Middle East.[38] Cooper is thus also the subject of Bradley's sonnet 'Onycha', a draft of which precedes the diary entries just given, the poem itself being included in *Wild Honey from Various Thyme*:

> There is a silence of deep gathered eve,
> There is a quiet of young things at rest;
> In summer, when the honeysuckles heave
> Their censer boughs, the forest is exprest.
> What singeth like an orchard cherry-tree
> Of its blown blossom white from tip to root,
> Or solemn ocean moving silently,
> Or the great choir of stars for ever mute?
> So falleth on me a great solitude;
> With miser's clutch I gather in the spell
> Of loving thee, unwooing and unwooed;
> And, as the silence settles, by degrees
> Fill with thy sweetness as a perfumed shell
> Sunk inaccessible in Indian seas.[39]

We have already seen ample evidence of perfume as an expression of love in the Michael Field relationship. Understanding that perfume, although silent, can still be an eloquent communication, not least because it is a concentrate containing the spirit of a substance, Bradley finds particular meaning in the natural scent of

---

[35] Roy Genders, *The Scented Wild Flowers of Britain* (London: Collins, 1971), p. 97.

[36] Works and Days, Add MS 46789, fols 178ᵛ, 179ᵛ (Christmas 1900).

[37] Works and Days, Add MS 46789, fol. 178ᵛ. Stacte, like onycha, an ingredient in the holy incense, is usually understood to be an aromatic gum-resin, with ancient classical sources identifying it as myrrh oil and modern sources favouring storax.

[38] There is now some considerable debate as to what material might be signified by the Greek word *onycha* (literally 'fingernail') used to translate the Hebrew *scheceleth*. Various commentators point out that an aromatic material derived from a sea-snail was not likely to be used in Temple services as it would contravene Mosaic teaching that the mollusc was an unclean animal.

[39] Works and Days, Add MS 46789, fol. 177ᵛ; 'Onycha', in *Wild Honey*, p. 14.

honeysuckle as expressing the very essence of the forest. A hint of fragrant communication also informs the ensuing visual analogy in which the spectacle of massed white cherry blossom 'voices' the beauty of the cherry tree at its best. These natural speaking silences are ranged alongside others of a larger kind, the eternal movement of the sea and the star-studded skies that tell of sublimity. In the octave the speaker reflects on the experience of loving the beloved and the eloquent silence of their relationship. If we concede this is Bradley speaking of Cooper, someone she has known and loved since birth, then there exists so much implicit understanding between them that neither has need to woo or court the other. Instead, the speaker savours her uniquely private experience of her beloved's essential nature and her loving. That unspoken but pervasive love permeates the speaker as scent does a 'perfumed shell', and it is present only to her, remaining out of reach or 'inaccessible' to others. The religious significance of onycha, an ingredient in the holy incense of the Old Testament, consecrates this private essence of love, and makes onycha a partner to the pagan sacred myrtle of Aphrodite.

In writing this sonnet Bradley seems to have assumed that the 'onycha' is a perfume that pervades the whole shell rather than an element, the operculum or 'lid', which is extracted and processed to make incense. She may have been subconsciously influenced by the Victorian vogue for artificially scented shells, used 'for perfuming jewel-cases and work-boxes'. Piesse's *Art of Perfumery* (1862) explains how the shells are first cleaned with weak muriatic acid till they assume a pearly lustre. Once selected essential oils have been prepared, 'The shells are then steeped into the scent, which ascends into their convolving tube'—a picturesque image of the 'perfumed shell' that fills with sweetness 'by degrees'.[40]

Of course, there is something paradoxical about voicing in verse the sanctity of a mutually understood unspoken love and we might wonder if Bradley's allusion to the grasping 'miser's clutch' betrays some underlying anxiety, some lack of confidence in the reciprocity of love as explored in the poem. Is she quite as sure of her beloved's love as she claims or is this sonnet wishful thinking? Since at least 1892, Cooper had nursed a long-standing infatuation for the art critic Bernard Berenson, a narcissist who cruelly toyed with her affections. As he was the lover and, from 1900, the husband of Mary Costelloe (née Pearsall Smith), a friend of both women, Cooper transmuted her feelings for him into a spiritualized platonic relationship.

As Martha Vicinus and Sarah Parker have shown, Cooper's feelings of thwarted love, while no doubt painfully real to her, nonetheless helped fuel her creativity, with Parker identifying Berenson as a male muse. Clearly, at some level, it suited her to have an unattainable love object. While it seems incontrovertible that Bradley remained her primary love, and while it is true that Berenson, in Parker's words 'was always, at least partly, a construction of Cooper's imagination', it must have been galling to Bradley to see her partner periodically unhappy on his account.[41] A rift with the Berensons in November 1895, which lasted till 1901,

---

[40] Piesse, *Art of Perfumery*, 3rd edn (1862), pp. 236–7.
[41] Martha Vicinus, '"Sister Souls": Bernard Berenson and Michael Field (Katharine Bradley and Edith Cooper)', *Nineteenth-Century Literature* 60 (2005), 326–54; see also Vicinus's later version of

may have dented Cooper's output as a poet, although she poured her energies into her work as a dramatist. Bradley was once again the focus of Cooper's love but the experience of sharing her may well have caused her to hold onto that love with a 'miser's clutch'.

When the newly-wed Berensons did visit the women at their Richmond home, The Paragon, for the first time on 30 June 1901, Berenson and Cooper had an intense meeting *à deux* in which they confirmed their still vital feelings for each other. Cooper breathlessly recorded this momentous encounter in a lengthy diary entry.[42] She and Bradley received the couple in the 'Sun Room' or white drawing room, which she had previously 'stack[ed] [...] at each end with lilies'. At one point after lunch Bradley took Mary Berenson upstairs to inspect the view from the guest bedroom, but Berenson followed Cooper back to the drawing room where she had 'escaped' to light a fire. When she rose at his entrance, they joined hands, and both exclaimed rapturously how the other was just 'the same'.[43] The next day she added 'I can only dwell on the most wonderful day of my life—that exclamation from him & me of the same, the same, our clasping hands, our peace, & the sheaves of long-flowered lilies in the White Room.'[44]

Bradley knew all about this almost immediately and her way of dealing with it was to transform the account of this meeting into the exquisite poem 'Chalices'. The experience was Cooper's and she swiftly wrote her own poem about it—'Eros of the Summits'—but Bradley is the one who masters it and presumably her own feelings by almost instantly turning the experience into art and winning Cooper's admiration. Cooper acknowledged: 'In Eros of the Summits I stammer the remembrance, but in Chalices Michael enters into my joy & peace, creating them again as they had been & wd be ever. A gift indeed that in her hand I receive the divinest moments in my life living & to endure.'[45]

'Chalices', though extremely beautiful, makes little sense without the journal account. The line 'Those twain, each dearer than our liberty' refers to Katharine Bradley and Mary Berenson who were absent during the final charged encounter. However, by creating the poem and taking over Cooper's voice, indeed by representing the tryst more effectively than Cooper could herself, Bradley writes herself back into the scene, becoming an active agent. This action manages simultaneously to demonstrate that she is not threatened by Cooper's other love, that she can transform and distance that love through art, and that she has a better knowledge of Cooper than Cooper does herself (and moreover a knowledge that Berenson can never attain). Cooper's acknowledgement hints that she sees 'Michael' as a priest-like

this essay 'Faun Love: Michael Field and Bernard Berenson', *Women's History Review* 18 (2009), 753–64; Sarah Parker, *The Lesbian Muse and Poetic Identity, 1889–1930* (London: Pickering & Chatto, 2013), p. 67.

[42] Works and Days, Add MS 46790, fols 84ᵛ–88ᵛ (30 June 1901).

[43] Works and Days, Add MS 46790, fol. 88ʳ.

[44] Works and Days, MS Add 46790, fol. 89ʳ⁻ᵛ (1 July 1901).

[45] Works and Days, MS Add 46790, fol. 89v (1 July 1901). For 'Eros of the Summits', see *A Shorter Shīrāzād: 101 Poems of Michael Field*, ed. Ivor C. Treby (Bury St Edmunds; De Blackland Press, 1999), p. 80.

figure dispensing the transformed 'divinest moments' as a sustaining sacrament from her chalice of art. This sacramental or religious imagery seems to have been absorbed from Bradley's poem for it does not exist in Cooper's original account. Nor does she mention perfume, merely noting how after lunch 'The sky is more threatening & the great sheaves of lilies only look the whiter & more dominant.' It is Bradley alone who writes of 'quires' (choirs) and 'chalices' and who describes the part played by the lilies and their scent in this scene:

> Tall lilies ranged in quires around us in the room
> Where of Fate's careful hands at last we came to meet;
> After long years we rose as spirits of fresh plume,
> And standing, side by side, smiled at our love's defeat:
>
> Beside us, yet, it seemed, below us and removed,
> Freeing us as the slave that keeps his master free,
> Those twain, each dearer than our liberty,
> Of whom Love breaking on us found us fast beloved.
>
> We were among our dreams; and fearless, seal on seal,
> We opened them; the lilies breathed about our heads;
> More keen of sword those incorrupt and fresh-pierced beds
> Swung tingling on our souls perfumes of strange appeal.
>
> An instant left alone, I lit a little fire.—
> Thou with they open hands! I rose beside the flame:
> Murmur there was between us of 'The same!'—'The same!'
> Then regally we turned back to that lilied quire.[46]

The first three stanzas chart how 'after long years' the estranged couple meet in the flower-filled room in the presence of their life partners. (Indeed, it is implied that it is the partners' generous compliance that allows the couple space to revisit their former emotions.) Yet, although physically present, the partners, 'those twain', seem almost 'removed' in the face of the couple's pressing rekindled 'dreams' that hang in the air as potently as the lilies' perfume.[47] As in 'Onycha', Bradley emphasizes the silent eloquence of perfume as the powerful lily scent seems to inspire and contain an unspoken exchange of fantasy, desire, and nostalgia. In the final stanza, briefly left alone, the couple take the opportunity to declare the continuity of their feelings for each other, seemingly requiring no further proof of their bond.

In choosing her title Bradley plays on the derivation of the word 'chalice', the cup or goblet used for the consecrated wine of the Eucharist, from 'calyx', the protective covering, outermost whorl, or floral envelope that protects the flower and which can be thought of as a cup. (Sometimes in fact the word 'chalice' is directly

---

[46] 'Chalices', in *Wild Honey*, p. 74. Vicinus, when discussing this poem in both her articles, does not seem to realize that Bradley is drawing directly on Cooper's diary account of her encounter with Berenson. See '"Sister Souls"', pp. 350–2; 'Faun Love', pp. 761–2.

[47] The phrase 'seal on seal' seemingly refers to another earlier Berenson-inspired poem 'Meeting at Bergamo' (*Wild Honey*, pp. 117–18), composed in 1893, in which the speaker, meeting her lover again, declares, '"Oh, what seals there are to open—not to open them is sin!"' (p. 118).

employed to signify the calyx or a cuplike blossom.) The image of the lilies—flowers commonly used at weddings—is complex, fusing connotations of purity and eroticism. The perfume of lilies is sultry, languorous, and intoxicating—often overpowering indoors—and intimates sensuality. However, *Lilium candidum*, the white or Madonna lily, is a symbol of the purity of the Virgin Mary, who is regularly portrayed alongside or holding these flowers, or receiving them from the Angel Gabriel.

Bradley does not specify that the lilies are white, although, as Michael Ferber says, 'the lily has long been a synonym for "white"', and the word 'incorrupt' implies this, especially when allied with the image of the flower as a (presumably) white-sheeted 'bed'.[48] The flower-decked room, along with the religious associations of 'quires' and 'chalices', evokes church ritual. Certainly the lilies, gathered as an attendant 'quire', look as if they accompany some kind of nuptial mass, an association reinforced by the faint resonance of celebratory bells as the lilies 'Swung tingling on our souls perfumes of strange appeal', a line that recalls Shelley's hyacinth in 'The Sensitive-Plant' 'Which flung from its bells a sweet peal anew | Of music so delicate, soft and intense, | It was felt like an odour within the sense' (*SPP*, p. 211).

Emulating the synaesthesia of Shelley, one of her favourite poets, Bradley makes flower perfume musical and tactile so that it speaks on more than one level. At lunch during his visit, Berenson had declared provocatively to her '"O Michael, poetry is about the dumbest thing I know"', with Cooper glossing his subsequent explanation: 'It has to use words, but it only begins beyond them, in what they suggest.'[49] In the eloquent perfume diffused in the air, Bradley's poem multiplies poetic suggestiveness through the richness of synaesthesia so that we wonder what type of union is signified, and just what the couple absorb when drinking in the heady perfume of the lily's chalice? The suggestive soul-tingling perfume 'of strange appeal' sounds as if it belongs to the recognizable class of decadent and seductive 'curious odours'. With more than a hint of phallic eroticism it penetrates like a keen sword, yet the flowers or white-petalled 'beds'—source of that penetrating scent—are represented as simultaneously pure and sexually initiated, 'incorrupt' and 'fresh-pierced', this last adjective presumably referring to the erect stamens of the newly opened flower.

However, it *is* the 'soul' that is stimulated rather than the body and there is a long-standing tradition that uses the language of erotic love to describe the mystical marriage between Christ and the soul, or Christ and his church, so it is likely that Bradley follows suit in using such language to reinforce what is essentially a platonic bond between these rarefied 'spirits of fresh plume'. Indeed, for the imagined speaker (Cooper), we can assume this symbolic wedding of souls is her consolation prize—for her, the elevated spiritual bond ranking above the carnal union of the recently married Berensons.[50] As Cooper loftily remarked in her diary account after this encounter, 'Bernhard & I are ~~just~~ one & the same to each other, & I don't

---

[48] Ferber, *A Dictionary of Literary Symbols*, p. 117.

[49] Works and Days, Add MS 46790, fol. 87ʳ (30 June 1901).

[50] It is possible that at a subliminal level the lilies also evoke those other witnesses, Bradley and Mary Berenson, the absent-present 'twain', whose own 'incorrupt and fresh-pierced beds' are a subtle reminder of primary bonds that cannot be broken.

want to be anything more or other.'[51] At the poem's conclusion the couple, now satisfied by a mutual declaration of enduring affinity that lifts them above the common level of alliances, 'regally' turn to the lilies as if to receive some sort of acknowledgement of their reaffirmed spiritual connection.

This was far from the only occasion when Bradley would transform a diary account of Cooper's into a poem, as is the case with another earlier perfumed memory. Gathering lilies of the valley in the French Ermenonville Woods in May 1897, Cooper writes that 'the slender sylph-lilies breathe a fragrance, not of the country, straight from the Boulevards of the Land of Magic. Anything so voluptuous I have never smelt as the lily-fragrance below & the pine-fragrance above—both received together.'[52] And in her customary end-of-year review she listed the places they had visited together in the past twelve months: 'We have seen Senlis, fairy-land & land of my love [...] where the lilies shake in the under-breeze & reveal themselves between their leaves, milky drops & a fragrance that thrills all the pleasure one is capable of.'[53]

As its name suggests, lily of the valley or *Convallaria majalis*, deriving from Latin word *convallis*, 'a valley', and a word meaning 'of the May', is found in leafy vales and shady woodland, appearing in the late spring, and for that reason was also known as the May lily. Its racemes of tiny white bell-shaped flowers are noted for their fragrance, having a delicate, green, rosy-sweet scent that cannot be extracted for perfumery, and thus can only be imitated by the perfumer, the most famous recreation being Edmond Roudnitska's Diorissimo (1956).[54] Reminded by her partner of that magical spring-time experience and the lilies' delightful 'dew of fragrance', Bradley is inspired to write the following poem:

> Lilies are come, & they are green & white,
> And full of angels' gladness is their glee,
> The more they breathe, the deeper my delight,
> And all their perfume I would give to thee.
> Yet how shall I present this lily-braid,
> This dew of fragrance, these fair drops of light,
> Seeing that thou so far away art laid,
> So far away, & in Death's utter night?
> I will myself receive them, so receive
> The rush of their white ardour through my soul
> That straightway I new numbers shall conceive
> And in their sweetness give thee back the whole,
> All of the lilies & their woods, & more
> Than they have been, or we have dreamed before.[55]

[51] Works and Days, Add MS 46790, fol. 88ᵛ (30 June 1901).

[52] Works and Days, Add MS 46786, fol. 62ʳ (May 1897).

[53] Works and Days, Add MS 46786, fol. 163ʳ (December 1897).

[54] Lily of the Valley was a favourite fragrance of Victorian women and still a bestseller in Selfridges in 1910 when the first dedicated perfume and cosmetics hall on the ground floor of any department store was opened. See Adburgham, *Shops and Shopping 1800–1914*, p. 278.

[55] Works and Days, Add MS 46786, fol. 162ᵛ. Reproduced in *Binary Star: Leaves from the Journal and Letters of Michael Field 1846–1914*, ed. Ivor Treby (Bury St Edmunds: De Blackland Press, 2006), p. 208.

In her May diary entry Cooper suggests that the fragrant lilies, gathered by the couple in the 'land of my love', are an expression of their feelings for each other. Both women were probably aware of the French custom of giving friends and loved ones posies of the flowers on May Day. However, when Bradley's speaker declares 'And all their perfume I would give to thee', this is no straightforward love poem. Rather she makes it clear that the flowers and their fragrance are now a love-offering of another kind, a funerary tribute intended for one 'laid, | So far away, & in Death's utter night'.

The dear departed is James Cooper, Edith's father, and Katharine Bradley's brother-in-law. Both women lived with Edith's parents and sister Amy until Edith's mother died in 1889. James subsequently bought Durdans, their new Reigate home, where they continued to live together as a family from March 1891. However, to his family's shock, he disappeared suddenly in late June 1897 during a holiday with Amy in the Swiss resort of Zermatt. Having apparently lost his way in the woods, he died after falling from a steep rock and his body lay undiscovered until 25 October. Five days later it was interred in a spot chosen by Bradley and Cooper in the graveyard at Zermatt.

Even before his remains were found and, as the grieving women struggled to come to terms with their loss, Bradley began to produce 'The Viewless Fields', an early version of the extraordinary elegiac sonnet sequence 'The Longer Allegiance' that would assume a prominent position in *Wild Honey from Various Thyme*. Titled 'The Viewless Fields Lilies XV' and dated 'The last day of the old year 1897', the sonnet just reproduced precedes Cooper's end-of-year diary entry. A revised version retitled 'Muguet' (the French name for lily of the valley, from the Old French word 'mugue' for 'musk') is as follows but was not included in *Wild Honey*, and both versions remained unpublished until Ivor Treby included them in his collection *Binary Star*:

> Lilies are come, & they are green & white
> With deeper shining green & white behind
> Unfathomable, & I set my mind
> To make a votive gift of my delight.
> This dew in fragrance, these fair drops of light
> This touch of music on the ear, divined
> As the incense pierces, how shall they be shrined
> For thee, withdrawn into Death's utter night?
> I will myself receive them, so receive
> The flush of their white ardour through my soul
> That, as thou broodest there, thou mayst conceive
> All of the lilies & their woods, the whole
> Oblation of their beauty, more, far more
> Than they present, or we have dreamed before.[56]

---

[56] Bodleian MS Eng. poet e. 137, fol. 32ʳ, reproduced in *Binary Star*, p. 11. (For another draft of this version with slightly variant punctuation and the subscription 'The last day of the Old Year 1897', see Bodleian MS Eng. poet e. 64, fol. 18ʳ.) I have emended Treby's transcription 'withdrawn unto' to 'withdrawn into' and added in an omitted comma in 'more far more'. 'Muguet' was originally Sonnet XV and then XVI in 'The Longer Allegiance'.

In both of these very beautiful sonnets the speaker ponders how she can give the fragrant flowers she loves so much to the deceased who is unable to appreciate their beauty or their perfume. She solves this problem by literally 'becoming a medium', absorbing the flowers' loveliness, and then transmitting it to the dead through the additional spiritualized medium of her verse.

Verse has traditionally been seen as perennial, outlasting other manmade forms, and transmitting the preserved words of dead poets across time. In so doing, it also makes those commemorated or addressed by the poet live again.[57] For Bradley, the traffic proceeds in the other direction, as verse becomes her way of communicating with the dead, a means of sending the departed gifts and messages. Unlike Wordsworth who, in his sonnet 'Surprized by Joy', suddenly realizes that he cannot share the 'transport' he has just experienced with the loved one 'long buried in the silent Tomb', Bradley, relishing the lilies' beauty, is determined to send a gift of their perfume to one 'laid, | So far away, & in Death's utter night'.[58]

Perfume in the form of balms, resins, and spices has often accompanied the dead as a form of preservative, as precious tokens of honour and respect, and to disguise the malodour of decay. These last two functions are also served by perfumed flowers like violets, lilies, and tuberose, which, along with other cut flowers placed on or in the coffin or the grave, are a symbol of life's brevity. Yet Bradley wants the departed to share in the pleasure of smelling what in the second sonnet she calls her 'votive offering', a gift of living flowers. In the first sonnet she achieves this through the poetic image of the flowers' perfume as 'breath', possibly recalling James Thomson's lines 'Where scatter'd wild the Lily of the Vale | Its balmy Essence breathes' from *The Seasons* (1728).[59] Herself inhaling the scent of the flowers and thus receiving 'the rush of their white ardour through my soul', her spirit absorbs their essence. This in turn *inspires* or generates her 'numbers' or verses, which, spoken as sweet or melodious words of exhaled breath, carry the distilled perfume of lyricism.

As in the later 'Chalices', the savour of perfume is synaesthetic, effecting its communication through more than one sense. Combining with scent and visual impression is touch, sensed in words like 'dew', 'rush', 'drops', and the 'piercing' incense of the second sonnet. The lilies' 'white ardour', which the speaker declares will 'rush' or 'flush' through her soul, is a tantalizing near echo of 'white odour', and their 'sweetness' is both smelt and heard. In the second sonnet, it is directly experienced as music—'This touch of music on the ear, divined | As the incense pierces'—again a tribute to the musical flower fragrance of Shelley's 'The Sensitive-Plant', a poem which also features the 'Naiad-like' lily of the valley—'so pale, | That the light of its tremulous bells is seen | Through their pavilions of tender green' (*SPP*, p. 211).

[57] See the famous example of Shakespeare's Sonnet 55.

[58] William Wordsworth, 'Surprized by Joy', in *Selected Poetry*, ed. Stephen Gill and Duncan Wu (Oxford: Oxford University Press, 1997), p. 152.

[59] James Thomson, 'Spring', *ll.* 447–8, in *The Seasons*, p. 24.

The great Elizabethan herbalist John Gerard declared of the lily of the valley that: 'The flowers [...] distilled with wine [...] restoreth speech unto those that hath the dumb palsie.'[60] While her poem cannot restore speech to the dead, Bradley's perfumed flowers distilled as poetry allow her a way of speaking to the dead, a means of communication that exploits 'the dumbest thing I know', poetry's power to go beyond the mere words to what they suggest and their capacity to release a perfume or essence that gives us 'the whole | Oblation of their beauty, more far more | Than they present, or we have dreamed before'.

'AN INFLUENCE, A PERFUME IN MY LIFE': THE FRAGRANCE OF *WILD HONEY*

Bradley's fragrant imagination, which enfolded those dearest to her, received a new source of inspiration from 1894 onwards. On St Stephen's Day 1900, in her end-of-year summation, she reflected: 'And there has been an influence, a perfume in my life—a trail on the wind, intoxicating, perilous—if it should pass away, it would pass away as a perfume, meanwhile it exhilarates.'[61] A page later Cooper casts light on this remark with her comment that 'two great influences [...] have been on us—The influence of the New Forest & the influence of the Painters.' Bradley's 'influence, a perfume in my life' is almost certainly the artist and sculptor, Charles de Sousy Ricketts, the more extrovert and charismatic of 'the Painters', his quieter fellow being the illustrator and lithographer Charles Shannon. A witty, lively raconteur and conversationalist, Ricketts was especially attractive to the vivacious Bradley, who loved spirited talk. Cooper, enlarging on the importance of the painters' friendship to them, noted: 'it gives Michael converse, her choicest demand on life'. Significantly, she also praised her partner's productivity that same year: 'Michael has written 17 Sonnets of high excellence—a few of the highest beauty. [...] Also some strange, new-moulded little poems—<u>In Persian Gardens</u>.'[62] Two years later she would observe, 'Unlike Bernhard, Ricketts has been a stimulating influence on our Work [...] The "drang" of his mind toward it has always been in favour of what is great & poetic & of the chosen mood.'[63]

Bradley and Cooper had first met the painters in January 1894 and they soon became key figures in the women's lives, especially after the rift with the Berensons in November 1895. The women immediately recognized the painters as kindred spirits, seeing in their devoted partnership a reflection of their own. With all four of them sharing a deep love of beauty, they enjoyed intense conversations about art, literature, and their creative pursuits, and where Berenson had shown himself hostile to Michael Field's dramas, Ricketts took a warm interest, providing astute critical feedback, and publishing four of their plays with the Vale Press, the small

---

[60] Gerard, *Herball*, p. 332.
[61] Works and Days, Add MS 46789, fol. 180ʳ (26 December 1900).
[62] Works and Days, Add MS 46789, fols 181ʳ, 181ᵛ, 182ʳ.
[63] Works and Days, Add MS 46791, fol. 71ᵛ (7 May 1902).

publisher's press created by himself and Shannon. The poets also contributed to *The Dial*, the painters' occasional art journal. Possessed of exquisite taste, Charles Ricketts in particular would exert a pervasive influence over both women, refining their visual sensibility, initially expressed in the more conventional aesthetic interiors of Durdans, to the more subtle and elegant decor of The Paragon, their Richmond home from 1899. As J. G. Paul Delaney notes, The Paragon became filled with works, 'early woodcuts, bronzes by Ricketts, lithographs by Shannon, drawings by both artists', some given as gifts, some purchased. Moreover, from the start of the relationship, 'Gifts of an aesthetic nature were exchanged, discussed, written about: amber, crystal, exquisite shells, aromatic gums, profusions of flowers.'[64]

As might be guessed from the mention of aromatic gums and flowers, Ricketts was an *olfactif*. Cooper described how, during a walk on 24 October 1899:

> Ricketts conversed on Smell & how intense & enjoyable the difference between the dead leaves at the feet of the different trees in spring: Now they are confused sweetness—then rich with character. Language is still in its infancy with regard to the sense of smell, itself hardly developed. Shannon has the English suspicion that any smell in a room is a stink & dangerous whereas even many strong odours in small quantities are delightful.[65]

Ricketts loved flowers and spent prodigious amounts of money on them, confessing to Cooper in May 1912 that he spent more on flowers in a year than the rent of his former house in Richmond.[66] His acute sense of smell and relish of different scents are lovingly recorded by both women in their diary. Thus, on 30 November 1897, Cooper noted: 'Ricketts [...] speaks eloquently of the fragrance of snow, an actual smell like the breath of the yellow tulips, crisp & full of possibilities, so that one thinks of buds & growing roots.'[67] On Easter evening 1900 Bradley took him two plover Easter eggs in a nest of maidenhair fern. She watched him spread out the maidenhair fronds on the satinwood tables: 'It is beautiful to watch him touching the delicate, little yellow spheres, & snuffing, snuffing. The smell is that of gauze—& reminds him of a certain bluish veil worn by an aunt of his—& of veils generally in the seventies.'[68]

Ricketts's olfactory imagination meant that he was aware of how scent might be used to please and surprise others. Unlike Bradley who was robust and vigorous, Cooper was frail and often unwell. When she was ill in April 1900, Bradley reported that 'Ricketts brings flowers—violets, lilies, freesias, & mignonette—the four great scents—brings them to my sick fellow.'[69] When Cooper was bed-bound

---

[64] *Letters from Charles Ricketts to 'Michael Field'*, p. iv.

[65] Works and Days, Add MS 46788, fol. 115r (24 October 1899).

[66] Cooper, cited in *Binary Star*, p. 195. See also J. G. P. Delaney, *Charles Ricketts: A Biography* (Clarendon Press: Oxford, 1990), p. 333.

[67] Works and Days, Add MS 46786, fols 154v–155r (30 November 1897).

[68] Works and Days, Add MS 46789, fol. 50r (Easter Evening [14 April] 1900).

[69] Works and Days, Add MS 46789, fol. 43r (1900). This offering inspired the short poem 'Gifts', first published by Treby in Michael Field, *Uncertain Rain: Sundry Spells of Michael Field*, ed. Ivor C. Treby (Bury St Edmunds: De Blackland Press, 2002), p. 149.

in 1912, stricken with the cancer that would kill her, he visited her almost weekly, bringing her expensive gifts, including wonderful exotic flowers, and 'lent her a translation of *Boris Godunof*, between each page of which he had put a fragrant leaf of lemon verbena'.[70]

A talented jewellery designer, Ricketts had several beautiful pieces made for both women, designing for Bradley the splendid 'Sabbatai Ring', whose substantial bezel took the form of a gold mosque with pierced doors and windows and a blue dome made of a large cabochon star-sapphire (see Plate 11).[71] Inside the mosque was a small loose emerald, '& the tinkle of it is heard like a God inside', wrote Cooper. Bradley declared of the ring that 'Its doors are to be smeared with ambergris, so that it may appeal to all the five senses.'[72] Delighted with her gift, she wrote Ricketts a sonnet 'On beholding a ring set with a star-sapphire', with the following sestet:

> It is a shrine, and from the fourfold tier
> Of solemn towers that bind its cupola,
> From the high windows and the golden doors,
> Glimpses there are that fall and disappear:
> The passing of trailed spices and the stir
> Of a god moving secret 'mid the floors.[73]

In response Ricketts wrote 'I like the sonnet immensely', enquiring, facetiously, 'I trust the ambergris has cured your fellow of a tendency to feel "piert" [lively, in good spirits]; this is an old Lancashire word in use in America.' The women evidently gave or promised him some of the ambergris they had bought, for he adds,

> I thank you for the morsel of ambergris. It will start me on a scheme I have long pondered upon, i.e., that of devoting a separate drawer of a piece of furniture to a separate scent, and thereby having a pleasure house or palace of perfume with a chamber for each odour.[74]

Mindful of his enjoyment of perfume, the women would regularly give Ricketts scented flowers and fragrant gifts as, for example, in October 1906, when they presented him with a birthday present of 'Sicilian Amber', accompanied by 'Persian rose-leaves & lumps of the real myrrh & frankincence [sic], & storax'.[75] So closely

[70] Delaney, *Charles Ricketts*, p. 275. Ricketts gave Cooper this scented translation on 1 July 1912.
[71] The ring was named after Sabbatai Sebi, a seventeenth-century Sephardic rabbi who claimed to be the Jewish messiah. He was the protagonist of Michael Field's drama *A Messiah* (1911), already being composed in 1903. Ricketts's ring, now in the Fitzwilliam Museum, Cambridge, commemorates one given to Sabbatai to make him change his religion to Islam. For a more in-depth account of the ring's creation, see Diana Scarisbrick, 'Charles Ricketts and his Designs for Jewellery', *Apollo* 116 (September 1982), 163–9.
[72] Works and Days, Add MS 46793, fols 22ʳ and 28ʳ (25 January and 10 February 1904); also cited by Treby in Field, *Uncertain Rain*, p. 177. Strictly the ring appeals to four rather than five senses, although ambergris can be consumed and has for centuries been grated or melted into food and drink as an exotic flavouring.
[73] Field, *Uncertain Rain*, p. 177; Bodleian Library MS Eng. poet, e. 66, fol. 3.
[74] Letter of 18 February 1904, in *Letters from Charles Ricketts to 'Michael Field'*, p. 14. He seems to have actually received the ambergris on 24 February. See Cooper, Works and Days, Add MS 46793, fol. 37ʳ⁻ᵛ.
[75] Works and Days, Add MS 46795, fol. 188ʳ (early October 1906). There is some confusion here because, although 'amber' is commonly used to mean 'ambergris', 'Sicilian Amber' ('simetite') generally

was he associated in Bradley's mind with scent that it is not surprising that she imagined him as a perfume. In the year she noted the 'influence, a perfume in my life' that 'exhilarates', she earlier recorded how, during 'A golden visit' from Ricketts, 'His soul is quivering forth her odour', and, of his conversation, 'I cannot recall the words, the perfume of them is too strong.'[76] Cooper, too, picked up on the association, observing on a later occasion that Ricketts's 'face looks like a flower you know by its appearance to be fragrant'.[77]

As their relationship had evolved and become closer, Bradley conceived a love for Ricketts that bears comparison to Cooper's for Berenson. However, while Cooper's feelings for Berenson were recognized, and to a certain extent encouraged by him, Bradley's were not openly acknowledged by Ricketts, although he was certainly aware of them. For a while it seems that she and Cooper thought that he returned her feelings but she came to believe that she had misread the signs. She never directly declared herself, presumably realizing that Ricketts could not and would not reciprocate; nonetheless, she expressed her love though her poetry.

One suspects that, like Cooper, it suited Bradley to love a man who was unavailable—one who, in this instance, had amatory feelings only for men—and perhaps she had from Ricketts quite as much as she needed or really wanted. He clearly enjoyed her company, took a keen interest in her work, and liked the special attention she gave him, though he found her overbearing at times. However, he could be cold, moody, and aloof, and often wounded her by his insensitivity. Presumably identifying with Bradley's experiences, Cooper was a sympathetic ally, wryly noting the evasive behaviour or subterfuges of her fellow in their joint diary. When Bradley produced another 'Onycha' sonnet, this time for Ricketts ('I would be dumb to thee, I would be dumb'), he proposed the sonnet be read aloud but, as Cooper noted, 'Something this side of the perfectly abstract makes him say "Let your Fellow read".' She adds, '& I put on the whole armour of the Abstract, securing every buckle, and read <u>Onycha</u>. [...] I conclude, "And of thy busy brain left desolate"—without panting. (Michael has been standing in the blackness against the twilit window, & her cigarette is vaporous for her screen.)'[78]

She also indignantly recorded Ricketts's cruelty, which seems to have caused Bradley particular pain in the late spring of 1906 when he refused to sympathize with the women's grief over the recent death of their pet chow. Cooper complained: 'for a year or more he has been freezing her life under a despotism that at last has made the witty & charming dull. He has taken from her the air that is her element.' And shortly after this she protested

> He has lost Michael's heart by his brutal gibes. [...] Now he will lose Michael. She will never give him another chance & his legend is over. Who now will ripple <u>bandinage</u> [*sic*] around his doings; who will touch his moods & appearances with poetry—& the

---

signifies a variety of the gemstone, red to orange in colour and usually dark in tone. However, Cooper specifically refers to seeing 'the Sicilian Ambergris' on 2 November at Ricketts's flat (fol. 200ʳ).

[76] Works and Days, Add MS 46789, fol. 24ᵛ (13 February 1900).
[77] Works and Days, Add MS 46795, fols 136ᵛ–137ʳ (19 July 1906).
[78] Works and Days, Add MS 46793, fol. 21ᵛ (25 January 1904). This second fine 'Onycha' sonnet, composed on 22 December 1903, was first published in *A Shorter Shīrazād*, p. 94.

plastic sonnet, who mould it for him? Where will he find another listener co-equal with his discourse, & who will bring him blue shells & white shells & rare flowers yet fresh of stalk?[79]

Nonetheless, the breach was healed and cordial relations were resumed by the end of May.

Like Berenson for Cooper, Ricketts acted as a male muse, generating some of Bradley's finest verse, much it collected in *Wild Honey from Various Thyme*. In spite of her tongue-in-cheek declaration to Ricketts—'And, Painter, remember! This book is Henry's [Cooper's]; what it is excellent in its ordering and distribution is Henry's. Attribute also to Henry all that is comfortable in the Art'—the majority of the poems were Bradley's.[80] In fact diary evidence suggests that the volume was intended as a love letter of sorts and the women's anxiety was rather that Ricketts might not recognize himself or, worse, be led to think his poems intended for Berenson. The teasing letter Bradley wrote about *Wild Honey* to the poet Thomas Sturge Moore, a close friend and her future executor, makes her purpose clear. In appraising the volume, Sturge Moore, who had 'noticed the presence of Berenson', declared 'I decidedly cannot find Ricketts behind the rhymes', to which Bradley replied:

> Dear St Thomas,
> you cannot find the Painter behind the rhymes? 'But when fair Cressid comes into my thoughts, | So, traitor, when she comes? When she is [*sic*] thence?' The thyme is 'various'— one cannot pass all the flowers, & yet it is to one secret, cleft-hid, stealthy, curiously small & delicate little binding plant of Basil-Thyme the fragrance of Michael's honey is owed. Poet, in this you must not blunder—<u>you may miss worlds</u>. Of course, Painter has his own sonnet among the <u>sonnet libres</u>, but which of the sonnets (not included in the sets as Longer Allegiance & those manifestly to 'Old Ivories' &c) wh: is not concerning him? Oh, read deeper & rectify![81]

She writes to similar effect and with a dig at Sturge Moore in one of her notebooks where, prefaced by the same Shakespeare quotation, is this quirky verse dated January 1908:

> I have written a Honey-Book,
> And I have made a song—
> That a friend on the page should look

---

[79] Works and Days, Add MS 46795, fol. 76ʳ (20 April 1906); fol. 85ᵛ (12 May 1906).

[80] Works and Days, Add MS 46798, fol. 3ʳ⁻ᵛ (4 January 1908). Ricketts does not seem to have been fooled, with Cooper reporting on 11 January: 'A disquieting thing he said to Michael à propos of "Wild Honey": "You are heartless and I am shameless." I did not hear it said, so cannot conjecture its intonations nor fathom it' (Add MS 46798, fol. 10ᵛ). Ursula Bridge speculates that Ricketts consciously transposed the adjectives: 'the inference is that he knew the poems were about him'. Bridge, typescript MS, unpublished biography of Michael Field, vol. 4: 1906–1914; Bodleian MS Eng. misc. d. 986, fol. 106.

[81] Letter from T. S. Moore copied in Works and Days, Add MS 46798, fol. 16ʳ⁻ᵛ. In response Cooper expostulated on fol. 18ᵛ: 'Not a trace of Fay [Ricketts]! But this Prophet is blind, white-blind! [...] And Fay! He will hear that Berenson is all in the Sonnets!' Bradley's letter to Moore is copied on fol. 17ʳ. Her (slightly inaccurate) quotation is from Shakespeare's *Troilus and Cressida* 1. 1. 28–9. Ricketts evidently is 'Cressid'. By 'sonnet libres' she probably means the freestanding sonnets as opposed to those in named sets, although various of her sonnets are irregular in form.

Nor find thee there in a single rhyme!
What of the fragrant flower-beds?
All the honey I have gathered is from one deep cleft nook,
Where the Basil-Thyme binds & spreads,
There can be in the Honey-Book no other rhyme
Than the buzzing that hung over the minute
Crafty, blossoms, whispering mute
Of the Basil-Thyme.[82]

Basil-thyme (*Acinos arvensis*), also known as spring savory, is a perennial herb with hairy leaves and purplish flowers that grows on rocky outcrops, ridged slopes, meadows, and river banks. In spite of its name it is actually a kind of mint with a strong pleasant fragrance. An alternative name, calamint (*Calamintha acinos*), comes from the Greek meaning 'beautiful mint', while the Greek word *akinos* means 'of good fragrance'. Bradley seems to have used 'Basil-Thyme' as a private nickname for the fragrant Ricketts, who is also linked to two other sonnets in *Wild Honey* named after herbs, 'Mintha' and 'Sweet-Basil'.[83] Basil (*Ocimum basilicum*) is a culinary herb of the larger mint family, with a pungent, often sweet smell. There are many different types but Italian 'Sweet Basil' is the most popular variety. The Greek word *basileus* means 'king', and basil is believed to be an abbreviation of *Basilikon phuton*, or 'kingly herb'. Through these names Bradley may be alluding—not wholly seriously—to Ricketts's 'kingly status', for the women referred to Lansdowne House, Ricketts and Shannon's home in Holland Park, as 'The Palace'.

A number of the poems in *Wild Honey* that touch on Bradley's feelings for Ricketts deal with the theme of suppression, muteness, or a love that cannot declare itself. These include 'Penetration', 'Violets', 'To the Winter Aphrodite', and 'Embalmment'.[84] Fragrance, as we have seen earlier in this chapter, is a form of silent communication. In 'Mintha', a sonnet written in April 1900, the speaker identifies with the mint plant, originally a naiad or water nymph of Cocytus, a river in the Underworld, who was beloved by Hades, the ruler of the Underworld and god of Death. Mintha is changed into the herb by Hades' Queen, Persephone.

Dusk Mintha, purple-eyed, I love thy story—
    Where was the grove,
Beneath what alder-strand, or poplar hoary
Did silent Hades look to thee of love?
Mute wert thou, ever mute, nor did'st thou start
Affrighted from thy doom, but in thy heart
Did'st bury deep thy god. Persephone
Passed thee by slowly on her way to hell;
And seeing Death so sore beloved of thee
She sighed, and not in anger wrought the spell

---

[82] See Bodleian MS Eng. poet e. 66, fol. 22. (Notebook containing poems dated 1904–8.)

[83] For 'Mintha' and 'Sweet-Basil', see *Wild Honey*, pp. 11, 20.

[84] See *Wild Honey*, pp. 13, 16, 23, 26. Although it is the first 'Onycha', written for Cooper, that appears in *Wild Honey* (p. 14), that poem, in the context of the others close by in the volume that deal with muteness and suppressed emotion, can be made to read as if addressed to Ricketts.

> Fixed thee a plant
> Of low, close blossom, of supprest perfume,
> And leaves that pant
> Urgent as if from spices of a tomb.[85]

In Bradley's interpretation the love relationship between Mintha and Hades seems to hinge more on longing looks rather than consummated passion. Mintha reciprocates the presumably unspoken love of 'silent Hades' but also remains 'mute', keeping her own feelings for the god deep buried. Persephone appears to transform Mintha into a herb less out of jealous spite (as in the standard version of the myth) than out of pity for her consort's desperate love. Mintha thus becomes a herb of Death or Hades, a plant used at ancient Greek funeral ceremonies to ward off the smell of decay. Although her 'purple-eyed' flowers have little or 'supprest perfume', her aromatic leaves are eloquent in their fragrance, silently but effectively communicating her association with her lover Death. Here Bradley may also be making a punning reference to the fragrant leaves of her own 'Honey-Book' that 'pant urgent' aromatic missives of love.

In contrast, the later sonnet 'Sweet-Basil', composed in 1902, refers to a time in a relationship where the speaker finds that the actual presence or reality of the lover seems diminished or insubstantial and, more specifically, no longer brings pleasure or perfume into her life: 'As a sad, languorous wind thou art to me, | As a wind thwarted from the beds of spice.'[86] Bidding him begone, she demands that:

> Some potent semblance creep into thy stead,
> Like that Sweet-Basil of the buried head,
> A thing that I might brood and dote upon!

The allusion is to a story in the late medieval collection *The Decameron* by Giovanni Boccaccio (1313–1375), although Bradley is most likely thinking of the version given by Keats, one of her favourite poets, in his 'Isabella and the Pot of Basil' (1818). Isabella, alerted by a dream to her brothers' murder of her lover Lorenzo, exhumes his body and buries his severed head in a pot of basil. She tends this plant devotedly and, forgetting all besides, 'Hung over her sweet basil evermore, | And moistened it with tears unto the core.' The basil, repaying such loving attention, produces an unrivalled scent: 'thick and green, and beautiful it grew, | So that it smelt more balmy than its peers | Of basil-tufts in Florence' (*PJK*, p. 348).

Isabella, given the chance, would rather have had her living lover than the basil, but Bradley's speaker, implied as female through her identification with the brooding Isabella, asserts a preference for the 'potent semblance' over the lover, a semblance that will doubtless provide the perfumed spice that her lover now lacks. With surprisingly cool detachment, she ponders the symbolic significance of the lover as muse, and considers how the images that double for him and replace him

---

[85] *Wild Honey*, p. 11. For draft and variants, see Works and Days, Add MS 46789, fol. 51ᵛ. 'Mintha' was originally one of the poems in the 'In Persian Gardens' group written by Bradley during 1900. For Ricketts's praise of 'Mintha', specifically given to him, see fol. 56ʳ (Low Sunday [22 April] 1900).

[86] 'Sweet-Basil', p. 20.

might come to assume more importance than his actual person. By assiduously cultivating her art of semblances, the speaker as poet is the one who will create the perfume she craves.

Those semblances enter another poem in *Wild Honey* inspired by Ricketts—'What is thy Belovéd more than another Belovéd?' Although prompted by Bradley and Cooper's admiration of a photograph of Ricketts, this sonnet playfully celebrates the male beloved's beauty through images of perfume.[87] Composed in April 1904, two months after the women had given Ricketts the 'morsel of ambergris', the sonnet envisages the beloved as precious and exotic fragrance:

> 'But what is thy Belovéd to behold
> More than another?'—He is pure
> As substances that grain on grain endure,
> As ambergris eternal in its gold.
> More wonderful and in aloofness bold
> His looking forth, more sensuously sure
> Than Pan's, when from great caverns that immure
> He looks abroad with all his flocks to fold.
>
> More than another he is beautiful,
> Nor is there any balm that gathereth
> His sweetness up, or flower that you can pull:
> From his own ecstasy he incenses,
> Even as a camel feeding on myrrh trees
> Blows from his nostrils aromatic breath.[88]

While the questioner asks 'what is thy Belovéd to behold [...]?', the respondent uses visual images only as analogies, appealing to smell as the dominant means of attesting the beloved's beauty. In expressing the soul or essence of the beloved as an enduring perfume, the poem evades the more traditional itemization of physical graces. 'Pan' was one of the women's nicknames for Ricketts and in her diary account Cooper drew lengthy comparisons between his portrait and the pagan god. However, while a visual analogy occurs in the octave when the beloved is compared to Pan, the emphasis is on manner, the beloved's confident hauteur and allure, rather than his actual appearance. In the sestet the arresting image of the camel's aromatic breath conveys how the beloved's essence, his unrivalled sweetness, is diffused through his dynamic and charismatic personality.

Taking its title from the Old Testament Song of Solomon (5:9 AV) and a question asked of the Song's female lover, the poem's mythical and Middle Eastern references and somewhat archaic diction mimic the translation of an ancient text. Eight of the seventeen references to myrrh in the Bible come from the Song of Solomon,

---

[87] Bradley's first attempt at the sonnet—'I have written 4 lines of the second sonnet on Painter's picture'—can be found in Works and Days, Add MS 46793, fol. 57ᵛ (Good Friday, 1 April 1904). A long appreciation (fols 58ᵛ–59ʳ) by Cooper starts: 'The portrait of Fay is a wonderful thing. It is Pan' (Easter Day, 3 April 1904). The complete sonnet appears on fol. 60ʳ with the note 'Finished Easter Even'. The photograph, notable for Ricketts wearing a ring given him by Bradley, is almost certainly the 1903 portrait by George Beresford reproduced in Delaney, *Charles Ricketts*, p. 189.

[88] 'What is thy Belovéd more than another Belovéd?', in *Wild Honey*, p. 27.

and Bradley's charming if curious image of the camel feeding on myrrh trees certainly recalls the Song, whose picturesque analogies sound quaintly odd to modern ears: 'Thy teeth are like a flock of sheep, that are even shorn, which came up from the washing; whereof every one bear twins, and none is barren among them' (4:2); 'His eyes are the eyes of doves, by the rivers of waters, washed with milk and fitly set' (5:12). Bradley, like Swinburne and others before her, was evidently influenced by the richly perfumed ambience of this Biblical text in which both the male and female lovers are compared to the odour of precious gums and spices. The male lover tells his beloved that she is like a garden and orchard where can be found 'Spikenard and saffron, calamus and cinnamon, with all trees of frankincense; myrrh and aloes, with all the chief spices' (4:14), while she declares of him that 'His cheeks are as a bed of spices, as sweet flowers; his lips like lilies, dropping sweet smelling myrrh' (5:13).

According to Roy Genders, 'Myrrh was from earliest times recognized as the most valued possession of civilized man, for the use of alcohol in which to dissolve the essential oil of flowers was then unknown, and myrrh was the only substance which could provide a powerful and lasting scent.'[89] Nigel Groom corroborates: 'Myrrh-oil or stacte had the longest life of any perfume known. Once applied to the person, the scent of stacte was one of the longest lasting.'[90] A warm spicy scent, myrrh is used as incense, anointing oil, or skin salve, and was traditionally worn by Middle Eastern women in a scented sachet beneath their clothes. Derived from the Arabic word *murr* meaning 'bitter', myrrh is astringent but can be mixed with wine, ingested as a medicine, or used as an antiseptic mouthwash. Myrrh resin comes from *Commiphora myrrha*, a small thorny South Arabian tree. It is obtained by tapping the shrub through incisions in the bark; however, it was also traditionally gathered from the beards of the goats that feast on the tree, the thorns proving no obstacle to them or to camels which also enjoy it. Bradley's image of the camel also evokes the ancient trade routes where camels were the only means of transporting the valuable commodities of spice and incense from the southern Arabian peninsula through desert lands of Saudi Arabia and Jordan to Israel and the port of Gaza, where they could be shipped to other countries.

Although not mentioned in the Bible, ambergris, the other precious perfume referred in the sonnet, was 'first introduced into medicine, cookery, and perfume by the Arabs who called it *anbar*. In Middle French this became *ambre gris*, or grey amber, to distinguish it from yellow amber, the petrified resin, or *ambre jaune*'.[91] Ambergris is a product of the sperm whale's intestines, which builds up around ingested squid beaks.[92] Initially faecal-smelling, it has to be weathered by sea and sun for years, possibly decades, before it acquires its distinctive and ineffable aroma variously described as sweet, earthy, woody, marine, and animalic. Sometimes

---

[89] Genders, *A History of Scent*, p. 13.

[90] Nigel Groom, *Frankincense and Myrrh: A Study of the Arabian Incense Trade* (London and New York: Longman, 1981), p. 17.

[91] Karl H. Dannenfeldt, 'Ambergris: The Search for its Origin', *Isis* 73 (1982), 382–97; 382.

[92] As noted in Chapter 1, ambergris is excreted rather than vomited by the whale. See Kemp, *Floating Gold*, pp. 11–13, 15.

referred to as 'floating gold' because of its great value, ambergris is traditionally used as a fixative in perfumes where it harmonizes and enhances the different notes and provides longevity. Like musk, it clings to fabric through repeated washings. Carefully preserved, a piece of ambergris will retain its odour for at least a hundred years and is said to remain fragrant for three hundred years.[93]

If the beloved's pervasive charm radiates and lingers like these costly long-lasting fragrances then, like them, it also endures and tantalizes after he is gone and out of sight, permeating the imagination of his female lover and impregnating her verse.

While the longevity of these perfumes fascinates, so does their long history, the fact that they charmed people in the distant past as they do today. Bradley and Ricketts were both intrigued by perfumes of ancient lineage. In the unpublished 'Benjamin', composed in 1907 and annotated 'A sonnet in January and a sonnet to Painter! What happiness!', Bradley writes about the balsamic resin benzoin, also known as 'gum benjamin' or storax, obtained from trees of the *styrax* species native to tropical Asia.[94] A common incense ingredient, it is employed in perfumery to give body and permanence and can also be used medicinally. However, according to Esther Katz, the first written references to benzoin appeared in ninth-century Chinese sources and the resin was later 'exported from Sumatra to India and the Middle East, where it was first mentioned in the fourteenth century'.[95] As Bradley is writing about a much older perfume, she has made the common error of confusing benzoin with the styrax or storax mentioned in classical texts, a perfume ingredient whose identity or botanical origin has not been ascertained by modern commentators.

Nonetheless, balsamic resins have a 'venerable' history. Roy Genders explains that 'sweetly scented balsams were the first scents to be appreciated by man. [...] They were the earliest plants to inhabit the earth, being thornless and reproducing themselves by wind pollination as there were few insects to do the work.'[96] In Bradley's sonnet the speaker addresses a friend (Ricketts) who brings her an antique pot 'to hold the storax yesterday I offered you—| A breath that steeps the air'. This ancient vessel is fitting for benjamin because:

> you knew
> The venerable perfume is so old
> That the whole time of the whole universe
> Is recent to its lovely spiceries.

---

[93] Kemp, *Floating Gold*, p. 79. Kemp describes smelling museum samples of ambergris over a hundred years old (pp. 150–1). The *Chemist and Druggist* for 1904 lists 'weak' and 'fair' quality ambergris selling at between 21 and 25 shillings per oz (10 December and 16 April 1904), pp. 961, 630. Supply and demand determines the price of this rare substance and good quality ambergris could command much higher prices. For example, Kemp notes that 'In the summer of 1891 the price of ambergris was unusually high, 108 shillings per ounce' (*Floating Gold*, p. 31).

[94] For 'Benjamin' (dated 31 January 1907), see Works and Days, Add MS 46796, fol. 32ʳ. See also Bodleian MS Eng. poet e. 66, fol. 20ʳ, and Bodleian MS Eng. poet d. 68, fol. 174ʳ (with variants). The second to last line suggests this poem may have originally been intended for *Wild Honey*.

[95] Esther Katz, 'Benzoin', in *Perfume: A Global History*, ed. Marie-Christine Grasse (Paris: Somogy Art Publishers, 2007), p. 241. See also the entry 'Styrax' by Élisabeth Dodinet, in *Perfume: A Global History*, p. 67.

[96] Genders, *A History of Scent*, p. 199.

The evocative archaism 'spiceries' ('spicery' in the singular), meaning spices considered as a group, or the aromatic or pungent quality of spices, is used in older translations of the Bible such as the Wycliffe Bible (Exod. 30:23; 35:28) and the Authorized Version where we find 'camels bearing spicery and balm and myrrh' (Gen. 37:25). It can also be used as an umbrella term that includes aromatics other than spices. This revival of a rare, even obsolete term itself adds an exotic touch of spice, brings something of the aroma of the past into the poem.

As mentioned, balsamic resins have a long history, although the line about the 'whole time of the whole universe' is a poetic exaggeration. (That said, there were many in the nineteenth century who, bucking the emerging trends in mainstream science, held to traditional beliefs that the earth and universe were of relatively recent creation and less than ten thousand or even seven thousand years old.) The speaker ends the sonnet by suggesting that, breathed in, the 'venerable perfume' of benjamin or storax, a perfume that encompasses ancient history, is something that will feed the imagination of herself and her companion:

> Let us not flee from it as from a curse
> Let us not wrestle with it as with sin
> But feed on it, in secret, honey-wise
> And of our finest senses breathe it in.

This nourishment by the perfume of the past is also a shared secret that unites the two of them and sustains their relationship.

Feasting on odours is a theme connected with the final perfume poem associated with Charles Ricketts explored in this chapter. In a diary entry dated Thursday, 27 October 1904, Edith Cooper detailed the presents she had bought for Katharine Bradley's birthday:

I give my Loved A Smoked Fox Stole. An old silver chain of 4 rows to fasten it—A single-row chain of oldest silver to match for the neck; A blue case from Piesse & Lubin containing at my caprice:

Holy Basil
Bergamotte
Civit [*sic*]

A bottle of Sweet Briar & a box of Frangipanni Incense. [...] We open our scents— Michael is fugitive from Civet, Birgamotte [*sic*] has the hair & stings of hedge-flowers in its rusticity—holy Basil has taken Salvia to its nectarous coolness. But we do not only feast on Odours—Mrs Johnson has made us a birthday cake [...] We end by throwing frangipanni on a live coal—& making a sweet-smelling savourness [*sic*] in honour of this most sweet birthday.[97]

While Cooper might have bought her gifts from Piesse and Lubin's main shop at 2 New Bond Street, the company's products were widely available and even purchasable by mail order. As seen in Chapter 1 (Figure 1.3), the company stocked a wide range of 'Concentrated Essences of Flowers for Perfuming the Handkerchief'.

---

[97] Works and Days, Add MS 46793, fols 163ʳ⁻ᵛ, 164ᵛ (27 October 1904).

The 1861 almanac includes 'Bergamotte', 'Civet', and 'Sweetbriar' among these.[98] Presumably 'Holy Basil' was later added to this or another list, as in his *Art of Perfumery* (1879), Septimus Piesse declares 'Under the name of HOLY BASIL, I have made a perfume which appears, by its extensive sale, to give much satisfaction.'[99] Following a lengthy quotation on 'Holy Basil'—'the most sacred plant in the whole indigenous materia medica of India'—Piesse provides a list of ingredients used in the composition of the perfume, which includes extracts of tonquin bean, vanilla, and essences of geranium, tolu, orange flower, cassie, jasmine, and tuberose, but apparently no basil.[100]

From at least 1861 it had also been possible to buy Piesse and Lubin gift cases containing a variety of products selected by the customer, or alternatively, wooden 'Toilet Cases' made of scented woods that could hold between two and six 'Elegant Bottles' filled with perfumes of the customer's choice.[101] Cooper possibly included 'Holy Basil' among the eclectic and rather unusual group of perfumes she selected for Bradley because of the association with Ricketts's nickname. 'Civet' would contain in a much diluted form a small portion of the strong-smelling substance secreted from the perineal glands of the civet cat, which, up to the mid-twentieth century, was widely used in perfumes as a fixative, and in the nineteenth century also used to scent writing paper. Diluted, civet smells honeysweet with a slight feline aroma that Bradley ('fugitive'), evidently found repellent.

'Bergamotte' contains an essential oil expressed from the peel of the bergamot orange (*Citrus bergamia*), grown in Calabria, southern Italy. It has a fresh, fruity, uplifting smell and is a major component in eau de cologne, a common ingredient in men's and women's perfumes, and a flavouring in Earl Grey tea. 'Sweetbriar', as seen earlier in this chapter, is the eglantine rose and had special significance for Bradley being associated with her love for Cooper; in 1902 she called it one of the 'symbols dearest to me on earth'.[102] Piesse explains that it cannot be extracted from the plant, but because the perfume 'is in demand by the public, a species of fraud is practised upon them, by imitating it', this essence containing 'French rose pomatum, cassie, fleur d'orange, esprit de rose, oil of neroly, and oil of lemon grass (verbena oil)'.[103] The 1861 almanac also lists 'Frangipanni Incense, price 1s 6d per Box' and instructs purchasers 'Take a hot cinder between the tongs, put a pinch of the Incense upon it, and the apartment will be delightfully perfumed' (see Figure 6.1). This seems to be exactly the procedure followed by Bradley and Cooper.

After Bradley's birthday supper the women played a game with some child guests: 'we smell scents blindfold & pay forfeits for ill-success in naming them'.[104] This game was repeated in November when Ricketts came to pay a visit. On the whole this was not an enjoyable occasion because he was in a bad mood. Cooper wrote:

---

[98] *Piesse & Lubin's Toilet Almanack for 1861*, p. 4. John Johnson Collection, Bodleian Library, Oxford. See Figure 1.3.

[99] Piesse, *Art of Perfumery*, 4th edn (1879), p. 96.

[100] Ibid., p. 97. Piesse cites 'Dr. George Birdwood', also Sir George Birdwood (1832–1917), Anglo-Indian official, naturalist, and writer.

[101] *Piesse & Lubin's Toilet Almanack for 1861*, pp. 29, 30.

[102] Works and Days, Add MS 46791, fol. 61ʳ (30 April 1902).

[103] Piesse, *Art of Perfumery* (1855), p. 34.

[104] Works and Days, Add MS 46793, fol. 164ᵛ (27 October 1904).

The Philosophical Fragrant Lamp. This is a most ingenious device for perfuming apartments. An ordinary Spirit Lamp is filled with Hungary Water, or other scented spirit, and "trimmed" with a wick in the usual way. Over the centre of the wick, and standing about the eighth of an inch above it, is placed a small ball of platinum; the Lamp being lighted, the platinum becomes red hot; the flame may then be blown out, nevertheless, the ball continues hot for an indefinite time, diffusing fragrance around. 7s. 6d. to 21s.

Frangipanni Incense, price 1s. 6d. per Box.

Take a hot cinder between the tongs, put a pinch of the Incense upon it, and the apartment will be delightfully perfumed.

Eau Bruler or Fumigating Water, for Perfuming Apartments. It is also a prophylactic, and is useful to correct the *mal odeur* of an office. 2s., 3s., and 4s. 6d.

Vaporizing Ladles. When heated and perfume is poured into the bowl the scent is very rapidly diffused, for use in a sick chamber, 9s.

Ribbon of Bruges, for Fumigating. Draw out of the Vase a piece of the Ribbon, light it, blow out the flame, and as it smoulders, a fragrant vapour will rise into the air, enough for a months' daily use, 1s.

Ivory Hair Brushes, Wood Hair Brushes, Cloth Brushes, Nail Brushes, Tooth Brushes, Tortoiseshell Combs, Horn Combs, Ivory Combs, Ladies' Extra Superfine Cut Pocket Combs, Smoothing and Tail Combs, Extra Superfine Teeth.

Glove Cleaning Paste, in 1s. Jars, enough to clean one dozen pairs of Gloves beautifully, and at the same time impart the sweetest fragrance.— Rub the Paste on the Glove with clean flannel, as the dirt disappears use more clean flannel to brighten them. If the Paste gets hard add hot water.

Perfumery Factors,

Figure 6.1 'Frangipanni Incense', *Piesse and Lubin's Toilet Almanack for 1861*, p. 28. John Johnson Collection: Labels 3 (88) (courtesy of The Bodleian Libraries, The University of Oxford)

Fay's visit was very long—he was disenchanting in looks & speech [...] Only once did he enchant, when he shut his eyes for Michael to put her scents to his nostrils that he might guess their names. Then all the coast-lines of his unsentried face lay open to admiration in their excellence, in their undefended lure—a territory of Sirens with the sirens whelmed under the eyelids—a coast safe & magic.[105]

By 'unsentried' Cooper means 'unguarded'. The word recurs in Bradley's sonnet 'Sirenusa' that recasts this episode:

> Caught unawares the moments that enchant!
> 'Civet or bergamot, or holy basil?—
> But close your eyes!'...And while the nostrils pant,
> With the kaleidoscopic sweets a-dazzle,
> 'Oh stay, you strive; draw in a deeper breath:
> You cannot fail: do not too quick reply!'
> And the great lids before me, not in death,
> But vivid as one feels the sea, being by,
> Are stretched unsentried. Lovely Gorgon mask,
> Kind betwixt me and doom! White siren coast,
> And all the sirens whelmèd, in their host
> Trembling unseen their perilous harps! Secure,
> I leave the chafing senses to their task,
> And profit of those brows serene and pure.[106]

Smelling the perfumes, the speaker's companion is made to close his eyes, which gives her the luxury of surveying him, gazing on his face without embarrassment—an 'enchantment' she prolongs by instructing him 'do not too quick reply!' Absorbed in the task of olfaction, her companion's face is unguarded and exposed; the act of inhaling and meditating on the perfume removes his regular defences, allowing his relaxed, contemplative, 'purer' self or essence to permeate through and be appreciated by her.

With his closed eyes and reflective expression, the man's face might momentarily evoke a death mask, but the speaker reassures us of the vital intelligence that underlies the shut lids. His stilled face is nonetheless compared to another type of mask, a 'Kind' one screening her from the mythic Gorgon's petrifying gaze. Paradoxically, the man's more vulnerable unguarded expression is itself a welcome defence against his usual persona; for, with his eyes veiled, his power over the speaker is interrupted and she is protected from his characteristic aggressive scrutiny. Thus she briefly evades 'doom', his unsparing judgement or her fateful submission to him.

Continuing the mythic theme, the contours of the man's pale brows suggest the place that provides the title of this sonnet—Sirenusa or Land of the Sirens. In Greek myth the Sirens were dangerous but beautiful female creatures who, with their enchanting song, lured passing sailors to shipwreck on the rocky shore of their island. Subsequently, 'siren' has come to denote a femme fatale, a beautiful seductive woman who is dangerously attractive to men. Something of an *homme*

---

[105] *Works and Days*, Add MS 46793, fols 176ʳ–177ʳ (11 November 1904).
[106] 'Sirenusa', in *Wild Honey*, p. 116.

fatal, the companion, temporarily tamed, is like that Siren land with all the sirens 'whelmèd', overcome or disempowered of their malevolent beguilements. The speaker uses perfume to disarm her companion, thereby unseating the primacy of his gaze; in so doing she mischievously redeploys mythic images of conquered femmes fatales—the thwarted Medusa and the 'whelmèd' sirens. The lure of perfume, 'the kaleidoscopic sweets a-dazzle', has momentarily enchanted or seduced him, allowing the speaker to escape his aggressive seduction and experience a different kind of enchantment, the pleasure of seeing him 'serene and pure', deprived of his need to perform or dominate.

As a young woman Bradley had declared: 'I think the difference between me, & a true poet, is this—a true poet gives out his poetry, it is of him, as much as the fragrance is of the flower: I suck a bit of sweetness here & there, & make honey of it, bee-fashion.'[107] Yet anyone reading Bradley's Honey-Book, published when she was sixty-one, and containing some of her most accomplished poems and a honey fragrant with basil-thyme and other scents, could not consider her other than a true poet. Moreover, the volume is already touched by another love that will in turn receive the tribute of Bradley's fragrant imagination.

By the end of 1906 Bradley and Cooper had begun to explore the Catholic faith, with both entering the church in 1907, and a number of poems in *Wild Honey*, particularly those in the final section of the book, indicate this new commitment. Both women go on to celebrate their devotion to God, Christ, and the Church in the volumes of religious verse each of them produced under the name 'Michael Field'—Cooper in *Poems of Adoration* (1912) and Bradley in *Mystic Trees* (1913). However, readers who have admired the freshness and originality of the earlier poetry often find a disappointing diminution in power in the religious verse, where the women tend to adopt more conventional sentiments and forms of expression. Thus Cooper in 'A Gift of Sweetness' opines 'never will a mould-born violet-bed | Smell like the violets from the Sacred Head'.[108] Bradley's devotional verse, in spite of its dimmed lustre, still retains a little more magic, especially when touched by her passion for perfume. For example, her poem 'O Trinity, that art a Bank of Violets', declares 'Where there is no more Time, in Trinity | The Holy Ghost begets, | Breathing as from a bank of violets, | That sweetness blowing through the Word'. And it concludes by seeing Christ 'to his Father offereth | Himself from the deep spiceries of death'.[109]

Her lyric 'A Profession' speaks fondly of olfactory pleasures:

> I have loved odours well,
> Loved frankincense and hydromel:
> The Angels know I have been very far
> After where wild roses are;
> And celled morsels of ambergris
> Have risen up to my heart in peace.[110]

[107] Bradley, cited in *Binary Star*, p. 43 (28 February 1868).
[108] 'A Gift of Sweetness', p. 108.   [109] 'O Trinity, that art a Bank of Violets', p. 13.
[110] 'A Profession', in *Poems of Adoration*, p. 135. Bradley adopts the English pronunciation 'amber-grease'. Hydromel, literally 'honey-water', is a fermented honey drink like mead; 'hydromel' is also the French word for mead.

The speaker of this poem reflects on the statement '"The Cross shall be on her breast as a bundle of myrrh"', which urges embracing the ideal of suffering represented by Christ's cross and holding it as close to one's heart as the myrrh sachet worn by Middle Eastern women. She concludes 'This would be, if I would let', that is, 'permit it', but significantly her very imagining of submission replaces the Eastern myrrh with the 'English Violet', introducing an expression of individuality at odds with a prescribed piety:

> Will the Cross confer
> One day with my breast as a bundle of myrrh?
> This would be, if I would let,
> Rather as an English Violet,
> That would make all my bosom's room
> A very murmur of perfume—
> This would be, if I would suffer it.

Moreover, the Cross as English Violet, true to Bradley's synaesthetic perception of scent, is envisaged as murmuring its perfume, holding an idiosyncratic private dialogue with its wearer.

Thus, when Bradley taps into her fragrant imagination, sporadic resurgences of energy lift her verse, one outstanding example being 'Gethsemane', a poem that pictures the place where Christ prayed the night before his crucifixion as a mystical rose garden:

> There is a garden of deep roses spread
> A garden of deep roses: red and red
> The culminating buds unclose:
> I cannot find upon the bed a leaf of fallen rose. [...]
>
> Why are they here? So large of volume, great—
> As swans from other birds take new estate—
> Magnificent! Their glow confutes,
> As they had plucked up rubies by the roots.
>
> What fête do they attend, holding their dense
> Profusion back as unburnt frankincense?
> A dark created round their blooms
> Falleth, a loving dark to give their spices tombs. [...][111]

Yet the mystic perfumed roses of 'Gethsemane' are potent because they feed in secret upon the fragrant honey and 'loving dark' of other earlier roses portrayed by Bradley and Cooper. The coda to this chapter thus returns to the image of the perfumed rose as a foundational figure or generating matrix of their creative imagination, and contemplates, in particular, one imperious rose whose identity becomes intimately bound up with the poetic identity of Michael Field.

---

[111] 'Gethsemane', in *Mystic Trees*, pp. 23–4; 23. The poem was first published in *The Academy* (7 November 1908), 473, and was admired by the poet and priest John Gray, a friend of Michael Field. See Works and Days, Add MS 46798, fol. 203ᵛ.

'ROSE-LEAVES FROM THE ROSE OF YOUR IMAGINATION'

At the back of the women's diary for 1898, Edith Cooper copied out under the heading 'Poetry: Smell' an extract from *The Omen*, a gothic novel by the Scottish novelist John Galt (1779–1839) containing this observation: 'I have sometimes thought that the faculty of the poet was liveliest in his smell, for no other revels so luxuriously in the reveries and ruminations of the aromatic summer, nor finds in the perfume of leaves & flowers such delicious reminiscences of wisdom & beauty.'[112] The perfumed leaves and flowers providing Bradley and Cooper with the most 'delicious reminiscences of wisdom & beauty' were undoubtedly those of the rose, and from early on Cooper treasured Bradley's 'fine thoughts [...] as rose-leaves from the rose of your imagination'.[113]

Roses and rose leaves are a fitting symbol for the Fieldian imagination because of their special significance for both women. In an exquisite passage copied by Bradley into their joint diary 'Works and Days', Cooper describes their trip in May 1888 to see Lawrence Alma-Tadema's masterpiece *The Roses of Heliogabalus* (see Plate 12):

> Ah, how I have been kindled by no picture save <u>The Roses of Heliogabalus</u>, Tadema's <u>chef-d'oeuvre</u> in the Academy. On Monday last Sim and I did battle with the fair & polished crowd that nearly removed all air from one's lungs with heat & gentle but firm pressure at Burlington House. Suddenly we were faced by 'a rain & ruin of roses'—a red-rose picture with flakes of cream petals. It has a divine power of endowing the mind with fragrance, & with that delicate transporting joy that roses alone can give. The sweetness, the muffling softness, the unutterable pink—ah, it is a picture that makes one's heart-blood leap delightedly.[114]

Here Cooper's own vibrant imagination supplies the fragrance suggested by the painted pink blossoms, and in the following June her imagination enters into the thoughts of the rose itself when she says 'The fragrance of a red rose is like rain as the flower imagines it (or as that has passed into the imagination of the flower).'[115] For Bradley, Tadema's painting induces 'a fervour to crown the rose with praise', making her recollect a saying by Philostratus: 'Sappho loves the Rose & always crowns it with some praise, likening beautiful maidens to it; she likens it also to the arms of the Graces, when she describes their elbows bare.' This results in Lyric 58 in *Long Ago* (1889), which opens 'What are these roses like? Oh, they are rare, | So balmy pink | I will not shrink | Them to the Graces to compare'.[116] Another artwork, a drawing by Leonardo in the Venetian Accademia seen the following year, inspires a poem in *Sight and Song* (1892) in

---

[112] Works and Days, Add MS 46787, fol. 145ᵛ (1898); extract taken from John Galt, *The Omen* (Blackwood: Edinburgh, 1825), p. 119.

[113] Cooper to Bradley (September 1880), *The Fowl and the Pussycat*, p. 37.

[114] Works and Days, Add MS 46777, fol. 5ʳ (9 May 1888).

[115] Works and Days, Add MS 46777, fol. 76ᵛ (June 1889).

[116] Works and Days, Add MS 46777, fol. 4ʳ; Field, *Long Ago*, p. 105.

which Bradley depicts Leonardo's rose 'Mystic, shining on the tufted bowers |
[That] burns its incense to the summer hours'.[117]

Roses recur repeatedly in the pages of *Underneath the Bough* (1893) but Bradley
and Cooper's use of the rose is no poetic commonplace but arises out of a deep
love and knowledge of the flower. There are many references throughout 'Works and
Days' to specific kinds of roses such as the white moss rose, the sweetbriar or
eglantine rose, and named types such as Banksiae, Malmaison, Maréchal Niel, and
Marie Van Houtte. In November 1893, two years after moving into their Reigate
home, Durdans, Bradley writes to the art historian John Miller Gray: 'Oh but, did
I tell you of the excitement of our rose garden? Two hundred rose-bushes my
brother has bought—so come in June, & it will be "roses, roses all the way".'[118] By
'brother' Bradley means her brother-in-law, James Cooper, who was a keen
amateur gardener. By the following summer the new roses were happily bedded in.
On 3 July Cooper reports how she and Bradley return from a brief trip to town:

> Father is working in the garden. We go out to him, & the roses swell up to our eyes
> like blood from the veins, blood from the arteries of summer, dark & carmine, used
> & adolescent, glowing in the noon. I have never seen such a sight before—every bush
> had a dozen or more roses on it, & the sweet-pea hedge took up their colours and cried
> them out with an airy insolence—as if in a popular song.[119]

In June she had enthused: 'Our chief balm is the presence on our desk of Marshall
Niel roses, with snow-green shadows on their warmest yellow petals & a breath
coming from their heart that lulls like sinking into a velvet couch.'[120] Apart from
Maréchal Niel, the diaries reveal that the rose garden included the light pink tea
rose Souvenir d'un Ami and the first hybrid tea La France, both heavily fragrant.
Bradley writes on the 4 June 1894: 'Among the <u>Sensations de Durdans</u> just now
is the joy of seeing the new tea roses come out. Michael is beginning to have a
bowl on his desk always, & the tumbling-over of their leaves almost drives him
mad. What miracles!' She adds: 'One must see the light through not on them, &
how they understand labyrinths. One would never find one's way out of the heart
of a rose.'[121]

The heart of the rose that seems to have most entranced Bradley is the one she
explores in 'The Grand Mogul', a poem dated 11 July 1894, composed a month
after that diary entry, and included only in the revised American edition of
Underneath the Bough published by Thomas B. Mosher in 1898.[122] The poem is
there untitled, although all the drafts and typescripts use the title 'The Grand Mogul'.
Many readers, including the critic Chris White, who has written about it on more
than one occasion, have encountered this poem either through A. J. A. Symons's

---

[117] 'Drawing of Roses and Violets', p. 5. Draft in Works and Days, Add MS 46778, fols 80ᵛ–81ᵛ
(August 1890).

[118] Bradley to John Miller Gray, BL Add MS 45854, fol. 195ʳ⁻ᵛ (November 1893).

[119] Works and Days, Add MS 46782, fol. 84ʳ (3 July 1894).

[120] Works and Days, Add MS 46782, fol. 52ʳ (1 June 1894).

[121] Works and Days, Add MS 46782, fol. 52ʳ (4 June 1894).

[122] Field, *Underneath the Bough* (1898), pp. 85–6. I use this edition for the 'The Grand Mogul' as
cited in my text.

An Anthology of 'Nineties' Verse (1928) where it is titled after its first line 'Your rose is dead', or in subsequent anthologies which also give the poem this title.[123] Noting the original title, Ivor Treby includes the poem as 'The Grand Mogul' in his annotated Michael Field collection *Uncertain Rain* (2002) but writes 'Since no rose called "The Grand Mogul" has proved traceable [...] this may be another apposite coinage of Michael's.'[124]

But there *is* a Grand Mogul rose, which at the time Bradley wrote her poem was relatively new. In his authoritative work *The Rose Garden in Two Divisions* (9th edn, 1888), the Victorian rose expert William Paul lists Grand Mogul, a rose supplied by his own company, among the hybrid perpetuals, a group he describes as 'fine roses, quite hardy, and very sweet'.[125] He indicates that Grand Mogul was introduced between 1876 and 1886, and notes its origins as 'a seedling from A. K. Williams, producing flowers of a deep brilliant crimson, shaded with scarlet and black; in dull weather and in Summer the flowers are darker, approaching to maroon. They are large, full, of symmetrical shape, and produced in great profusion; the foliage is large and massive.' He also adds that the rose won a 'First-Class Certificate from the Royal Horticultural Society', a detail surely attractive to anyone planning a new rose garden in the early 1890s.[126] The colour-illustrated version of his book (10th edn, 1903) also includes an artist's impression of the rose, which, on the left-hand margin, bears the attribution 'J. L. Goffart, Brussels' (see Plate 13).[127]

That Bradley is describing a particular rose, one whose colours are true to the description provided by Paul—'deep brilliant crimson, shaded with scarlet and black', and one most likely growing in her own garden, does make a difference to the way we read the poem:

> *Your rose is dead,*
>   They said,
> *The Grand Mogul*—for so her splendour
> Exceeded, masterful, it seemed her due
> By dominant male titles to commend her:
>   But I, her lover, knew
> That myriad-coloured blackness, wrought with fire,
> Was woman to the rage of my desire.
>   My rose was dead? She lay
> Against the sulphur, lemon and blush-gray
> Of younger blooms, transformed, morose,

---

[123] *An Anthology of 'Nineties' Verse*, ed. A. J. A. Symons (London: Elkin Mathews & Marot, Ltd, 1928), pp. 55–6. See, most recently, *Victorian Women Poets: An Anthology*, ed. Angela Leighton and Margaret Reynolds (Oxford: Blackwell, 1995), pp. 503–4.

[124] Field, *Uncertain Rain*, p. 121.

[125] William Paul, FLS, *The Rose Garden in Two Divisions*, 9th edn (London: Kent & Co., 1888), p. 260.

[126] Ibid., pp. 187, 272.

[127] Colour plate, in William Paul, *The Rose Garden in Two Divisions, Illustrated with Twenty-one Coloured Plates and Numerous Engravings in the Text*, 10th edn (London: Simpkin, Marshall & Co., 1903), opposite p. 55. There is apparently a colour-illustrated version of the ninth edition but I have not been able to trace a copy.

Her shrivelling petals, gathered round her close,
    And where before,
Coils twisted thickest at her core
A round, black hollow: it had come to pass
Hints of tobacco, leather, brass,
Confounded, gave her texture and her colour.
I watched her, as I watched her, growing duller,
    Majestic in recession,
    From flesh to mould.
My rose is dead—I echo the confession,
    And they pass to pluck another;
While I drawn on to vague, prodigious pleasure,
    Fondle my treasure.
O sweet, let death prevail
Upon you, as your nervous outlines thicken
And totter, as your crimsons stale,
I feel fresh rhythms quicken,
Fresh music follows you. Corrupt, grow old,
Drop inwardly to ashes, smother
Your burning spices, and entoil
My senses till you sink a clod of fragrant soil!

In the late spring and summer of 1894, Bradley and Cooper hosted two visits by Charles Ricketts and Charles Shannon, whom they had first met in January. The first visit of 22 May was a success, with Cooper recording the painters' pleasure in the garden: 'Every herb is examined with eyes that discover quality in the leaves. [...] Ricketts knows a great deal about flowers.'[128] However, with regard to the second visit of 9 July, the women felt they had failed to please their guests' fastidious tastes, with Cooper lamenting:

> Our flowers went wrong—we got too many kinds in the room—we lost the tact of decoration: [...] & when we went into the damp garden sweet-peas were found to be 'violent' & roses, we felt, were silently dubbed 'fat'—although La France, with her outer pyramids of silver & her inner core of fresh pink won Ricketts' attention.[129]

Bradley's lyric, dated just two days after this visit, features the speaker in the company of a group viewing her roses. This coincidence suggests that the speaker's response to the comment 'Your rose is dead' may have been triggered by a similar disparaging comment passed by one of the women's exacting guests.[130]

My reading then is different from those of Chris White, who disregards the specificity of the rose to argue that 'the text pursues a celebration of a woman who has been loved for a very long time, and whose aged appearance has made no difference to the love, even when compared to younger, more perfect, alive blooms'.[131]

---

[128] Works and Days, Add MS 46782, fol. 46ᵛ (22 May 1894).
[129] Works and Days, Add MS 46782, fol. 85ᵛ (9 July 1894).
[130] For MS drafts annotated 'Wednesday 11 July', see Works and Days, Add MS 46782, fols 78ᵛ, 79ʳ, 81ᵛ.
[131] The same sentence occurs in identical passages in Chris White, 'The Tiresian Poet: Michael Field', in *Victorian Women Poets: A Critical Reader*, ed. Angela Leighton (Oxford: Blackwell, 1996),

Clearly the rose is both feminized and eroticized—though not, as I would see it, to provide a primary allegory of enduring love for an ageing beloved. The name 'Grand Mogul' is a term coined by Europeans for the ruler of the Mughal Empire, a domain that extended over large parts of the Indian subcontinent during the early sixteenth to the early eighteenth centuries when the Empire was at its peak, with Mughal rule continuing after that in a diminished way till the mid-nineteenth century. 'Grand Mogul' is an appropriate name for a fragrant rose because, according to legend, otto of roses or rose essential oil was supposedly discovered during the Mughal rule in India, a discovery popularly attributed to Nur Jehan, wife of the Emperor Jahangir (1569–1627; ruled 1605–27), but recounted by him as being the work of her mother, Asmat Begum, who skimmed off and preserved the strongly scented froth that formed on rosewater.[132] Amina Okada comments 'Of all the fragrances, rosewater and rose essence [...] were the most closely associated with the refined way of life upheld at the Mogul court, where an elegant and civilised custom involved sprinkling the hands and clothes of guests with rosewater to welcome them.'[133] Given the 'dominant male title' of 'Grand Mogul' as commendation of her 'splendour', this commanding bloom, in an elegant implied 'sub rosa' pun, is to her knowing owner and lover emphatically female—'woman to the rage of my desire'. It is a masquerade that parallels Bradley and Cooper's own claim to poetic power under the male title 'Michael Field', with White herself noting how the poem's opening signals 'the mixed gender identity that is shared by the name of Michael Field'.[134]

For me this extraordinary lyric is about the romantic poetic imagination, or the moment of poetic inspiration as Bradley sees it, something that is strongest and most characteristically itself at the very moment when it is about to die, embracing death or the 'dying fall' as the very nature of lyric itself. In another exquisite pun the rose is 'morose', a dead or dying rose, but in dying also 'more rose', more itself, strangely more of a rose than it has ever been. Bradley's poem is clearly in dialogue with Blake's 'The Sick Rose', another lyric that apostrophizes the flower. A traditional interpretation sees Blake's rose as feminized beauty destroyed by the phallic and masculine evil of 'the invisible worm', although, as Elizabeth Langland points

---

pp. 148–61; 159, and Chris White, 'Flesh and Roses: Michael Field's Metaphors of Pleasure', *Women's Writing* 3.1 (1996), 47–62; 57. White's analysis in an earlier essay is handicapped by the fact that she reproduces only the first eleven lines under the mistaken belief that these constitute the whole poem. See Chris White, 'The One Woman (in Virgin Haunts of Poesie): Michael Field's Sapphic Symbolism', in *Volcanoes and Pearl Divers: Essays in Lesbian Feminist Studies*, ed. Suzanne Raitt (London: Only Women Press, 1995), pp. 74–102; 98–9.

[132] Amina Okada, 'India and Perfume in the Mughal Period, Sixteenth to Nineteenth Centuries', in *Perfume: A Global History*, pp. 172–3; 172. See also Jennifer Potter, *The Rose: A True History* (London: Atlantic Books, 2010), p. 348. Potter nominates Geronimo Rossi of Ravenna as the first to develop a technique for separating rose oil from rosewater as 'described in a European source dated 1574' (p. 348).

[133] Okada, 'India and Perfume in the Mughal Period', p. 172.

[134] Chris White, 'The Tiresian Poet', p. 158; 'Flesh and Roses', p. 57.

out, twentieth-century male critics have perpetuated misogynist readings that see the rose as deceptive and blamed for her own sickness.[135]

In contrast, for Bradley's speaker, there is no blame for the rose, only love, and admiration is undimmed in celebration of a demise that is 'Majestic in recession'. The dying but still potent rose is a decadent variant of other key nineteenth-century tropes of triumphant deaths like those lyric swans and nightingales that sing most sweetly in their dying throes. It is a daring *fin-de-siècle* revision of Shelley's image of poetry as the perfect rose in his 'Defence', where he declares poetry 'the perfect and consummate surface and bloom of things; it is as the odour and colour of the rose to the texture of the elements which compose it, as the form and splendour of unfaded beauty to the secrets of anatomy and corruption' (*SPP*, p. 503). In Bradley's lyric the unsparing willed anatomy of the disintegrating rose endorses decay and corruption, as the beloved poetic image pushed to crisis dissolves to induce a fresh new lyricism: 'as your crimsons stale, | I feel fresh rhythms quicken, | Fresh music follows you'. Moreover, words and phrases like 'wrought with fire', 'ashes', and 'burning', hint at a possible ghostly resurrection, the spectre of a rose, that famous Renaissance wonder the 're-individualling of an incinerated plant' or the rose that the alchemist Paracelsus boasted he could raise from its ashes.[136] Indeed, fresh generation is implied by the 'fragrant soil', that, unlike dust, suggests a growing medium enriched for the next flowering cycle.

Yet those shrivelled falling petals, what Cooper calls 'the rose-leaves of your imagination', would still hold fragrance like Shelley's 'Rose leaves, when the rose is dead' (*SPP*, p. 442). As the aromatherapist Julia Lawless observes, 'Rose petals have a very tenacious scent which actually increases when they are kept (just as rose oil improves with age) which is why they form the basis for many pot pourri recipes.'[137] The poem produces another ghost in the guise of perfume that lives on after the rose itself has expired, or as Cooper writes in another lyric: 'The roses wither and die, | But their fragrance is not dead.'[138] In Bradley's lyric, as the petals shrivel and fall, they expose the heart or 'core' of the rose, 'A round, black hollow', suggestive of female sexuality but also more generally a figure of the poetic or imaginative unconscious where images coalesce or decompose.

Interestingly, just as we encounter the feminine core of the poem a tantalizing aroma of masculinity appears in the 'hints' of 'tobacco, leather, brass' said to give the dead rose 'her texture and her colour'. Yet the word 'hints' irresistibly suggests the idea of fragrance; indeed, 'texture' and 'colour', though keyed to tactile and visual impression, are words that might well be used by a perfumer. Karen Gilbert, advising the perfume student how to build up an olfactory vocabulary, writes, 'Think on

---

[135] Elizabeth Langland, 'Blake's Feminist Revision of Literary Tradition in "The Sick Rose"', in *Critical Paths: Blake and The Argument of Method*, ed. Dan Miller, Mark Bracher, and Donald Ault (Durham, NC, and London: Duke University Press, 1987), pp. 225–43.

[136] Cited in Walter Pater, 'Sir Thomas Browne', in *A*, p. 151.

[137] Julia Lawless, *Rose Oil: The New Guide to Nature's Most Precious Perfume and Traditional Remedy* (London: HarperCollins, 1995), p. 80.

[138] 'The roses wither and die', in *Underneath the Bough* (1893), pp. 117–18. Cooper echoes Shelley's 'Rose leaves, when the rose is dead | Are heaped for the beloved's bed', 'To ———' (*SPP*, p. 442).

different levels. Consider whether the fragrance recalls a color, texture, or weight?'[139] The perfumer Jean-Claude Ellena, recording his desire to express the 'tactile aspect' of a particular perfume, observes, 'A perfume never speaks to one sense alone, but offers itself to all the senses', and the poetic speaker urges the Grand Mogul rose to 'entoil' or entangle '[her] senses'.[140]

'[T]obacco, leather, brass' is an unusual trio to find in a lyric by a Victorian woman; Chadwyck-Healey's poetry database reveals no other use of the word 'tobacco' by a woman poet in the period 1880–1900.[141] Such odorous 'hints' seem to anticipate twentieth-century perfumes where it is not uncommon to encounter masculine 'leather', 'tobacco', or metallic notes combined with florals such as rose—rose oil being the most common floral ingredient in modern perfume.[142] Early influential tobacco and leather perfumes such Tabac Blond (1919), Habanita (1921), Cuir de Russie (1924), and Bandit (1944)—the last three containing rose—are daring perfumes, specifically designed for the twentieth-century emancipated woman who smoked.[143] Some later rose perfumes are also said to have a metallic aspect because certain essential oils and synthetic molecules used to create a rose fragrance, such as rose otto, geranium oil, palmarosa oil, rose oxide, and geraniol, have metallic notes. And indeed botanical roses themselves offer a huge range of notes, often varying with temperature and time of day, and reminiscent of many fruits, spices, and what the horticultural historian Jennifer Potter calls 'sundry substances' that include moss, damp earth, musk, rancid butter, face-powder, and Russian leather.[144] Bradley and Cooper were clearly aware of such variety; in 'Festa', a later poem from *Wild Honey*, written by Bradley on 15 July 1900, the speaker portrays her beloved 'with me in the bloom of roses' laughingly trying to identify the notes of different rose scents with descriptions such as 'A cedar-coffer, a miasma dense | With suck of honey.'[145]

Although 'The Grand Mogul' anticipates the avant-garde leather and tobacco-rose perfumes to come, it also evokes scents nearer at hand that could be combined with rose. The leather note in perfume is actually an old one dating from the Renaissance, when perfume was applied to gloves and other items of leather apparel to disguise the unpleasant smell of the tanning process. This eventually evolved into the perfume peau d'espagne or 'Spanish leather', a popular unisex handkerchief and sachet perfume in the late nineteenth and early twentieth centuries that contains leather notes, spices, and florals, including rose. It seems less surprising that tobacco appears in this poem when one recalls that Bradley and Cooper were respectively the daughter and granddaughter of Charles Bradley, a Birmingham tobacconist and snuff-manufacturer who died when Bradley was two but whose money effectively financed their independent lifestyle and writing career. Tobacco might be considered a subtle aromatic reminiscence of the absent enabling father

---

[139] Gilbert, *Perfume: The Art and Craft of Fragrance*, p. 60.
[140] Ellena, *The Diary of a Nose*, p. 136.
[141] This is, of course, a very partial mode of assessment and it should be said 'The Grand Mogul' itself does not appear in the database.
[142] See Lawless, *Rose Oil*, p. 81.   [143] Herman, *Scent and Subversion*, pp. 29, 33, 37, 79.
[144] Potter, *The Rose: A True History*, p. 338.   [145] 'Festa', in *Wild Honey*, p. 176.

who infiltrates the poem alongside the poetic fathers of Blake and Shelley. Moreover, both women were smokers, with Bradley in particular daring to smoke in male company. Smoking was another olfactory pleasure for them, with Bradley recording how, as presents on Easter Day 1904, 'We give each other, not eggs,—fine cigarettes & liquid ambergris.'[146]

As Penny Tinkler points out, smoking among middle and upper-class women in the period 1880 to 1920 can be regarded as 'a gendered statement of modernity' and 'a sign of gender rebellion', although a concession to femininity might be made in the form of ladies' cigarettes 'very dainty in appearance', which gave off 'the sweet odours of violets and roses'.[147] From the Regency period, snuff, finely ground tobacco for inhalation, had been scented with essential oils, with rose a popular note in varieties such as Macouba.[148] Brass—a metal that gives off a distinct smell in contact with human skin—was used during the nineteenth century for the buttons on men's uniforms but also for snuff boxes, cigarette cases and holders, perfume bottles and stoppers, becoming an additional element in the olfactory experience. Thus, if the Grand Mogul rose forges an identity of masculine command and authority fused with an underlying feminine desire, pleasure, and imaginative inspiration, this is echoed in a ghostly smell-signature, an emancipated fragrance of rose with masculine notes of tobacco, leather, brass, a sort of 'essence of Michael Field' that is left lingering at the poem's close.

---

[146] Works and Days, Add MS 46793, fol. 68ʳ (Easter Day [3 April] 1904).
[147] Penny Tinkler, 'Sapphic Smokers and English Modernities', in *Sapphic Modernisms: Sexuality, Women and National Culture*, ed. Laura Doan and Jane Garrity (Basingstoke: Palgrave Macmillan, 2006), pp. 75–90; 79; Penny Tinkler, *Smoke Signals: Women, Smoking and Visual Culture* (Oxford: Berg, 2006), p. 21.
[148] Arlott, *The Snuff Shop*, p. 34.

7

Dandies and Decadents
Oscar Wilde and Arthur Symons

In early June 1898, following his release from prison the previous year, Oscar Wilde was in Paris with his lover Lord Alfred Douglas. Given tickets by the soprano singer and actress Georgette Leblanc, they attended a performance of Jules Massenet's *Sapho*, at the Opéra Comique. Writing to Robbie Ross about their evening, Wilde, dismissive of the music though admiring of Leblanc's acting, commented on an unanticipated demand on another of their senses:

> Bosie was seated next a *German* who exhaled in strange gusts the most extraordinary odours, some of them racial; (it is smell that differentiates races); others connected with all kinds of trades from leather-dressing and carpentry, to vitriol-works and the keeping of an Italian warehouse; others such as are found only among '*les mangeurs des choses immondes*' [the eaters of unclean things]; others connected with gas, fuel, and candles. In the last act he became like a petroleum lamp: Bosie bore it very well indeed: but had practically to sit in my pocket. (*CL*, p. 1083)[1]

Manifesting the olfactory acuity expected of the aesthete, Wilde humorously lists the odours emitted by their neighbour that breach the habits of good society: he offends not only by smelling unacceptably 'foreign', but also by reeking of trade, of repellent food, and of utilitarian substances. His invasive malodour is an affliction to the more sensitive Douglas and Wilde, with Bosie portrayed as stoically bearing it 'very well' yet simultaneously shrinking away towards his sympathetic partner.

The decadent dandy cultivates and inhabits a refined olfactory space that bears little or no taint of worldly or utilitarian influences. He may derive pleasure from natural floral scents, although he typically favours the stronger, more exotic fragrances thought oppressive or dangerously intoxicating by others. Yet he also attempts to improve on nature, and his pursuit, creation, or acquisition of pleasing odours for pleasure's sake inevitably involves bought or manufactured perfume. As mentioned in my Introduction, the artifice of perfumery makes it a perfect partner for decadent culture, which coincides with the discovery and use of synthetic fragrance materials and the concomitant birth of the modern perfume industry. This chapter examines the decadent *olfactif* as represented by Oscar Wilde and the less well-known poet and critic Arthur Symons, both of whom make scents and

---

[1] The phrase '*les mangeurs des choses immondes*' comes from Flaubert's *Salammbô* (1862), where it is applied by the Carthaginians to their barbarian neighbours whose 'unclean' foods include molluscs and serpents.

scented atmospheres a notable feature of their work. However, unlike other the male *olfactifs* examined in this book, both Wilde and Symons show a more evident personal appreciation of manufactured perfume, which they clearly enjoyed wearing, aware of its invisible but influential role in shaping the sexual and social identity of the decadent dandy or sophisticated man about town. Both writers have a connection to the origins of modern perfumery in that they allude to perfumes that contain synthetic ingredients. In Symons's case one particular scent, made popular by its greater availability due to its use of a synthetic aroma chemical, contributes to one of his best-known lyrics, a poem that is itself a harbinger of modernity. This chapter begins by discussing the ways in which Wilde explores the importance of perfume to the decadent in *Dorian Gray*, and shows how he links it to homosexual identity and desire. Unlike John Addington Symonds who associated his version of a healthy virile homosexual desire with fresh outdoor natural scents, Wilde emphasizes heavier fragrances and the artifice of perfume as the preferred choice for the urbane dandy who is sexually attracted to other men. Such a choice reflects Wilde's own perfumed lifestyle abruptly curtailed by his imprisonment in 1895, and this chapter also shows how during his incarceration, perfume conspicuous by its absence, nonetheless remains a vital symbol both of consolation and the promise of a longed-for future life beyond bars.

INTOXICATING ODOURS: OSCAR WILDE AS DECADENT *OLFACTIF*

Oscar Wilde is almost certainly the writer whom most people will think of in relation to perfume in the late Victorian period. *The Picture of Dorian Gray* (1890, 1891) perhaps the most widely read *fin-de-siècle* text, famously includes perfume as one of the fads Dorian indulges in when he is experimenting with sensuous experience and connoisseurship:

> And so he would now study perfumes, and the secrets of their manufacture, distilling heavily-scented oils, and the burning odorous gums from the East. He saw that there was no mood of the mind that had not its true counterpart in the sensuous life, and he set himself to discover their true relations, wondering what there was in frankincense that made one mystical, and in ambergris that stirred one's passions, and in violets that woke the memory of dead romances, and in musk that troubled the brain, and in champak that stained the imagination; and seeking often to elaborate a real psychology of perfumes, and to estimate the several influences of sweet-smelling roots, and scented pollen-laden flowers, of aromatic balms, and of dark and fragrant woods, of spikenard that sickens, of hovenia that makes men mad, and of aloes that are said to be able to expel melancholy from the soul.   (*DG*, p. 111)[2]

Although this passage is relatively well known, compared with the catalogues of Dorian's other passions for music, jewels, and embroidered textiles, it is actually

---

[2] Gillespie's Norton edition (*DG*) usefully contains both the original 1890 *Lippincott's Magazine* version and the text of the novel of 1891. Unless otherwise stated, I refer to the latter throughout.

quite short and is quoted here entire. It is inspired by a much longer and richer treatment of perfume by Joris-Karl Huysmans in *A Rebours* (1884), one of the most significant French literary decadent texts and the thinly disguised real-life analogue of the infamous novel read by Dorian that helps determine his subsequent direction in life.[3] The collecting and experimentation of Huysmans's decadent hero Des Esseintes influences both Dorian and part of Wilde's narrative, but, befittingly in a novel about influence, the presence of the precursor text is obliquely acknowledged. Wilde's narrator characterizes the pseudo-*A Rebours* as a pervasive and dangerous perfume—'It was a poisonous book. The heavy odour of incense seemed to cling about its pages and to trouble the brain' (*DG*, p. 104)—and later Dorian complains to Lord Henry Wotton, who has lent him the book: 'you poisoned me with a book once. I should not forgive that. Harry, promise me that you will never lend that book to anyone. It does harm' (p. 180). Indeed, earlier Lord Henry, musing on the 'terribly enthralling' nature of influence, finds 'joy' in the thought of 'convey[ing] one's temperament into another as though it were a subtle fluid or a strange perfume' (p. 34), while Dorian, stimulated by Henry's influence to a 'mad curiosity' about the people he sees in the streets and a new 'passion for sensations', experiences an 'exquisite poison in the air' (p. 44). Dorian's brief flirtation with the study of perfume has charm, but perfume-as-influence is the more intriguing and pervasive topic and indeed is diffused throughout the novel's opening pages.

For a writer like Wilde, who is so very visual, it is striking that the novel starts with an appeal to smell rather than sight: 'The studio was filled with the rich odour of roses, and when the light summer wind stirred amidst the trees of the garden there came through the open door the heavy scent of the lilac, or the more delicate perfume of the pink-flowering thorn' (p. 5). Signalling that that we are entering a domain of refined sensory pleasure, these alluring, intoxicating flower scents stir sub-rational impulses, trigger associations, and evoke a languorous, though expectant, mood. They will be joined in the 'languid air' by the suggestion of other odours: the 'honey-sweet [...] laburnum', the 'straggling woodbine', and the 'thin blue wreaths of smoke' from Lord Henry Wotton's 'heavy opium-tainted cigarette' (pp. 5–6). The reader, like Dorian, is about to be seduced. Wilde plays with the relation of inside and outside, artifice and nature. Natural scents enter Basil Hallward's studio, a place of artistic and perceptual transformation, are subtly refined by aesthetic evaluation, and, combined with more artificial odours, become part of a seductive perfumed atmosphere.

Moving from the studio back into the garden, something of that atmosphere moves too, so that the garden with its 'polished' and 'green lacquer leaves' (pp. 8, 15) is tinged with artifice. Dorian, escaping the 'stifling' air of the studio and Lord Henry's verbal blandishments, takes refuge by 'burying his head in the great cool lilac-blossoms, feverishly drinking in their perfume as if it had been wine' (p. 21); but that febrile desire for intoxication shows that this is no longer a simple, unalloyed,

---

[3] For Des Esseintes's experiments with perfume, see Huysmans, *Against Nature*, ch. 10 (pp. 118–29), helpfully printed as a supplementary document in Gillespie's edition.

natural pleasure. Dorian is already under the influence, and influence, literally 'a flowing into', is a matter of atmosphere—that 'stifling' air—as well as words. He has already breathed in, been inspired by Henry's intoxicating words, which, like the 'opium-tainted' cigarette have altered the ambience of Basil's more benign aestheticism. Later in the novel there is a nice understated moment in Lord Henry's library, when Dorian, having announced to Henry his passion for Sibyl Vane and preparing to leave, affects a dandyish manner by casually 'putting some perfume on his handkerchief out of a large, gold-topped bottle that stood on the table' (p. 50). That he insouciantly helps himself shows his newfound confidence—he is now completely at home in Lord Henry's domain—but he is also, perhaps unconsciously, putting on another man's scent, heading out into the city with Henry's aura around him.

Wilde himself, highly aware of perfume's ability to create an ambience and influence mood, was keen to manipulate the atmosphere in which his dramas were performed. Planning the stage design for *Salome*, he wanted '"in place of an orchestra braziers of perfume. Think—the scented clouds rising and partly veiling the stage from time to time—a new perfume for each emotion."' This imaginative, though rather impractical, plan was not carried out because, as his friend, the artist Graham Robertson, 'pointed out [...] the theatre could not be aired between each emotion'.[4] Wilde was more successful with the première of *The Importance of Being Earnest*. Ada Leverson noted the 'perfumed atmosphere' that resulted from Wilde's request to his supporters—both men and women—to wear lily of the valley on the opening night: 'nearly all the pretty women wore sprays of lilies against their large puffed sleeves, while rows and rows of young elegants had buttonholes of the delicate bloom of lily of the valley'.[5]

In his early critical study of Wilde (1912), Arthur Ransome referenced *Dorian Gray*'s themes of perfume culture and esoteric connoisseurship when classing the novel among those 'mysterious' books, 'kept, like mysteries, for peculiar moods':

> We keep them for rare moments, as we keep in a lacquer cabinet some crystal-shrined thread of subtle perfume, or some curious gem, to be a solace in a mood that does not often recur, or, perhaps, to be an instrument in its evocation. *Dorian Gray*, for all its faults, is such a book. It is unbalanced; and that is a fault. [...] But in it there is an individual essence, a private perfume, a colour whose secret has been lost. There are moods whose consciousness that essence, perfume, colour, is needed to intensify.[6]

Fin-de-siècle readers of *Dorian Gray* also experienced its influence as odorous: reprising the image Wilde used of Lord Henry's book, the *Daily Chronicle* called the novel a 'poisonous book, the atmosphere of which is heavy with the mephitic odours of moral and spiritual putrefaction'.[7] Wilde, responding to this review in a

[4] Richard Ellmann, *Oscar Wilde* (London: Penguin, 1988), p. 351.

[5] Ada Leverson, 'The First Last Night' (1926), in *Oscar Wilde: Interviews and Recollections*, ed. E. H. Mikhail, 2 vols (London and Basingstoke: Macmillan, 1979), 2. 267. Nick Freeman kindly informs me that this was a tribute to the absent Bosie, whom Wilde associated with the lily.

[6] Arthur Ransome, *Oscar Wilde: A Critical Study* (London: Martin Secker, 1912), p. 98.

[7] Unsigned review, *Daily Chronicle* (30 June 1890), 7, reprinted in Karl Beckson, ed., *Oscar Wilde: The Critical Heritage* (London: Routledge & Kegan Paul, 1970), p. 72. This denunciatory language of

letter to the *Chronicle*, ended with the declaration that his novel was 'poisonous, if you like, but you cannot deny that it is also perfect, and perfection is what we artists aim at' (*CL*, p. 436; 30 June 1890). Alfred Douglas, who read the novel fourteen times running, wrote about the 'intoxicating' effect it had on him.[8] For many, like Ransome, the atmosphere of the book was not 'mephitic' but perfumed, if oppressively so. The anonymous reviewer for the journal *Theatre* complained: 'Reading it, we move in a heavy atmosphere of warm incense and slumbering artificial light. [...] We long to push on to the light, and the blowing wind, and the clean air of honest commonplace that Mr Wilde's cultured puppets cry faugh! to.'[9] As mentioned in Chapter 4, John Addington Symonds, who found *Dorian Gray* 'unwholesome in tone, but artistically and psychologically interesting', nonetheless 'resent[ed] the unhealthy, scented, mystic, congested touch which a man of this sort has on moral problems', and was disturbed by 'the morbid & perfumed manner of treating such psychological subjects' (*LJAS* 3. 477, 478; 22 July 1890). Conversely, the French poet Stéphane Mallarmé wrote to Wilde (who had given him a copy): 'I am finishing the book, one of the few that can take hold of the reader, since from an inner revery and the strangest perfumes of the soul it stirs up a storm.'[10] In their different ways, these views attest to perfume's relation with deeper concerns, with psychology or even the soul. For Mallarmé, interestingly, *Dorian Gray*, rather than imposing its own fragrance, appears to activate and release the reader's 'soul'-perfume—presumably his repressed or unconscious thoughts—while Symonds finds the book's influence invasive and contaminating, and experiences it as the unsolicited 'touch' of an undesirable 'scented' man. It is an image reminiscent of Lord Henry's continuing temptation of Dorian in Basil's garden, when he comes upon him drinking in the lilac: 'He came close to him and put his hand upon his shoulder. "You are quite right to do that", he murmured, "Nothing can cure the soul but the senses, just as nothing can cure the senses but the soul." The lad started and drew back' (p. 21).

The touch that makes Dorian start and Symonds shudder emphasizes a difference in style. Wilde's literary 'manner', identified by Symonds as 'morbid and perfumed', is—in other words—'decadent'. Perfume as an attribute of literary and, in particular, decadent style, is something that recurs repeatedly in the criticism of the late Victorian period. However, for Symonds, that style is here indivisible from its 'decadent' content, a certain unhealthy treatment of a psychosexual disposition. This is not to put Symonds in the same company as the reactionary social commentator Max Nordau, who thought that 'The predominance of the sense of smell and its connection with the sexual life is very striking among many degenerates.

'malodorous putrefaction' is also present in a review in the *St James's Gazette* (24 June 1890), included in Gillespie's edition (*DG*, p. 360).

   [8] See Douglas's letter of 8 July 1935 to A. J. A. Symons, quoted in Neil McKenna, *The Secret Life of Oscar Wilde* (London: Century, 2003), p. 201.

   [9] Unsigned review, *Theatre* 8 (1 June 1891), 245, in Beckson, ed., *Oscar Wilde: The Critical Heritage*, p. 81.

   [10] Cited in Ellmann, *Oscar Wilde*, p. 319 (Ellmann's translation).

Scents acquire a high importance in their work.'[11] Symonds shies away from what he finds effete and decadent as opposed to his own preference for a virile homosexuality. To another correspondent he wrote: 'I do not like this touch upon moral psychological problems, wh[ich] have for myself great actuality, & ought I think to be treated more directly. I am afraid that Wilde's work in this way will only solidify the prejudices of the vulgar' (*LJAS* 3. 479; 24 July 1890). Symonds was himself extremely scent-sensitive (although very particular in his preferred fragrances), and while he would undoubtedly have gibed at Nordau's verdict of 'degeneracy', he probably would not have disagreed with his friend and collaborator, the psychologist Havelock Ellis, who, in his psychosexual analysis of smell published in 1905, claimed that 'It is certain also that a great many neurasthenic people, and particularly those who are sexually neurasthenic, are peculiarly susceptible to olfactory influences. A number of eminent poets and novelists—especially, it would appear, in France—seem to be in this case.'[12]

Already, from this initial brief consideration of *Dorian Gray*, we see scent and perfume emerge not only as metaphors for influence but as markers of style and sexuality. While perfume can arouse appetite and increase sensuous pleasure, it also has the ability to create mood, reflect psychology, and stir the soul. Indeed, Lord Henry's axiom—'Nothing can cure the soul but the senses, just as nothing can cure the senses but the soul'—reminds us of the senses' inextricable relation with spiritual health. Later in the novel, Lord Henry will return to this relationship: 'Soul and body, body and soul—how mysterious they were! There was animalism in the soul, and the body had its moments of spirituality. The senses could refine, and the intellect could degrade. Who could say where the fleshly impulse ceased, or the psychical impulse began?' (p. 52). The relationship between soul and senses is explored throughout the novel, with smell having its own important role. Dorian's actual dalliance with perfume experimentation might be an abbreviated version of Des Esseintes's connoisseurship, but Wilde's novel nonetheless shows how scent permeates his aesthetic existence.

In this Dorian takes his lead from his mentor, Lord Henry, an olfactory epicure who not only wears scented buttonholes (pp. 50, 85) and keeps perfume in his study to scent his handkerchiefs, but weaves the refined pleasures of fragrance seamlessly into his everyday life; in one scene we see him casually 'dipping his white fingers into a red copper bowl filled with rose-water' (p. 172), and a few minutes later 'passing beneath his nostrils the gilt trellis of an open vinaigrette-box' (p. 175). Shortly after this, in mid-conversational flow, he turns round 'taking his handkerchief out of his pocket' (p. 176), this seemingly inconsequential gesture almost certainly a gestural flourish to scatter fragrance. In this same scene, he also reveals that for him particular perfumes have become associated with key experiences, and can thus reactivate 'subtle memories': 'There are moments when the

---

[11] Nordau, *Degeneration*, p. 500.

[12] Ellis, 'Section II: Smell', pp. 72–3. Ellis's view is not so different from a modern observation: 'people with emotionally unstable personalities, sometimes called *neurotic*, tend to be more sensitive to noise, pain, unpleasant scenes, and bitter tastes than emotionally stable individuals. [They] are also more responsive and sensitive to odors.' See Herz, *The Scent of Desire*, pp. 53–4.

odour of *lilas blanc* passes suddenly across me, and I have to live the strangest month of my life over again' (p. 179).

After his seduction by Lord Henry, a drinking-in of both fragrance and influence, perfume also becomes an integral part of Dorian's life, from the scent on his handkerchief and his fragrant buttonholes such as Parma violets (p. 145), to the 'delicately scented chamber' where he sleeps (p. 106), and his sitting room fragranced by furniture of 'dark perfumed wood' (p. 102). After his incineration of Basil's clothes and bag, he banishes the 'horrible' smell by burning pastilles and soothes himself by bathing his face with 'with a cool musk-scented vinegar' (p. 152). Seeking 'oblivion', he is allured by the 'curiously heavy and persistent' smell of opium (p. 153) and encountering the 'heavy odour' of its fumes at a dockside drug-den, 'his nostrils quivered with pleasure' (p. 156). At specific moments Dorian's mood is responsive to ambient smells: loitering in Covent Garden after his rejection of Sibyl Vane, he finds 'The air was heavy with the perfume of the flowers, and their beauty seemed to bring him an anodyne for his pain' (pp. 75–6). Once home, standing in front of the subtly changed portrait, he resolves to make amends with Sibyl, and 'The fresh morning air seemed to drive away all his sombre passions' (p. 78). The next day, unaware of her suicide, he enjoys a leisurely late breakfast in his library where 'The warm air seemed laden with spices. A bee flew in and buzzed round the blue-dragon bowl that, filled with sulphur-yellow roses, stood before him. He felt perfectly happy' (p. 79). Much later, while staying at Selby Royal, his country house, he manages to suppress his anxiety about Sibyl's vengeful brother, and relishes 'something in the clear, pine-scented air of that winter morning that seemed to bring him back his joyousness and his ardour for life' (p. 166).

The Decadent Scent of Desire

That Dorian's developing sensitivity to scent and perfume is an indicator of his decadent sexual identity, cultivated by Lord Henry from the novel's opening seduction scene, can be even more clearly appreciated if we place alongside it the far more explicit contemporary narrative of *Teleny*, an anonymous homoerotic novel written by several hands and published in 1893, with Wilde often proposed as one of its contributors. *Teleny* opens with the narrator, Camille Des Grieux, relating to a friend how he met the eponymous hero, a handsome and talented pianist, at a charity concert. Des Grieux is clearly interested in René Teleny from the start, carefully observing his appearance and noting his somewhat eccentric choice of buttonhole: 'a bunch of white heliotrope, although camellias and gardenias were then in fashion'.[13] It soon transpires that there is a magnetic attraction and

---

[13] Oscar Wilde and Others, *Teleny*, ed. John McRae (London: Gay Men's Press, 1986), pp. 28–9. Subsequent references appear in the text. The novel was first published in a run of two hundred copies by Leonard Smithers, a publisher known for his erotica, and was priced at four guineas a copy. Smithers allegedly (p. 11) transferred the action of the novel from London to Paris. During his American tour, Wilde, interviewed by a journalist in San Francisco in March 1882, was described as wearing 'a boutonnnière, somewhat withered, made up of heliotrope, a brightly foliated daisy and a tuberose'. Mikhail, ed., *Oscar Wilde: Interviews and Recollections*, 1. 59.

quasi-telepathic sympathy between the two young men that has also an olfactory dimension. Des Grieux describes Teleny's first piece as 'a favourite *gavotte* of mine—one of those slight, graceful and easy melodies that seem to smell of *lavande ambrée*' (p. 27). *Lavande ambrée* is a lavender water, popular throughout the nineteenth century and beyond, that contains ambergris to bring out the scent of the flowers.[14] It is a gentle, old-fashioned scent that, as Des Grieux suggests of the music, 'put[s] you in mind of Lulli and Watteau, of powdered ladies dressed in yellow satin gowns, flirting with their fans' (p. 27).

However, Teleny's rendition of a 'wild, Hungarian rhapsody' causes Des Grieux to feel unstrung by a deepening sensation of lust and longing, all the while imagining a succession of exotic scenes and locations that ends with a hallucination of Teleny with a dagger in his breast. Still reeling from this vision, he encounters the pianist in the company of some other young men. Praised for his performance, Teleny declares that he plays at his best when he has a 'sympathetic listener' in the audience who sees the same visions that he does (p. 34). When Des Grieux hints at one of the visions he himself experienced, Teleny is clearly moved, wiping his perspiring forehead with 'a strongly-scented lawn handkerchief' (p. 37), and soon after suggests that they leave the concert together. Once alone, they share their experience of the visions, but it turns out that this visual transmission was not the only sensory communication between them. Teleny asks Des Grieux if he smelt a scent when he was playing the gavotte, and when he admits he did, tells him it was *lavande ambrée*:

'Which you do not care for, and which I dislike; tell me which is your favourite scent?'
'*Heliotrope blanc.*'
Without giving me an answer, he pulled out his handkerchief and gave it to me to smell.
'All our tastes are exactly the same, are they not?' And saying this, he looked at me with such a passionate and voluptuous longing that the carnal longing depicted in his eyes made me feel faint.
'You see, I always wear a bunch of white heliotrope; let me give this to you, that its smell may remind you of me to-night, and perhaps make me dream of you.'   (p. 39)

Heliotrope blanc or white heliotrope is a vanilla-sweet, almond-smelling, powdery floral that was, as will be corroborated later in this chapter, an immensely popular *fin-de-siècle* fragrance. Here, however, for Des Grieux it is the sign of the 'same' tastes he shares with Teleny and the scent that evokes Teleny himself—indeed Des Grieux will go on to experience an erotic heliotrope-scented dream influenced by his longing for his new friend. Moreover, when the long-awaited consummation scene occurs, it is in Teleny's apartment in a white chamber specially designed by him and scented with white heliotrope, and afterwards the lovers bathe together in 'warm water, scented with essence of heliotrope' (pp. 117, 121).

This far more explicit treatment of sexual desire and attraction between men nonetheless alerts us to the significance of the scent cues that subtly pervade the

---

[14] A receipt can be found in C. F. Bertrand, *Le Parfumeur imperial, or l'art de préparer les odeurs, essences, parfums* (Paris: Brunot-Labbé, 1809), p. 113.

narrative of *Dorian Gray*. If its 'scented' or 'perfumed' manner alerted knowing
though disapproving readers like Symonds to its 'psychological' content, it also
unsettled less sophisticated readers who registered something of the oddity or
'queerness' of this carefully cultivated masculine olfactory sensitivity. Certainly
the popular suspicion of men who wear or use perfume can be seen in the Wilde
trials when the landlady of Wilde's associate Alfred Taylor was asked whether he
had any scent in his rooms and replied that 'Mr Taylor used to burn scent'.
Taylor himself, asked why he burnt incense in his rooms, replied, 'Because
I liked it.' Montgomery Hyde comments that most of the jurymen were no doubt
adversely influenced by the description of Taylor's darkened candlelit rooms 'the
languorous atmosphere heavy with perfume'.[15] Robert Sherard, Wilde's friend
and biographer, comments:

> [B]e it noted *en passant* how even the most innocent practices of his were made weapons
> against him. For instance the burning of perfumes in his rooms and those of his
> friends: of this much was made. It was a habit he had no doubt contracted at Oxford.
> I remember very well that when I was at the University a number of undergraduates
> used to burn that scented ribbon which one pulls out of a little round, red, cardboard
> box, which is made I fancy by the House of Rimmel and which is supposed to coun-
> teract the unpleasant odour of stale tobacco smoke.[16]

In fact, the popular product known as 'Ruban de Bruges' (Ribbon of Bruges) made
by Piesse and Lubin (see Chapter 6, Figure 6.1), or 'Persian Fumigating Ribbon'
made by Rimmel, was widely available from at least the 1860s and was evidently
used in many British homes.[17] However, even without the imputation of sexual
degeneracy, 'incense' might well have negative connotations being associated controversial ritualistic Roman Catholic or High Church practices on the one hand,
and dubious oriental cultures and customs on the other, though both have possible
homoerotic implications. Indeed, Dorian, like his creator and other aesthetes of
the period, is strongly attracted to the theatre of the Catholic mass with its picturesque young acolytes: 'The fuming censers, that the grave boys, in their lace and
scarlet, tossed into the air like great gilt flowers, had their subtle fascination for him'
(p. 110). Dorian would also have encountered Arabic incense in the Mediterranean
city of Algiers, a favourite destination for well-to-do homosexual men, where he

---

[15] H. Montgomery Hyde, *Oscar Wilde: A Biography* (London: Eyre Methuen, 1976), pp. 242, 261, 235.

[16] Robert Harborough Sherard, *The Real Oscar Wilde* (London: T. Werner Laurie, 1916), pp. 26–7.
Robert Sherard (1861–1943) was briefly an undergraduate at New College, Oxford, in 1880, but left
for financial reasons after a quarrel with his father, who cut him off from an expected family
inheritance.

[17] 'Ruban de Bruges' is mentioned in Piesse and Lubin's 1861 catalogue (p. 28), and a receipt for
its manufacture, which includes benzoin, myrrh, orris, musk, and rose otto, can be found in Piesse's
Art of Perfumery, 3rd edn (1862), pp. 246–7. 'Persian Fumigating Ribbon' can be found in various
Rimmel advertisements in theatrical programmes from the 1870s archived in the John Johnson
Collection, Oxford. The Rimmel adverts stipulate that the ribbon is priced at 1s. in 'paper boxes' and
at 1s. 6d 'in neat Parian boxes'. A programme advertising a production of *Antony and Cleopatra*
announces that the perfume in Act 1, scene iii ('Cleopatra's Barge') is 'produced by means of Rimmel's
Persian ribbon' (John Johnson Collection, London Playbills Drury Lane Box 2 (3)).

spends more than one winter with Lord Henry (p. 118).[18] Later, when ousting the smell of Basil's incinerated effects, he lights 'Algerian pastilles in a pierced copper brazier' (p. 152).

For conservative readers Dorian's slide into decadence might seem to be marked by his adoption of exotic olfactory practices, beginning in his experimental phase with the burning of 'odorous gums from the East'. Wilde himself implied there was something suspect about the use of incense, balking at the word when it was suggested to him that this was what Taylor burnt in his rooms; and he also hinted at its decadent connotations when he noted of Dorian's 'poisonous' book that 'the heavy odour of incense seemed to cling about its pages and to trouble the brain'. But readers might also have been discomposed by the way floral epithets, commonly used in the Victorian era to describe feminine charm and beauty, are conspicuously applied to an attractive young man. Those familiar with classical literature would recognize, not necessarily approvingly, that such usage followed in the homoerotic tradition of the Greek Anthology, a tradition, as mentioned in Chapters 4 and 5, emulated by John Addington Symonds and Mark André Raffalovich, who used images of flowers, especially scented flowers, to hymn the youthful male beloved.[19] However, neither of these writers exposed themselves to public comment in the way Wilde did with his novel, Symonds's letters being private and Raffalovich's poems being restricted to a select readership. Wilde's use of such classically influenced language undoubtedly contributed to the charge of 'frank Paganism' brought against him by the *St James's Gazette* (*DG*, p. 360). Thus Dorian Gray, with his 'gold hair, blue eyes, and rose-red lips' (p. 99), is described by Lord Henry as 'made of ivory and rose-leaves', possessing both a complexion of 'lilies and [...] roses' and a 'rose-red youth and rose-white boyhood' (pp. 7, 23, 20). His pact with his portrait ensures miraculous preservation of his 'flowerlike bloom' (p. 115).

Wilde used this floral language of his lover Alfred Douglas, famously writing of him to Robert Ross in the early summer of 1892, 'Bosie [...] lies like a hyacinth on the sofa, and I worship him' (*CL*, p. 526). He gave Douglas a copy of his story collection *A House of Pomegranates* (1891) inscribed with the words: 'Pomegranates for a pomegranate flower'.[20] Such endearments would cause problems for him in another context, the letter that he wrote to Douglas in January 1893 being cited and used against him in his trial: 'it is a marvel that those red rose-leaf lips should have been made no less for music of song than for madness of kisses. [...] I know Hyacinthus, whom Apollo loved so madly, was you in Greek days' (*CL*, p. 544). In April 1895, from Holloway Prison where he was waiting for his first trial to open, Wilde assured Ada and Ernest Leverson of Bosie's supportive presence—'He moves in the gloom like a white flower' (*CL*, p. 641)—referring in subsequent letters

---

[18] Wilde and Douglas would visit Algiers in January 1895 just before Wilde's libel case against the Marquess of Queensbury.

[19] Wilde declared his enthusiasm for the Greek Anthology in a letter of February 1886 to the Editor of the *Pall Mall Gazette*, complaining that it had been unaccountably omitted from a list of 'The Hundred Best Books' and declaring it 'necessary for a complete understanding of the Greek spirit' (*CL*, p. 277).

[20] Thomas Wright, *Oscar's Books: A Journey around the Library of Oscar Wilde* (London: Vintage Books, 2009), p. 194.

to Bosie by the nicknames of 'Fleur de-Lys' and 'Jonquil' (*CL*, p. 648).[21] Writing to Douglas on 20 May 1895, just before he was convicted, Wilde calls him 'My sweet rose, my delicate flower, my lily of lilies' (*CL*, p. 651), and, evoking the amatory olfactory symbolism of the Biblical Song of Solomon, declares: 'my heart is a rose which your love has brought to bloom, my life is a desert fanned by the delicious breeze of your breath [...] the odour of your hair is like myrrh, and wherever you go you exhale the perfumes of the cassia tree' (*CL*, pp. 651–2).[22]

While Wilde undoubtedly loved flowers, and in particular scented flowers, his love of them is consciously mediated by literary reference. In 'The Critic as Artist', a dialogue that asserts the primacy of art over nature, it is the everlasting flowers of literature and their associations that delight the imagination:

> And then, when you are tired of these flowers of evil, turn to the flowers that grow in the garden of Perdita, and in their dew-drenched chalices cool your fevered brow, and let their loveliness heal and restore your soul; or wake from his forgotten tomb the sweet Syrian, Meleager, and bid the lover of Heliodore make you music, for he too has flowers in his song, red pomegranate-blossoms, and irises that smell of myrrh, ringed daffodils and dark-blue hyacinths, and marjoram and crinkled ox-eyes. Dear to him was the perfume of the bean-field at evening, and dear to him the odorous eared-spikenard that grew on the Syrian hills, and the fresh green thyme, the wine-cup's charm. The feet of his love as she walked in the garden were like lilies set upon lilies. Softer than sleep-laden poppy petals were her lips, softer than violets and as scented.[23]

To relinquish the 'poisonous honey' of Baudelaire's *Les Fleurs du mal* for Shakespeare and the Greek Anthology is not to privilege nature over artifice, because these more bucolic texts, while they may have a more naturalistic charm, are, as compositions, just as artificial in their own way. Wilde would later speak of himself as 'me, to whom flowers are part of desire' (*CL*, p. 777), but that 'desire' is one undoubtedly stimulated by literary reminiscence. Literature has its own special scents which in turn then infiltrate the scents of nature, making them all the dearer.

Wilde's own taste in perfume reveals a preference for strong scents that are in keeping with decadent fashion. The young poet Theodore Wratislaw describes a trip to see Wilde at Goring-on-Thames in August 1893: 'Oscar proposed to spend the morning on the river and later on joined me, clearly spraying himself with a scent which filled the room. I inquired its name. "It is white lilac", he said. "A most insidious and delightful perfume."'[24] Lilac is one of a number of perfumes that are never or very rarely manufactured from the actual flower, either because, like lily of the valley, it is impossible to do so, or because the natural extracts are too laboursome and expensive to obtain, making perfume production impractical on a commercial scale. Lilac belongs to this second category. According to Piesse, lilac essential oil

---

[21] These names are taken from 'Jonquil and Fleur de Lys', a poem by Douglas.

[22] Cassia is a spice, obtained from the bark of an East Asian tree (*Cinnamomum cassia*) that is very similar to cinnamon (*Cinnamomum verum*), and indeed often marketed as cinnamon as it is less costly.

[23] Wilde, 'The Critic as Artist', in *Oscar Wilde: The Major Works*, p. 273. Wilde alludes to Perdita's flowers in Shakespeare's *The Winter's Tale* (4. 4. 118–27) and to the poems of Meleager in the Greek Anthology, a number of which are addressed to a female lover, Heliodora.

[24] Theodore Wratislaw, *Oscar Wilde: A Memoir*, foreword by John Betjeman, intr. and notes by Karl Beckson (London: Eighteen Nineties Society, 1979), p. 13; Ellmann, *Oscar Wilde*, p. 378.

could be obtained by maceration or enfleurage, although an imitation essence of white lilac might be made with its principal ingredient being 'Spirituous extract from tuberose pomade'.[25] A much cheaper alternative after 1885 was the use of the synthetic terpineol, which had a recognizable lilac odour, and which could be combined with natural ingredients to make a convincing scent.[26] While all perfume is a matter of artifice, Wilde's 'white lilac' accentuates this and its decadent character by, most likely, incorporating this new synthetic ingredient.

The description of his perfume—'insidious and delightful'—that Wilde casually tosses out to Wratislaw is a typically paradoxical decadent formula rather like Arthur Symons's famous description of decadence as 'a new and beautiful and interesting disease'.[27] However, Wilde may have had an additional reason for describing lilac in this way. In common with other heavier flower scents such as jasmine, tuberose, and orange flowers, admired by many decadents including Wilde, lilac contains indole, that tarry-smelling molecule also found in human faeces and decomposing human bodies.[28] As the chemist and perfume writer Paul Jellinek writes: 'It is precisely the odor of indol [*sic*], reminiscent of decay and faeces, that lends orange blossom, jasmine, tuberose, lilac and other blossoms that putrid-sweet, sultry-intoxicating nuance which has led to the use of these flowers and of their extracts as delicate aphrodisiacs, today as in the past.'[29] An authentic-smelling lilac, which for the perfume critic Chandler Burr evokes 'soiled underwear', will thus reproduce this indolic 'putrid-sweet' smell, which could quite feasibly be called 'insidious and delightful'.[30] Lilac is, of course, also one of the flower scents that suffuse the opening scene of *Dorian Gray*, and Lord Henry later mentions 'the odour of *lilas blanc*' as responsible for reviving memories of 'the strangest month of my life' (p. 179). Flower scents mentioned by Walter Pater as actually giving him pain—the white jonquil, the gardenia, and the syringa (lilac)—are all indolic, but, true to his decadent credentials, Wilde seems to have had a particular liking for these heavier scented, 'sultry-intoxicating' flowers.[31]

Indoles are essential to creating complex and beautiful perfumes, with the most important of the indolic flowers for perfumery being jasmine. Mandy Aftel explains that 'Jasmine flower is one of the essential elements, and sometimes the main pillar, in the structure of the greatest perfumes [...] everyone in perfumery knows the adage, "No perfume without jasmine".'[32] Wilde mentions jasmine in a number of

[25] Piesse, *Art of Perfumery* (1855), p. 49.   [26] Williams, *Perfumes of Yesterday*, p. 305.
[27] Arthur Symons, 'The Decadent Movement in Literature', *Harper's New Monthly Magazine* 87 (November 1893), 859, reprinted in *Dramatis Personæ* (London: Faber & Gwyer, 1925), p. 97, and *The Symbolist Movement in Literature*, ed. Matthew Creasy (Manchester: Fyfield Books, Carcanet Press, 2014), p. 169.
[28] Indoles, according to Luca Turin (*Secret of Scent*, p. 61), are 'an essential component of raspy-voiced white flowers', and can also be found in lilies, lilies of the valley, gardenias, honeysuckle, hyacinth, philadelphus, freesia, and osmanthus.
[29] Jellinek, *The Psychological Basis of Perfumery*, p. 42.
[30] Burr, *The Perfect Scent*, p. 214. Perfume critics routinely compare scents to soiled or dirty underwear. This is far from being an insult.
[31] Sharp, 'Some Personal Reminiscences of Walter Pater', p. 807.
[32] Mandy Aftel, 'Perfumed Obsession', in *The Smell Culture Reader*, pp. 206–11, 206. Aftel reprises much of this article in her recent book *Fragrant: The Secret Life of Scent* (New York: Riverhead Books, 2014), pp. 203–7.

poems and prose texts including 'Athanasia', 'The Burden of Itys', *Dorian Gray*, and 'The Young King', but he is more famously associated with the lily, another indolic decadent flower. In 1877, he listed his favourite flower as the 'Lilium Auratum' in an American 'Confession Album'; and he announced to an American reporter in 1882 that 'I have always loved lilies. At Oxford I kept my room filled with them, and I had a garden of them where I used to work very often.'[33] The literary cult of the lily, popularized by Wilde, had reached such a pitch by the 1890s that the poet Victor Plarr proposed to his fellow members of the Rhymers' Club 'that in future a levy of sixpence be imposed by the Club upon mention of the word lily, singular or plural'.[34]

In his 'Confession Album' entry Wilde listed his favourite perfume as 'almond blossom', incidentally one of the heavy scents, along with musk and rose saffron that the American beauty adviser Harriet Hubbard Ayer lists as 'dangerous', being 'almost hypnotic to some sensitive organizations'.[35] Almond blossom is a sweet floral scent with a touch of almond in it, a note that in the nineteenth century might be recreated using small quantities of either essential oil of bitter almonds or nitrobenzol (aka nitrobenzene), a synthetic 'otto of almonds' patented under the name 'Essence of Mirbane'. Wilde evidently liked that almond note in perfume—there is an almond nuance in heliotrope scent as well—writing of 'the almond-scented vale' in his early poem 'By the Arno' and of the wind-borne perfume of almond blossom in his early essay 'The Women of Homer'.[36] However, he might have been intrigued to know that both the natural and synthetic substances used to produce that note in scents like almond blossom or cherry blossom are poisonous.[37]

Wilde also enjoyed wearing fragrant flowers—his fondness for buttonholes is well known; in his financial heyday, says Robert Sherard, he had a standing order with a florist in the Burlington Arcade who sent him two *boutonnières* daily, one for himself and one for his driver (see Figure 7.1).[38] Favourite scented buttonholes included Parma violets and carnations, the white carnation artificially coloured green—a badge of decadence and possibly homosexual identity—being worn by Wilde at the premières of both *Lady Windermere's Fan* and *The Importance of*

---

[33] Merlin Holland, *The Wilde Album* (London: Fourth Estate, 1997), p. 44; 'A Talk with Wilde: The Apostle of the Aesthetes Enunciates his Views', *Philadelphia Press* (17 January 1882), 2, rpt. in Mikhail, ed., *Oscar Wilde: Interviews and Recollections*, 1. 44.

[34] Cited in Roger Lhombreaud, *Arthur Symons: A Critical Biography* (London: Unicorn Press, 1963), p. 87.

[35] Ayer, *Harriet Hubbard Ayer's Book*, p. 454.

[36] Wilde, 'By the Arno', in *Poems* (London: David Bogue, 1881), p. 162; *The Women of Homer*, ed. Thomas Wright and Donald Mead (London: Oscar Wilde Society, 2008), p. 56.

[37] Piesse, *Art of Perfumery* (1855), p. 20, warns that 'essential oil of [bitter] almonds' is 'exceedingly *poisonous*'. It is a source of hydrogen cyanide, also known as 'prussic acid', and deemed by Lord Henry as the poison most likely to have killed Sibyl Vane (*DG*, p. 83). However, 'Oil of Mirbane', first synthesized in 1834, was also extremely poisonous, and recognized as such from 1876. See 'Nitro-Benzol Poisoning', *California State Journal of Medicine* 16.5 (May 1918), 252–3. The almond note in modern perfume is produced by benzaldehyde, first synthesized in 1832, which, being not only considerably safer, is superior in smell. David Williams in *Perfumes of Yesterday*, pp. 110–11, speculates that 'Oil of Mirbane' was widely used because it was cheaper to produce than benzaldehyde.

[38] Sherard, *The Real Oscar Wilde*, p. 57.

Figure 7.1 Oscar Wilde wearing a characteristic carnation buttonhole (Granger Historical Picture Archive/Alamy Stock Photo)

Being Earnest (1892 and 1895).[39] It was probably Wilde's fondness for the large, clove-scented Malmaison carnation, which comes in a range of shades including white, that has led to the apocryphal story that his favourite perfume was Malmaison by Floris, which smells of carnations and clove oil and is described rather engagingly as a 'closet musk', meaning a fragrance which does not officially identify itself as a musk but whose musky nature and erotic power lie hidden within the folds of the perfume.

Robert Sherard, recalling his first dinner with Wilde in Paris in 1883, remarks that:

> He had spent an hour that evening at a hairdresser's, as was his daily custom, and I found him curled and resplendent. This delight in beautifying himself proceeded entirely from the most innocent joyousness of life. It was a token of triumph in happy vitality, and in somewise also the defiance of an artist to the moneyed bourgeoisie. To show amazingly, was to impress the Philistines with due respect for letters, ragged and pitiable no longer, but curled and scented, and in costly raiment.[40]

[39] *The Artist and Journal of Home Culture*, an aesthetic periodical with a homoerotic slant, explained how white carnations could be so transformed using the aniline dye malachite green. See Anon., 'From Month to Month: A Summary', *The Artist and Journal of Home Culture* 13.1 (April 1892), 114–15, and also cited in McKenna, *The Secret Life of Oscar Wilde*, p. 229. See also Karl Beckson, 'Oscar Wilde and the Green Carnation', *English Literature in Transition* 43.4 (2000), 387–97. Beckson is sceptical about some of the supposed homoerotic associations of the green carnation but does not cite *The Artist and Journal of Home Culture* as one of his sources.

[40] Robert Sherard, *Oscar Wilde: The Story of an Unhappy Friendship* (London: Greening & Co., 1905), pp. 32–3.

Though not visible in his 'resplendent' appearance, perfume formed an integral part of Wilde's identity and his public display as decadent artist, symbolically extending by his choice of scents the aura of his personality and drawing his interlocutors into the seductive atmosphere of the urbane and the exotic. Along with the rest of his artfully composed self-presentation, Wilde's perfume aura was abruptly terminated by his sentencing in May 1895 to two years' hard labour for 'acts of gross indecency'.

Prison and the Scent of Redemption

The antithesis of Wilde's perfumed existence was prison with its inadequate sanitary arrangements, bad food, and stifling fetid air. According to Frank Harris, Wilde recalled:

> At first it was a fiendish nightmare; more horrible than anything I had ever dreamt of; from the first evening when they made me undress before them and get into some filthy water they called a bath and dry myself with a damp, brown rag and put on this livery of shame. The cell was appalling: I could hardly breathe in it, and the food turned my stomach; the smell and sight of it were enough: I did not eat anything for days and days, I could not even swallow the bread; and the rest of the food was uneatable.[41]

Harris is not the most reliable of sources, but Wilde made similar complaints in two separate letters to the *Daily Chronicle*. Shortly after his release, he wrote on 27 May 1897 protesting about the treatment of child prisoners: 'The dark, badly ventilated, ill-smelling prison cells are dreadful for a child, dreadful indeed for anyone. One is always breathing bad air in prison' (*CL*, p. 852). A year later on 28 March 1898 he wrote again in a letter urging prison reform:

> The foul air of the prison cells, increased by a system of ventilation that is utterly ineffective, is so sickening and unwholesome that it is no uncommon thing for warders, when they come in the morning out of the fresh air, and open and inspect each cell, to be violently sick. (*CL*, p. 1046)

In 'The Ballad of Reading Gaol', also written shortly after his release, Wilde contrasts the literal and figurative stench of the prison regime with the holy fragrance of compassion:

> Each narrow cell in which we dwell
>   Is a foul and dark latrine,
> And the fetid breath of living Death
>   Chokes up each grated screen,
> And all, but Lust, is turned to dust
>   In Humanity's machine.
>   [...]
> And every human heart that breaks,
>   In prison-cell or yard,
> Is as that broken box that gave

---

[41] Frank Harris, *Oscar Wilde: His Life and Confessions*, 2 vols (New York: Brentano's, 1918), 2. 331.

> Its treasure to the Lord,
> And filled the unclean leper's house
> With the scent of costliest nard.[42]

The human heart that, touched by suffering, breaks open and emits the sweetness of sympathy is compared to the alabaster perfume box of the King James Bible, which, broken open, has its precious contents poured out over the feet of Jesus. This story, related variously by the gospel writers, seems to have been a favourite of Wilde's that he alludes to on more than one occasion. In 'The Soul of the Man under Socialism', published first in the *Fortnightly Review* in February 1891, he retells it with his own interpretation:

> There was a woman who was taken in adultery. We are not told the history of her love, but that love must have been very great; for Jesus said that her sins were forgiven her, not because she repented, but because her love was so intense and wonderful. Later on, a short time before his death, as he sat at a feast, the woman came in and poured costly perfumes on his hair. His friends tried to interfere with her, and said that it was an extravagance, and that the money that the perfume cost should have been expended on charitable relief of people in want, or something of that kind. Jesus did not accept that view. He pointed out that the material needs of Man were great and very permanent, but that the spiritual needs of Man were greater still, and that in one divine moment, and by selecting its own mode of expression, a personality might make itself perfect. The world worships the woman, even now, as a saint.[43]

The story of a woman who anoints Christ with perfume is told with variations in all four gospels, although Wilde here mainly follows the version given by Mark (14:3–9) and Matthew (26:6–13). Both these writers explicitly mention an event that occurs in the house of Simon the Leper in Bethany, and narrate how a nameless woman poured precious perfume on Jesus's hair, and how he defended her against his disciples when they complained about the waste of a resource that could have been sold and the money given to the poor: 'And Jesus said, "Let her alone. Why trouble ye her? She hath wrought a good work on me"' (Mark 14:6). Wilde clearly relished what he undoubtedly saw as Jesus's championing of aesthetics above common sense and utility. Moreover, as a good Greek scholar, he knew that the Greek words καλὸν ἔργον that translate 'a good work' can be and frequently are translated as 'a beautiful work' or 'a beautiful thing', and his use of the phrase 'one divine moment' also emphasizes Jesus's aesthetic credentials by implying his appreciation of epiphanies, those peak moments of perceptual experience that Walter Pater in his Conclusion to *The Renaissance* famously singles out as giving our lives their *raison d'être*.

To the story as given by Mark and Matthew, Wilde also adds in elements from a similar account in Luke (7:36–50) where Jesus, having dinner at the house of a Pharisee named Simon, is anointed by a woman said to have lived a sinful life. In this version she wets with her contrite tears Jesus's feet, wipes them with her hair,

---

[42] Wilde, 'The Ballad of Reading Gaol', in *Oscar Wilde: The Major Works*, pp. 564, 565.
[43] Wilde, 'The Soul of the Man under Socialism', in *Plays, Prose Writings and Poems*, ed. Anthony Fothergill (London: Everyman and J. M. Dent, 1996), p. 24.

and then pours perfume on them. Simon is scandalized that Jesus lets himself be touched by a sinner, but Jesus points out she has shown him the loving attentions neglected by his host, and duly forgives the woman her sins—'Her sins, which are many, are forgiven; for she loved much' (7:47). He also observes that her actions show her grateful understanding of what is to have absolution for the burden of past errors. In his version Wilde supplies the specific detail that the woman was 'taken in adultery', something not mentioned by Luke, although sexual sin, such as fornication, adultery, or even prostitution, is strongly implied. Wilde adds a mischievous touch of decadence to his portrayal of Jesus by hinting, in a deliberate misprision of verse 47, that he forgives the woman her sins 'not because she repented, but because her love was so intense and wonderful'; that is, the woman's redeeming love is not the love she demonstrates to Christ himself, but the previously mentioned 'history of her love', the sexual love she manifested during her previous wayward life.[44] Typically, his interpretation of the story accents the importance of individualism and personality over rigid ethical codes of behaviour.

The final line of Wilde's story 'The world worships the woman, even now, as a saint' also intimates that the woman, far from being anonymous, now occupies an acknowledged place in the Christian tradition, and suggests he is making the traditional though Biblically unsupported link between the woman with the perfume and Mary Magdalen, regarded as a saint in the Catholic, Orthodox, Anglican, and Lutheran churches. In John's gospel (12:3), Jesus comes to stay with his friends at Bethany—Lazarus and his sisters Martha and Mary—all of whom feature in other gospel stories. While Jesus is having supper, Mary takes a jar of expensive perfume made from essence of nard, anoints his feet, and then wipes them with her hair. In an unforgettable verse that Wilde loved, the smell of the fragrance is said to fill the whole house (12:3).[45] At the end of the sixth century, Pope Gregory authoritatively endorsed the conflation of Mary of Bethany and the unnamed anointing woman (a sinner in Luke's account) with Mary Magdalen, a woman from whom Jesus cast out seven demons (Luke 8:1–3).[46] The gospel writers name Mary Magdalen as a key follower of Jesus who witnessed his crucifixion and was the first person to see him in his risen state. However, although there is nothing in the gospels to suggest she was ever a prostitute, she was commonly regarded as such by medieval commentators who agreed that she was the composite character established by Pope Gregory and identified her with the repentant anointing woman.[47] According to Susan Haskins, from the thirteenth century Mary Magdalen became 'the favourite

---

[44] In her seminal study *Mary Magdalen: Myth and Metaphor* (London and New York: HarperCollins, 1993), Susan Haskins indicates that this interpretation was not uncommon (p. 19). For a similar reading of Wilde's words about Jesus's forgiveness of Mary, see Guy Willoughby, *Art and Christhood: The Aesthetics of Oscar Wilde* (Rutherford, NJ, and London: Fairleigh Dickinson University Press and Associated University Presses, 1993), p. 57.

[45] Wilde alludes to this verse in 'De Profundis', *CL*, p. 743. Nard or spikenard is an aromatic essential oil derived from the flowering plant *Nardostachys jatamansi* from the Himalayas, and has been used as medicine, perfume, and in religious incense since ancient times, being mentioned in the Song of Solomon (1:12 and 4:13). However, it is worth noting that 'nardos', the ancient Greek word used in the gospels, can also signify lavender.

[46] Haskins, *Mary Magdalen*, p. 16.   [47] Ibid., p. 136.

saint of the Middle Ages', her story of 'prostitute to penitent' lending itself well to artistic representation and popular retellings of her life.[48] Moreover, from the 1690s, the term 'magdalen' would be used as a synonym for 'reformed prostitute', while 'magdalen homes' or reformatory houses for fallen women established in the mid-eighteenth century were a recognized feature of nineteenth-century urban life.[49]

A sensual foil to the purity of the Virgin Mary, Mary Magdalen was often portrayed in religious art as a sexualized or fallen woman. Typically holding or accompanied by an *alabastron*, her alabaster container of perfume, she was depicted as a weeping penitent beauty with long, flowing red or golden hair. Because of her identification with the anointing woman, she was often regarded as the patron saint of perfume and perfumers, her suitability for this role strengthened by the gospels of Mark (16:1) and Luke (24:10) where Mary Magdalen is named as one of two women who visit Jesus's tomb to anoint his dead body with spices. Touchingly, the medieval writer Pseudo-Rabanus Maurus in his *Life of Mary Magdalene* refers to her on several occasions as 'Christ's perfume-maker'.[50] In 'De Profundis', the long meditative letter that he wrote to Lord Alfred Douglas from prison, Wilde returned again to the gospel story of the anointing woman, this time specifically identifying her with Mary Magdalen:

> Those whom he saved from their sins are saved simply for beautiful moments in their lives. Mary Magdalen, when she sees Christ, breaks the rich vase of alabaster that one of her seven lovers had given her, and spills the odorous spices over his tired dusty feet, and for that one moment's sake sits for ever with Ruth and Beatrice in the tresses of the snow white rose of Paradise.   (*CL*, pp. 751–2)

Embroidering this version of the story with the fancy that the alabaster vessel is a present from one of Mary's seven lovers, Wilde again, even more explicitly than in 'The Soul of the Man under Socialism', emphasizes the importance of those uplifting Paterian 'beautiful moments', adding 'All that Christ says to us by way of a little warning is that *every* moment should be beautiful, that the soul should *always* be ready for the coming of the bridegroom' (*CL*, p. 752).[51]

Perfume seems to lend itself to the experience of 'the beautiful moment', saturating the present instant with sudden sensory éclat and rousing possible sensations of surprise, recognition, and pleasure. However, as memories like Lord Henry's attest, it may go deeper than the present moment, leaving a lasting memorial, even if only by report—Mary's perfume forever filling the house at Bethany and thus forever associated with her. In 'De Profundis', a text that shows Wilde extremely aware of the scented pleasures denied him, even non-perfumed incidents and events can exude fragrance, as we saw in the initial quotation from 'The Ballad of

---

[48] Ibid., pp. 134, 136.   [49] Ibid., pp. 297, 309–15, 317–19.

[50] Rabanus Maurus was a ninth-century German teacher and scholar but the *Life of Mary Magdalene* attributed to him is now generally thought to be the work of an anonymous twelfth-century Cistercian author. See Pseudo-Rabanus Maurus, *The Life of Mary Magdalene and her Sister Saint Martha*, tr. and ed. David Mycoff, Cistercian Studies Series 108 (Kalamazoo, MI: Cistercian Publications, 1989), pp. 54, 65, 73, 81. See also Haskins, *Mary Magdalen*, p. 218.

[51] Wilde was clearly fascinated by the figure of the sanctified harlot, returning to her in his play *La Sainte Courtisane*, composed in 1893, a text that exists now only as a fragment.

Reading Gaol' where human sympathy and acts of charity manifest themselves as
sweetness, a kind of odour of sanctity. Wilde relates how after his conviction he
was obliged to attend the bankruptcy court mired in disgrace, and he tenderly
recalls as a sustaining scented memory the redemptive moment when his friend
Robert Ross publicly raised his hat to him: 'I store it in the treasury-house of my
heart. [...] It is embalmed and kept sweet by the myrrh and cassia of many tears'
(*CL*, p. 722). Interestingly, although Ross's gesture is a compassionate one and
therefore 'sweet', Wilde here represents *himself* as a weeping Magdalen, preserving
the precious memory by the sweetness of his own tears. Weeping, especially the
weeping that commemorates painful or precious experiences, is a constant theme
throughout 'De Profundis', with Wilde asserting 'To those who are in prison, tears
are a part of every day's experience' (*CL*, p. 757). In visual depictions Mary's *alabastron*
or perfume container may also do duty as a lachrymatory, a bottle that preserves the
tears of mourners, and here Wilde's 'heart' seems to take on both these functions.[52]

His interest in Mary Magdalen seems to have dated at least from his undergraduate years when he was a student at Magdalen, Oxford, a college that takes
its name directly from the saint. (The names of the colleges of Magdalen, Oxford,
and Magdalene, Cambridge, are pronounced 'maudlin', a late Middle English
pronunciation—with the word 'maudlin', meaning lachrymose and over-emotional,
derived from 'Magdalen', being associated with the iconic images of Mary weeping.[53]) According to biographical sources, photographs of artworks displayed in
Wilde's college room around 1876 included a *Christ and Magdalen* by the Pre-
Raphaelite painter Edward Burne-Jones (possibly the image pictured in Figure 7.2).[54]
Iconic representations of the Magdalen that Wilde would have encountered on a
daily basis as an undergraduate include the statue originally on the Pugin Gate
(demolished 1883) and now located on the north end of the Grove Buildings, the
two stained glass windows in the chapel, the dramatic sculptural tableau of Christ
and Mary that tops the reredos, and the carved panels dating from 1541 situated
behind the High Table in the Hall that depict scenes from her life. Other less
common images include the figurine on the Founder's Cup, and image of Mary
on the college seal.[55] Wilde may possibly have known that the medieval *Life of*

[52] See Diane Apostolos-Cappadona, '"Pray with Tears and your Request will Find a Hearing": On
the Iconology of the Magdalene's Tears', in *Holy Tears: Weeping in the Religious Imagination*, ed.
Christine Kimberly Patton and John Stratton Hawley (Princeton, NJ: Princeton University Press,
2005), pp. 201–28; 218, 219.

[53] Haskins, *Mary Magdalen*, pp. 275–6.

[54] See Ellmann, *Oscar Wilde*, p. 66. Wilde was an undergraduate at Oxford from 1874 to 1878.
There is no painting by Burne-Jones of Christ and Mary Magdalen of this period or earlier (my thanks
to Stephen Wildman for confirming this) so Wilde must have owned a photograph of one of his car-
toons for stained glass. A possible contender is *Christ and St Mary Magdalene* (1872), a cartoon for St
Chad's, Rochdale, reproduced in Malcolm Bell, *Edward Burne-Jones: A Record and Review* (London:
George Bell & Sons, 1892), between pp. 104–5, in an (undated) photograph by Frederick Hollyer
(1837–1933). Another is a design of 1863, *The Magdalen at Christ's Feet*, also photographed by
Hollyer, reproduced as Fig. 289 in Colin Cruise, *Pre-Raphaelite Drawing* (London: Thames &
Hudson), p. 194. Hollyer photographed the work of the Pre-Raphaelites from the mid-1860s onwards.

[55] See David Roberts and Richard Sheppard, eds., *Hidden Magdalen* (Oxford: Magdalen College,
2008), pp. 40, 136–7, 80. My thanks to Robin Darwall-Smith, Archivist at Magdalen College, for
kindly supplying additional information.

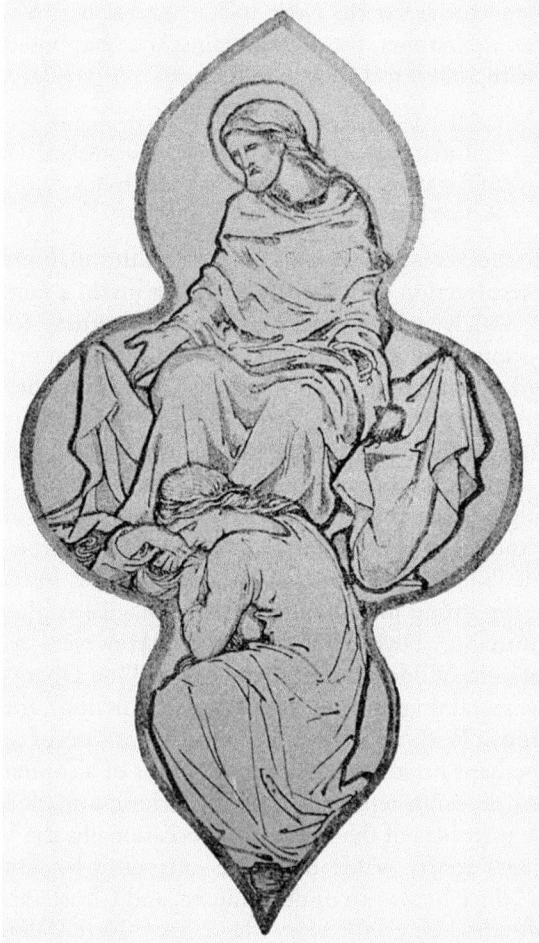

Figure 7.2 Frederick Hollyer, photograph of *Christ and St. Mary Magdalene*, a cartoon for stained glass by Edward Burne-Jones for Rochdale Church, from Malcolm Bell, *Edward Burne-Jones* (1892). (Photo: Daichi Ishikawa, courtesy of the London Library)

Mary Magdalene by the Pseudo-Rabanus Maurus that describes Mary as 'Christ's perfume-maker' was one of the treasures of his college, the manuscript published for the first time in 1848.[56]

As an undergraduate Wilde alluded to Mary Magdalen in his sonnet 'On the Massacre of the Christians in Bulgaria', a poem that indignantly recalled the recent wholesale butchering of Christians by Turkish Muslim troops in May 1876.

---

[56] Magd. MS Lat. 89(1). See Maurus, *Life of Mary Magdalene*, p. 21. The Catholic historian Étienne-Michel Faillon used the Magdalen College MS, the only MS that names Rabanus Maurus as author, as the source for the version of the text that appears in the second volume of his *Monuments inédits sur l'apostalat de Sainte Marie-Madeleine en Provence*, 2 vols (Paris: J.-P. Migne, 1848). There is a copy of Faillon's book in Magdalen Old Library, although it is uncertain when the College acquired this.

Probably composed during his 1877 trip to Italy and sent to W. E. Gladstone in May the same year, this sonnet, protesting against the unopposed slaughter of the innocent, opens with a daring challenge to Christ:

> Christ, dost thou live indeed? or are thy bones
> Still straightened in their rock-hewn sepulchre?
> And was thy Rising only dreamed by Her
> Whose love of thee for all her sin atones?[57]

The impassioned speaker suggests that Christ's failure to protect his followers indicate that his resurrection and afterlife may be a myth, a fantasy generated by Mary Magdalen, widely acknowledged as the first witness to his risen body. (Notably in this sonnet the youthful Wilde provides a more orthodox interpretation of the Magdalen's atoning 'love' for Christ, something he will revise in his more provocative interpretation in 'The Soul of the Man under Socialism'.) Glossing these lines for Gladstone, Wilde wrote: 'the allusion is of course to *Mary Magdalen* being the first to see our Lord after his Resurrection, and bringing the news to the Disciples; Renan says somewhere this was the divinest lie ever told' (*CL*, p. 48).[58] Actually the French humanist Ernest Renan, whose popular *Vie de Jésus* (1863) Wilde follows here, does not use the word 'lie', instead writing of the resurrection that 'the strong imagination of Mary Magdalen played an important part in this circumstance. Divine power of love!'[59] However—as signalled by his adjective 'divinest'—to Wilde, the future author of 'The Decay of Lying' (a text that celebrates the sustaining or beautiful imaginative fiction), the lie attributed to Mary is no calumny. Thus, in spite of adopting a position of apparent religious scepticism, and perhaps honouring her as the creator of a supreme fiction, Wilde capitalizes the first pronoun representing Mary ('Her'), a mark of respect usually accorded only the members of the Trinity and, occasionally, the Virgin Mary.[60]

Sceptical gestures apart, Wilde had been entranced by what he called 'the perfume of belief' since he was an undergraduate, and Christ appears as a fragrant figure in 'De Profundis' along with Mary Magdalen.[61] Here Wilde revisits the issue of the supernatural and the miraculous somewhat differently; although he alludes respectfully to the *Vie de Jésus* as 'that gracious Fifth Gospel, the Gospel according to St Thomas one might call it', he does not, like Renan, regard Christ's miracles as a barrier to modern minds, 'a violence done to him by his age, a concession forced on him by necessity', finding another way to explain them.[62] When Wilde celebrates

[57] Wilde, 'On the Massacre of the Christians in Bulgaria', in his *Poems*, p. 13.

[58] In this letter of 17 May 1877, Wilde alludes to ch. 26 of Ernest Renan's immensely popular *La Vie de Jésus* (1863), which depicted Jesus as man not God and denies his miracles.

[59] Ernest Renan, *Life of Jesus* (London: Watts & Co., 1935), p. 215. Renan continues: 'Sacred moments in which the passion of one possessed gave to the world a resuscitated God!'

[60] As Ellis Hanson points out, Wilde also identifies with the Magdalen in his early poem 'Quia Multum Amavi' (translation: 'Because I loved much'), this title a variant of Luke 7:47. See Hanson, *Decadence and Catholicism* (Cambridge, MA, and London: Harvard University Press, 1997), p. 95.

[61] Wilde used the phrase of Ruskin's writing which he said was 'like a violet filling the whole air with the ineffable perfume of belief', Harris, *Oscar Wilde*, 1. 47.

[62] Renan, *Life of Jesus*, p. 144.

the unrivalled 'charm' of Christ, he explains his miracles as a 'natural' result of his personal charisma as experienced by those around him:

> when he taught on the hillside the multitude forgot their hunger and thirst and the cares of the world, and that to his friends who listened to him as he sat at meat the coarse food seemed delicate, and the water had the taste of wine, and the whole house became full of the odour and sweetness of nard. (*CL*, p. 743)

Delight in Christ's transformative presence exalts the senses of those around him, so that all who take pleasure in him experience him and their surroundings in enhanced and beautiful ways in which olfaction plays a by-no-means minor role. In 'De Profundis', Christ is an aesthete who makes aesthetes of all who truly love him. Fittingly, for Wilde, Christ's life also becomes an aesthetic document, being 'the most wonderful of poems', ending with the unrivalled tragic drama of his death and 'his final burial in the tomb of the rich man, his body swathed in Egyptian linen with costly spices and perfumes as though he had been a king's son' (*CL*, pp. 742, 743). Wilde's own tragic drama and the suffering he experienced after his conviction and imprisonment helped him identify with Christ's suffering and rekindled interest in his personality and teaching. In place of Alfred Douglas, it is Christ, reconceived as an individualist and aesthete, who is now associated with flowers. In Wilde's eyes, Christ is 'the first person who ever said to people that they should live "flower-like lives"' (*CL*, p. 750), and 'We owe to him [...] the love of children and flowers—for both of whom, indeed, there was in classical times but little place' (*CL*, p. 747), for Christ reveals 'the real beauty of the lilies of the field as none, either on Cithareon or at Enna had ever done it' (*CL*, p. 746).

Indeed, after enduring the squalor and privations of prison, Wilde turned, albeit temporarily, against Douglas. To the incarcerated Wilde prison is characterized by its lack of flowers—'But neither milk-white rose or red | May bloom in prison air'—while Douglas is bitterly perceived as walking 'free among the flowers' (*CL*, p. 685).[63] Flowers are associated with a simple life of liberty beyond the prison walls that Wilde longs for and idealizes: 'With freedom, books, flowers, and the moon, who could not be happy?' (*CL*, p. 755). In the Conclusion to 'De Profundis' he vividly imagines the scented pleasures that await him after his release: 'both the laburnum and the lilac will be blooming in the gardens [...] so that all the air shall be Arabia for me' (*CL*, p. 777). Aligning himself with Linnaeus, one of the founding figures of modern botany, he also suggests that he, too, is not above being moved by the simple pleasure of scented, coloured blooms:

> Linnaeus fell on his knees and wept for joy when he saw for the first time the long heath of some English upland made yellow with the tawny aromatic brooms of the common furze; and I know that for me, to whom flowers are part of desire, there are tears waiting in the petals of some rose. (*CL*, p. 777)

---

[63] 'The Ballad of Reading Gaol', p. 561. This state of affairs ended when Wilde was reconciled with Douglas after his release when Bosie is once more sentimentally associated with flowers: See *CL*, pp. 886, 898, 902.

The scented rose becomes a lachrymatory, receiving the tears of one not too proud to admit his emotions on being readmitted to the beauty of the natural world. Moreover, Robert Ross, in a description of the newly released Wilde, reports how he accompanied him on a walk at Arques, observing: 'He enjoyed the trees and the grass and country scents and sounds in a way I had never known him to do before, just as street-bred child might enjoy them.'[64]

Yet although Wilde may have found new pleasure in the simple scents of nature, perfume for him was an essential component of his urbane cultivated self-presentation, something he was understandably anxious to reclaim on his departure from prison. Preparing to leave Reading Gaol in May 1897, he was particular in his requests to More Adey, asking him to obtain for him for 'Some nice French soap, Houbigant if you can get it for me: either "Peau d'Espagne" or "Suc de Laitue" [sic] would do: a case of three. Also, some scent; Canterbury Wood Violet I much like, and also some "Eau de Lubin" for the toilet, a large bottle.' And, understandably, he added: 'I want, for psychological reasons, to feel entirely physically cleansed of the stain and soil of prison life' (*CL*, p. 809).[65] Perfume, especially French perfume, the odour of sophistication, must have seemed transformative, the ultimate antidote to the grim institutional smells of prison, magically restoring the comfort of an once-familiar aura, and that happy time when, according to the poet Edith Cooper, he seemed to 'exhale Paris'.[66] Wilde was also delighted when his friend Reggie Turner presented him with a new silver dressing-case on his release. A letter of thanks written later from Dieppe on 27 May 1897 is a witty piece of theatre in which the luxury of perfume represents the acme and essence of desire:

> The population came to look at my dressing-case. I showed it to them, piece of silver by piece of silver. Some of the old men wept for joy. Robbie detected me at Dieppe in the market place of the sellers of perfumes, spending all my money on orris-root and the tears of the narcissus and the dust of red roses. He was very stern and led me away. I have already spent my entire income for two years. I see now that this lovely dressing-case with its silver vials thirsty for distilled odours will gradually lead me to the perfection of poverty. But it seemed to me to be cruel not to fill with rose-petals the little caskets shaped so cunningly in the form of a rose. (*CL*, p. 855)

---

[64] Robert Ross, unfinished and unpublished preface (MS Clark) to a proposed collection of Wilde's letters to him, included in *CL*, p. 844.

[65] Houbigant, founded in Paris in 1775, is sometimes said to be the oldest perfume house still operating today, though both Farina and Floris are older. For 'Peau d'Espagne', see the poem by Symons discussed later in this chapter. Misrendered 'Suc de Laitue' by Wilde's editors, 'Sac de Laitue' is lettuce juice. Lettuce-juice soap, still available today from a number of different manufacturers, is said to be gentle on dry, delicate, or aged skin. By 1897 the violet perfume Wilde requests would probably contain synthetic violet fragrance in the form of ionones (discovered in 1893). Eau de Lubin, created in 1798 by Pierre-François Lubin, was a very popular toilet water containing clove oil and benzoin, which, seen as hygienically cleansing, might be added to bath water. For a reproduction of a highly decorative poster of 1897 advertising 'Eau de Lubin' in which the product is described as 'La Reine des Eaux de Toilette' (The Queen of Toilet Waters), see Stamelman, *Perfume*, p. 173.

[66] Edith Cooper, in Mikhail, ed., *Oscar Wilde: Interviews and Recollections*, 1. 199. Also Works and Days Add MS 46781, fol. 30ʳ (25 March 1893).

For Wilde, always prodigal with money, the acquisition of perfume is worth impoverishment. In this, he is like his heroine Mary Magdalen, who achieves sainthood through a gesture of reckless perfumed extravagance, although she empties a vessel of perfume while Wilde in a spirit of gleeful improvidence fills his 'thirsty' vials and caskets. Robert Ross, here portrayed as the 'stern' guardian who polices Wilde's spending, would write to Adela Schuster after Wilde's death on 30 November 1900, observing that 'Two things were absolutely necessary for him, contact with comely things, as Pater says, and social position.' Sadly, for Wilde, his social position was irretrievably lost. However, Ross explained that 'Comely things meant for him a certain standard of living, and this, since his release, he *was able to have* except for a few weeks at a time, or perhaps months' (*CL*, p. 1229). Perfume, one of the 'comely things' 'absolutely necessary' to him, represents that 'standard of living' he craved, and thus justifies a profligate expenditure. Its purchase helped transform Wilde once more into the semblance of a decadent man about town, re-establishing him as an *olfactif* and arbiter who could pronounce on and adjudicate the 'extraordinary odours' of others. Little wonder that, for Edith Cooper, perfume was the inevitable symbol of his inimitable spirit: 'I have met most of the "moderns". None of them blew a breeze or had any fragrance like Oscar at his best.'[67]

ARTHUR SYMONS AND THE SCENT OF DECADENT MODERNITY

In the work of the poet and critic Arthur Symons strong or recognizable perfumes of the period are evoked for scrutiny or contemplation or they permeate the memory, calling attention to themselves as markers of decadent modernity. The most famous example of this is Symons's 'Being a Word on Behalf of Patchouli', the Preface to the second edition of his verse collection *Silhouettes* (1896), and an essay that reveals a cultivated, dandified love of fragrance. Responding to a pejorative assessment of his verse as inappropriately perfumed, Symons follows one of his own critics in using, as a synonym for artifice and decadence, patchouli (*Pogostemon cablin*)—a strong woody perfume made from the leaves and flowers of a bushy plant of the mint family native to Indonesia whose odour is described by Piesse as 'the most powerful of any derived from the botanic kingdom'.[68]

Fashionable in France from the middle of the nineteenth century, patchouli was imported into Britain from around 1850. It first became popular after leaves from the patchouli plant, a natural insect repellent, were included in the expensive cashmere shawls exported from India, permeating the fabric with their fragrance. In Elizabeth Gaskell's *North and South* (1855) Margaret Hale goes upstairs to fetch her cousin's costly Indian wraps to display to visitors and 'went down laden with shawls, and snuffing up their spicy Eastern smell'.[69] In 1866 Arnold James Cooley

---

[67] Edith Cooper, Works and Days Add MS 46789, fol. 162ᵛ (30 November 1900).
[68] Piesse, *Art of Perfumery* (1855), p. 61.   [69] Gaskell, *North and South*, p. 9.

pronounced 'Essence of Patchouli' 'A very fashionable perfume, particularly for personal use', declaring the version made to his specification 'has largely been used at Court and by the nobility generally'.[70] However, as it grew in popularity and became more cheaply available, patchouli became debased as a perfume and was disapproved of by many Victorians as a heavy fragrance associated with 'loose women'. In the authoritative words of Harriet Hubbard Ayer in 1899: 'A high-bred woman does not associate herself with musk or patchouly.'[71] In the 1890 *Lippincott's Magazine* version of *Dorian Gray*, Lord Henry Wotton's wife exits the room leaving behind her 'a faint odor of patchouli' (*DG*, p. 210), a scent which Wilde changed to 'frangipani' in his 1891 novel (p. 42), presumably because he had become aware of patchouli's connection with prostitutes. Symons makes the connection himself in 'Love and Art', a poem published in *The Second Book of the Rhymers' Club* in 1894, in which the speaker describes returning home after dark to his lodgings in The Temple, the residential district in the City of London favoured by lawyers, where Symons had his own rooms. As he enters through the gateway, he finds that 'strangely, comes to me | The odour of patchouli'. He has caught the sillage or perfume-wake of a prostitute visiting a client, and looking up, sees 'Ah, there she flits before me, whose gay scent | Betrays the way she went'.[72]

Symons was thus more than aware when he wrote his critical rejoinder that patchouli had by the 1890s a decidedly downmarket reputation, being considered cheap, louche, and unsubtle, but he gamefully decides to defend it anyway:

> An ingenuous reviewer once described some verses of mine as 'unwholesome,' because, he said, they had 'a faint smell of Patchouli about them'. I am sorry he chose Patchouli, for that is not a particularly favourite scent with me. If he had only chosen Peau d'Espagne, which has a subtle meaning, or Lily of the Valley, with which I have associations! But Patchouli will serve. Let me ask, [...] why art should not, if it please, concern itself with the artificially charming, which, I suppose, is what my critic means by Patchouli? All art, surely, is a form of artifice, and thus to the truly devout mind, condemned already, if not as actively noxious, at all events as needless. [...] Patchouli! Well, why not Patchouli? Is there any 'reason in nature' why we should write exclusively about the natural blush, if the delicately acquired blush of rouge has any attraction for us? Both exist; both, I think, are charming in their own way; and the latter as a subject, has, at all events, more novelty. If you prefer your 'new-mown hay' in the hayfield, and I, it may be in a scent-bottle, why may not my individual caprice be allowed expression as well as yours? Probably I enjoy the hayfield as much as you do; but I enjoy quite other scents and sensations as well, and I take the former for granted, and write my poem, for a change, about the latter. There is no necessary difference in artistic value between a good poem about a flower in a hedge and a good poem about a scent in a sachet.[73]

---

[70] Cooley, *The Toilet and Cosmetic Arts in Ancient and Modern Times*, p. 589.

[71] Ayer, *Harriet Hubbard Ayer's Book*, p. 454.

[72] Symons, 'Love and Art', in *The Second Book of the Rhymers' Club* (London and New York: Elkin Mathews & John Lane and Dodd, Mead & Co., 1894), p. 45.

[73] Arthur Symons, Preface to *Silhouettes*, 2nd edn (London: Leonard Smithers, 1896), pp. xiii–xv; xiii, xiv–xv. Also reprinted as an essay in *Studies in Prose and Verse* (London: J. M. Dent, 1904), pp. 279–82; 279, 281, where the word 'ingenuous' is rendered as 'ingenious'.

Symons responds with panache, unabashedly embracing the perfume metaphor by presenting himself as a literary *olfactif* and playfully discriminating his preferred perfumes in a way that suggests his critic's 'insult' is far from subtle. The original review is untraced but the word 'unwholesome' suggests that Symons's critic was making a moral judgement, presumably about the sexual content of the verse. Doubtless aware of this, Symons cheerfully transforms that moral objection into a supposed repudiation of 'artifice', allowing himself a philosophical right of reply. His unflappable reclamation of the illicit fragrance as a symbol for artifice—'But Patchouli will serve'—shows a new confidence in adopting and imaginatively recycling labels and descriptors formerly perceived as negative. It is a typically decadent manoeuvre.

'All art, surely, is a form of artifice', writes Symons, understanding that perfumery which represents the scents of nature through approximation and illusion is no exception. As he may have known, lily of the valley, mentioned as one of his favourite scents, is a perfume that belies its seeming naturalism. No essence can be extracted from the actual flowers, meaning that any perfume called 'Lily of the Valley' is always an artificial affair. At the time when Symons was writing, imitation lily of the valley perfume would be made from a blend of other essences but may possibly have been created using synthetic ingredients. Piesse's *Art of Perfumery* (1855) provides a receipt containing essences of tuberose, jasmine, orange flowers, vanilla, cassie, rose, and otto of almonds, and in the 1891 edition adds that 'An artificial otto of Lily of the Valley is now in the market. Its odour closely resembles that of the flower.'[74] Terpineol, mentioned as helping create lilac fragrances, is the most likely contender for this 'artificial otto' or synthetic, as hydroxycitronellal, the synthetic accepted as producing an authentic odour of lily of the valley, is usually understood to be a very early twentieth-century discovery dating to around 1905.[75]

Although, as we have seen in the first part of this chapter, synthetics play their part in a number of the fragrances worn or liked by Wilde, they really come into their own in the twentieth century when advances in aroma chemistry allow perfumers to take things to another level and create innovative sophisticated perfumes that aim to evoke more of a mood or impression. However, while the most dramatic

---

[74] Piesse, *Art of Perfumery* (1855), p. 50; 5th edn (1891), p. 153.

[75] According to Pybus, 'History of Aroma Chemistry', p. 22, hydroxycitronellal was prepared and marketed in 1905–8. David Williams, *Perfumes of Yesterday*, p. 57, attributes its synthesis to the House of Chuit Naef, although he suggests that 'it may well have been in use as a perfume ingredient within the originating company for some time before' (p. 197). In his online blog, the perfumer Chris Bartlett states that it was also manufactured by Givaudan and from 1906 sold under the name of Laurine. See http://pellwall-perfumes.blogspot.co.uk/2014/07/lily-of-valley-mystery-manufacture.html. Hydroxycitronellal is the key aroma chemical used in Edward Roudnitska's Diorissimo (1956), widely acknowledged as the most distinguished lily of the valley perfume. Eugénie Briot suggests the synthesis of terpineol as a factor of the increase in both lilac and lily of the valley perfumes in the 1890s. See her paper for the Economic History Society Annual Conference, Exeter University, 2007, 'Perfume Sprayed and Displayed', p. 4, freely downloadable at http://www.ehs.org.uk/dotAsset/29e9625d-a48c-49bd-9188-c9fdf83b6536.doc. Regarding muguet or lily of the valley, Ernest Parry, in *The Chemistry of Essential Oils and Artificial Perfumes*, pp. 504–5, writes 'A mixture of terpineol (90 per cent.) along with palmarosa oil (10 per cent.) will serve the purpose of this perfume.' In the twentieth century, terpineol with hydroxycitronellal was a standard base in lily of the valley fragrance.

synthetic innovations do not really impinge on the period reviewed in this chapter, synthetics certainly add another dimension to one of the most famous impressionist lyrics of the 1890s, Arthur Symons's 'White Heliotrope', written on 20 June 1893 and first published in his collection *London Nights* (1895).[76] A poem that looks like a harbinger of modernity, it is short enough to be quoted entire:

> The feverish room and that white bed,
>   The tumbled skirts upon a chair,
>   The novel flung half-open, where
> Hat, hair-pins, puffs, and paints are spread;
>
> The mirror that has sucked your face
>   Into its secret deep of deeps,
>   And there mysteriously keeps
> Forgotten memories of grace;
>
> And you, half dressed and half awake,
>   Your slant eyes strangely watching me,
>   And I, who watch you drowsily,
> With eyes that, having slept not, ache;
>
> This (need one dread? nay, dare one hope?)
>   Will rise, a ghost of memory, if
>   Ever again my handkerchief
> Is scented with White Heliotrope.[77]

The title of this poem, referring to the name of the perfume with which Symons's bohemian man-about-town speaker scents his handkerchief, seems on closer examination to have an almost facetious arbitrariness about it. Apart from the fact that it provides a useful rhyme word ('hope'), there appears to be nothing specific about white heliotrope that suggests that it, rather than any other perfume, should figure here. What at first seems very specific, is, it transpires, a matter of mere serendipity, as if the perfume was simply one that came to hand at a particular moment in time. Apart from the title, the scent is mentioned only in the final stanza where the speaker, having experienced what is obviously a one-night stand, imagines it as a mnemonic that may possibly evoke the experience at some later date. The perfume could be his own, worn for an evening out but, as it seems associated with this particular encounter, it is probable that, like Dorian in Lord Henry's library, he has casually helped himself to the woman's scent from a dressing table where 'Hat, hair-pins, puffs, and paints are spread'. She and the uncomplicated pleasure of a casual sexual encounter will, he hopes, come to mind—evoked by a reapplication of the same fragrance—as an enjoyable fleeting memory only. The poem's title signifies the perfume, and the perfume becomes synonymous with the mood and

---

[76] The date of composition is given in Symons's *Poems*, 3 vols, in his *Collected Works* (London: Martin Secker, 1924).

[77] Arthur Symons, 'White Heliotrope', in *London Nights* (London: Leonard C. Smithers, 1895), p. 49. For modern editions, see Arthur Symons, *Selected Writings*, ed. Roger Holdsworth (Manchester: Fyfield Books, Carcanet Press, 1989), p. 47, and Arthur Symons, *Selected Early Poems*, ed. Jane Desmarais and Chris Baldick (London: Modern Humanities Research Association, 2017), p. 115.

essence of the poetic narrative, and the potential to re-present it, thus fulfilling one of the characteristics Symons accredited to impressionistic writing—its ability to 'convey to us [...] the revelation of just that landscape, just that significant moment'.[78]

As mentioned earlier in this chapter, white heliotrope is a vanilla-sweet, almond-smelling, powdery floral. As such it has no evident erotic or sensual cachet; in itself it is not the kind of perfume one might expect a 'good-time girl' to wear. Indeed, its comparative 'innocence' is something that would seem to add to its arbitrariness—it is the speaker's whim, not any inherent quality in the perfume, that makes it a marker, a mere figure, the flower-become-trope for a random erotic memory. And yet perhaps there is more to it than that. As we saw, white heliotrope is the favourite scent of Teleny and Des Grieux, and a perfume that plays a key role in their erotic relationship. Assuming he could get his hands on a copy, Symons might just conceivably have read this novel of 1893, published by Leonard Smithers, the future publisher of his own *London Nights*, although the price of four or five guineas for the volume would seem prohibitive.[79] He had almost certainly read Edmond de Goncourt's *Chérie* (1883) in which the eponymous young upper-class heroine, an avid lover of perfumes, sprays white heliotrope scent under the covers of her bed each morning and then luxuriates in the fragrance.[80] These two novels might provide a sensual association not suggested by the perfume itself. More importantly, however, Symons had read the 1890 *Lippincott's Magazine* version of *Dorian Gray* in which Lord Henry's remark about the mnemonic power of 'the odour of *lilas blanc*' (p. 179) is originally made about heliotrope: 'There are moments when the odor of heliotrope passes suddenly across me, and I have to live the strangest year of my life over again' (p. 298).[81] In his mind Symons may have combined Wilde's earlier allusion to heliotrope with the '*blanc*' of the later '*lilas blanc*'. Fittingly then, his decadent lyric that flirts with the idea of perfume memory may itself remember an earlier decadent allusion to perfume memory, as well as other 'scented' texts.

Nonetheless, as these literary references attest, white heliotrope was a popular perfume in the *fin de siècle* and the early years of the twentieth century, and Symons undoubtedly also selected it as a widely available, inexpensive scent that in 1893 was

---

[78] Arthur Symons, 'Impressionistic Writing', in *Dramatis Personæ*, p. 345.

[79] As Amanda Caleb writes: 'The original price of *Teleny* is still debated. Smithers's prospectus advertised it at four guineas, but Hirsch insists that the original price was five guineas.' See her edition of *Teleny* (Kansas City, MO: Valancourt Books, 2010), p. xxii, note 2. Charles Hirsch was a French bookseller who issued a French translation of *Teleny* in 1934.

[80] Edmond de Goncourt, *Chérie* (Paris: Ernest Flammarion et Eugène Fasquelle, 1883), pp. 225–6. *Chérie* is not available in English translation and the novel is usually dated to 1884, but Stamelman gives this earlier reference in his *Perfume* (p. 357), where he also provides a valuable overview of Chérie's passion for perfume (p. 298). Symons refers to *Chérie* in 'The Decadent Movement in Literature', *Harper's*, pp. 859, 860, some months after the composition of 'White Heliotrope'. (See also *Dramatis Personæ*, p. 141, and *The Symbolist Movement in Literature*, Appendix 1, pp. 171, 172.) However, he had first met Edmond de Goncourt in Paris in 1890 and paid him a visit at his home in Auteuil in May 1892. See Symons's essay 'A Literary Causerie: On Edmond de Goncourt', *The Savoy* 5 (September 1896), 85–7.

[81] Symons reports reading the magazine version of *Dorian Gray* in July 1890. See 'An Actress in Whitechapel', in *The Memoirs of Arthur Symons*, p. 75.

very up-to-the-minute. It is also worn by another good-time girl in his unpublished story 'The Life and Adventures of Lucy Newcome', most likely written between 1896 and 1898, which features Lucy, a former and still occasional prostitute, and the mistress of Sebastian, a minor literary man. While Sebastian is away, their mutual friend Cecil meets her in a pub and spends some time in her company. When, having escorted her home, he comes to say goodbye: 'As he stooped down and put his lips against her cheek, a sharp scent of white heliotrope, that scent he remembered, came into his nostrils.'[82]

In the 1890s the ubiquity of the perfume was a consequence of aroma-chemical advances, as heliotrope scent is made either by combining other perfume essences or by synthetic means, which give the impression or the illusion of the flower.[83] Synthetic heliotropin (also known as piperonal), which would be widely used in a variety of perfumes, was first discovered in 1869.[84] Examining the variety of different makes of the perfume, one notices a sudden proliferation of brands from 1890 onwards, suggesting that the greater availability of the synthetic substantially increased production of this fragrance.[85] In her discussion of the production and marketing of French perfume in the nineteenth century Eugénie Briot indeed confirms that 'piperonal began to be produced industrially in 1874, and in quantities in 1886', adding that 'the scent of heliotrope was first listed in perfumers' catalogues in the 1880s', and that 'between 1879 and 1899 the price of one kilogram of piperonal dropped dramatically, to 37.5 francs, one hundredth of its former price'.[86] With respect to the English market, Piesse's *Art of Perfumery* (1891) corroborates Briot's findings:

> A substance prepared chemically, and sold under the name of Heliotropine, in the form of a white, light, crystalline powder, is now a regular article of commerce: its price is about 8s. per oz. It has the most perfect resemblance to the odour of heliotrope blossoms. It is extensively used abroad for making the so-called 'Heliotrope blanc' essence, and also for perfuming toilet powders, sachet powders, and soaps.[87]

Briot suggest that 'twelve or fifteen years' after heliotrope was first worn by Edmond de Goncourt's well-to-do Chérie, the affordability of the perfume meant that it was

[82] Alan Johnson, 'Arthur Symons' "The Life and Adventures of Lucy Newcome": Preface and Text', *English Literature in Transition* 28.4 (1985), 33–45; 332, 344. Also included in Arthur Symons, *Spiritual Adventures*, ed. Nicholas Freeman (London: Modern Humanities Research Association, 2017), pp. 74–87; 86. My warm thanks to Nick Freeman for drawing Symons's story to my attention. Johnson explains that Lucy is based on Muriel Broadbent, a former prostitute, whom Symons met in 1892 and who became the mistress of his friend, the writer Herbert Horne. She told Symons her life story 'in and around 1896'. Johnson remarks that in 'The Life and Adventures of Lucy Newcome', 'according to Symons himself, "Sebastian is Horne. I am Cecil"' (p. 332).

[83] Piesse's *Art of Perfumery* (1855) explains that it is possible to obtain essential oil from heliotrope flowers by maceration or enfleurage but that these processes are not used commercially (pp. 36–9).

[84] Pybus, 'History of Aroma Chemistry', p. 21; Turin and Sanchez, *Perfumes: The A–Z Guide*, p. 36.

[85] See the website http://www.perfumeintelligence.co.uk, which lists alphabetically the many different makes and issue dates of specific perfumes.

[86] Eugénie Briot, 'From Industry to Luxury: French Perfume in the Nineteenth Century', *British History Review* 85 (2011), 273–94; 281–2.

[87] Piesse, *Art of Perfumery*, 5th edn (1891), p. 130.

'adopted by populations whose taste was more questionable', citing a drunken character in Alfred Jarry's *Ubu roi* (1896) as evidence.[88] The year 1893, the date of Symons's poem, most likely marks the point when the perfume had reached a popular high and was just beginning to lose its former cachet.

Like the popular new fragrance that gives it its title, Symons's poem is of its moment. Poets, like perfumers, are illusionists, and in its portrayal of a 'modern' man's sexual manners, the poem, too, is a clever piece of artifice that tries to look 'natural', and, as such, is an illusion. Though the composition is masterly, the speaker is somewhat too studied in his pose of insouciance, and there is something rather awkward about that final stanza:

> This (need one dread? nay, dare one hope?)
> Will rise, a ghost of memory, if
> Ever again my handkerchief
> Is scented with White Heliotrope.

The speaker's hope that he will be so nonchalant about the episode as to remember it only by chance necessitates the somewhat art-ful projection of a desired future recollection. The very contrivance of this militates against the impression of casualness he hopes to achieve. He is still too conscious, as well as too self-congratulatory about breaking taboos, to be as relaxed about his sexual behaviour as he would like. (There is also a reactionary whiff of old-fashioned Victorian morality and a hint of the double standard in the second stanza, when he imagines his sexual partner's 'forgotten memories of grace', presumably a reference to her once-unsullied 'innocence'.) Moreover, the desired impulse towards transience and ephemerality translates into something strangely indelible, the ghost of a perfume or a poetic memory that can never be erased. Indeed, the speaker who effortlessly imagines his partner's 'forgotten' grace does not seem the type who will forget things easily.[89]

For today's readers the poem is both dated and oddly contemporary. On the one hand, nothing dates as quickly as presentations of 'modernity'. 'White Heliotrope', no longer a title that immediately conveys to its readers the contemporary moment, instead preserves the inherently synthetic nature of all attempts to pass oneself off as current or even avant-garde. For twenty-first-century readers, the title is not a modish marker of modern urban manners but a stopper that, once lifted, releases

---

[88] Briot, 'From Industry to Luxury', p. 282.

[89] My reading of 'White Heliotrope' contrasts with that of Jane Desmarais in her suggestive essay 'Perfume Clouds: Olfaction, Memory, and Desire in Arthur Symons's *London Nights* (1895)', in *Economies of Desire at the Victorian Fin de Siècle*, ed. Jane Ford, Kim Edwards, and Patricia Pulham (London: Routledge, 2016), pp. 62–9. Her essay includes a response to the earlier, shorter version of this chapter 'Scents and Sensibility: The Fragrance of Decadence', published in *Decadent Poetics: Literature and Form at the British Fin de Siècle*, ed. Jason David Hall and Alex Murray (Basingstoke and New York: Palgrave Macmillan, 2013), pp. 201–25. Desmarais tends to emphasize the transient fleeting nature of perfume and memory as she sees it in Symons's poems, whereas I am struck by Symons's insistence on the imperishability of perfume, something explored in more depth in the subsequent part of this chapter. In a late letter, probably dating to 1931, Symons cites the final stanza of 'White Heliotrope' as evidence of the idiosyncratic working of his own 'extraordinary memory', implying that it responded to olfactory cues. See *Arthur Symons: Selected Letters 1880–1935*, ed. Karl Beckson and John M. Munro (London and Basingstoke: Macmillan, 1989), p. 257.

'off' notes, the slightly stale but nonetheless intriguing atmospheric fragrance surrounding the formation of sexual identity in the 1890s. On the other hand, Symons's impressionistic narrative is curiously prescient in that it bears a strong resemblance to much modern perfume advertising, which typically downplays the olfactory experience but uses striking visual imagery to represent an emotionally charged tryst, brief encounter, or sexual scenario between a man or a woman that encapsulates a mood identified with the perfume.

This strategy is also true of Symons's somewhat later poem 'Peau d'Espagne', which celebrates a favourite perfume mentioned in his Preface to *Silhouettes*. The presentation is modern although the scent itself takes us way back into the past. Also known as 'Spanish skin' or 'Spanish leather', peau d'espagne has a long history being, as the perfumer Mandy Aftel explains:

> [A] highly complex and luxurious perfume originally used to scent leather in the sixteenth century. Chamois was steeped in neroli, rose, sandalwood, lavender, verbena, bergamot, cloves, cinnamon, and subsequently smeared with civet and musk. Bits of the leather were used to perfume stationery and clothing. It was a favorite of the sensuous because of the musk and civet, and also because of the leather itself, which may have stirred ancestral memories of the sexual stimulus of skin odor.[90]

Peau d'espagne, the precursor of modern leather fragrances, was adapted for wearing as a perfume in the late nineteenth century.[91] (We may recall that Wilde also liked it in the form of a scented soap made by Houbigant, who had brought out a perfume of that name around 1894.) Like many of the perfumes liked by Wilde and Symons, peau d'espagne has a strong, penetrating smell. In his Preface to *Silhouettes* Symons declares teasingly that the scent 'has a subtle meaning', a somewhat arch comment that makes us suspect that the meaning is perhaps not so very subtle. Indeed, Havelock Ellis, a good friend of Symons, remarks in his discussion of smell that peau d'espagne 'is often the favorite scent of sensuous persons', and that 'It is said by some, probably with a certain degree of truth, that "Peau d'Espagne" is of all perfumes that which most nearly approaches the odor of a woman's skin.'[92] Written on 18 October 1896, 'Peau d'Espagne' was published in Symons's 1913 collection *Knave of Hearts*, where the meaning of the perfume is made explicit:

> Insinuating monotone,
> Why is it that you come to vex,
> With your one word, a heart half grown
> Forgetful of you, scent of sex?
>
> With that warm overcoming breath
> You flow about me like the sea,

---

[90] Aftel, *Essence and Alchemy*, p. 35. Aftel leans heavily on Havelock Ellis's description of the perfume in *Studies in the Psychology of Sex*, p. 99. David Williams offers a receipt for the perfume in *Perfumes of Yesterday*, p. 292.

[91] A number of perfumes still retail under the name of 'Peau d'Espagne' or 'Spanish Leather', including a powerfully animalic tarry one sold by Santa Maria Novella, reputedly dating from 1901.

[92] Ellis, *Studies in the Psychology of Sex*, pp. 99–100.

And down to some delicious death
Your waves are swift to hurry me.

It is the death of her desire;
The prelude of sleep-heavy sighs,
The pulsing ecstasy of fire,
The wet lips and the closing eyes.

And, Peau d'Espagne, I breathe again,
But, in this ultimate eclipse
Of the world's light, I breathe in vain,
The flower's heart of the unseen lips.

Peau d'Espagne, scent of sex, that brings
To mind those ways wherein I went,
Perhaps I might forget those things
But for that infamy, your scent![93]

The speaker of this poem is in the actual situation fantasized by the narrator of 'White Heliotrope'; a re-encounter with a particular perfume evokes a sexual episode, indeed, here perhaps, a series of sexual trysts. However, while in the earlier poem the floral perfume serves somewhat tangentially and perhaps artificially as a mnemonic marker for the sexual scenario, in 'Peau d'Espagne', the perfume, presumably worn by one or other partner at the time recalled, evokes sex itself and the unmistakable sexual scent of a woman—'The flower's heart of the unseen lips'. Far more blatant than 'White Heliotrope', 'Peau d'Espagne' revels in its excess, challenging sexual taboos via perfume, which allows Symons's speaker to mention the unmentionable, connecting the musky sensual spiciness of the scent with the aroma of sex itself. The speaker selects what he wants to take from the sexual experience—not intimacy itself, but a particular scent or aura of intimacy, the extractible essence of the occasion, something vividly conveyed by the fact that he apostrophizes not the woman but the perfume, peau d'espagne. (Indeed, it is unclear whether the woman mentioned is a specific individual or a composite sexual archetype.) Symons uses an old perfume for a modern perception about the enduring timelessness of sexual impulses. Sexual desire and its pervasive memories have been age-old constants, he implies, but it is now that that they can be openly acknowledged and celebrated. 'Peau d'Espagne' is a considerably less refined and nuanced poem than 'White Heliotrope', but if the earlier poem had a troubling self-consciousness about its modernity that made it seem dated, this is also true of 'Peau d'Espagne' with its over-exuberant relish and its unabashed desire to unleash the shock of the new.

The language of this poem may appear somewhat overblown to twenty-first-century readers of poetry, although its self-conscious provocative 'decadence' means that select quotation would not look out of place in modern advertising copy. Moreover, Symons's sophisticated impressionistic medium has strong analogies with modern advertising visuals. The blurriness, opacity, and layering of the images, which move from the oceanic imagery connected with the scent to a hazy

---

[93] Symons, 'Peau d'Espagne', in *Knave of Hearts: 1894–1908* (London: William Heinemann, 1913), p. 46. See also *Selected Writings*, pp. 64–5; *Selected Early Poems*, p. 179.

close-up erotic vignette of the rapt orgasmic woman, the 'eclipse' of remembered sexual climax giving way to the tantalizingly veiled image of the sexually suggestive 'flower'—these fade outs, segues, and ambiguous superimpositions are reminiscent of cinematic sequences and photographic stills used to communicate the erotic allure of modern perfumes.

Finally, both of Symons's perfume poems could be said to be 'modern' in that they anticipate Proust's link between smell and memory in the famous madeleine episode in the first volume of *Remembrance of Things Past* (1913), although, as detailed in Chapter 2, the notion of smell-memory has a literary history that stretches back via figures like Tennyson, Gaskell, Wordsworth, and Lamb to the eighteenth century at least.[94] Moreover, as shown with the scent of violets, texts that allude to smell memory tend to remember the odours of earlier texts, as Symons perhaps does with Wilde's *Lippincott's* version of *Dorian Gray* in 'White Heliotrope', and Wilde himself does in *Dorian Gray* when Lord Henry describes how the life-defining moment owes much to memory, and in recounting this, remembers Pater's discussion of the epiphanic moment in the Conclusion to *The Renaissance*:

> [A] chance tone of colour in a room or a morning sky, a particular perfume that you once had loved and that brings subtle memories with it, a line from a forgotten poem that you had come across again, a cadence from a piece of music you had ceased to play—I tell you Dorian, it is on moments like these that our lives depend.   (p. 179)

> While all melts under our feet, we may well catch at any exquisite passion, or any contribution to knowledge that seems, by a lifted horizon, to set the spirit free for a moment, or any stirring of the senses, strange dyes, strange flowers, and curious odours, or work of the artist's hands, or the face of one's friend.   (*SR*, p. 120)

Relished for its intensity and then stored as a memory to infuse or irradiate the future, the Paterian moment recycled as the Wildean 'beautiful moment' (*CL*, p. 751) is like a precious perfume preserved in a bottle that can be applied to our pulse points when our lives begin to flag.

It is interesting then that a claim to be 'modern' should be founded on a 'remembrance of things past', but Wilde and Symons, along with their peers, are masters of evocation, and especially sensitive to the fragrance of the past as revived and remembered in the present moment. The final part of this chapter continues an exploration of Symons, perfume, and memory, to show how the influence of strong, tenacious perfumes conditions his idea of what endures in literature and, in particular, poetry.

Perfumed Thoughts, Fragrant Memories, and the Imperishability of Perfume

> As a perfume doth remain
> In the folds where it hath lain,
>   So the thought of you, remaining
> Deeply folded in my brain,

---

[94] See Gilbert, *What the Nose Knows*, pp. 189–204.

Will not leave me: all things leave me:
You remain.

Other thoughts may come and go,
Other moments I may know
    That shall waft me, in their going,
As a breath blown to and fro,
    Fragrant memories: fragrant memories
Come and go.

Only thoughts of you remain
In my heart where they have lain,
    Perfumed thoughts of you, remaining,
A hid sweetness, in my brain.
    Others leave me: all things leave me:
You remain.[95]

There is something rather curious about Symons's lyric 'Memory', dated 15 February 1895, and published in his collection *London Nights* in June that same year. The notion of smell or perfume as a mnemonic trigger that cues a remembrance of things past is a literary commonplace, but for Symons's speaker, memory itself is like a perfume, specifically a perfume that clings to the fabric it has impregnated. Symons, moreover, is undoubtedly remembering his own earlier poem 'Perfume', written on 20 September 1891, and printed in *Silhouettes* in October 1892, in which the scent of a woman's hair remains on the speaker's pillow after he and his lover, most likely a one-night stand or prostitute, have said their goodbyes:

'Farewell' between our kisses creeps,
    You fade, a ghost, upon the air;
Yet ah! the vacant place still keeps
    The odour of your hair.[96]

The perfume of the woman's hair will probably last longer than the brief encounter. She 'fades' like a ghost but her perfume endures, although we assume it too will vanish before much time has passed.

We assume this because we usually associate perfume with ephemerality, yet if we consider the later poem, 'Memory', the perfumed fabric is presented as the symbol of something enduring. The speaker compares the perfume lingering on in the fabric's folds with his abiding remembrance of the absent addressee, apparently a former lover. As in 'Perfume', their relationship may have been brief, yet the impression she leaves upon him is—perhaps surprisingly—long-lasting. Other thoughts and memories, possibly of other lovers, 'come and go' and seem pleasant enough, indeed are described as 'fragrant', yet are more transient, lacking the staying power of the 'perfumed thoughts' that have saturated the speaker's heart and brain.

---

[95] Arthur Symons, 'Memory' (Poem 8 in the sequence 'Bianca'), in *London Nights*, p. 98; *Selected Early Poems*, p. 144. The poem was first published in the *Athenæum* (2 March 1895), 281.
[96] Symons, 'Perfume', in *Silhouettes*, p. 41; *Selected Early Poems*, p. 62.

As Symons was undoubtedly aware, while most fragrances and perfumes once applied have a fairly short life, others can be remarkably tenacious. Musk, for example, that animalic substance derived from the gland of the musk deer and named by Roy Genders in his *History of Scent* as 'the most powerful of perfumes', is known for its longevity.[97] He writes that musk's 'penetrating smell will affect anything near it, and the East India Company during Victorian times refused to include musk in any shipment of tea'.[98] This detail also appears in the second edition of Piesse's *Art of Perfumery* (1856), supplementing a statement about musk found in the first edition that confirms that 'everything in its vicinity soon becomes affected by it, and long retains its odour, although not in actual contact with it'.[99] In his third edition (1862), Piesse introduced one of the most famous apocryphal tales about musk concerning the Empress Josephine, who loved its odour, and whose her dressing room at Malmaison was supposed to smell of it over forty years after she had died.[100] However, by his fourth edition of 1879, Piesse had become more sceptical and disparages this 'evidence' of musk's longevity as well as the 'oft-repeated fable' that '"A grain of musk will perfume an apartment for a whole year without sensibly losing weight"', although he appears more tolerant of the tale of the 'extravagant Turk, who built a harem and had the cement of its walls mixed with musk, which is fragrant to this day'.[101] A better-known variant of this story with a probable basis in fact is that various Arab mosques were built with musk incorporated into the mortar so that, warmed by the sun, the scent would permeate the interior for decades to come.[102]

An overt smell of musk was supposedly frowned on in polite Victorian society although, as mentioned in Chapter 1, musk was far more widely used than might be assumed. Still, like a number of other stronger-smelling perfumes that respectable Victorian ladies were urged to avoid, musk, in common with fragrances like patchouli, opopanax, and frangipani, seems to have been especially favoured by women who wanted to draw attention to themselves or their sexuality, such as actresses, dancers, models, demi-mondaines, and prostitutes. We have already seen how Symons exploits the louche associations of patchouli in his 'Being a Word on Behalf of Patchouli' and his poem 'Love and Art'. Patchouli occurs along with musk in 'The Old Women', a poem published in *The Savoy* in 1896 and later included in *Ideas of Good and Evil* (1899), which portrays—grown old, tired, and impoverished—former dancers, singers, and good-time girls who wistfully recall their glory days. Now reduced to scraping a living by such means as selling 'little bags of lavender', they remember their more decadently scented pasts:

[97] Genders, *A History of Scent*, p. 218.   [98] Ibid.

[99] Piesse, *Art of Perfumery*, 2nd edn (1856), p. 156. See also *Art of Perfumery* (1855), p. 100.

[100] Piesse, *Art of Perfumery*, 3rd edn (1862), pp. 185–6. This legend endures. Roy Genders claims that Josephine's dressing room 'still carries the smell' (*A History of Scent*, p. 218). In a more credible version, Josephine is supposed to have splashed her musk-based perfume around the imperial apartments to bring her to Napoleon's mind long after he divorced her in order to remarry and produce an heir. See Stamelman, *Perfume*, p. 56.

[101] Piesse, *Art of Perfumery*, 4th edn (1879), pp. 257–8.

[102] Genders, *A History of Scent*, p. 101. See also Nigel Groom, *The New Perfume Handbook*, 2nd edn (London: Blackie Academic Publishing, 1997), p. 219.

> In their shaking heads
> A dancer of old carnivals yet treads
> The measure of past waltzes, and they see
> The candles lit again, the patchouli
> Sweeten the air, and the warm cloud of musk
> Enchant the passing of the passionate dusk.[103]

Musk and patchouli, the strong-smelling perfumes of their youth, have saturated and live on in the memories of the 'Old Women'.

Thus, in comparing the absent lover to a still pervasive perfume, Symons was certainly aware of the time-defying effects of certain fragrances, as well as the way in which persons, episodes, and activities strongly associated with a particular perfume might become absorbed into one's consciousness as an indelible perfume memory. We saw how 'White Heliotrope' explores, albeit somewhat disingenuously, the idea of the casually encountered scent that acts as a random mnemonic trigger, although I suggested that, in spite of a willed impulse towards transience, the speaker—too self-conscious to forget things easily—is haunted by the ghost of a perfume memory that will not fade. However, the self-protective attitudinizing of 'White Heliotrope' is absent from 'Memory', which openly acknowledges how a significant scent penetrates deeply, becoming a 'hid sweetness' and shaping both olfactory and emotional recall.

It is this enduring aspect of perfume, its capacity to pervade and entrance the mind, which stays with Symons when he turns to literature. It is what he alludes to when he describes the poetry of Robert Bridges in a review of 1901, later collected in *Studies in Prose and Verse* (1904). Discussing Bridges in relation to his peers, he writes:

> [W]hile all these men have been singing themselves, and what they have counted most individual in themselves, this man has put into his verse only what remains over when all the others have finished. It is a kind of essence; it is what is imperishable in perfume; it is what is nearest in words to silence.[104]

Symons styles Bridges 'a writer of purely lyric poetry', and his conception of lyric poetry owes much to his appreciation of the lyrics of Shelley and Keats, which for him epitomize this genre.[105] For example, in reviewing Byron's poetry he complains:

> [T]here is not a single poem, [...] perhaps not a single stanza, which can be compared as poetry with a poem or passage or stanza of Keats or Shelley, such as any one will find by merely turning over the pages of those poets for five minutes at random. What is not there is precisely the magic which seems to make poetry its finer self, the perfume

---

[103] Symons, 'The Old Women', *The Savoy* 5 (1896), 55–6, and *Ideas of Good and Evil* (London: William Heinemann, 1899), p. 57; *Selected Early Poems*, p. 167. These arresting perfumes were evidently not restricted to use by women, as a 'strong scent—if the noxious odour of musk or of patchouli can be called a scent' is worn by one of the male prostitutes Des Grieux encounters in *Teleny* (p. 106).

[104] Symons, 'Robert Bridges', in *Studies in Prose and Verse*, p. 207.   [105] Ibid.

of the flower, that by which the flower is remembered, after its petals have dropped or withered.[106]

Symons's conception of the imperishability of perfume and of lyric poetry—'that by which the flower is remembered, after its petals have dropped or withered'—was almost certainly influenced by Shelley's 'Music, when soft voices die', an important lyric already quoted more than once in this book:

> Music, when soft voices die,
> Vibrates in the memory.—
> Odours, when sweet violets sicken,
> Live within the sense they quicken.   (*SPP*, p. 442)

Just as music lives on in our auditory memory, significant fragrant odours are absorbed by, preserved in, and indeed help constitute our olfactory memory. The link with Symons's poem 'Memory' is evident, especially as Shelley's second stanza draws an analogy with Love:

> Rose leaves, when the rose is dead,
> Are heaped for the beloved's bed—
> And so thy thoughts, when thou art gone,
> Love itself shall slumber on....   (*SPP*, p. 442)

For Shelley, the thoughts mentioned here, compared to heaped rose leaves, are usually taken to signify the words or writings of Emilia (Teresa) Viviani, though may perhaps be his own if he addresses himself, or even those of his reader addressed as 'thou'. The 'thoughts' (fragrant like rose leaves that retain and intensify their scent as they are preserved) outlast the death or absence of their author, consoling and sustaining the meditative dreams of the loved one left behind. Again we see something similar in Symons's poem and the perfumed 'thoughts of you [that] remain | In my heart where they have lain'. Symons thus suggests that the true lyric poem, the lyric poem of the kind written by Keats and Shelley, is a space that retains the perfumed essence of the poet's perceptions, long after the things that actually inspired him have gone or even after the poet himself is dead—his thoughts lingering on to pervade the life of others.

Symons said that the poet Ernest Dowson possessed 'a certain engaging quality, which seemed unconscious of itself, which was never anxious to be or to do anything, which simply existed, as perfume exists in a flower'.[107] The charm of perfume that is integral or essential to the flower also characterizes Symons's idea of literary value. '[W]ithout charm there can be no fine literature, as there can be no perfect flower without fragrance', he writes in an essay on Zola.[108] Perfume is often understood to be the soul of a flower. Christina Rossetti's lyric poems are said to have 'the very music of Ariel, and yet with all the intimacy of a perfume, the

---

[106] Symons, 'Byron' (1900), in *The Romantic Movement in English Poetry*, p. 245.

[107] Ernest Dowson (1900), in *Studies in Prose and Verse*, p. 272.

[108] Symons, 'A Note on Zola's Method', in *Studies in Two Literatures* (London: Leonard Smithers, 1897), p. 311.

perfume of a flower; the soul of something living and beautiful, with its roots in the earth'.[109] In Symons's own poem 'The Dance of the Seven Sins' 'the wandering odours' that 'come and go' 'All day within a pleasant house' are said to be 'the souls of flowers that grow | Too faint with ecstasy to live'.[110] Wittily Symons plays with the Greek origins of 'ecstasy', literally 'a standing outside oneself': the flower's perfume emanates beyond its transient blossom, perhaps impregnating the memory, or perhaps captured and distilled as liquid essence, enduring long after the flower.

For him, the imperishability of perfume, the unforgettable soul of the flower, seems one with lyric poetry itself, where the souls of things, their essences, are preserved through language and symbol. Discussing the way in which rhythm gives words of lyrical utterance an indefinable reverberation and resonance, he writes in the Introduction to *The Romantic Movement in English Poetry* (1909): 'Call it atmosphere, call it magic; say, again with Joubert: "Fine verses are those that exhale like sounds or perfumes".'[111] In the same book he cites Coleridge's declaration 'Poetry is the identity of all other knowledges', 'the blossom and fragrance of all human knowledge, human thoughts, human passions, emotions, language', while in *The Symbolist Movement in Literature* (1899), he singles out Gérard de Nerval as someone who had divined 'before all the world, that poetry should be a miracle; not a hymn to beauty, nor the description of beauty, nor beauty's mirror; but beauty itself, the colour, fragrance, and form of the imagined flower, as it blossoms again out of the page'.[112]

As poets, Shelley in England and Verlaine in France seem to be those most often associated by Symons with perfumed lyricism. He described Shelley as one to whom 'The scent or music of love came [...] like a flower's or bird's speech', noting that 'His poetry, more than that of any poet, is the poetry of the soul, and nothing in his poetry reminds us that he had a body at all, except as a nerve sensitive to light, colour, music, and perfume.' Quoting from *Prometheus Unbound*, he asks 'Can syllables turn to more delicate sound and perfume than in such lines as these?'[113] When he praises Christina Rossetti's 'exquisite lyrics', which are as 'immaterial as perfume', he declares them as being 'in the most ethereal and quintessential elements of song, the most perfect we have had since Shelley'.[114] Of Verlaine he wrote in *Colour Studies in Paris* (1918): 'His verse is as lyrical as Shelley's, as fluid, as magical—though the magic is a new one. It is a twilight art, full of reticence, of perfumed shadows, of hushed melodies.'[115] In an essay on Huysmans, he notes how his decadent hero Des Esseintes discovers 'the fine perfume,

---

[109] Symons, 'Christina Rossetti', in *Studies in Two Literatures*, p. 137.

[110] Symons, 'The Dance of the Seven Sins' (composed December 1896–February 1897), in *Ideas of Good and Evil*, p. 7.

[111] Symons, Introduction, in *The Romantic Movement in English Poetry*, p. 6.

[112] Symons, 'Samuel Taylor Coleridge' (1904), in *The Romantic Movement in English Poetry*, p. 136; 'Gérard de Nerval' (1898), in *The Symbolist Movement in Literature*, ed. Creasy, p. 21. Creasy's edition also includes the essays Symons added to the 1919 edition of his book.

[113] Symons, 'Percy Bysshe Shelley' (1907), in *The Romantic Movement in English Poetry*, pp. 273, 281, 283.

[114] Symons, 'Christina Rossetti', p. 147. Unlike the quotation from this essay referenced in note 109, this quotation occurred in the original *London Quarterly Review* essay of July 1887.

[115] Symons, 'Notes on Paris and Paul Verlaine', in *Colour Studies in Paris* (London: Chapman & Hall, 1918), pp. 171–2.

the evanescent charm, of Paul Verlaine'.[116] Both Shelley and Verlaine are known for their use of synaesthesia, that mixing of the senses in which perception is refined and heightened to another level. Both show awareness of how fragrance could be experienced as music, something most evident in Shelley's 'The Sensitive-Plant' and also integral to Verlaine's 'À Clymène' from *Fêtes galantes* (1869)—a lyric translated by Symons—in which the whole being of the beloved woman, including her scent, is absorbed by her lover as a music that penetrates his heart.[117] Synaesthesia seems especially suited to what Symons identifies as the fluid, magical nature of lyric, where the fine nuances of sense perception are easily transposed into each other.

Symons himself uses olfactory synaesthesia in a number of his own lyrics. Imitating Baudelaire and Swinburne, both synaesthetic poets who revel in the scent of the beloved's hair, he links perfume with touch as if he could absorb it from the woman's tresses: 'Shake out your hair about me, so, | That I may feel the stir and scent', says the speaker of 'Perfume'.[118] 'I feel the perfume of your hair', says the speaker of 'Stella Maris'; 'Only shake loose the perfume of thy hair, | And let me bathe in those delirious streams', entreats the speaker of 'Stellae Figura'.[119] Sound and music are implicated with scent in other poems. In the 1902 version of 'Maquillage' the woman adorned with make-up has a 'voice of violets', presumably because she is wearing violet powder, a popular Victorian cosmetic made from cornflour or farina scented with ground orris-root. She is said to have 'A voice of violets that speaks | Of perfumed hours of day, and doubtful night'.[120] The lyric 'On an Air of Rameau' opens with a tune played on a harpsichord: 'A melancholy desire of ancient things | Floats like a faded perfume out of the wires'.[121]

Smell's alliance with the other senses reinforces the way in which perfume penetrates memory and consciousness, as well as emphasizing lyric poetry's finer shades or nuances of sense and sensibility that raise it above all other literature. Among the poems by Verlaine that Symons translated was 'Art Poétique', his manifesto poem that instructs the poet to revel in his use of 'la nuance', or the subtle shade, and whose final stanza exhorts:

> *Que ton vers soit la bonne aventure*
> *Eparse au vent crispé du matin*
> *Qui va fleurant la menthe et le thym …*
> *Et tout le reste est littérature.*

[116] Symons, 'Joris-Karl Huysmans' (1892), in *Figures of Several Centuries*, p. 287, reprinted in *The Symbolist Movement in Literature*, p. 102.

[117] See Paul Verlaine, *Choix de Poésies*, ed. Michel Dansel (Paris: Librairie Larousse, 1973), pp. 36–7; Symons, 'À Clymène', in *Silhouettes*, p. 76, and in *Selected Early Poems*, pp. 79–80, also included in *The Symbolist Movement in Literature*, Appendix 2, p. 196.

[118] Symons, 'Perfume', p. 41; *Selected Early Poems*, p. 62.

[119] Symons, 'Stella Maris', in *London Nights*, p. 41 (first published in the *Yellow Book* in April 1894) and in *Selected Early Poems*, p. 110; 'Stellae Figura' (composed 26 May 1889), from 'Stella Maligna', in *Lesbia and Other Poems* (New York: E. P. Dutton & Co., 1920), p. 37.

[120] Symons, 'Maquillage', in *Poems*, 2 vols (London: William Heinemann, 1902), 1. 24; cf. *Silhouettes*, p. 14 and *Selected Early Poems*, p. 47. The subject of this poem may have been using violet-scented cachous, but, as the poem is about make-up, violet powder seems more likely.

[121] Symons, 'On an Air of Rameau', in *Ideas of Good and Evil*, p. 113; *Selected Early Poems*, p. 172.

Let your verse be the luck of the lure
Afloat on the winds that at morning hint
Of the odours of thyme and the savour of mint ...
And all the rest is literature.[122]

Reviewing Symons's *London Nights* in *The Bookman* for August 1895 in a piece titled 'That Subtle Shade', W. B. Yeats evidently had Verlaine's poem in mind when he said of his friend's collection that it was 'sometimes crude' and 'clumsy' in its brooding on upon 'common accidents and irrelevant details', but 'wholly distinguished and beautiful when it tells of things an artist loves—of faint perfume, of delicate colour, of ornate and elaborate gesture'.[123]

The notion of perfumed memory and the lyric that retains both memory and perfume clearly stayed with Symons throughout his career. The words of his speaker in 'Mundi Victima' would prove prescient: 'My letters keep the scent of days that were, | My verses keep the perfume that was yours'.[124] I conclude this chapter by looking at a late lyric titled simply 'Song' from his collection *Lesbia and Other Poems* published in 1920. Although many of the poems in this collection date from the 1890s and earlier, 'Song' is dated 1915 in the *Collected Works* of 1924:

My silks I put away
Into a scented room
Where the night-moths can play
With their own perfume.

And then away I went
But left a lovely cloth
To perfume with its scent
The perfumed moth.[125]

Although ultimately indebted to Shelley, this lyric has a Blakeian simplicity, which, as in Blake, proves to be deceptive.[126] By way of preface to my interpretation, I offer a few contextual remarks about the poem's key terms.

Silk, although produced by the silk moth, is, along with wool, one of the natural fabrics vulnerable to attack by moths that are customarily stored with odorants that act as deterrents. Products with names such as 'Alabastrine' or 'Camphylene', containing naphthalene made from coal tar, which kills moths and their larvae with its fumes, were available from the early 1890s, and naphthalene mothballs were widely used in the twentieth century but have the disadvantage of giving

---

[122] Paul Verlaine, 'Art Poétique', from *Jadis et naguère* (1884), in *Choix de Poésies*, p. 67. Symons's translation was first included in *Knave of Hearts* (1913), pp. 120–1, and then in the 1919 edition of *The Symbolist Movement in Literature*. See Creasy's edition, Appendix 2, pp. 210–11.

[123] W. B. Yeats, 'That Subtle Shade', *The Bookman* 8 (August 1895), 144.

[124] Symons, 'Mundi Victima' (Section X), originally published in *The Savoy* 8 (December 1896), then *Amoris Victima* (London: Leonard Smithers, 1897), p. 69.

[125] Symons, 'Song', in *Lesbia and Other Poems*, p. 108.

[126] Symons spent a large part of 1906 in the British Museum working on his book *William Blake*, published in September 1907. Behind 'Song' perhaps lurk the more malign predations of the 'The invisible worm that flies in the night' of 'The Sick Rose' as well as, on a more positive note, the injunction 'Kill not the Moth nor Butterfly | For the Last Judgment draweth nigh' of 'Auguries of Innocence'.

Figure 7.3 Advertisement for Mikado Moth Paper, *Graphic* (1 June 1898), Summer number, p. 2 (detail), N. 2288 b. 7 (vol. 57) (courtesy of The Bodleian Libraries, The University of Oxford)

clothes and the ambient environment a distinctively unpleasant tell-tale smell (Figure 7.3). A more aromatic traditional alternative is camphor, a waxy crystalline substance deriving from the resin of the Asian camphor laurel (*Cinnamomum camphora*) or from the Malaysian Kapur tree (*Dryobalanops aromatica*), which might be used in the form of large lumps or mothballs, although some might still find the strong odour too pervasive or overly medicinal.[127] Lavender bags or cedar balls or shavings might offer a gentler, less penetrating odour; indeed, well-to-do Victorians often stored their clothes in wardrobes and chests made of cedar, which imparted a pleasant fragrance to the fabric.[128] Other aromatic deterrents are cinnamon, cloves, and herbs such as rosemary and southernwood, while more exotic repellents coming from India include vetiver root and patchouli.

Although there are many day-flying moths, we tend to think of moths as a nocturnal species, pollinators of those flowers that release their strongest perfume after dark. Many female moths emit a pheromonal scent in order to attract mates, a phenomenon documented by Charles Darwin in the 1850s and subsequently by the French naturalist Jean-Henri Fabre; hence Symons's allusion to the night-moths'

---

[127] Camphor can also be obtained by synthesizing turpentine.
[128] See Baroness Staffe, *The Lady's Dressing Room*, tr. Lady Colin Campbell, p. 344.

'own perfume'.[129] In an essay almost contemporary with Symons's poem, the early twentieth-century novelist Mary Webb writes that 'Insects are the artists of fragrance', observing that 'moths call each other by scent'.[130]

Symons plays with the paradox of the cloth that, impregnated with scent, ends up perfuming the moths who would devour it. The moths might well seem to embody the threatened ravages of time, while the silken cloth, a valuable textile, is almost certainly a text, perhaps akin to the precious poetic dream-cloths of Symons's friend W. B. Yeats.[131] Saturated with indelible perfumed memory, the cloth defies and deters attack, moreover fragrancing the days and years to come. However, Symons, who elsewhere writes of 'Time, that cannot mar one triumphant rose's scent', may also have been recalling a passage in Shelley's 'A Defence of Poetry'.[132] Here the potentially adversarial moths are not Time, for Shelley sees Time as actually enhancing true poetry, which is of its nature immortal. Rather the moth is what Shelley calls the 'epitome' or 'story of particular facts', which has no inherent beauty and is antithetical to true poetry:

> Time, which destroys the beauty and the use of the story of particular facts, stripped of the poetry which should invest them, augments that of poetry, and forever develops new and wonderful applications of the eternal truth which it contains. Hence epitomes have been called the moths of just history; they eat out the poetry of it. A story of particular facts is as a mirror which obscures and distorts that which should be beautiful; poetry is a mirror which makes beautiful that which is distorted.   (*SPP*, p. 485)

If we set this passage by Shelley alongside Pater's comments on 'fact' in his essay on 'Style' (1888), true poetry might, to use Pater's phrase, contain an author's expanded or supplementary 'imaginative sense of fact', 'fact as connected with soul', rather than a dry summary of particular fact (*A*, pp. 8, 9). Facts destroy poetry but 'imaginative facts' can become part of the textual fabric, and, in Symons's eyes, that very poetic fabric might be by its nature transformative. The moths of fact exposed to the perfumed ambience of the poetic cloth might absorb its influence, and, taking up its perfume and loveliness, become of the same imaginative substance and henceforth no longer a danger to its integrity.

Both of these interpretations assume that the moths do not consume the cloth, something not ultimately guaranteed by the poem. A third reading might see the cloth, so tantalizing to the moths, as eaten by their offspring, which then hatch into adult moths impregnated with the cloth's perfume. This version would have also the additional charm of the implied metamorphosis with the newly-born perfumed moth a symbol of the *psyche* or winged soul, something that might be

---

[129] *Charles Darwin's Natural Selection being the Second Part of his Big Species Book Written from 1856 to 1858*, ed. R. C. Stauffer (Cambridge: Cambridge University Press, 1987), p. 381. See J. H. Fabre, *Social Life in the Insect World*, tr. Bernard Miall (London: T. Fisher Unwin, 1912), ch. 14: 'The Great Peacock or Emperor Moth', pp. 179–201.

[130] Mary Webb, 'The Joy of Fragrance', in *The Spring of Joy: A Little Book of Healing* (London, Toronto, and New York: J. M. Dent and E. P. Dutton, 1917), p. 56.

[131] W. B. Yeats, 'He Wishes for the Cloths of Heaven', in *Collected Poems* (London: Macmillan & Co., 1963), p. 81.

[132] Symons, 'Song', in *Knave of Hearts*, p. 40.

especially appealing to Symons, whose stated purpose was the 'endeavour to disengage the ultimate essence, the soul, of whatever exists and can be realised by the consciousness'.[133] The moth, made beautiful by the perfumed cloth it consumes, then itself becomes another version of lyric poetry, like that ideal poetic style Symons found in Verlaine, 'a winged soul in flight "toward other skies and other loves"'.[134]

Symons's little lyric could thus also be read as a poem about legacy in which aspiring poets or writers consume the poetry, the perfumed silken cloth made by their predecessors, this being the precious text that helps them metamorphose into the writers they want to be. Yet even as they explore 'other skies and other loves', they still give off the ingrained scent of ancestral poetic memory that marks their unmistakable lineage. This theme continues into Chapter 8, which looks at specifically at perfumed inheritance in a number of twentieth-century writers, concentrating in particular on two almost diametrically opposed figures: Virginia Woolf and Compton Mackenzie.

[133] Symons, Introduction, in *The Symbolist Movement in Literature*, p. 8. Both Aristotle and Theophrastus use the Greek word 'psyche' to signify 'moth' or 'butterfly' in their writings. The moth or butterfly is used in classical art to represent the soul, and Psyche in the myth of Cupid and Psyche is often portrayed with butterfly wings. The *Psychidae* are a moth family of the order of *Lepidoptera* that encompasses butterflies and moths.

[134] Symons, 'The Decadent Movement in Literature', *Harper's*, p. 860, in *Dramatis Personæ*, p. 103, and in *The Symbolist Movement in Literature*, Appendix 1, p. 173.

8

Victorian Drydown and Sillage
Virginia Woolf and Compton Mackenzie

WHO'S AFRAID? VIRGINIA WOOLF AND PERFUME

'Did Virginia Woolf dislike perfume altogether?' writes Antony Alpers, Katherine Mansfield's biographer, with reference to Woolf's now infamous diary response to meeting Mansfield on 10 October 1917:

> The dinner last night went off: the delicate things were discussed. We could both wish that ones [sic] first impression of K.M. was not that she stinks like a—well civet cat that had taken to street walking. In truth, I'm a little shocked by her commonness at first sight, lines so hard & cheap. However, when this diminishes, she is so intelligent & inscrutable that she repays friendship.[1]

Defending Mansfield against this slur and Leonard Woolf's subsequent gibe about her 'cheap scent and cheap sentimentality', Alpers remarks that she was unlikely to be wearing cheap scent as she favoured 'a rather expensive French perfume called Genêt Fleuri'.[2] As he and other critics have pointed out, Woolf's comments about Mansfield—she repeatedly uses the word 'cheap' of her and her writing, for instance about her short story 'Bliss'—reveal her anxious suspicion of a confident, expressive, and sensuous female sexuality. Patricia L. Moran observes that, for Woolf, 'the woman who writes openly about sexual desire—as Mansfield, for example, does in "Bliss"—makes herself and her work "cheap"; that is, she turns herself into a

---

[1] Antony Alpers, *The Life of Katherine Mansfield* (London: Jonathan Cape, 1980), p. 254; *The Diary of Virginia Woolf*, ed. Anne Olivier Bell with Andrew McNeillie, 5 vols (London: The Hogarth Press, 1977–84), vol. 1: *1915–1919*, 58 (Entry of 11 October 1917, re: a meeting on 10 October).

[2] Alpers, *The Life of Katherine Mansfield*, p. 254; Leonard Woolf, *Beginning Again: An Autobiography of the Years 1911–1918* (London: The Hogarth Press, 1964), p. 205. 'Genêt' is the French name for 'broom', a term used for shrubs of the *Cytisus* or *Genista* genera. An absolute made from the yellow fragrant flowers of the related shrub *Spartium junceum* (or Spanish broom) is used in perfumery. Mansfield was undoubtedly familiar with common or Scotch broom (*Cytisus scoparius*), which also has yellow fragrant flowers, flourishes in dry soil and sunny sites, and is now an invasive weed in her native New Zealand. However, broom is related to the thorny shrub gorse (*Ulex europaeus*) and she evidently thought 'Genêt Fleuri' meant 'Flowering Gorse'. See *The Collected Letters of Katherine Mansfield*, ed. Vincent O'Sullivan and Margaret Scott, 5 vols (Oxford: Oxford University Press, 1984–2008), vol. 1: *1903–1917*, 210; letter of 12–13 December 1915. Mansfield also mentions Genêt Fleuri in *Letters of Katherine Mansfield*, vol. 2: *1918–1919* (1987), 130 (19 March 1918), and vol. 3: *1919–1920* (1993), 24, where she calls it 'a heavenly scent'. Genêt Fleuri is not among the perfumes listed in the online encyclopaedia *Perfume Intelligence*, although there are several early (now discontinued) twentieth-century 'Genêt' perfumes.

whore'.[3] That said, Woolf, who admitted that Mansfield was the only writer she was jealous of, was undoubtedly impressed by the immediacy of her rival's physical responses, noting that 'Her senses are amazingly acute.'[4] Antony Alpers reflects 'Katherine, with a hint of Lawrence's "good animal" in her, did go in for the life of the senses, and Virginia shied away from it—which is why she had such curiosity in this regard.'[5] Later Woolf uses, not the malodorous civet, but the more positive image of the lone cat to describe Mansfield's perceptive detachment: 'It struck me that she [KM] is of the cat kind: alien, composed, always solitary & observant.'[6]

However, Mansfield was not the only woman that Woolf condemned for wearing perfume. She had previously tried out her civet cat insult on the wealthy women who frequented Days, a circulating library in Mayfair: 'A more despicable set of creatures I never saw. They come in furred like seals & scented like civets, condescend to pull a few novels about on the counter, & then demand languidly whether there is *anything* amusing.'[7] To the self-conscious, physically ill-at-ease Woolf, who admitted her horror of mirrors, the pleasure-seeking woman or the woman who draws attention to herself and her body by wearing perfume, make-up, or flamboyant dress, was threatening and repellent, seeming, by her scent, to encroach on Woolf's own space. Thus in September 1920 she remarks of her friend Mary Hutchinson 'Then I didn't like Mary; scented, tinted, lewd lipped, & blear eyed.'[8] When the modernist writer Hope Mirrlees came to visit in August 1919, she complained that 'powder fell about in flakes; and the scent was such we had to sit in the garden'.[9] The following November she recorded in her diary: 'Hope (Mirrlees) has been for the weekend—over-dressed, over elaborate, scented, extravagant, yet with thick nose, thick ankles; a little unrefined, I mean.'[10] After a visit from the writer Mary Butts, she mused on the trappings of writers' success such as good reviews, declaring loftily, 'I want to be quit of all this. It hangs about me like Mary Butts' scent.'[11]

There is undoubtedly a class element to this by which Woolf maintains her sense of intellectual and social superiority. She confessed to inheriting 'a streak of the puritan of the Clapham sect' from her father, Leslie Stephen, whom she described as 'spartan, ascetic, puritanical'.[12] She had picked up something of that high-minded, plain-living attitude which disdained any show or self-display as vulgar, and regarded any obviously perfumed woman as underbred. Thus T. S. Eliot's first wife, Vivienne, nervously excitable, broke all the rules and offended Woolf's

[3] Patricia L. Moran, *Word of Mouth: Body Language in Katherine Mansfield and Virginia Woolf* (Charlottesville, VA: University Press of Virginia, 1996), p. 78.
[4] *Diary of Virginia Woolf*, vol. 2: *1920–1924* (1982), 227 (16 January 1923); 62 (25 August 1920).
[5] Alpers, *The Life of Katherine Mansfield*, p. 254.
[6] *Diary of Virginia Woolf*, 2. 43; 31 May 1920.   [7] Ibid., 1. 17; 13 January 1915.
[8] Ibid., 2. 63; 8 September 1920.
[9] *The Letters of Virginia Woolf*, ed. Nigel Nicolson with Joanne Trautmann, 6 vols (London: The Hogarth Press, 1975–80), vol. 2: *1912–1922* (1976), 384; 17 August 1919.
[10] *Diary of Virginia Woolf*, 2. 75; Tuesday, 23 November 1920.
[11] Ibid., 2. 209; 29 October 1922.
[12] Virginia Woolf, 'Sketch of the Past', in *Moments of Being: Autobiographical Writings*, ed. Jeanne Schulkind, with a new introduction by Hermione Lee, rev. edn (London: Pimlico, 2002), pp. 81, 82.

sense of propriety by drawing attention to herself at a social gathering 'Mrs Eliot—this last almost making me vomit, so scented, so powdered, so egotistic, so morbid, so weakly.'[13]

'Powdered' often accompanies 'scented' in Woolf's damning litanies, face powder then, as now, being mostly scented. In fact Woolf writes to her lover, Vita Sackville-West, in July 1927, enquiring anxiously about how she can get hold of unscented powder: 'Once you gave me some which didn't smell; but I dont know what it was: I bought some which permeates every pore and I daren't stink like that.' Answering Alpers's question, she then exclaims 'I loathe scents', adding diplomatically, 'except on you, when they are merely the ripeness of the apricot'.[14] The words 'powdered' and 'scented' tend to function for Woolf as terms of difference.[15] She disdainfully notes 'a few scented American girls' at Shakespeare's birthplace when she and Leonard visit Stratford-on-Avon in May 1934, but becomes charged with venom when class barriers are breeched and outsiders impinge on her.[16] Hence her outburst when she eavesdropped on lower-class women gossiping in the lavatory at the Sussex Grill, Brighton, in February 1941: 'They were powdering & painting, these common little tarts.' Later that same day she sees in Fuller's tearoom 'A fat, smart woman [...] consuming rich cakes' with a 'shabby dependant also stuffing', and pronounces 'Something scented, shoddy, parasitic about them', asking 'Where does the money come to feed these fat white slugs?'[17]

Mansfield, a woman who loved perfume and whose stories are full of reference both to natural scents and scented women, passed her own olfactory judgement on Leonard and Virginia. '"I'm sorry you have to go to the Woolves", she wrote to her partner John Middleton Murry in February 1918. "I don't like them either. They are *smelly*."'[18] Her view chimes with Alison Light's later assessment of Monk's House as 'messy, dusty, and smelly'.[19] Mansfield seems to have bonded with Lady Ottoline Morrell, a prominent member of Woolf's circle, over their shared love of perfume. In her memoirs, Ottoline recalls how Mansfield helped her with the collecting and drying of lavender at Garsington, the Morrells' country house—'How we both loved the strong aromatic smell which would permeate the house when it was brought in'—and she remembers how she 'would linger round me when I was collecting the herbs, sweet geranium and verbena, the rose leaves and

---

[13] *Diary of Virginia Woolf*, 2. 304; 21 June 1924.

[14] *Letters of Virginia Woolf*, vol. 3: *1923–1928* (1977), 402–3; 24 July 1927. Sackville-West's teasing reply can be found in *The Letters of Vita Sackville-West to Virginia Woolf*, ed. Louise DeSalvo and Mitchell A. Leaska (London: Hutchinson, 1984), p. 237; 25 July 1927.

[15] The young gay men in Woolf's circle, being 'pretty and ladylike', also come in for some mockery: 'They paint and powder, which wasn't the style in our day at Cambridge', *Letters of Virginia Woolf*, 3. 155; 24 January 1925. In another letter we find that social gatherings of gay men make Woolf reach for a different category of malodour: 'When I go to what we call a Buggery Poke party I feel as if I had strayed into a male urinal; a wet, smelly, trivial kind of place.' *Letters of Virginia Woolf*, vol. 4: *1929–1931* (1978), 200; 15 August 1930.

[16] *Diary of Virginia Woolf*, vol. 5: *1936–1941* (1984), 219; 9 May 1934.

[17] Ibid., 5. 357; 26 February 1941.

[18] *Letters of Katherine Mansfield*, 2. 77; 16 and 17 February 1918.

[19] Alison Light, *Mrs Woolf and the Servants: An Intimate History of Domestic Life in Bloomsbury* (London: Fig Tree, 2007), p. 232.

rosemary for *pot-pourri*'.[20] When Mansfield's partner John Middleton Murry falsely claimed that Ottoline had tried to seduce him, Mansfield's letter to her is elegaic rather than reproachful, evoking the women's perfumed idyll and turning the supposed incriminating scented 'evidence' into a kind of love token:

> The strangest part was that my memory of the days we had just spent were as perfect as ever—as bright as untroubled. I still see the blue spikes of lavender—the trays of fading, scented leaves, you in your room, and your bed with the big white pillow. [...] Murry came to see me this evening. He showed me a handkerchief you had given him. I took it in my hands and the scent of it shook my heart—Yes, just as if I had been a young person profoundly in love with you.[21]

Her misapprehension corrected, she continued to write to Ottoline in this lyrical mode, with scent still a charged communication between them. Many of Mansfield's letters contain thanks for gifts of fragrant flowers and dwell on shared memories of fragrance.[22] Responding to a scented letter from Ottoline in December 1921, she exclaims: 'Isn't it astonishing how a scent can carry one back— — —when I opened your envelope the delicious strange perfume quite overwhelmed me.'[23]

In the early days of their acquaintance Woolf compared Ottoline Morrell to an oppressively seductive exotic flower: 'It is like sitting under an Arum lily; with a thick golden bar in the middle, dropping pollen, or whatever it is that seduces the male bee.'[24] Ottoline's aristocratic status may have prevented Woolf from denigrating her perfume as 'cheap', but her description of the Morrells' house at Bedford Square is nonetheless mocking as she details 'the drawing room full of people, [...] the embroideries, the tassels, the scent, the pomegranates, the pugs, the pot pourri', and how one was 'made to sign one's name in a little scented book'.[25] David Garnett, another Bloomsbury Group member, explains that

> The characteristic of every house in which Ottoline lived was its smell and the smell of Garsington was stronger than that of Bedford Square. It reeked of the bowls of pot-pourri and orris-root which stood on every mantel-piece, side table and window-sill and of the desiccated oranges, studded with cloves, which Ottoline loved making.[26]

Robert Gathorne-Hardy, a friend of Ottoline's, refers to 'the faint delicious smell about the house of fine incense', and mentions how when staying in a hotel bedroom she made it 'her own [...] pervading everything with her personal, delicious perfume'.[27] Visiting Garsington for the first time in December 1917,

---

[20] *Ottoline at Garsington: Memoirs of Lady Ottoline Morrell, 1915–1918*, ed. Robert Gathorne-Hardy (London: Faber & Faber, 1974), p. 186.

[21] *Letters of Katherine Mansfield*, 1. 323; 11 August 1917.

[22] See, for example, *Letters of Katherine Mansfield*, 2. 274 (5 September 1918); 329 (12 June 1919); 338 (13 July 1919); 346 (13 August 1919).

[23] *Letters of Katherine Mansfield*, vol. 4: *1920–1921* (1996), 355–6; 27 December 1921.

[24] *Letters of Virginia Woolf*, vol. 1: *1888–1912* (1975), 392; ?13 May 1909.

[25] Virginia Woolf, 'Old Bloomsbury', in *Moments of Being*, p. 60.

[26] David Garnett, *The Flowers of the Forest* (London: Chatto & Windus, 1953), p. 109.

[27] *Ottoline: The Early Memoirs of Lady Ottoline Morrell*, ed. Robert Gathorne-Hardy (London: Faber & Faber, 1963), pp. 20, 39. Mansfield also wrote about the scent of Ottoline's home: 'There is a delicious, delicate perfume I remember.' See *Letters of Katherine Mansfield*, 2. 336; 1 July 1919.

Woolf wrote disparagingly of 'too many scents, & silks, & a warm air which was a little too heavy'.[28] And in June 1923 she wrote to Barbara Bagenal about another visit in May, complaining of the artificiality of her hostess and her home: 'one receives impressions merely from her drawl and crawl and smell which might be harmless in the stir of normal sunlight. Only is the sunlight ever normal at Garsington? No, I think even the sky is done up in pale yellow silk, and certainly the cabbages are scented.'[29]

Mansfield loved the gardens at Garsington, immediately seeing them as a source of inspiration. On 15 July 1917, only a few days after intimating that Ottoline Morrell had seduced Murry, she wrote to her:

> Your glimpse of the garden—all flying green and gold made me wonder again *who* is going to write about that flower garden. It might be so wonderful, do you know *how* I mean? There would be people walking in the garden—several *pairs* of people—their conversation their slow pacing—their glances as they pass one another—the pauses as the flowers 'come in' as it were—as a bright dazzle, an exquisite haunting scent, a shape so formal and fine, so much a 'flower of the mind' that he who looks at it really is tempted for one bewildering moment to stoop & touch and make sure. The 'pairs' of people must be different and there must be a slight touch of enchantment—some of them seeming so extraordinarily 'odd' and separate from the flowers, but others quite related and at ease. A kind of, musically speaking, conversation *set* to flowers.[30]

She also wrote a very similar letter (now lost) to Woolf, before arriving on 17 August to spend a long weekend with her. Woolf herself wrote to Ottoline Morrell on 15 August just before Mansfield's arrival: 'Katherine Mansfield describes your garden, the rose leaves drying in the sun, the pool, and long conversations between people wandering up and down in the moonlight.'[31] Mansfield's appreciation of Garsington is thought to have helped inspire Woolf's 'Kew Gardens', published in 1919, a story marking an important evolution in her style that seems to have been written very close to Mansfield's letter and visit. Certainly Woolf's painterly vignette emulates the impressionist suggestiveness of Mansfield's epistolary sketch to Ottoline Morrell, although, interestingly, while Mansfield writes of 'an exquisite haunting scent', there is no olfactory reference whatsoever in Woolf's story.

In writing her letters about Garsington Mansfield may have recalled her own short story 'In the Botanical Gardens', composed when she was seventeen and published in 1907 in *Native Companion*, a Melbourne monthly magazine. In this piece her narrator sees 'a great stretch of foam-like cowslips': 'As I bend over them, the air is heavy and sweet with their scent, like hay and new milk and the kisses of children', and she later notices 'everywhere that strange, indefinable scent. As I breathe it in, it seems to absorb, to become part of me—and I am old with the age of centuries, strong with the strength of savagery.'[32]

---

[28] *Diary of Virginia Woolf*, 2. 78; 19 December 1917.
[29] *Letters of Virginia Woolf*, 3. 50; 24 June 1923.
[30] *Letters of Katherine Mansfield*, 1. 325; 15 August 1917.
[31] *Letters of Virginia Woolf*, 2. 174; 15 August 1917.
[32] Mansfield, 'In the Botanical Gardens', in *The Collected Fiction of Katherine Mansfield*, ed. Gerri Kimber and Vincent O'Sullivan, 2 vols (Edinburgh University Press, 2012), vol. 1: *1898–1915*, pp. 84–5.

The absorption of scent, something other or alien, an influence that then becomes part of oneself, can be part of a seduction, and in Mansfield scent is a seduction, often of one woman by another. In 'Carnation', a story about adolescent schoolgirls based on Mansfield's own experience at Queen's College, London (1903–6), 'curious Eve', a temptress like her namesake, teases 'Katie' by playing flirtatiously with perfumed flowers—roses and then a carnation—in class. On a hot afternoon as their French master reads to his inattentive pupils, Eve 'made a warm, white cup of her fingers, the carnation inside. Oh, the scent! It floated up to Katie. It was too much. Katie turned away to the dazzling light outside the window.'[33] Katie then watches a young workman pumping water outside the window 'his chest bare, all splashed with water', her intense visual impressions in concert with the sound of her teacher's rising voice, the heat of the day, and 'Oh, the scent of Eve's carnation!' The class suddenly breaks up, and Eve 'popped the carnation down the front of Katie's blouse'.[34]

As Mansfield probably knew, the word 'carnation' has a popular etymology that links it to Middle French *carnation*, signifying 'a person's colour or complexion', deriving ultimately from the Latin *caro* for 'flesh'. In her story, the carnation's rich scent is certainly linked to the drama of Katie's emergent physical desires. Interestingly, in Woolf's short story 'Moments of Being: "Slater's Pins have no Points"' (1928), a story she described to Vita Sackville-West as 'a nice little story about Sapphism, for the Americans', a dropped rose that turns into a carnation, fondled by one woman and watched by another, sets up a sympathetic erotic charge between them. 'And [Julia] picked up the carnation which had fallen on the floor, while Fanny searched for the pin. She crushed it, Fanny felt, voluptuously in her smooth, veined hands stuck about with water-coloured rings set in pearls.'[35] However, although the description is sensual and sensuous, there is, as in 'Kew Gardens', no allusion to the flower's scent, so powerful in Mansfield's story.[36]

One of the reasons that Woolf leaves out flower scent in these stories and also undoubtedly contributes to her dislike of perfume is that she associated the scent of flowers with the death of her mother, Julia Stephen. She writes of the terrible days preceding her mother's funeral: 'People were coming to the house all the time. We were all sitting in the drawing room round father's chair sobbing. The hall reeked of flowers. They were piled on the hall table. The scent still brings back

---

[33] Mansfield, 'Carnation', in *The Collected Fiction of Katherine Mansfield*, vol. 2: *1916–1922*, pp. 160–3; 160, 162.

[34] Ibid., 2. 162.

[35] *Letters of Virginia Woolf*, 3. 397; ?8 July 1927; 'Moments of Being: Slater's Pins Have No Points', in *The Complete Shorter Fiction of Virginia Woolf*, ed. Susan Dick (London: The Hogarth Press, 1985), pp. 209–10; 211.

[36] Janet Winston has also written interestingly about the link between these stories by Mansfield and Woolf in her essay 'Reading Influences: Homoeroticism and Mentoring in Katherine Mansfield's "Carnation" and Virginia Woolf's "Moments of Being: 'Slater's Pins Have No Points'"', in *Virginia Woolf: Lesbian Readings*, ed. Eileen Barrett and Patricia Cramer (New York and London: New York University Press, 1997), pp. 57–77.

those days of astonishing intensity.'[37] In an essay on flowers in Woolf, Elisa Kay Sparks notes how

> This memory appears in several novels including in *The Voyage Out* where the smell of broom brings back to Rachel 'the sickly horrible sensation' of her mother's funeral, in *The Waves* where Bernard imagines Percival covered over with lilies and exuding 'this lily-sweet glue', and in *The Years* where, after her mother's death, Delia is 'pent up' for days 'in the half-lit house which smelt of flowers', lilies, white tulips, white lilac, and even more lilies.[38]

However, another reason for Woolf's ambivalence about scent and perfume might be her lack of direct contact with the heady, sensate culture of the *fin de siècle*.

Mansfield's ease with perfume was encouraged by her love of aesthetic and *fin-de-siècle* literature—Pater, Symons, and especially Oscar Wilde—a literature she encountered while a schoolgirl at Queen's College and which she associated with the senses and sensuality. In an early notebook she writes, regarding Wilde's *The Picture of Dorian Gray*,

> 'Soul & senses, senses & soul'—here is the innate spirit of Henry Wotton, here is the quintessence of Wilde's life, <of Dowson, and of Arthur Symons two most vitally interesting books of Poems. To Pater this did not so exactly apply>, yet there is a very real sensuousness in his early Portraits—a certain voluptuous pleasure in garden scents.[39]

For Mansfield, Wilde is imagined as a sympathetic friend and ally and humorously apostrophized: 'O Oscar! Am I peculiarly susceptible to sexual impulse?'[40]

Woolf, who was not 'peculiarly susceptible to sexual impulse', did not have the same marked attraction to the culture of the *fin de siècle*. In contrast, her view of Victorianism is that of an imprisoning monolithic conservatism. Although she read and enjoyed Pater in the early 1900s, and in 1916 wrote appreciatively about Symons's essays, the drama, colour, and perfume of decadence and the 1890s seems to have passed her by. She says of her formative years at Hyde Park Gate, 'we lived under the sway of a society that was about fifty years too old for us', writing of her father and half-brothers 'they were living in 1860'.[41] Visitors to the house tended to be from an older generation of Victorians. Woolf explains that 'This was partly, of course, due to father's deafness, which had cut off his intercourse with the younger generation of writers. Young writers, young painters never came to Hyde Park Gate.' However, even with the older 'Great figures' like George Meredith, George Frederic Watts, Henry James, Edward Burne-Jones, John

---

[37] Woolf, 'Sketch of the Past', p. 104.

[38] Elisa Kay Sparks, '"Everything tended to set itself in a garden": Virginia Woolf's Literary and Quotidian Flowers: A Bar-Graphical Approach', in *Virginia Woolf and the Natural World: Selected Papers from the Twentieth International Conference on Virginia Woolf, Georgetown College, Georgetown, Kentucky 3–June 2010*, ed. Kristin Zarnecki and Carrie Rohman (Clemson, SC: Clemson University Digital Press, 2011), pp. 42–57; 44.

[39] *The Katherine Mansfield Notebooks*, ed. Margaret Scott, 2 vols (Canterbury, NZ: Lincoln University Press, 1997), 1. 165. Entry probably of 1909.

[40] Ibid., 1. 10; 1 June 1907.   [41] Woolf, 'Sketch of the Past', pp. 149, 150.

Addington Symonds (the last two with some aestheticist credentials), 'we had no close connection. My memories of them are strong; but only of figures booming large in the distance.'[42]

Woolf's parents, Leslie and Julia Stephen, had stayed with Symonds at Davos, but her only recollection was of his 'crinkled yellow face' and unusual cord tie.[43] However, in 1898, five years after Symonds's death, the two families became related when his favourite daughter, Madge, married William Wyamar Vaughan, a cousin of the Stephens. Woolf, devoted to Madge as an adolescent, visited her with Leonard Woolf shortly before her own marriage in 1912, when Symonds's widow, Catherine, and his biographer Horatio Brown were present. Leonard Woolf's comments on the occasion are pertinent for their dismissal of the scented, crumbling relics of aestheticism and decadence:

> Madge too was charming and Virginia was fond of her. But she, her mother, and Horatio Brown oozed the precious, incense-laden Italianate culture of Walter Pater and the eighties and nineties. I don't suppose anyone still reads Symonds but he had a reputation in the last decade of the nineteenth century, which still existed, in a rather decrepit state, in 1912.[44]

'Our intelligence domineers over our senses', observed Woolf in an essay of 1930, noting how

> in illness, with the police off duty, [...] the words give out their scent and distil their flavour, and then, if at last we grasp the meaning, it is all the richer for having come to us sensually at first, by way of the palate and the nostrils, like some queer odour.[45]

Although Woolf's ostensible references here are Mallarmé and Donne, there is perhaps a whiff of Pater's incense here, a reminiscence of his 'Style' and the writer's 'soul perfume'. Three years later, she finds another way to let 'the police off duty', finally achieving a rapprochement with the scented world of Victorian literature through *Flush* (1933), her narrative account of the married life of Elizabeth Barrett Browning and Robert Browning as viewed by EBB's pet spaniel. There are obvious links between Barrett Browning and Woolf, not least the experiences of early maternal bereavement, an overbearing father, debilitating illness and confinement, and a sympathetic husband, but Woolf is also clearly invested in the dog Flush. Although inspired by her own spaniel Pinker, a gift from Vita Sackville-West, Woolf's novel is no dog-lover's rhapsody, but a chance for her to explore her own 'good animal' self in the guise of a dog, perhaps a foil to Mansfield, the 'composed' perceptive cat. As Quentin Bell observes of his aunt and her novel: 'Her dog was the embodiment of her own spirit, not the pet of an owner. Flush in fact was one of the routes which Virginia used, or at least examined, in order to escape from her own human corporeal existence.'[46]

---

[42] Ibid., pp. 158, 159.   [43] Ibid., p. 159.   [44] Woolf, *Beginning Again*, pp. 72–3.
[45] Virginia Woolf, 'On Being Ill', in *The Moment and Other Essays* (London: The Hogarth Press, 1947), p. 22. Many thanks to Michèle Barrett for providing this reference.
[46] Quentin Bell, *Virginia Woolf: A Biography*, 2 vols (St Albans: Triad Paladin, 1976), 2. 175–6.

A dog primarily interprets the world by smell and a dog's sense of smell is estimated to be a thousand to ten thousand times more sensitive than a human's. 'The human nose', writes Woolf in a telling sweeping statement, 'is practically non-existent. The greatest poets in the world have smelt nothing but roses on the one hand, and dung on the other. The infinite gradations that lie between are unrecorded.'[47] Nonetheless, while Woolf's earlier fiction is predominantly concerned with visual impressions, *Flush* gives her the opportunity to access the under-explored olfactory dimension of experience, for 'it was in the world of smell that Flush mostly lived'.[48] Woolf scrupulously imagines the indoors and out-of-doors aspects of Flush's olfactory world—the countryside where he is raised, London where he lives with the invalid poet Elizabeth Barrett, and Italy where he accompanies the Brownings after their marriage. Interestingly, Flush, echoing Woolf's own dislike of scent, shows a marked distaste for the smell of eau de cologne, that popular Victorian restorative, which pervades Elizabeth Barrett's oppressively close bedroom: 'only the sensations of such an explorer into the buried vaults of a ruined city can compare with the riot of emotions that flooded Flush's nerves as he stood for the first time in an invalid's bedroom, in Wimpole Street, and smelt eau-de-Cologne', and some weeks after this we learn that 'the smell of eau-de-Cologne still affected his nostrils disagreeably'.[49]

Although the period explored in the novel ends with Flush's death in 1854, there are narratorial divergences from strict chronology. For example, in detailing Flush's olfactory experience, the narrator invokes Swinburne—one of the founding figures of Victorian aestheticism and a notable *olfactif*—even though he did not publish his first texts until 1860, and the famously spiced *Poems and Ballads* until 1866: 'Not even Mr Swinburne could have said what the smell of Wimpole Street meant to Flush on a hot afternoon in June.'[50] Moreover, following on from this, in a well-known passage in which the narrator describes Flush savouring the smells of Florence, Woolf resorts to synaesthesia, something strongly associated with Swinburne, himself influenced by both Shelley and Baudelaire:

> He slept in this hot patch of sun—how sun made the stone reek! He sought that tunnel of shade—how acid shade made the stone smell! He devoured whole bunches of ripe grapes largely because of their purple smell; he chewed and spat out whatever tough relic of goat or macaroni the Italian housewife had thrown from the balcony— goat and macaroni were raucous smells, crimson smells. He followed the swooning sweetness of incense into the violet intricacies of dark cathedrals; and sniffing, tried to lap the gold on the window-stained tomb.[51]

---

[47] Virginia Woolf, *Flush*, ed. Kate Flint (Oxford University Press, 2009), p. 86.
[48] Ibid.   [49] Ibid., pp. 16, 20.   [50] Ibid., p. 86.
[51] Ibid., p. 87. Synaesthesia involving odorous colour is uncommon in Swinburne, but can be found, for example, in the sonnet 'To William Bell Scott', from *Tristram of Lyonesse and Other Poems* (1882), which describes gorse flowers: 'their glorious gold | With odour like the colour' (*Poems* 5. 232). In 'Correspondances' Baudelaire famously referred to perfumes 'verts comme les prairies' ('green as meadows'), something Swinburne emulates in 'the grasses round | Have odours in them of green bloom', in 'Tiresias', *Songs before Sunrise* (1871) (*Poems* 2. 177) and 'The green smell of thickets drenched with dawn', *Tristram of Lyonesse* (4. 140).

Yet while Woolf seems very aware of the smell of other women and ranks them accordingly, the novel, perhaps rather oddly, does not mention Flush's impressions of the smell of the other dogs he encounters in England and Italy. Still, Woolf's narrator informs us, 'For many years now Flush had been taught to consider himself an aristocrat.' When the Brownings settle temporarily in Pisa, Flush realizes 'though dogs abounded, there were no ranks at all; all—could it be possible?—were mongrels'. Yet he proudly retains his own status: 'Flush felt himself like a prince in exile. He was the sole aristocrat among a crowd of *canaille*.' And the narrator comments 'There was an element, it must be admitted, of the snob in Flush.'[52] Woolf, it will be remembered, wrote a short, self-mocking essay titled 'Am I a Snob?' (1936), admitting to her love of a certain kind of English aristocrat, 'I want [...] old coronets [...]; coronets that breed simplicity, eccentricity, ease.'[53] It is, after all, only the scent of her lover, the aristocratic Sackville-West, that she claimed she could tolerate.

Woolf was ambivalent about *Flush*, referring to it with some embarrassment as 'that silly book', and 'a waste of time', apparently resenting the labour of researching, writing, and correcting the novel, which she also found hard to 'despatch'.[54] In October 1933, contemplating its imminent publication, she anticipated being 'much depressed' by 'the kind of praise' she thought it would attract: 'I shall very much dislike the popular success of *Flush*.'[55] Perhaps some of the discomfort she felt may have stemmed from the threatened public exposure of a private fantasy, the imagining of a physical self that revels in one of the 'lower senses', and her disavowal of the book was a way of refusing to admit it to the cadre of her more cerebral 'serious' fictions.

However, *Flush* does seem to have released something in Woolf. In August 1933, she writes 'What a vast fertility of pleasure books hold for me! I went in & found the table laden with books. I looked in & sniffed them all.'[56] As she 'sniffs' the books like her canine hero, Woolf's 'vast fertility of pleasure' encompasses her relish of the material smell of books, her sensual enjoyment of odorous words and style, and the tantalizing scent or foretaste of the literary treats in store. Her greater receptivity to smell is also obvious if one compares the memoirs that Woolf wrote before and after *Flush*; 'Sketch of the Past', written in 1939–40, is a far more sensory text and contains much more olfactory detail than, say, the earlier 'Reminiscences' of 1907–8. In 'Reminiscences' Woolf mentions how, when a child, 'great satisfaction was to be had from impersonal things. There were smells and flowers and dead leaves and chestnuts, by which you distinguished the seasons, and each had innumerable associations, and power to flood the brain in a second', but she does not name or describe any of the smells.[57] In 'Sketch of the Past' Woolf

[52] Woolf, *Flush*, pp. 74, 75.   [53] Woolf, 'Am I a Snob?', in *Moments of Being*, p. 65.

[54] *Diary of Virginia Woolf*, vol. 4: *1931–1935* (1982), 153 (29 April 1933); 144 (21 January 1933).

[55] Ibid., 4. 181; 2 October 1933. *Flush* was published on 5 October 1933.

[56] Ibid., 4. 173; 24 August 1933. My warm thanks to Michèle Barrett for kindly locating this reference.

[57] Woolf, 'Reminiscences', in *Moments of Being*, p. 2.

mentions a 'highly sensual' early memory of St Ives, where the Stephen family holidayed every summer:

> It still makes me feel warm; as if everything were ripe; humming, sunny; smelling so many smells at once; and all making a whole that even now makes me stop [...]. The buzz, the croon, the smell, all seemed to press voluptuously against some membrane; not to burst it; but to hum round one in such a complete rapture of pleasure that I stopped, smelt; looked.[58]

The humming synaesthetic 'rapture of pleasure' expressed here bears comparison with the odorous warmth and ripeness of Flush's Florentine 'rapture of smell', which he enjoys with 'his nose in the air vibrating with the aroma'.[59] Much later in her essay, and after the allusion to the reek of her mother's funeral flowers, Woolf includes other olfactory impressions of her London childhood scattered piecemeal through her text: her father, back from 'a Sunday tramp, smelling airy and muddy in his rough suit', the dining room at Hyde Park Gate that 'smelt slightly of wine, cigars, food', the 'different smells on different landings of that tall dark house', with one smelling of 'candle grease', her father's study that 'smelt perpetually of cigar smoke', the underground at Kensington High Street or Gloucester Road, 'a sulphur smelling steam clouded tunnel', and the street that 'rocked with horses and smelt of horses'.[60] From Cornwall she recalls 'the fishy smells in the steep little streets' of St Ives, the escallonia hedges surrounding Talland House, 'whose leaves, pressed, gave out a very sweet smell', the pilchard boats that 'made the beach always smell slightly of tar', a nearby wood that 'smelt of oak apples', and the smell of Halestown Bog. A final impression commemorates a coming to maturity, as she remembers the fixative used by her sister Vanessa as an art student to preserve her drawings, 'a spray of odd smelling mixture'.[61] None of these smells (apart from the sweet escallonia leaves) strikes one as a particularly perfumed smell, although notes of earth, tar, and tobacco might certainly find their way into a perfume.

Writing *Flush* may have helped Woolf come to terms with her sensory self, but her belated appreciation of smell and somewhat random olfactory memories are in stark contrast with the confident, unabashed responses of a near contemporary who needed no mediating animal presence to record his responses to the perfume, literature, and culture of the Victorian *fin de siècle*.

COMPTON MACKENZIE: THE WRITER AS AROMANCER

Woolf's olfactory memories bear comparison with a more sustained passage of olfactory reminiscence by the novelist Edward Montague Compton Mackenzie (1883–1972), born the year after her and also brought up in London. He recorded

---

[58] Woolf, 'Sketch of the Past', p. 80.   [59] Woolf, *Flush*, pp. 86, 87.
[60] Woolf, 'Sketch of the Past', pp. 119–20, 124, 125, 126, 127, 128.
[61] Ibid., pp. 133, 134, 135, 138, 139, 150.

his early sensory impressions in an essay titled 'The Vanished Colour and Scent of London':

> What I miss most of London's vanished colour are the window-boxes [...] of every house from Kensington to Mayfair [...]. And in the dusk the smell of the fresh-watered earth wafted along the stale streets, the very staleness of which had a half-rustic smell in those days when horses drew the traffic. It has vanished with the smell of the oranges and gas in Drury Lane Theatre, with the perfume of the lavender cried at the end of our summer holidays by girls in grey shawls and big hats, with the smell of the dust laid by leisurely watering-carts on a fine May morning, and with the scent of the musk [plant] that once upon a time made fragrant the dingiest room in the dingiest slum, but which now all the world over is scentless.[62]

Although Woolf and Mackenzie were close in age, their experience of *fin-de-siècle* London was quite different. While they both mention street smells relating to horses, it is unlikely Woolf had much knowledge of dingy rooms in dingy slums. Mackenzie's allusion to 'oranges and gas in Drury Lane Theatre' is also indicative, as he was born into a theatrical family, spending the first two and a half years of his life on tour with his father's company. After that, although his family was considerably less well-to-do than the Stephens, who lived in Kensington and had seven maids, his parents acquired a house in West Kensington, a much cheaper, less prestigious, but still respectable suburb. There, he and his siblings were brought up by a tyrannical nanny in a household with a maid and a colourful cook who entertained the young Mackenzie with bawdy stories. Once he went to school and escaped his nanny, he had more liberty to explore his immediate neighbourhood. As an adolescent, he possessed a freedom unknown to the young Virginia Stephen, roaming the city on his own or with friends to buy books and cigarettes, attend Anglo-Catholic services and meetings, hang out with bohemian types, and seek out attractions like the Earl's Court Exhibition where he observed prostitutes plying their trade.[63]

Like Woolf, Mackenzie was distantly related to John Addington Symonds, although in his case it was a blood connection.[64] However, his personal links with literary aestheticism and decadence were much stronger than hers. While Woolf regarded the whole Victorian period as one of stifling conservatism, he had a different perspective: 'My own view of the 'nineties may be coloured by the fact that they coincided with my 'teens, on which that sense of life awakening from the

---

[62] Compton Mackenzie, *Echoes* (London: Chatto & Windus, 1954), p. 80. The musk that Mackenzie mentions here is not animalic musk, but a popular Victorian flowering plant (*Mimulus moschatus*), which, by the twentieth century, had lost its fragrance. In 1931, the garden writer Eleanour Sinclair Rohde lamented that 'for many years past it has been impossible for anyone to find a [musk] plant with anything more than the faintest suspicion of scent'. See her *The Scented Garden*, p. 11. In the first volume of his compendious biography, *My Life and Times*, 10 vols (London: Chatto & Windus, 1963–71), Mackenzie laments 'the sudden fading of the scent from musk everywhere is a botanical mystery nobody has been able to explain' (Octave 1: *1883–1891*, p. 211).

[63] The standard biography, which draws extensively on Mackenzie's *My Life and Times*, is Andro Linklater, *Compton Mackenzie: A Life* (London: The Hogarth Press, 1992). See pp. 48–9 for a digest of Mackenzie's adolescence, covered more extensively in *My Life and Times*, Octave 2: *1891–1900* (1963).

[64] Mackenzie, *My Life and Times*, 1. 18–20. Mackenzie's great-grandmother, Elizabeth Symonds, was John Addington Symonds's great-aunt.

snores of latter-day Victorianism cast an intoxicating spell.'[65] A bohemian journalist friend, Philip Sergeant, introduced him to decadent literature and lent him Huysmans's *A Rebours*, he eagerly bought Swinburne for himself, and he thought Wilde's *Intentions* (1891) 'the *ne plus ultra* of sophisticated wit'.[66] As a sixteen-year-old he met and dined with Lord Alfred Douglas, who presented him with a volume of his poems and issues of the *Spirit Lamp*, the decadent Oxford magazine he had edited as an undergraduate. Shortly after that Mackenzie also associated with two other key members of Wilde's circle, Robbie Ross and Reggie Turner. (Much later, in 1930, he would become a member of the Edinburgh salon of Mark André Raffalovich and his partner, Father John Gray.[67])

Mackenzie had been twelve when Wilde was sentenced, and later observed that 'Newspapers were cheap, and no amount of care by father to keep them out of reach availed to preserve the innocence of the younger generation. We knew every detail of the case.'[68] He also declared that 'when the bad behaviour of schoolboys became a criminal offence for which they could be sent to gaol as they thought, then bad behaviour became a magnificent fashion. The result was that indulgence in it became a mark of intellectual pre-eminence.'[69] However, he was adamant that he was 'not at all physically interested in homosexuals', although he enjoyed their company and was 'fascinated' by their belief that they were superior to normal people.[70]

In later life Mackenzie was irritated by popular accounts such as William Gaunt's *The Aesthetic Adventure* (1945), which claimed a decisive break between the culture of the 1890s and the Edwardian period, summarizing this in wild caricature:

> The trial and conviction of Oscar Wilde had seemingly brought the aesthetic movement in Britain to a halt. It had caused a wholesale literary and social fumigation. An exaggerated robustness was one of the consequences. Poets, no longer velvet-collared, absinthe sipping, were now a hearty and virile race, tweed-clad, pipe-smoking, beer-drinking, Sussex-downs-tramping. They broke into rousing choruses, discarded subtlety for the sake of a cheery lilt, and proclaimed that Philistines could also sing.[71]

Alluding to Gaunt's book, Mackenzie firmly noted 'there was no desire in my generation to disown the "nineties"', citing a breakfast he organized for Max Beerbohm 'at my Oxford digs in 1903': 'To us he was the incarnation of that dazzling decade of the 'nineties'.[72] Elsewhere he stated: 'the 'nineties, far from being a sunset, were a sunrise, and to regard them as anything else is as absurd as to regard the French revolution as a political sunset and to find the political sunrise in Chartism'. And he reflected:

> Looking back at that period now, we should be able to discern in it a miniature of the state of the world to-day, and it is only if we regard the literature of the 'nineties as a

---

[65] Compton Mackenzie, *Literature in My Time* (London: Rich & Cowan, 1933), p. 67.
[66] Mackenzie, *My Life and Times*, 2. 257, 274.
[67] Ibid., Octave 6: *1923–1930* (1967), 222.   [68] Mackenzie, *Literature in My Time*, p. 80.
[69] Ibid., p. 82.   [70] Quoted in Linklater, *Compton Mackenzie: A Life*, p. 48.
[71] William Gaunt, *The Aesthetic Adventure* (London: Jonathan Cape, 1945; repr. Cardinal/Sphere Books, 1975), p. 176.
[72] Mackenzie, 'The Nineties', in *Echoes*, pp. 87, 86, 87.

forerunner of literature to-day and not as a coloured footnote to the literature of yesterday that we can hope to appreciate the significance of that exciting decade.[73]

Mackenzie relates that 'when I went up to Oxford in the autumn of 1901 [...] I was buying *Yellow Books* and *Savoys*, plays by Maeterlinck, symbolist poets like Mallarmé, and binding up a complete edition of Verlaine in a special shade of green buckram that took a week to meditate over'. And he adds:

> I had already started on Walter Pater; but I now bought his complete works, and read and re-read them until I could quote pages by heart of *Marius the Epicurean* and all the others. What had formerly attracted by its strangeness and richness and partial incomprehensibility now attracted as an ordered system of æsthetics which seemed to offer a key to an understanding of all the arts.[74]

Copies of Leonardo's *Mona Lisa* and Botticelli's *Primavera* also adorned the walls of his college room at Magdalen, with the Mona Lisa also gracing the rooms of the arty young men who featured in his early novels.

Compton Mackenzie would produce over forty novels, as well as books on historical topics, and diverse essays and numerous articles on books, music, and gardening. His œuvre also includes many books of memoirs detailing his extraordinary rich and varied life as an actor, Catholic convert, master-spy, early Scots nationalist, and serial purchaser of islands. Although now best known for the comic novels *The Monarch of the Glen* (1941) and *Whisky Galore* (1947), the last filmed as a 1949 Ealing comedy with a cameo appearance by Mackenzie himself, he was a protean writer whose many novels are written in a number of distinct styles.[75] Those he produced up to and including the early part of the First World War have a luxuriant, elaborate style partly influenced by literary decadence. It was this early work, principally the best-selling novels *Carnival* (1912) and *Sinister Street* (1913–14), that launched his reputation as one of the most promising young writers of the age, with Henry James, who admired *Sinister Street*, acknowledging him as 'very much the greatest talent of the new generation'.[76]

Both *Carnival* and *Sinister Street* show an acute awareness of olfactory sensations and impressions and also an unusual attention to actual perfumes worn at the times represented, a period spanning the 1880s through to 1911. That olfactory awareness, already glimpsed in Mackenzie's essay on the vanished scents of London, reflects his own sensitivity to the way in which smell and memory are connected, especially in early life. In his biography he vividly recalls how as an infant he detested the rubbery smell of the hood of his pram: 'people have questioned my ability to remember pram transport but the power of a smell to stimulate the memory is a commonplace, and it should be borne in mind that the child's response to smell and to colour is much stronger than it will be when he is grown up'.[77] A committed gardener who loved plants and flowers, he also remembers the pleasure

---

[73] Mackenzie, *Literature in My Time*, pp. 67, 70.   [74] Ibid., p. 129.
[75] A film remake of *Whisky Galore* (2016) has recently been released.
[76] Cited by Linklater, *Compton Mackenzie: A Life*, p. 130.
[77] Mackenzie, *My Life and Times*, 1. 92.

he took in floral scent from the age of two: 'the first daisies smelt marvellously sweet to that nose of childhood whose percipience and power of scent we who have lost it do not always realise'.[78] Jenny Pearl and Michael Fane, the lead protagonists in *Carnival* and *Sinister Street*, share Mackenzie's keen olfactory sensitivity and his tendency to associate key moments and strong emotion and desire with scent. As such, they are important examples of characters whose olfactory experience is an integral part of their identity and whose biographies can be charted through a series of scented or odorous events and encounters, confirming Mackenzie's power as an aromancer, a storyteller who uses scent to conjure up the past.

Sinister Street as Olfactory Autobiography

Although Mackenzie denied that *Sinister Street* was thinly veiled autobiography, it is evident that Michael Fane is his contemporary, sharing a sizeable number of impressions and experiences with his creator.[79] This means that even though *Carnival* was published first, the action of *Sinister Street* opens at an earlier date, and so, for reasons of historical continuity, I shall start with a discussion of *Sinister Street* before considering its predecessor.

Michael Fane and his younger sister Stella are the illegitimate children of the married Earl of Saxby, but grow up believing their father to be dead. They each meet Lord Saxby only once, Stella when she is too young to remember. Mrs Fane, the Earl's mistress, spends long periods of time away with her lover, so the children are brought up by a bullying nanny in West Kensington, with Michael, who worships his mother, always longing for her return. As a schoolboy he attends the nearby St James's School (based on Mackenzie's own public school, St Paul's) and later goes up to Oxford, where he is an undergraduate at St Mary's College, a replica of Mackenzie's Magdalen. Lord Saxby dies of enteric fever in the Transvaal during the Boer War just before Michael starts Oxford, but leaves his unofficial family well provided for. As an adolescent schoolboy with a knowledge and experience of London similar to Mackenzie's, Michael falls in love at the age of seventeen with Lily Haden, a graceful but flighty and superficial young woman from a 'vulgar' family whom he first meets in Kensington Gardens. Although they separate before he goes to Oxford, his obsession with her lasts into his adult life. After he finishes university, he hears rumours that she has been seen soliciting and he searches for her in vain in the slums of London. When they finally meet again, he persuades her to marry him against the advice of his friends and family, but she cheats on him shortly before the wedding and they part for good. *Sinister Street* is famous for its lyrical evocation of Michael's time at Oxford that opens volume 2;

---

[78] Ibid., 1. 101. Other cherished scents remembered from early childhood include the musk plant, honeysuckle, pink convolvulus, and lady's bedstraw. See ibid., 1. 211, 242.

[79] It is clear from the internal chronology of *Sinister Street* that Michael is born the same year as Mackenzie, i.e. 1883. In his Foreword to the 1949 edition of *Sinister Street*, reprinted in subsequent editions, Mackenzie wrote '*Sinister Street* is so exactly dated that it remains alive.' See Mackenzie, *Sinister Street* (Harmondsworth: Penguin, 1960), p. 12.

however, it is the first volume detailing his childhood and adolescence that is my focus here.[80]

Strikingly, Michael's formation as a character is marked by a series of olfactory milestones. Like Mackenzie, he has a warm appreciation for scent from an early age. As a small boy, scared when lost in Kensington Gardens, he finds that 'With waves of scent the beds of hyacinths impressed themselves upon his memory.'[81] At home he plants seeds in his window-box and, 'when the mignonette bloomed, he almost sniffed it away, so lovely was the perfume of it during the blue days of June'. The perfume of Michael's flowers is linked with the pleasure of his mother's return:

> But, best of all, when the pansies were still a-blowing and the Virginia stocks were fragrant, and when from his mother's window below he could see his nasturtium flowers, golden and red and even tortoiseshell against the light, his mother came home suddenly for a surprise [*sic*], and the house woke up.[82]

From the start Michael's adored mother and his time with her are associated with perfume. During one of her absences he imagines her close to him: 'His sleepy eyelids uncurled to the scented vision of his beautiful mother.'[83] When she is at home he relishes 'the firelit confidences, the scented good mornings and good nights'.[84] This ambience is due not only to the perfume she wears but also to the fact that the house, made especially comfortable for her arrival, is decked out with fragrant flowers during her visits:

> About a week before Christmas his mother came back, and Michael was happy. All the rooms that were only used when she was at home changed from bare beeswaxed deserts to places of perfect comfort, so rosy were the lampshades, so sweet was the smell of flowers and so soft and lovely were his mother's scattered belongings.[85]

When Stella begins to takes up more of their mother's time, we learn that 'Michael did not exactly feel jealous of his sister, but he had an emotion of disappointment that no longer could he be alone with his mother in a fragrant intimacy from which the perpetually sleeping Stella was excluded.'[86] Later, when Mrs Fane takes him in a hansom cab to visit his father, the Earl, he is proud be 'in his Eton suit and top-hat sitting beside his mother scented sweetly with delicious perfumes and very silky to the touch'.[87] The fragrant presence of Mrs Fane is in sharp contrast to the 'stuffy nursery' and Michael's bad-tempered, often tipsy nurse who mocks the sensitive boy's fears, and 'would blow cheesescented breath at him' when

---

[80] Compton Mackenzie, *Sinister Street*, 2 vols (London: Martin Secker, 1913–14). Mackenzie divides vol. 1 into two 'Books', 'The Prison House' and 'Classic Education', which detail, respectively, Michael's childhood and adolescence. Subsequent references are to vol. 1 (1913), specifying the book and chapter titles for readers using other editions.

[81] Ibid. (bk 1, ch. 4 'Bittersweet'), p. 24.

[82] Ibid. (bk 1, ch. 4 'Unending Childhood'), p. 69.

[83] Ibid. (bk 1, ch. 1 'The New World'), p. 9.

[84] Ibid. (bk 1, ch. 5 'The First Fairy Princess'), p. 70.

[85] Ibid. (bk 1, ch. 4 'Bittersweet'), p. 36.

[86] Ibid. (bk 1, ch. 4 'Unending Childhood'), p. 52.

[87] Ibid. (bk 1, ch. 8 'Siamese Stamps'), p. 125.

she staggers drunkenly to bed.[88] The happy perfumed interludes that Michael enjoys with his mother undoubtedly set up positive associations, allowing him to link smell and fragrance to other pleasurable pursuits and activities.

A good example of this is a subsequent olfactory episode that seems to determine Michael's encounter with religion. As a small child he attends a High Church service while staying at the seaside and is fascinated by the operations of the boy acolyte and thurifer:

> How he longed to be the little boy in scarlet who carried a sort of silver sauce-boat and helped to spoon what looked like brown sugar into the censer. Once during a procession, Michael stepped out into the aisle and tried to see what actually was carried in the boat. But the boat-boy put out his tongue very quickly, as he walked piously by, and glared at Michael very haughtily, being about the same size.[89]

The 'brown sugar' Michael sees is grains or beads of frankincense resin (also known as olibanum), the major ingredient in church incense, which may also contain other resins such as myrrh, benzoin, and styrax. On another seaside holiday during his teens a dawning interest in Anglo-Catholicism is part-triggered by the recollection of this incident: 'Michael felt a craving to go somewhere and smell that powerful odour again.'[90] The title of the chapter in which this craving occurs is 'Incense', the smell of which communicates Michael's newfound attraction. Although 'he had never before wanted to go to church', he searches out St Bartholomew's, an Anglo-Catholic establishment, where 'The air was pungent with the smell of wax and the stale perfume of incense on stone', and 'waiting for a spiritual experience, communed that night with the saints of God, as during the Magnificat his soul rose to divine glories on the fumes of the aspiring incense'.[91] He has a brief but intense flirtation with Anglo-Catholicism, turning his bedroom into an ornate religious shrine:

> Michael slept in an oriental atmosphere, because he had formed the habit of burning during his prayers cone-shaped pastilles in a saucer. The tenuous spiral of perfumed smoke carried up his emotional apostrophes through the prosaic ceiling of the old night-nursery past the stars, beyond the Thrones and Dominations and Seraphim to God.[92]

But incense provides continuity to his next passion, the literature and culture of decadence, when 'Incense was still burnt, not as once to induce prayers to ascend, but to stupefy Michael with scent and warmth into an imitation of a drug-taker's listless paradise.'[93]

Michael is set on his path towards decadence by Brother Aloysius, a disreputable monk he meets while on retreat, who corrupts him by telling him about his seedy past on the Seven Sisters Road in squalid North London. So vivid are his tales that

---

[88] Ibid. (bk 1, ch. 2 'Bittersweet'), p. 38; (ch. 3 'Fears and Fantasies'), p. 40.
[89] Ibid. (bk 1, ch. 2 'Bittersweet'), pp. 27–8.   [90] Ibid. (bk 2, ch. 5 'Incense'), p. 214.
[91] Ibid. (bk 2, ch. 5 'Incense'), pp. 214, 215, 217.   [92] Ibid. (bk 2, ch. 6 'Pax'), pp. 233–4.
[93] Ibid. (bk 2, ch. 9 'The Yellow Age'), p. 297.

the fifteen-year-old Michael imagines himself as the protagonist in a series of insalubrious scenes complete with olfactory effects:

> Michael came to know this street as one comes to know the street of a familiar dream. [...] On summer dusks he pushed his way through the fetid population that thronged it, smelling the odour of stale fruit exposed for sale [...] And not only was Michael cognizant of the sordid street's exterior. He heard the creak of bells by blistered doors, he tripped over mats in narrow gloomy passages and felt his way up stale rickety stairs. Michael knew many rooms in this street of dreams: but they were all much alike with their muslin and patchouli, their aspidistras and yellowing photographs.[94]

By this date—1898—the mention of patchouli, very much associated with prostitutes and perceived as 'cheap', makes clear the sexual nature of these borrowed fantasies.[95] Michael's re-imaginings of down-at heel, seamy London are vaguely reminiscent of the sexualized urban encounters popularized by decadent poets like Arthur Symons, Theodore Wratislaw, and Ernest Dowson. As another new friend, Arthur Wilmot, a minor decadent poet, reassures Michael in due course: "'Squalor is the Parthenope of the true Romantic. You'll find it in all the poets you love best—if not in their poetry, certainly in their lives. Even romantic critics are not without temptation. One day you shall read of Hazlitt and Sainte-Beuve.'"[96]

Wilmot, who nonetheless represents the more refined and elevated aspect of decadence, speaks in an amusing parody of Wildean discourse and tempts his would-be disciple with Wildean-scented beguilements. He meets Michael, whom he salutes as 'Hyacinthus', in a Hammersmith second-hand bookshop, befriends him, and insists on buying him 'some exquisite book full of strange perfumes and passionate courtly gestures', eventually selecting Pater's *Imaginary Portraits*.[97] Moreover, he invites him to dinner, and after the other guests have gone, plies him with cigarettes and liqueurs, and questions him about his interests:

> 'Crème-de-Menthe?'
> 'Yes, please', said Michael, who would have accepted anything in his present receptive condition.
> 'And what do you think of life?' enquired Mr. Wilmot, taking his place on a divan opposite Michael. 'Do you mind if I smoke my Jicky-scented hookah?' he added.
> 'Not at all', said Michael. 'These cigarettes are jolly ripping. I think life at school is frightfully dull—except, of course, when one goes out. Only I don't often.'[98]

[94] Ibid. (bk 2, ch. 7 'Cloven Hoofmarks'), p. 259.

[95] By 1898 patchouli was most definitely a 'cheap' smell. A brief article in the *Soapmaker and Perfumer* (15 September 1896) relates the tale of a lady who, complaining that 'everything cooked in her establishment had tasted of patchouli', traced that flavour to 'a cake of cheap scented soap in possession of the cook' (p. 94).

[96] Mackenzie, *Sinister Street* (bk 2, ch. 9 'The Yellow Age'), p. 287. In Greek mythology Parthenope is one of the Sirens, seductive singers who lure seafarers to shipwreck.

[97] Ibid. (bk 2, ch. 8 'Mirrors'), p. 278.

[98] Ibid. (bk 2, ch. 9 'The Yellow Age'), p. 283. Mackenzie was an enthusiastic smoker and a tobacco connoisseur since boyhood. In *Sublime Tobacco*, his history of smoking and the tobacco industry, he firmly denies that the olfactory sensitivity of smokers is impaired by their habit, declaring that various floral scents 'smell the sweeter to me because I am a smoker'. See *Sublime Tobacco* (London: Chatto & Windus, 1957), p. 331. Luca Turin points out that many perfumers are smokers and provides a scientific account of why smoking might help with olfaction. See Burr, *The Emperor of Scent*, p. 401.

In an exotic gesture Wilmot appears to have added Guerlain's Jicky to the tobacco he is smoking through his waterpipe. Jicky, created in 1889, with the lavender and coumarin (tonka bean) accord now regarded as typifying classic fougère fragrances, is one of the earliest perfumes to contain a synthetic, here vanillin or synthetic vanilla. It was considered a daring perfume because of its hefty dose of civet, and is just the sort of edgy avant-garde perfume that would have pleased a bohemian dandy like Wilmot. Smoking Jicky is not as bizarre as it at first sounds, as the coumarin, present in Jicky, has a tobacco facet and indeed has often been added as an aromatic flavouring to tobacco.[99]

Thus, appropriately, Jicky and the smell of exotic cigarettes accompany the lecture on decadent literature that Wilmot gives Michael when he confesses that his interest in the Church has gone stale. For this Wilmot prepares 'by lighting a very long cigarette wrapped in brittle fawn-coloured paper, whose spirals of smoke Michael followed upward to their ultimate evanescence, as if indeed they typified with their tenuous plumes and convolutions the intricate discourse that begot them'.[100] Too long to cite in full, the flavour or perfume of Wilmot's lecture is given in this brief sample, which echoes the tones of the elegant aesthetic young men who speak Wilde's dialogues, cigarette in hand:

> You must read your Latin authors well, for, since you must be decadent, it is better to decay from a good source. And neglect not the Middle Ages. You will glide most easily into them from the witches and robbers of Apuleius. You will read Boccaccio, whose tales are intaglios carved with exquisitely licentious and Lilliputian scenes. Neither forget Villon, whose light ladies seem ever to move elusively in close-cut gowns of cloth-of-gold and incredibly tall steeple-hats. But even with Villon the world becomes complicated, and you will soon reach the temperamental entanglements of the nineteenth century, for you may avoid the coarse, the beery and besotted obviousness of the Georgian age.[101]

Michael subsequently mingles with the homerotically inclined bohemian crowd that frequents Wilmot's 'perfumed house' in Edwardes Square, although he treats any sexual advances towards him with 'virginal disdain'.[102] However, his absorption of decadent influence can be detected by his wearing one of Wilmot's perfumes, an occurrence that mimics Dorian's casual application of Lord Henry's scent, except in this instance Michael is reproved by a priest-friend, Mr Viner, who acts as a more down-to-earth mentor:

> Michael's next encounter was with Mr. Viner, on the occasion of his producing in the priest's pipe-seasoned sitting-room a handkerchief inordinately perfumed with an Eastern scent lately discovered by Wilmot.

---

[99] Moreover, as mentioned in the Introduction and Chapter 6, perfumed cigarettes were available during the 1890s, and, later, in 1921, Habanita was first available as a scented liquid applied to cigarettes before they were smoked. In the original MS of *Sinister Street*, preserved in Walpole Collection at the King's School, Canterbury, Wilmot refers to 'my wallflower-scented Hookah' (2. 308).

[100] Mackenzie, *Sinister Street* (bk 2, ch. 9. 'The Yellow Age'), p. 285.

[101] Ibid. (bk 2, ch. 9. 'The Yellow Age'), p. 288.

[102] Ibid. (bk 2, ch. 9. 'The Yellow Age'), pp. 298, 299.

'Good heavens, Michael, what Piccadilly breezes are you wafting into my respectable and sacerdotal apartment?'

'I rather like scent', explained Michael lamely.

'Well, I don't, so, for goodness' sake don't bring any more of it in here. Pah! Phew! It's worse than a Lenten address at a fashionable church. Really, you know, these people you're in with now are not at all good for you, Michael.'[103]

Mr Viner's allusion to 'Piccadilly breezes' may refer to perfumes purchased by dandies in the fashionable shops of Piccadilly. At this time reputable perfumers like Floris and Penhaligon's had shops in nearby Jermyn Street.[104] Well-known perfumes with an 'Eastern' aura like Penhaligon's Hammam Bouquet (1872), inspired by the Turkish bath next door, or Grossmith's supposedly Japanese-inspired Hasu-No-Hana (1888), promoted as 'A realised dream of the Æsthete' (see Figure 8.1) and the same firm's Phūl-Nānā (1891), are probably too mainstream and well established to have attracted Wilmot, but show the burgeoning interest in 'oriental' fragrance.[105] However, Viner may also allude to the area's many prostitutes, the 'Piccadilly ladies' and possibly rent boys, who would wear strong perfumes to draw attention to themselves.[106] His reaction to Michael's handkerchief scent is typical of a more conservative Victorian man who adheres to traditional markers of manliness like pipe-smoking and shuns scent-wearing as effeminate. He immediately deciphers Michael's scent as an indicator of the company he keeps and deprecates its unwholesome influence.

Michael's dalliance with the more effete or camp ambience of decadence quickly wanes, although he will take his aesthetic and decadent literary and artistic tastes with him when he goes up to Oxford. However, his liking for scent continues, and my final illustration shows how another perfume reflects his transition from the hothouse fragrance of effeminate decadence to heterosexuality, as scent and sentiment combine in commemorating his first real crush.

While on holiday at Bournemouth with his mother the now seventeen-year-old Michael takes a fancy to an older pretty girl, Kathleen McDonnell, who is staying at the same hotel. Disconcerted to find out she is secretly engaged, he nonetheless meets her fiancé and supports the couple in their decision to marry while enjoying romantic fantasies of his own self-sacrifice. After the newly-weds leave, he enters the room recently occupied by his inamorata: 'He looked round hastily for one souvenir of Kathleen, and perceived still moist from her last quick

---

[103] Ibid. (bk 2, ch. 9. 'The Yellow Age'), p. 291.

[104] Floris still retains its Jermyn Street shop although Penhaligon's was destroyed in the Blitz in 1941, along with the Hammam next door. Penhaligon's shop nearest to its original site is now in the Burlington Arcade.

[105] The slogan for Hasu-No-Hana is taken from a back section advertisement in *The Lady* (12 November 1891), xvi.

[106] See Robert Machray, *The Night Side of London* (Philadelphia, PA: J. Lippincott Co., 1902). On the opening page of his book, in a chapter on Piccadilly which mainly deals with its streetwalkers, Machray writes, regarding the name 'Piccadilly', 'the famous Circus and street by any other name might have had just as special an aroma, as exotic a bouquet as they undoubtedly possess (particularly at certain hours), but somehow the foreign-sounding tag seems to have an appropriateness of its own' (p. 1). However, he also mentions the 'faint fragrance that perfumes the wandering air' exuded by aristocratic ladies exiting the theatre (p. 11).

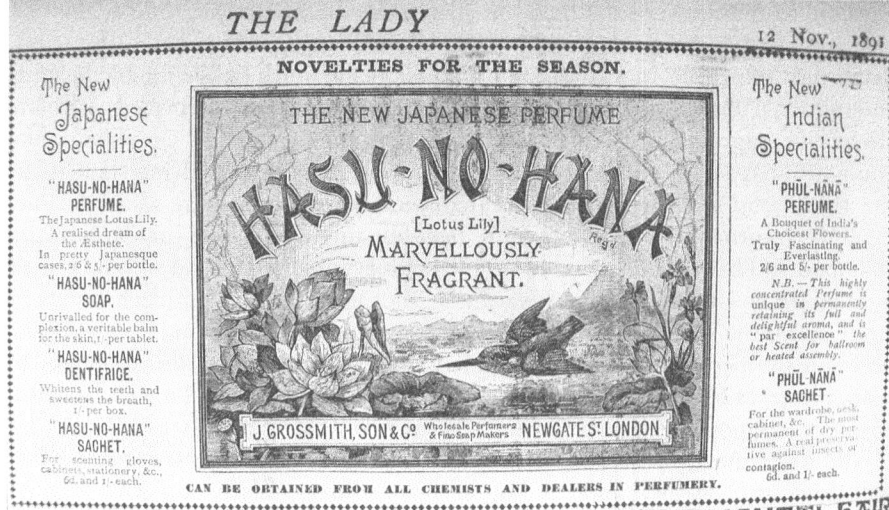

Figure 8.1 Advertisement for Grossmith's Hasu-No-Hana (1888) and Phūl-Nānā (1891) in *The Lady* (12 November 1891), p. xvi. (Photo: Daichi Ishikawa, courtesy of the London Library)

ablution a piece of soap. He seized it quickly and surrendered the room to the destructive personality of the housemaid.'[107] When his mother teasingly asks him if Kathleen left him a keepsake, 'he blushed, thinking of the soap that was even now enshrined in a drawer and scenting his handkerchiefs and ties. He wondered if Alan [his best friend] would understand the imperishable effluence from that slim cenotaph of soap.'[108]

Mackenzie's narrator gently mocks Michael's calf-love, showing how, in spite of his boasts to his friends of undying ardour, Kathleen's image fades over the next few months. In the end, when he finds the maid has neglected 'to put a fresh cake of soap in the dish', he 'callously' decides to use 'Kathleen's commemorative tablet':

> [A]s he slowly washed his hands, he washed from his mind the few insignificant out-lines of Kathleen that were printed there. The soap was Trèfle Incarnat, and somewhat cynically Michael relished the savour of it, and even made up his mind to buy a full fat cake when this one should be finished. Kathleen, however, even in the fragrant moment of her annihilation, had her revenge, for Michael experienced a return of the old restlessness and discontent.[109]

Michael washes his hands of Kathleen, the memory associated with her scented soap erased by his pleasure in the scent alone, with the clean soapy smell also an

---

[107] Mackenzie, *Sinister Street* (bk 2, ch. 13 'Sentiment'), p. 377.

[108] Ibid. (bk 2, ch. 13 'Sentiment'), p. 377. In *My Life and Times*, Mackenzie admits that the soap incident is based on his own crush as a seventeen year old, though his Kitty 'was infinitely more attractive than the Kathleen McDonnell of *Sinister Street* and shared nothing with her except Irish nationality'. See Octave 3: *1900–1907* (1964), p. 19.

[109] Mackenzie, *Sinister Street* (bk 2, ch. 14 'Arabesque'), pp. 381–2.

antidote to the heavier vapours of decadence. Le Trèfle Incarnat, one of the first synthetic perfumes, was launched in 1897 by the French perfumer L. T. Piver and, being very affordable, quickly became popular, being much publicized by the Paris International Exhibition of 1900.[110] It contains the newly discovered synthetic chemical compound amyl salicylate that imitates the smell of red clover, and, like coumarin, has a clean, fresh, green, hay-like or cut-grass aroma. As was standard at the time, soap and face powder scented with the perfume were also available. Le Trèfle Incarnat is now long discontinued, but amyl salicylate is present in many shampoo and bath products as well as men's fougère fragrances and so is identified by modern consumers as a clean smell.[111] Michael's crush on Kathleen occurs in April 1900, the same month that the Paris Exhibition started, and therefore just precedes the perfume's boom in popularity, ensuring that his 'slim cenotaph of soap' preserves for the moment its cachet.[112] However, as we will see in *Carnival*, the increased popularity of Le Trèfle Incarnat will substantially alter its status.

The restlessness Michael experiences after the ghost of his romance disappears will drive him on to a more profound and enduring infatuation with another woman, but one that still fails to afford him any true satisfaction. The second volume of *Sinister Street* is noticeably less fragrant than its predecessor, and many of its olfactory references evoke the stale unpleasant odours of the streets and houses which Michael will visit during his long search for the elusive Lily Haden who, in spite of a flowery name that promises perfume, is never mentioned as possessing a scent of her own.[113] However, rather than follow Michael's pursuit of his vapid lover, we turn to the earlier *Carnival*, and a heroine who, even more than Michael, experiences her life through strong and persuasive olfactory cues and markers.

CARNIVAL: A LIFE IN SCENT

In *Carnival* Mackenzie explores a world he knew well—this being the world of the London 'ballet girl' in an era when ballet frequently meant more of a revue-type legshow. While waiting for the publication of his first novel *The Passionate Elopement* (1911), Mackenzie had been employed by the theatrical producer Harry Pélissier to write lyrics for a new show for his cabaret revue troupe, the Follies, and to rehearse the chorus girls. When the show moved to the larger Alhambra Theatre in Leicester Square, known for its ballet performances, Mackenzie met a dancer called Chrissie Maude who would inspire him to create Jenny Pearl, the vivacious, witty, sharp-tongued heroine of *Carnival*. Jenny's scathing put-downs of would-be

[110] As is the case with many older perfumes, the date of creation for Le Trèfle Incarnat is not precise and is given in different sources as 1896, 1897, and 1898.

[111] The sample of Le Trèfle Incarnat provided at the Osmothèque, the Perfume Museum at Versailles, has a delightfully fresh, soapy, vibrant smell.

[112] The Paris Exhibition ran from 15 April to 12 November 1900.

[113] The one time Michael associates Lily with fragrance is by analogy: 'To find Lily like this after a tantalizing fortnight was like being in a room heavily perfumed with flowers.' It is a moment that recalls the fragrant homecomings of his mother after her long absences. See Mackenzie, *Sinister Street*, vol. 2 (bk 4, ch. 6 'Tinderbox Lane'), p. 1011.

male suitors—'Who cares?' and 'You must be potty'—became the fashionable catchphrases of the day.[114]

Independent, spirited, Jenny Pearl, originally Jenny Raeburn, born into a modest but respectable working-class home in Islington, has ambitions to be a dancer. Trained as a 'ballet girl', she is engaged at the Orient Palace of Varieties where she meets Maurice Avery, a slightly older Oxford graduate and self-confessed dilettante. They become a couple, fall in love, and enjoy socializing with their circle of friends, but tensions surface when Jenny is unwilling to enter a sexual relationship with Maurice. After she refuses to join him on a trip to Spain, he ends their romance. She becomes increasingly depressed and has a one-night stand with a man who means nothing to her. Following the death of her mother, she accepts a marriage proposal from Zachary Trewhella, a Cornish farmer visiting London, agreeing to the marriage only because she is disenchanted with the stage and sees no other real prospects for herself and her younger disabled sister, May. After the wedding, Trewhella whisks Jenny and May away to his farm in Cornwall. Although the change is a culture shock, Jenny gradually learns to appreciate her surroundings and becomes a doting mother, but finds her husband increasingly repellent. Maddened by jealousy when an old friend of Maurice's pays Jenny an innocent call, Trewhella has her spied on by one of his retainers. Four years after leaving her, Maurice himself turns up and encounters Jenny and May walking on the beach. She agrees to meet him alone to hear him out, but on doing so, responds to his penitent account of his actions with an impassioned speech of dismissal. She has just bade him goodbye when Trewhella, who has been tracking the pair, murders her by shooting her through the throat.

Throughout *Carnival* Jenny's memories, desires, and aspirations are expressed through smell, perfume, and fragrance, which are also strongly redolent of class and social status. Jenny is the daughter of a good-natured but dull and unsuccessful joiner who 'smelt of sawdust and furniture polish' and a more vital and intelligent mother who is conscious of having married beneath her.[115] Early on Jenny becomes aware of her mother's marital disappointment as well as temptation in the form of Mr Timpany, a prosperous gentleman caller whose visits are announced by 'the smell of a good cigar'. The narrator comments that Jenny 'did not know it was a good cigar, but the perfume hung about the dark hall of Number Seventeen with a strange richness never associated in her mind with the smell of her father's smoke'.[116] She overhears Mr Timpany urging her mother to go away him and bring Jenny with them, but Mrs Raeburn turns him down. After he is gone, Jenny firmly tells her mother she would much prefer Mr Timpany to occupy her father's place, adding as corroborating evidence 'he smelt nice'.[117]

---

[114] The married Mackenzie had a brief relationship with Chrissie Maude—full name Christine Maude Humphreys (1886–1971). In 1914 she married his friend, John Mavrogordato, a writer and academic, and later the Bywater and Sotheby Professor of Byzantine and Modern Greek at Oxford. Mavrogordato was the dedicatee of volume 2 of *Sinister Street*.

[115] Mackenzie, *Carnival* (London: Martin Secker, 1912). I use the text of the first edition but provide chapter titles in brackets for readers using other editions. See *Carnival* (ch. 1 'Birth of Columbine'), p. 5.

[116] Ibid. (ch. 5 'Pretty Apples in Eden'), p. 47.

[117] Ibid. (ch. 5 'Pretty Apples in Eden'), p. 53.

Pleasant odours pervade Jenny's own ambitions. As a little girl she shows a flair for dancing. Mr Vergoe, a lodger in her family home, soon recognizes her talent, introducing the six-year-old Jenny to his granddaughter, a 'second-line girl in the Corps de Ballet of the Oriental Palace of Varieties', who takes an interest in her and teaches her to dance:

> Miss Lilli Vergoe, all chiffon and ostrich plumes, took her upon a *peau de soie* lap, and clasped her to a Frangipani breast. Jenny thought she had never experienced any sensation half so delicious. Amid the heavy glooms and fusty smells of the old house in Hagworth Street, Miss Lilli Vergoe blossomed like an exotic flower, or rather, in Jenny's own simile, like lather. [...] She woke in Jenny a cooing affection such as had never been by her bestowed upon a living soul.[118]

Up to this point Jenny may only have experienced perfume through scented toilet soap—hence her simile of 'lather'. Scented soap, though still considered a luxury product, would be more affordable than bottled perfume as an aspirational purchase for respectable working- or lower-middle-class households, though would be probably tucked into drawers to fragrance clothing rather than used to wash with. Frangipani was certainly one of many perfumes used to scent soap, although Lilli Vergoe's Frangipani is most likely out of a bottle or possibly from a sachet used to fragrance clothes.[119]

A heady mix 'of every known spice', ground orris-root, musk, and civet, and named after the nobleman who first concocted it, frangipani supposedly smells like the fragrance of the flowers of the tropical and sub-tropical plumeria (*Plumeria alba*), itself later known as 'frangipani'.[120] A very popular exotic scent in the *fin de siècle*—witness the sillage left by Lord Henry Wotton's wife in *The Picture of Dorian Gray* (1891)—frangipani could also be burnt as incense of the kind supplied by Piesse and Lubin and used by Michael Field.[121] However, the growing popularity of perfumes often suggests a fall in prestige or status, and other evidence implies that frangipani had already begun to attract more downmarket associations by 1893, approximately the year that Jenny meets Lilli Vergoe.[122] Although stronger perfumes became more fashionable towards the end of the nineteenth century, those wanting to advertise their presence or send out a message of availability often

---

[118] Ibid. (ch. 4 'The Ancient Mischief'), p. 43.

[119] A recipe for 'Frangipanne Soap' ('Frangipanni' in subsequent editions) can be found in Piesse's *Art of Perfumery* (1855), p. 172. Piesse and Lubin's 1861 catalogue lists 'Frangipanni Scented Soap' available at 1s., 1s. 6d., and 2s. 6d., and a 'Frangipanni Sachet' at 1s. 6d. (pp. 20, 22). The same catalogue also lists 'Frangipanni Bouquet' perfume available in bottles, starting at 2s. 6d. to 40s.

[120] Piesse, *Art of Perfumery* (1855), p. 13. For more on the background to frangipani, see Kettler's article, 'Making the Synthetic Epic', pp. 13, which points out that the discovery of the plant by Charles Plumier in the 1690s occurs after the creation of the perfume, and that the plant was known as 'frangipani' because it was thought to smell like the perfume. See also Piesse, *Art of Perfumery*, 3rd edn (1862), p. 83.

[121] *DG*, p. 42. As mentioned in Chapter 7, Wilde changed the 'patchouli' of the 1890 *Lippincott's Magazine* version, to 'frangipani' in his 1891 novel, presumably because of patchouli's connection with prostitutes. However, by 1893, frangipani also seems to have acquired some dubious associations.

[122] Harrods catalogue for 1895 lists several well-known brands of Frangipani perfume, made respectively by Bertrand Frères, Atkinson's, The Royal Perfumery, Hendrie's, and Piesse and Lubin. See Adburgham, *Victorian Shopping: A Facsimile of the Harrod's Stores 1895 Issue of the Price List*, pp. 1108–9.

adopted more obtrusive scents. Theodore Wratislaw's poem 'Frangipani', from his 1893 collection *Caprices*, associates the perfume with demi-mondaines or prostitutes who use it as an erotic body scent:

> Thou leavest on the languid skin
> Outworn with nights of amorous toil,
> A spice of health that blossoms in
> Hot lands that tropic fragrance win
> From marvellous flowers and scented oil.[123]

There is no indication that Lilli is free with her sexual favours, and Mackenzie's narrator is keen to scotch the rumour that dancers are loose women, referring acerbically to 'the vulgar and baseless tradition of frailty still sedulously propagated'.[124] However, Lilli's powerful perfume aura, so attractive to Jenny, is compatible with the less than totally respectable reputation of the stage, and also hints at the downward movement of frangipani, something we shall see again when Jenny becomes a young adult.

Unsurprisingly then, Jenny identifies perfume with the world of the stage and her ambition to become a dancer: 'She must go on the stage. She must dance for all the world to gaze at her. She would. She would. She must. What a world it was, this wonderful world of the stage—an existence of colour and scent and movement and admiration.'[125] By association perfume also becomes evocative of dancers' dressing rooms and female camaraderie. After her dance training is complete, Jenny goes off to her first stage role in Glasgow by train with a group of other girls: 'She was glad to be in the powdered, scented, untidy compartment in warmth and light.'[126] At home, her toilet-table, 'inhabited by a collection of articles that presented the most sudden and amazing contrasts', shows her aspirations: 'Next to a comb that might easily have been rescued from a dustbin was a brush backed with silver repoussé. Beside seven broken pairs of nail-scissors was a scent-bottle with golden stopper.'[127] Tiring of short-term appointments at the more respectable Covent Garden and Drury Lane, she secures a permanent position at the Orient Palace of Varieties, Piccadilly (based on the Alhambra), which Mackenzie's narrator describes with teasing grandiloquence: 'the Orient was alluring, blazed upon the vision like an enchanted cave, or offered to the London wanderer a fancy of the scents and glossy fruits and warblers of the garden where Camaralzaman lost Badoura'.[128]

However, as becomes clear, some of those wanderers are attracted by something other than the performances, as the Orient's famous Promenade, like that of the Alhambra, is a key pick-up spot for well-dressed prostitutes:

> Under the stars they achieve a pictorial romance; but on the carpet of the Promenade, they are hard and heartless and vile. Their eyes are coins; their hands are purses.

---

[123] Wratislaw, 'Frangipani', p. 35.
[124] Mackenzie, *Carnival* (ch. 11 'The Orient Palace of Varieties'), p. 140.
[125] Ibid. (ch. 7 'Ambition Wakes'), p. 75.   [126] Ibid. (ch. 9 'Life, Art and Love'), p. 101.
[127] Ibid. (ch. 9 'Life, Art and Love'), p. 114.
[128] Ibid. (ch. 11 'The Orient Palace of Varieties'), p. 135.

At their heels patter old men like unhealthy lap-dogs; beefy provincials stare at them, their foreheads glistening. Above all the Frangipani and Patchouli and Opoponax and Trèfle Incarnat steals the rank odour of goats.[129]

The soliciting women advertise themselves with strong perfumes. Here frangipani definitely seems to have a more dubious reputation, while, as mentioned, patchouli is another heavy perfume that well before this date had lost its cachet and was associated with prostitutes and light women. Opoponax, also known as sweet myrrh, and like myrrh derived from trees and shrubs of the *Commiphora* genus, is a gum resin with a warm, honey-sweet balsamic odour used in incense and perfumery. It was an enormously popular late Victorian perfume, with Septimus Piesse remarking in 1879, 'No perfume ever made, eau de Cologne excepted, has ever had a larger sale.'[130] Because of its popularity, it too became debased. Theodore Wratislaw's 'Opoponax' specifically makes a link between this scent and seductive women, most likely prostitutes, met at balls or in music-halls:

> Blonde perfume of the painted girl!
> You where the heated dancers whirl
> In mazes of the midnight ball
> Or in the glittering music-hall,
> Uplift your rich and cloying scent
> Until the banal blandishment
> Of whispers and inviting eyes
> Seems tempting even to the wise.[131]

We last encountered Le Trèfle Incarnat in *Sinister Street* where in 1900 it had been on the market for only a few years. By my calculation, the year Jenny joins the Orient must be approximately 1905, so Le Trèfle Incarnat is about eight years old, and at a point when it had lost its early exclusivity and had gathered mass-market appeal.[132] The perfume blogger Chantal-Hélène Wagner identifies Le Trèfle Incarnat as a 'widely accessible' perfume that came 'to be associated with easy virtue and after a while lost all luster by being derogatorily qualified as "common"'.[133]

---

[129] Ibid. (ch. 11 'The Orient Palace of Varieties'), p. 137. The historian Jerry White explains that from 1880s onwards 'the music-hall promenades were the premier showcase of well-dressed prostitutes in London'. See his *London in the Nineteenth Century* (London: Jonathan Cape, 2007), p. 305. In 1913, one commentator noted that 'the *demi-mondaines* who nightly frequent the back of the dress-circle of certain houses of entertainment' compared very favourably in dress, toilet, and manners with the 'tawdry' creatures of 'thirty years ago'. See 'A Journalist', *Bohemian Days in Fleet Street* (London: John Long, 1913), p. 162.

[130] Piesse, *Art of Perfumery*, 4th edn (1879), p. 169.

[131] Wratislaw, 'Opoponax', in *Caprices*, p. 36.

[132] Jenny is about seventeen and a half when she joins the Orient and nineteen when she meets her boyfriend, Maurice Avery, who also features as one of Michael Fane's fellow students in *Sinister Street*. Assuming Maurice and Michael are born, like Mackenzie, in 1883, then Maurice meets Jenny roughly around 1907. In his Foreword to the 1951 edition of *Carnival*, reprinted in subsequent editions, Mackenzie reports that the original germ of inspiration for the story took place in 1907. See *Carnival* (London: Mayflower Books/Granada Publishing, 1972), p. 7.

[133] Chantal-Hélène Wagner, 'The Popularity of Clover Aroma and L. T. Piver Trèfle Incarnat in Literature and Perfume since the 19th Century: Part 1'. See http://www.mimifroufrou.com/scentedsalamander/2010/03/the_popularity_of_clover_aroma.html. Wagner does not mention Mackenzie's novel.

Although her references suggest a later date for this fall from grace, Mackenzie implies the perfume's reputation had degraded very quickly. The more or less debased perfumes named in this passage, further compromised by the real or imagined rank goat-like smell of licentious male clients, will contrast with the more romantic descriptions of scent used to communicate Jenny's feelings.

When Jenny is a teenager at dancing school, we learn that 'There was no sentiment about her, and an attempted kiss would have provoked spitfire rage. There was something of Atalanta about her, and in Hellas Artemis would have claimed her, running by the thyme-scented borders of Calydon.'[134] Once she becomes a dancer, she is happy to receive gifts and treats from men, but remains contemptuous of their attempts to woo or ensnare her. She now offers token kisses to her suitors, but despises male 'selfishness and grossness', and is wary of losing her self-respect and independence through pregnancy or a shotgun marriage.[135] However, at nineteen she decides that 'she wanted to fall in love'. The antiseptic, even anti-erotic, smell of thyme that the narrator jokily associated with the virginal mythic huntress Atalanta and Jenny's fierce maidenhood is now replaced by the heady fragrance of lilac: 'Desire, winged with the scent of lilac blossom, stole in through the sapphire window. Desire flooded her soul with ineffable aspirations.'[136]

Shortly after this, during one of her performances, she sees in the audience the man who will become her first and only real love. His admiration is like the 'almost visible' scent of the tributary bouquets whose perfume accompanies her dawning romantic interest:

> The curtain fell, rising again at once to let the bouquets fall softly round the silver shoes of the Ballerinas. The odour of stephanotis, mingled with the sharper perfume of carnations, seemed almost visible. The emotion of the audience struck the emotion of the dancers and kindled a triumph. The man in the stalls leaned forward, and the intensity of his gaze was to Jenny as real an offering as a bouquet.[137]

She soon meets her admirer, Maurice Avery, a comfortably off, twenty-four-year-old Oxford graduate, living in a shared flat in Westminster, writing occasional critical reviews, and trying his hand at sculpture and drawing. They embark on a love affair and enjoy a succession of lively social events that bring together their respective London circles—her fellow dancers and his old college friends. However, class differences begin to tell when, scared of disillusion and disappointment, Jenny is reluctant to sleep with or live with Maurice, who is painfully aware of the social awkwardness involved in making her his wife. Tension enters the relationship around Jenny's twentieth birthday in October 1907, but there is a lull when Maurice inherits a small legacy from an aunt, and spends the lot on taking their group of friends to a Covent Garden costume ball.

With tickets at a guinea apiece, the ball, which takes place in January 1908, is more obviously more glamorous and exclusive than a regular dance-hall event, yet, as Mackenzie's narrator makes apparent, it is also different from a society ball in

---

[134] Mackenzie, *Carnival* (ch. 8 'Ambition Looks in the Glass'), p. 86.
[135] Ibid. (ch. 9 'Life, Art and Love'), p. 118.   [136] Ibid. (ch. 12 'Growing Old'), p. 149.
[137] Ibid. (ch. 13 'The Ballet of Cupid'), p. 160.

that there is 'neither host nor hostess', and no carefully vetted invitation list, no 'chaperons', debutantes, 'old men', or parents.[138] The youthful participants are there simply to enjoy themselves and pursue their romances.[139] At one point when Jenny and Maurice are talking between waltzes, the next dance starts up to the Eton Boating Song, a tune Maurice immediately recognizes, and the couple resume dancing amid wafts of perfume that both reflect and yet unify the ball's socially mixed clientele. Through its transformative exoticism the scent also seems to mask the class element in this public school anthem, turning it into a more romantic melody that suits the couple's mood:

> 'Hark! They're playing the Eton Boating Song. Come along. We mustn't miss a bar of it.'
> In the scent of Frangipani and Jicky and Phulnana the familiar tune became queerly exotic. The melody, charged with regret for summer elms and the sounds of playing-fields, full of the vanished laughter of boyhood, held now the heart of romantic passion. It spoke of regret for the present rather than the past and, as it reveled in the lapse of moments, gave expression to the dazzling swiftness of such a night in a complaint for flying glances, sighs and happy words lost in their very utterance.[140]

Although the scents mentioned here include the somewhat dubious Frangipani—perhaps worn by some of the ballet girls—the other two fragrances have more cachet and indeed are still available today as prestige perfumes. Guerlain's Jicky, already encountered in Wilmot's hookah in *Sinister Street*, was originally a unisex fragrance, but because of the sexual provocation of its powerful civet, was not widely worn by women till after 1912. In the context of this scene, it is likely to be worn by the bohemian dandies attending the ball.[141]

Phūl-Nānā, meaning 'lovely flower' in Hindi, was created in 1891 by the reputable British perfume house J. Grossmith & Son, and was resourcefully marketed as an Indian perfume, purporting to be 'distilled from the choicest blossoms of the exotic east'.[142] While there is nothing specifically Indian about the fragrance, it contains bergamot, orange, neroli, geranium, tuberose, ylang ylang, patchouli, benzoin, cedar, sandalwood, opoponax, tonka bean, and vanilla, and helped set the trend for the oriental fragrances that would flourish in the twentieth century till

---

[138] As Mackenzie indicates, the Orient ballet girls can attend Covent Garden balls for free, presumably to help attract male customers, but Maurice needs money to pay for himself and his friends, as well as costumes, supper, and taxis. See *Carnival* (ch. 11 'The Orient Palace of Varieties'), pp. 141–2; (ch. 20 'Fête Galante'), p. 225. In 1902 Machray writes about Covent Garden balls in *The Night Side of London* (pp. 135–41), where he suggests that, while the male guests come from a variety of middle- and lower-middle-class backgrounds, 'the ladies for the most part belong to the Half-World' (p. 146), although this is not the impression given by *Carnival*'s ball of 1908.

[139] Mackenzie, *Carnival* (ch. 20 'Fête Galante'), p. 228.

[140] Ibid. (ch. 20 'Fête Galante'), p. 229. The words of the Eton Boating Song are by William Johnson Cory, the great-uncle of Mackenzie's wife, Faith. The tune is by Cory's pupil, Algernon Drummond.

[141] Stamelman, *Perfume*, p. 185. In the (incomplete) 1911 holograph manuscript of *Carnival* (Special Collections, Senate House Library, University of London) SLV/63, fol. 172, Mackenzie originally included Jicky in the list of perfumes worn by the prostitutes at the Orient Palace (*Carnival*, p. 137), but then replaced it with Opoponax, presumably because Jicky was a scent worn mainly by men and was more exclusive than the other scents listed.

[142] Phūl-Nānā, illustrated advertisement, *The Graphic* (Summer number, June 1896), 2.

today. It was also available as a powder, soap, and sachet.[143] An early advertisement in *The Lady* for November 1891 (see Figure 8.1) declares '*This highly concentrated Perfume is* unique *in permanently retaining its full and delightful aroma, and is* "par excellence" *the best Scent for ballroom or heated assembly*', something that would certainly recommend its use to the female dancers at the Covent Garden ball. A similarly worded advert in the *Graphic* for June 1896, featuring a female Indian dancer, pressed the message home, as well as assuring readers that 'The very pleasant thing about **Phūl-Nānā** is that, *though powerful, it is not heavy*.'[144] The perfume also secured an apparent royal seal of approval: a Grossmith advertising card depicts 'The Presentation of the Phūl-Nānā Perfume to H.R.H. the Princess of Wales at the "Orient" Exhibition, 1895.'[145] Phūl-Nānā became a top-selling perfume and, although well out of the range of a working-class woman, was not overly expensive—the Army and Navy Stores catalogue for 1907 lists two sizes of bottle at two shillings and three shillings and sixpence respectively, prices that are cheaper than when it was launched in 1891, suggesting that increased production may have cut costs.[146] Even though some of the female dancers in *Carnival* might not be considered respectable, wearing Phūl-Nānā represents an aspiration to be perceived as 'lady-like'. Indeed, a contemporary advertisement in *The Lady* for December 1907, declares Phūl-Nānā as 'Unrivalled as Perfume for Ladies of Taste', and 'Fragrant, Powerful & Entrancing'.[147]

The exotic perfumed idyll of the ball with its temporary suspension of class differences is followed by a quarrel between Jenny and Maurice about their relationship, 'the wet and dreary morning [...] destroying romantic enchantments and accentuating the plain and ugly facts'.[148] When Maurice, sent to Spain on a family matter, writes to Jenny asking her to come out and stay with him, she is tempted but, as she reads his letter on a tram, 'over her senses stole the odour of a cigar that carried her mind racing back to the past'. Triggered by smell, a tender memory of her mother's long-ago renunciation touches her emotions and influences her decision.[149] Having already quarrelled with her family, who have accused her of immoral behaviour, and not wishing to cause a further breach with her mother, she refuses Maurice's request though later privately resolves to become his lover on his return.

---

[143] Phūl-Nānā was available from 1891 to the mid-1970s, though latterly in a debased form. It is now restored to a near approximation of its original identity, being one of three classic perfumes recreated from the original formulae when Grossmith was relaunched by Simon Brooke, great-great-grandson of the founder, with his wife, Amanda Brooke, in November 2009. See Bailey et al., eds., *British Perfumery: A Fragrant History*, p. 167, and *Grossmith London, Overview* (Winter 2014) PDF booklet, kindly supplied by Amanda Brooke of Grossmith.

[144] Phūl-Nānā, illustrated advertisement, *The Graphic* (Summer number, June 1896), 2.

[145] Illustrated advertising card (*c*.1896), kindly supplied as PDF image by Amanda Brooke of Grossmith. This card also states 'Latest Award Gold Medal, Amsterdam, 1895'.

[146] See Adburgham, *Yesterday's Shopping: The Army & Navy Stores Catalogue 1907*, p. 529. The 1891 prices for Phūl-Nānā—two shillings and sixpence and five shillings—make it unattainable for those on low incomes. A laundress, like Symons's Lucy Newcome, might be paid only eight shillings a week. See 'Pages from the Life of Lucy Newcome' (1896), in Symons, *Spiritual Adventures*, p. 65.

[147] Advertisement for Phūl-Nānā, *The Lady* (5 December 1907), 1069.

[148] Mackenzie, *Carnival* (ch. 20 'Fête Galante'), p. 238.

[149] Ibid. (ch. 23 'Two Letters'), p. 265.

But Maurice, angry at her refusal, decides not to return to England. Dispirited by his abandonment of her and the break-up of her family home after her mother's death, Jenny, now twenty-two, accepts a marriage proposal from Zachary Trewhella, a Cornish farmer. Possessed of a primitive 'force' and described 'a little more than fox, a little less than wolf', Trewhella is besotted with her although he knows she has no feelings for him.[150] Jenny's unease with her fiancé is foreshadowed by olfactory ambivalence. Before he proposes, May asks if Jenny likes him and she replies, "'Yes, all right. Only his clothes smell funny. Lavingder or something. I suppose they've been put away for donkey's years."'[151] Her discomfort with her suitor's smell and the ominous feeling that he is too old for her is reinforced by association when she sorts her mother's 'relics' and packs them away in a 'big trunk', also referred to as 'a lavendered tomb'.[152]

In Cornwall the smells of the city and manufactured perfume are replaced by natural scents. As Trewhella drives Jenny and her sister to the farm in the evening twilight, May ingenuously makes comparisons with the things more familiar to her:

'It smells like the inside of a flower-shop, doesn't it?' said May. 'You know, sort of bathroom smell. It must be glorious in the daytime.'

'Yes, 'tis grand in summer time, sure enough', Trewhella agreed.[153]

Mackenzie resists the lure of an oversimplified contest between urban or manufactured smells and rural scents, understanding that pleasure in the one does not preclude enjoyment of the other. Although Jenny has occasional olfactory reminders of London—a letter from a dancer friend pervaded with 'a faint theatre scent' or a memory of the smell of the city's 'wood-pavement'—she comes to relish the sights and fragrance of the countryside about her, reminiscent of a happy year she spent staying with relatives in rural Hampshire as a small child.[154] Mackenzie's own love of flowers is amply reflected in the descriptions of the colours and scents of 'escallonias aromatic in the sunlight', 'almond-scented' gorse, 'Brompton stocks in a sweetness of pink and gray [that] scented the rich Cornish winter', a 'slope [...] fragrant with white sea-campion', 'Bluebells [...] a blue mist of perfume', 'the scent of the tobacco plants', 'the delicious odour of pinks in full June bloom'.[155] Jenny finds herself ever more in harmony with her surroundings when she gives birth to her much-cherished son, Frank, and she is delighted to see her frail sister bloom in the country air. However, she finds her husband increasingly repugnant; his smell, once mildly disturbing, now becomes positively detestable: '[he] was perpetually an intrusion on any final serenity. She could not bear the way he ate, the grit and soil and raggedness of his face; she loathed the grimy scars upon his hands, his smell of corduroy.'[156] The smell psychologist Rachel Herz writes 'There is something

---

[150] Ibid. (ch. 34 Mr Z. Trewhella), p. 348.   [151] Ibid. (ch. 34 Mr Z. Trewhella), pp. 350–1.
[152] Ibid. (ch. 34 Mr Z. Trewhella), pp. 358, 359.
[153] Ibid. (ch. 35 'The Marriage of Columbine'), pp. 368–9.
[154] Ibid. (ch. 43 'Bow Bells'), p. 413; (ch. 44 'Picking Up Threads'), p. 420. For Jenny's childhood visit to the country, see ch. 6 'Shepherd's Calendar', pp. 62–7.
[155] Ibid. (ch. 38 'The Alien Corn'), pp. 385, 386, 389; (ch. 39 'Intermezzo'), pp. 396, 401; (ch. 47 'Nightlight Time'), p. 437.
[156] Ibid., (ch. 46. 'May Morning'), p. 430.

very important and biologically sound going on when a woman finds a man's smell delicious or distasteful', adding 'I have been told by several marital therapists that one of the most common complaints made by women is a current repulsion for their husband's smell.'[157] It is hard to resist the feeling that in accepting her suitor Jenny should have trusted to the sound olfactory instincts that made her prefer Mr Timpany to her feckless father.

The final chapter of the novel is titled 'Carni Vale' or 'farewell to flesh' as Mackenzie ironically invokes a popular etymology connected with the festivities that precede Lenten renunciation, this darker meaning being the shadow-side of the celebratory spectacle commonly associated with 'carnival'. Symbolically, the mist that 'shrouds' Jenny as she walks to her fatal meeting with Maurice, brings about 'an annihilation of shape and colour and scent and sound', this sensory deprivation hinting at the doom that awaits her.[158] Poignantly her final walk is interrupted by just two flashes of colour—a ruddy fox, a creature associated with the animalistic Trewhella and which Jenny momentarily mistakes for his dog, and a solitary blue columbine, a flower associated with Jenny herself, as Columbine was the dance role she longed for as a child.[159] Moreover, the scentless landscape of the novel's denouement is in sharp contrast to the balmy 'perfumed silence' of the previous night, which a meditative Jenny spends with her baby, where crimson roses and 'the delicious odour of pinks' outside her bedroom window recall the same flowers that fragranced the room she stayed in when a child in Hampshire. The ominous scentlessness of Jenny's final walk is a foil to all the many other perfumes and odours that have charted her life and expressed her longings and emotions.[160]

There is no evidence of any conscious intention on Mackenzie's part to be an aromancer and track fictional biography through smell, and readers unalerted to an olfactory thread might easily pass it by amid the descriptive richness of *Carnival* and *Sinister Street*. Yet my close examination of these novels reveals that that such a thread, whether intentional or simply reflecting the author's own strong unconscious investment in smell, certainly exists. In these two important novels of development, Mackenzie demonstrates that it is possible to use the sense of smell, olfactory memory and impressions, and the social and cultural contexts of perfume, to underscore the key moments and experiences in an individual's life. Unlike Woolf, he shows that olfactory experience is not merely the preserve of animals, but is also an integral part of being human, with smell appealing not just to our sensual nature but also playing a major part in our understanding of the world around us, being deeply entwined with our notions of personal identity.

[157] Herz, *The Scent of Desire*, pp. 120, 140.

[158] Mackenzie, *Carnival* (ch. 48 'Carni Vale'), pp. 439, 440.

[159] Ibid. (ch. 12 'Growing Old'), p. 150. Mackenzie originally wanted to call his novel 'Columbine' but the title had been taken by another recently published novel. Several chapter titles refer to Jenny as 'Columbine', an artist friend of Maurice's paints her as 'Columbine Asleep', and Maurice attempts to sculpt her in the same pose. In *My Life and Times*, Octave 4: *1907–1915* (1965), p. 84, Mackenzie indicates that the traditional meaning of the columbine flower (or aquilegia) is 'false vows', which, in the context of his novel, may represent Maurice's abandonment of Jenny.

[160] Mackenzie, *Carnival* (ch. 47 'Nightlight Time'), p. 437.

Moreover, he proves remarkably sensitive to the class and social associations of manufactured perfume. Both these early twentieth-century novels inherit and respond to the fragrant legacy of the *fin de siècle*, with *Carnival* in particular revealing that there is no abrupt break between the nineties and the decades that succeeded them, but rather a perfumed evolution.

We have already seen Katherine Mansfield alive to the decadent alliance of 'Soul & senses', and exhibiting, like Pater, 'a certain voluptuous pleasure in garden scents', but there are other continuities. The scent of tuberose, associated with 'dangerous' or 'voluptuous pleasures' by Raffalovich, Robinson, and Wratislaw, permeates the popular erotic novel *Three Weeks* (1907) by Elinor Glyn, where it is the signature scent of the seductive femme fatale, as well as contributing to the queer ambience of the avant-garde Parisian salon of Valérie Seymour depicted by Radclyffe Hall in *The Well of Loneliness* (1927): 'The odour of somebody's Oriental scent was mingling with the odour of tuberoses in a sixteenth-century chalice.'[161] Seymour is the fictional counterpart of Natalie Barney, the expatriate American writer and Left Bank *salonnière*, famous for her many lesbian affairs, and tuberose was indeed one of her favourite flowers. In her old age she disconcerted her future biographer Jean Chalon by presenting him with a spray: 'I didn't know what to do with it. You don't take the métro with a tuberose branch in your hand.'[162]

Symons's decadent mnemonic perfumes do not completely fade away but become the ghosts of fragrance in one of his grudging inheritors, informing the lilacs of *The Waste Land* that help mix 'Memory and desire', the hyacinths of 'Portrait of Lady' that recall 'things that other people have desired', or the 'perfume from a dress', that makes J. Alfred Prufrock 'digress'.[163] While Eliot recoils at 'female smells', shying away from Symons's delight in the 'scent of sex', those natural odours are openly relished by James Joyce, a friend and admirer of Symons, who also remembers his 'Peau d'Espagne' in *Ulysses* (1918–20) where it is worn by Molly Bloom, while Gerty MacDowell wears a perfume that makes Leopold Bloom think of heliotrope.[164] Molly also wears opopanax, that heady *fin-de-siècle* perfume hymned by Theodore Wratislaw. But more austere versions of modernism also take their inspiration from the less obviously voluptuous perfumes of aestheticism. Swinburne's love of sharp green fragrances, astringent marine smells, and the scents of the 'quiet sea-flower moulded by the sea' are echoed by his admirer, the

[161] Elinor Glyn, *Three Weeks* (New York: Duffield & Co., 1907), pp. 15, 24, 38, 46, 47, 198–9, 282. Thanks to Shahidha Bari for the reference. Radclyffe Hall, *The Well of Loneliness* (London: The Falcon Press, 1949), p. 274 (ch. 31).

[162] Jean Chalon, *Portrait of a Seductress: The World of Natalie Barney*, tr. Carol Barko (London: Blond and Briggs, 1979), p. 199.

[163] Eliot, *The Poems* 1. 55, 12, 7.

[164] My thanks to Katy Mullin for suggesting a link between Joyce, Symons, and *Ulysses*. See also Karl Beckson and John M. Munro, 'Letters to Arthur Symons from James Joyce', *James Joyce Quarterly* 4.2 (Winter 1967), 91–101. Laura Frost gives a good overview of Joyce and perfume (though without the link to Symons) in *The Problem with Pleasure: Modernism and Its Discontents* (New York: Columbia University Press, 2013), pp. 33–62.

modernist Imagist poet H.D., in her first collection *Sea Garden* (1916). In 'Sheltered Garden' she reveals her frustration with conventional garden scents:

> I have had had enough—
> border-pinks, clove-pinks, wax-lilies,
> herbs, sweet-cress.
>
> O for the some sharp swish of a branch—
> there is no scent of resin
> in this place,
> no taste of bark, of coarse weeds,
> aromatic, astringent—
> only border on border of scented pinks.[165]

More recently, with the rise of neo-Victorian fiction, the evocation of smell, scent, and perfume has become an effective means of creating period atmosphere, conjuring the nineteenth-century past into the present, as seen in novels as diverse as Joanne Harris's *Sleep, Pale Sister* (1994), Sarah Waters's *Tipping the Velvet* (1998), *Affinity* (1999), and *Fingersmith* (2002), and Michel Faber's *The Crimson Petal and the White* (2002), in which the male protagonist is the inheritor of a perfumery business.[166] Heirs to their Victorian predecessors, these contemporary novelists are modern aromancers, channelling 'Smell', the 'potent wizard', not to transport us 'across thousands of miles and all the years you have lived' but to take us into a past we never knew but still think we recognize through our familiarity with the traces of its sillage.[167]

---

[165] Hilda Doolittle (H.D.), *H.D.: Collected Poems: 1912–1944*, ed. Louis L. Martz (Manchester: Carcanet Press, 1984), p. 19. Thanks to Claire Preston for suggesting the link. 'Sheltered Garden', copyright © 1982 by The Estate of Hilda Doolittle. reprinted by permission of New Directions Publishing Corp (US) and Carcanet Press Limited (UK).

[166] See Silvana Colella's fine exploration of Faber's novel in 'Olfactory Ghosts: Michel Faber's *The Crimson Petal and the White*', in *Haunting and Spectrality in Neo-Victorian Fiction: Possessing the Past*, ed. Rosario Arias and Patricia Pulham (Basingstoke: Palgrave, 2010), pp. 85–110.

[167] Keller, 'Smell, the Fallen Angel', p. 64.

APPENDIX

Tuberose and Meadowsweet

Of tuberose I sing, and meadowsweet:
One flower much whiter than the fervent dove,
Whose scent in living pulses seems to beat:
Magnetic ardour, drowsy scent of love,
O memory, O presence odorous,
Thy life's perfume, my perfect tuberose!

O meadowsweet, my passion's purity,
O distant echo, faintness rapt and fresh,
That means my soul to thee, and thine to me,
O symbols flowersoft of soul and flesh,
My hands on my love's knees, at my love's feet,
Of tuberose I sing and meadowsweet.

I sing for one we love, my rhymes and I,
Who loves my song for me, me for my song,
   One whom we love we know well why,
       My song and I.
O love do you love us for short, for long,
       Me and my song?
Of meadowsweet I sing, of meadowsweet!

    O mine, my meadowsweet,
     O slender grace to me,
    O fairness made to meet
     With slimness loftily,
    And white but rose-delighted,
    And pink but pale-affrighted,
    With gazing unreserved
     On love's most steep abysses!
    Spreading smiles many curved!
     Soft dreamful skin and kisses,
    O mouth not meant to speak
    The riddle of thy cheek!
    What can be whispered lower,
     Hardly with words to-day,
    (But flower-leaf touching flower)
      O do not stir to say.
    Silence, for silence knows best.
    Be mute: the amorous best!

Of meadowsweet I sing, of meadowsweet.
Slender and sweet, like honey, like thy hair,

O like my words to thee, like meadowsweet,
    Stainless and tender, tall and fair,
       Fair like thy hair,
Tender and sweet like grasses to thy feet,
      Like meadowsweet,
Of meadowsweet I sing, of meadowsweet!

O flower, O love, most mystical and fresh,
Whose breath can thrill us with a breath most sweet,
As with the touch of warm seraphic flesh,
Of meadowsweet I sing, of meadowsweet!

Of tuberose, O love, of tuberose,
I sing of tuberose, of tuberose!
It may be summer in the woods to-day,
Or winter with the trees, or spring, who knows?
It may be pleasant on the new-mown hay
Or near the sea-rock where the wet wind goes,
And happy lovers find their kisses salt.
It may be summer in the woods to-day
Or spring unfolding such a perfect rose
That it would not be fairer for a fault;
If you have me, and I have you, then say
What should we do, who love with empty shows?
It may be summer in the woods to-day,
Or winter with the trees, or spring, who knows?
Of tuberose I sing, of tuberose!

Behind the soft green curtains half undone,
The fluttering paleness, is it morn or eve,
To-day that ends, to-morrow that's begun?
While through the cream white muslin like a sieve,
Some precious light is shed like powdered amber
Between the soft green curtains half undone,
Enough of light to see you nor to grieve—
Glimpses and whispers outside of our chamber,
Inadequate beneath a useless sun,
What sight or sound can one of us receive?
Behind the soft green curtains half undone
The fluttering paleness, is it morn or eve?

Here in the vague and close confined room
All senses are as one acutely blent,
When speechless, touching not, in silent gloom
We yearn and languish with a single scent,
Relentlessly and subtly odorous.
Here in the vague and close confined room
And of Lethean pleasures redolent,
The strong inevitable tuberose
Surrounds irradiating to a tomb,
Where half-unconsciousness is well content.

Here in the vague and close confined room
All senses are as one acutely blent.

If this be death, then we are dead indeed!
O do not stir lest we find life again:
What should we have of life? There is no need
For us to fill the hollow hours in vain
Or lengthen out the sobbing of our breath.
If this be death, then we are dead indeed,
Or waiting for the whole of life to wane,
After the last sigh, love, the first kiss, death!
I think that on some battlefield we bleed,
And I would live once more to be so slain.
If this be death, then we are dead indeed.
O do not stir lest we find life again!

Of tuberose I sing, of tuberose!
O love, O flower, whose name I may not tell
Save unto one alone who is not here,
But who perhaps like me remembers well
One flower, one scent, one hour and one called dear.
For this perfume since then a grave profound,
Wherein is laid of life the perfect whole,
Has undivided from desire been wound
About the inmost longings of my soul.
And when I sicken of my living now
This wizard flower brings back again thy breath,
Touches my mouth and hands: how far art thou?
For I do feel thee like delight or death,
Thy shoulders and thy arms, thy shadowed hair,
Thy speechless lips and thy unaltered stare.
Of tuberose, desirous tuberose,
Of tuberose I sing, of tuberose,
Of tuberose I sing and meadowsweet.

Too much has my desire been heard to moan
Within the narrow cavity of rhyme,
And made poor music in a place of stone,
For loved henceforth or unbeloved, time
No longer may deny for all his wrong,
One worth my rapture, rapture worth my song.
And if my kisses have been strangely red
You must ask meadowsweet and tuberose,
Or pale like them and mutely sung instead;
If each flower cannot tell, at least each knows,
And either scent remembers, white and strong,
One worth my kisses, kisses worth my song.

Give me thy voice, thy breath, thy lids, thy presence,
Thy arm, thy neck, and much too sweet, thy breast;
And bruise my life until thou find its essence,

Love's deepest poppy for my soul's dear guest.
Let them be crushed beneath thy darling feet,
Darling, my tuberose and meadowsweet![1]

Tuberoses

The Tuberose you left me yesterday
  Leans yellowing in the glass we set it in;
It could not live when you were gone away,
  Poor spike of withering sweetness changed and thin.

And all the fragrance of the dying flower
  Is grown too faint and poisoned at the source,
Like passion that survives a guilty hour,
  To find its sweetness heavy with remorse.

What shall we do, my dear, with dying roses?
  Shut them in weighty tomes where none will look
—To wonder when the unfrequent page uncloses
  Who shut the wither'd blossoms in the book?—

What shall we do, my dear, with things that perish,
  Memory, roses, love we feel and cherish?

II.

Alive and white, we praised the Tuberose,
  So sweet it fill'd the garden with its breath
A spike of waxy bloom that grows and grows
  Until at length it blooms itself to death.

Everything dies that lives—everything dies;
  How shall we keep the flower we lov'd so long?
O press to death the transient thing we prize,
  Crush it, and shut the elixir in a song.

A song is neither live nor sweet nor white.
  It hath no heavenly blossom tall and pure,
No fragrance can it breathe for our delight,
  It grows not, neither lives; it may endure.

Sweet Tuberose, adieu! you fade too fast!
  Only a dream, only a thought, can last.

III.

Who'd stay to muse if Death could never wither?
  Who dream a dream if Passion did not pass?
But, once deceived, poor mortals, hasten hither
  To watch the world in Fancy's magic glass.

---

[1] Mark André Raffalovich, from *Tuberose and Meadowsweet* (London: David Bogue, 1885), pp. 37–43.

Truly your city, O men, hath no abiding!
　Built on the sand it crumbles, as it must;
And as you build, above your praise and chiding,
　The columns fall to crush you to the dust.

But fashion'd in the mirage of a dream,
　Having nor life nor sense, a bubble of nought,
The enchanted City of the Things that seem
　Keeps till the end of time the eternal Thought.

Forswear to-day, forswearing joy and sorrow,
Forswear to-day, O man, and take to-morrow.[2]

---

[2] A. Mary F. Robinson, from *Songs, Ballads and a Garden Play* (London: T. Fisher Unwin, 1888), pp. 22–4.

Bibliography

MANUSCRIPTS

Bridge, Ursula, typescript MS, unpublished biography of Michael Field, 4 vols, vol. 4: 1906–1914, Bodleian Special Collections.

Field, Michael, MS materials, Bodleian Special Collections.

Field, Michael, Works and Days (Add. MS. 46777–467798, Add. MS. 46804A) and other MS materials, British Library Special Collections.

Mackenzie, Compton, *Carnival* (published 1912) (incomplete) holograph manuscript (Special Collections, Senate House Library, University of London) SL V/63.

Mackenzie, Compton, *Sinister Street*, vol. 1 (published 1913) holograph manuscript, 2 vols, Walpole Collection, The King's School, Canterbury.

OTHER ARCHIVAL MATERIALS

Army and Navy Stores Catalogues (1899, 1900, and 1901), British Library Special Collections.

Piesse & Lubin's Toilet Almanack for 1861, 32 pp. John Johnson Collection, Bodleian Library Special Collections, Oxford.

Programme for *Antony and Cleopatra* advertising Rimmel's Persian Ribbon (John Johnson Collection, London Playbills Drury Lane Box 2 (3).

Trade card for J. C. and J. Field, Samphire Soap (*c*.1885), Evanion 4192, British Library Special Collections.

NEWSPAPERS AND PERIODICALS

Aberdeen Weekly Journal
Birmingham Daily Post
Bristol Mercury
Chemist and Druggist
Graphic
Illustrated London News
The Lady
London Gazette
Modern Man
Myra's Journal
New York Times
Pall Mall Gazette
The Smoker
Soapmaker and Perfumer
The Times

SOURCES

Ackerman, Diane, *A Natural History of the Senses* (London: Chapmans, 1990).

Adburgham, Alison, intr. *Yesterday's Shopping: The Army & Navy Stores Catalogue 1907: A Facsimile of the Amy & Navy Co-operative Society's 1907 Issue of Rules of the Society and Price List of Articles Sold at the Stores* (Newton Abbot: David & Charles, 1969).

Adburgham, Alison, intr. *Victorian Shopping: A Facsimile of the Harrod's Stores 1895 Issue of the Price List* (Newton Abbot: David & Charles, 1972).

Adburgham, Alison, *Shops and Shopping 1800–1914: Where, and in What Manner the Well-dressed Englishwoman Bought her Clothes*, 2nd edn (London: George Allen & Unwin, 1981).

Addleshaw, Stanley, 'A Short Note upon a New Volume of Poems' (Review of Arthur Symons, *Silhouettes*), *The Spirit Lamp* 2.4 (6 December 1892), 118.

Aftel, Mandy, *Essence and Alchemy: A Natural History of Perfume* (New York: North Point Press, 2001).

Aftel, Mandy, 'Perfumed Obsession', in *The Smell Culture Reader*, ed. Jim Drobnick (Oxford and New York: Berg, 2006), pp. 206–11.

Aftel, Mandy, *Fragrant: The Secret Life of Scent* (New York: Riverhead Books, 2014).

'A Journalist', *Bohemian Days in Fleet Street* (London: John Long, 1913).

Allen, Grant, *Physiological Æsthetics* (London: Henry S. King, 1877).

Alpers, Antony, *The Life of Katherine Mansfield* (London: Jonathan Cape, 1980).

Anon., *The Habits of Good Society: A Handbook of Etiquette* (London: John Hogg, 1859).

Anon., 'Britannia's Smelling Bottle', *Once a Week* (8 December 1860), 665–8.

Anon., 'Flower Farming', *Cornhill Magazine* 10.58 (October 1864), 427–33.

Anon., 'Flower Framing and Perfume Manufacturing', *Illustrated Review* 2.137 (August 1874), 90–1.

Anon., *Etiquette for Ladies and Gentlemen* (London and New York: Frederick Warne & Co., 1876).

Anon., *The Gentleman's Art of Dressing with Economy by a Lounger at the Clubs* (London: Frederick Warne, 1876).

Anon., *Our Deportment, or the Manners, Conduct and Dress of the Most Refined American Society* (Detroit, MI: F. B. Dickerson, 1879).

Anon., 'From Month to Month: A Summary', *The Artist and Journal of Home Culture* 13.1 (April 1892), 114–15.

Anon., *Practical Perfumery by An Expert*, 3rd edn (London: The British and Colonial Druggist, 1896).

Anon., 'Nitro-Benzol Poisoning', *California State Journal of Medicine* 16.5 (May 1918), 252–3.

Anson, Peter F., 'Random Reminiscences of John Gray and André Raffalovich', in *Two Friends: John Gray and André Raffalovich: Essays Biographical and Critical*, ed. Brocard Sewell (Aylesford: St Albert's Press, 1963), pp. 134–41.

Apostolos-Cappadona, Diane, '"Pray with Tears and your Request will Find a Hearing": On the Iconology of the Magdalene's Tears', in *Holy Tears: Weeping in the Religious Imagination*, ed. Christine Kimberly Patton and John Stratton Hawley (Princeton, NJ: Princeton University Press, 2005), pp. 201–28.

Arlott, John, *The Snuff Shop* (London: Michael Joseph, 1974).

Arnold, Sir Edwin, *Japonica* (London: James R. Osgood, McIlvaine & Co., 1891).

Arnold, Sir Edwin, *Seas and Lands: Reprinted by Permission of the Proprietors of the 'Daily Telegraph' from Letters Published under the Title 'By Sea and Land' in that Journal* (London: Longman & Co., 1891).

Arnold, Sir Edwin, *East and West: Being Reprinted from the 'Daily Telegraph' and Other Sources* (London: Longmans, Green, & Co., 1896).

Arnold, Matthew, *Culture and Anarchy*, ed. J. Dover Wilson (Cambridge: Cambridge University Press, 1960).

Austin, Alfred, *The Autobiography of Alfred Austin*, 2 vols (London: Macmillan, 1911).

Ayer, Harriet Hubbard, *Harriet Hubbard Ayer's Book: A Complete and Authentic Treatise on the Laws of Health and Beauty* (New York: Home Topics Book Company, 1899).

Bacon, Francis, *The Major Works*, ed. Brian Vickers (Oxford: Oxford University Press, 2002).

Bailey, John, Helen Hill, Yvonne Hockey, and Matthew Williams, eds., *British Perfumery: A Fragrant History: Celebrating 50 Years of the British Society of Perfumers* (Frome: British Society of Perfumers, 2013).

Bailey, Philip James, *The Mystic and Other Poems* (London: Chapman & Hall, 1855).

Banks, Elizabeth, *Campaigns of Curiosity: Journalistic Adventures of an American Girl in London* (Chicago and New York: F. Tennyson Neely, 1894).

Banks, Elizabeth, 'How the Other Half Lives: The Flower Girl', *English Illustrated Magazine* (June 1894), 925–31.

Barbey d'Aurevilly, Jules-Amédée, *Les Bas-bleus* (Paris: Société Générale de Librarie Catholique, 1878).

Barolsky, Paul, *Walter Pater's Renaissance* (University Park, PA, and London: Pennsylvania University Press, 1987).

Barrett, Elizabeth, *The Letters of Robert Browning and Elizabeth Barrett Barrett 1845–1846*, ed. Elvan Kintner, 2 vols (Cambridge, MA: The Belknap Press of Harvard University Press, 1962).

Bartlett, Chris, 'Lily of the Valley: Mystery, Manufacture and Murder', http://pellwall-perfumes. blogspot.co.uk/2014/07/lily-of-valley-mystery-manufacture.html (accessed 17 April 2017).

Baudelaire, Charles, *Les Fleurs du mal*, tr. Arthur Symons (London: The Casanova Society, 1925).

Baudelaire, Charles, *The Complete Verse*, intr. and tr. Francis Scarfe (London: Anvil Press Poetry, 1986).

Beals, Katharine M., *Flower Lore and Legend* (New York: Henry Holt & Co., 1917).

Beardsley, Aubrey, 'Under the Hill: A Romantic Story' (Chapters 1, 2, and 3), *The Savoy* 1 (January 1896), 151–70.

Beaulieu, Denyse, *The Perfume Lover: A Personal History of Scent* (London: HarperCollins, 2012).

Beckson, Karl, ed., *Oscar Wilde: The Critical Heritage* (London: Routledge & Kegan Paul, 1970).

Beckson, Karl, 'Oscar Wilde and the Green Carnation', *English Literature in Transition* 43.4 (2000), 387–97.

Beckson, Karl, and John M. Munro, 'Letters to Arthur Symons from James Joyce', *James Joyce Quarterly* 4.2 (Winter 1967), 91–101.

Bell, Malcolm, *Edward Burne-Jones: A Record and Review* (London: George Bell & Sons, 1892).

Bell, Quentin, *Virginia Woolf: A Biography*, 2 vols (St Albans: Triad/Paladin, 1976).

Bertrand, C. F., *Le Parfumeur imperial, or l'art de préparer les odeurs, essences, parfums* (Paris: Brunot-Labbé, 1809).

Betts, Hannah, 'Let us Spray', *Guardian* (6 December 2008), https://www.theguardian. com/lifeandstyle/2008/dec/06/perfume-ingredients (accessed 17 April 2017).

Binyon, Laurence, *Lyric Poems* (London: Elkin Mathews & John Lane, 1894).

Binyon, Laurence, *Porphyrion and Other Poems* (London: Grant Richards, 1898).

Bloch, Iwan, *Odoratus Sexualis: A Scientific and Literary Study of Sexual Scents and Erotic Perfumes* (New York: American Anthropological Society, 1933).

Bloch, Iwan, *Odoratus Sexualis: A Scientific and Literary Study of Sexual Scents and Erotic Perfumes* (North Hollywood, CA: Brandon House, 1967).

Blodgett, Bonnie, *Remembering Smell* (Boston, MA, and New York: Houghton Mifflin Harcourt, 2010).

Boase, Frederick, *Modern British Biography containing Many Thousand Concise Memoirs of Persons who have Died since the Year 1850*, 2 vols (Truro: Netherton & Worth for the author, 1897).

Bose, T., and Paul Tiessen, eds., *A Bookman's Catalogue: The Norman Colbeck Collection of Nineteenth-Century and Edwardian Poetry and Belles Lettres*, 2 vols (Vancouver: UBC Press, 1987).

Boyer, Jacques, 'The Perfume Trade', *The Idler* 23 (September 1903), 434–41.

Boyle, E. V., *Days and Hours in a Garden* (London: Elliot Stock, 1884).

Boyson, Rowan, 'Wordsworth's Anosmia', *La Questione Romantica* 3.2 (2014), 63–80.

Braddon, Mary Elizabeth, *Lady Audley's Secret*, ed. David Skilton (Oxford: Oxford University Press, 1987).

Bradstreet, Christina, '"Wicked with Roses": Floral Femininity and the Erotics of Scent', *Nineteenth-Century Art Worldwide* 16.1 (2007), http://www.19thc-artworldwide.org/46-spring07/spring07article/144-qwicked-with-rosesq-floral-femininity-and-the-erotics-of-scent (accessed 17 April 2017).

Bradstreet, Christina, 'A Trip to Japan in Sixteen Minutes: Sadakichi Hartmann's Perfume Concerts', in *Art, History and the Senses: 1830 to the Present*, ed. Patrizia di Bello and Gabriel Koureas (Farnham and Burlington, VT: Ashgate, 2010), pp. 51–64.

Brant, Clare, 'Fume and Perfume: Some Eighteenth-Century Uses of Smell', *Journal of British Studies* 43 (2004), 444–63.

Brewer, Emma, 'Petal to Perfume', *Strand Magazine* 16.92 (August 1898), 232–5.

Bright, Henry A., *A Year in a Lancashire Garden* (London: Macmillan & Co., 1879).

Briot, Eugénie, 'Perfume Sprayed and Displayed', Paper presented at Economic History Society Annual Conference, Exeter University, 2007. http://www.ehs.org.uk/events/assets/ConfBook2007.pdf (accessed 17 April 2017).

Briot, Eugénie, 'From Industry to Luxury: French Perfume in the Nineteenth Century', *Business History Review* 85 (Summer 2011), 273–94.

Brontë, Charlotte, *Jane Eyre*, ed. Margaret Smith (Oxford: Oxford University Press, 2000).

Brooks, Van Wyck, *John Addington Symonds: A Biographical Study* (London: Grant Richards, 1914).

Brown, Horatio F., *John Addington Symonds: A Biography*, compiled from his Papers and Correspondence by Horatio F. Brown, 2nd edn (London: Smith, Elder, & Co., 1908.)

Browning, Robert, *Dearest Isa: Robert Browning's Letters to Isa Blagden*, ed. Edward C. McAleer (Austin, TX, and Edinburgh: University of Texas Press and Edinburgh University Press, 1951).

Browning, Robert, *The Poems of Browning*, ed. John Woolford and Daniel Karlin, 4 vols to date (London and New York: Longman, 1991–).

Buchanan, Robert, 'The Fleshly School of Poetry: Mr. D. G. Rossetti' (1871), in *Critical Essays on Dante Gabriel Rossetti*, ed. David Riede (New York: G. K. Hall & Co., 1992).

Buchanan, Robert, *The Fleshly School of Poetry and Other Phenomena of the Day* (London: Strahan & Co., 1872).

Bulwer, Edward, *Pelham; or, The Adventures of a Gentleman*, 3 vols (London: Henry Colburn, 1828).

Bump, Jerome, 'Seeing and Hearing in *Marius the Epicurean*', *Nineteenth-Century Fiction* 37 (1982), 188–206.

Burbidge, F. W., *Domestic Floriculture: Window-Gardening and Floral Decorations* (Edinburgh and London: William Blackwood & Sons, 1874).

Burbidge, F. W., *The Book of the Scented Garden* (London and New York: John Lane, 1905).

Burr, Chandler, *The Emperor of Scent: A Story of Perfume, Obsession, and the Last Mystery of the Senses* (London: Arrow Books, 2004).

Burr, Chandler, *The Perfect Scent: A Year Inside the Perfume Industry in Paris and New York* (New York: Picador, 2007).

Butter, Peter, *Shelley's Idols of the Cave* (Edinburgh: Edinburgh University Press, 1954).

Calè, Luisa, and Patrizia di Bello, eds., *Illustrations, Optics and Objects in Nineteenth-Century Literary and Visual Cultures* (London and Basingstoke: Palgrave Macmillan, 2010).

Carlisle, Janice, *Common Scents: Comparative Encounters in High-Victorian Culture* (New York: Oxford University Press, 2004).

Carruthers, Miss, *Flower Lore: The Teaching of Flowers, Historical, Legendary, Poetical and Symbolical* (Belfast: McCaw, Stevenson & Orr, 1879).

Carter, Tom, *The Victorian Gardener* (London: Bell & Hyman, 1984).

Cassell's Household Guide, 2 vols (London: Cassell, Petter, & Galpin, 1869).

Chalon, Jean, *Portrait of a Seductress: The World of Natalie Barney*, tr. Carol Barko (London: Blond & Briggs, 1979).

Chamberlain, Basil Hall, *Things Japanese* (London: Kegan Paul, Trench, Trübner & Co., Ltd, 1890).

Chambers Dictionary (Edinburgh: Chambers Harrap Ltd, 1993).

Chantraine, Pierre, *Dictionnaire étymologique de la langue grecque: Histoire des mots* (Paris: Librarie Klincksiek, 2009).

Charteris, Evan, *The Life and Letters of Sir Edmund Gosse* (London: W. Heinemann, 1931).

Chico, Tita, *Designing Women: The Dressing Room in Eighteenth-Century English Literature and Culture* (Lewisburg, PA: Bucknell University Press, 2005).

Chitty, Susan, *The Beast and the Monk: A Life of Charles Kingsley* (London: Hodder & Stoughton, 1975).

Classen, Constance, *Words of Sense: Exploring the Senses in History and Across Cultures* (London and New York: Routledge, 1993).

Classen, Constance, *The Color of Angels: Cosmology, Gender and the Aesthetic Imagination* (New York and London: Routledge, 1998).

Classen, Constance, David Howes, and Anthony Synott, *Aroma: The Cultural History of Smell* (New York: Routledge, 1994).

Clements, Elicia, 'Pater's Musical Imagination: The Aural Architecture of "The School of Giorgione" and *Marius the Epicurean*', in *Victorian Aesthetic Conditions: Walter Pater across the Arts*, ed. Elicia Clements and Lesley J. Higgins (Basingstoke: Palgrave Macmillan, 2010), pp. 152–66.

Clements, Patricia, *Baudelaire and the English Tradition* (Princeton, NJ: Princeton University Press, 1985).

Cockaigne, Emily, *Hubbub: Filth, Noise and Stench in England, 1600–1770* (New Haven, CT, and London: Yale University Press, 2007).

Cohen, William A., *Embodied: Victorian Literature and the Senses* (Minneapolis, MN: University of Minnesota Press, 2009).

Cohen, William A., and Ryan Johnson, eds., *Filth: Dirt, Disgust and Modern Life* (Minneapolis, MN: University of Minnesota Press, 2005).

Colella, Silvana, 'Olfactory Ghosts: Michel Faber's *The Crimson Petal and the White*', in *Haunting and Spectrality in Neo-Victorian Fiction: Possessing the Past*, ed. Rosario Arias and Patricia Pulham (Basingstoke: Palgrave, 2010), pp. 85–110.

Coleridge, Samuel Taylor, *Samuel Taylor Coleridge: Poems*, ed. John Beer (London and Melbourne: Everyman's Library, J. M. Dent, 1974).

Colette, *Claudine s'en va* (Paris: Société d'Éditions littéraires et artistiques, Librairie Paul Ollendorff, 1903).

Cooley, Arnold J., *The Toilet and Cosmetic Arts in Ancient and Modern Times* (London: Robert Hardwicke, 1866).

Coombs, Roy E., *Violets: The History and Cultivation of Scented Violets* (London: B. T. Batsford, 2003).

Coon, Nelson, and Georgianne Giffen, *The Complete Book of Violets* (South Brunswick, NJ, New York, and London: A. S. Barnes & Co. and Yoseloff Ltd, 1977).

Corbin, Alain, *The Foul and the Fragrant: Odour and the Social Imagination* (London and Basingstoke: Papermac, 1996).

Corelli, Marie, *The Sorrows of Satan* (Oxford: Oxford University Press, 1998).

Cotes, Rosemary A., *Dante's Garden, with Legends of the Flowers* (London: Methuen & Co., 1898).

Cott, Jonathan, *Wandering Ghost: The Odyssey of Lafcadio Hearn* (Tokyo, New York, and London: Kodansha International, 1992).

Crane, Walter, *An Artist's Reminiscences* (London: Macmillan & Co., 1907).

Cross, Victoria, 'Theodora', *Yellow Book* 4 (January 1895), 156–88.

Cruise, Colin, *Pre-Raphaelite Drawing* (London: Thames & Hudson, 2012).

Dannenfeldt, Karl H., 'Ambergris: The Search for its Origin', *Isis* 73 (1982), 382–97.

Darwin, Charles, *Charles Darwin's Natural Selection being the Second Part of his Big Species Book Written from 1856 to 1858*, ed. R. C. Stauffer (Cambridge: Cambridge University Press, 1987).

Davies, Jennifer, *The Victorian Flower Gardener* (London: BBC Books, 1991).

Debay, A., *Les Parfums et les fleurs, leur histoire et leurs diverses influences sur l'économie humaine* (Paris: Moquet, Libraire-Éditeur, 1846).

Delaney, J. G. P., *Charles Ricketts: A Biography* (Oxford: Clarendon Press, 1990).

De Nicolai, Patricia, 'A Smelling Trip into the Past: The Influence of Synthetic Materials on the History of Perfume', *Chemistry and Biodiversity* 5 (2008), 1137–46.

De Quincey, Thomas, *Suspiria de Profundis, Confessions of an English Opium-Eater and Other Writings*, ed. Barry Milligan (London: Penguin, 2003).

Desmarais, Jane, 'Perfume Clouds: Olfaction, Memory, and Desire in Arthur Symons's *London Nights* (1895)', in *Economies of Desire at the Victorian Fin de Siècle*, ed. Jane Ford, Kim Edwards, and Patricia Pulham (London: Routledge, 2016), pp. 62–79.

Detienne, Marcel, 'The Hunt and the Erotic', *Diogenes* 96 (1976), 110–31.

Detienne, Marcel, *Dionysos Slain*, tr. Mireille Muellner and Leonard Muellner (Baltimore, MD, and London: Johns Hopkins University Press, 1979).

Dickens, Charles, *Pickwick Papers*, ed. James Kinsley (Oxford: Oxford University Press, 1988).

Dickens, Charles, *Barnaby Rudge*, ed. Clive Hurst (Oxford: Oxford University Press, 2003).

Dickens, Charles, *Great Expectations*, ed. Margaret Cardwell (Oxford: Oxford University Press, 2008).

Disraeli, Benjamin, *The Young Duke*, 3 vols (London: H. Colburn & R. Bentley, 1831).

Disraeli, Benjamin, *Benjamin Disraeli: Letters*, vol. 6: *Letters 1852–1856*, ed. M. G. Wiebe, Mary S. Millar, and Ann Robson (Toronto and London: University of Toronto Press, 1997).

Dobson, Austin, *Vignettes in Rhyme and Vers de Société* (London: Henry S. King, 1873).

Dobson, Mary, *Medieval Muck* (Oxford: Oxford University Press, 1997).

Dobson, Mary, *Tudor Odours* (Oxford: Oxford University Press, 1997).

Dobson, Mary, *Victorian Vapours* (Oxford: Oxford University Press, 1997).

Dobson, Mary, *Reeking Royals* (Oxford: Oxford University Press, 1998).

Donne, John, *The Complete English Poems*, ed. A. J. Smith (Harmondsworth: Penguin Books, 1973).

Doolittle, Hilda (H.D.), *H.D.: Collected Poems: 1912–1944*, ed. Louis L. Martz (Manchester: Carcanet Press, 1984).

Dove, Roja, *The Essence of Perfume* (London: Black Dog Publishing, 2008).

Doyle, Sir Arthur Conan, *The Complete Adventures of Sherlock Holmes* (Harmondsworth: Penguin, 1981).

Drobnick, Jim, 'Toposmia: Art, Scent and Interrogations of Spatiality', *Angelaki* 7.1 (April 2002), 31–46.

Drobnick, Jim, ed., *The Smell Culture Reader* (Oxford and New York: Berg, 2006).

Dugan, Holly, *The Ephemeral History of Perfume: Scent and Sense in Early Modern England* (Baltimore, MD: Johns Hopkins University Press, 2011).

Eastham, Andrew, 'Walter Pater's Acoustic Space: "The School of Giorgione", Dionysian *Anders-streben*, and the Politics of Soundscape', in guest ed. Stefano Evangelista and Catherine Maxwell, *The Yearbook of English Studies* 40.1 and 40.2 *The Arts in Victorian Literature*, (2010), 197–216.

Eckstein, Markus, *Eau de Cologne: Farina's 300th Anniversary* (Cologne: J. P. Bachem Verlag, 2009).

Eliot, George, *The Mill on the Floss*, ed. Gordon S. Haight (Oxford: Oxford University Press, 1996).

Eliot, T. S., *The Use of Poetry and the Use of Criticism* (London: Faber, 1933).

Eliot, T. S., *The Sacred Wood: Essays on Poetry and Criticism* (London and New York: Methuen, 1960).

Eliot, T. S., *The Varieties of Metaphysical Poetry*, ed. Ronald Schuchard (London: Faber & Faber, 1993).

Eliot, T. S., *The Letters of T. S. Eliot*, vol. 1: *1898–1923*, rev. and ed. Valerie Eliot and Hugh Haughton (London: Faber & Faber, 2009).

Eliot, T. S., *The Poems of T. S. Eliot*, ed. Christopher Ricks and Jim McCue, 2 vols (London: Faber & Faber, 2015).

Ellacombe, Henry N., *The Plant-Lore and Garden Craft of Shakespeare* (London: W. Satchell & Co., 1884).

Ellena, Jean-Claude, *Perfume: The Alchemy of Scent*, tr. John Crisp (New York: Arcade Publishing, 2011).

Ellena, Jean-Claude, *The Diary of a Nose: A Year in the Life of a Parfumeur*, tr. Adriana Hunter (London: Particular Books, 2012).

Ellenbogen, Eileen, *English Vinaigrettes* (Cambridge: The Golden Head Press, 1956).

Ellis, Aytoun, *The Essence of Beauty: A History of Perfume and Cosmetics* (London: Secker & Warburg, 1960).

Ellis, Havelock, *Studies in the Psychology of Sex: Sexual Inversion* (Philadelphia, PA: F. A. Davis Company, Publishers, 1901).

Ellis, Havelock, *Studies in the Psychology of Sex: Sexual Selection in Man* (Philadelphia, PA: F. A. Davis Company, 1906).

Ellis, Havelock, and J. A. Symonds, *Studies in the Psychology of Sex: Sexual Inversion* (London: Wilson & Macmillan, 1897).

Ellis, Havelock, and J. A. Symonds, *Sexual Inversion: A Critical Edition, Havelock Ellis and John Addington Symonds (1897)*, ed. Ivan Crozier (Basingstoke and New York: Palgrave Macmillan, 2008).

Ellmann, Richard, *Oscar Wilde* (London: Penguin, 1988).

Evangelista, Stefano, *British Aestheticism and the Greeks* (Basingstoke and New York: Palgrave Macmillan, 2009).

Eveleigh, David J., *Bogs, Baths and Basins: The Story of Domestic Sanitation* (Stroud: Sutton Publishing, 2002).

Fabre, J. H., *Social Life in the Insect World*, tr. Bernard Miall (London: T. Fisher Unwin, 1912).

Faillon, Étienne-Michel, *Monuments inédits sur l'apostolat de Sainte Marie-Madeleine en Provence*, 2 vols (Paris: J.-P. Migne, 1848).

Fairley, Josephine, and Lorna McKay, *The Perfume Bible* (London: Kyle Books, 2014).

Fanning the Senses, 13 March 2007–1 July 2007, preface by H. E. Alexander (London: The Fan Museum, 2007).

Fenwick-Miller, Mrs, 'Ladies' Column', *Illustrated London News* (1 December 1894), 686.

Ferber, Michael, *A Dictionary of Literary Symbols*, 2nd edn (Cambridge: Cambridge University Press, 2007).

Feynman, Richard P., *Surely You're Joking, Mr Feynman! Adventures of a Curious Character as Told to Ralph Leighton*, ed. Edward Hutchings (New York: W. W. Norton & Co., 1985).

Field, Michael, *Long Ago* (London: George Bell & Sons, 1889).

Field, Michael, *Sight and Song* (London: Elkin Mathews & John Lane, 1892).

Field, Michael, *Underneath the Bough* (London and New York: George Bell & Sons, 1893).

Field, Michael, *Underneath the Bough* (Portland, ME: Thomas B. Mosher, 1898).

Field, Michael, *Wild Honey from Various Thyme* (London: T. Fisher Unwin, 1908).

Field, Michael, *Poems of Adoration* (London and Edinburgh: Sands & Co., 1912).

Field, Michael, *Mystic Trees* (London: Eveleigh Nash, 1913).

Field, Michael, *A Shorter Shīrazād: 101 Poems of Michael Field*, ed. Ivor C. Treby (Bury St Edmunds: De Blackland Press, 1999).

Field, Michael, *Music and Silence: The Gamut of Michael Field*, ed. Ivor C. Treby (Bury St Edmunds: De Blackland Press, 2000).

Field, Michael, *Uncertain Rain: Sundry Spells of Michael Field*, ed. Ivor C. Treby (Bury St Edmunds: De Blackland Press, 2002).

Field, Michael, *Binary Star: Leaves from the Journal and Letters of Michael Field 1846–1914*, chosen and annotated by Ivor C. Treby (Bury St Edmunds: De Blackland Press, 2006).

Field, Michael, *The Fowl and the Pussycat: Love Letters of Michael Field 1876–1909*, ed. Sharon Bickle (Charlottesville, VA, and London: University of Virginia Press, 2008).

'Filomena', 'Christmas Presents', *Illustrated London News* (10 December 1898), 884.

Flint, Kate, *The Victorians and the Visual Imagination* (Cambridge and New York: Cambridge University Press, 2000).

Foerster, Norman, 'Whitman as a Poet of Nature', *PMLA* 31.4 (1916), 736–58.

Foster, Charles, *Being a Beast* (London: Profile Books Ltd, 2016).

Franklin, George, 'Instances of Meeting: Shelley and Eliot: A Study in Affinity', *ELH* 61 (1994), 955–90.

Fraser, Amy Stewart, *Roses in December: Edwardian Reflections* (London: Routledge & Kegan Paul, 1981).

Frazer, Sir James George, *Adonis, Attis, Osiris: Studies in the History of Oriental Religion* (London: Macmillan & Co. Ltd, 1906).

Freedman, Jonathan, *Professions of Taste: Henry James, British Aestheticism, and Commodity Culture* (Stanford, CA: Stanford University Press, 1990).

Frost, Laura, *The Problem with Pleasure: Modernism and Its Discontents* (New York: Columbia University Press, 2013).

Galopin, Augustin, *Le Parfum de la femme et le sens olfactif dans l'amour* (Paris: Saint-Germain, 1886).

Garnett, David, *The Flowers of the Forest* (London: Chatto & Windus, 1953).

Gaskell, Elizabeth, *Ruth: A Novel*, 3 vols (London: Chapman & Hall, 1853).

Gaskell, Elizabeth, *Letters of Mrs Gaskell*, ed. J. A. V. Chapple and A. Pollard (Manchester: Manchester University Press, 1966).

Gaskell, Elizabeth, *Cranford*, ed. Elizabeth Porges Watson (Oxford: Oxford University Press, 1980).

Gaskell, Elizabeth, *North and South*, ed. Angus Easson (Oxford: Oxford University Press, 1982).

Gaskell, Elizabeth, *Ruth*, ed. Alan Shelston (Oxford: Oxford University Press, 1983).

Gaskell, Elizabeth, *Wives and Daughters*, ed. Angus Easson (Oxford: Oxford University Press, 1987).

Gaskell, Elizabeth, *My Lady Ludlow and Other Stories*, ed. Edgar Wright (Oxford: Oxford University Press, 1989).

Gaskell, Elizabeth, *A Dark Night's Work and Other Stories*, ed. Suzanne Lewis (Oxford: Oxford University Press, 1992).

Gaskell, Elizabeth, *Mary Barton*, ed. Shirley Foster (Oxford: Oxford University Press, 2006).

Gaskell, Elizabeth, *Cousin Phillis and Other Stories*, ed. Heather Glen (Oxford: Oxford University Press, 2010).

Gaskell, Elizabeth, *Sylvia's Lovers*, ed. Francis O'Gorman (Oxford: Oxford University Press, 2014).

Gaunt, William, *The Aesthetic Adventure* (1945; London: Cardinal/Sphere Books, 1975).

Gautier, Théophile, 'Honoré de Balzac', in *Œuvres complètes de H. de Balzac*, 20 vols (Paris: A. Houssiaux, 1855), 1. 1–16.

Gautier, Théophile, *Honoré de Balzac* (Paris: Poulet Malassis et de Broise, 1859).

Gautier, Théophile, *Portraits contemporains* (Paris: Charpentier et Cie, 1874).

Gautier, Théophile, 'Honoré de Balzac' in *The Works of Théophile Gautier*, vol. 6: *Portraits of the Day*, tr. and ed. F. C. de Sumichrast (London: G. G. Harrap, 1900), 16–137.

Gautier, Théophile, *Charles Baudelaire: His Life [...] with Selections from His Poems*, tr. Guy Thorne (London: Greening & Co., 1915).

Gautier, Théophile, *Selected Lyrics*, tr. Norman A. Shapiro (New Haven, CT, and London: Yale University Press, 2011).

Genders, Roy, *Perfume in the Garden* (London: The Garden Book Club, 1954).

Genders, Roy, *The Scented Wild Flowers of Britain* (London: Collins, 1971).

Genders, Roy, *A History of Scent* (London: Hamish Hamilton, 1972).

Genders, Roy, *Bulbs: A Complete Handbook of Bulbs, Corms and Tubers* (London: Robert Hale & Co., 1973).

Gerard, John, *The Herball or Generall Historie of Plants* (London: Printed by John Norton, 1597).

Gilbert, Avery, *What the Nose Knows: The Science of Smell in Everyday Life* (New York: Crown Publishers, 2008).

Gilbert, Karen, *Perfume: The Art and Craft of Fragrance* (London and New York: Cico Books, 2013).

Glyn, Elinor, *Three Weeks* (New York: Duffield & Co., 1907).

Goncourt, Edmond de, *Chérie* (Paris: Ernest Flammarion et Eugène Fasquelle, 1883).

Goodman, Ruth, *How to be a Victorian: A Dawn-to-Dusk Guide to Everyday Life* (London: Viking, 2013).

Goodman, Ruth, *How to be a Tudor: A Dawn-to-Dusk Guide to Everyday Life* (London: Viking, 2015).

Gosse, Edmund, *On Viol and Flute* (London: Henry S. King & Co., 1873).

Gosse, Edmund, *Questions at Issue* (London: William Heinemann, 1893).

Gosse, Edmund, *Portraits and Sketches* (London: William Heinemann, 1912).

Gosse, Edmund, 'Algernon Charles Swinburne (1837–1909)', in *The English Poets: 1880–1918*, vol. 5: *Browning to Rupert Brooke*, ed. Thomas Humphry Ward (London: Macmillan & Co., 1918), 368–75.

Gosse, Edmund, *Father and Son*, ed. Michael Newton (Oxford: Oxford University Press, 2004).

Gould, George M., *Concerning Lafcadio Hearn*, with a Bibliography by Laura Stedman (London and Leipzig: T. Fisher Unwin, 1908).

Grasse, Marie-Christine, ed., *Perfume: A Global History* (Paris: Somogy Art Publishers, 2007).

Greek Lyric Poetry, tr. David Campbell, Loeb Classical Library, 5 vols (Cambridge, MA, and London: Harvard University Press, 1982–93).

Green, Annette, and Linda Dyett, *Secrets of Aromatic Jewelry* (Paris: Flammarion, 1998).

Greenwell, Dora, *Carmina Crucis* (London: Bell & Daldy, 1869).

Griffiths, Mark, 'Sweet Tenants of the Shade', *The Garden* 125 (February 2001), 88–91.

Grigson, Geoffrey, *The Goddess of Love: The Birth, Triumph, Death and Return of Aphrodite* (London: Constable, 1976).

Groom, Nigel, *Frankincense and Myrrh: A Study of the Arabian Incense Trade* (London and New York: Longman, 1981).

Groom, Nigel, *The New Perfume Handbook*, 2nd edn (London: Blackie Academic Publishing, 1997).

Grosskurth, Phyllis, 'Swinburne and Symonds: An Uneasy Literary Relationship', *Review of English Studies* 14.55 (1963), 257–68.

Grosskurth, Phyllis, *John Addington Symonds: A Biography* (London: Longmans, Green & Co., Ltd, 1964).

Grossmith, London, *Overview* [advertising booklet] (Winter 2014).

Hall, Radclyffe, *The Well of Loneliness* (London: The Falcon Press, 1949).

Halliday, Stephen, *The Great Stink of London: Sir Joseph Bazalgette and the Cleansing of the Victorian Metropolis* (Stroud: Sutton, 1999).

Halliday, Stephen, *The Great Filth: The War against Disease in Victorian London* (Stroud: Sutton, 2007).

Hanson, Ellis, *Decadence and Catholicism* (Cambridge, MA, and London: Harvard University Press, 1997).

Harad, Alyssa, *Coming to My Senses: A Story of Perfume, Pleasure, and an Unlikely Bride* (New York: Viking, 2012).

Hardy, Thomas, *The Complete Poems of Thomas Hardy*, ed. James Gibson (London and Basingstoke: Papermac, 1981).

Harris, Frank, *Oscar Wilde: His Life and Confessions*, 2 vols (New York: Brentano's, 1918).

Harrison, Frederic, 'Culture: A Dialogue', *Fortnightly Review* 2 (November 1867), 603–14.

Harrison, John, *Synaesthesia: The Strangest Thing* (Oxford: Oxford University Press, 2001).

Haskins, Susan, *Mary Magdalen: Myth and Metaphor* (London and New York: HarperCollins, 1993).

Hassard, Anne, *Floral Decorations for the Dwelling House: A Practical Guide for the Home Arrangement of Plants and Flowers* (London: Macmillan, 1875).

Hastings, Somerville, *Summer Flowers of the High Alps* (London and New York: J. M. Dent & Sons and E. P. Dutton, 1910).

Hathaway, Anne, 'Scent and Scent Bottles', *Woman's World* 2 (1889), 321–5.

Hatt, Michael, 'Near and Far: Homoeroticism, Labour and Hamo Thornycroft's Mower', *Art History* 26 (2003), 26–55.

Hawthorne, Nathaniel, *The House of the Seven Gables* (Boston, MA: Ticknor, Reed, & Fields, 1851).

Hawthorne, Nathaniel, *Tales and Sketches* (New York and Cambridge: The Library of America, 1982).

Hearn, Lafcadio, 'An Odorous Subject', *Item* (12 August 1878), 1.

Hearn, Lafcadio, 'The Physiology of Smells', *Item* (3 January 1880), n.p.

Hearn, Lafcadio, *Stray Leaves from Strange Literature* (Boston, MA: James R. Osgood & Co., 1884).

Hearn, Lafcadio, *Glimpses of Unfamiliar Japan*, 2 vols (London: Osgood McIlvaine & Co., 1894).

Hearn, Lafcadio, *Kokoro: Hints and Echoes of Japanese Inner Life* (London: Gay & Bird, 1895).

Hearn, Lafcadio, *In Ghostly Japan* (Boston, MA: Little, Brown, & Co., 1899).

Hearn, Lafcadio, *Letters from the Raven: Being the Correspondence of Lafcadio Hearn with Henry Watkin*, ed. Milton Bronner (New York: Brentano's, 1907).

Hearn, Lafcadio, *Life and Letters of Lafcadio Hearn*, ed. Elizabeth Bisland, 2 vols (London, Boston, MA, and New York: Archibald Constable & Co., and Houghton, Mifflin & Co., 1907).

Hearn, Lafcadio, *The Japanese Letters of Lafcadio Hearn*, ed. Elizabeth Bisland (Boston, MA, and New York: Houghton Mifflin Co., 1910).

Hearn, Lafcadio, *Exotics and Retrospectives* (Boston, MA: Little, Brown, & Co., 1914).

Hearn, Lafcadio, *Fantastics and Other Fancies*, ed. Charles Woodward Hutson (Boston, MA, and New York: Houghton Mifflin, 1914).

Hearn, Lafcadio, *Appreciations of Poetry*, ed. John Erskine (New York: Dodd, Mead & Co., 1916).

Hearn, Lafcadio, *Karma and Other Stories* (New York: Boni & Liveright, 1918).

Hearn, Lafcadio, *Books and Habits from the Lectures of Lafcadio Hearn*, ed. John Erskine (New York: Dodd, Mead & Co., 1921).

Hearn, Lafcadio, *Pre-Raphaelite and Other Poets: Lectures by Lafcadio Hearn*, ed. John Erskine (New York: Dodd, Mead & Co., 1922).

Hearn, Lafcadio, *Miscellanies*, ed. Albert Mordell, 2 vols (London: William Heinemann, 1924).

Hearn, Lafcadio, *Occidental Gleanings: Sketches and Essays*, ed. Albert Mordell, 2 vols (London: W. Heinemann, 1925).

Hearn, Lafcadio, *Editorials by Lafcadio Hearn*, ed. Charles Woodson Hutson (Boston, MA, New York, and Cambridge: Houghton Mifflin Co., The Riverside Press, 1926).

Hearn, Lafcadio, *Complete Lectures on Poets by Lafcadio Hearn*, ed. Ryuji Tanabé, Teisaburo Ochiai, and Ichiro Nishizaki (Tokyo: The Hokuseido Press, 1934).

Hearn, Lafcadio, *Literary Essays by Lafcadio Hearn*, ed. Ichiro Nishizaki (Tokyo: The Hokuseido Press, 1939).

Hearn, Lafcadio, *The New Radiance and Other Scientific Sketches by Lafcadio Hearn*, ed. Tchiro Nishizaki (Tokyo: The Hokuseido Press, 1939).

Hearn, Lafcadio, 'Fantasy of a Fan', *Ye Giglampz* 6 (26 July 1874), 2–3, in *Ye Giglampz: A Weekly Illustrated Journal devoted to Art, Literature and Satire*, ed. *Lafcadio Hearn and*

Henry Farny, ed. Jon Christopher Hughes (Cincinnati, OH: Crossroads Books with the Public Library of Cincinnati and Hamilton County, 1983).

Hearn, Lafcadio, *Period of the Gruesome: Selected Cincinnati Journalism of Lafcadio Hearn*, ed. Jon Christopher Hughes (London and New York: University Press of America, 1990).

Hearn, Lafcadio, *Inventing New Orleans: Writings of Lafcadio Hearn*, ed. S. Frederick Starr (Jackson, MI: University Press of Mississippi, 2001).

Hearn, Lafcadio, *The New Orleans of Lafcadio Hearn: Illustrated Sketches from the Daily City Item*, ed. Delia LaBarre (Baton Rouge, LA: Louisiana State University Press, 2007).

Hearn, Lafcadio, *Lafcadio Hearn: American Writings*, ed. Christopher Benfey, The Library of America (New York: Literary Classics of the United States, Inc., 2009).

Hemans, Felicia, *The Poetical Works of Mrs Hemans* (London: Henry Frowde, n.d.).

Herman, Barbara, *Scent and Subversion: Decoding a Century of Provocative Perfume* (Guildford, CT: Lyons Press, 2013).

Herrick, Robert, *The Hesperides and Noble Numbers*, ed. Alfred Pollard, The Muses' Library, 2 vols (London: Lawrence & Bullen, 1891).

Herz, Rachel, *The Scent of Desire: Discovering Our Enigmatic Sense of Smell* (New York and London: Harper Perennial, 2008).

Hibbert, Christopher, *Disraeli: A Personal History* (London: HarperCollins, 2004).

Hogg, Thomas Jefferson, *The Life of Percy Bysshe Shelley*, 2 vols (London: Edward Moxon, 1858).

Holland, Merlin, *The Wilde Album* (London: Fourth Estate, 1997).

Holman-Hunt, Diana, *My Grandfather, His Wives and Loves* (1969; London: Columbus Books, 1987).

Holmes, Oliver Wendell, *The Autocrat of the Breakfast-Table* (Boston, MA: Phillips, Sampson & Company, 1858).

Howard, Lady Constance, *Etiquette: What to Do, and How to Do It* (London: F. V. White, 1885).

Hughes, Jon Christopher, 'Introduction', in *Ye Giglampz: A Weekly Illustrated Journal devoted to Art, Literature and Satire, ed. Lafcadio Hearn and Henry Farny*, ed. Jon Christopher Hughes (Cincinnati, OH: Crossroads Books with the Public Library of Cincinnati and Hamilton County, 1983), pp. 7–18.

Huneker, James, *Visionaries* (New York: Charles Scribner's Sons, 1905).

Hunt, Leigh, 'Ronald of the Perfect Hand', *The Indicator* 20 (Wednesday, 23 February 1820), 153–60.

Huysmans, J. K., *Against Nature*, tr. Robert Baldick (Harmondsworth: Penguin, 1959).

Huysmans, J. K., *Parisian Sketches: A Translation of Croquis Parisiens*, tr. Richard Griffiths (London: The Fortune Press, 1962).

Hyde, H. Montgomery, *The Other Love: An Historical and Contemporary Survey of Homosexuality in Britain* (London: Heinemann, 1970).

Hyde, H. Montgomery, *Oscar Wilde: A Biography* (London: Eyre Methuen, 1976).

Hyder, C. K., ed., *Swinburne: The Critical Heritage* (London: Routledge & Kegan Paul, 1970).

Ingram, John, *Flora Symbolica or the Language and Sentiment of Flowers* (London and New York: Frederick Warne & Co., 1870).

International Exhibition 1862: Reports of the Juries on the Subjects of the Thirty-Six Classes into which the Exhibition was Divided (London: Printed for the Society of Arts, 1863).

Irvine, Susan, *Perfume: The Creation and Allure of Classic Fragrances* (New York and Avenel, NJ: Crescent Books, 1995).

Irvine, Susan, *The Perfume Guide* (London: Haldane Mason, 2000).

Jackson, Holbrook, *The Eighteen Nineties: A Review of Art and Ideas at the End of the Nineteenth Century* (London: Grant Richards, 1912).

Jackson, Lee, *Dirty Old London: The Victorian Fight against Filth* (New Haven, CT: Yale University Press, 2014).

Jacox, Francis, 'Scent Memories', *Bentley's Miscellany* 54 (1863), 360–6.

Jäger, Gustav, *Dr Jaeger's Health-Culture*, tr. and ed. Lewis R. S. Tomalin, rev. and greatly enlarged edn (London: Waterlow & Sons Ltd, 1887).

Jäger, Gustav, *Problems of Nature: Researches and Discoveries by Gustav Jaeger, Selected from his Published Writings*, tr. and ed. Henry G. Schlicter (London, Edinburgh, and Oxford: William & Norgate, 1897).

James, Lionel, *A Forgotten Genius: Sewell of St Columba's and Radley* (London: Faber & Faber, 1945).

Jashemski, Wihelmina Feemster, and Frederick G. Meyer, eds., *The Natural History of Pompeii* (Cambridge: Cambridge University Press, 2002).

Jekyll, Gertrude, *Wood and Garden: Notes and Thoughts, Practical and Critical, of a Working Amateur* (London: Longmans, Green & Co., 1899).

Jellinek, Paul, *The Psychological Basis of Perfumery*, tr. and ed. J. Stephan Jellinek, 4th edn (London: Blackie Academic & Professional, 1997).

Jenner, Mark, 'Civilization and Deodorization? Smell in Early Modern English Culture', in *Civil Histories: Essays Presented to Sir Keith Thomas*, ed. Peter Burke, Brian A. Harrison, and Paul Slack (Oxford: Oxford University Press, 2000), pp. 127–44.

Jesse, Jill, 'Perfume', in William Kaufmann, *Perfume*, A Dutton Visual Book (New York: E. P. Dutton, 1974), pp. 109–12.

Johnson, Alan, 'Arthur Symons' "The Life and Adventures of Lucy Newcome": Preface and Text', *English Literature in Transition* 28.4 (1985), 33–45.

Kaiser, Matthew, 'Pater's Mouth', *Victorian Literature and Culture* 39 (2011), 1–18.

Keats House Committee, *The John Keats Memorial Volume* (London: John Lane, The Bodley Head, 1921).

Keats, John, *The Poems of John Keats*, ed. Miriam Allott (London and New York: Longman, 1970).

Keats, John, *John Keats: The Major Works*, ed. Elizabeth Cook (Oxford: Oxford University Press, 2001).

Keller, Helen, *The World I Live In* (New York: The Century Co., 1908).

Kelley, Victoria, *Soap and Water: Cleanliness, Dirt and the Working Classes in Victorian and Edwardian Britain* (London: I. B. Tauris, 2010).

Kelly, Ian, *Beau Brummell: The Ultimate Dandy* (London: Sceptre, 2005).

Kemp, Christopher, *Floating Gold: A Natural (and Unnatural History) of Ambergris* (Chicago and London: University of Chicago Press, 2014).

Kernahan, Coulson, *In Good Company: Some Personal Recollections* (London and New York: John Lane, The Bodley Head and John Lane Company, 1917).

Kettler, Andrew, 'Making the Synthetic Epic: Septimus Piesse, the Manufacturing of Mercutio Frangipani, and Olfactory Renaissance in Victorian England', *The Senses and Society* 10.1 (2015), 5–25.

Kingsford, Anna, *Health, Beauty, and the Toilet: Letters to Ladies from a Lady Doctor* (London and New York: Frederick Warne & Co., 1886).

Kipling, Rudyard, *The Five Nations* (London: Methuen, 1903).

Knight, David, 'Chemistry on an Onshore Island: Britain 1789–1840', in *The Making of the Chemist: The Social History of Chemistry in Europe, 1789–1914*, ed. David Knight and Helge Kragh (Cambridge: Cambridge University Press, 1998), pp. 95–106.

Koizumi, Setsuko (Mrs Hearn), *Reminiscences of Lafcadio Hearn*, tr. Paul Kiyoshi Hisada and Frederick Johnson (Boston, MA, and New York: Houghton Mifflin Co., 1918).

Koller, Theodor, *Cosmetics: A Handbook of the Manufacture, Employment, and Testing of all Cosmetic Materials and Cosmetic Specialities*, tr. Charles Salter (London: Scott, Greenwood & Co., 1902).

Krueger, Cheryl, 'Decadent Perfume under the Skin and through the Page', *Modern Languages Open*, http://www.modernlanguagesopen.org/index.php/mlo/article/view/36 (accessed 17 April 2017).

Kuhn, William, *The Politics of Pleasure: A Portrait of Benjamin Disraeli* (London: Free Press, 2006).

Landon, Letitia [L.E.L.], *Traits and Trials of Early Life* (London: H. Colburn, 1836).

Landon, Letitia, *Letitia Elizabeth Landon: Selected Writings*, ed. Jerome McGann and Daniel Riess (Peterborough, ON: Broadview Press, 1997).

Langland, Elizabeth, 'Blake's Feminist Revision of Literary Tradition in "The Sick Rose"', in *Critical Paths: Blake and The Argument of Method*, ed. Dan Miller, Mark Bracher, and Donald Ault (Durham, NC, and London: Duke University Press, 1987), pp. 225–43.

Lawless, Alec, *Artisan Perfumery or Being Led by the Nose* (Stroud: Baronia Souk, 2009).

Lawless, Julia, *Rose Oil: The New Guide to Nature's Most Precious Perfume and Traditional Remedy* (London: HarperCollins, 1995).

Le Gallienne, Richard, *The Romance of Perfume* (New York and Paris: Richard Hudnut, 1925).

Leighton, Angela, 'Pater's Music', *Journal of Pre-Raphaelite Studies* 14 (2005), 67–79.

Leighton, Angela, and Margaret Reynolds, eds., *Victorian Women Poets: An Anthology* (Oxford: Blackwell, 1995).

Leland, Charles Godfrey, *The Music-Lesson of Confucius* (London: Trübner & Co., 1872).

Leverson, Ada, 'The Quest of Sorrow', *Yellow Book* 5 (April 1895), 325–35.

Lewis, Wyndham, *Men without Art*, ed. Seamus Cooney (Santa Rosa, CA: Black Sparrow Press, 1987).

Lhombreaud, Roger, *Arthur Symons: A Critical Biography* (London: Unicorn Press, 1963).

Light, Alison, *Mrs Woolf and the Servants: An Intimate History of Domestic Life in Bloomsbury* (London: Fig Tree, 2007).

Linklater, Andro, *Compton Mackenzie: A Life* (London: The Hogarth Press, 1992).

Linton, Eliza Lynn, 'Perfumes', *Household Words* 15.363 (7 March 1857), 236–40.

Linton, Eliza Lynn, *The Girl of the Period*, 2 vols (London: Richard Bentley & Son, 1883).

Lutterman, James B., *The Tobacco Manufacturers' Manual: A Vade-Mecum for the Allied Industries* (London: [The author], 1887).

Machray, Robert, *The Night Side of London* (Philadelphia, PA: J. Lippincott Co., 1902).

McCormack, Derek, interview with Kilian Hennessy, *National Post* (8 March 2008). http://hisnherperfumes.blogspot.co.uk/2008/06/all-in-stink-about-perfume.html (accessed 17 April 2017).

McCormack, Jerusha Hull, *John Gray: Poet, Dandy, Priest* (Hanover, NH, and London: Brandeis University Press, 1991).

McDermott, Edward, *The Popular Guide to the International Exhibition of 1862* (London: W. H. Smith & Son, 1862).

McDonald, Donald, *Sweet-Scented Flowers and Fragrant Leaves* (New York: Charles Scribner's Sons, 1895).

McKenna, Neil, *The Secret Life of Oscar Wilde* (London: Century, 2003).

Mackenzie, Compton, *Carnival* (London: Martin Secker, 1912).

Mackenzie, Compton, *Sinister Street*, 2 vols (London: Martin Secker, 1913–14).

Mackenzie, Compton, *Literature in My Time* (London: Rich & Cowan, 1933).

Mackenzie, Compton, *Echoes* (London: Chatto & Windus, 1954).

Mackenzie, Compton, *Sublime Tobacco* (London: Chatto & Windus, 1957).

Mackenzie, Compton, *Sinister Street* (Harmondsworth: Penguin, 1960).

Mackenzie, Compton, *My Life and Times*, 10 vols (London: Chatto & Windus, 1963–71). Octave 1: *1883–1891* (1963), Octave 2: *1891–1900* (1963), Octave 3: *1900–1907* (1964), Octave 4: *1907–1915* (1965).

Mackenzie, Compton, *Carnival* (London: Mayflower Books/Granada Publishing, 1972).

McKenzie, Dan, *Aromatics and the Soul* (London: William Heinemann, 1923).

Madden, Ed, 'Say it with Flowers: The Poetry of Marc-André Raffalovich', *College Literature* 24 (1997), 11–27.

Malone, Jo, *My Story* (London and New York: Simon and Schuster, 2016).

Mansfield, Katherine, *The Collected Letters of Katherine Mansfield*, ed. Vincent O'Sullivan and Margaret Scott, 5 vols (Oxford: Oxford University Press, 1984–2008). vol. 1: *1903–1917* (1984), vol. 2: *1918–1919* (1987), vol. 3: *1919–1920* (1993), vol. 4: *1920–1921* (1996).

Mansfield, Katherine, *The Katherine Mansfield Notebooks*, ed. Margaret Scott, 2 vols (Canterbury, NZ: Lincoln University Press, 1997).

Mansfield, Katherine, *The Collected Fiction of Katherine Mansfield*, ed. Gerri Kimber and Vincent O'Sullivan, 2 vols (Edinburgh: Edinburgh University Press, 2012). vol. 1: *1898–1915*, vol. 2: *1916–1922*.

Marks, Amber, *Headspace: Sniffer Dogs, Spy Bees and One Woman's Adventures in Surveillance Society* (London: Virgin Books, 2009).

Marks, Elaine, '1929 "Odor di Femina" [*Sic*]', in *A New History of French Literature*, ed. Denis Hollier (Cambridge, MA: Harvard University Press, 1994), pp. 887–91.

Marsh, Peter T., *Joseph Chamberlain: Entrepreneur in Politics* (New Haven, CT: Yale University Press, 1994).

Marston, Philip Bourke, *The Collected Poems of Philip Bourke Marston*, ed. Louise Chandler Moulton (Boston, MA: Roberts Bros, 1892).

Matthews, Samantha, *Poetical Remains: Poets' Graves, Bodies, and Books in the Nineteenth Century* (Oxford: Oxford University Press, 2004).

Maurus, Pseudo-Rabanus, *The Life of Mary Magdalene and her Sister Saint Martha*, tr. and ed. David Mycoff, Cistercian Studies Series 108 (Kalamazoo, MI: Cistercian Publications, 1989).

Maxwell, Catherine, *The Female Sublime from Milton to Swinburne: Bearing Blindness* (Manchester: Manchester University Press, 2001).

Maxwell, Catherine, *Swinburne*, Writers and their Work Series (Tavistock: Northcote House, 2006).

Maxwell, Catherine, *Second Sight: The Visionary Imagination in Late Victorian Literature* (Manchester: Manchester University Press, 2008).

Maxwell, Catherine, 'Shelley's Alchemy, Pater's Transformations', in *Legacies of Romanticism: Literature, Culture, Aesthetics*, ed. Carmen Casaliggi and Paul March Russell, Routledge Studies in Romanticism (London: Routledge, 2012), pp. 85–100.

Maxwell, Catherine, 'Scents and Sensibility: The Fragrance of Decadence', in *Decadent Poetics: Literature and Form at the British Fin de Siècle*, ed. Jason David Hall and Alex Murray (Basingstoke and New York: Palgrave Macmillan, 2013), pp. 201–25.

Mikhail, E. H., ed., *Oscar Wilde: Interviews and Recollections*, 2 vols (London and Basingstoke: Macmillan, 1979).

Miller, William Ian, *The Anatomy of Disgust* (Cambridge, MA: Harvard University Press, 1997).

Milnes, Richard Monckton, *The Life, Letters, and Literary Remains of John Keats* (London: Edward Moxon, 1848).

Mitford, Mary Russell, *Our Village: Sketches of Rural Character and Scenery* (London: G. & W. B. Whittaker, 1824).

Moers, Ellen, *The Dandy: Brummell to Beerbohm* (London: Secker & Warburg, 1960).

Moore, Thomas, *Odes of Anacreon, Translated into English Verse, with Notes* (London: John Stockdale, 1800).

Moore, Thomas, *Lalla Rookh: An Oriental Romance* (London: Longman, Hurst, Rees, Orme & Brown, 1817).

Moran, Patricia L., *Word of Mouth: Body Language in Katherine Mansfield and Virginia Woolf* (Charlottesville, VA: University Press of Virginia, 1996).

Morita, Kiyoko, *The Book of Incense* (Tokyo: Kodansha International Ltd, 1992).

Morrell, Ottoline, *Ottoline: The Early Memoirs of Lady Ottoline Morrell*, ed. Robert Gathorne-Hardy (London: Faber & Faber, 1963).

Morrell, Ottoline, *Ottoline at Garsington: Memoirs of Lady Ottoline Morrell, 1915–1918*, ed. Robert Gathorne-Hardy (London: Faber & Faber, 1974).

Muddiman, Bernard, *Men of the Nineties* (London: Henry Danielson, 1920).

Murray, Paul, *A Fantastic Journey: The Life and Literature of Lafcadio Hearn* (Folkestone: Japan Library, 1993).

Nesbit, Edith, *Leaves of Life* (London and New York: Longmans, Green & Co., 1888).

Newman, Sally, 'The Archival Traces of Desire: Vernon Lee's Failed Sexuality and the Interpretation of Letters in Lesbian History', *Journal of the History of Sexuality* 14 (2005), 51–75.

Nordau, Max, *Degeneration*, tr. George L. Mosse (Lincoln, NE, and London: University of Nebraska Press, 1993).

Norton, Charles Eliot, *Letters of Charles Eliot Norton*, ed. Sara Norton and M. A. De Wolfe Howe, 2 vols (Boston, MA, and New York: Houghton Mifflin Co., 1913).

Oakes, John, *The Perfume Zodiac* (London: Prion, 2000).

Østermark-Johansen, Lene, *Walter Pater and the Language of Sculpture* (Farnham and Burlington, VT: Ashgate, 2011).

Ostrom, Lizzie, *Perfume: A Century of Scents* (London: Hutchinson, 2015).

Ovid, *Metamorphoses*, tr. Frank Justus Miller, rev. G. P. Goold, 2 vols, 3rd edn (London and New York: W. Heinemann and G. P. Putnam's Sons, 1977–84).

Parker, Sarah, *The Lesbian Muse and Poetic Identity, 1889–1930* (London: Pickering & Chatto, 2013).

Parry, Ernest J., *The Chemistry of Essential Oils and Artificial Perfumes*, 2nd edn (London: Scott, Greenwood & Co., 1908).

Pater, Walter, 'Poems by William Morris', *Westminster Review* 34 (October 1868), 300–12.

Pater, Walter, 'The School of Giorgione', *Fortnightly Review* 22 (October 1877), 526–38.

Pater, Walter, 'Æsthetic Poetry', in *Appreciations with an Essay on Style* (London: Macmillan, 1889), pp. 213–27.

Pater, Walter, *Appreciations with an Essay on Style* (London: Macmillan, 1910).

Pater, Walter, *Essays from 'The Guardian'* (London: Macmillan, 1910).

Pater, Walter, *Greek Studies* (London: Macmillan, 1910).

Pater, Walter, *Miscellaneous Studies* (London: Macmillan, 1910).

Pater, Walter, *Plato and Platonism* (London: Macmillan, 1910).

Pater, Walter, 'Imaginary Portraits 2: An English Poet', ed. May Ottley, *Fortnightly Review* 129 (April 1931), 433–48.

Pater, Walter, *The Renaissance: Studies in Art and Poetry (The 1893 Text)*, ed. Donald L. Hill (Berkeley, CA: University of California Press, 1980).

Pater, Walter, *Gaston de Latour: The Revised Text*, ed. Gerald Monsman (Greensboro, NC: ELT Press, 1995).

Pater, Walter, *Marius the Epicurean*, ed. Gerald Monsman (Kansas City, MO: Valancourt Books, 2008).

Pater, Walter, *Studies in the History of the Renaissance* (1873), ed. Matthew Beaumont (Oxford: Oxford University Press, 2010).

Pater, Walter, *Imaginary Portraits*, ed. Lene Østermark-Johansen (London: Modern Humanities Research Association, 2014).

Paul, William, FLS, *The Rose Garden in Two Divisions*, 9th edn (London: Kent & Co., 1888).

Paul, William, FLS, *The Rose Garden in Two Divisions, Illustrated with Twenty-one Coloured Plates and Numerous Engravings in the Text*, 10th edn (London: Simpkin, Marshall & Co., 1903).

Pausanias, *Description of Greece*, tr. W. H. S. Jones, 4 vols (Cambridge, MA, and London: Harvard University Press and W. Heinemann, 1918).

Picker, John M., *Victorian Soundscapes* (Oxford: Oxford University Press, 2003).

Piesse, Charles H., 'Perfumery', in *Encyclopædia Britannica*, 9th edn, 25 vols (Edinburgh: Adam & Charles Black, 1875–89), vol. 18 *ORN–PHT* (1885), 525–7.

Piesse, Charles H., *Olfactics and the Physical Senses* (London: Piesse & Lubin, 1887).

Piesse, G. W. Septimus, *The Art of Perfumery and the Methods of Obtaining the Odours of Plants* (London: Longman, Brown, Green, & Longmans, 1855).

Piesse, G. W. Septimus, *The Art of Perfumery and the Methods of Obtaining the Odours of Plants*, 2nd edn (London: Longman, Brown, Green, Longmans, & Roberts, 1856).

Piesse, G. W. Septimus, *The Art of Perfumery and the Methods of Obtaining the Odours of Plants*, 3rd edn (London: Longman, Green, Longman, & Roberts, 1862).

Piesse, G. W. Septimus, *The Art of Perfumery and the Methods of Obtaining the Odours of Plants; The Growth and General Flower Farm System of Raising Fragrant Herbs*, 4th edn (London: Longmans, Green, & Co., 1879).

Piesse, G. W. Septimus, *Piesse's Art of Perfumery and the Methods of Obtaining the Odours of Plants; The Growth and General Flower Farm System of Raising Fragrant Herbs*, ed. Charles H. Piesse, 5th edn (London: Piesse & Lubin, 1891).

Poe, Edgar Allan, 'Marginalia (Part 2)', *Democratic Review* 15 (December 1844), 580–94.

Poe, Edgar Allan, *Essays and Reviews* (New York: Literary Classics of the United States, 1984).

Potter, Jennifer, *The Rose: A True History* (London: Atlantic Books, 2010).

Poucher, William A., *Perfumes, Cosmetics and Soaps with Especial Reference to Synthetics*, 2 vols (London: Chapman & Hall, 1925–6).

Proust, Marcel, *In Search of Lost Time*, vol. 1: *Swann's Way*, tr. C. K. Moncrieff and Terence Kilmartin, rev. D. J. Enright (London: Vintage, 2002).

Pybus, David, *Kodo: The Way of Incense* (Boston, MA: Turtle Publishing, 2001).

Pybus, David, 'The History of Aroma Chemistry and Perfume', in *The Chemistry of Fragrances*, ed. Charles Sell, 2nd edn (Cambridge: Royal Society of Chemistry 2006), pp. 3–23.

Pybus, David, ed., *Transports of Delight: An Aromatic Journey in Verse from East to West on the Wings of Perfume* (Folkestone: Global Oriental Ltd, 2007).

Raffalovich, Mark André, *Tuberose and Meadowsweet* (London: David Brogue, 1885).

Raffalovich, Mark André, *The Thread and the Path* (London: David Nutt, 1895).

Raffalovich, Mark André, *Uranisme et Unisexualité* (Paris: Storck, Lyons & Masson, 1896).

Ramond, Louis-François, *Travels in the Pyrenees*, tr. F. Gold (London: Longman, Hurst, Rees, Orme & Browne, 1813).

Ransome, Arthur, *Oscar Wilde: A Critical Study* (London: Martin Secker, 1912).

Reckford, Kenneth J., *Recognizing Persius* (Princeton, NJ, and Oxford: Princeton University Press, 2009).

Reinarz, Jonathan, *Past Scents: Historical Perspectives on Smell* (Urbana, Chicago, and Springfield, IL: University of Illinois Press, 2014).

Renan, Ernest, *Life of Jesus* (London: Watts & Co., 1935).

Rhind, Jennifer Peace, *Fragrance and Wellbeing: Plant Aromatics and their Influence on the Psyche* (London and Philadelphia, PA: Singing Dragon, 2014).

Rhymers' Club, *The Second Book of the Rhymers' Club* (London and New York: Elkin Mathews & John Lane and Dodd, Mead & Co., 1894).

Ricketts, Charles, *Letters from Charles Ricketts to 'Michael Field' (1903–1913)*, ed. J. G. Paul Delaney (Edinburgh: The Tregara Press, 1981).

Ridge, William Pett, *69 Birnam Road* (London: Hodder & Stoughton, 1908).

Rindisbacher, Hans J., *The Smell of Books: A Cultural-Historical Study of Olfactory Perception in Literature* (Ann Arbor, MI: University of Michigan Press, 1992).

Rimmel, Eugene, *The Book of Perfumes* (London: Chapman & Hall, 1865).

Rimmel, Eugene, *Recollections of the Paris Exhibition of 1867* (London: Chapman & Hall, 1868).

Rimmel, Eugene, *Le Livre des Parfums* (Paris: E. Dentu, 1870).

Roberts, David, and Richard Sheppard, eds., *Hidden Magdalen* (Oxford: Magdalen College, 2008).

Roberts, Harry, *The Book of Old-Fashioned Flowers: A Handbook of Practical Gardening* (London and New York: John Lane, 1901).

Roberts, John R., *New Perspectives on the Life and Art of Richard Crashaw* (Columbia, MO: University of Missouri Press, 1990).

Robinson, A. Mary F., *The Crowned Hippolytus* (London: C. Kegan Paul, 1881).

Robinson, A. Mary F., *Songs, Ballads, and a Garden Play* (London: T. Fisher Unwin, 1888).

Rohde, Eleanour Sinclair, 'Primroses and Violets', *Spectator* (22 February 1930), 12.

Rohde, Eleanour Sinclair, *The Scented Garden* (London: The Medici Society, 1931).

Rogers, William W., Robert David Ward, and Dorothy McLeod MacInerney, 'Oscar Wilde Lectures in New Orleans and Across the South in 1882', *Southern Studies* 11.3–4 (Fall–Winter 2004), 31–65.

Rosenberg, John D., 'Swinburne', *Victorian Studies* 11 (1967), 131–52.

Rossetti, Dante Gabriel, *The Collected Works of Dante Gabriel Rossetti* (London: Ellis, 1911).

Rossetti, Dante Gabriel, *The Correspondence of Dante Gabriel Rossetti*, ed. William Fredeman, 10 vols (Woodbridge and Rochester, NY: D. S. Brewer, 2002–15).

Rossi, Luigi, *Il Piemonte in Europa: 500 anni di emigrazione dalla Valle Vigezzo: La Famiglia Farina e L'Acqua di Colonia* (Novara: interlinea edizioni, 2009).

Ruskin, John, *The Library Edition of the Works of John Ruskin*, ed. E. T. Cook and A. Wedderburn, 39 vols (London: George Allen, 1903–12).

Sackville, Margaret, 'At Whitehouse Terrace', in *Two Friends: John Gray and André Raffalovich: Essays Biographical and Critical*, ed. Brocard Sewell (Aylesford: St Albert's Press, 1963), pp. 142–7.

Sackville-West, Vita, *The Letters of Vita Sackville-West to Virginia Woolf*, ed. Louise DeSalvo and Mitchell A. Leaska (London: Hutchinson, 1984).

Sagarin, Edward, *The Science and Art of Perfumery* (New York and London: McGraw Hill Book Company, 1945).

Sappho, *If Not, Winter: Fragments of Sappho*, tr. Anne Carson (Vintage Books, 2003).

Saunders, Captain L. H., 'The Outer Man', *Modern Man* (13 March 1909), 24.

Sawer, Charles, *Odorographia: A Natural History of Raw Materials and Drugs Used in the Perfume Industry*, 2 vols (London: Gurney & Jackson, 1892–4).

Scarisbrick, Diana, 'Charles Ricketts and his Designs for Jewellery', *Apollo* 116 (September 1982), 163–9.

Schülting, Sabine, *Dirt in Victorian Literature and Culture* (London: Routledge, 2016).

Seaton, Beverly, *The Language of Flowers: A History* (Charlottesville, VA: University Press of Virginia, 1995).

Seiler, R. M., ed., *Walter Pater: The Critical Heritage* (London: Routledge & Kegan Paul, 1980).

Seiler, R. M., ed., *Walter Pater: A Life Remembered* (Calgary, AB: University of Calgary Press, 1987).

Severn, Joseph, 'On the Vicissitudes of Keats's Fame', *Atlantic Monthly* 11.66 (April 1863), 401–7.

Severn, Joseph, *Joseph Severn: Letters and Memoirs*, ed. F. Grant Scott (Aldershot and Burlington, VT: Ashgate, 2005).

Sewell, Brocard, 'John Gray and André Sebastian Raffalovich: A Biographical Outline', in *Two Friends: John Gray and André Raffalovich: Essays Biographical and Critical*, ed. Brocard Sewell (Aylesford: St Albert's Press, 1963), pp. 7–49.

Sewell, Brocard, *Footnote to the Nineties: A Memoir of John Gray and André Raffalovich* (London: Cecil & Amelia Woolf, 1968).

Shakespeare, William, *Shakespeare's Sonnets*, ed. Stephen Booth (New Haven, CT, and London: Yale University Press, 2000).

Shakespeare, William, *The Norton Shakespeare, Based on the Oxford Edition*, ed. Stephen Greenblatt, Walter Cohen, Jean E. Howard, and Katharine Eisaman Maus, 2nd edn (New York and London: W. W. Norton & Co., 2008).

Shanks, Michael, *Art and the Early Greek State* (Cambridge: Cambridge University Press, 2004).

Sharp, William, *The Life and Letters of Joseph Severn* (London: Sampson Low, Marston & Co., 1892).

Sharp, William, 'Some Personal Reminiscences of Walter Pater', *Atlantic Monthly* 74 (December 1894), 801–14.

[Shaw, Donald], *London in the Sixties (with a Few Digressions) by One of the Old Brigade* (London: Everett & Co., 1908).

Shelley, Percy Bysshe, *Letters of Percy Shelley*, ed. F. L. Jones, 2 vols (Oxford: Oxford University Press, 1964).

Shelley, Percy Bysshe, *Shelley: Poetical Works*, ed. Thomas Hutchinson, rev. G. M. Matthews (Oxford: Oxford University Press, 1970).

Shelley, Percy Bysshe, *Shelley's Poetry and Prose*, ed. Donald H. Reiman and Sharon B. Powers (New York and London: Norton, 1977).

Shelley Society, *The Report of the Shelley Society for 1886–7* (London and Bungay: Printed by Richard Clay & Sons, 1887).

Sherard, Robert, *Oscar Wilde: The Story of an Unhappy Friendship* (London: Greening & Co., 1905).

Sherard, Robert Harborough, *The Real Oscar Wilde* (London: T. Werner Laurie, 1916).

Shewring, Walter, 'Two Friends', in *Two Friends: John Gray and André Raffalovich: Essays Biographical and Critical*, ed. Brocard Sewell (Aylesford: St Albert's Press, 1963), pp. 148–51.

Shoemaker, John V., *Heredity, Health and Personal Beauty* (London and Philadelphia, PA: F. A. Davis, 1890).

Showalter, Elaine, ed., *Daughters of Decadence: Women Writers of the Fin de Siècle* (London: Virago Press, 1993).

Sitwell, Osbert, *Noble Essences or Courteous Revelations: An Autobiography* (London: Macmillan, 1950).

Sivulka, Juliann, *Stronger than Dirt: A Cultural History of Advertising Personal Hygiene in America, 1875 to 1940* (New York: Humanity Books, 2001).

Skeat, Walter W., ed., *An Etymological Dictionary of the English Language*, 4th edn (Oxford: Clarendon Press, 1910).

Skinner, Charles M., *Myths and Legends of Flowers, Trees, Fruits and Plants in all Ages and all Climes* (Philadelphia, PA, and London: J. B. Lippincott, 1911).

Smith, Roly, *A Camera in the Hills: The Life and Work of W. A. Poucher* (London: Frances Lincoln Publishers, 2008).

Southey, Robert, *The Life and Correspondence of Robert Southey*, ed. C. C. Southey (London: Longmans, 1849–50).

Sparks, Elisa Kay, '"Everything tended to set itself in a garden": Virginia Woolf's Literary and Quotidian Flowers: A Bar-Graphical Approach', in *Virginia Woolf and the Natural World: Selected Papers from the Twentieth International Conference on Virginia Woolf, Georgetown College, Georgetown, Kentucky 3–June 2010*, ed. Kristin Zarnecki and Carrie Rohman (Clemson, SC: Clemson University Digital Press, 2011), pp. 42–57.

Stacpoole, Florence, *A Healthy Home and How to Keep It* (London: Wells Gardener, Darton & Co., 1905).

Staffe, Baroness, *The Lady's Dressing-Room*, tr. Lady Colin Campbell (London: Cassell & Co., 1892).

Staffe, Baroness, *My Lady's Dressing Room*, adapted from the French by Harriet Hubbard Ayer (New York: Cassell Publishing Company, 1892).

Staffe, La Baronne, *Le Cabinet de toilette* (Paris: Victor-Havard, 1891).

Stamelman, Richard, *Perfume: Joy, Obsession, Scandal, Sin* (New York: Rizzoli, 2006).

Stewart, Amy, *Gilding the Lily: Inside the Cut Flower Industry* (London: Portobello, 2009).

Stoddart, D. Michael, *The Scented Ape: The Biology and Culture of Human Odour* (Cambridge: Cambridge University Press, 1990).

Story, William Wetmore, *Poems* (Boston, MA: Little, Brown & Co., 1856).

Strauss, G. L. M., *England's Workshops* (London: Groombridge & Sons, 1864).

Stuart, Malcolm, *Encyclopedia of Herbs and Herbalism* (London: Orbis Publishing, 1979).

Swinburne, Algernon Charles, *William Blake* (London: Chatto & Windus, 1868).

Swinburne, Algernon Charles, *Essays and Studies* (London: Chatto & Windus, 1875).

Swinburne, Algernon Charles, *A Note on Charlotte Brontë* (London: Chatto & Windus, 1877).

Swinburne, Algernon Charles, *Miscellanies* (London: Chatto & Windus, 1886).

Swinburne, Algernon Charles, *A Study of Ben Jonson* (London: Chatto & Windus, 1889).

Swinburne, Algernon Charles, 'Preface', in Robert Herrick, *The Hesperides and Noble Numbers*, ed. Alfred Pollard, The Muses' Library, 2 vols (London: Lawrence & Bullen, 1891), 1. ix–xiv.

Swinburne, Algernon Charles, *Studies in Poetry and Prose* (London: Chatto & Windus, 1894).

Swinburne, Algernon Charles, *The Collected Poetical Works of Algernon Charles Swinburne*, 6 vols (London: Chatto & Windus, 1904).

Swinburne, Algernon Charles, *Love's Cross-Currents* (London: Chatto & Windus, 1905).

Swinburne, Algernon Charles, *The Bonchurch Edition of the Complete Works of Algernon Charles Swinburne*, ed. Edmund Gosse and Thomas James Wise, 20 vols (London and New York: William Heinemann and Gabriel Wells, 1925–27).

Swinburne, Algernon Charles, *Lucretia Borgia: The Chronicle of Tebaldeo Tebaldei*, ed. Randolph Hughes (London: Golden Cockerell Press, 1942).

Swinburne, Algernon Charles, *Lesbia Brandon*, ed. Randolph Hughes (London: The Falcon Press, 1952).

Swinburne, Algernon Charles, *The Swinburne Letters*, ed. Cecil Y. Lang, 6 vols (New Haven, CT, and London: Yale and Oxford University Presses, 1959–62).

Swinburne, Algernon Charles, *Swinburne as Critic*, ed. Clyde K. Hyder (London: Routledge & Kegan Paul, 1972).

Swinburne, Algernon Charles, *A Year's Letters*, ed. F. J. Sypher (London: Peter Owen, 1976).

Swinburne, Algernon Charles, *Poems and Ballads and Atalanta in Calydon*, ed. Kenneth Haynes (London: Penguin Books, 2000).

Swinburne, Algernon Charles, *Algernon Charles Swinburne: Major Poems and Selected Prose*, ed. Jerome M. McGann and Charles L. Sligh (New Haven, CT: Yale University Press, 2004).

Swinburne, Algernon Charles, *The Uncollected Letters of Algernon Charles Swinburne*, ed. Terry Meyers, 3 vols (London: Pickering & Chatto, 2005).

Swinburne, Algernon Charles, 'Supplementary Material to *The Uncollected Letters of Algernon Charles Swinburne*', ed. Terry Meyers, http://swinburnearchive.indiana.edu/swinburne/ (accessed 17 April 2017).

Symonds, J. A., *Studies of the Greek Poets*, 2 vols (London: Smith, Elder, & Co., 1873–6).

Symonds, J. A., *Sketches in Italy and Greece* (London: Smith, Elder, & Co., 1874).

Symonds, J. A., *Many Moods: A Volume of Verse* (London: Smith, Elder & Co., 1878).

Symonds, J. A., *Sketches and Studies in Italy* (London: Smith, Elder, & Co, 1879).

Symonds, J. A., *Vagabunduli Libellus* (London: Kegan Paul, Trench, & Co., 1884).

Symonds, J. A., *Shelley*, English Men of Letters, 2nd edn (London: Macmillan & Co., 1887).

Symonds, J. A., *Essays Speculative and Suggestive* (London: John Murray, 1890).

Symonds, J. A., *A Study of Walt Whitman* (London: John C. Nimmo, 1893).

Symonds, J. A., *Letters and Papers of John Addington Symonds*, ed. Horatio F. Brown (London: John Murray, 1923).

Symonds, J. A., *The Letters of John Addington Symonds*, ed. Herbert M. Schueller and Robert L. Peters, 3 vols (Detroit, MI: Wayne State University Press, 1967–9).

Symonds, J. A., *The Memoirs of John Addington Symonds*, ed. Phyllis Grosskurth (New York: Random House, 1984).

Symonds, J. A., *Soldier Love and Related Matter*, tr. and ed. Andrew Dakyns (Eastbourne: Andrew Dakyns, 2007).

Symonds, J. A., *John Addington Symonds (1840–1893) and Homosexuality: A Critical Edition of Sources*, ed. Sean Brady (London and Basingstoke: Palgrave Macmillan, 2012).

Symonds, J. A., and Margaret Symonds, *Our Life in the Swiss Highlands* (London and Edinburgh: Adam & Charles Black, 1892).

Symonds, J. A., and Margaret Symonds, *Our Life in the Swiss Highlands*, 2nd edn (London and Edinburgh: Adam & Charles Black, 1907).

Symonds, Margaret (Mrs W. V. Vaughan), *Out of the Past, with an Account of Janet Catherine Symonds by Mrs Walter Leaf* (London: John Murray, 1925).

Symons, A. J. A., ed., *An Anthology of 'Nineties' Verse* (London: Elkin Mathews & Marot, Ltd, 1928).

Symons, Arthur, 'The Decadent Movement in Literature', *Harper's New Monthly Magazine* 87 (November 1893), 858–67.

Symons, Arthur, *London Nights* (London: Leonard C. Smithers, 1895).

Symons, Arthur, 'A Literary Causerie: On Edmond de Goncourt', *The Savoy* 5 (September 1896), 85–7.

Symons, Arthur, 'The Old Women', *The Savoy* 5 (1896), 55–6.

Symons, Arthur, *Silhouettes*, 2nd edn (London: Leonard Smithers, 1896).

Symons, Arthur, *Amoris Victima* (London: Leonard Smithers, 1897).

Symons, Arthur, *Studies in Two Literatures* (London: Leonard Smithers, 1897).

Symons, Arthur, *Ideas of Good and Evil* (London: William Heinemann, 1899).

Symons, Arthur, *Poems*, 2 vols (London: William Heinemann, 1902).

Symons, Arthur, *Studies in Prose and Verse* (London: J. M Dent, 1904).

Symons, Arthur, 'Shelley', *Atlantic Monthly* 100 (September 1907), 347–56.

Symons, Arthur, *The Romantic Movement in English Poetry* (London: Archibald Constable & Co., 1909).

Symons, Arthur, *Knave of Hearts: 1894–1908* (London: William Heinemann, 1913).

Symons, Arthur, *Figures of Several Centuries* (London: Constable & Co., 1916).

Symons, Arthur, *Colour Studies in Paris* (London: Chapman & Hall, 1918).

Symons, Arthur, *Lesbia and Other Poems* (New York: E. P. Dutton & Co., 1920).

Symons, Arthur, *Poems:Collected Works*, 3 vols (London: Martin Secker, 1924).

Symons, Arthur, *Dramatis Personæ* (London: Faber & Gwyer, 1925).

Symons, Arthur, *The Memoirs of Arthur Symons*, ed. Karl Beckson (University Park, PA, and London: Pennsylvania University Press, 1977).

Symons, Arthur, *Arthur Symons: Selected Letters 1880–1935*, ed. Karl Beckson and John M. Munro (London and Basingstoke: Macmillan, 1989).

Symons, Arthur, *Selected Writings*, ed. Roger Holdsworth (Manchester: Fyfield Books, Carcanet Press, 1989).

Symons, Arthur, *The Symbolist Movement in Literature*, ed. Matthew Creasy (Manchester: Fyfield Books, Carcanet Press, 2014).

Symons, Arthur, *Selected Early Poems*, ed. Jane Desmarais and Chris Baldick (London: Modern Humanities Research Association, 2017).

Symons, Arthur, *Spiritual Adventures*, ed. Nicholas Freeman (London: Modern Humanities Research Association, 2017).

Tabb, John Banister, *Lyrics* (Boston, MA: Small Maynard & Co., 1897).

Tanner, Jeremy, *The Invention of Art History in Ancient Greece: Religion, Society and Artistic Rationalisation* (Cambridge: Cambridge University Press, 2006).

Taylor, Helen, '"The perfume of the past": Kate Chopin and Post-Colonial New Orleans', in *The Cambridge Companion to Kate Chopin*, ed. Janet Beer (Cambridge: Cambridge University Press, 2008), pp. 147–60.

Tennyson, Alfred, *Poems* (London: Edward Moxon, 1833).

Tennyson, Alfred, *Tennyson: A Selected Edition*, ed. Christopher Ricks (Harlow: Longman, 1989).

Thackeray, William Makepeace, *Stray Papers by William Makepeace Thackeray*, ed. Lew Melville (London: Hutchinson & Co., 1901).

Thackeray, William Makepeace, *Vanity Fair*, ed. John Sutherland (Oxford: Oxford University Press, 1983).

Thackeray, William Makepeace, *The History of Pendennis*, ed. John Sutherland (Oxford: Oxford University Press, 1994).

Thompson, C. J. S., *The Cult of Beauty: A Handbook of Personal Hygiene* (London: Walter Scott, 1894).

Thompson, C. J. S., *The Mystery and Lure of Perfume* (London: John Lane, 1927).

Thomson, James, *The Seasons*, ed. James Sambrook (Oxford: Clarendon Press, 1981).

Thwaite, Ann, *Edmund Gosse: A Literary Life* (Oxford: Oxford University Press, 1985).

Tilley, Heather, ed., 'The Victorian Tactile Imagination', *19: Interdisciplinary Studies in the Long Nineteenth Century* 19 (2014), http://www.19.bbk.ac.uk (accessed 17 April 2017).

Tinker, Edward Larocque, 'Lafcadio Hearn and the Sense of Smell', *The Bookman* (January 1924), 519–27.

Tinker, Edward Larocque, *Lafcadio Hearn's American Days* (New York: Dodd Mead, 1924).

Tinkler, Penny, 'Sapphic Smokers and English Modernities', in *Sapphic Modernisms: Sexuality, Women and National Culture*, ed. Laura Doan and Jane Garrity (Basingstoke: Palgrave Macmillan, 2006), pp. 75–90.

Tinkler, Penny, *Smoke Signals: Women, Smoking and Visual Culture* (Oxford: Berg, 2006).

Treby, Ivor C., ed., *The Michael Field Catalogue: A Book of Lists* (Bury St Edmunds: De Blackland Press, 1998).

Trefusis, Violet, *Don't Look Round* (London: Hamish Hamilton, 1952).

Trollope, Anthony, *Doctor Thorne*, ed. David Skilton (Oxford: Oxford University Press, 1980).

Trollope, Anthony, *Barchester Towers*, ed. John Sutherland (Oxford: Oxford University Press, 1996).

Trollope, Anthony, *An Autobiography*, ed. P. D. Edwards (Oxford: Oxford University Press, 1999).

Trueblood, Emily W. Emmart, '"Omixochitl": The Tuberose (*Polianthes tuberosa*)', *Economic Botany* 27 (1973), 157–73.

Tucker, Priscilla, 'Scented with Success', *New York Herald Tribune* (18 October 1964), section 2, p. 4.

Tullett, William, 'Review of Jonathan Reinarz's *Past Scents*', *Reviews in History* (2014), review no. 1648, http://www.history.ac.uk/reviews/review/1648 (accessed 17 April 2017).

Tullett, William, 'The Macaroni's "Ambrosial Essences": Perfume, Identity and Public Space in Nineteenth-Century England', *Journal for Eighteenth-Century Studies* 38 (2015), 163–80.

Turin, Luca, *The Secret of Scent: Adventures in Perfume and the Science of Smell* (New York: HarperCollins, 2006).

Turin, Luca, and Tania Sanchez, *Perfumes: The A–Z Guide* (London: Profile Books, 2009).

Verlaine, Paul, *Choix de Poésies*, ed. Michel Dansel (Paris: Librairie Larousse, 1973).

Vicinus, Martha, '"Sister Souls": Bernard Berenson and Michael Field (Katharine Bradley and Edith Cooper)', *Nineteenth-Century Literature* 60 (2005), 326–54.

Vicinus, Martha, 'Faun Love: Michael Field and Bernard Berenson', *Women's History Review* 18 (2009), 753–64.

Vivien, Renée, *The Muse of the Violets: Poems of Renée Vivien*, tr. Margaret Porter and Catharine Kroger, with a preface by Mme Louise Faure-Favier, tr. Jeanette Forster (Baltic City, MO: The Naiad Press, 1977).

Wagner, Chantal-Hélène, 'The Popularity of Clover Aroma and L. T. Piver Trèfle Incarnat in Literature and Perfume since the 19th Century: Part 1', http://www.mimifroufrou.com/scentedsalamander/2010/03/the_popularity_of_clover_aroma.html (accessed 17 April 2017).

Walker, Mrs A., *Female Beauty as Preserved by Regimen, Cleanliness and Dress* (London: Thomas Hood, 1837).

'Walter', *My Secret Life*, Wordsworth Erotic Classics, 2 vols (Ware: Wordsworth, 1995).

Watry, Maureen, *The Vale Press: Charles Ricketts, a Publisher in Earnest* (London: The British Library, 2004).

Watson, William, *The Poems of William Watson*, new edn (London and New York: Macmillan & Co., 1893).

Watts-Dunton, Clara, *The Home Life of Algernon Charles Swinburne* (London: A. M. Philpotts, 1922).

Webb, Mary, *The Spring of Joy: A Little Book of Healing* (London, Toronto, and New York: J. M. Dent and E. P. Dutton, 1917).

Welch, Evelyn, 'Scented Buttons and Perfumed Gloves: Smelling Things in Renaissance Italy', in *Ornamentalism*, ed. Bella Mirabella (Ann Arbor, MI: University of Michigan Press, 2011), pp. 13–39.

Wells, H. G., *The Stolen Bacillus and Other Incidents* (London: Macmillan & Co., 1904).

Wharton, Edith, *The Custom of the Country*, ed. Stephen Orgel (Oxford: Oxford University Press, 2008).

White, Chris, 'The One Woman (in Virgin Haunts of Poesie): Michael Field's Sapphic Symbolism', in *Volcanoes and Pearl Divers: Essays in Lesbian Feminist Studies*, ed. Suzanne Raitt (London: Only Women Press, 1995), pp. 74–102.

White, Chris, 'Flesh and Roses: Michael Field's Metaphors of Pleasure', *Women's Writing* 3.1 (1996), 47–62.

White, Chris, 'The Tiresian Poet: Michael Field', in *Victorian Women Poets: A Critical Reader*, ed. Angela Leighton (Oxford: Blackwell, 1996), pp. 148–61.

White, Jerry, *London in the Nineteenth Century* (London: Jonathan Cape, 2007).

Whitman, Walt, *Complete Poetry and Collected Prose*, ed. Justin Kaplan (New York: Literary Classics of the United States, 1982).

Wilde, Oscar, *Poems* (London: David Bogue, 1881).

Wilde, Oscar, *Plays, Prose Writings and Poems*, ed. Anthony Fothergill (London: Everyman/J. M. Dent, 1996).

Wilde, Oscar, *The Complete Letters of Oscar Wilde*, ed. Merlin Holland and Rupert Hart-Davis (London: Fourth Estate, 2000).

Wilde, Oscar, *Oscar Wilde: The Major Works*, ed. Isobel Murray (Oxford: Oxford University Press, 2000).

Wilde, Oscar, *The Picture of Dorian Gray*, ed. Michael Patrick Gillespie, Norton Critical Editions (New York and London: W. W. Norton, 2007).

Wilde, Oscar, *The Women of Homer*, ed. Thomas Wright and Donald Mead (London: Oscar Wilde Society, 2008).

Wilde, Oscar, *Teleny*, ed. Amanda Caleb (Kansas City, MO: Valancourt Books, 2010).

Wilde, Oscar, *The Complete Works of Oscar Wilde*, vol. 6: *Journalism Part 1*, ed. John Stokes and Mark Turner (Oxford: Oxford University Press, 2013).

Wilde, Oscar, and Others, *Teleny*, ed. John McRae (London: Gay Men's Press, 1986).

Wilder, Louise Beebe, *The Fragrant Path: A Book about Sweet Scented Flowers and Leaves* (New York: Macmillan Co., 1931).

Williams, David G., *Perfumes of Yesterday* (Port Washington, NY, and Weymouth: Micelle Press, 2004).

Williams, Tessa, *Cult Perfumes: The World's Most Exclusive Perfumes* (London and New York: Merrell, 2013).

Willoughby, Guy, *Art and Christhood: The Aesthetics of Oscar Wilde* (Rutherford, NJ, and London: Fairleigh Dickinson University Press and Associated University Presses, 1993).

Wilson, George, *The Five Gateways of Knowledge* (London and New York: Macmillan & Co., 1856).

Wilton, Richard, *Sungleams: Rondeaux and Sonnets* (London: Home Words, Publishing Office, 1882).

Winston, Janet, 'Reading Influences: Homoeroticism and Mentoring in Katherine Mansfield's "Carnation" and Virginia Woolf's "Moments of Being: 'Slater's Pins Have No Points' " ', in *Virginia Woolf: Lesbian Readings*, ed. Eileen Barrett and Patricia Cramer (New York and London: New York University Press, 1997), pp. 57–77.

Wood, Ellen, *East Lynne*, ed. Elisabeth Jay (Oxford: Oxford University Press, 2005).

Woolf, Leonard, *Beginning Again: An Autobiography of the Years 1911–1918* (London: The Hogarth Press, 1964).

Woolf, Virginia, 'On Being Ill', in *The Moment and Other Essays* (London: The Hogarth Press, 1947), pp. 14–24.

Woolf, Virginia, *The Letters of Virginia Woolf*, ed. Nigel Nicolson with Joanne Trautmann, 6 vols (London: The Hogarth Press, 1975–80). vol. 1: *1888–1912* (1975), vol. 2: *1912–1922* (1976), vol. 3: *1923–1928* (1977), vol. 4: *1929–1931* (1978).

Woolf, Virginia, *The Diary of Virginia Woolf*, ed. Anne Olivier Bell with Andrew McNeillie, 5 vols (London: The Hogarth Press, 1977–84). vol. 2: *1920–1924* (1982), vol. 4: *1931–1935* (1982), vol. 5: *1936–1941* (1984).

Woolf, Virginia, *The Complete Shorter Fiction of Virginia Woolf*, ed. Susan Dick (London: The Hogarth Press, 1985).

Woolf, Virginia, 'Sketch of the Past', in *Moments of Being: Autobiographical Writings*, ed. Jeanne Schulkind, with a new intr. by Hermione Lee, rev. edn (London: Pimlico, 2002).

Woolf, Virginia, *Flush*, ed. Kate Flint (Oxford: Oxford University Press, 2009).

Wordsworth, William, *Selected Poetry*, ed. Stephen Gill and Duncan Wu (Oxford: Oxford University Press, 1997).

Wratislaw, Theodore, *Caprices* (London: Gay & Bird, 1893).

Wratislaw, Theodore, *Orchids* (London: Leonard Smithers, 1896).

Wratislaw, Theodore, *Oscar Wilde: A Memoir*, foreword by John Betjeman, intr. and notes by Karl Beckson (London: Eighteen Nineties Society, 1979).

Wright, Thomas, *The Life of Walter Pater*, 2 vols (London: Everett & Co., 1902).

Wright, Thomas, *Oscar's Books: A Journey around the Library of Oscar Wilde* (London: Vintage Books, 2009).

Wyndham, Violet, *The Sphinx and her Circle: A Biographical Sketch of Ada Leverson 1862–1933* (London: André Deutsch, 1963).

Yeats, W. B., 'That Subtle Shade', *The Bookman* 8 (August 1895), 144.

Yeats, W. B., *Essays and Introductions* (London: Macmillan, 1961).

Yeats, W. B., *Collected Poems* (London: Macmillan & Co., 1963).

Young, Edward, *The Complete Works of Edward Young to which is Prefixed a Life of the Author by John Doran*, 2 vols (London: William Tegg, & Co., 1854).

Index